CW01332736

A TASTE OF PARIS IN
200 CULINARY DESTINATIONS

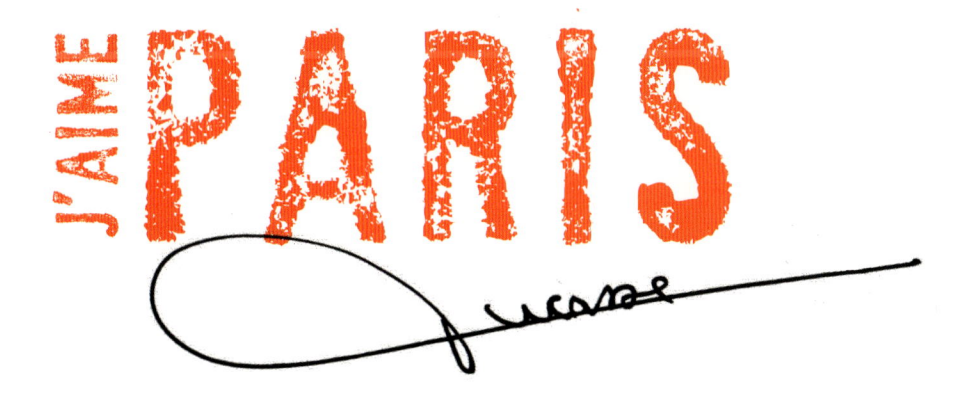

J'AIME PARIS

Ducasse

hardie grant books
MELBOURNE · LONDON

« To Gwénaëlle, who shares my love for Paris, and our son Arzhel. »

CO-AUTHOR
FRÉDÉRICK e. GRASSER HERMÉ

PHOTOGRAPHY
PIERRE MONETTA

ARTISTIC DIRECTION
PIERRE TACHON

PARIS

has been around for a long time! Steeped in a history with close ties to its great culinary tradition, it is known for its fashions and whims, as well as its authentic creations. It is a place where the art of entertaining and the science of gastronomy are actively encouraged by a public of discriminating tastes. Yet it is more than just the grand establishments of haute cuisine, the charming bistros and brasseries of yesteryear – Paris is the setting for new sensations and innovation. Paris breathes an atmosphere that inspires excellence, inventiveness and renewal. I love both the left and right banks of the city. I love Paris for its unpredictable diversity; it never ceases to surprise me. If only there were more hours in the day, it would be such a pleasure to stroll, shop and dine whenever the urge took me, in the miniature cities known as the quartiers. Paris is far from my origins in the south, but the ever-changing scenery, which invites you to go on imaginary journeys through time and space, makes it feel like home.

Ducasse

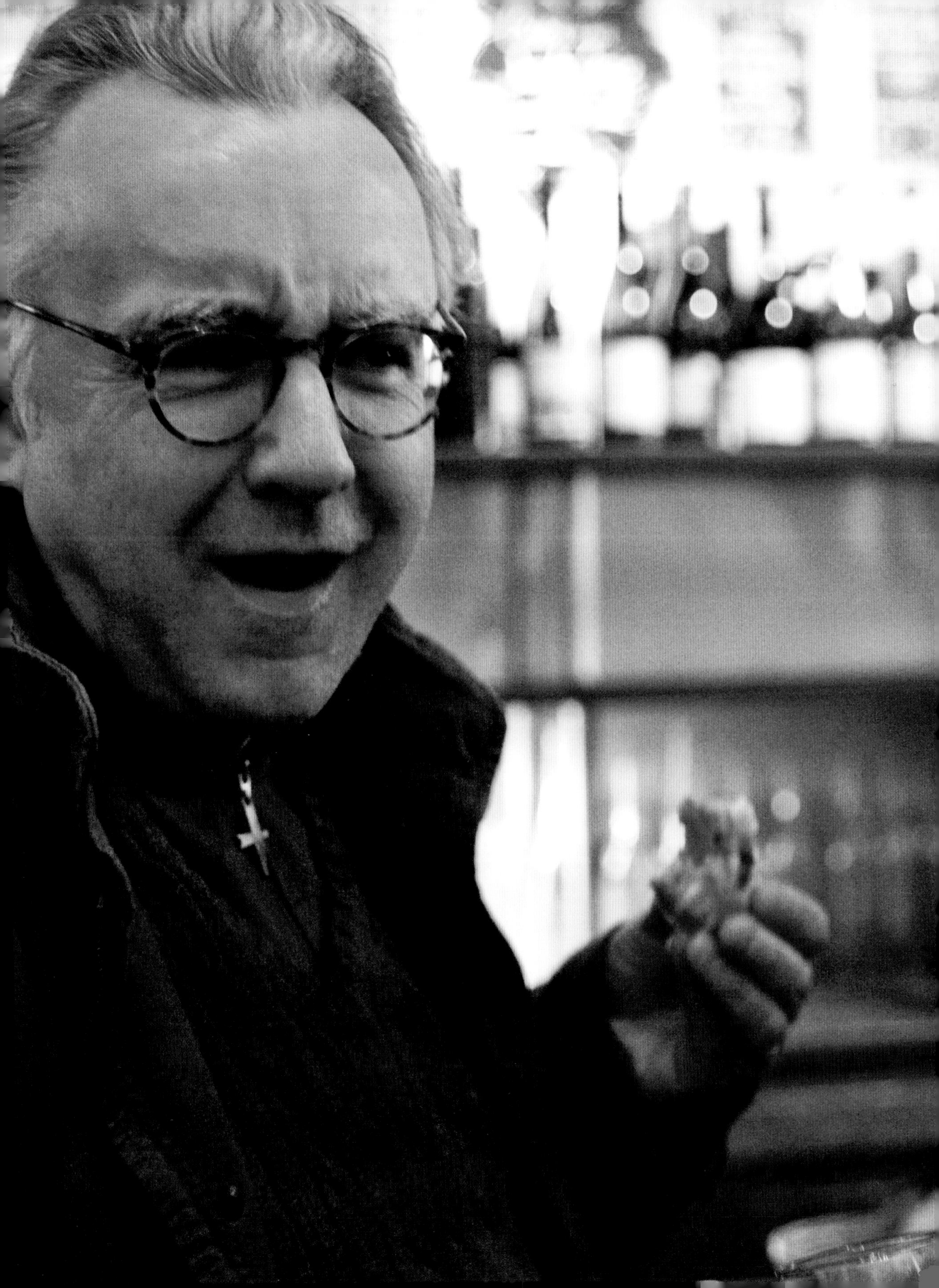

CONTENTS

Paris will always be Paris	11
Paris: Home to the regions	297
Paris: Where the world meets	399
Paris, sweet Paris	515
Index & Acknowledgements	586

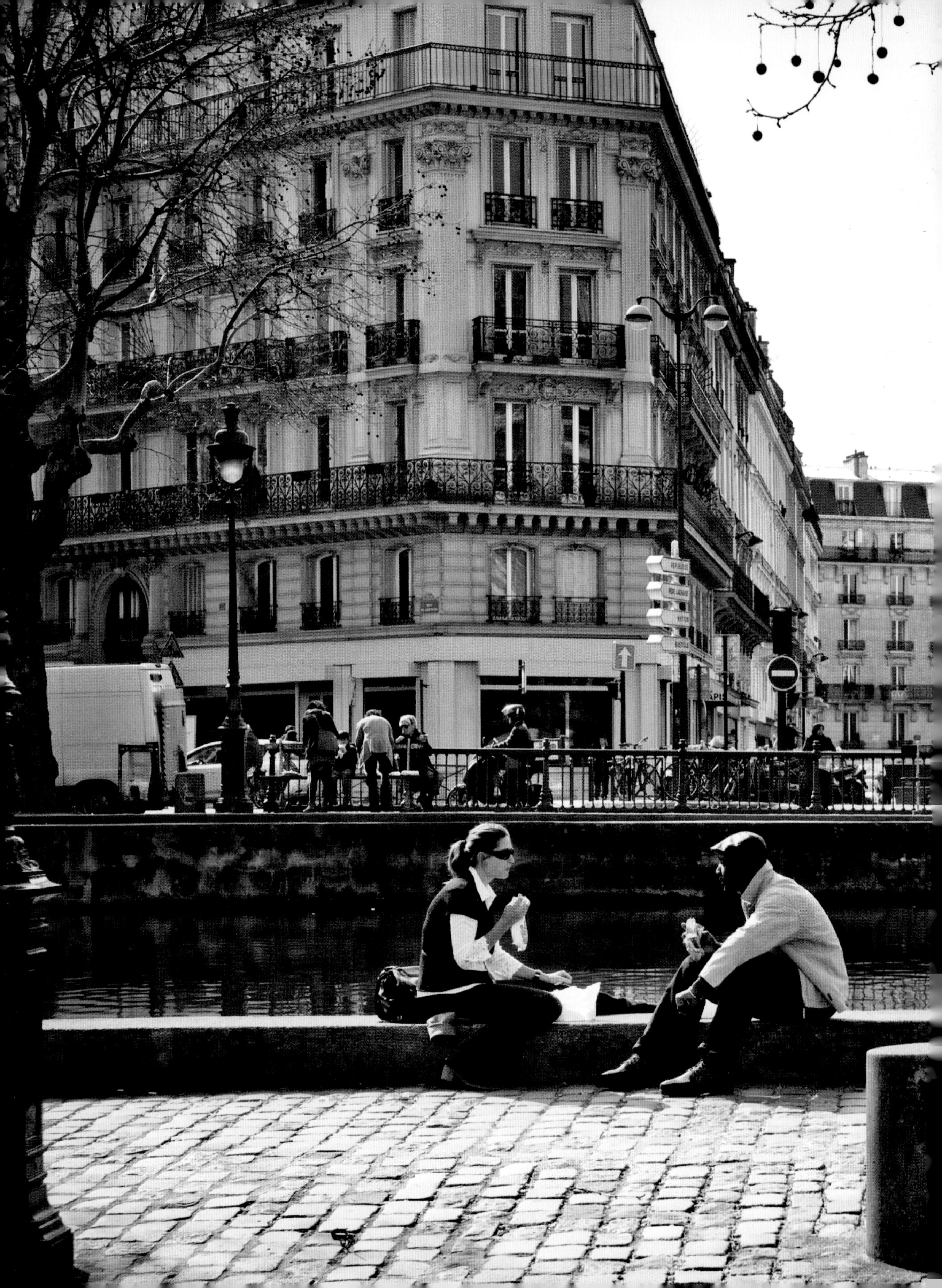

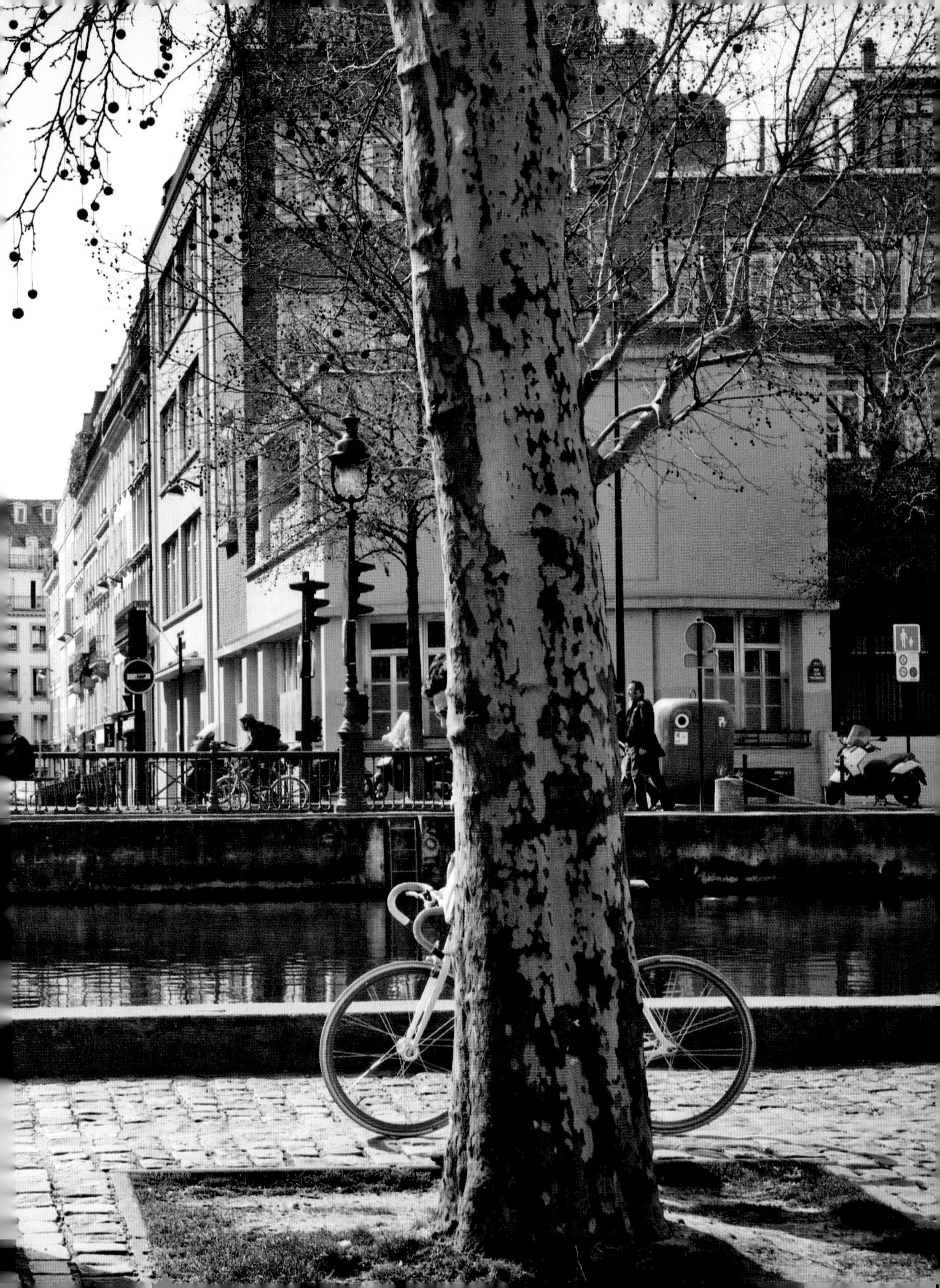

PARIS WILL ALWAYS BE PARIS

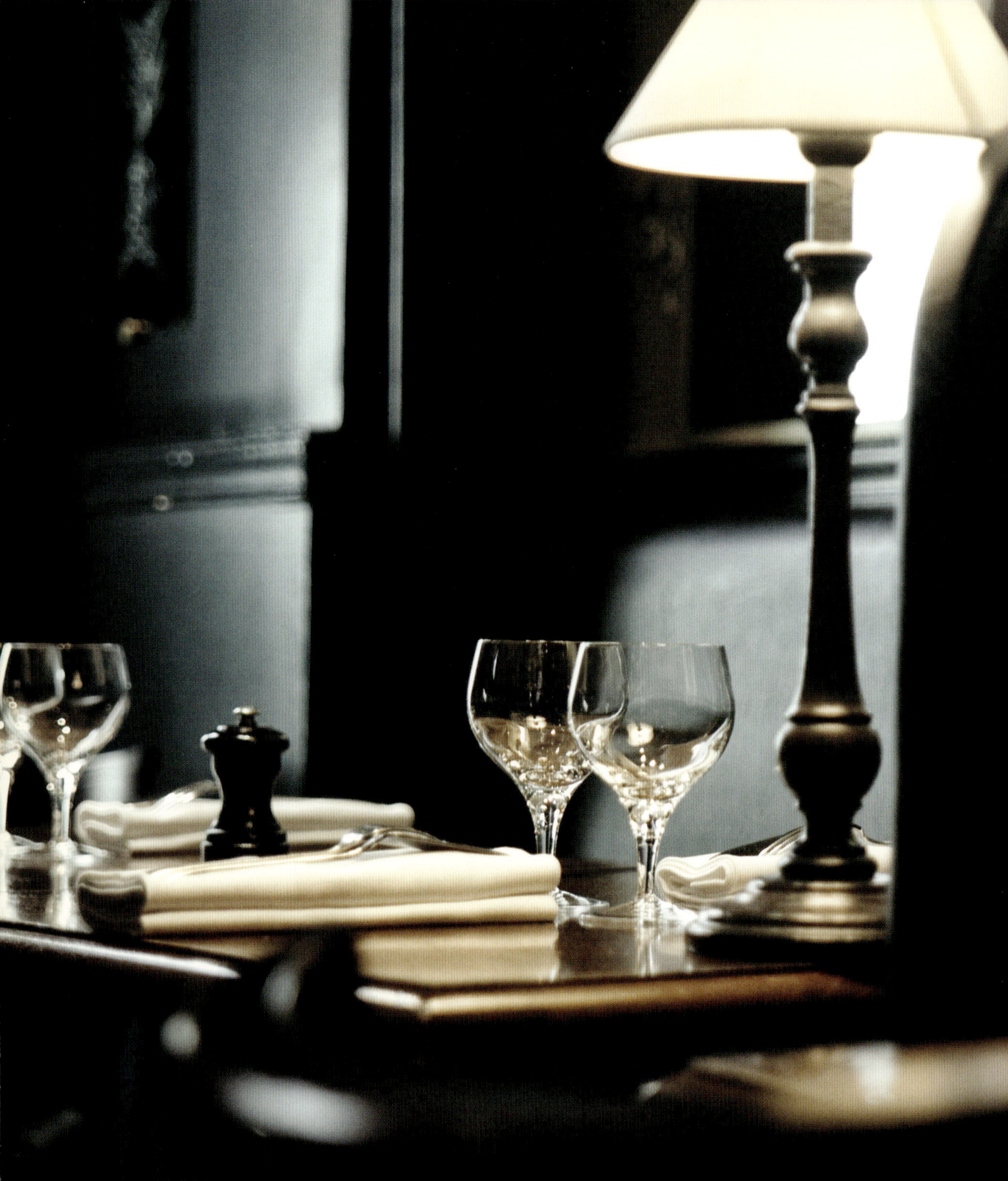

Mogettes à la boutargue 26
Tartare de bar et saumon 25
Hareng cousu main 13
Sardines confites Achards 20
Tartare de haddock, bacon 26
Soupe de poissons et crustacés 20
Émincé de haddock huile tomates confites 20
Lentilles à la Corse 22

Bar de ligne au sel 48
Fish & chips bacon & egg 36
Pasta Supions au noir 34
Sole poêlée, beurre salé
Haddock, œuf à cheval, bacon 38
Goujonnettes de joues de lotte curry Safran 37

21

As you eat, your eye is drawn to the jars of homemade preserves lining the big wall. But they aren't jams. They are Basque-style tuna fillets, vegetable relishes and lobster oil, and fresh sardines in olive oil in beautiful black tins with silver lettering. This restaurant is run by Paul Michelli, who is truly inventive with fish. On the menu that day were mogette beans with bottarga, sea bass and salmon tartare and *main cousu* ('hand-stitched') herring, followed by fish and chips with bacon and egg, pasta with small cuttlefish in its ink, monkfish cheek goujonettes and saffron curry. On the table was a copy of *Le Phare de Ré*, the newspaper 'of local interest with advertisements and miscellaneous notices', a souvenir from the island where the chef opened his first restaurant.

J'aime Paris

21 / 21 rue Mazarine / Paris VI

- 15

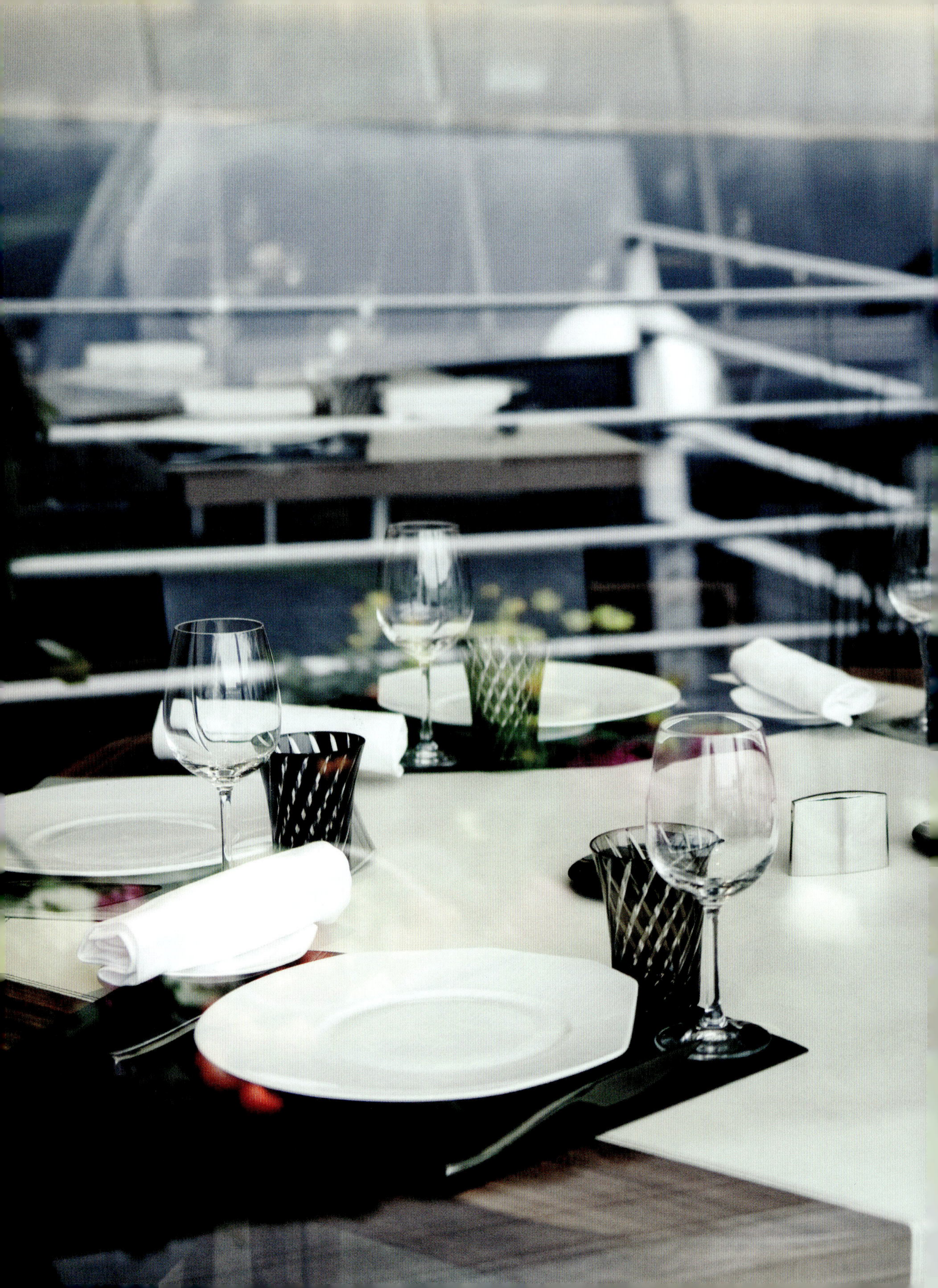

39 V / 39 avenue George V / Paris VIIIe

39V

'Above all, 39V is a wonderful story of harmony. I wanted to gather together in this place the ingredients to make my recipe for happiness: love, involvement, humanity, good humour, conversation, sharing, discipline, beauty, sensuality, respect... and to put hospitality back into the heart of our daily preoccupations, both in the dining room and the kitchen. Located at the centre of the triangle d'or and hidden away under the rooftops of Paris, 39V is a haven of peace that offers genuine and simple cuisine. Good produce is the result of a perfect agreement between nature and people who find inspiration in her...'

Frédéric Vardon

PARIS WILL ALWAYS BE PARIS / J'aime Paris

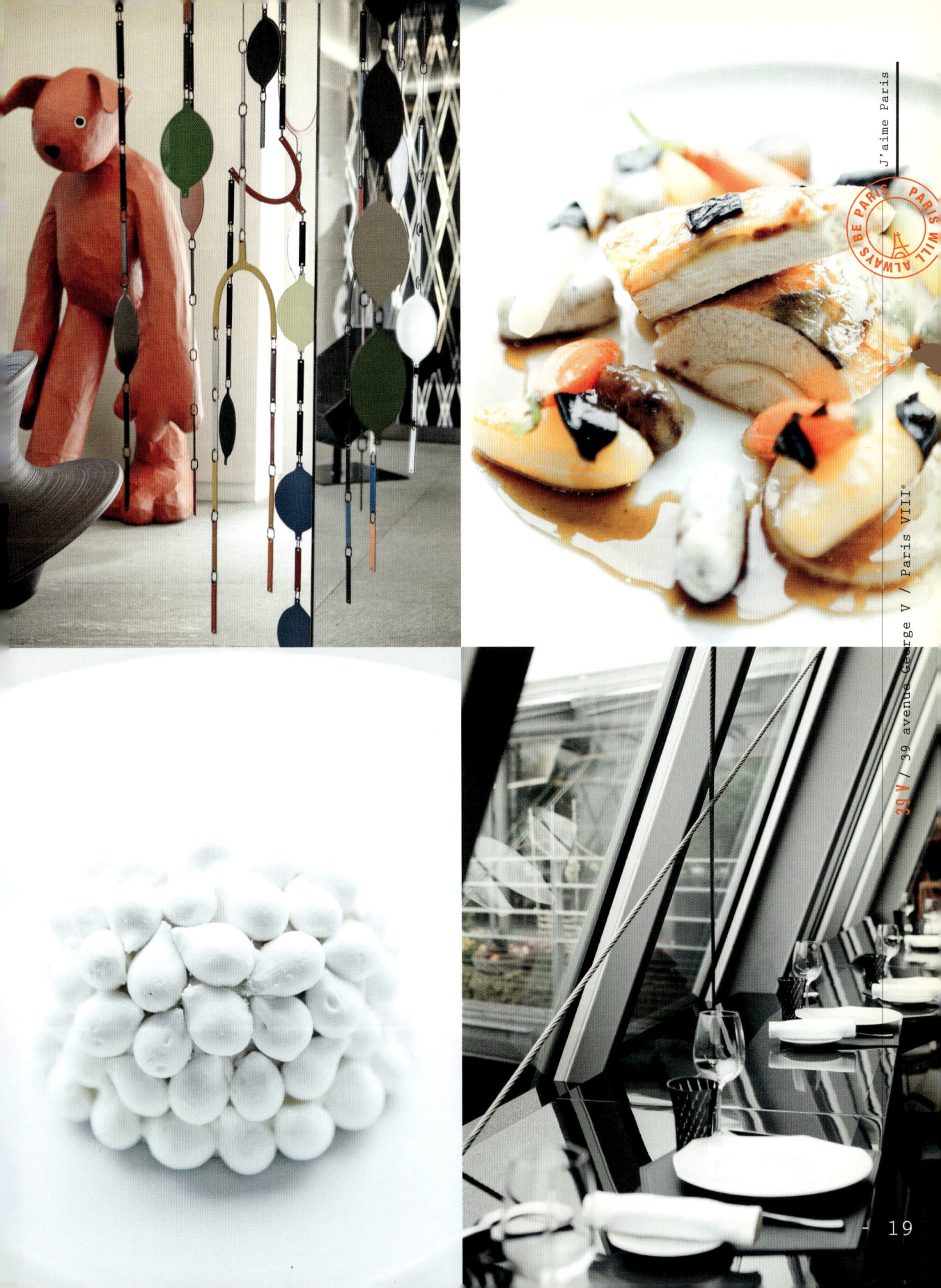

39 V / 39 avenue George V / Paris VIII⁰

19

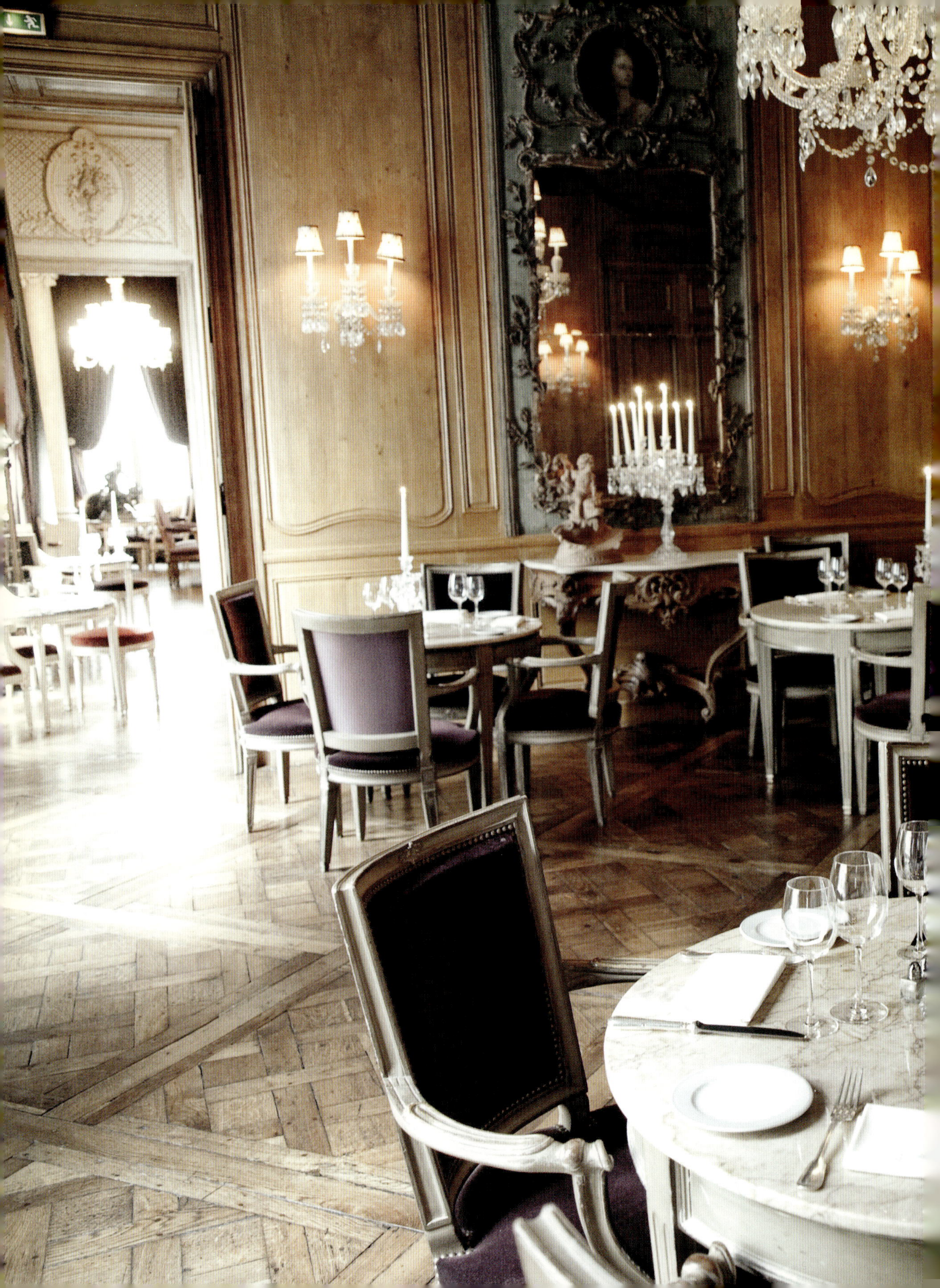

1728 / 8 rue d'Anjou / Paris VIIIe

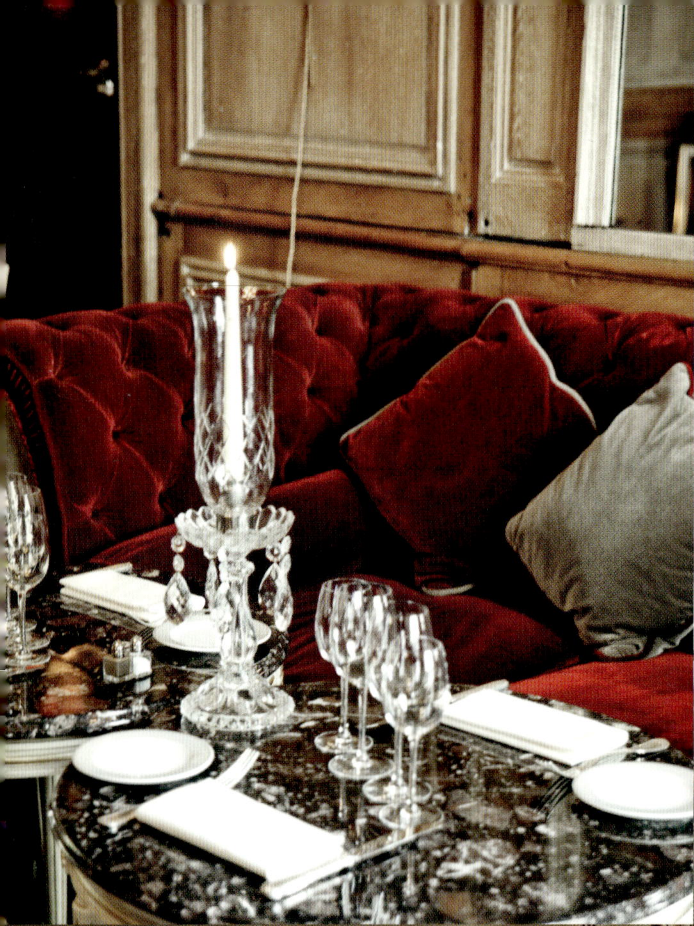
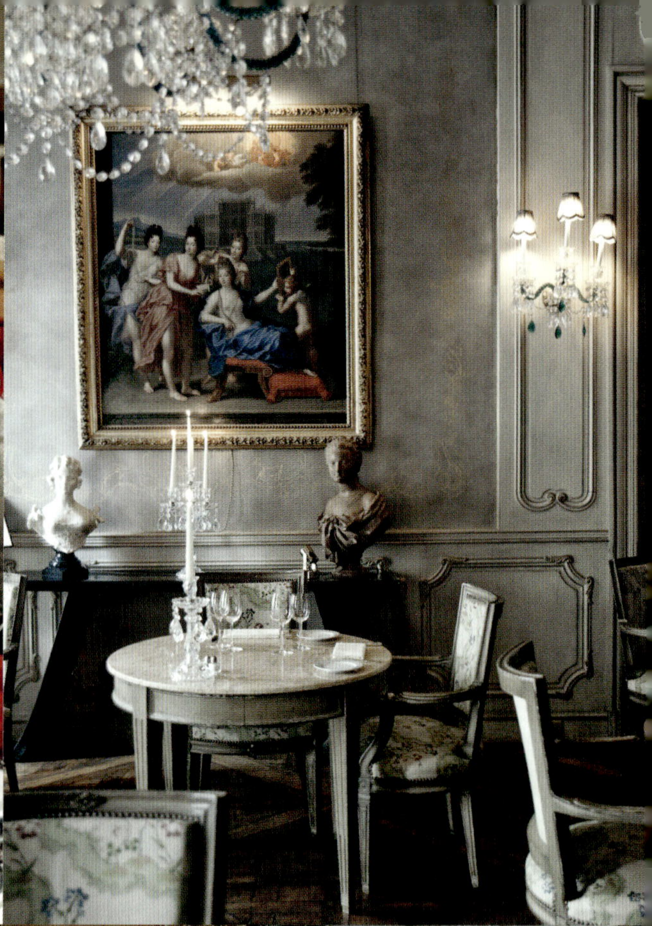
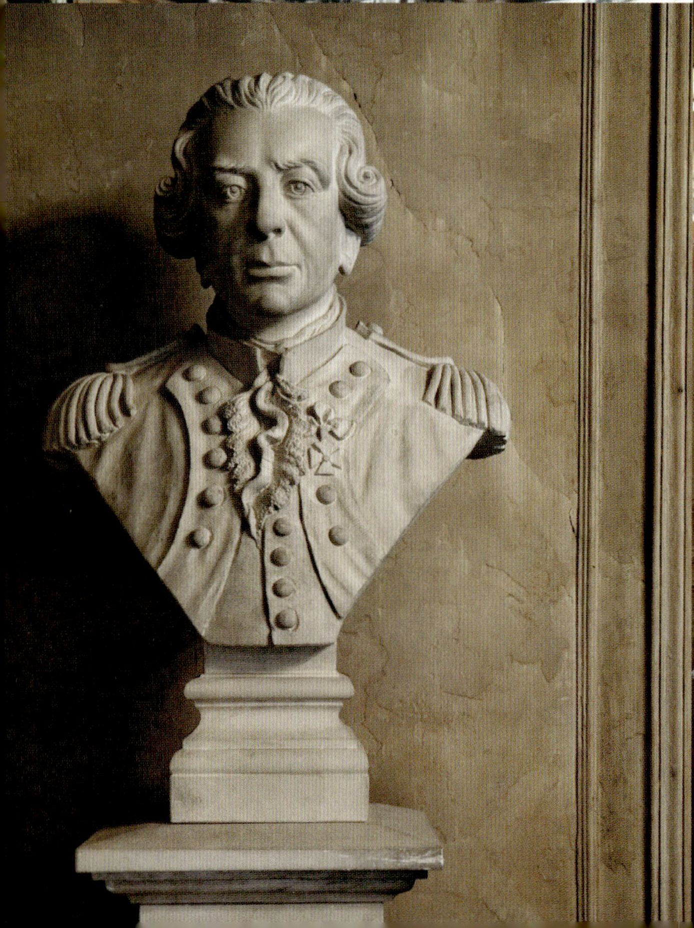
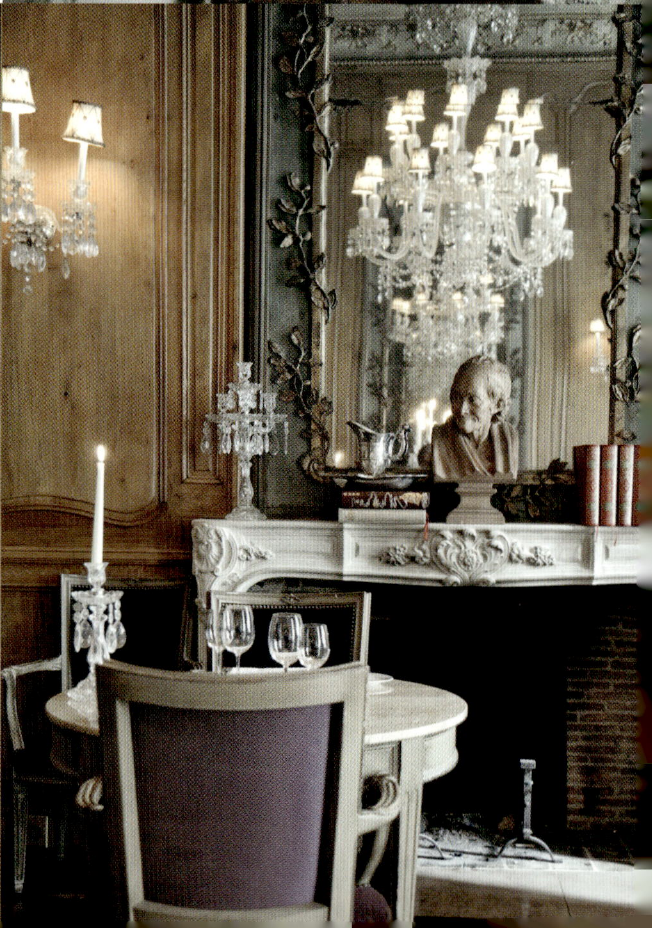

1728

Lafayette lived in this house and Madame de Pompadour held court here. The Asian-inspired cuisine served in the small and adorably quaint Trois Ors room is somewhat unusual but refreshingly different. More classic is the elegant tea menu, with pastries by Arnaud Larher, a disciple of Pierre Hermé.

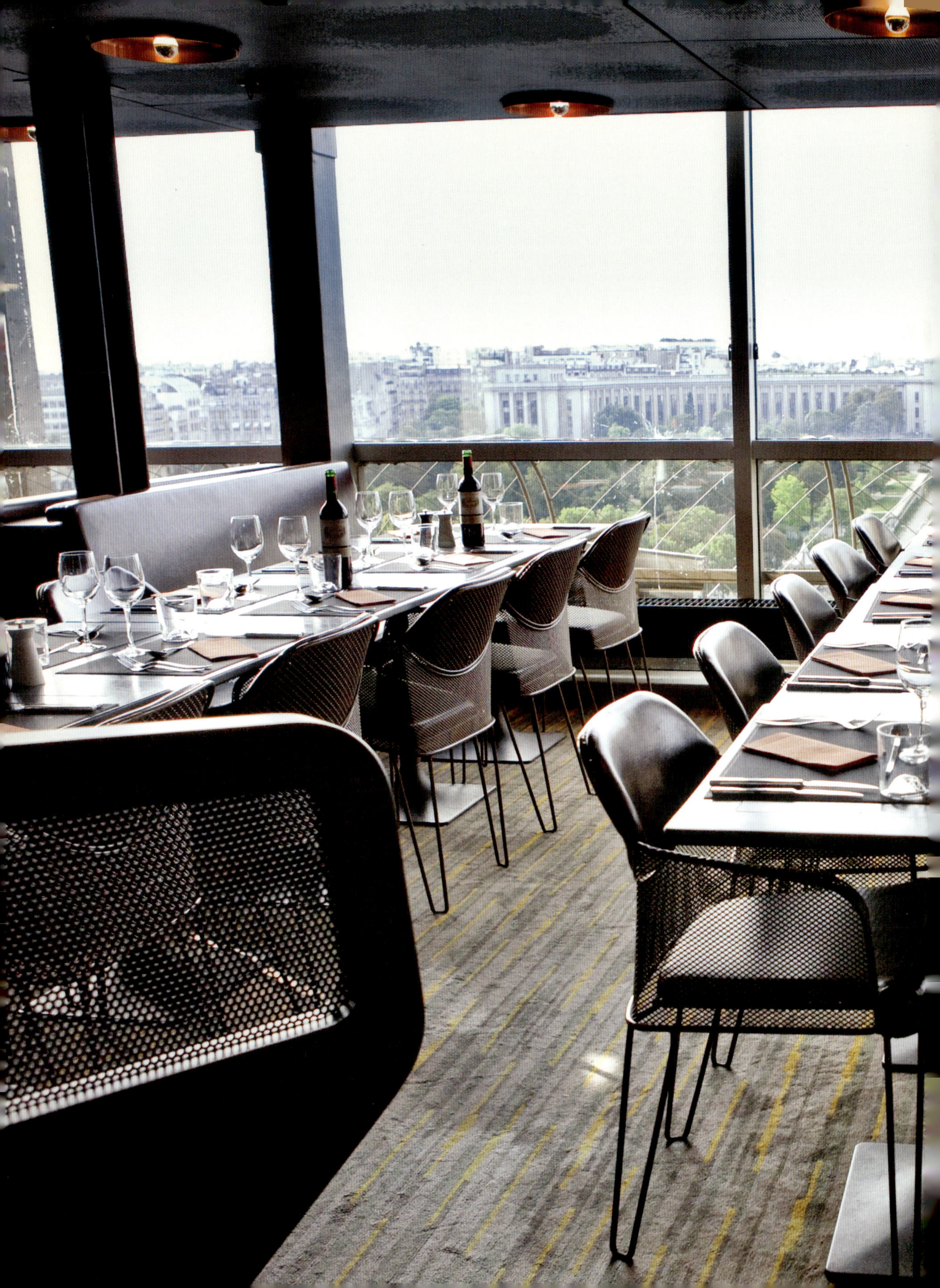

58 TOUR EIFFEL / 6 avenue Gustave Eiffel / Paris VII

J'aime Paris · PARIS WILL ALWAYS BE PARIS

58 TOUR EIFFEL

The giant sundial on the Champs de Mars tells you it's midday — time for a picnic on level one of the Eiffel Tower with all of Paris at your feet. Start with a cool drink in the sunny open-air bar and enjoy the view over the Chaillot Hill. Then head for the kitchen — your picnic basket awaits. When evening falls, feast on iced pea velouté or marbré de canard, a sautéed veal rib chop or beef fillet, and vacherin du jour or profiteroles. At night, Alain Soulard offers you a gastronomic experience 95 metres above the ground.

58 TOUR EIFFEL / 6 avenue Gustave Eiffel / Paris VIIe

J'aime Paris

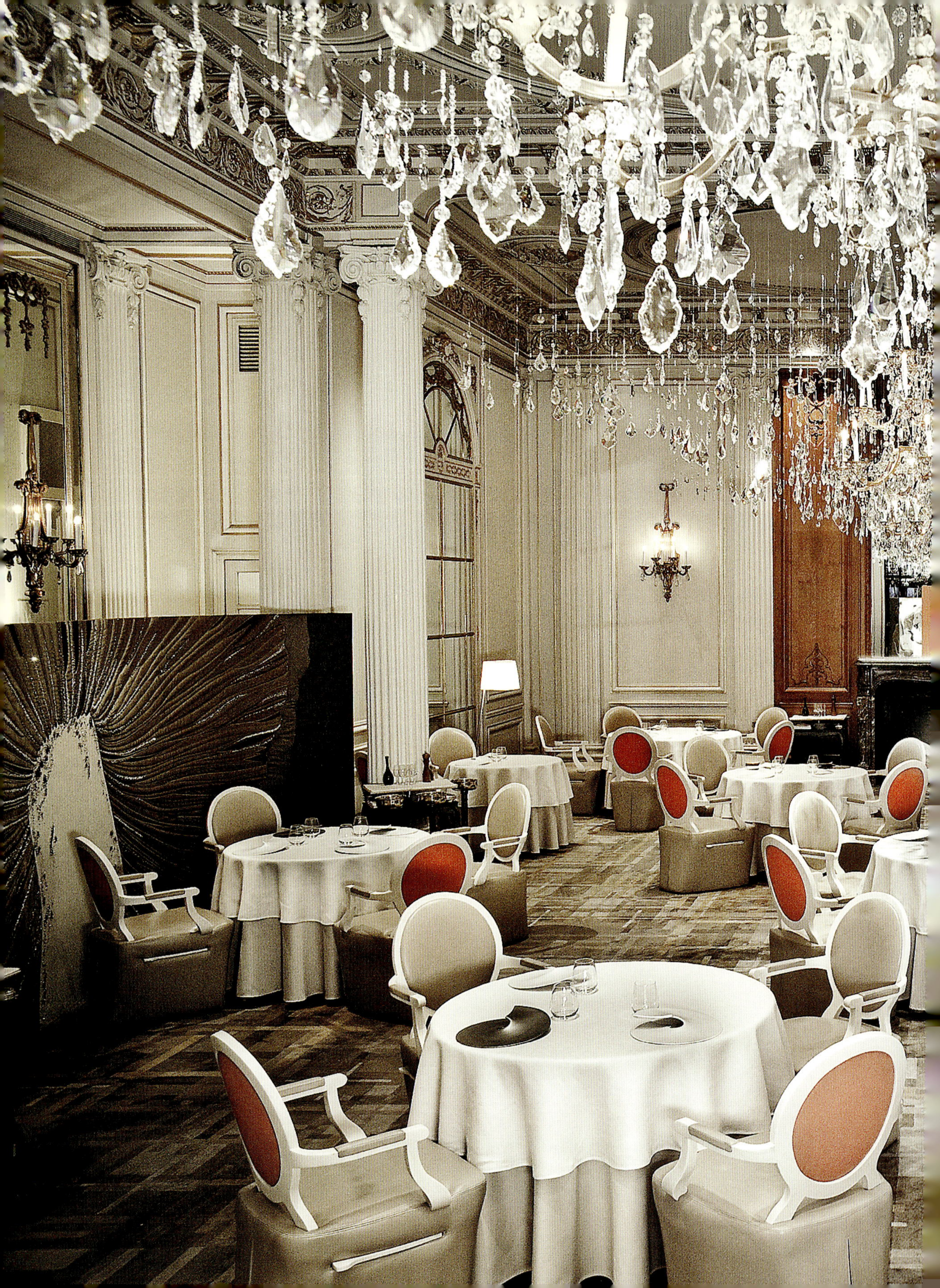

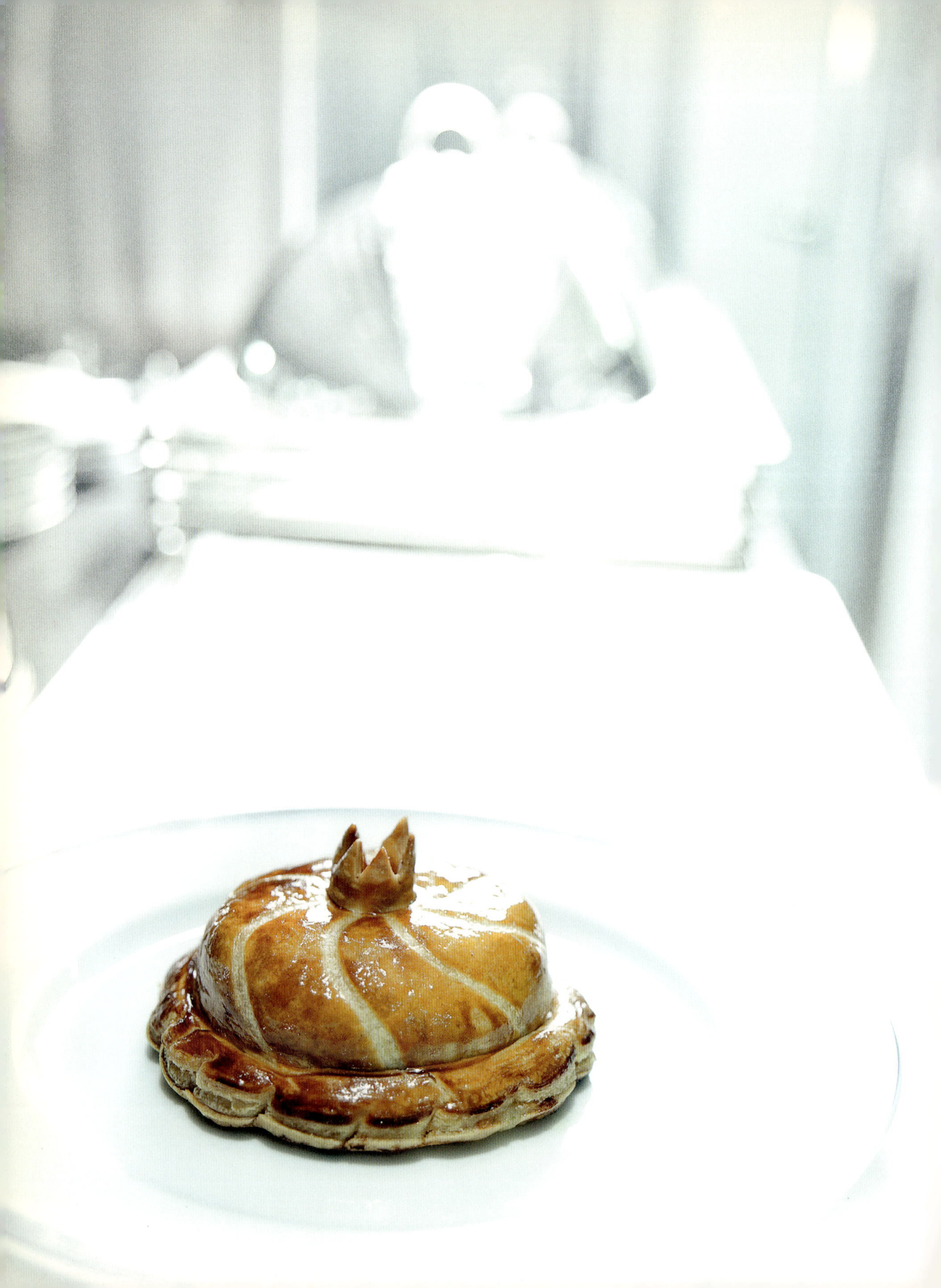

ALAIN DUCASSE AU PLAZA ATHÉNÉE / 25 avenue Montaigne / Paris VIIIe

J'aime Paris

- 31

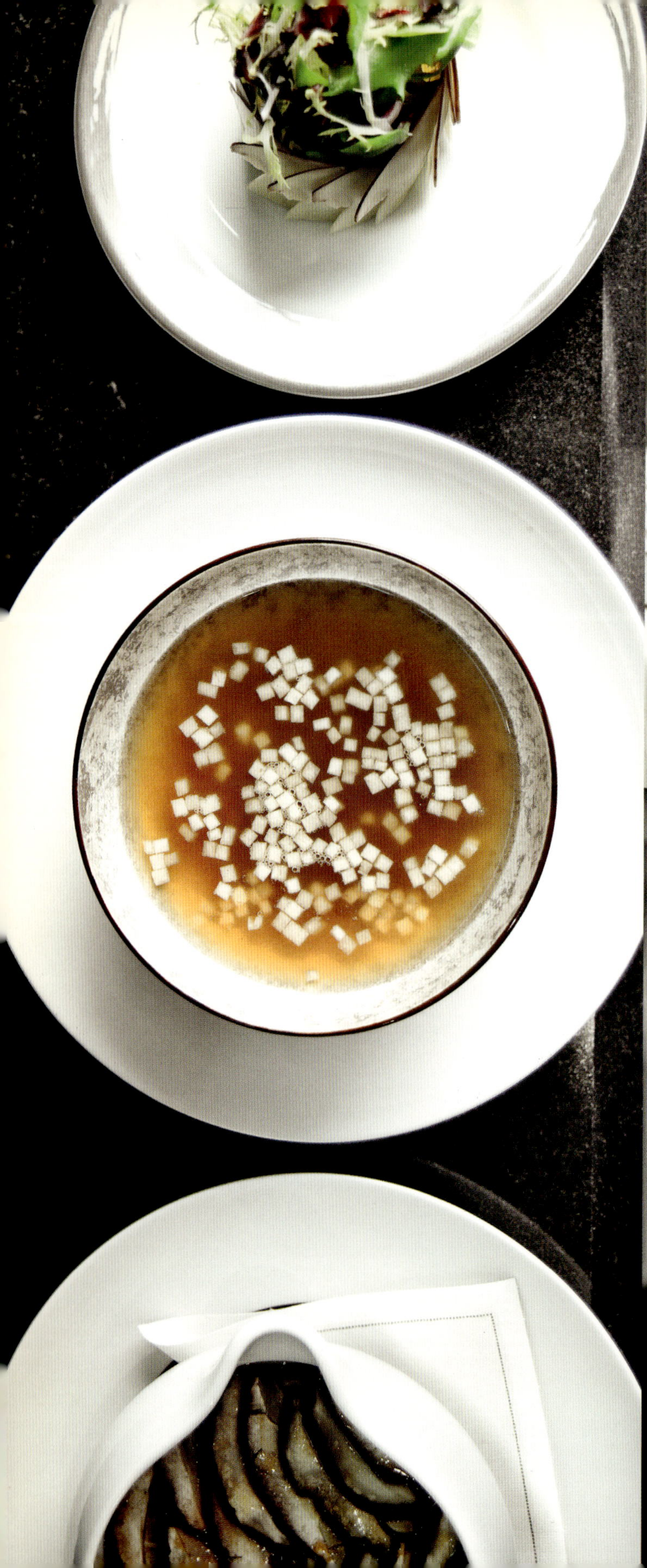

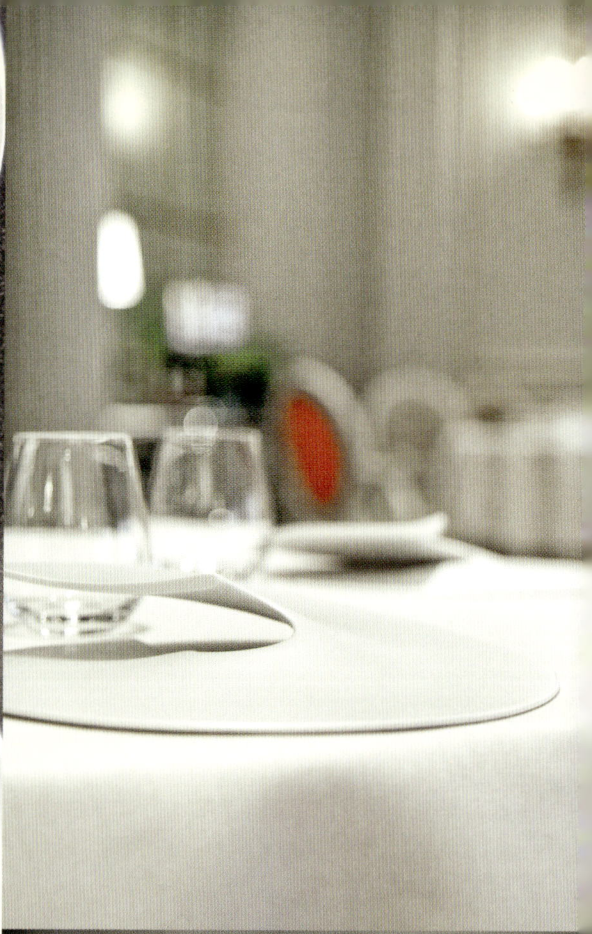

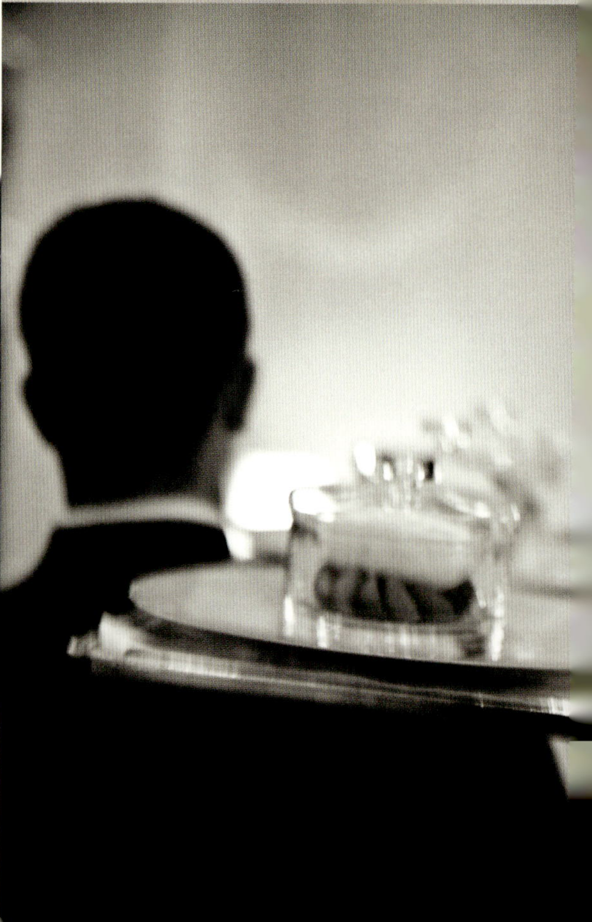

ALAIN DUCASSE AU PLAZA ATHÉNÉE / 25 avenue Montaigne / Paris VIIIe

J'aime Paris

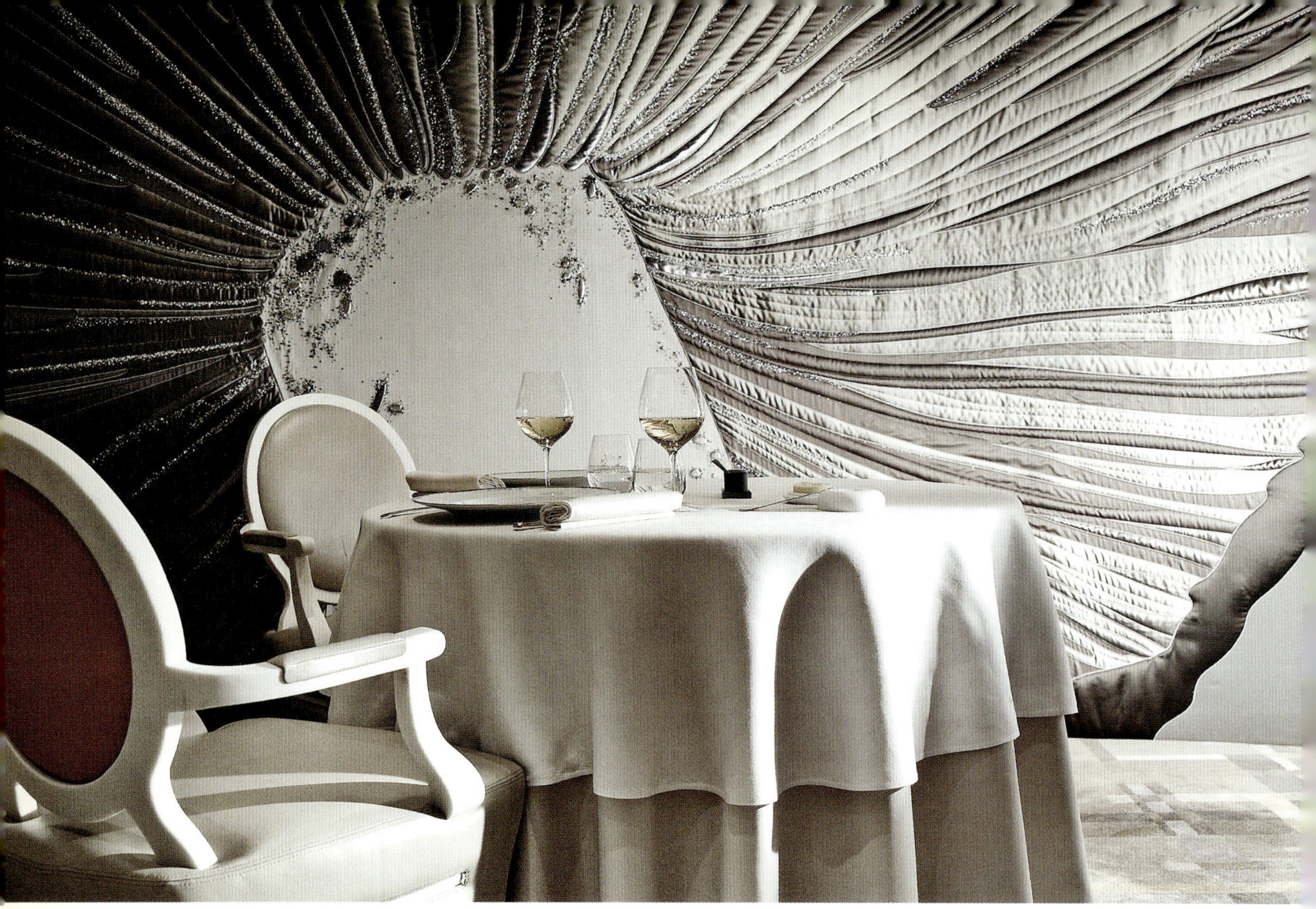

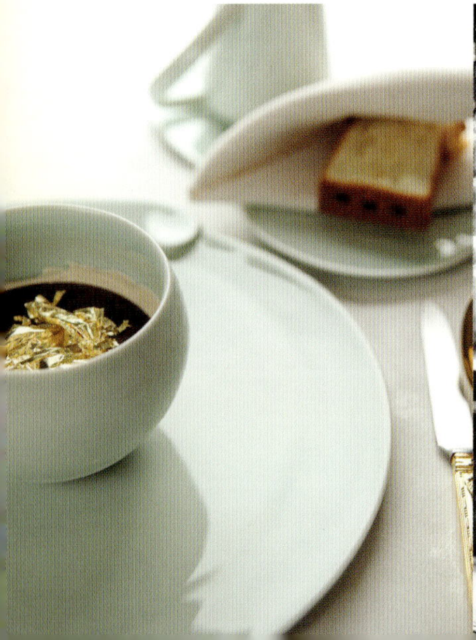

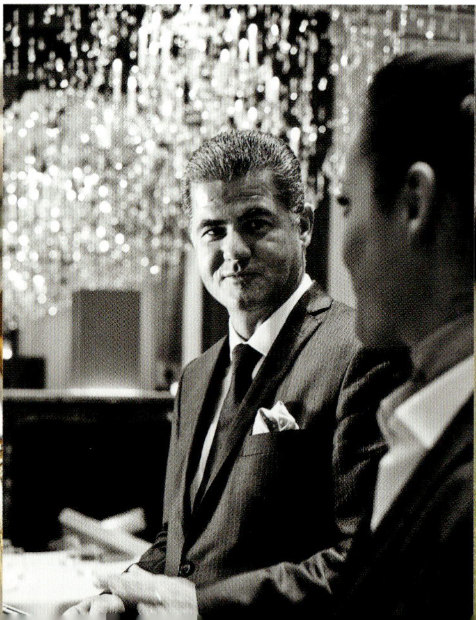

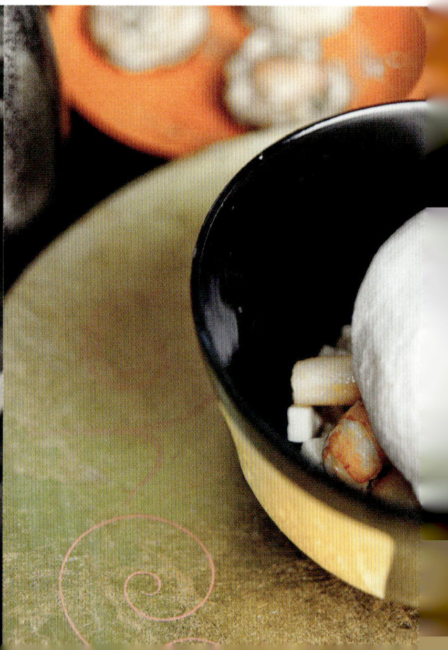

AD PA

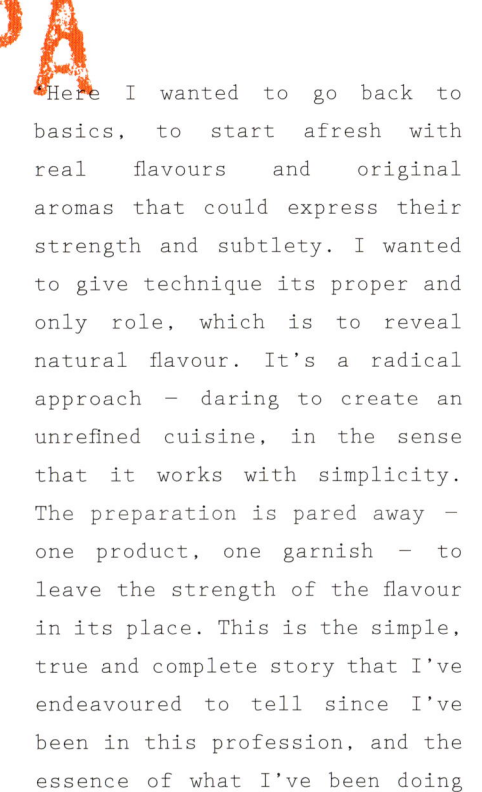

'Here I wanted to go back to basics, to start afresh with real flavours and original aromas that could express their strength and subtlety. I wanted to give technique its proper and only role, which is to reveal natural flavour. It's a radical approach — daring to create an unrefined cuisine, in the sense that it works with simplicity. The preparation is pared away — one product, one garnish — to leave the strength of the flavour in its place. This is the simple, true and complete story that I've endeavoured to tell since I've been in this profession, and the essence of what I've been doing at the Plaza Athénée, aided by Christophe Saintagne.'

Alain Ducasse

ALAIN DUCASSE AU PLAZA ATHÉNÉE / 25 avenue Montaigne / Paris VIIIe

J'aime Paris

ALFRED

A few steps down from the Palais Royal gardens is the establishment run by William Abitbol, where the charm can be felt the moment you tread the metal staircase, reminiscent of the Eiffel Tower. You are suspended, as if seated in the dress circle at the Opéra. The golden light shining through an old lampshade gives a soft glaze to the Gauloise chicken and the gilthead bream tartare with purslane. Though simple in appearance, each vegetable on the large plate is prepared differently to respect its individual flavour. The food is market-fresh every day, but the chocolate mousse is timeless.

ALFRED / 52 rue de Richelieu / Paris I⁽ᵉʳ⁾

J'aime Paris

- 37

On peut
APPORTER
son MANG

L'ASSIETTE / 181 rue du Château / Paris XIVe

J'aime Paris

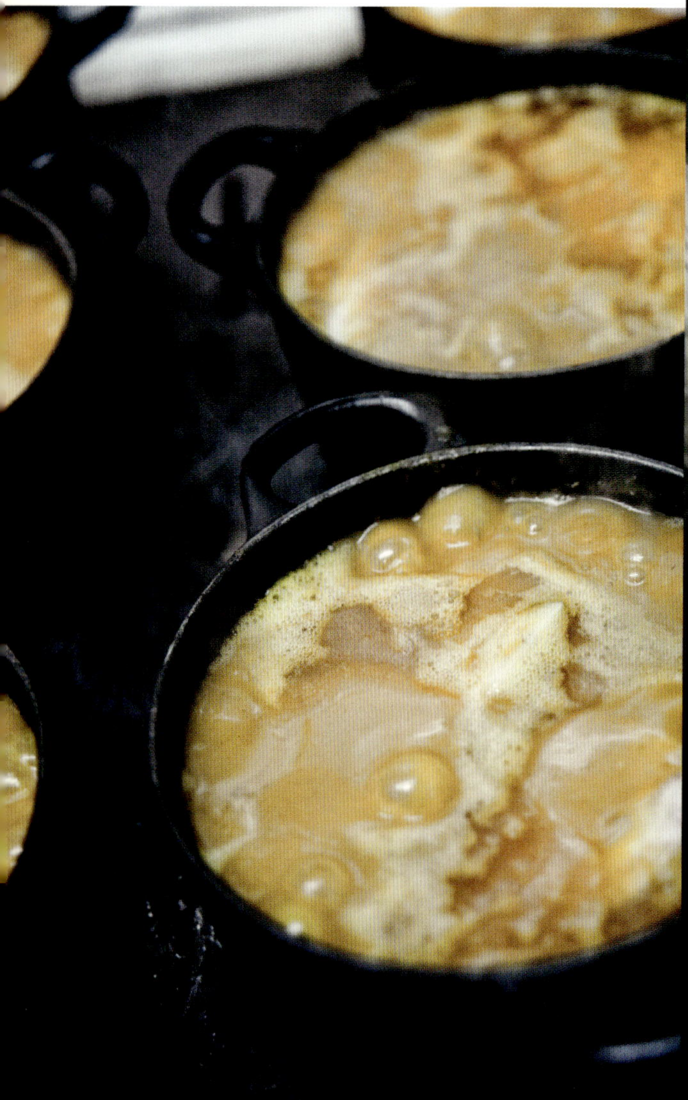
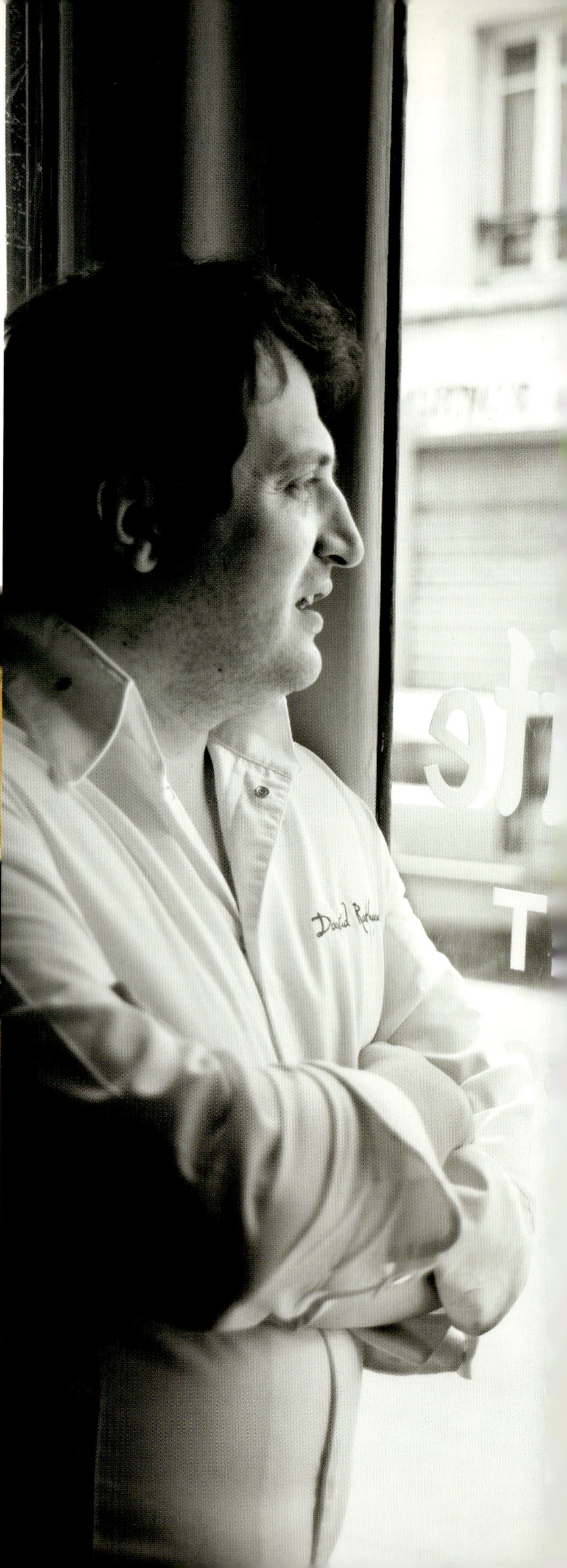

L'ASSIETTE

Alain Ducasse: David, after so many years by my side, I'm happy to see the success you're having with your bistro. Taking over from Lulu must have been a challenge. What are you going to let us try today?

David Rathgeber: My *sauté gourmand*: veal sweetbreads, crayfish, wild mushrooms and warm foie gras. I do large sweetbread escalopes in a *beurre mousseux*. I add the crayfish, the Saint George's mushrooms and a few asparagus tips. Then I deglaze with cognac. I cover lightly with the Nantua sauce before adding the foie gras escalopes, the *fleur de sel* and a good sprinkling of pepper... *À table!*

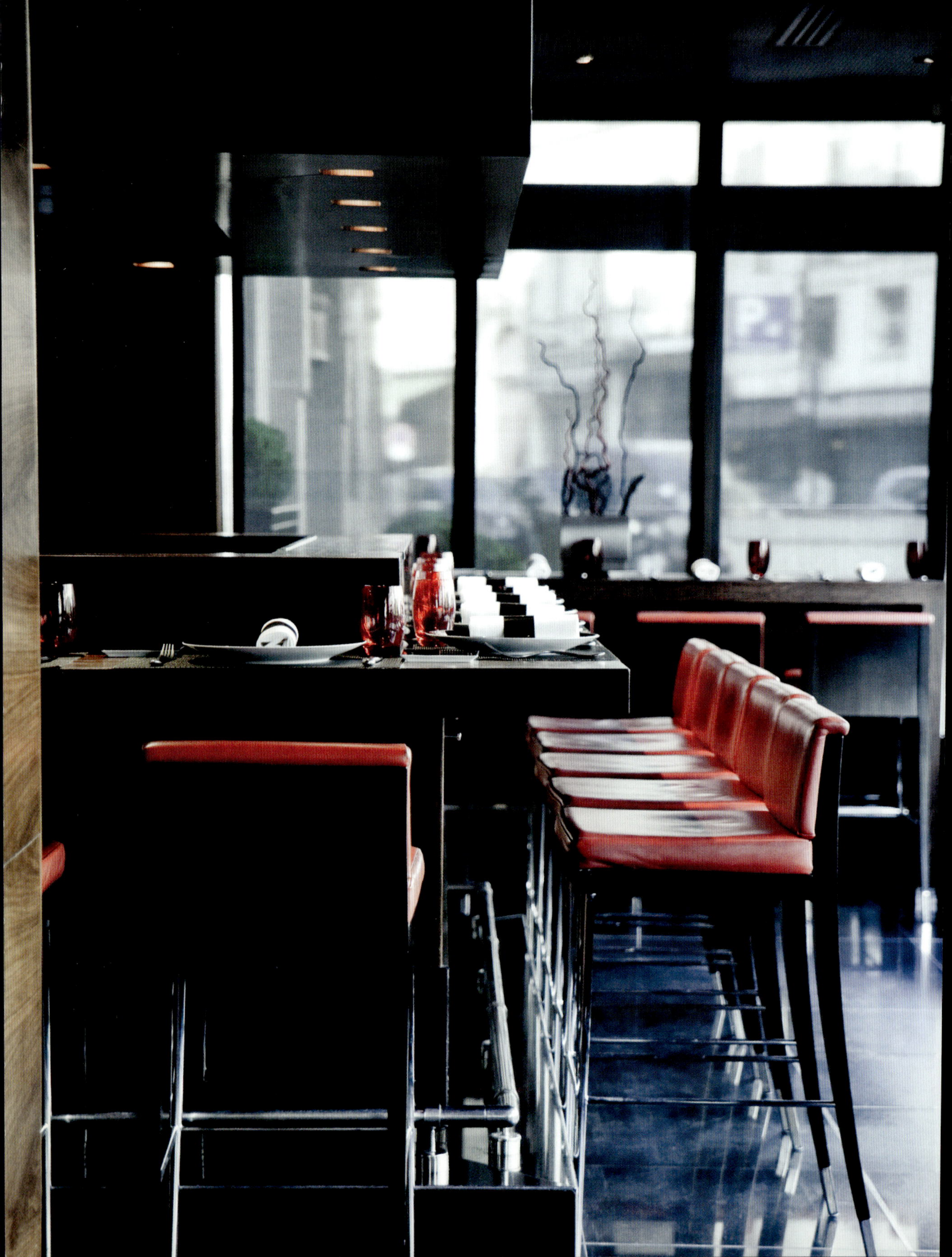

L'ATELIER DE JOËL ROBUCHON / 5 rue de Montalembert / Paris VIIe

43

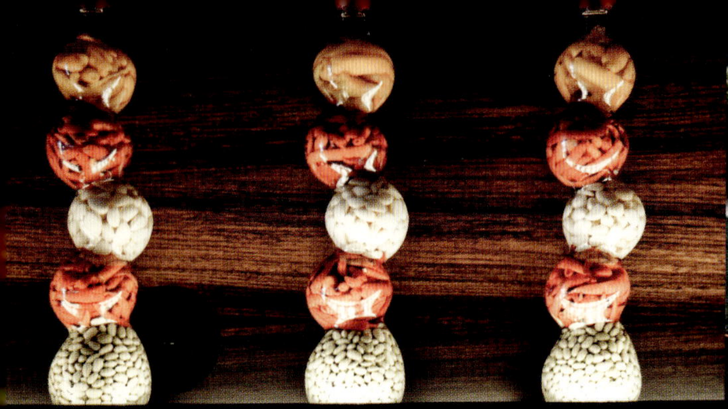
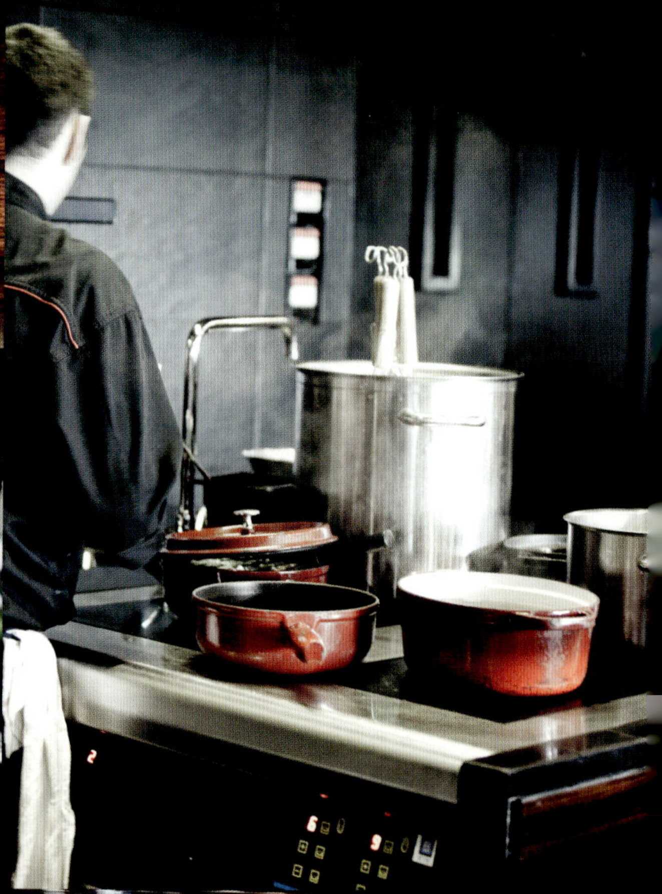
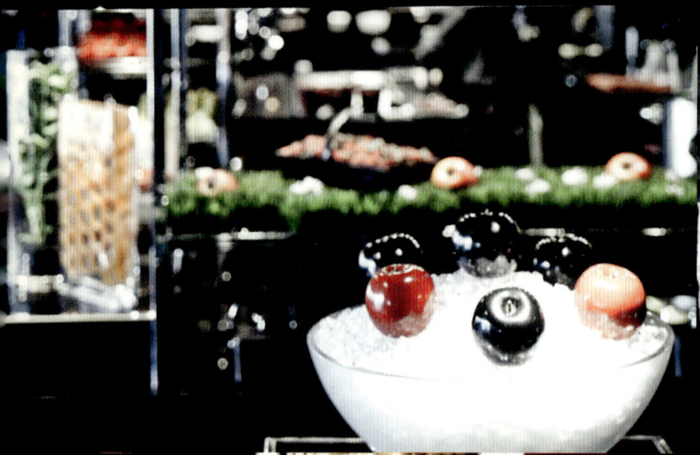
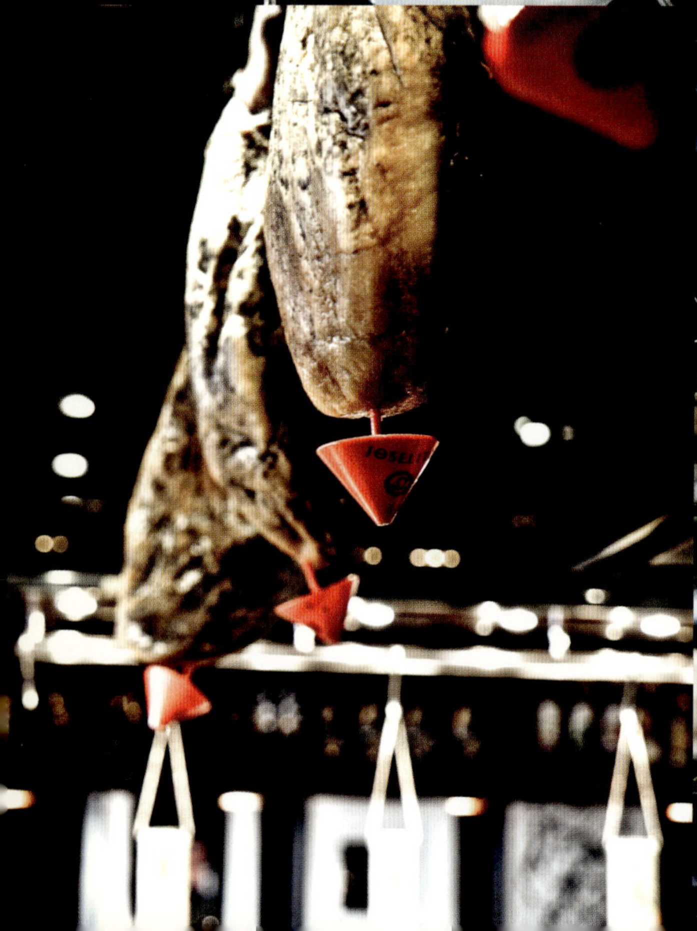
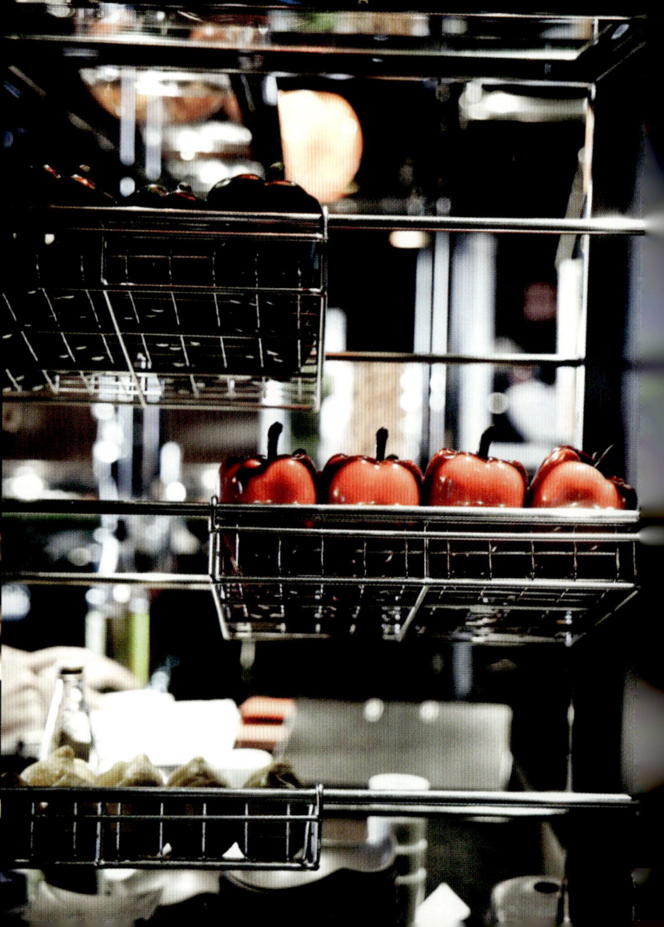

ATELIER JOËL ROBUCHON

'I've been working with Robuchon since 1982. When he wanted to create a new restaurant concept, in 2003, he naturally joined forces with his main associates. First, we didn't want to work under pressure, and, above all, we wanted to be physically closer to our patrons, which is why we have this open kitchen. The way the kitchen works has also evolved. We always use quality produce, reared or harvested directly by our suppliers, and prepared with great simplicity. Today we welcome our guests as friends; it's our finest reward.'

Éric Lecerf

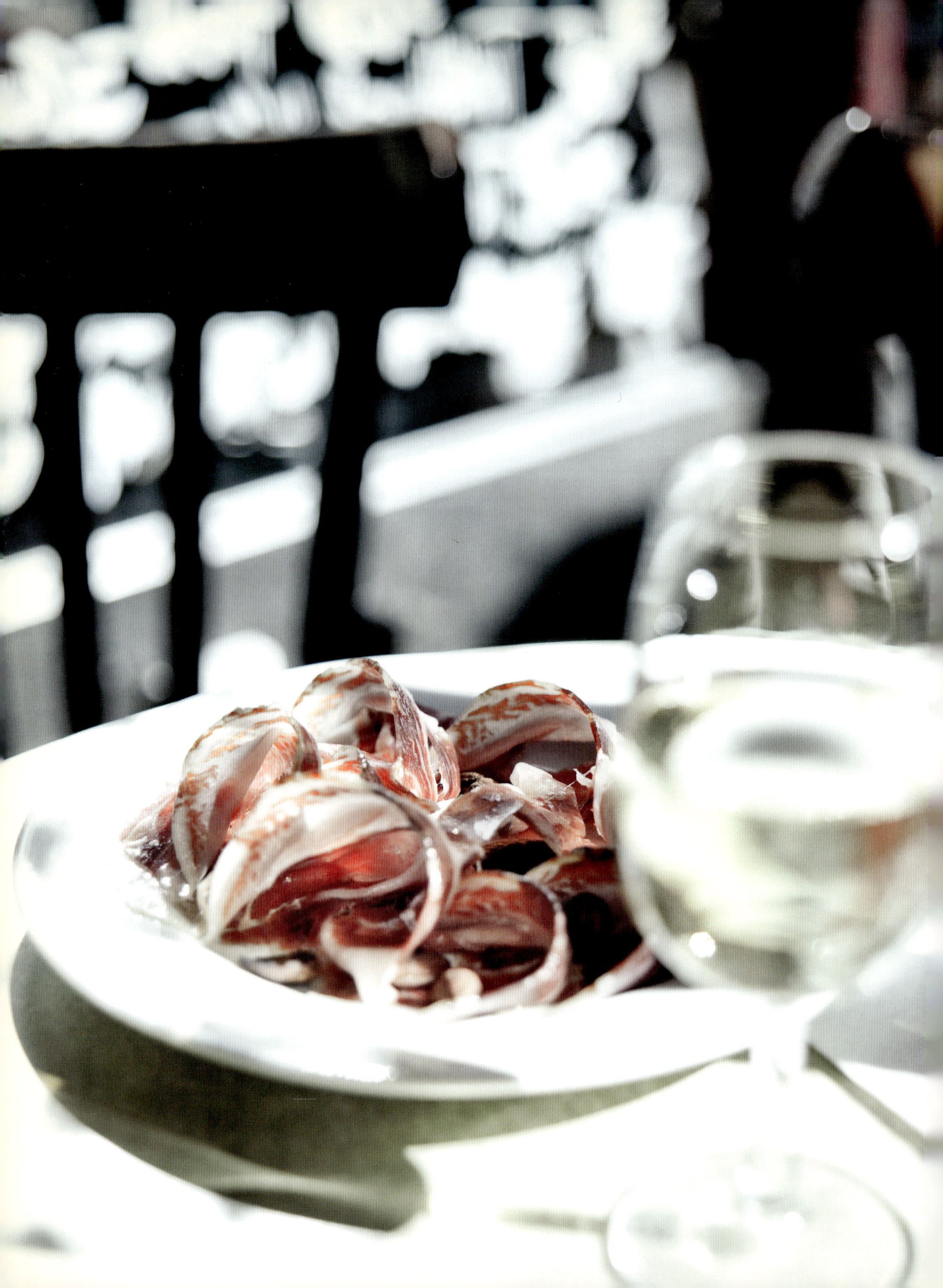

AUX DEUX AMIS / 45 rue Oberkampf / Paris XI°

CAFE AUX DEUX AMIS COMPTOIR

AUX DEUX AMIS

Aux Deux Amis has been rejuvenated. While the décor hasn't changed, the menu has been updated. Quench your thirst with a glass of *vin nature* before sitting under the neon lights to enjoy the daily specials. There is no need to make things complex for them to be good; just enjoy the moment. Don't forget to have your last drink outside on the terrace and take in the buzzing street atmosphere!

AUX DEUX AMIS / 45 rue Oberkampf / Paris XIe

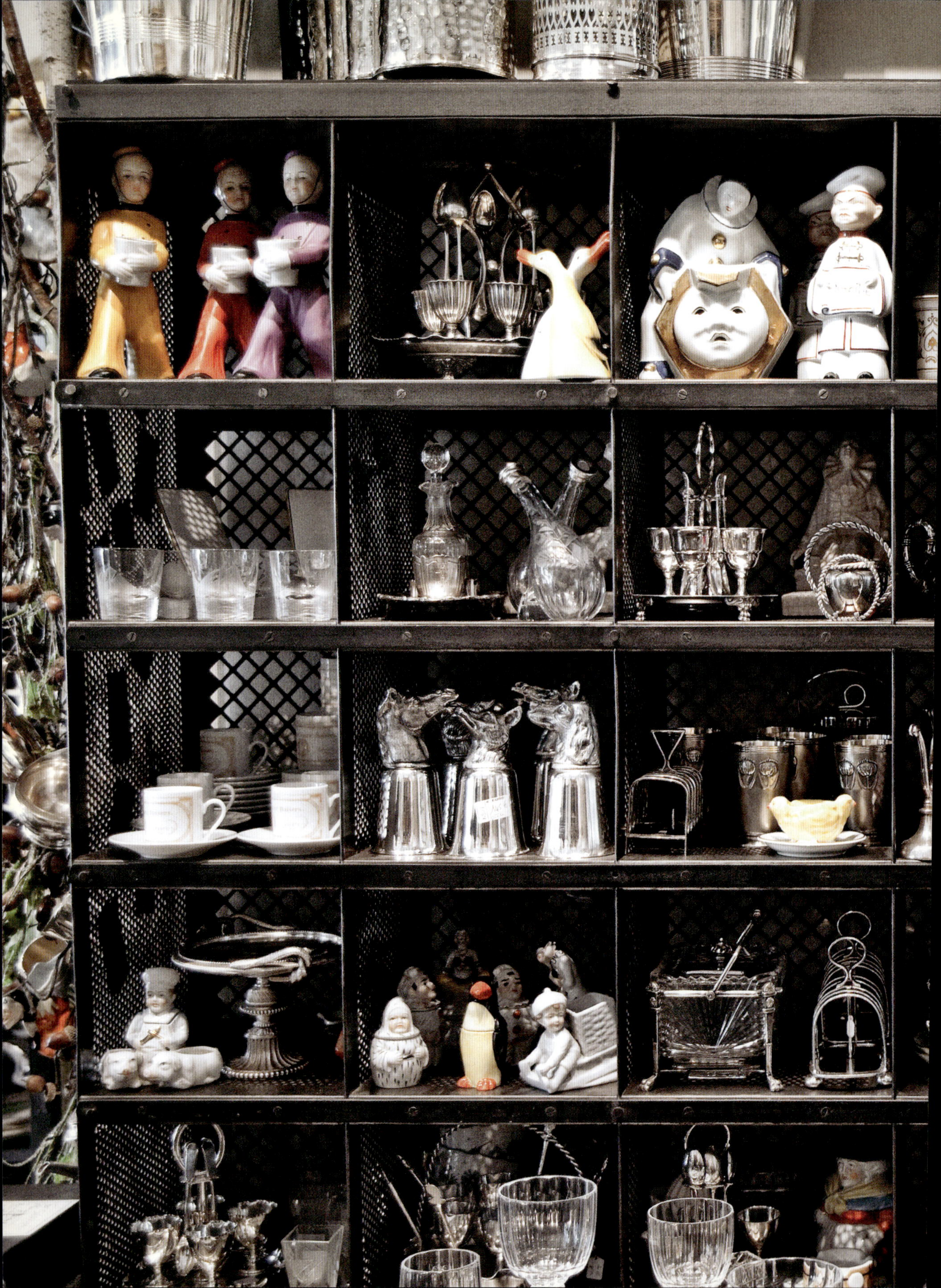

AU BAIN MARIE / 56 rue de l'Université / Paris VIIe J'aime Paris

- 51 -

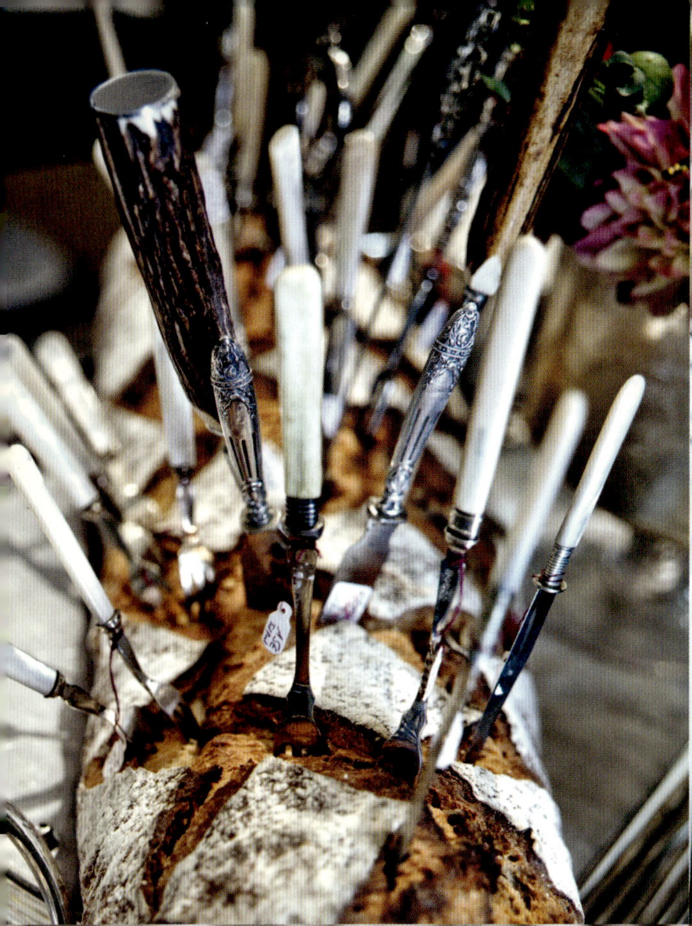
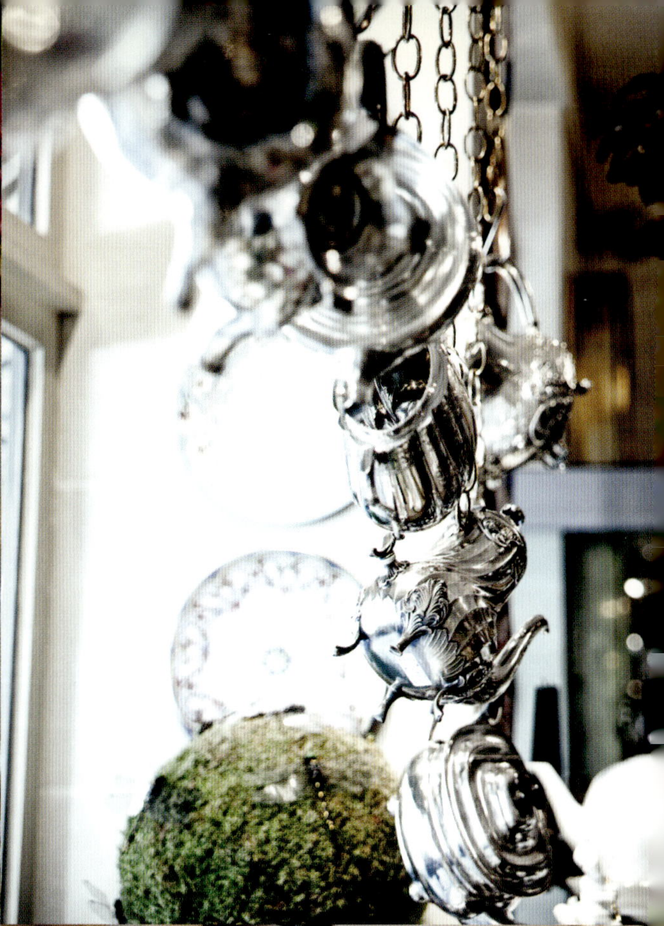
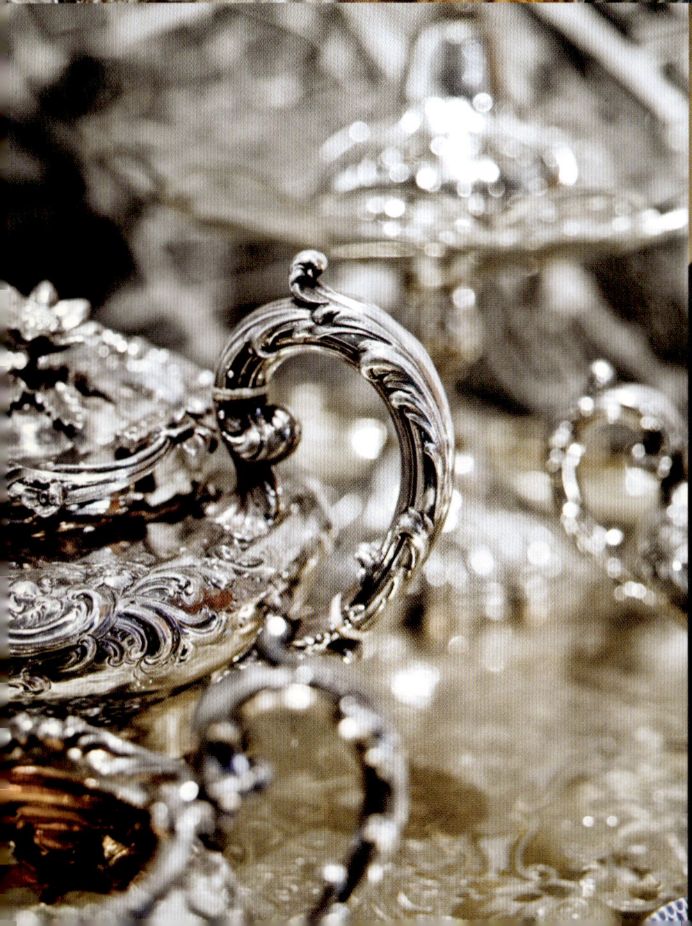
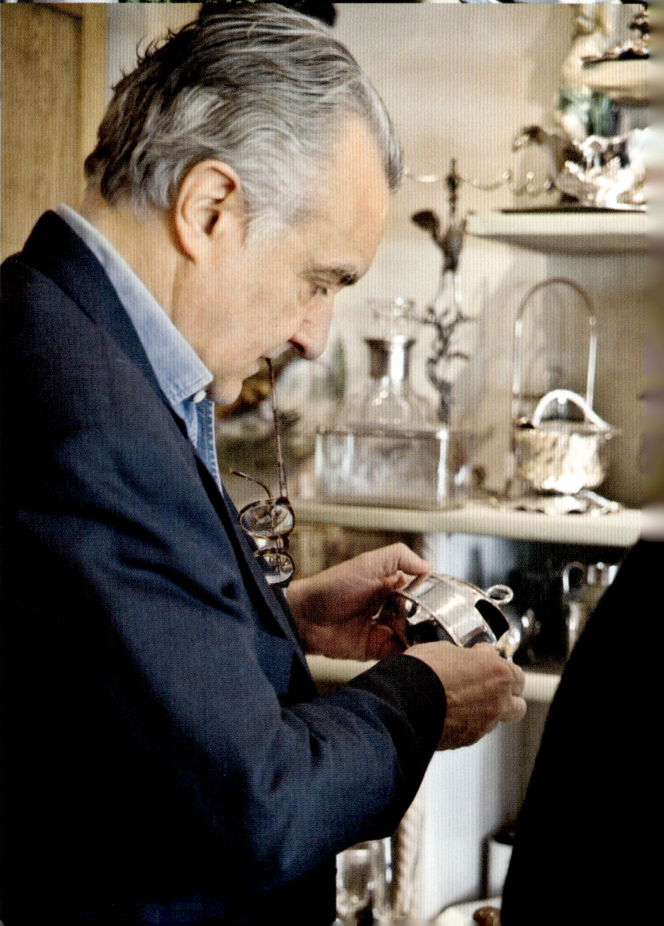

BAIN MARIE

AU BAIN MARIE / 56 rue de l'Université / Paris VIIe

An English duck press, the fine detail of a 1920s picnic case, a series of late 19th-century lemon-shaped bar citrus squeezers, an unusual ivory truffle grater... We're in the establishment run by Aude Clément, actually resembling the attic of a collector and traveller, where she has opened her chest full of extraordinary objects. With a flash of cloth, a genie is released from a soup tureen.

- 53

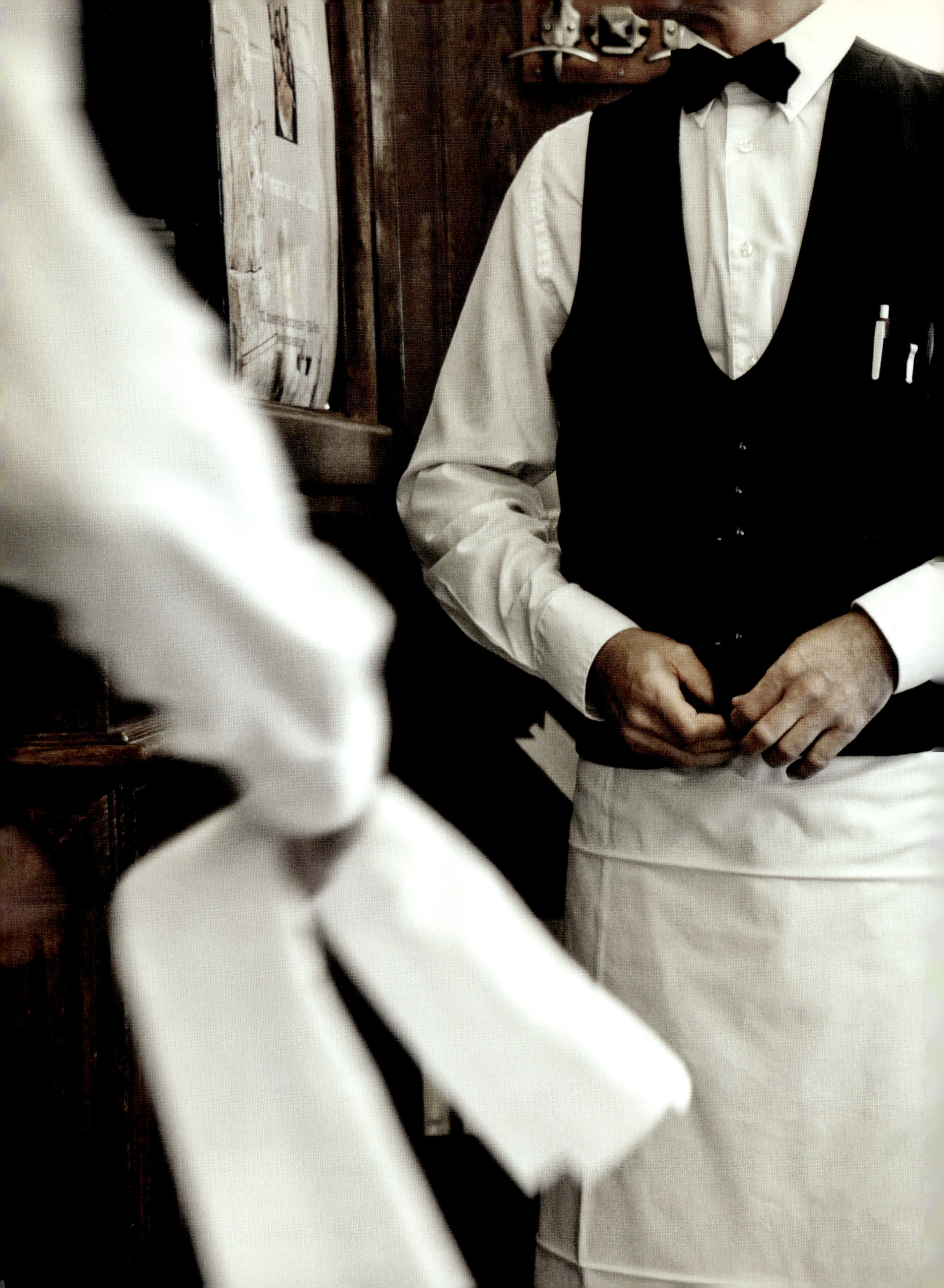

BALZAR / 49 rue des Écoles / Paris V

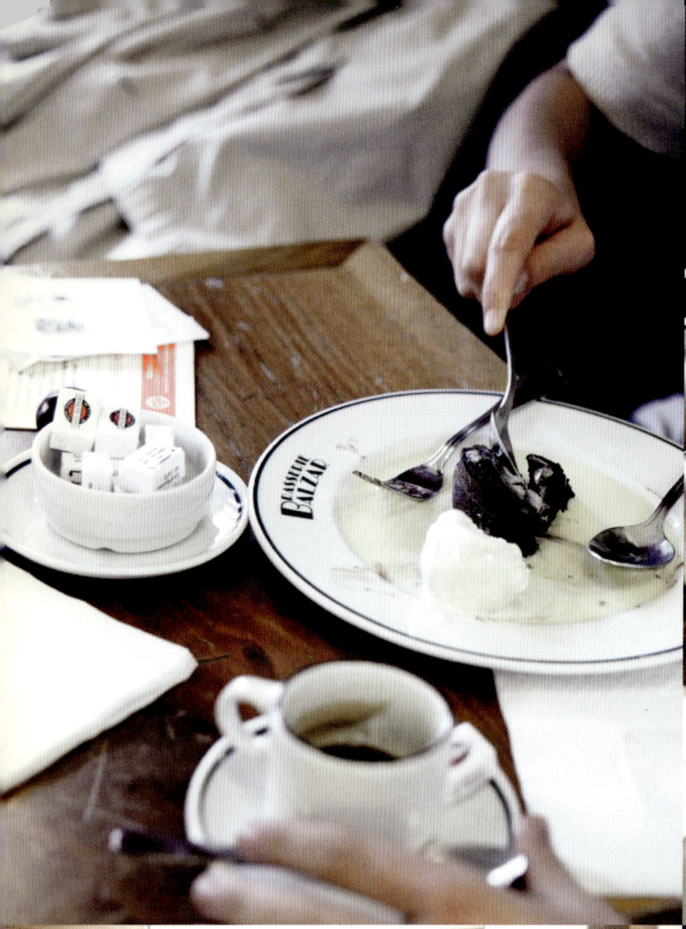
BRASSERIE BALZAC
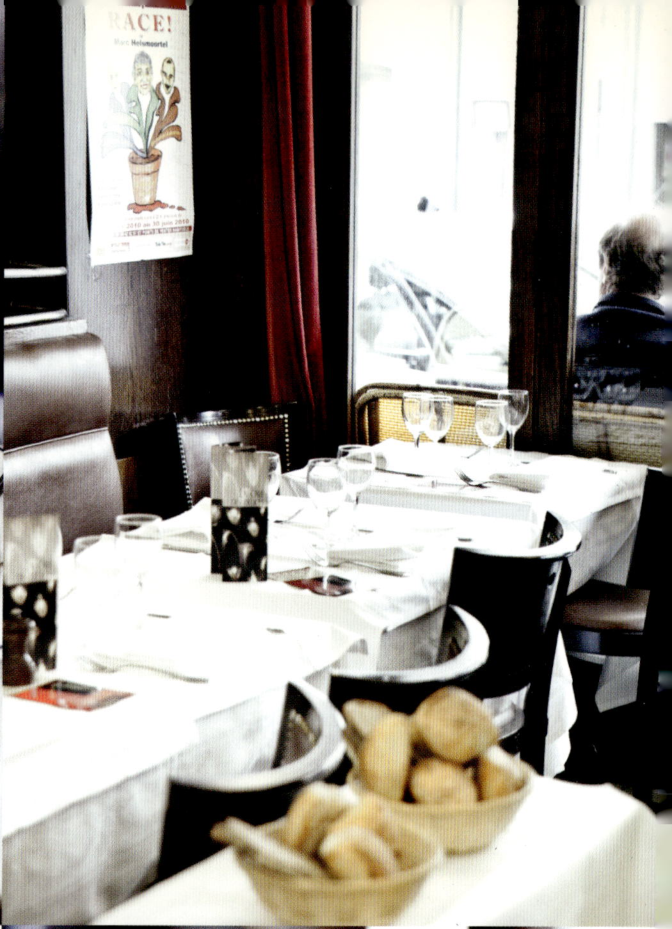
RACE!
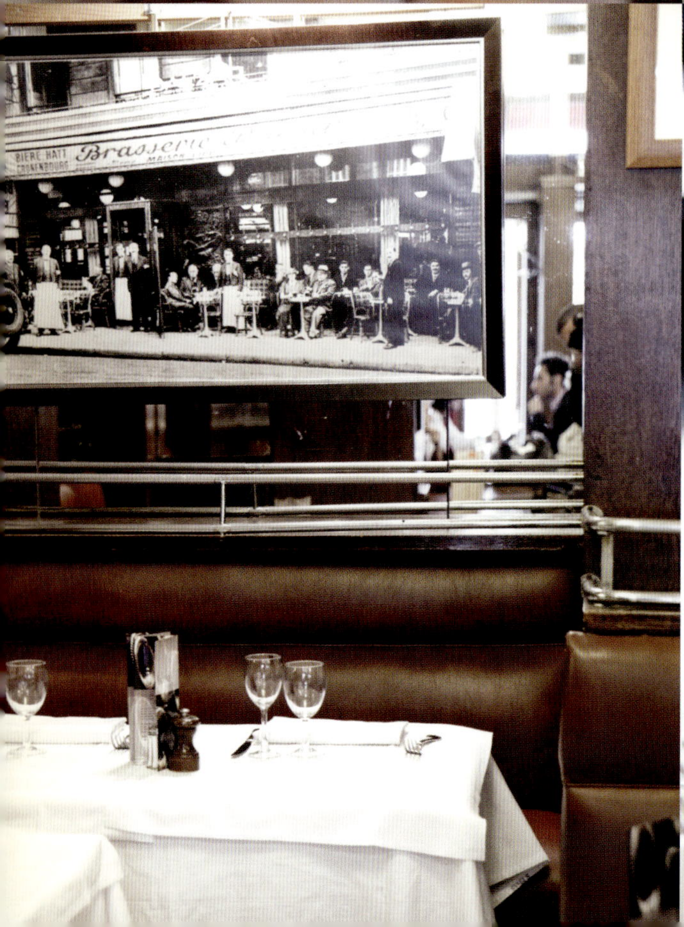
Brasserie
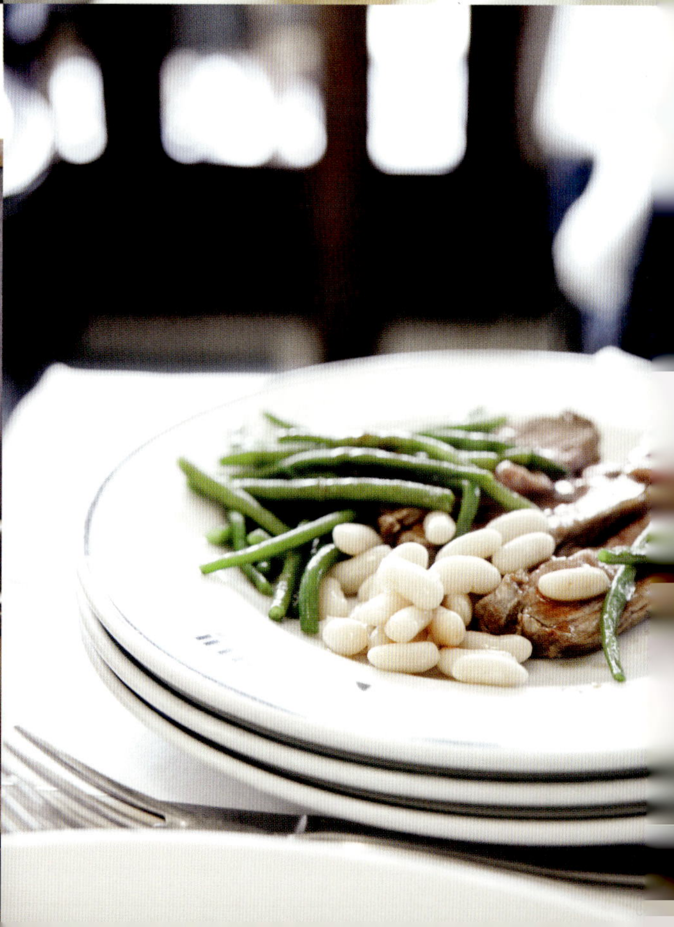

BAL ZAR

The terrace seems to have been set up for Smurfs! With your knees firmly wedged under your chin, you wonder if there might be other, less cramped, tables around the Sorbonne. But you go there for Sartre and Camus, or to wait until it's time for the cinema — where your seats will be even worse — and to be teased by the waiters who are more cultured than their patrons. You also go there to enjoy such classic bistro fare as celery remoulade and leeks vinaigrette. It's an institution.

BALZAR / 49 rue des Écoles / Paris Vᵉ

- 57

Vins
Rouges
Blancs
Chardonnay
CAFES RICHARD
CHINE
AUX FOLIES

BAR AUX FOLIES — rue de Belleville Paris / XXe

This place was once a cabaret where Piaf and Maurice Chevalier sang. It has retained the feel of a Parisian *café théâtre* with its columns and mosaic floor. You can have your coffee while standing at the counter like in the old days, avoiding the reflection of the coloured neon lights in the large mirror that runs along the bar. Or indulge in the pleasure of a beer on the terrace to watch the world stroll by. You'll suddenly feel completely at ease there, in the true Parisian spirit.

BAR AUX FOLIES

BAR AUX FOLIES / 8 rue de Belleville Paris XX

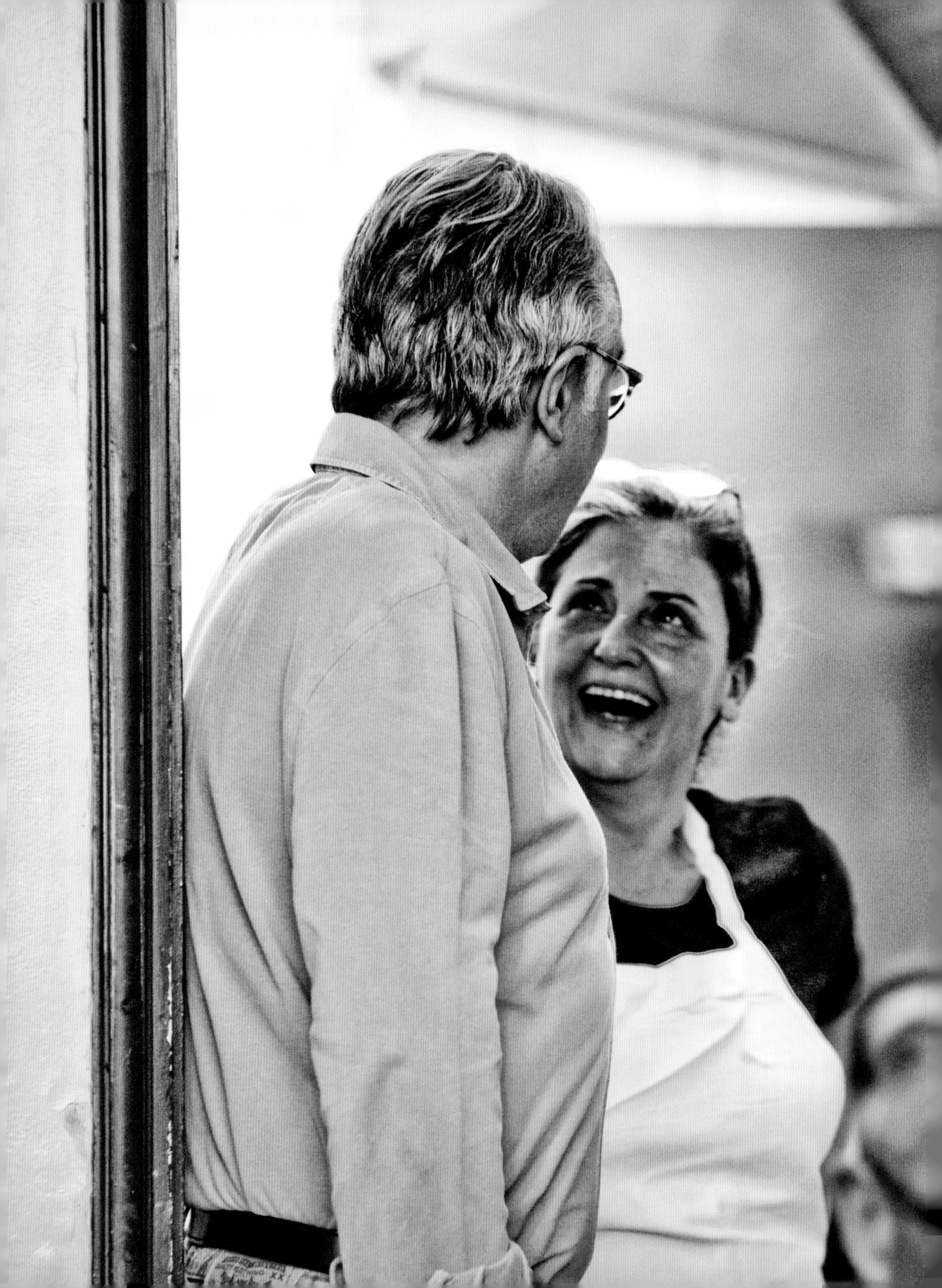

LE BARATIN / 3 rue Jouye-Rouve / Paris XXe

BAR ATIN

Raquel doesn't speak. She has no time, because time is of the essence. Simplicity is simmering gently in the serenity of her large shiny aluminium pans and the intimacy of her tiny kitchen. Regulars will want to sit under the photo by Willy Ronis — one of the first to be taken by him in Paris. It's actually quite moving! Sitting on the school benches, the exquisite veal shank and Spanish white beans melt in your mouth. The delicate monkfish liver terrine, mackerel sashimi, horseradish and fresh raspberries display the colours of her personal and perfectly disciplined cuisine. The list of *vins nature* chosen by Philippe Pinoteau, 'Pinuche' to his friends, are a real talking point, and will no doubt take care of conversation.

LE BARATIN / 3 rue Jouye-Rouve / Paris XXe

PARIS WILL ALWAYS BE PARIS

J'aime Paris

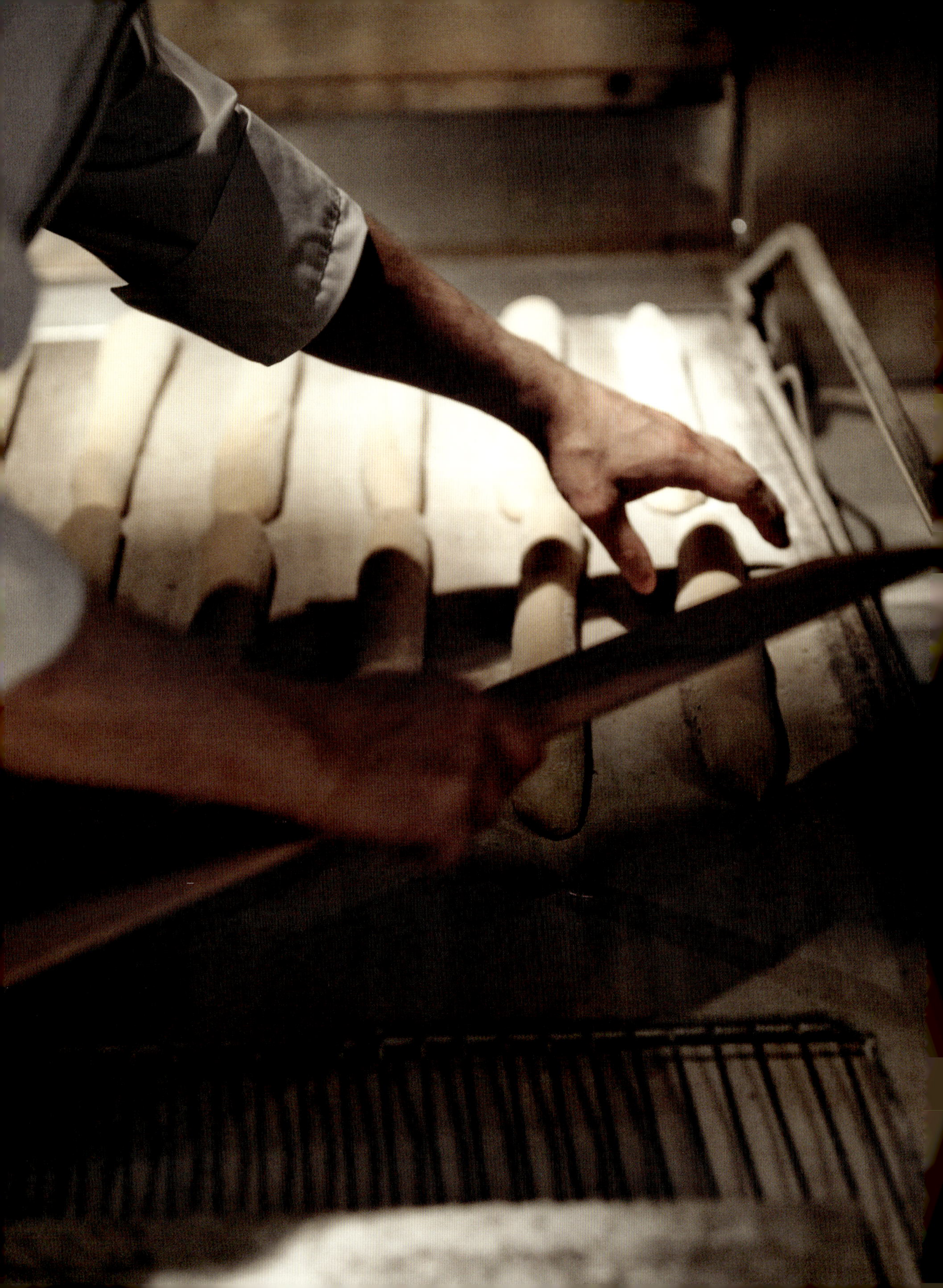

PARIS WILL ALWAYS BE PARIS · J'aime Paris

BF / 73 boulevard de Courcelles / Paris VIIIe

BE Just because you lead a hectic life doesn't mean you have to eat badly. Don't expect Chef Dominique to tell you otherwise. The bread here is made from scratch and baked in the oven that is the central fixture of this bakery-cum-grocery store. You have such a choice: bread with Périgord walnuts, with seaweed, with figs... The soup is fresh on the day, with seasonal vegetables. The sandwiches are made with the best fillings: tuna belly, sardines in oil, tomato confit, cured ham and rocket, among others. In five minutes your *be box*® is ready to take away. For your evening meal, have a blood sausage, a packet of good pasta and olive oil, which you'll find on the shelves. Just follow the instructions on the label. You will also find superb pastries and chocolate pizza.

BE / 73 boulevard de Courcelles / Paris VIIIe

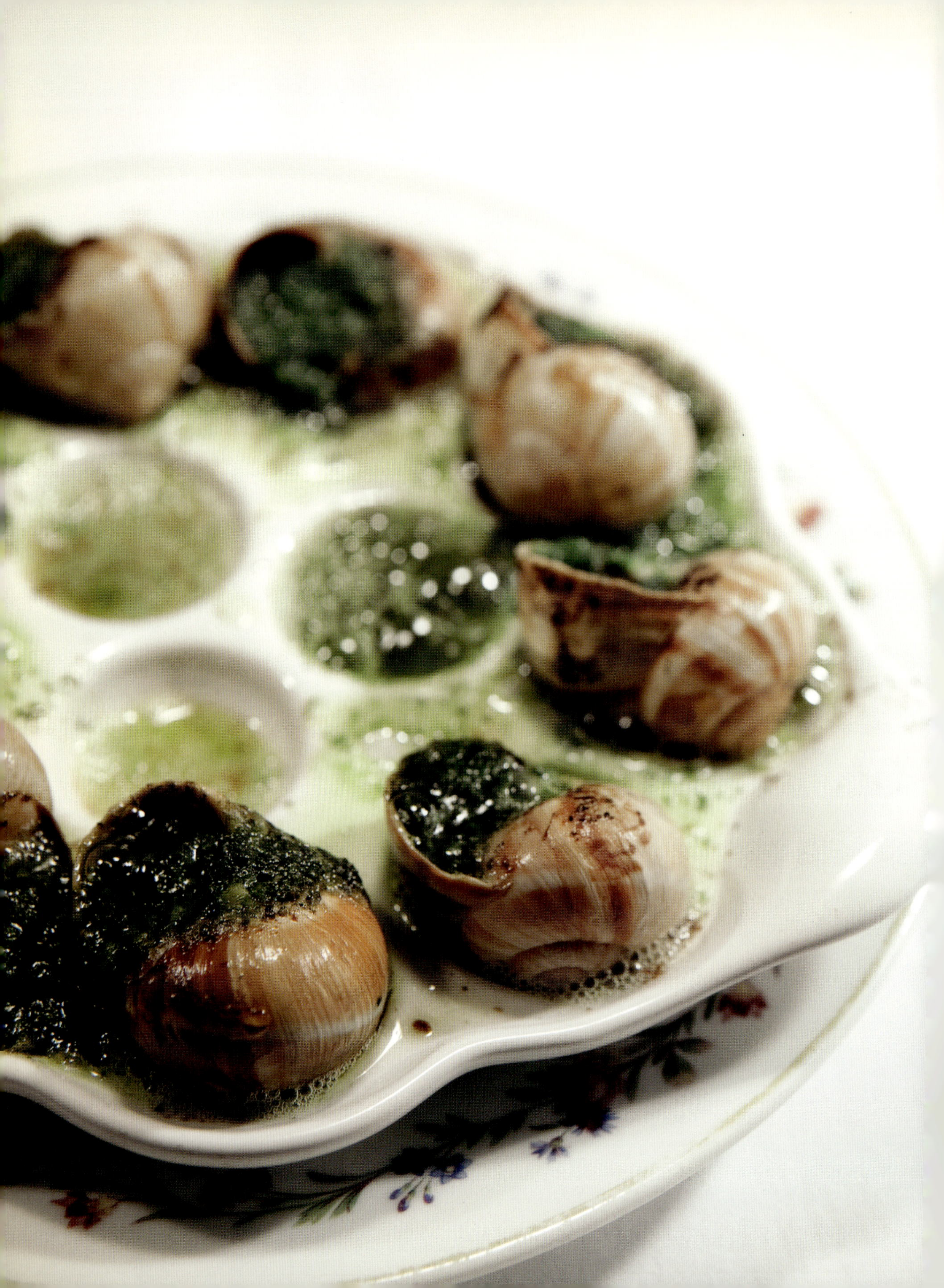

BENOIT / 20 rue Saint-Martin / Paris IV

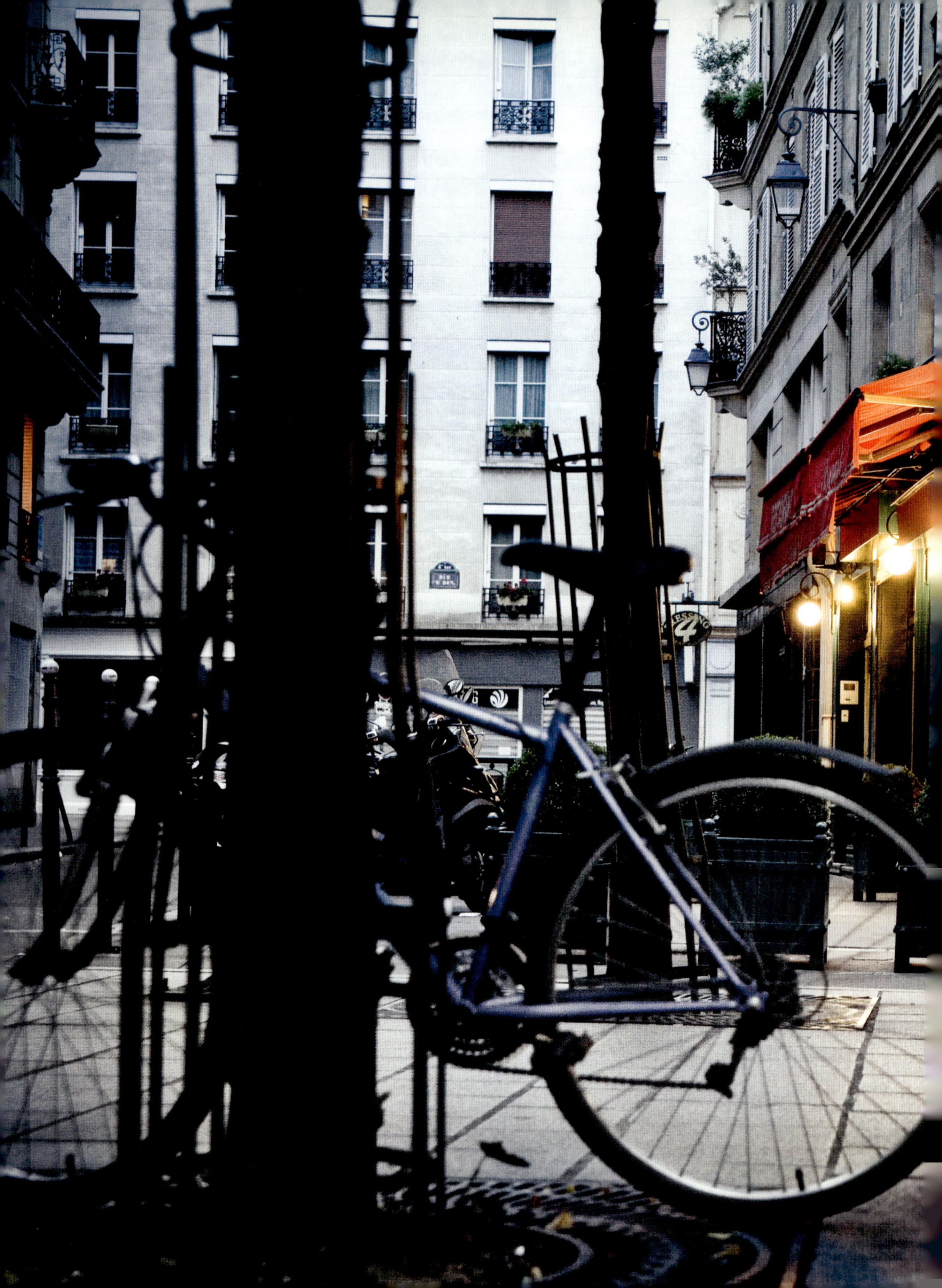

BENOÎT / 20 rue Saint-Martin / Paris IVe

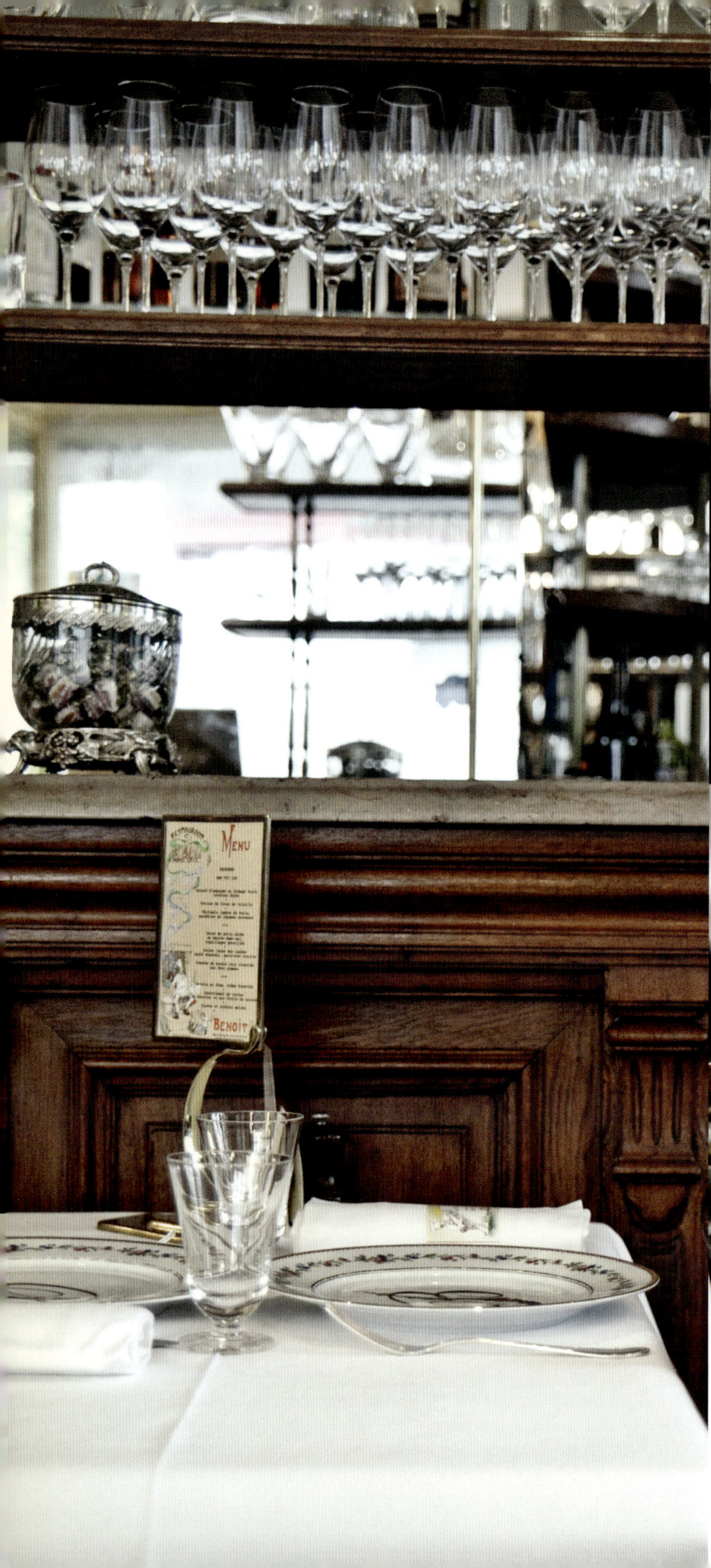
Menu
Benoit

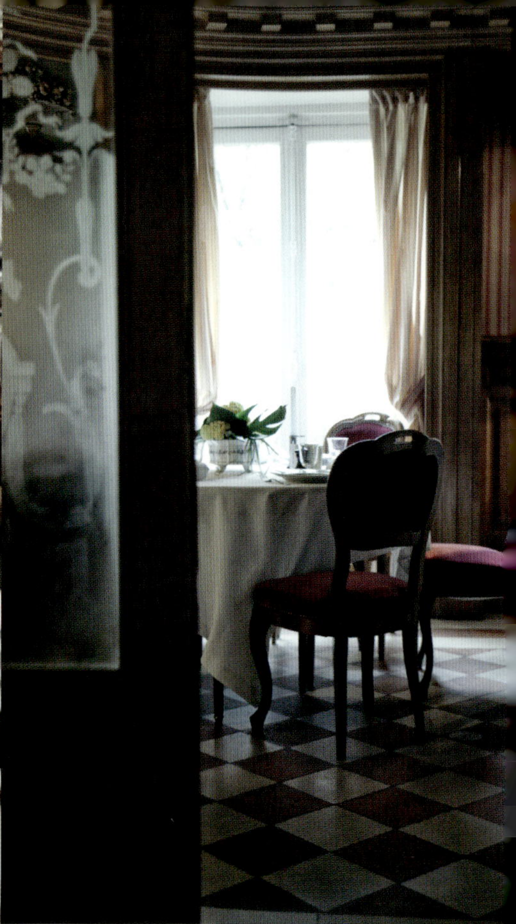

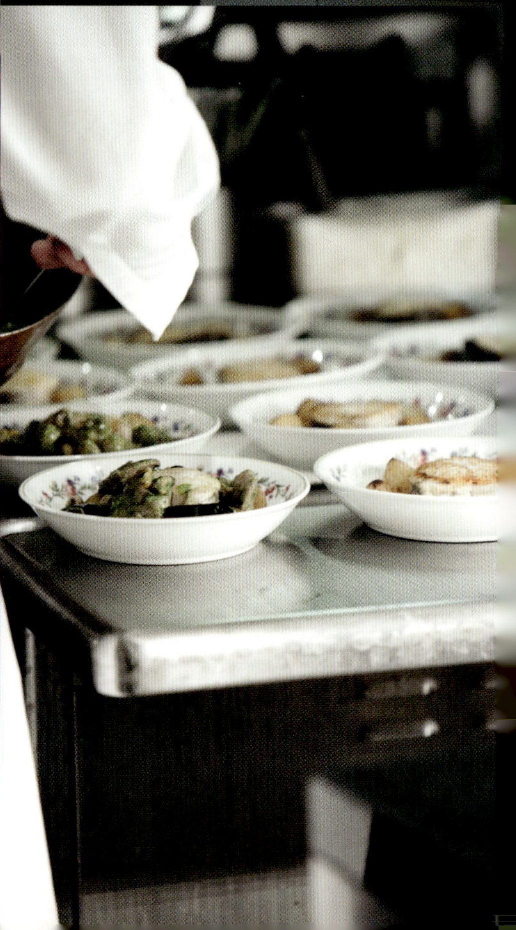

BENOIT

A landmark to the Parisian appetite for indulgence, Benoit has been treating the taste buds of the French capital since 1912. Wilfrid Hocquet offers traditional fare but with a modern twist – true Parisian cuisine. Depending on the season, enjoy stuffed tomatoes or asparagus in mousseline sauce, followed by sole à la Nantua or Lucullus-style veal tongue. Then there is the rare pleasure of authentic profiteroles. You don't need an accordion player; the bistro's spirit sings on your plate.

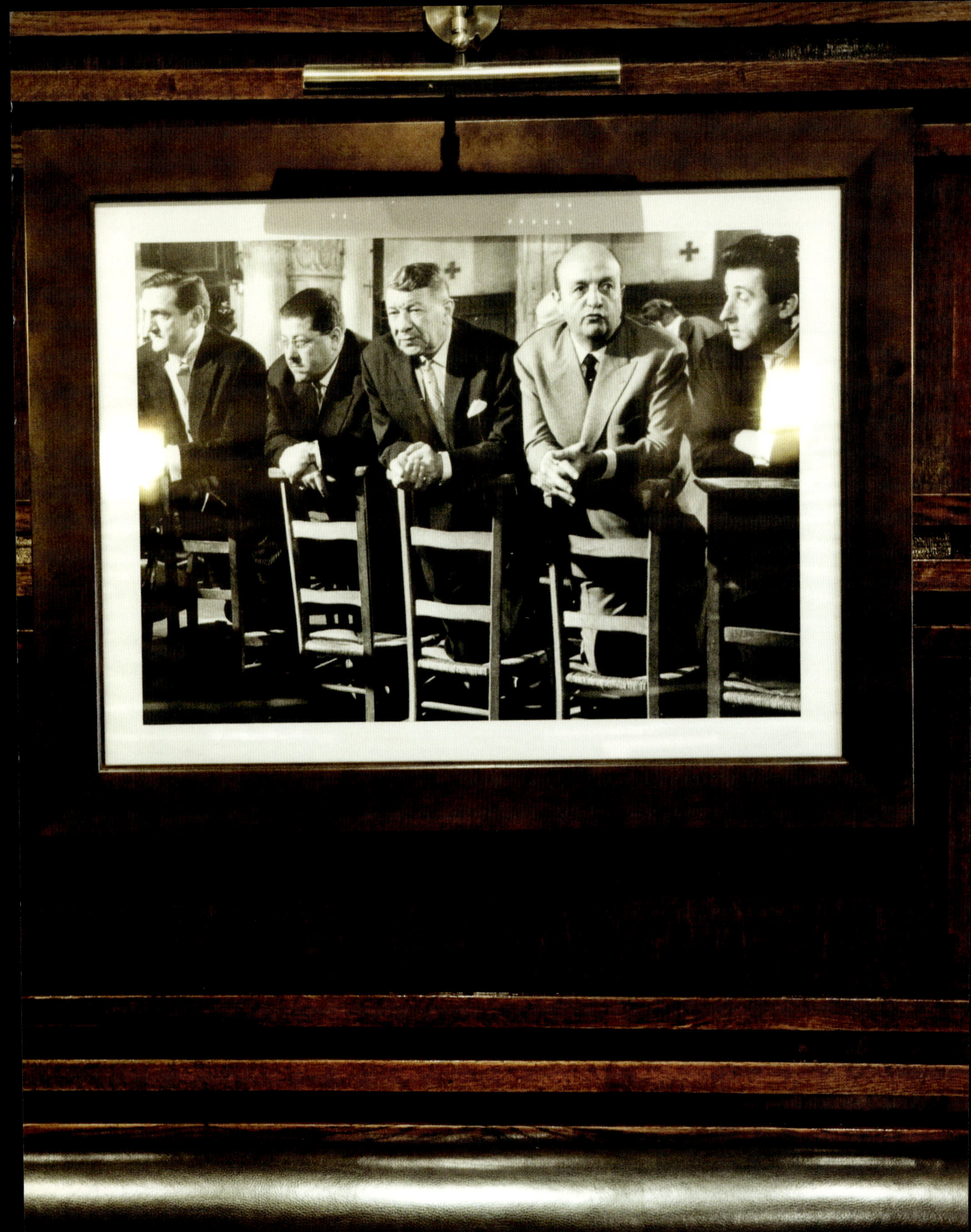

BIDOU BAR /12 rue Anatole de la Forge / Paris XVIIe

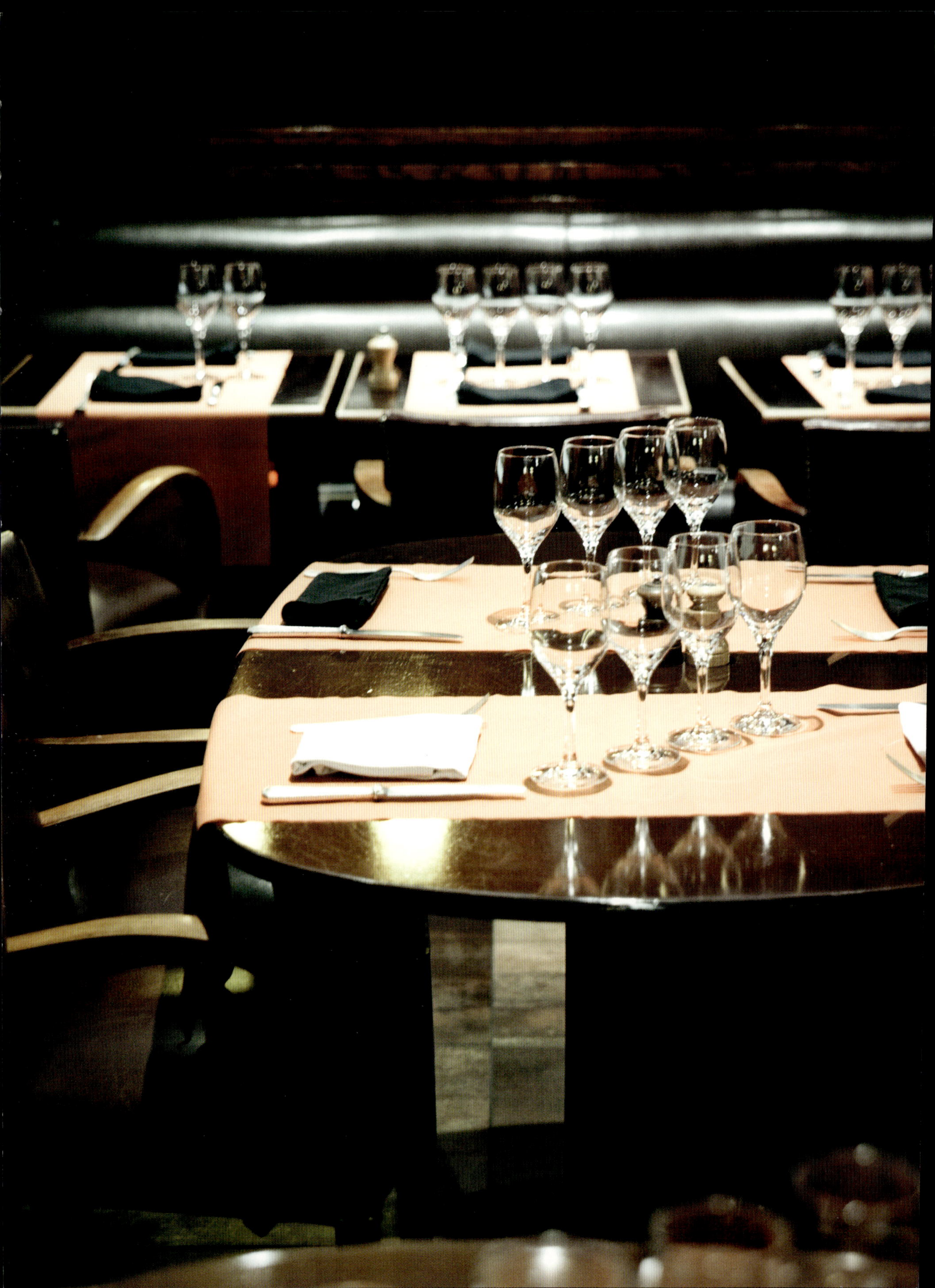

BI DOU BAR

Piaf is there, two stools away. She must have felt at home in this now legendary bar, among the carefully lined up bottles, the dark woodwork with rounded corners and the sleek leather banquettes. The atmosphere is laid-back. A portrait of *Les Tontons Flingeurs* watches over from the back wall between two old radios. Even today, the cuisine served here is in the typical *Parigot/tête de veau* (down-to-earth Parisian) style. Blackboard specials from 11 a.m. to 2 p.m. Good wine list. Champagne!

BIDOU BAR / 12 rue Anatole de la Forge / Paris XVIIe

J'aime Paris

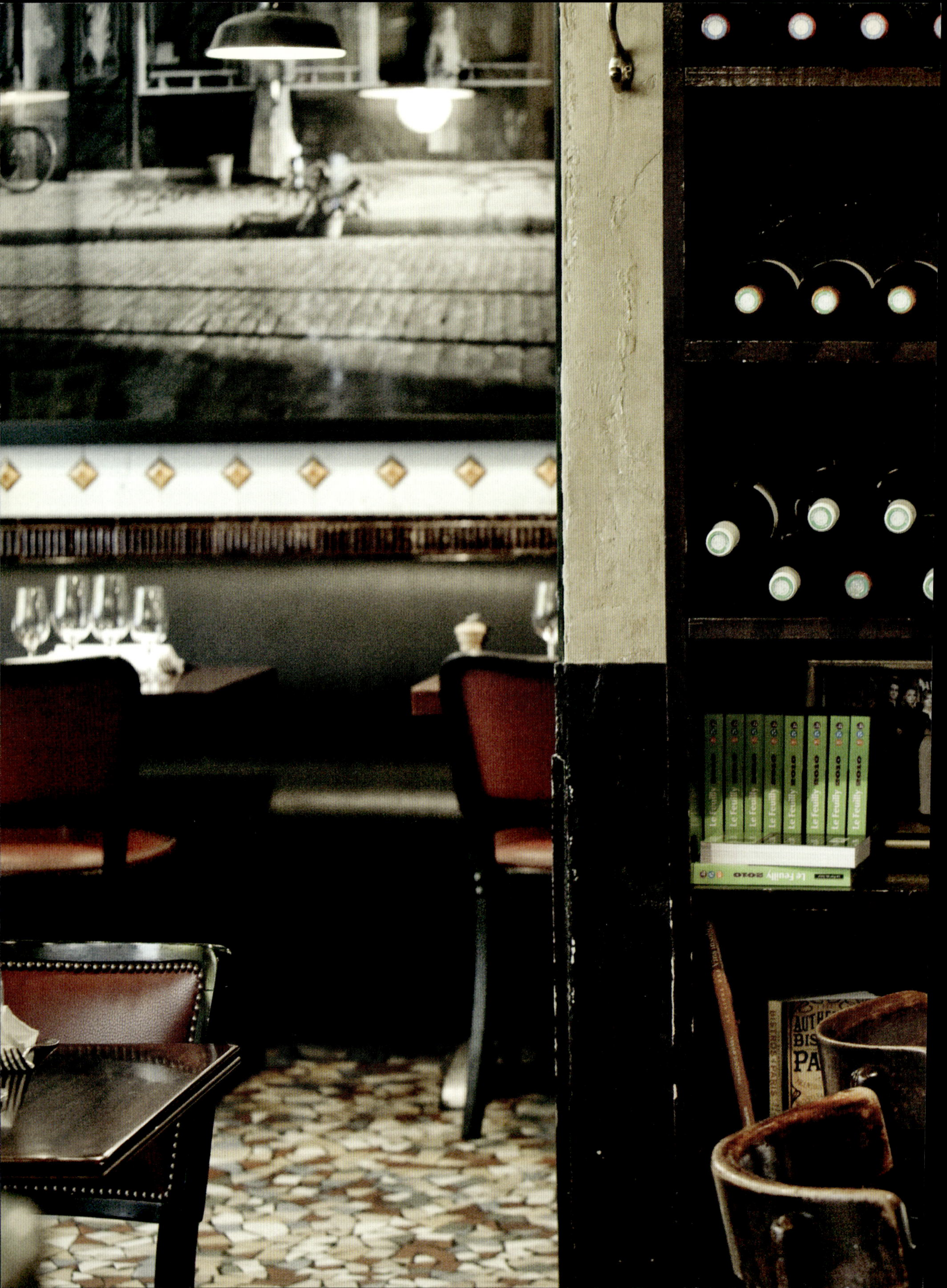
Le Feuilly 2010

MENU À : 34

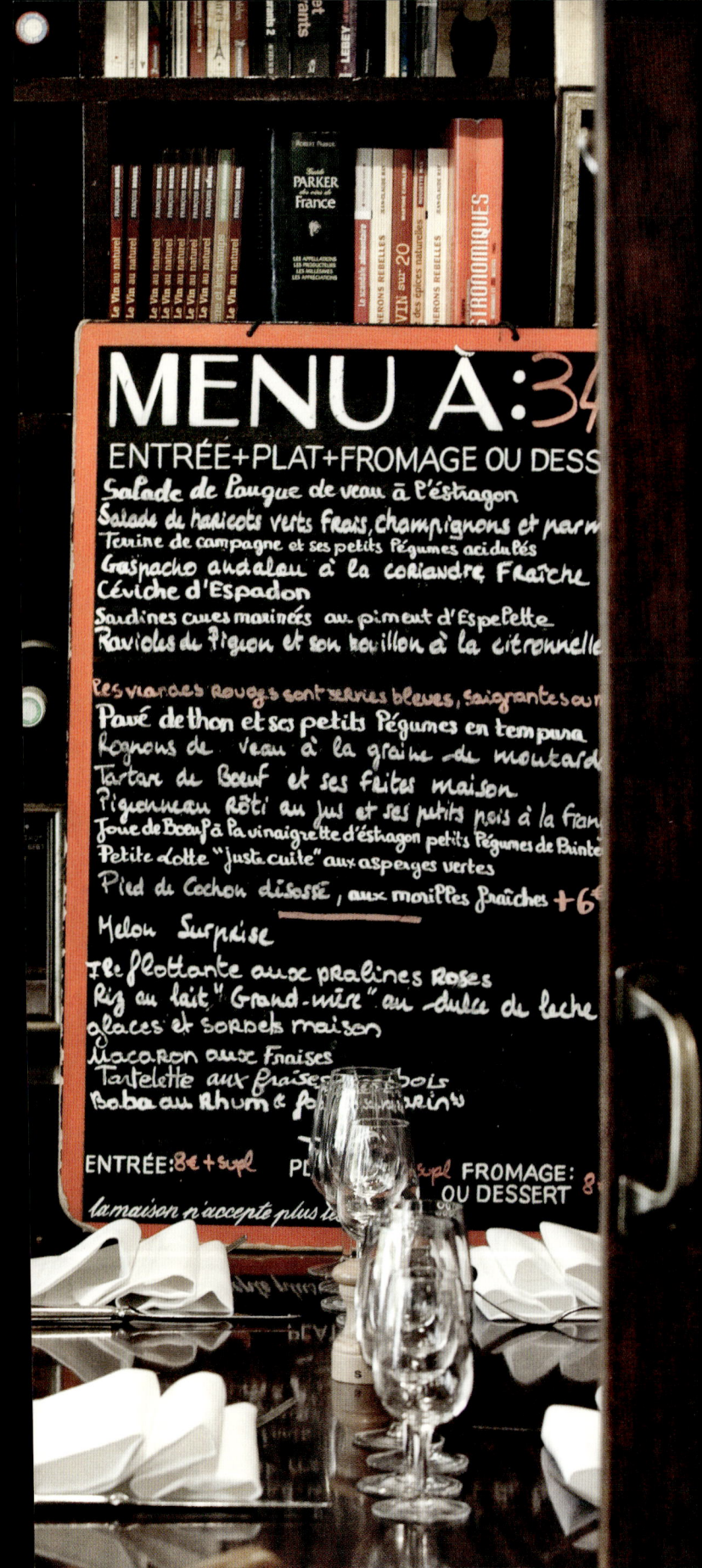

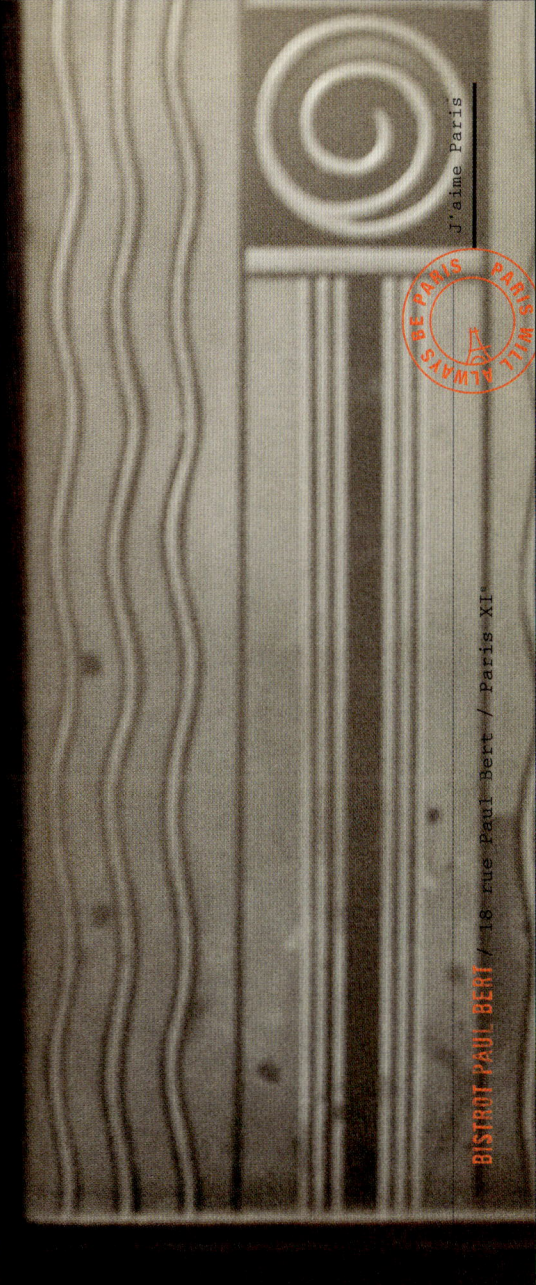

ENTRÉE + PLAT + FROMAGE OU DESSERT

Salade de langue de veau à l'estragon
Salade de haricots verts frais, champignons et parmesan
Terrine de campagne et ses petits légumes acidulés
Gaspacho andalou à la coriandre fraîche
Céviche d'Espadon
Sardines crues marinées au piment d'Espelette
Ravioles de Pigeon et son bouillon à la citronnelle

Les viandes rouges sont servies bleues, saignantes ou...
Pavé de thon et ses petits légumes en tempura
Rognons de veau à la graine de moutarde
Tartar de Bœuf et ses frites maison
Pigeonneau rôti au jus et ses petits pois à la française
Joue de Bœuf à la vinaigrette d'estragon petits légumes de printemps
Petite lotte "juste cuite" aux asperges vertes
Pied de Cochon désossé, aux morilles fraîches +6€

Melon Surprise
Ile flottante aux pralines roses
Riz au lait "Grand-mère" au dulce de leche
Glaces et sorbets maison
Macaron aux fraises
Tartelette aux fraises des bois
Baba au Rhum & ...

ENTRÉE : 8€ + suppl   PLAT : ... + suppl   FROMAGE : 8€ OU DESSERT

la maison n'accepte plus ...

BISTROT PAUL BERT / 18 rue Paul Bert / Paris XI·

J'aime Paris

- 81

BISTROT PAUL BERT

Jean Gabin is having problems with his son, a lad named Claude Brasseur, and with his daughter, Jeanne Moreau. Gabin is from the country, Brasseur is a racing cyclist and Jeanne Moreau is infatuated with an old beau. When you sit down in Bistrot Paul Bert, what you see is *Gas-oil (Hi-Jack Highway)*, Gabin's great films, Moreau's smile and Paris in black and white.

J'aime Paris

PARIS WILL ALWAYS BE PARIS

BISTROT PAUL BERT / 18 rue Paul Bert / Paris XIe

- 83

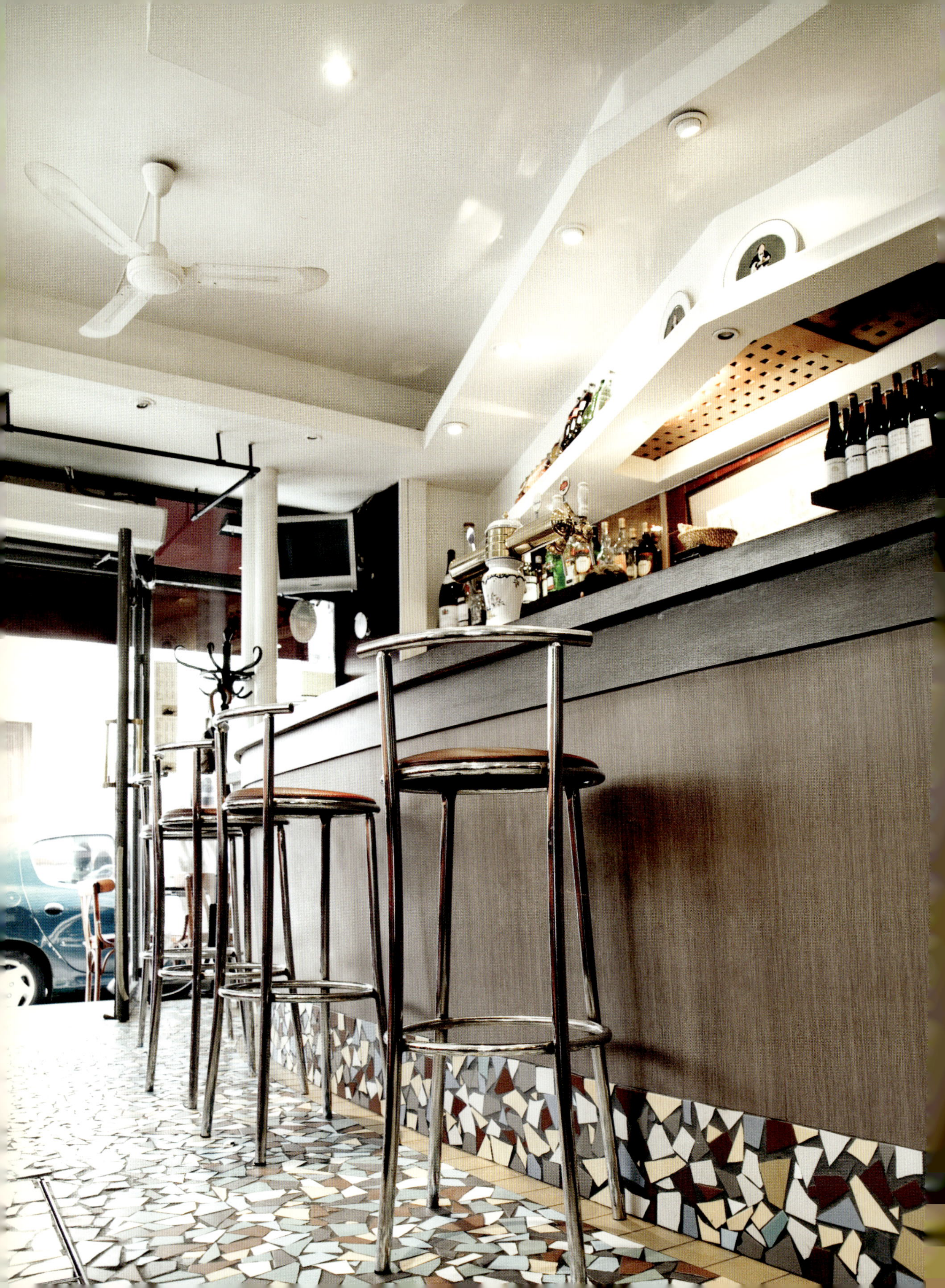

CAFÉ CONSTANT / 139 rue Saint-Dominique / Paris VIe

J'aime Paris

Suggestions du Chef

Entrées

* Salade de haricots verts, pêches et copeaux de foie gras   12€
* Queues d'écrevisses, gelée de homard et velouté de blette   12€
* Raviole de homard relevée au gingembre, sauce crustacés

Plats

* Tête, langue et cervelle de veau croustillante, pommes vapeurs et sauce gribiche   20€

Prix nets, service compris

CAFÉ CONSTANT

Christian Constant has entrusted the reins of this establishment to the former head chef of his Les Fables de La Fontaine restaurant. The brasserie food is inspired by Constant's mother and revisited by one who knows what he's doing. You are transported back to his childhood with roast berry chicken with herb butter and vanilla rice pudding. There are also forays into more modern dishes such as saddle of rabbit ballotine with artichoke carpaccio or crisp pastry-wrapped shrimp with basil. Come back the next morning for a chocolate croissant at the bar.

CAFÉ CONSTANT / 139 rue Saint-Dominique / Paris VIe

CATED

CAFÉ DE FLORE / 172 boulevard Saint Germain / Paris VI°

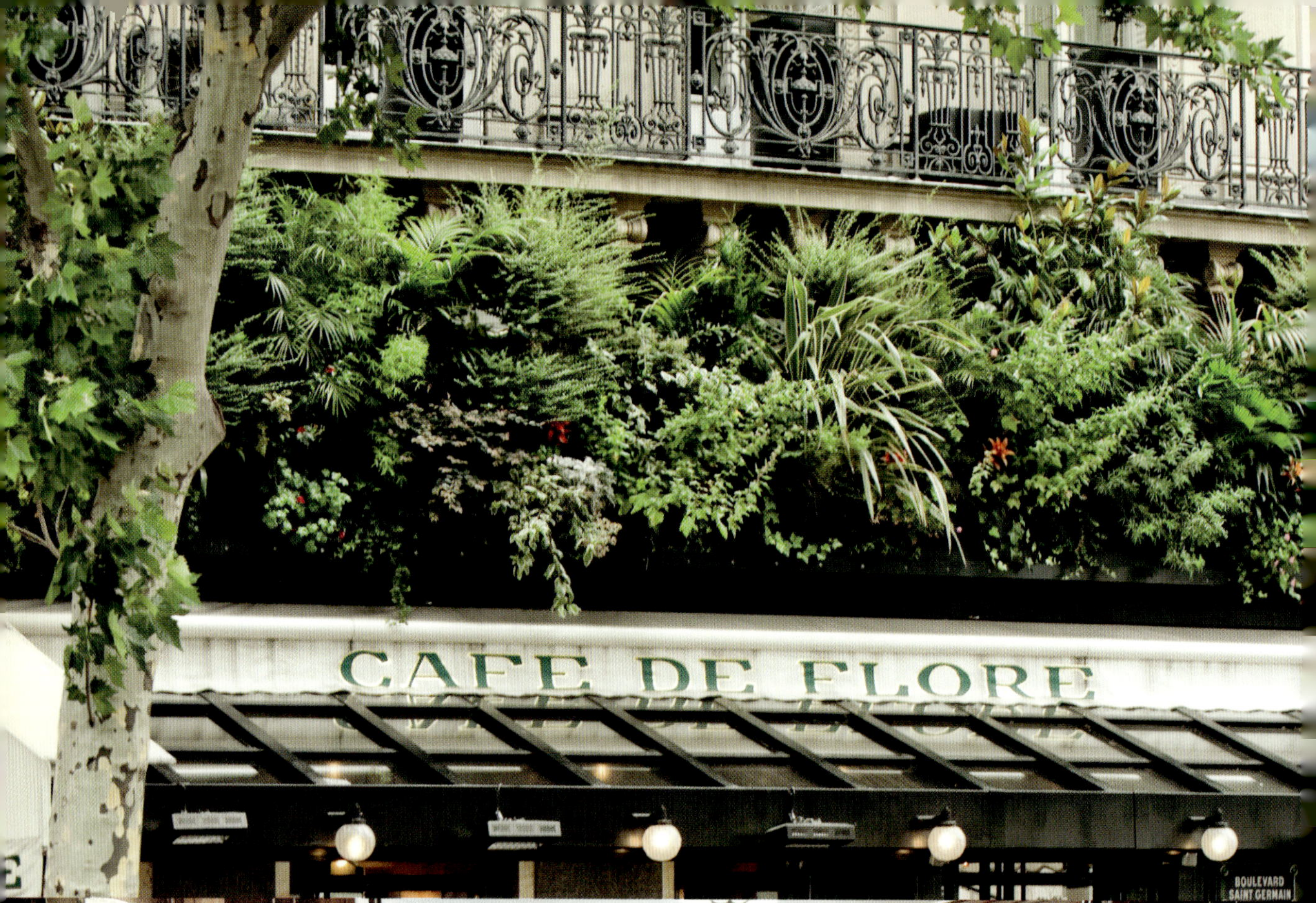
CAFE DE FLORE
BOULEVARD
SAINT GERMAIN

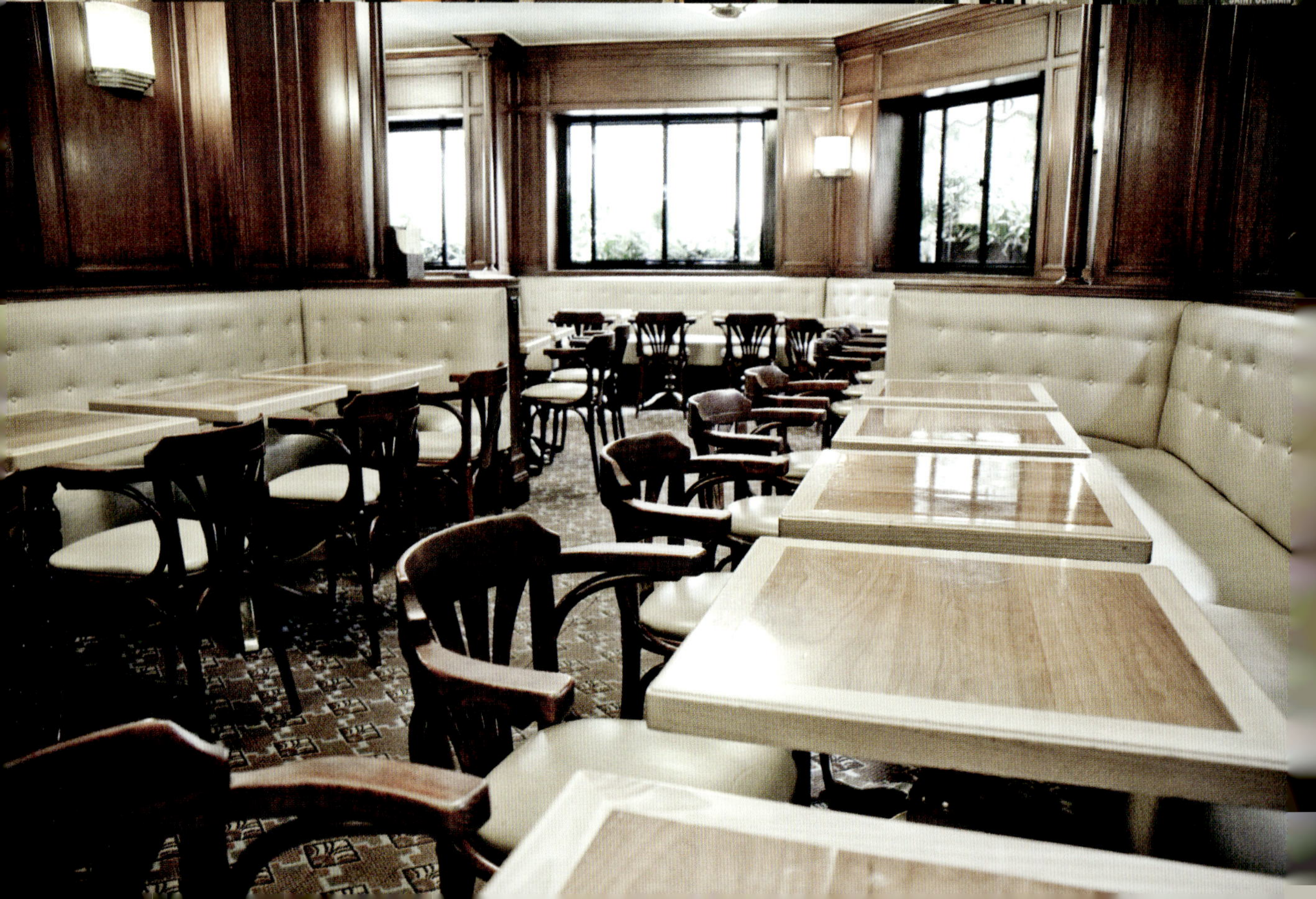

CAFÉ DE FLORE

CAFÉ DE FLORE / 172 boulevard Saint-Germain / Paris VIe

The dish arrives boiling hot and golden. The regular customer barely looks at his Welsh rarebit, a melted Cheddar treat. It consists of tasty morsels of bread under a creamy, beer-flavoured coating *au gratin*. On the terrace, in the shadow of Sartre and his 'Beaver', you trace the back of your spoon over the green writing on the saucer while enjoying life. A cappuccino with the froth rising like a soufflé and a buttered slice of Parisian baguette are just the thing to start the day.

- 91

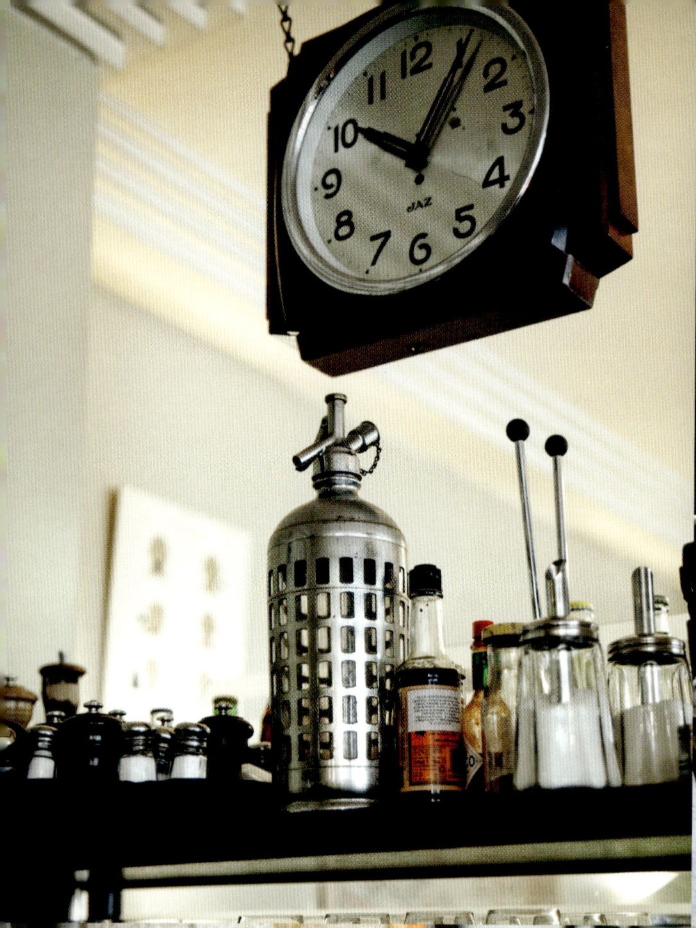
JAZ

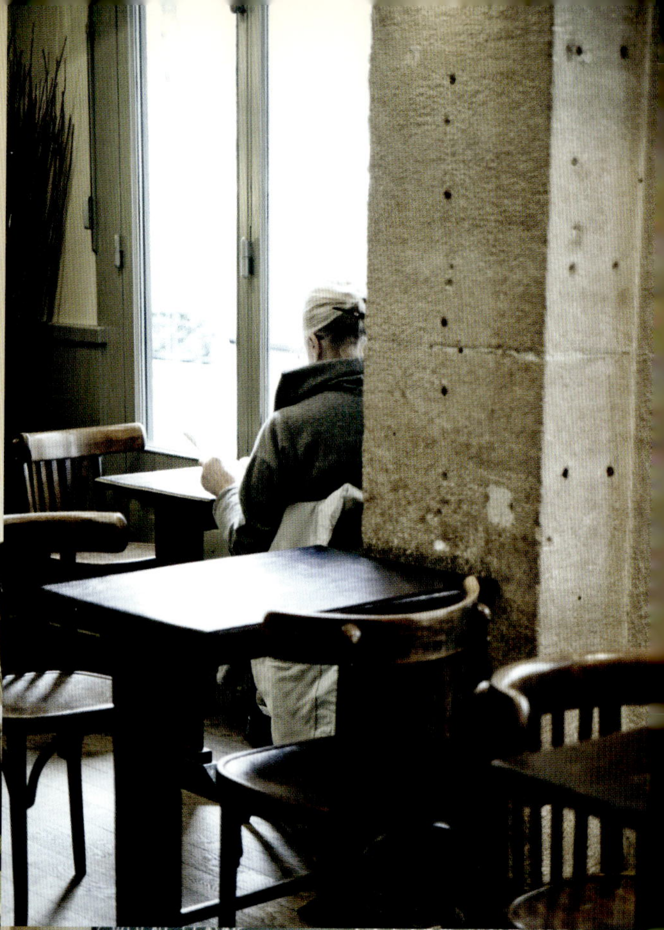

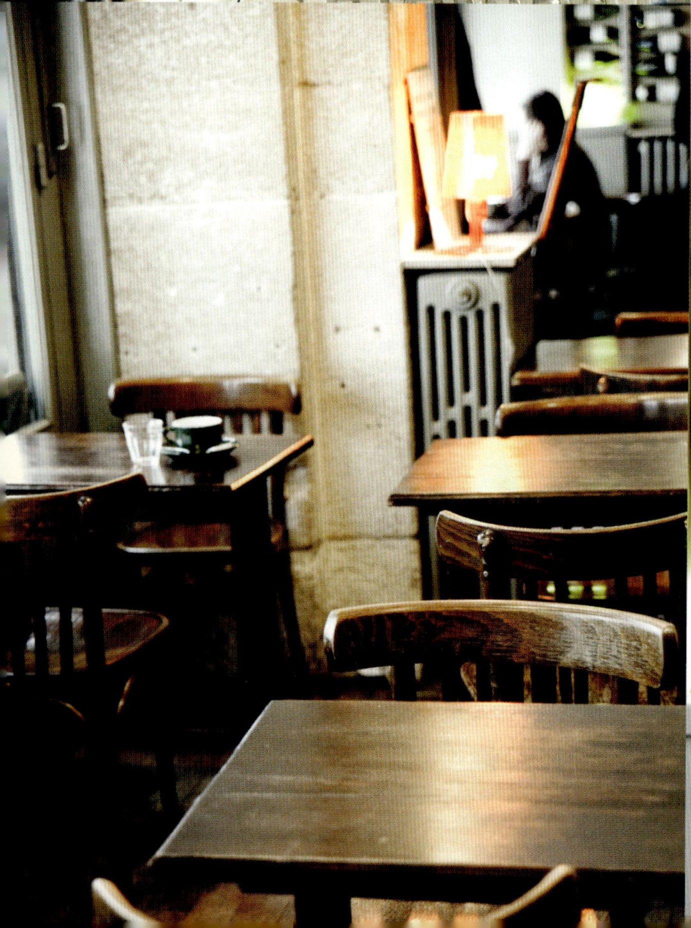

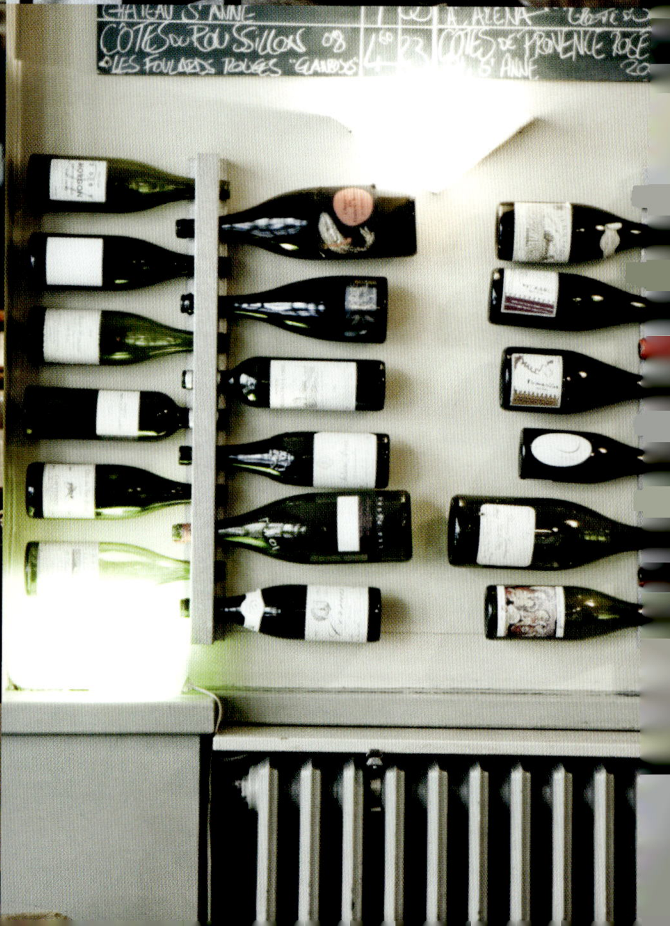
CÔTES DU ROUSSILLON 08
LES FOULARDS ROUGES

A stone's throw from the Panthéon, lunch is being served in a small shady square. The students have come from the Lycée Henri IV on the rue d'Ulm. They take their time, sporting moustaches from their almost solid hot chocolates. A pretty blonde girl flicks through the newspaper under a blackboard that reads 'Fine wines, *vins nature*'. After rabbit terrine and a glass of Anjou, it's back to school.

CAFÉ DE LA NOUVELLE MAIRIE

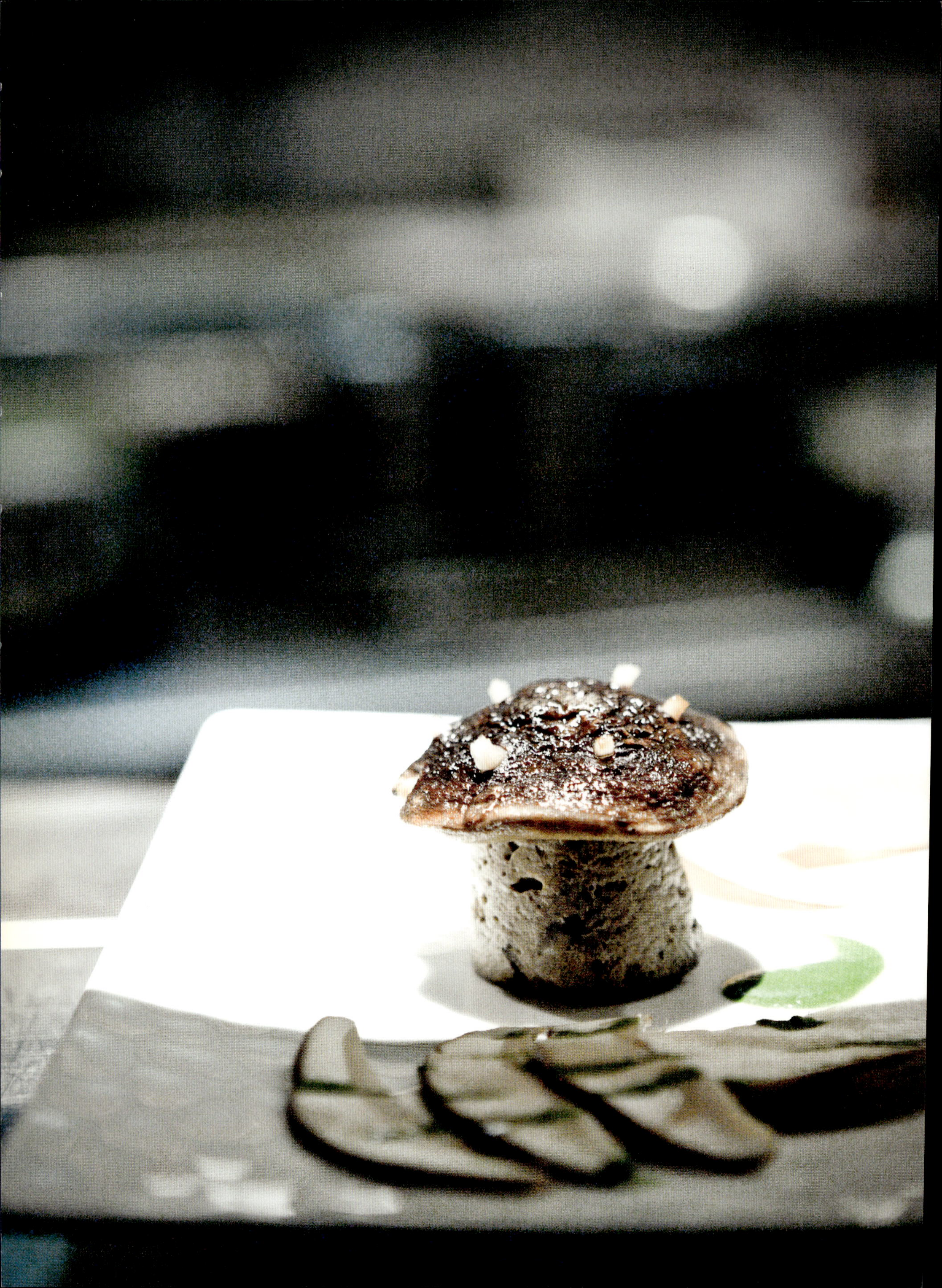

LE CARRÉ DES FEUILLANTS / 14 rue de Castiglione / Paris Ier

CARRÉ DES FEUILLANTS

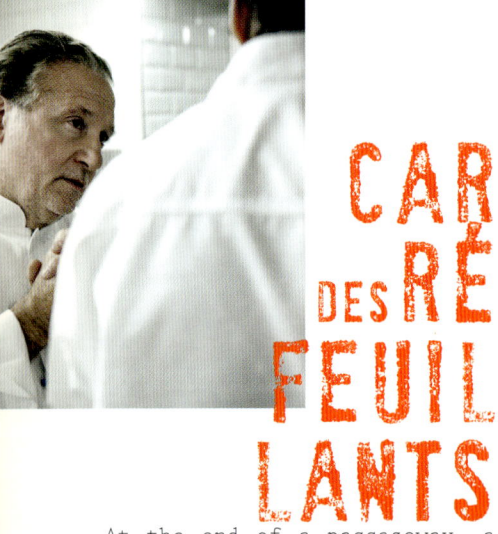

At the end of a passageway, a box-like building stands on the site of the former Feuillant monastery built in the time of Henri IV. Alain Dutournier has a keen sense of beauty, and he treats us to elegant and contemporary dishes influenced by the food of south-west France. People come to Le Carré des Feuillants to sample its generous, characterful cuisine: foie gras, langoustines with sweet garlic nougatine, veal sweetbreads with fresh morels, and wild strawberry, rose and lychee macaroons. Place Vendôme is nearby, yet we could almost be in the south.

LE CARRÉ DES FEUILLANTS / 14 rue de Castiglione / Paris Iᵉʳ

J'aime Paris · Paris will always be Paris

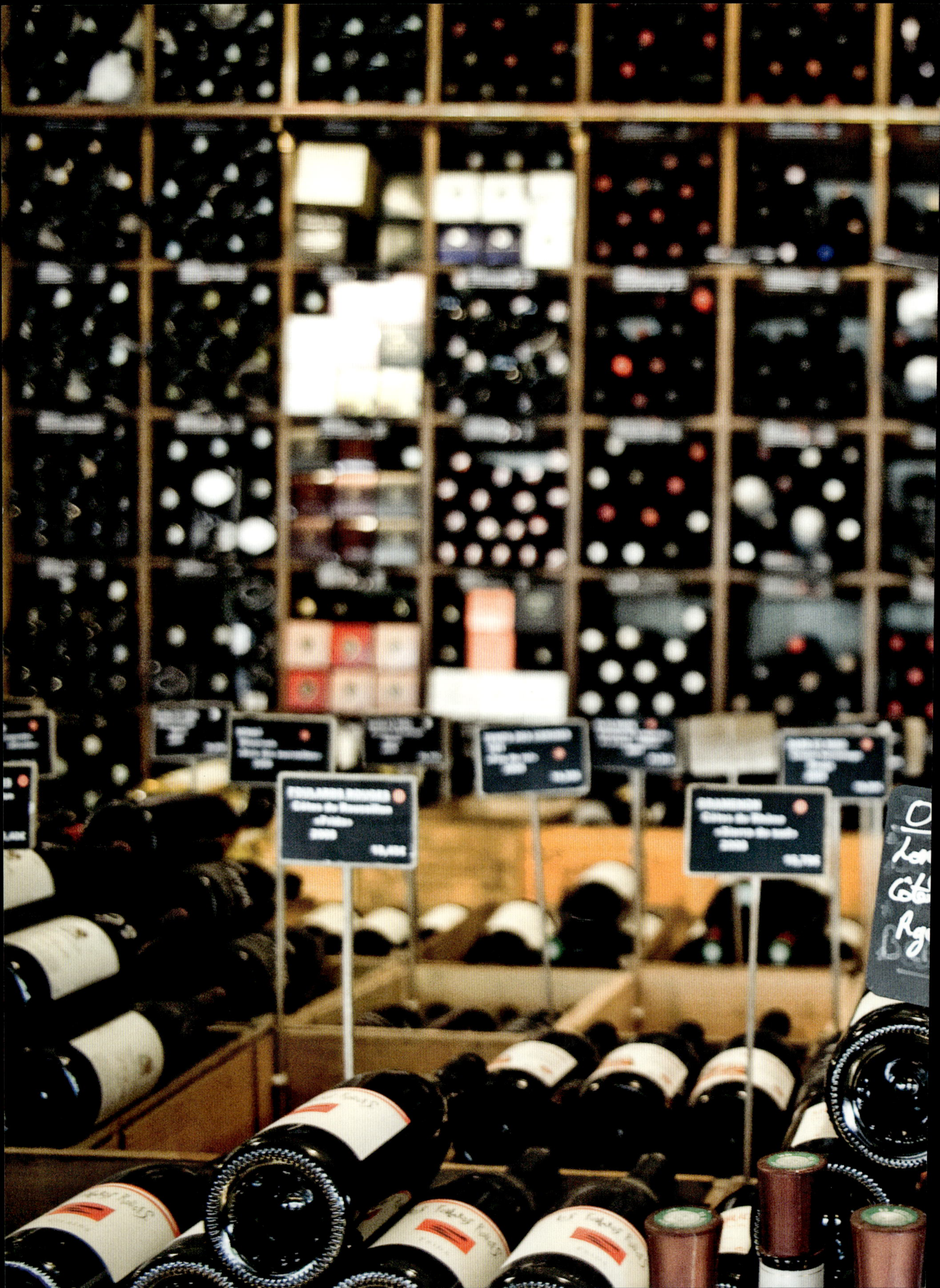

LES CAVES AUGÉ / 116 boulevard Haussmann / Paris VIII° / J'aime Paris

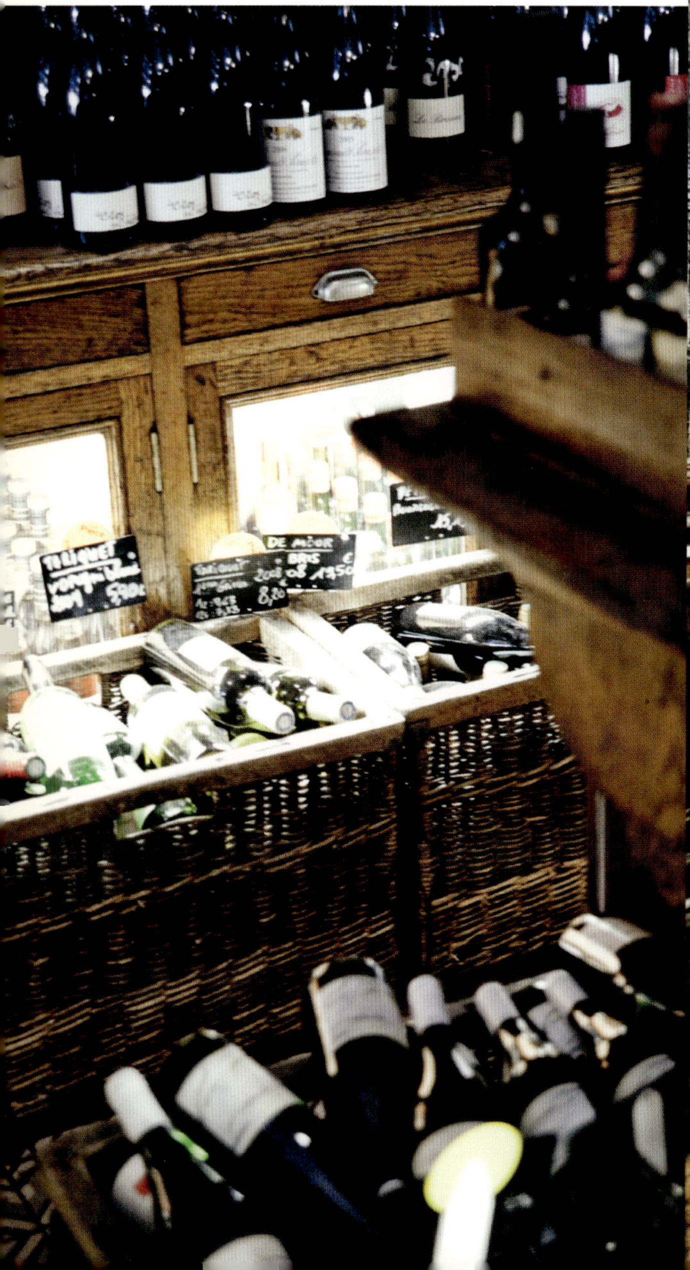

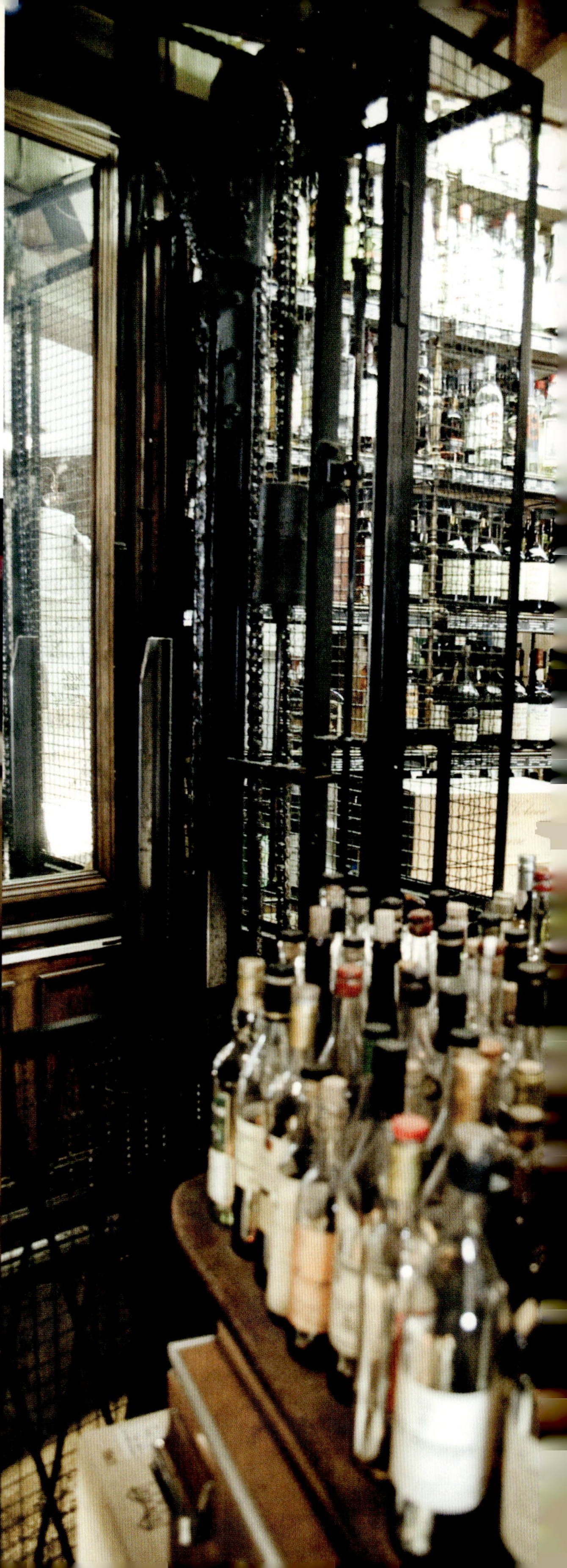

CAVES AUGE

The apostles of *vin nature* have been preaching here for over 20 years. The establishment's chirpy owner Marc Sibard, former head sommelier at Fouquet's, makes a stand in defence of the honour of small-scale producers. Inside his Ali Baba's cave, the goods lift comes to the surface with some very pretty bottles, uncompromisingly guaranteed from their *terroir* and free from chemical additives.

Maison

Chardenoux

Menu Déjeuner 25€

Billes de melon au jambon de pays
ou
Poireaux vinaigrette et mimosa d'œuf
ou
Filet de dorade orange verveine, fondue de choux pak-choï
ou
Tartare de bœuf au couteau, frites jambon

Tarte aux fruits rouges
ou
Éclair au caramel au beurre salé

LE CHARDENOUX / 1 rue Jules Vallès / Paris XIe

J'aime Paris — BE PARIS · PARIS WILL ALWAYS

CHAR DE NOUX

'I was looking for a very Parisian location, where I could create an easy and uncomplicated cuisine. A bistro is associated with the idea of a chef - timeless, charming, authentic, gourmet... I pushed open the door at Le Chardenoux and I said to myself: this is the place. We've been interpreting the great Parisian classics ever since: beef tartare, Landes asparagus with mimosa sauce, saddle of lamb cooked in a clay crust, chicken cooked in hay, French toast, waffles... But this doesn't mean we can't do other more exotic things, like curried clams, for instance.'

Cyril Lignac

LE CHARDENOUX / 1 rue Jules Vallès / Paris XIe

J'aime Paris

- 105

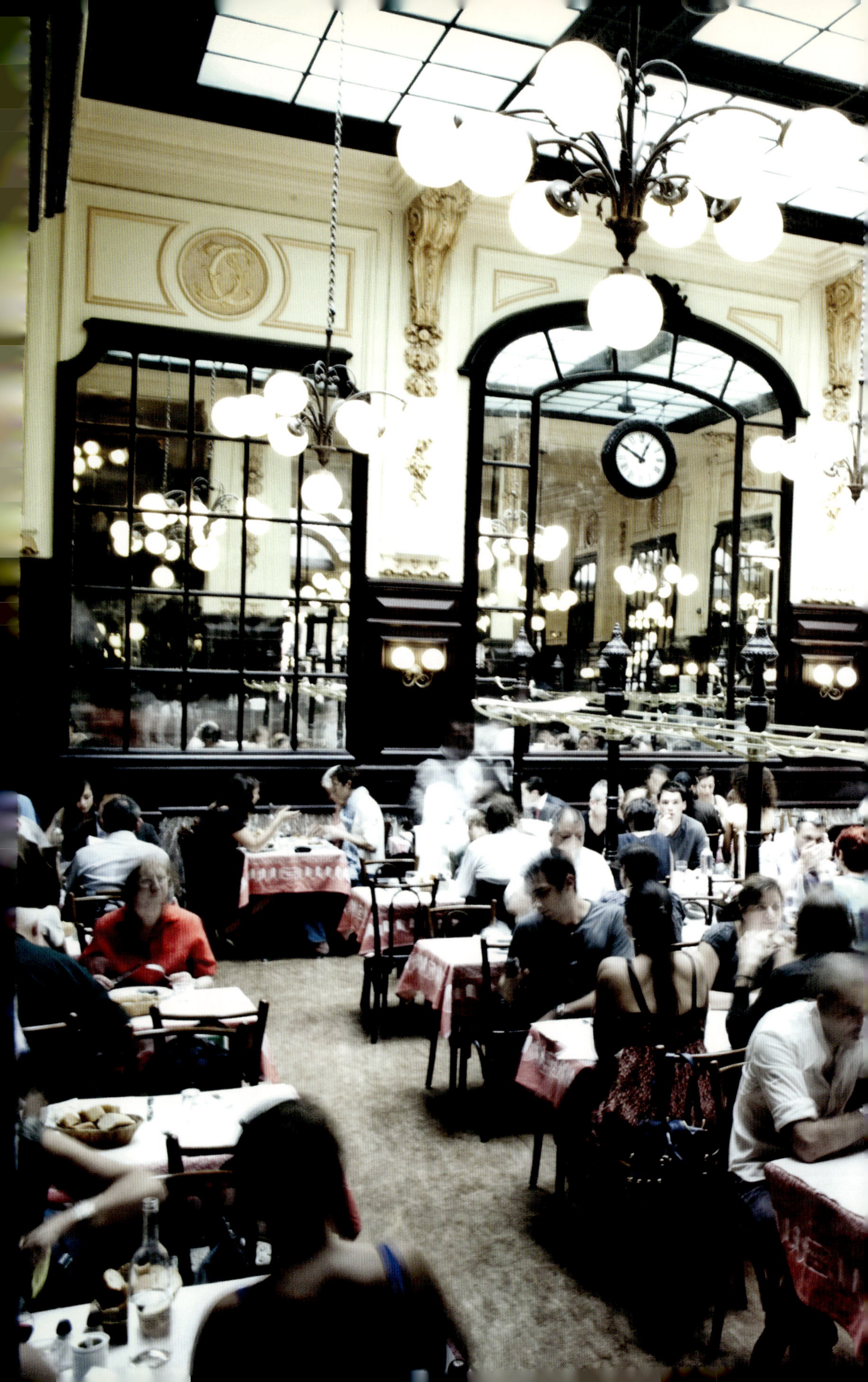

RESTAURANT CHARTIER / 7 rue du Faubourg Montmartre / Paris IXe

J'aime Paris

PARIS WILL ALWAYS BE PARIS

CHARTIER

This reasonably priced restaurant has always had *bouillon* as its signature dish, a broth made from meat and vegetables served directly at the table. Chartier is popular for its unusual mix of simple bistro cooking and opulent theatrical décor. As if seated in a velvet-lined box, you can appreciate this quality simply by biting into an egg with mayonnaise. Canteen-style dishes are the order of the day, with grated carrots and cucumbers in cream. The menu scrawled on the paper tablecloth is almost worth framing.

RESTAURANT CHARTIER / 7 rue du Faubourg Montmartre / Paris IXe

J'aime Paris

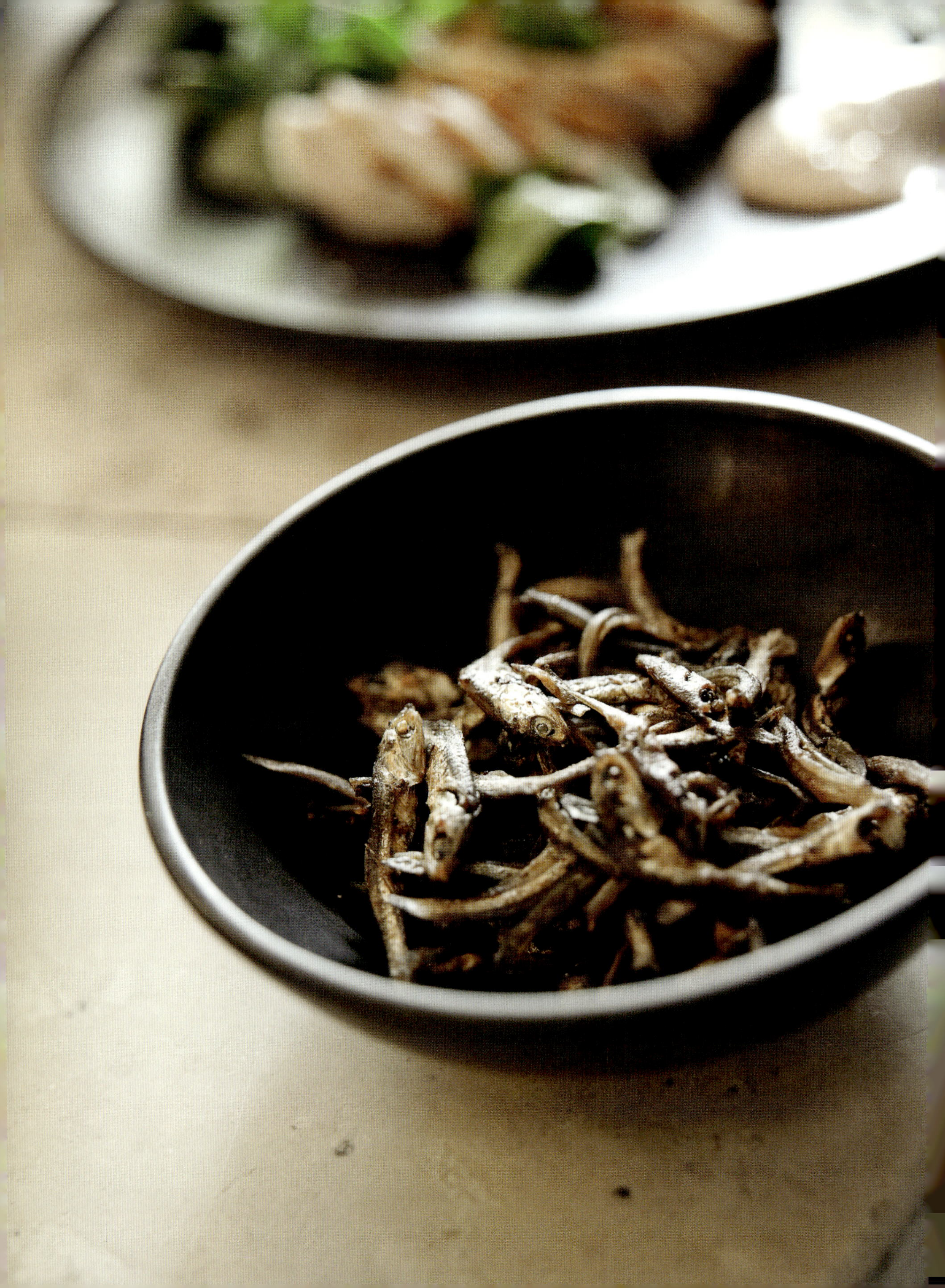

LE CHATEAUBRIAND / 129 avenue Parmentier / Paris XIe

- 111

CHATEAU BRIAND

Warning, cuisine on the move — frequent turbulence; chance of dizziness; unexpected encounters with shellfish and dashi; anchovies or mango coming aground on a carpaccio; the crash of orange on yellow pollock. The taste buds are liberated to explore the raw, the bare and the simple. At the helm, Inaki Aizpitarte smiles behind his beard. Drawing on his Basque roots, he creates a soft fruit piperade and a rose-flavoured fromage frais. For dessert, he is bold enough to serve his already famous *banane ecrasée* (mashed banana). You come back to land a little shaken after having discovered new horizons; it's as if you have just gone for a spin in a flying saucer.

LE CHATEAUBRIAND / 129 avenue Parmentier / Paris XIe / J'aime Paris

- 113

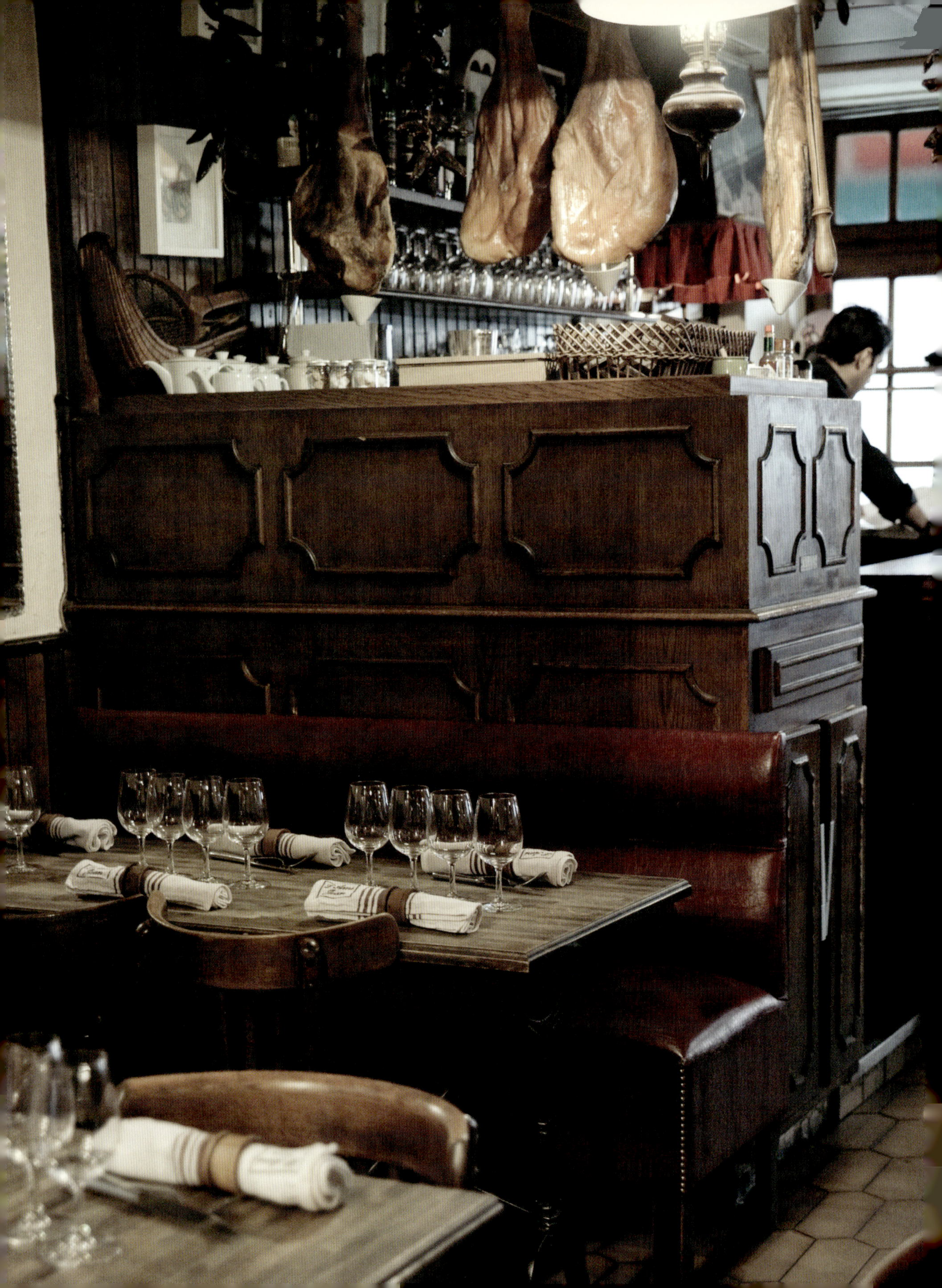

CHEZ L'AMI JEAN / 27 rue Malar / Paris VII

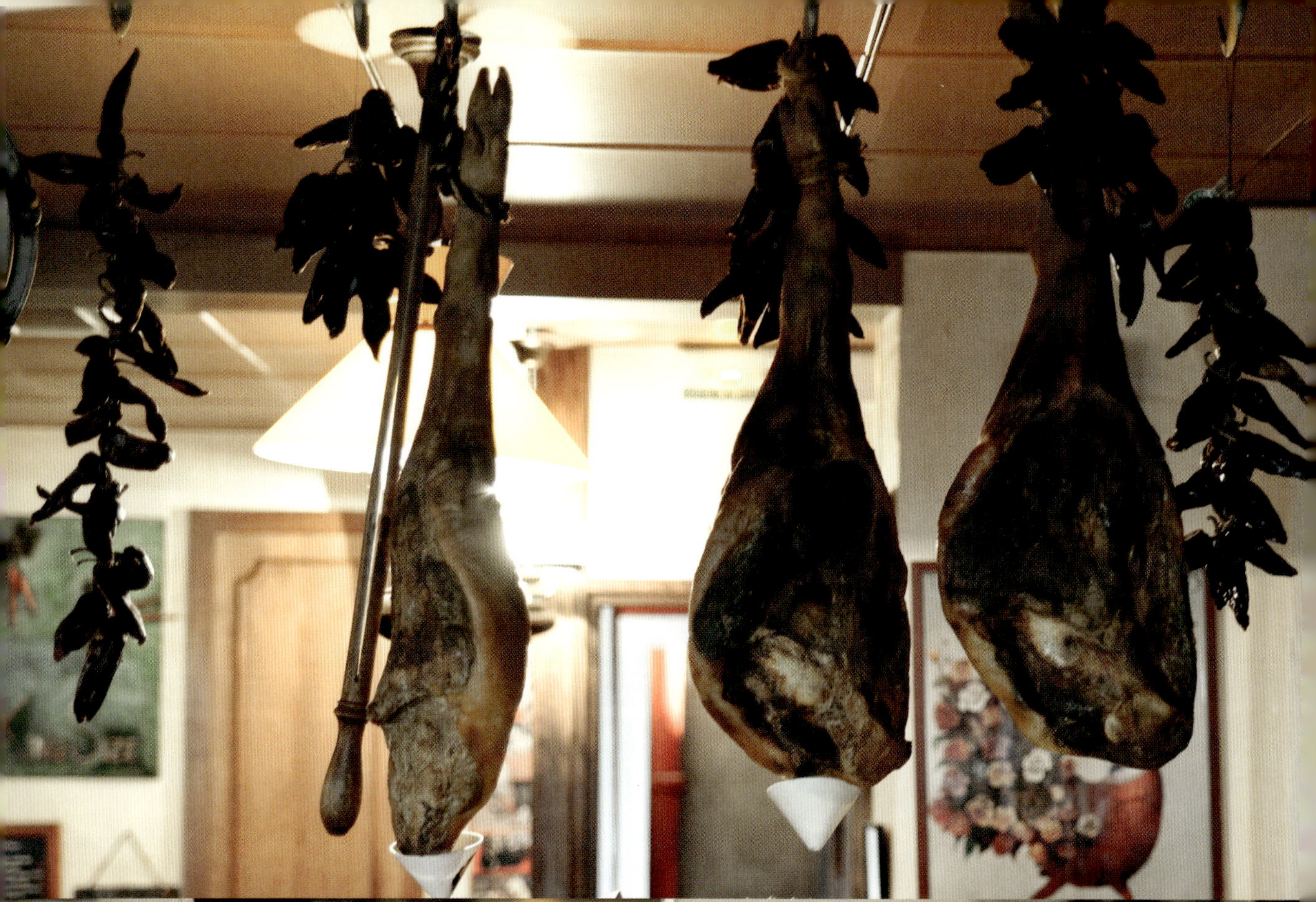
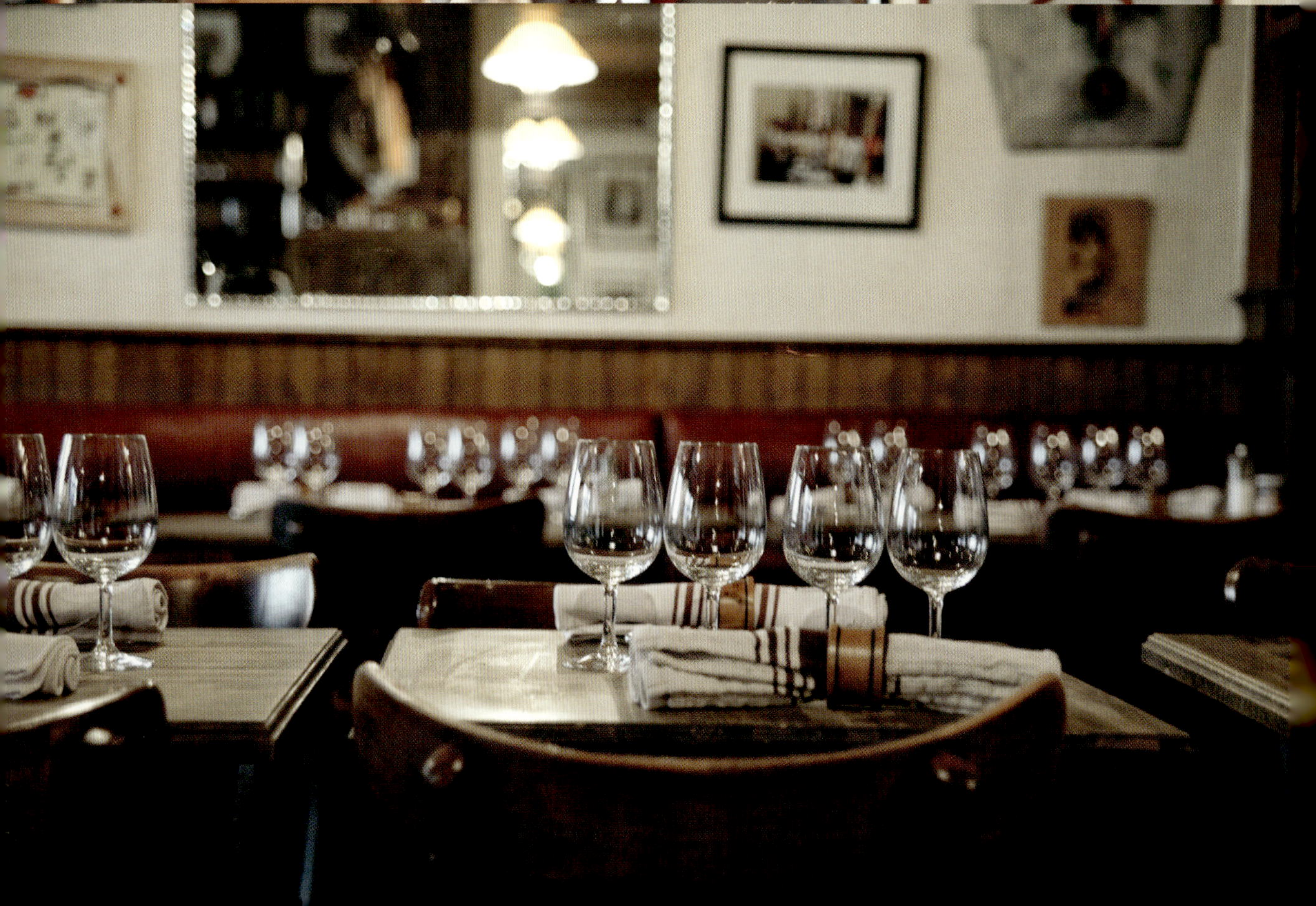

CHEZ L'AMI JEAN

'The philosophy behind my kitchen and cooking is simple: no partitions; no barriers; inspiration taken from tradition; being free... do you know what I mean? We do gastronomy; bistro-style, regional and country cooking; in fact just cooking! My strategy is to find the best produce, sourced from all over France, and then to do everything, from A to Z, something different every day. Today I've made this: octopus terrine with foie gras and smoked salt. That's for today; but I don't know about tomorrow. The easy thing would be to make it again, but that wouldn't be any fun... Freedom is what counts here!'

Stéphane Jego

CHEZ L'AMI JEAN / 27 rue Malar / Paris VIIe

J'aime Paris

PARIS WILL ALWAYS BE PARIS

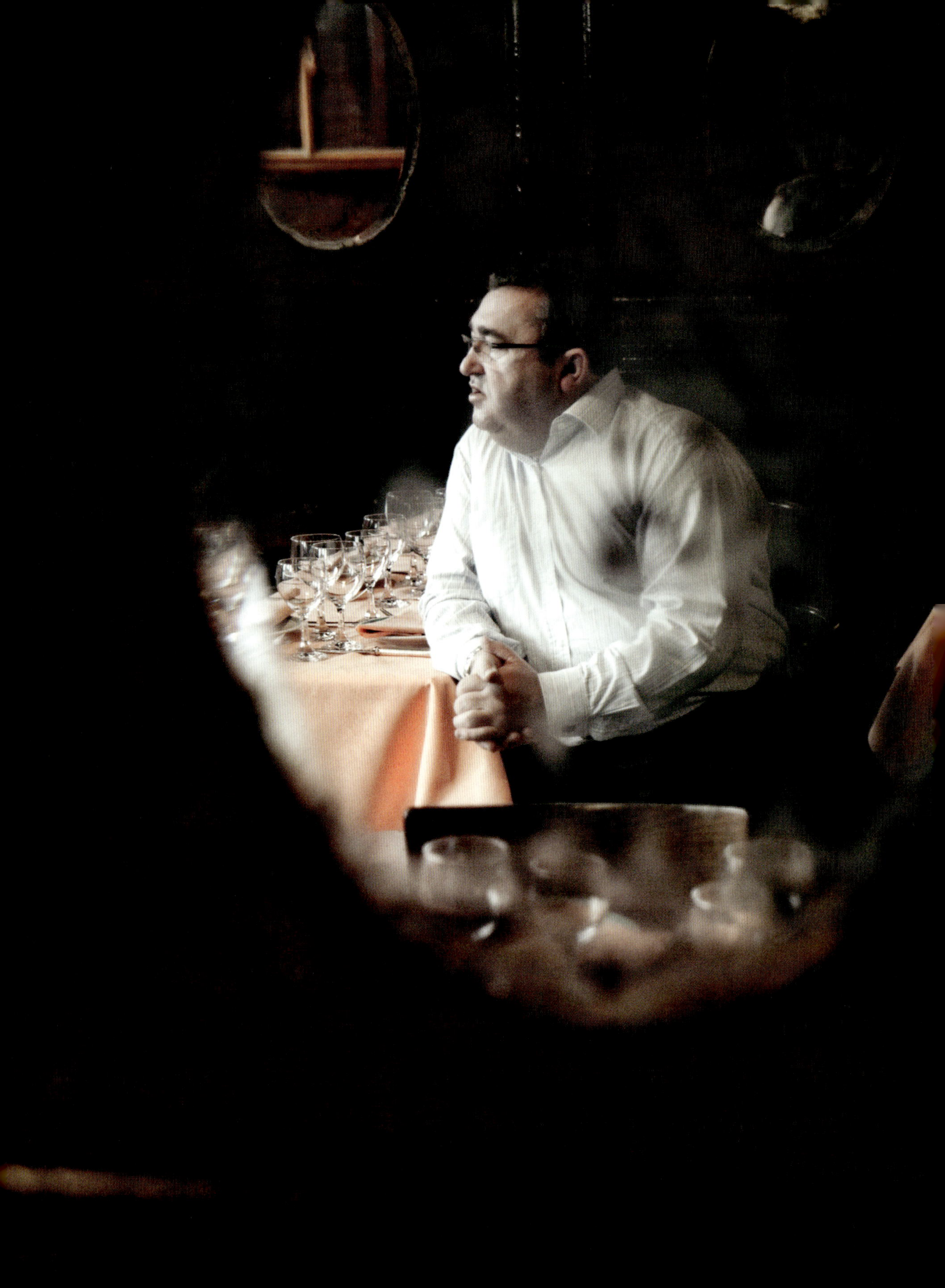

CHEZ L'AMI LOUIS / 32 rue du Vertbois / Paris III[e]

J'aime Paris

SANCERRE LES MONTS DAMNES 2008 H. BOURGEOIS 60 – TRONQUOY LALANDE 2005 81 –VIEUX
CHATEAU LANDON 2005 60 - M.A VENT MERLIN 2005 56 – MARIUS 2005 115 – RESERVE DE LOUIS 2006 80

   FOIE GRAS DES LANDES   57
   JAMBON PATA NEGRA   52
   CONFIT DE CANARD FROID   38
   ESCARGOTS DE BOURGOGNE LA DZ   39
   CUISSES DE GRENOUILLES A LA PROVENCALE   60

AGNEAU DE LAIT ROTI P. BEARNAISES 2 pers. 64 p. pers.
COTE DE BŒUF GRILLEE 2 pers. 60 p. pers.
ENTRECOTE POELEE 64
COTES DE MOUTON GRILLEES 45
CONFIT DE CANARD AUX POMMES BEARNAISE 47
COTE DE VEAU GRILLEE 47
COTE DE VEAU A LA CREME 53
ROGNON DE VEAU GRILLE 48
ROGNON DE VEAU FLAMBE 54
PIGEON ROTI AUX PETITS POIS 49
CAILLES D ELEVAGE AUX RAISINS 45
POULET ROTI (entier) 78 2pers
                                      SALADE

FRUITS DE SAISON
FRUITS ROUGES (selon arrivage) 24
GÂTEAU AU CHOCOLAT 24
NOUGATINE AU RHUM 24
ANANAS FRAIS 24 OU AU KIRSCH 24
PRUNEAUX A L ARMAGNAC 24
GLACES ET SORBETS AU CHOIX 24
       PRIX NETS SERVICE 15% COMPRIS

CHEZ L'AMI LOUIS

In 1924, this establishment, which served *bouillon* and fried dishes, was owned by Louis Pedebosq. Antoine Magnin bought the business in 1936 and continued to offer traditional cuisine. Several generations of customers frequent the restaurant today, each of whom has a particular emotional attachment to it. Its last owner, Thierry de La Brosse, perfectly preserved the spirit of the place. Now that he has joined the angels, it is certain that his successors will, under the benevolent supervision of Monsieur Louis, be able to carry on his legacy.

CHEZ L'AMI LOUIS / 32 rue du Vertbois / Paris IIIe

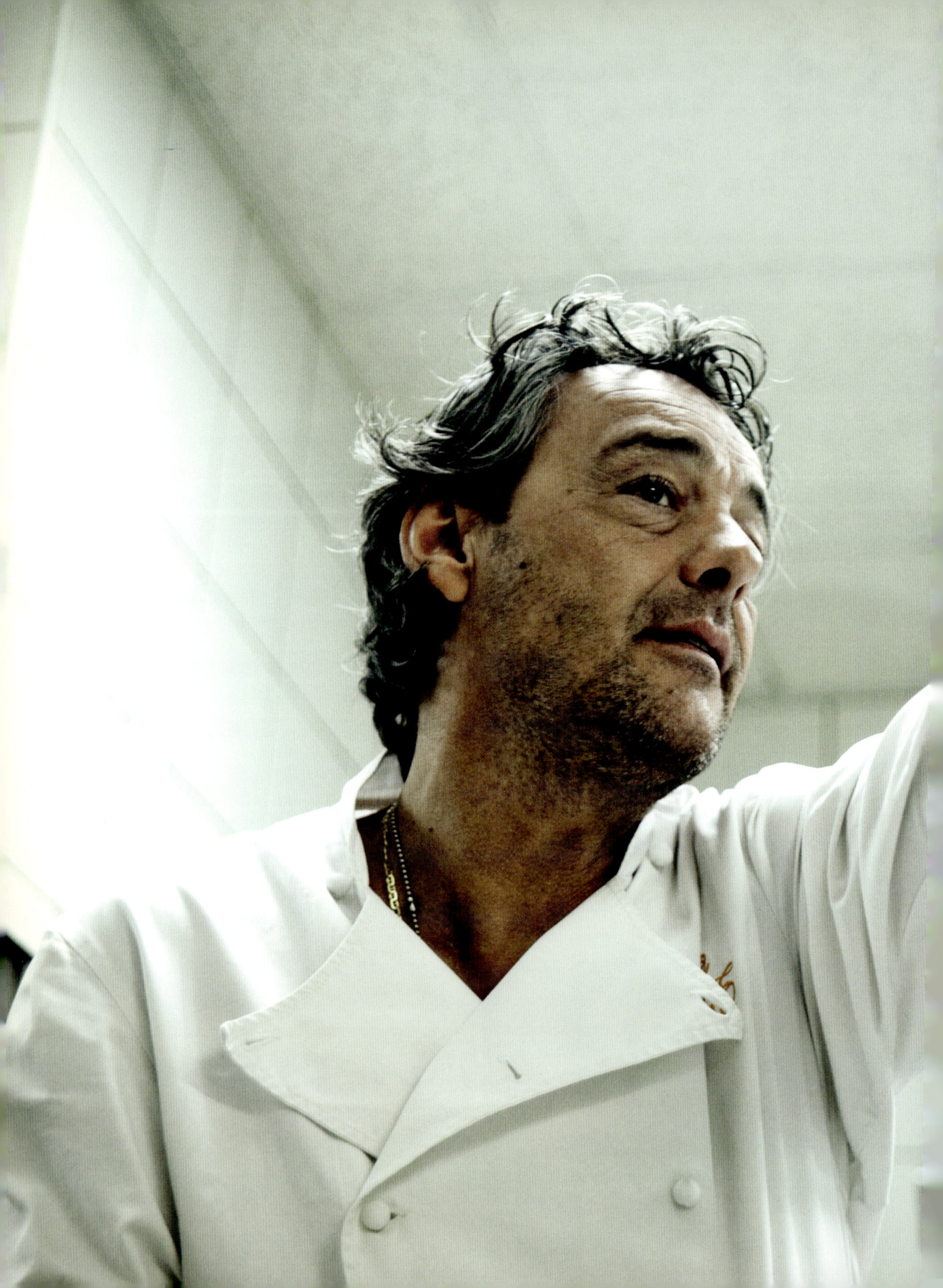

CITRUS ÉTOILE / 6 rue Arsène Houssaye / Paris VIIIe

PARIS WILL ALWAYS BE PARIS

J'aime Paris

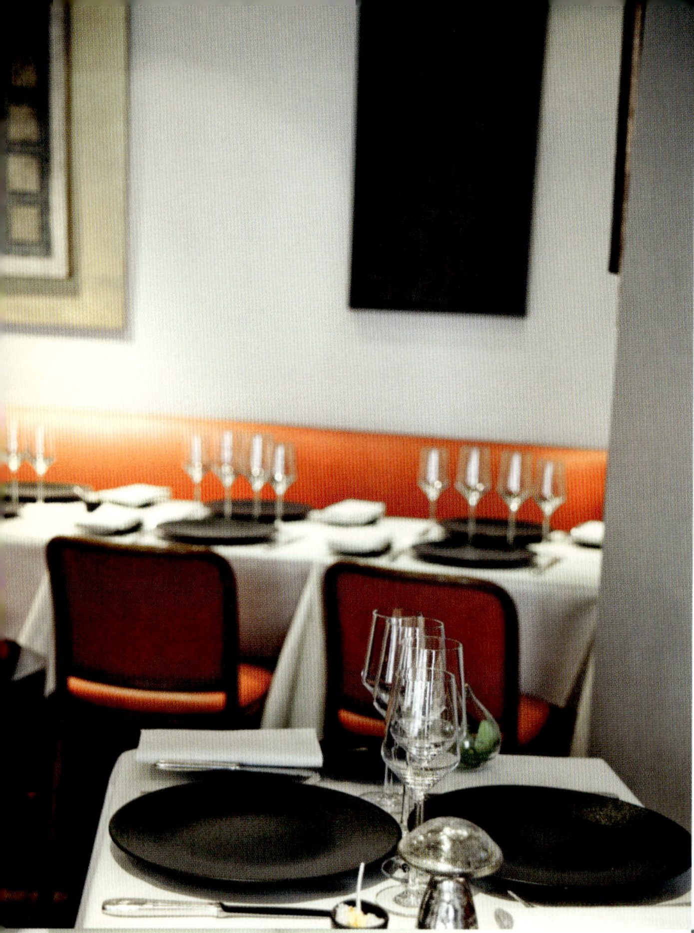

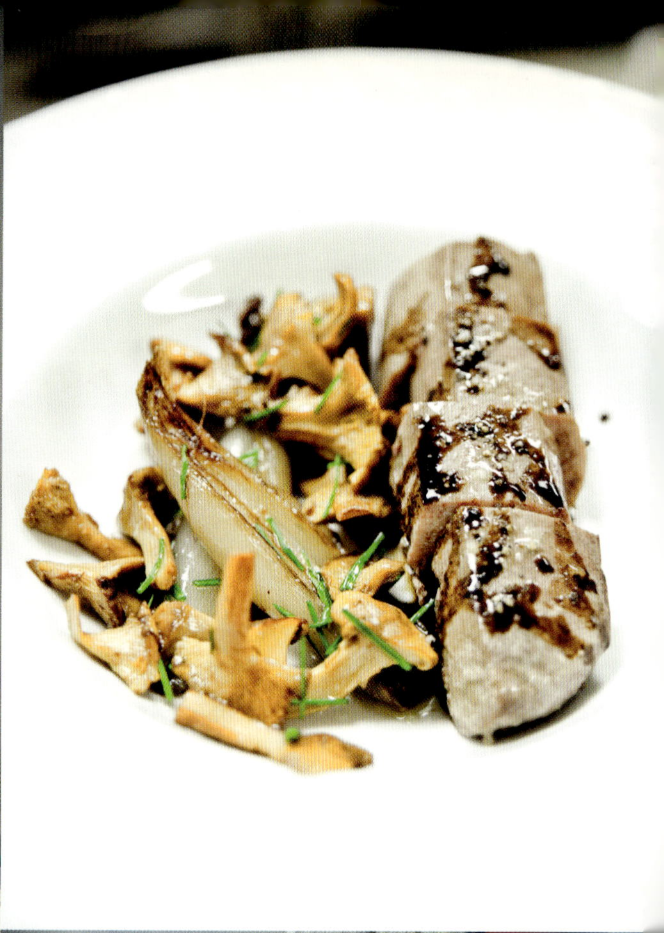

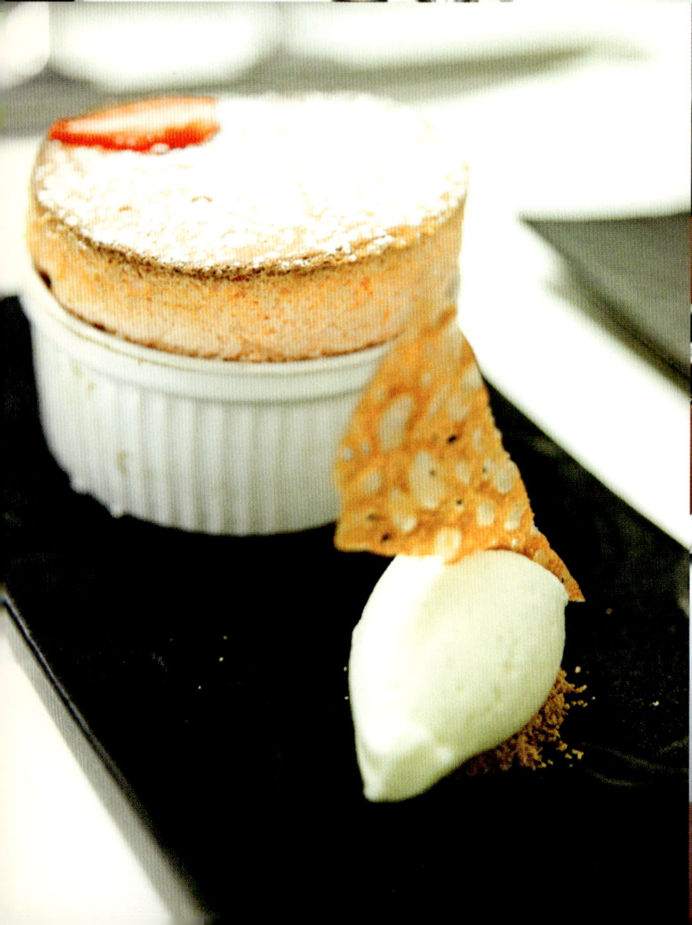

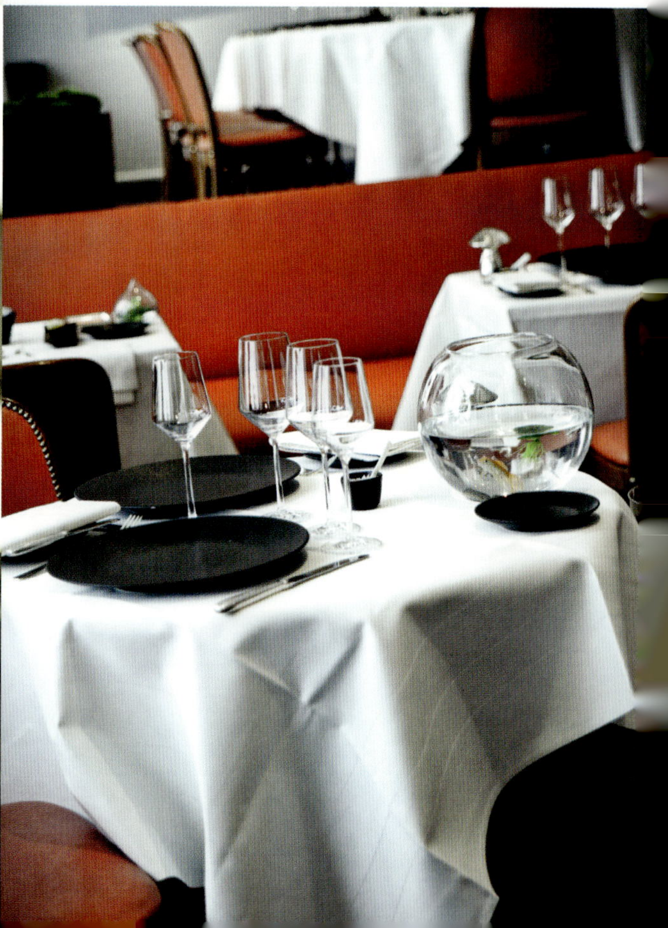

During his ten years in Hollywood, five of which were spent at L'Orangerie, Gilles Epié learned the lessons of lively and light cuisine without cream or butter. Steaming and lemon juice are enough to bring out the best in food and evidently work: duck foie gras ravioli with truffles and morels or steamed calf's liver with chanterelle mushrooms. The chic décor features a palette of electrifying citrus colours. Epié's wife Élizabeth, a former model he met in Los Angeles, supervises the front of house with enthusiasm and energy. She offers an extremely warm welcome to all customers.

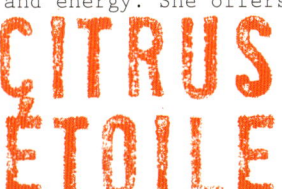

CITRUS ÉTOILE

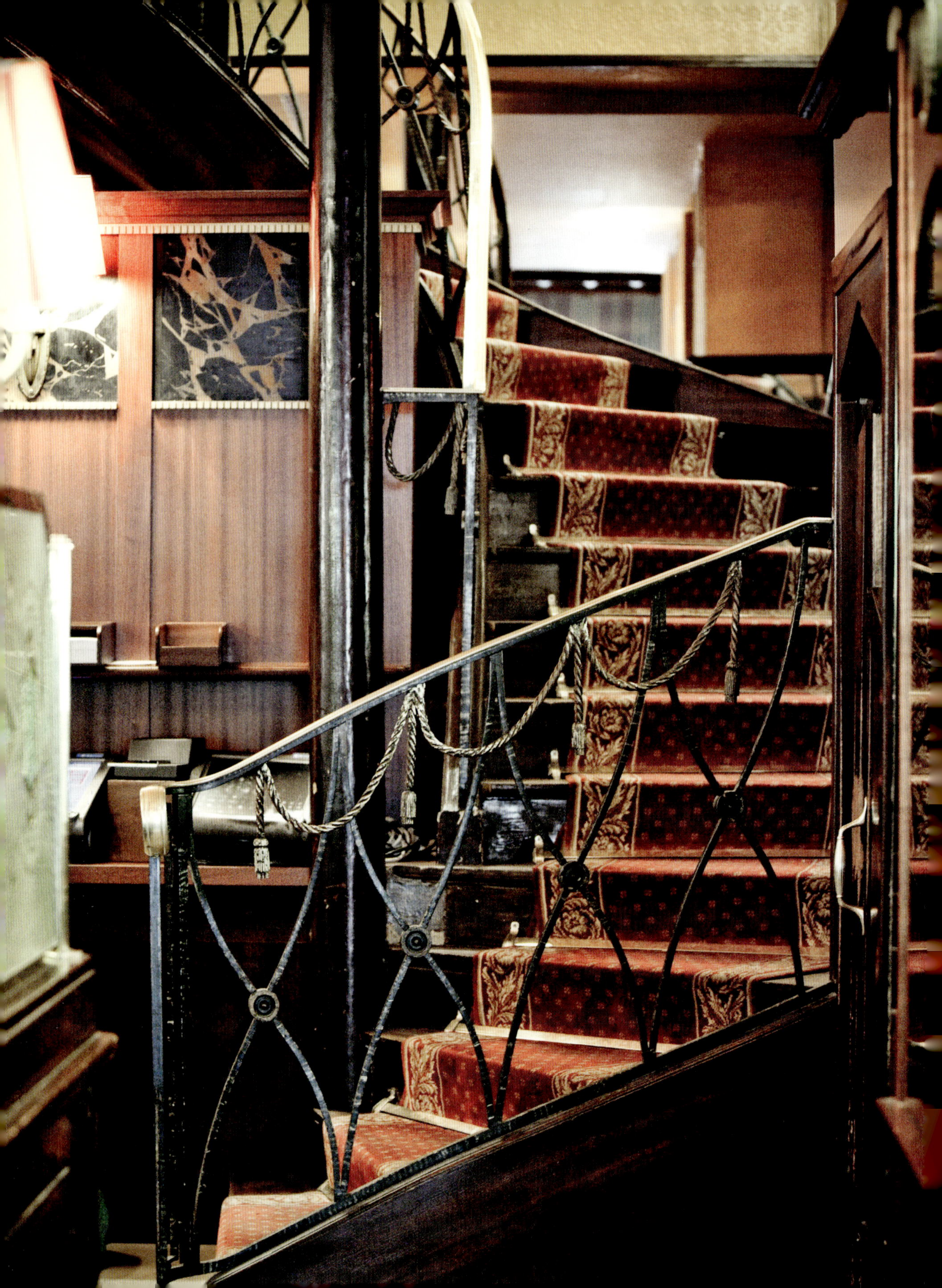

LA CLOSERIE DES LILAS / 171 boulevard du Montparnasse / Paris VI

DES LILAS

171, BOULEVARD DU MONTPARNASSE, PARIS

CLOSERIE DES LILAS

171 boulevard du Montparnasse / Paris VIe

You automatically look under the banquette in case Picasso left behind a splash of paint, Hemingway a page of one of his manuscripts or Rimbaud a free verse. Regulars who come here — even in Aragon's day — are in the know: you have to go to the brasserie; the restaurant is for the *bourgeois*. What matters is that you enjoy the arbour and its famous lilac trees while you let the legendary hand-cut steak tartare or haddock *à la crème* melt in your mouth and tantalise your taste buds.

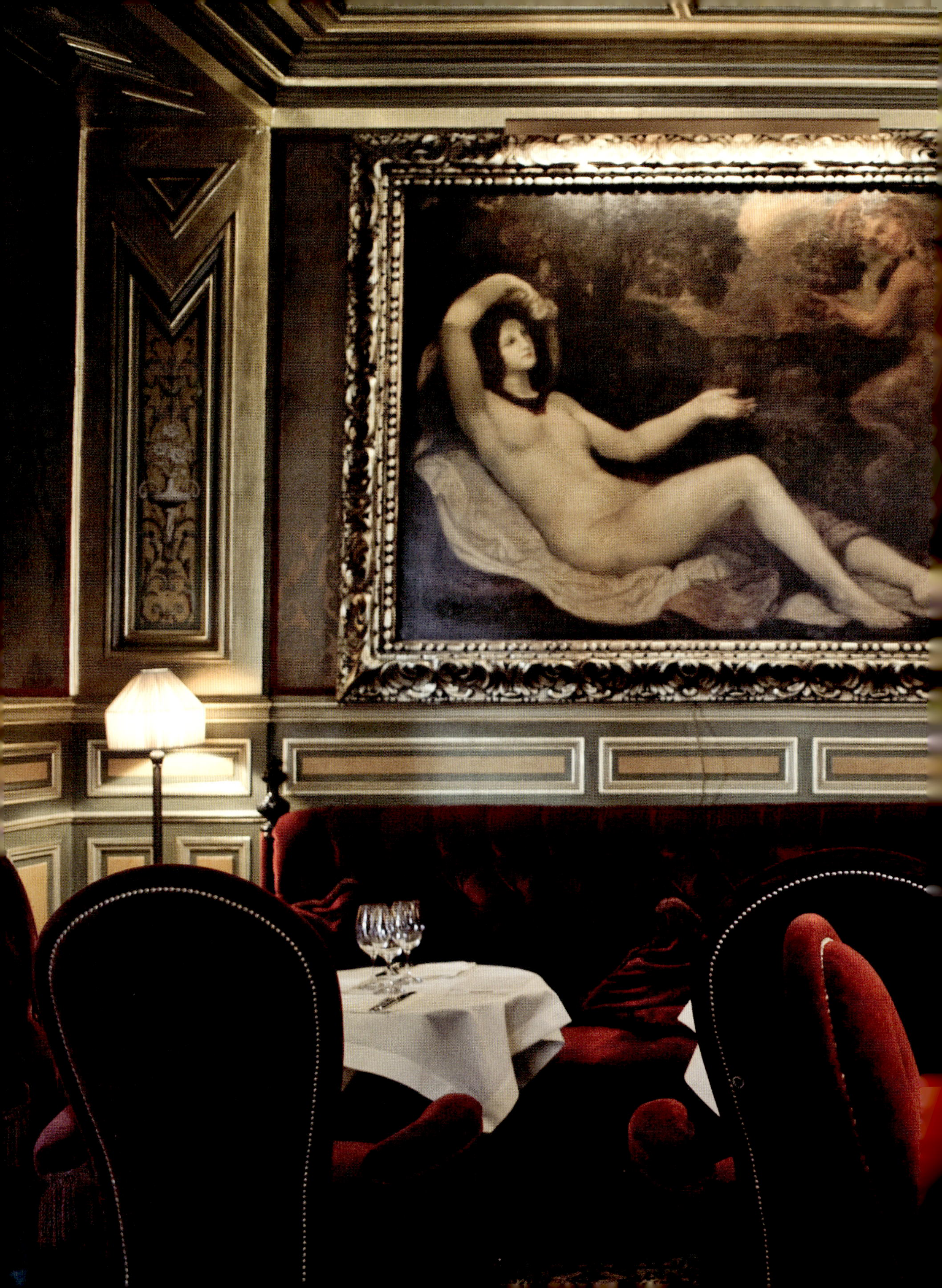

HÔTEL COSTES / 239 rue Saint-Honoré / Paris1er J'aime Paris

HŌTEL COSTES

Here is Costes, in the style of Jean-Louis. People go there to check out the scene and to be treated badly. Jacques García's neo-Napoleon III décor, with its cardinal red draperies and velvet, is worth seeing — and so are the clientele. But if you come back, it won't be by chance. The quality of the food is exacting and constant, almost obsessively so. The menu doesn't change often, but why alter something that works? Signature dishes include the famous 'Crying Tiger', a reworking of the Thai classic.

HÔTEL COSTES / 239 rue Saint-Honoré / Paris Ier

J'aime Paris

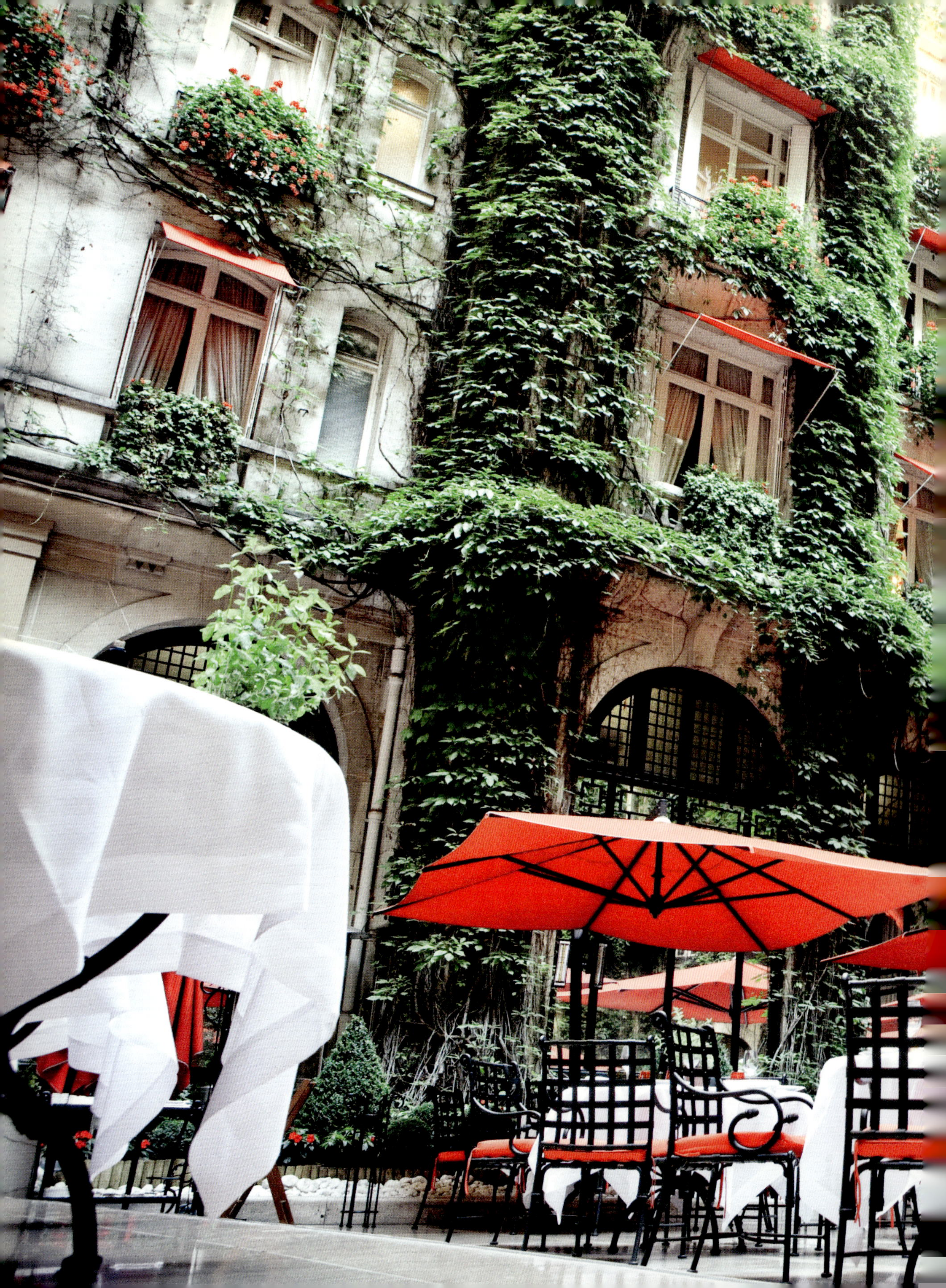

J'aime Paris

LA COUR JARDIN / 25 avenue Montaigne / Paris VIIIè

COUR JAR DIN

From May to September, the Hotel Plaza Athénée opens its courtyard and sets up a summer restaurant. Sheltered from view in the cool garden, you can enjoy a special moment with a Mediterranean feel. Heritage tomatoes, fava beans, artichokes, fennel, courgette flowers... vegetables dominate the menu. Enjoy listening to the birds in a chic rustic atmosphere.

LA COUR JARDIN / 25 avenue Montaigne / Paris VIIIe

J'aime Paris

- 137

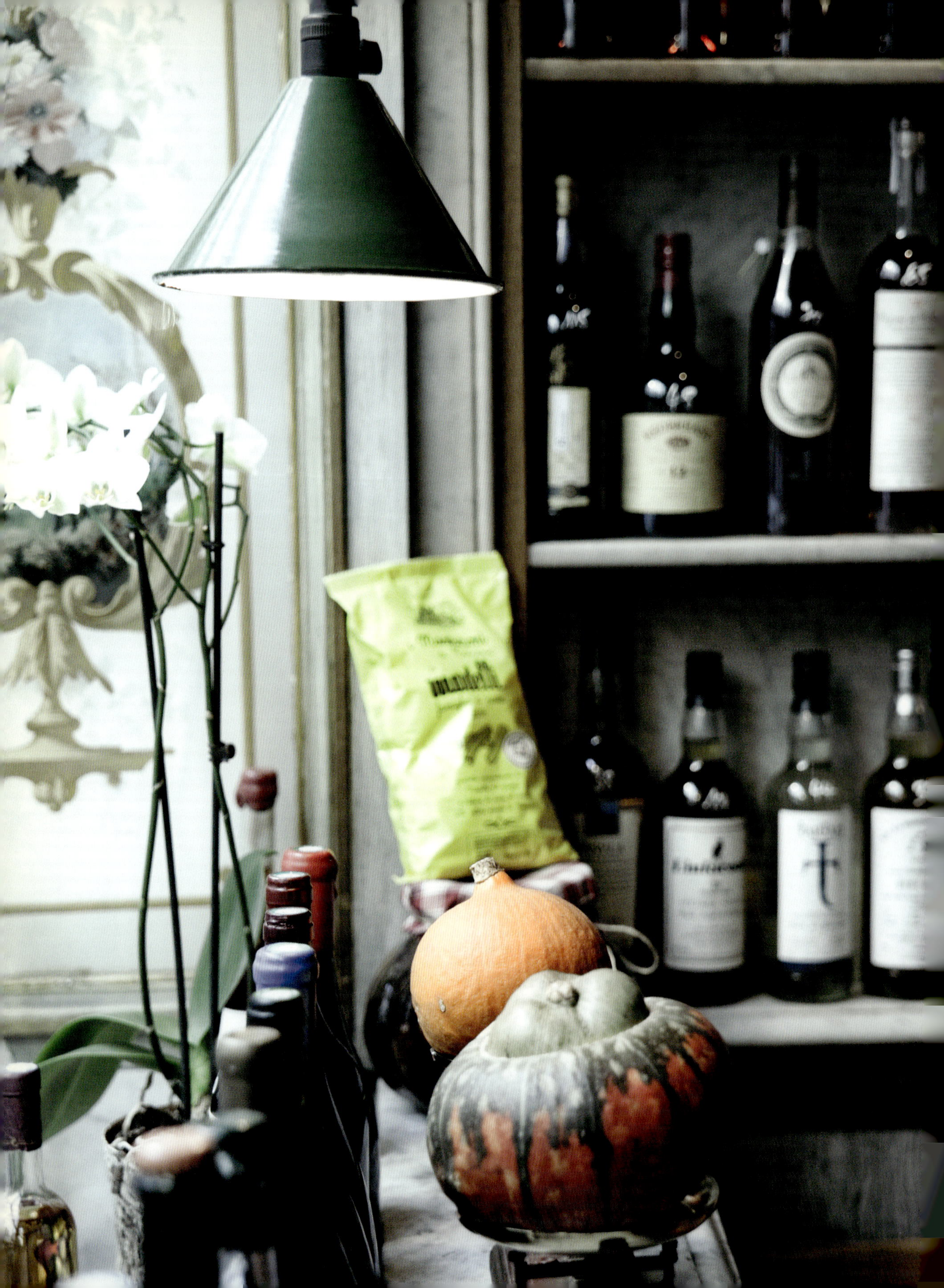

J'aime Paris

PARIS WILL ALWAYS BE PARIS

LA CRÉMERIE 9 rue des Quatre-Vents / Paris VIe

- 139

CRÉMERIE

It's always a magical moment when the scissor tip cuts the pouch, which opens like petals. Inside, happiness takes on the form of *burrata cremossissima*. A drizzle of olive oil, a few cherry tomatoes and a scant sprinkling of herbs are added. A spoon sinks into it and would like to stay there forever. While Serge cuts *prosciutto* on the Berkel slicer, Hélène prepares a vegetable tian. We're ready for the ripe Camembert, handsome Serge's pride and joy.

LA CRÉMERIE / 9 rue des Quatre-Vents / Paris VIe

J'aime Paris

Le Divellec

LE DIVELLEC / 107 rue de l'Université / Paris VIIe

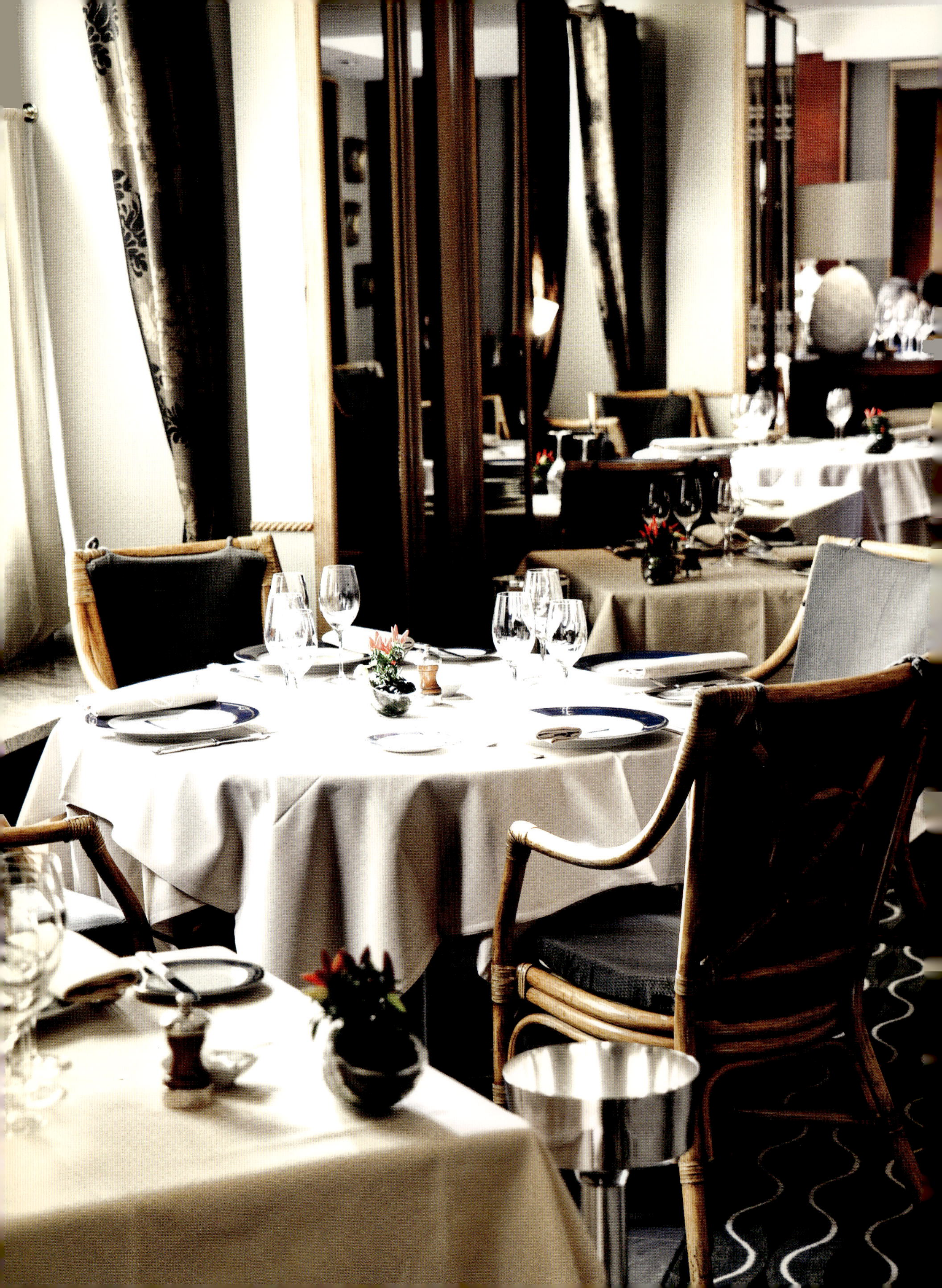

LE DIVELLEC

'Paris? I was born there. But my parents, both natives of Brittany, moved to La Rochelle when I was young. I spent 25 years there, preparing game in winter and fish in summer. I returned to Paris in 1983, and I brought back coastal cuisine with me — fish, crustaceans and shellfish... My cooking seems classic today. But back then there weren't many people who would dare to serve veal sweetbreads with langoustines or shellfish with foie gras. This morning I received these seven-kilo turbots, some wedge sole and mullets as wide as your arm from my wholesalers in Brittany. I taught my waiters to handle and bone fish in front of customers. This means a lot to me; it's the identity of the house.'

Jacques Le Divellec

LE DIVELLEC / 107 rue de l'Université / Paris VIIe

J'aime Paris — PARIS WILL ALWAYS BE PARIS

- 145

EDMOND et JULES DE GONCOURT

JOURNAL
MÉMOIRES
DE LA VIE
LITTÉRAIRE

DROUANT / 16-18 place Gaillon / Paris II

DROUANT

'One day during my life as a chef, I decided I needed a change. I told myself that I had to grow further in the art of cooking. So I gave back my three Michelin stars and I simplified my cuisine by removing it from the gastronomy scene. I focused on core values, on what I felt was essential, and on what I wanted to cook from that day forward. But there are certain pillars that are untouchable when cooking: pleasure, indulgence, warmth and generosity. Since 2006, Drouant, this monument in Parisian restaurant culture and literature, has allowed me to express myself and to spread my wings...'

Antoine Westermann

DROUANT / 16-18 place Gaillon / Paris II

PAIN A LA FARINE DE

ET DE CHAUSSONS

AUX POMMES FRAICHES

DU PAIN ET DES IDÉES / 34 rue Yves Toudic – Paris X

DU PAIN ET DES IDÉES

'Time makes the difference — time and the number of stages. Working slowly keeps the leavening wilder. But it's also more fragile. It's like wine. Certain types of leavening will express themselves if you aren't too aggressive with them. It's living beings that are transformed; you can only adapt to the material.'

Christophe Vasseur, baker

DU PAIN ET DES IDÉES / 34 rue Yves Toudic / Paris X^e

MENU

Salade de King-crabe frais 25€
Ormes de Tonneau Archiduc 14€
Sashimi de bar de ligne 16€
Asperges Verts tièdes et sauce fraîche 12€ — huitres Plates 000
Millefeuille de homard "bleu" et légumes Confits 18€   3 pièces 15€
Langoustines vivantes rôties au beurre d'algues 16€
Aiguille de Couteaux aux épices 10€
Langoustines Royales vivantes rôties au beurre d'algues, riz crémeux à la tomate 35€
Demi-homard "bleu" frais, macédoine de légumes 32€
Demi-homard "bleu" au Kari-Gosse, frites "maison" 32€
Sole "Petit Bateau" meunière, pommes ratte à l'échagne 36€
Blanc de turbot "Sauvage" et jeunes poireaux 36€
Joues de Lotte du Guilvinec aux petits légumes 22€
Petit de St Pierre aux girolles 36€
Turbotin "Sauvage" pour 3 personnes 36€/personne

Assiette de fromages fermiers affinés de chez Bacrot 9€
Fondant au chocolat, crème au bailli
Tapioca Vanille en granité 8€

MENU HOMARD
46€

12 Huîtres Plates du Belon N°5
―
½ Homard "Bleu" au Kari-Gosse
et ses Frites "Maison"
―
Émincé de Pommes et son Caramel

ÉCAILLER DU BISTROT

This is the seafood restaurant belonging to Bistrot Paul Bert, Edith Piaf's haunt that we liked so much. On the style side, it's definitely a notch above the other. On the food side, it's also good, and not without reason; the chef's father-in-law is a fisherman. There are a dozen seafood dishes on the blackboard featuring fish, shellfish and shelled crab. There's also a good-value lobster menu.

L'ÉCAILLER DU BISTROT / 22 rue Paul Bert / Paris XIe

J'aime Paris

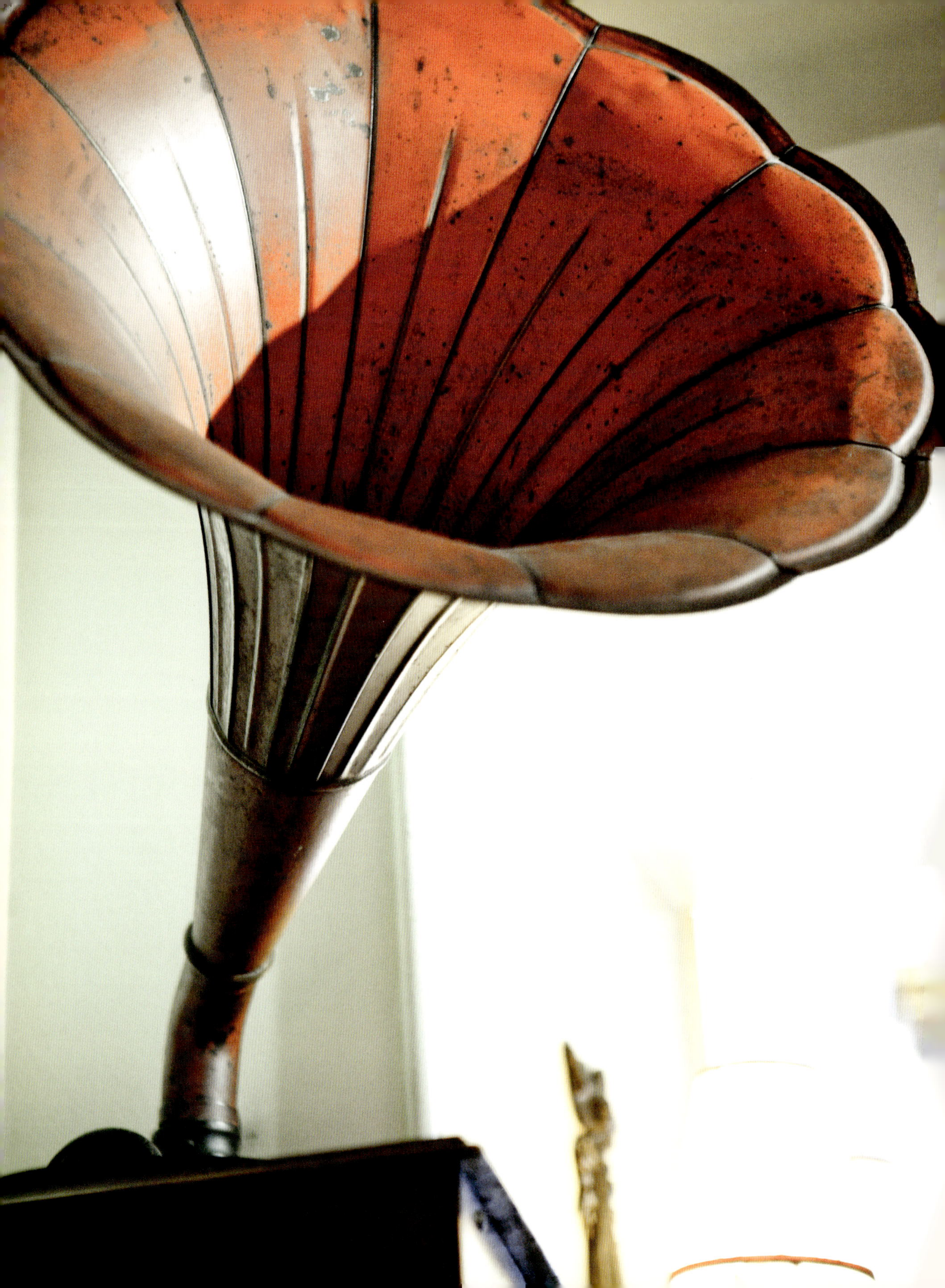

LA FONTAINE DE MARS / 129 rue Saint-Dominique / Paris VIIe

FONTAINE DE MARS

In the past, the horses of Napoleon's Imperial Guard came to drink from the fountain of Mars, god of war. The horses are now a thing of the past, but the fountain continues to murmur invitingly to passers-by and American presidents on official visits. In this traditional bistro — complete with checked tablecloths, moleskin banquettes and straw-bottom chairs — Christiane and Jacques Boudon showcase products from the south-west of France: cassoulet with Tarbes beans, Basque country blood sausage by Christian Parra and *tourtière landaise* prune pie, among others. However, they don't neglect the rest of the country with their charcuterie products from Mainon Laborie in the Auvergne region and Duval andouillette sausages. The eggs poached in Madiran wine are a highlight.

LA FONTAINE DE MARS (129, rue Saint-Dominique, Paris VII°) PARIS WILL ALWAYS BE PARIS — J'aime Paris

Hi-Fidelity

LE FORUM / 4 boulevard Malesherbes / Paris VIIIᵉ

FORUM

Why on earth is this so good? The spirits come in all colours with the most fashionable labels. There are more than 25 cocktail recipes and a third-millennium London ambience. The cocktails in this institution of Parisian nightlife, stirred not shaken by Josaine Biolatto, are true culinary concoctions. They radiate quality, inventiveness and humour. You could while the night away just enjoying them.

LE FORUM / 4 boulevard Malesherbes / Paris VIIIe

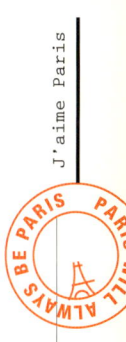

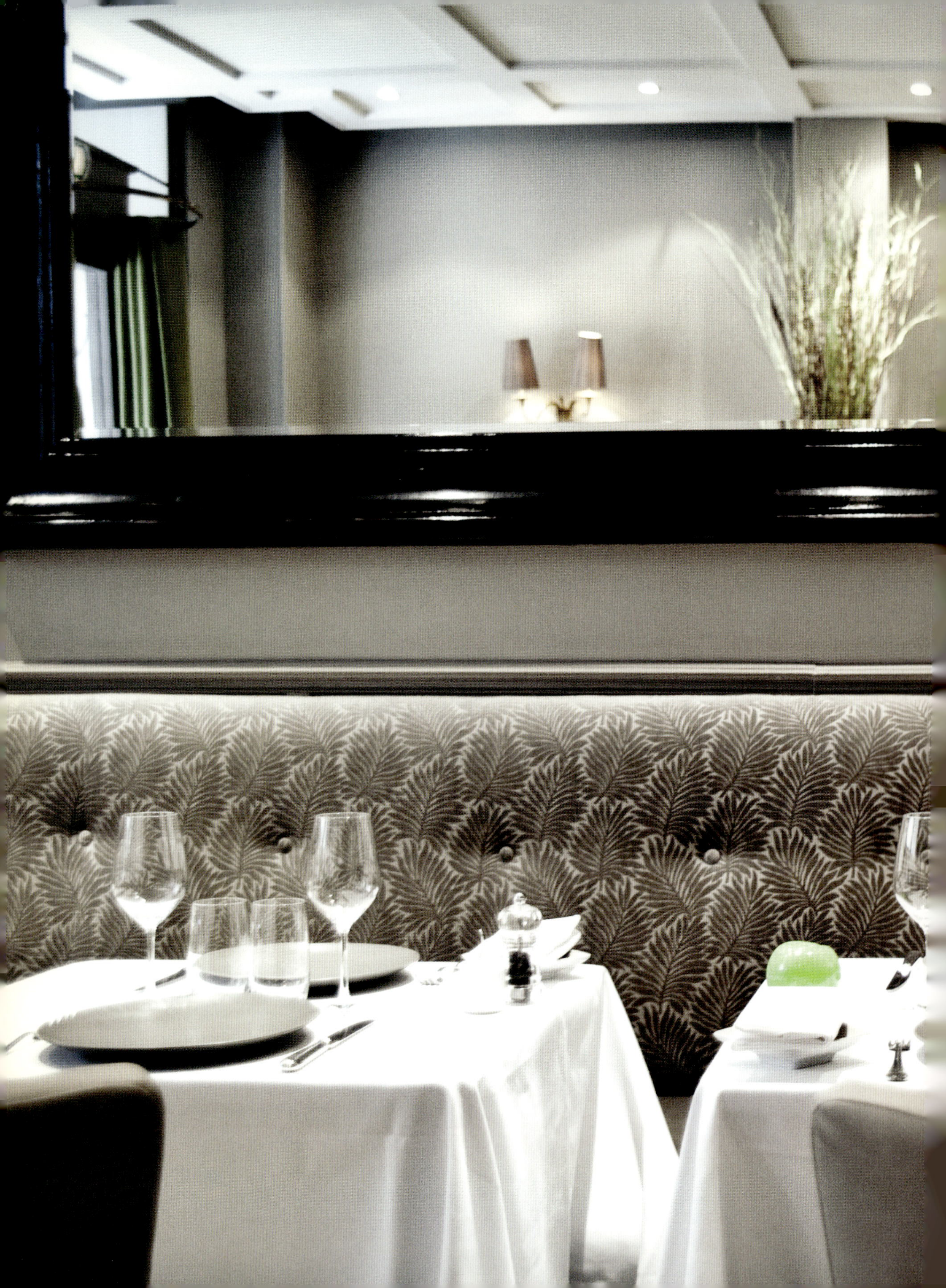

LES FOUGÈRES / 10 rue Villebois Mareuil / Paris XVIIe

J'aime Paris

PARIS WILL ALWAYS BE PARIS

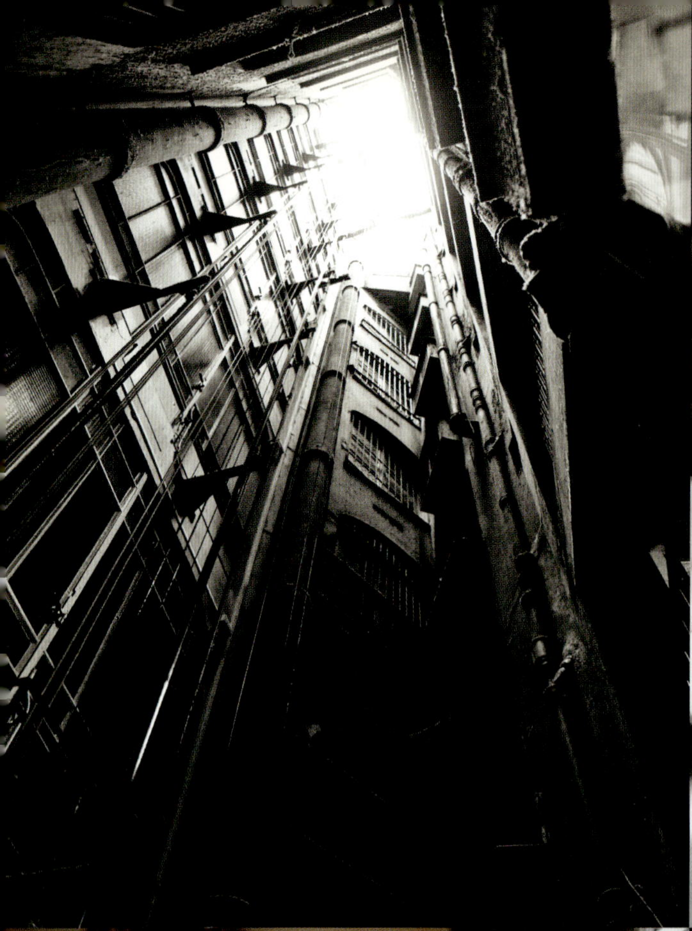
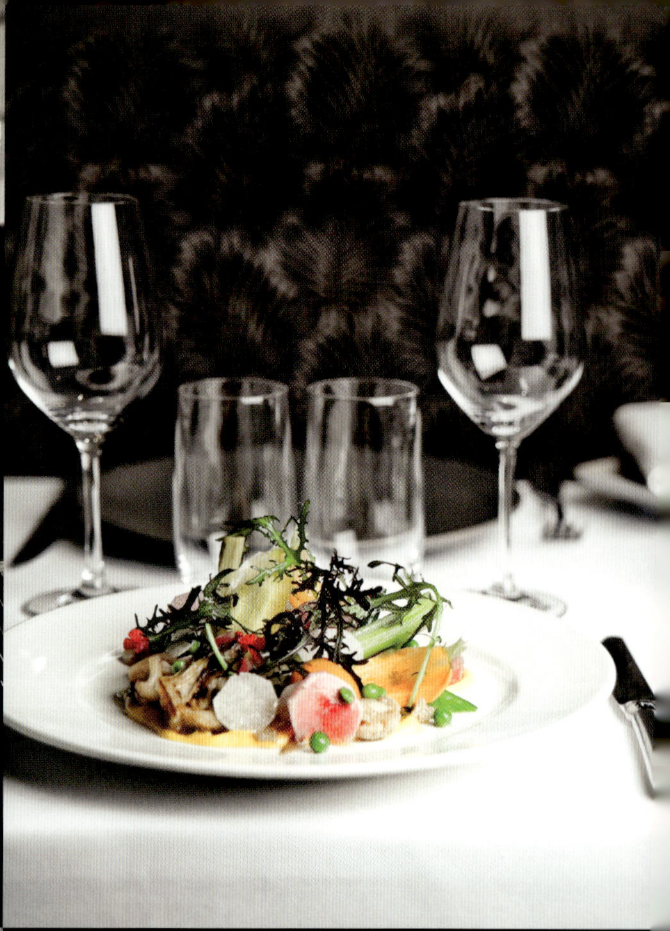
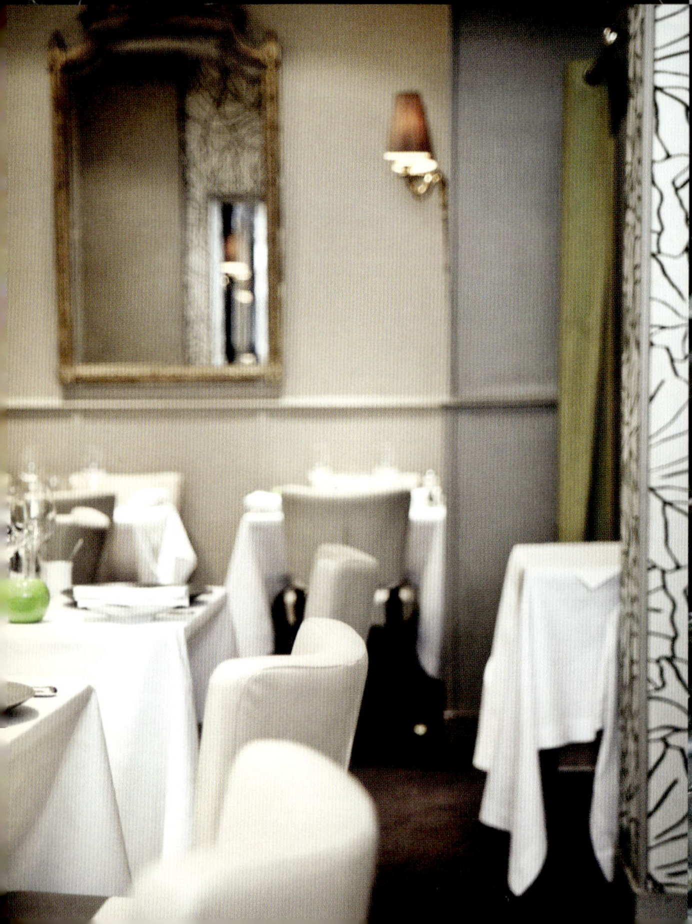
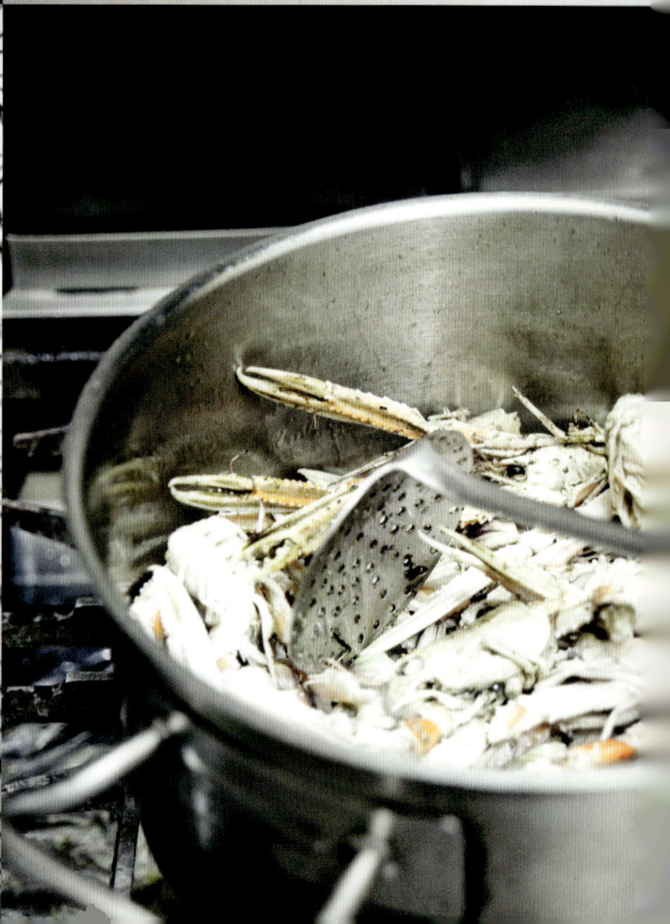

FOUGERES

LES FOUGÈRES / 10 rue Villebois Mareuil / Paris XVIIe

J'aime Paris — Paris will always be Paris

Stéphane Duchiron, chef of Les Fougères, explains: 'My favourite ingredient is mackerel. I like to start with a simple product that is available to everybody and reveal all its complexity in a dish that will surprise my guests. My favourite recipe is cuttlefish fillets with seasonal vegetables. Shiitake mushrooms are perfect in May, with their marked aroma of black truffles. What I like is to use unexpected ingredients like *écume de mer* sauce, *Juliette des Sables* potatoes and lemongrass to enhance regional produce like this sublime farmhouse pork.'

- 167

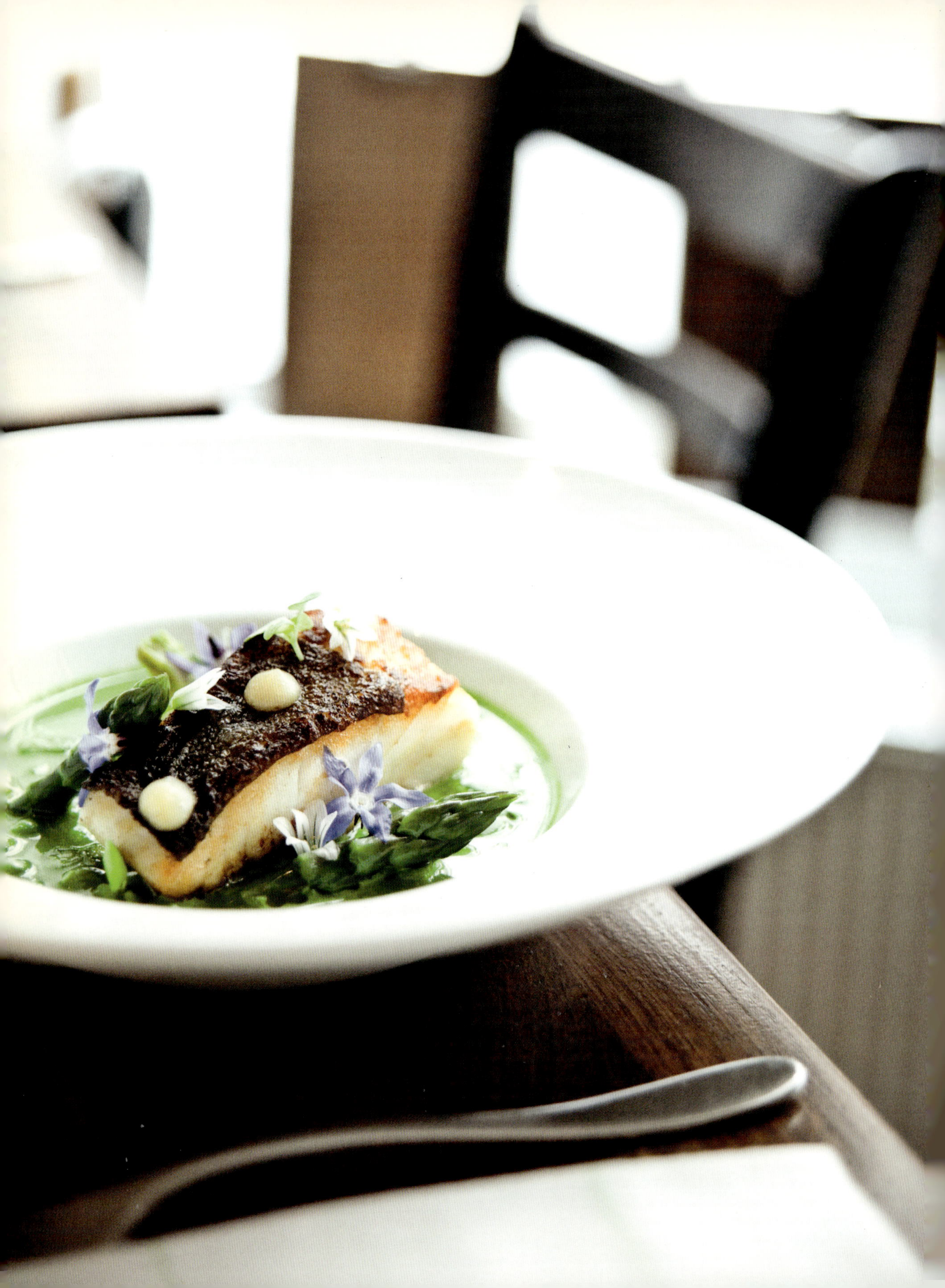

FRENCHIE / 5 rue du Nil / Paris II°

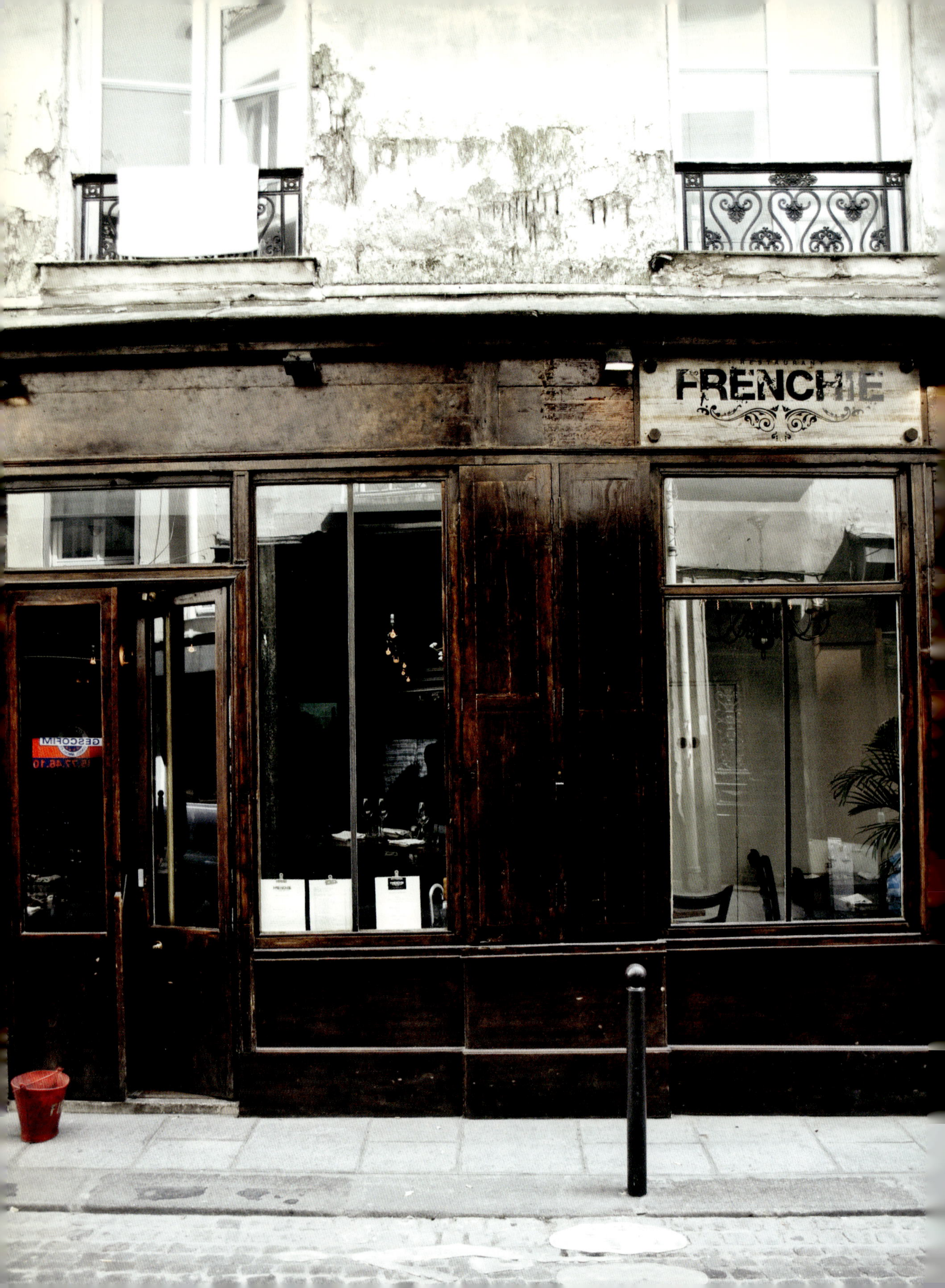
RESTAURANT
FRENCHIE

FR EW CH IE

'I went abroad at a very young age. I worked in New York and London. From what I learned during those years of training, I've tried to retain a spontaneous and honest way of cooking, and also flavours that are considered unusual in France: pickles, chutneys and citrus condiments. I do lots of freshly smoked fish... As I work alone in the kitchen, I have to get down to the essentials, to the flavour. Afterwards, for the garnish, you know there is a French school of classical garden... I'm more the English garden type; I go for an organised chaos, but one that's always harmonious!'

Grégory Marchand

PARIS WILL ALWAYS BE PARIS — J'aime Paris

FRENCHIE / 5 rue du Nil / Paris IIe

De père en fils   Les Gour

- 173

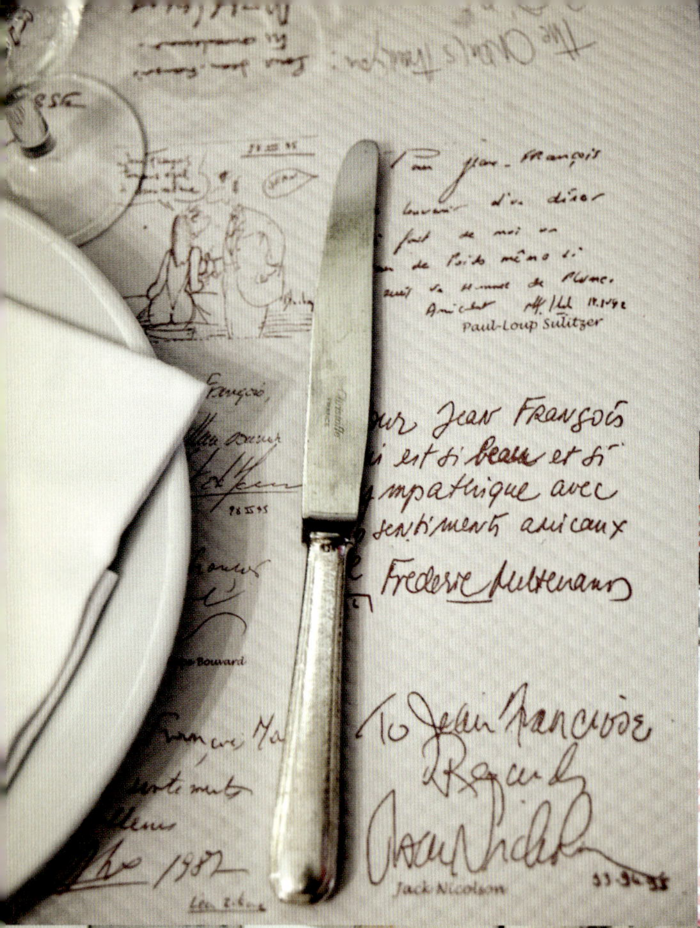
Paul-Loup Sulitzer
Jack Nicolson

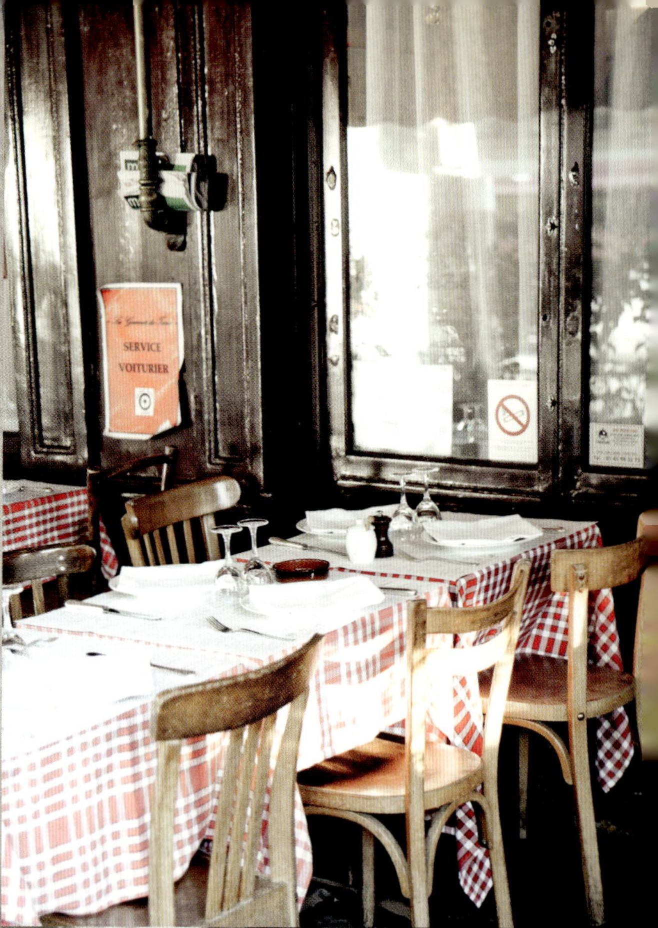
SERVICE
VOITURIER

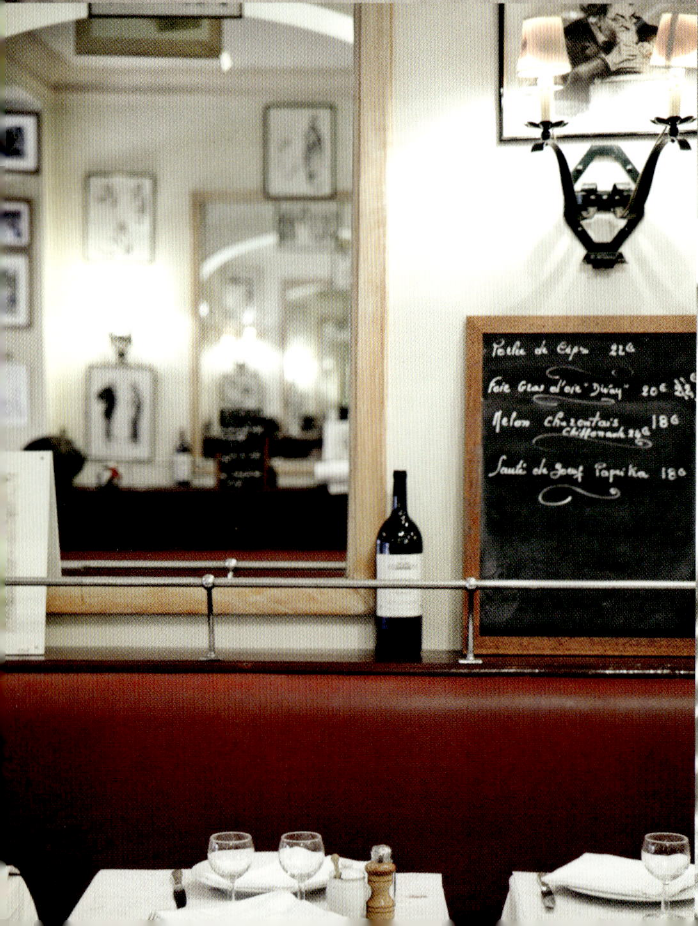

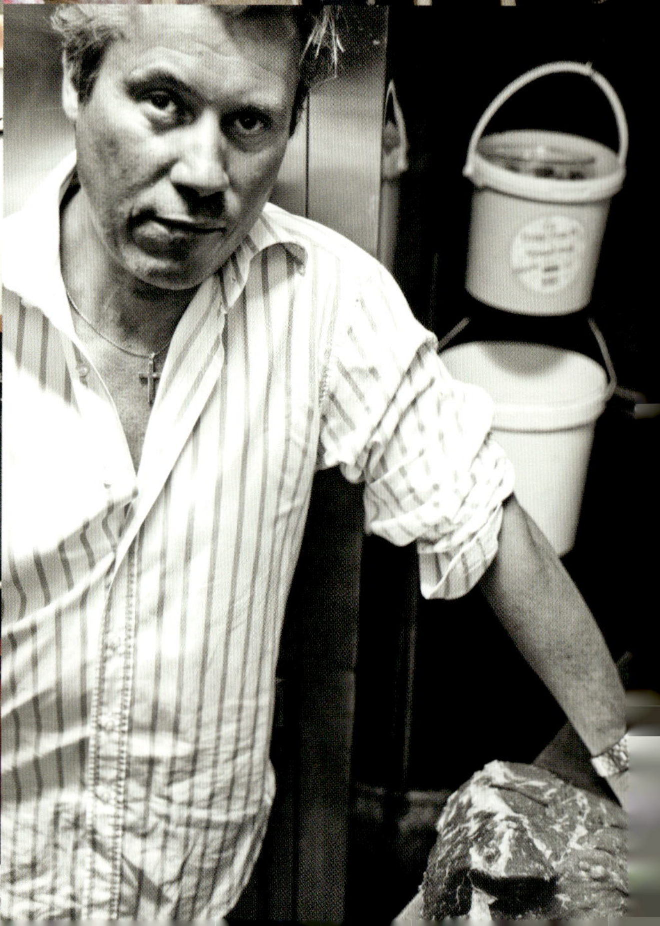

If you're a lover of straightforward cuisine and big servings, this is a really good bistro. You'll appreciate the brawn, the andouillette sausage and leeks vinaigrette. And you'll especially love the enormous 'special' steak with marrow. And you can't leave without having the *baba chantilly* dessert, which rhymes with yippee and arouses passions. Booking is recommended.

GOUR METS DES TERNES

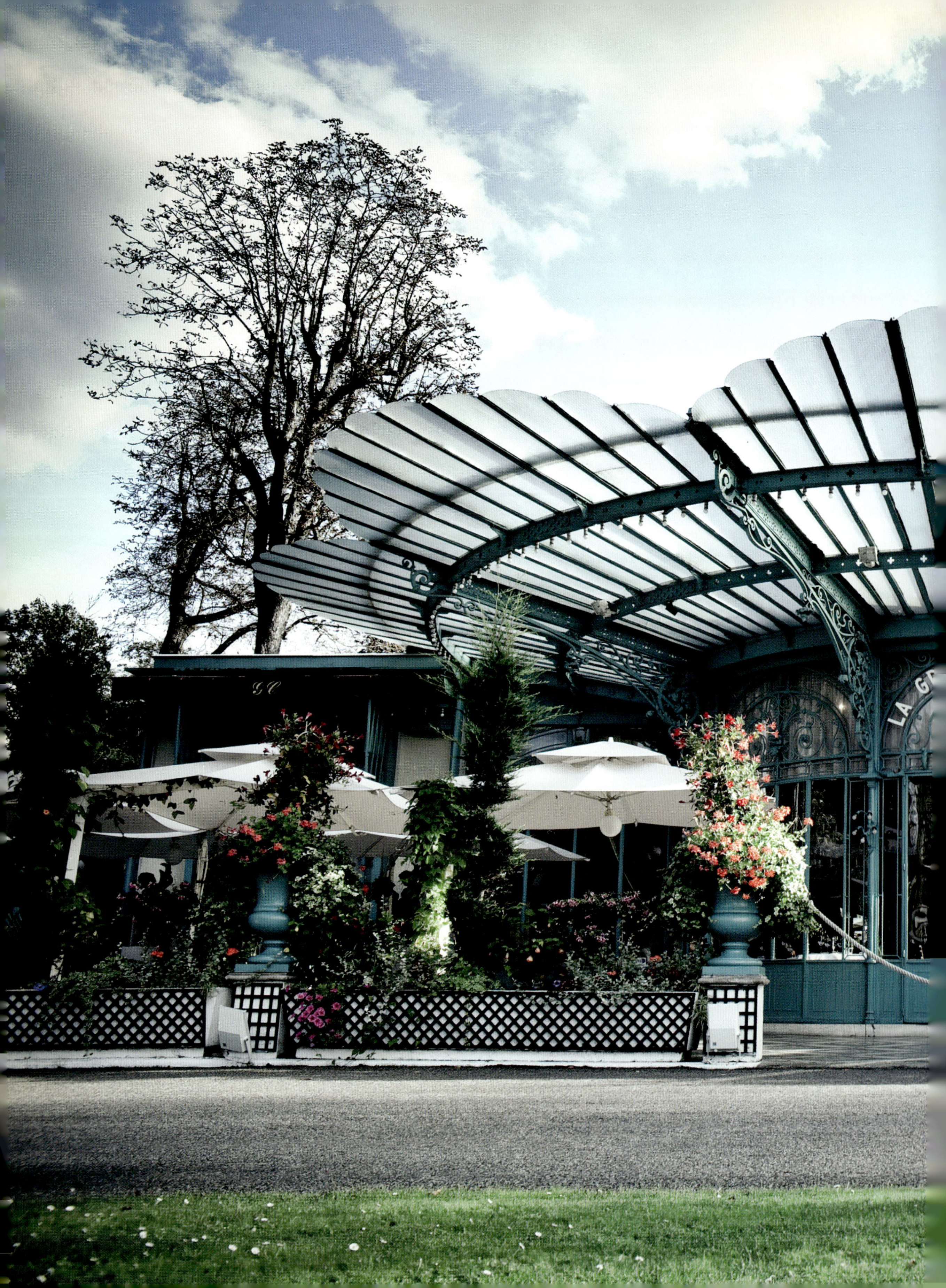

LA GRANDE CASCADE / Bois de Boulogne, Paris XVIe

GRANDE CASCADE

At midday, you are charmed by the décor, the Second Empire pavilion and the cool murmuring of the waterfall. At night, away from Paris and the notion of time, you enjoy the elegant cuisine at this, the Menut family's flagship restaurant. Here the classics are treated with a good dose of inventiveness: escargots with verbena butter, baked cod steak with butternut mousseline or horseradish *espuma* and toasted *kouglof* to go with duck foie gras. As impressionist as a Sunday in the country.

LA GRANDE CASCADE / Bois de Boulogne / Paris XVIe

J'aime Paris

PARIS WILL ALWAYS BE PARIS

- 179

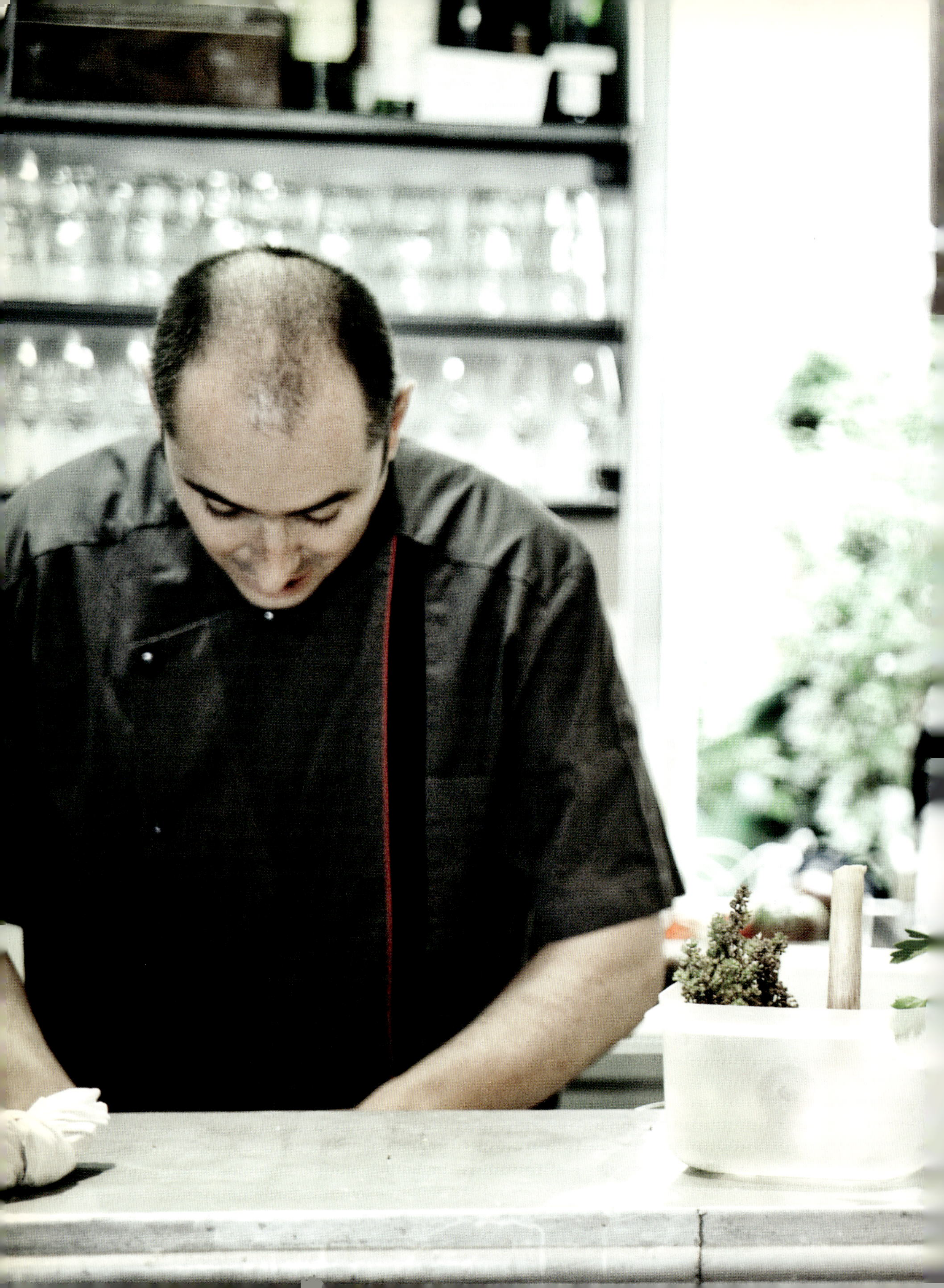

LE JEU DE QUILLES / 45 rue Boulard / Paris XIVe

PARIS WILL ALWAYS BE PARIS

J'aime Paris

- 181

JEU DE QUILLES

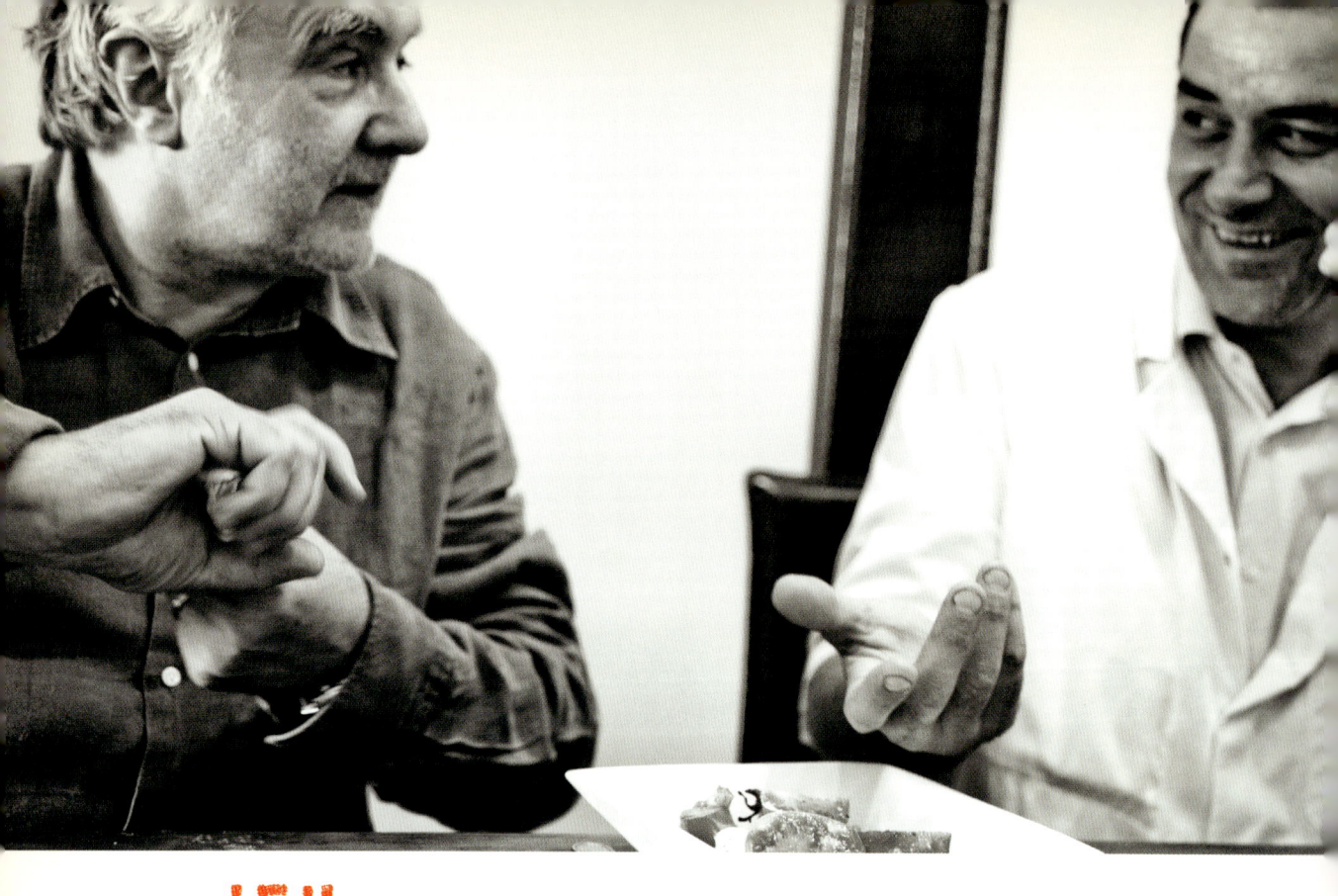

Here is a small grocery counter that is big on flavour. A superb selection of unprocessed products is served generously by Benoît Reix, who presides over the place from behind the bar. For our tasting pleasure that day: a *burrata* from Puglia, a soft mixture of cow's milk and creamy mozzarella, to be eaten with a teaspoon. It was matched to great effect with a freshly picked ripe tomato drizzled with a mild olive oil... *fleur de sel* would have been too much! Behind the bar, Benoît proposed good bio wines in classic styles.

LE JEU DE QUILLES / 45 rue Boulard / Paris XIVe

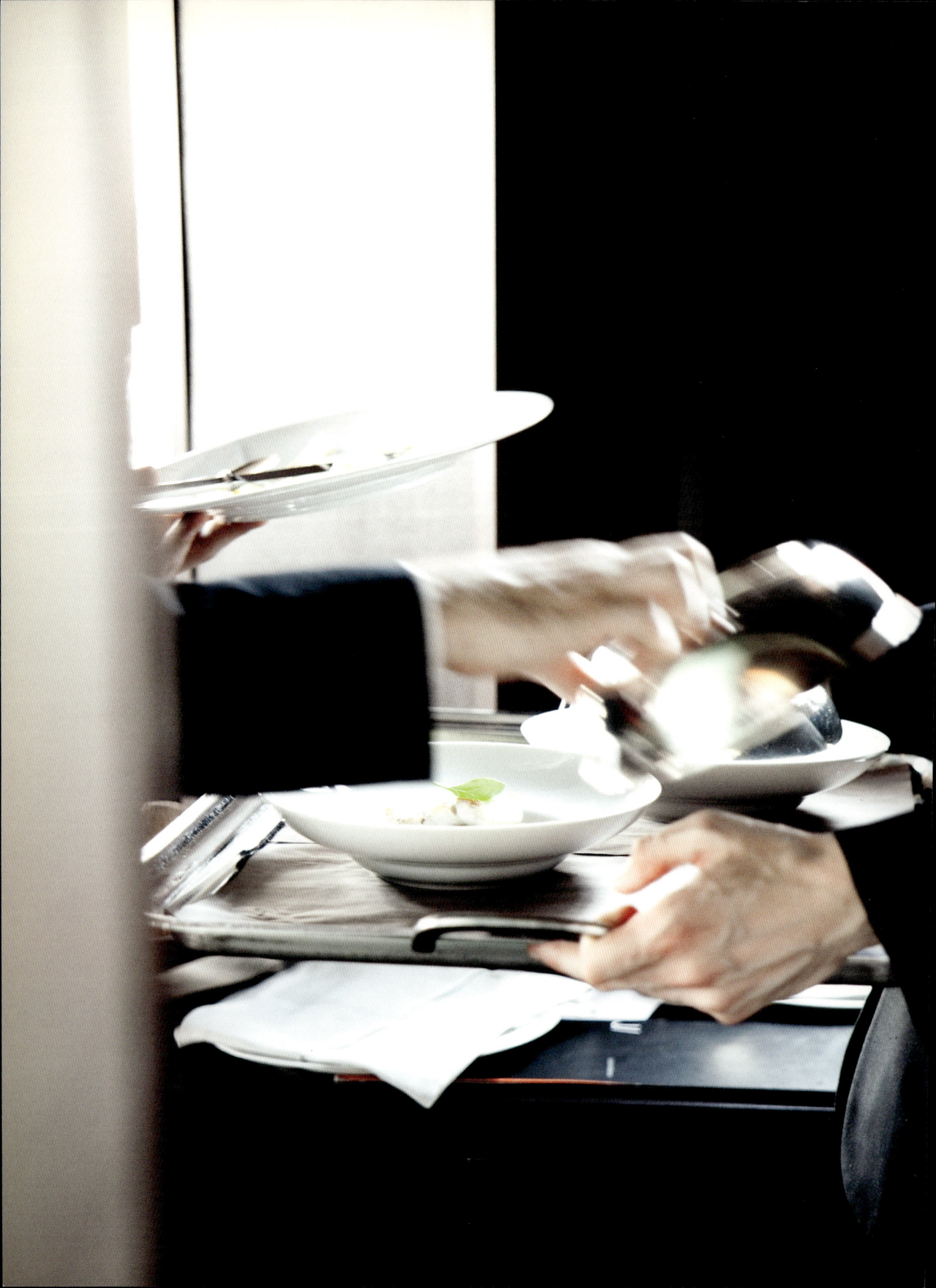

LE JULES VERNE / Altima – 6 avenue Gustave Eiffel / Paris VIIe

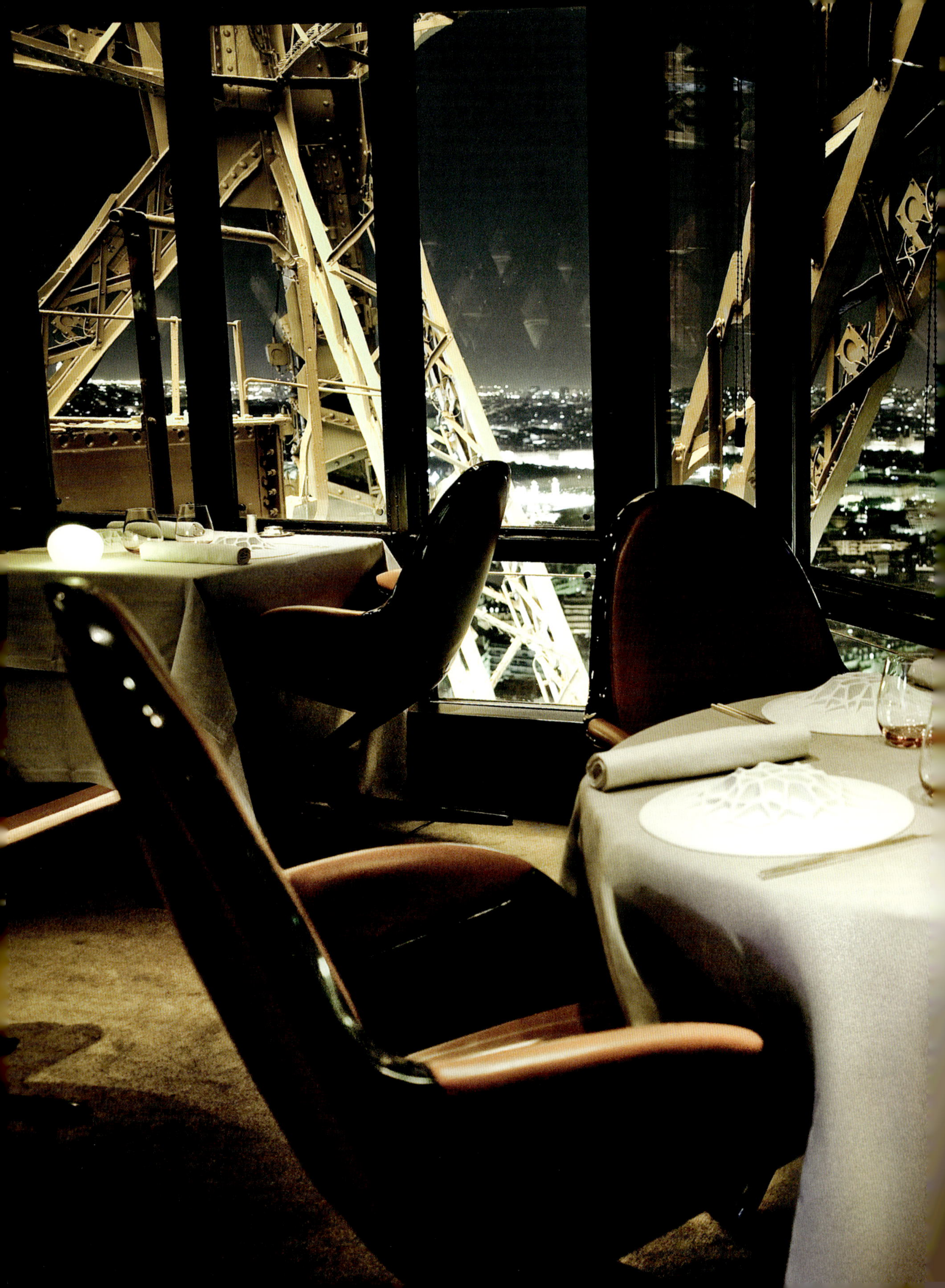

LE JULES VERNE / Alain Ducasse / 6 avenue Gustave Eiffel / Paris VII⁰

J/ LeJulesVerne

JULES VERNE

The Eiffel Tower — no Parisian can ever be indifferent about it. When it starts to sparkle the moment you look at it, and when you discover the lights of the city through the bay window, the Eiffel Tower offers you the magic of Paris as a gift. In this unique place, iconic landmark of France, the cuisine Pascal Féraud serves is 100 per cent French. From olive oil to morel mushrooms, it is a tricolour rainbow of the best products from the country's regions. Down-to-earth cooking to accompany a moment of weightlessness.

LE JULES VERNE / Altima – 6 avenue Gustave Eiffel / Paris VII

- 189

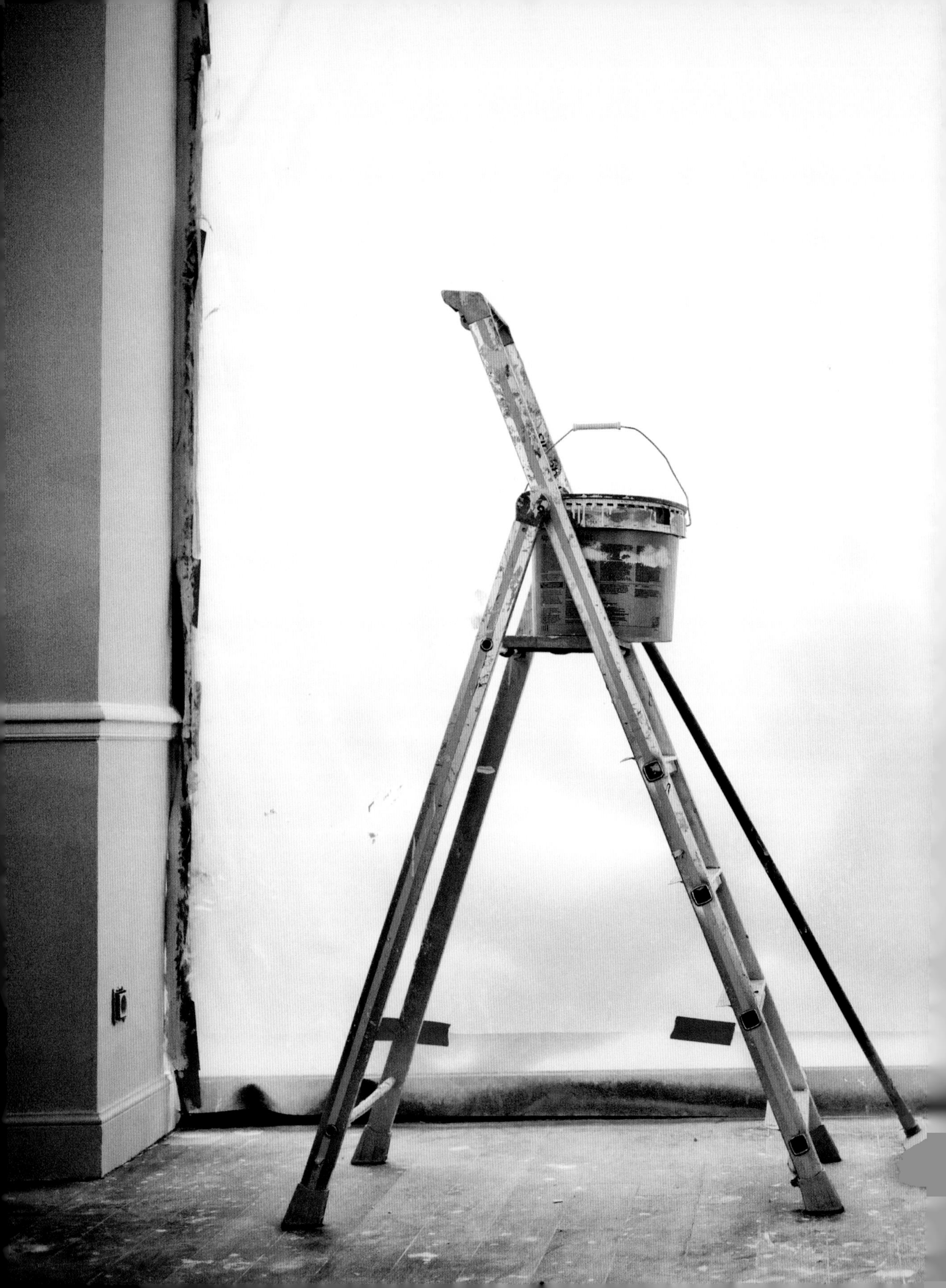

J'aime Paris

PARIS WILL ALWAYS BE PARIS

N°3 / 5 rue Coq-Héron / Paris Ier

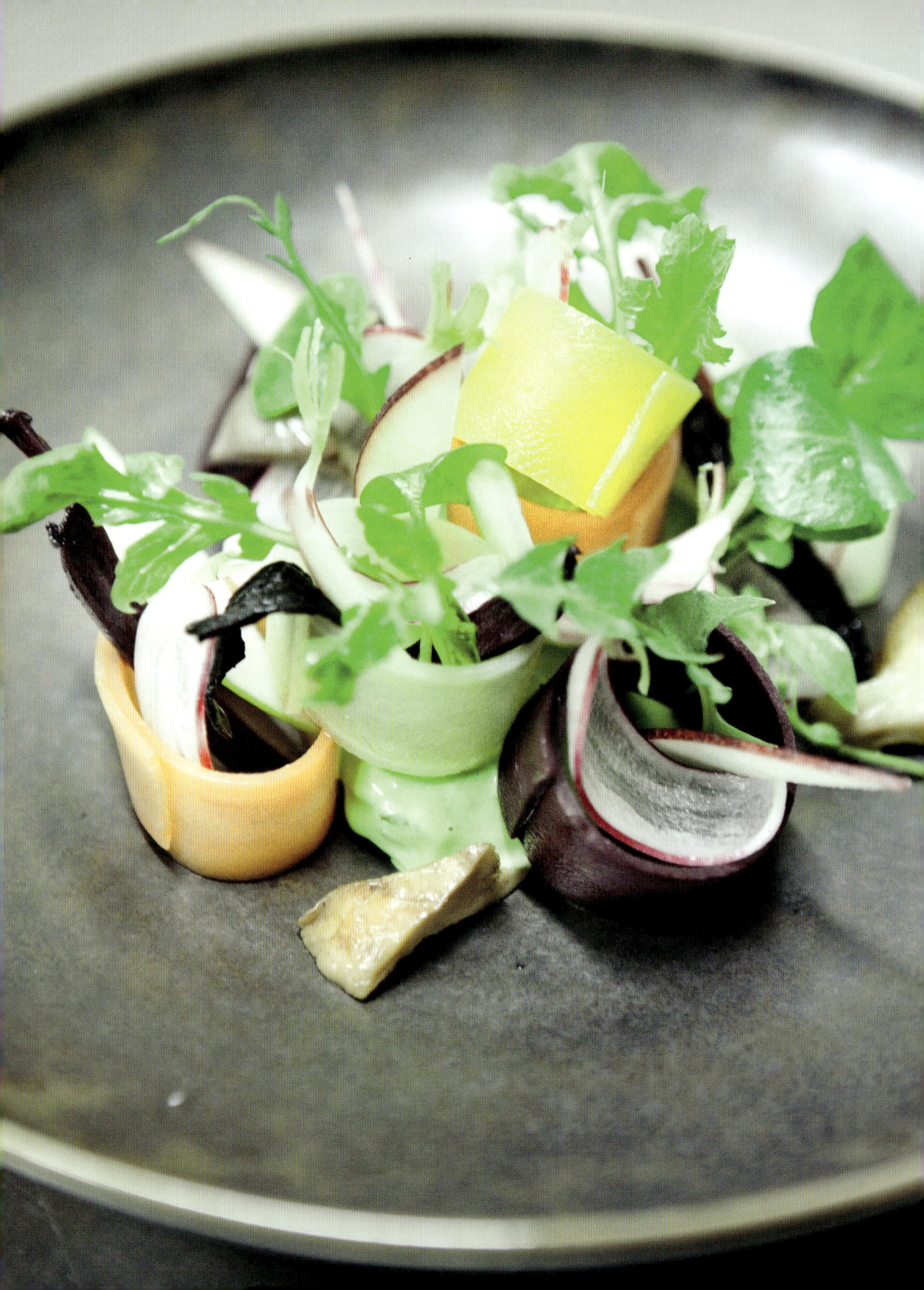

KEI

Kei Kobayashi is a very Japanese chef who is actually French! His influences are therefore mixed: the aestheticism, the verticality of his constructions, poetic harmony of colours and delicate flavours are inspired by Japan; while France has taught him the precision of actions and cooking times, meticulous finishing touches and respect for ingredients. The result is a rich and creative palette of subtle combinations where defined flavours culminate in a unique and perfectly executed cuisine.

KEI / 5 rue Coq-Héron / Paris Ier

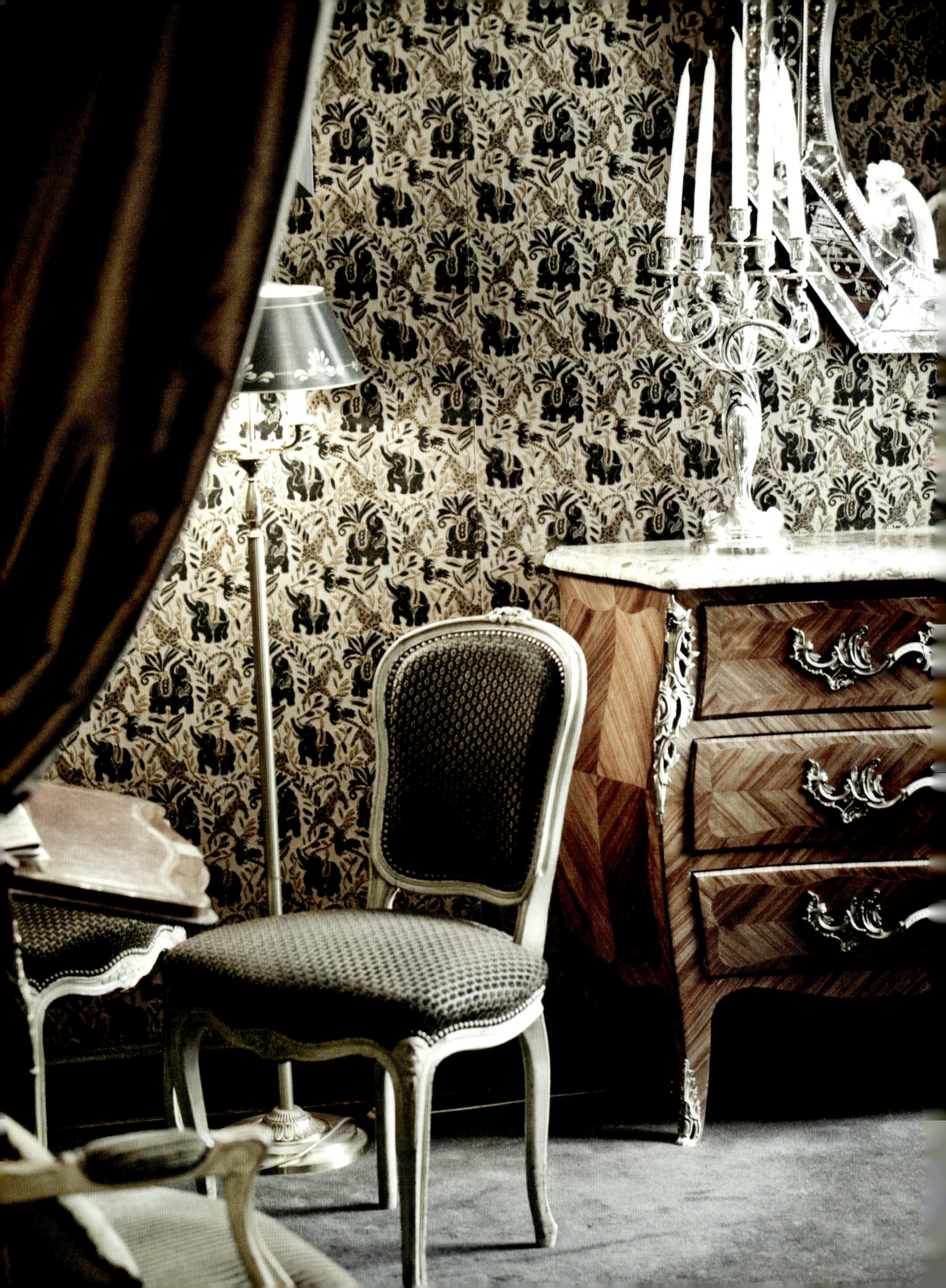

LASSERRE / 17 avenue Franklin Roosevelt / Paris VIIIe

LASSERRE

In 1942, René Lasserre acquired a small wooden restaurant building constructed for the 1937 World Fair. After the war, the modest bistro he founded moved into the adjacent mansion, which had been restored. This legendary restaurant is the fruit of the labours and passion of this man. Over the years, it earned him international renown and breathed life into a classic, delicate French cuisine. Today, Restaurant Lasserre has taken on a new impetus with the arrival of Christophe Moret, a chef with six years' experience at the Plaza Athénée. The opportunity was also taken to refresh the décor of the main dining room, where the retractable roof opens for dinner under the stars. Another page is being written in this particular story.

LASSERRE / 17 avenue Franklin Roosevelt / Paris VIII[e]

PARIS WILL ALWAYS BE PARIS — J'aime Paris

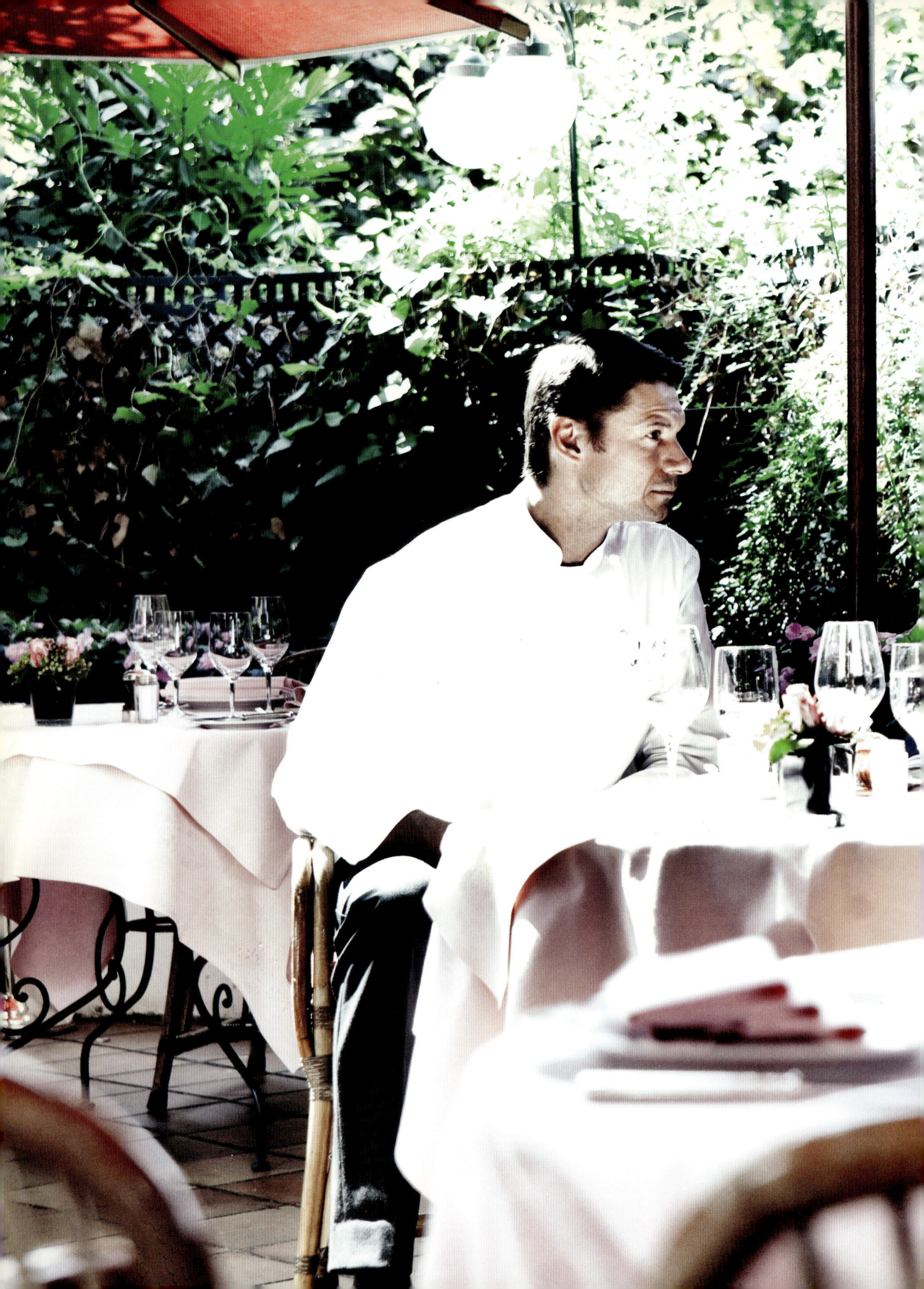

LE LAURENT / 41 avenue Gabriel / Paris VIIIe

LAURENT

LAU RENT

J'aime Paris

PARIS WILL ALWAYS BE PARIS

LE LAURENT / 41 avenue Gabriel / Paris VIII

'First of all we had to soak up the history of this place, to listen to it and feel it. Then we had to offer dishes suited to the sensitivity of Philippe Bourguignon, named best sommelier in France in 1978, who has managed this establishment since 1976. The benchmarks we set were subtlety, elegance and respect for the products we use. Today, the spider crab in lobster jelly and fennel crème, the winter vegetable *palette de couleurs*, the turbot in a salt crust and the milk-fed veal confit are part of the history of this house. We are very proud of that.'

Alain Pégouret

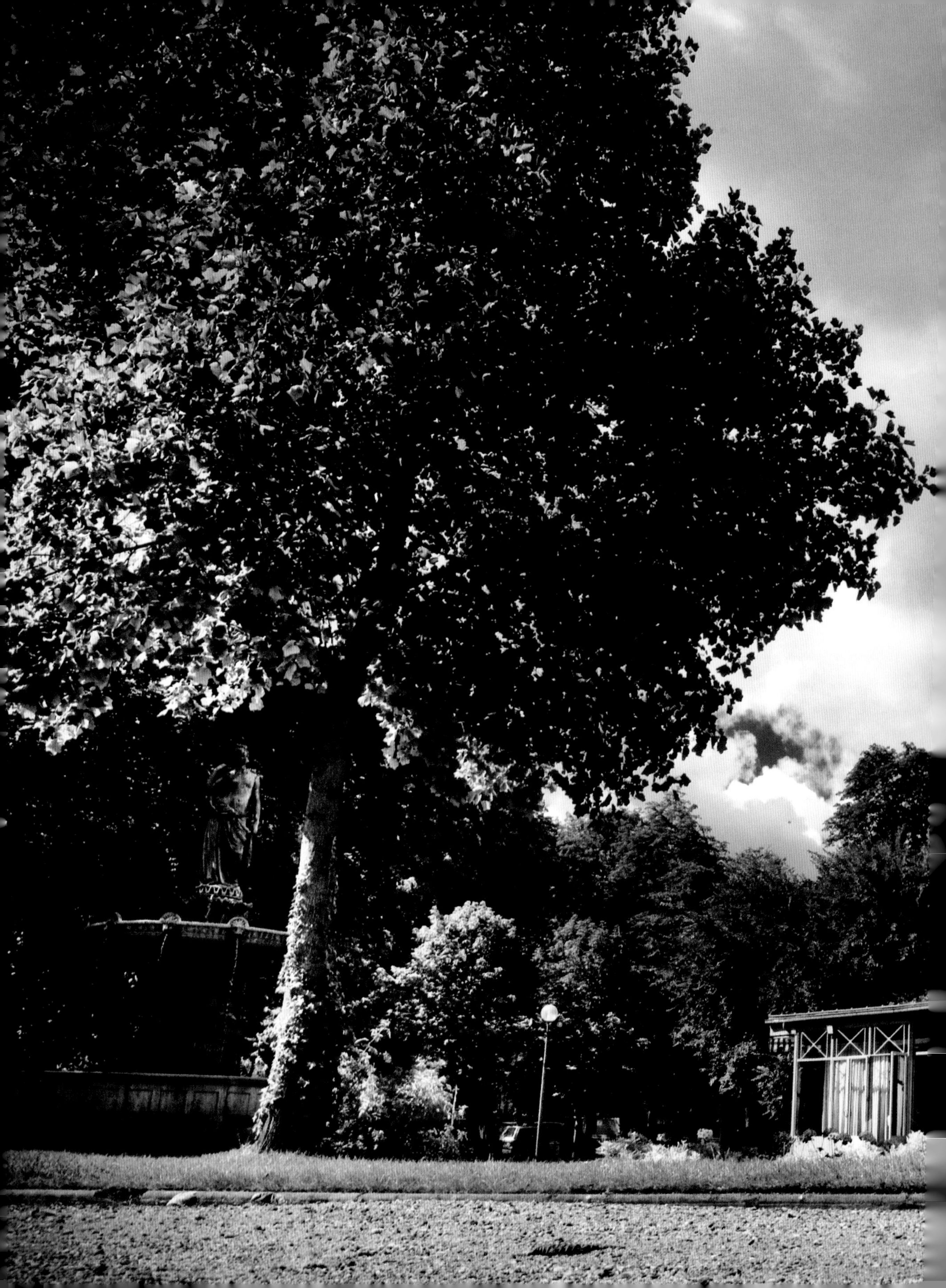

LEDOYEN / 1 avenue Dutuit / Paris VIII°

LEDOYEN
1792

LE DOYEN

'I grew up and started my training on the Gulf of Morbihan. My boss at the time would always tell me: "To become a good chef, you have to train in the great Parisian establishments." So, in 1988, I joined Pavillon Ledoyen as head chef. What cuisine do I create today? One that combines visual simplicity with complex flavours, while at the same time being elegant and full of freshness. Among the highlights are the veal sweetbreads with lemongrass, the turbot with truffle emulsion and the langoustines with citrus. It's always a pleasure to discover in the Carré des Champs Elysées district a legendary place in the midst of an oasis of greenery. This is Paris at its most magical!'

Christian Le Squer

LEDOYEN / 1 avenue Dutuit / Paris VIII

- 205

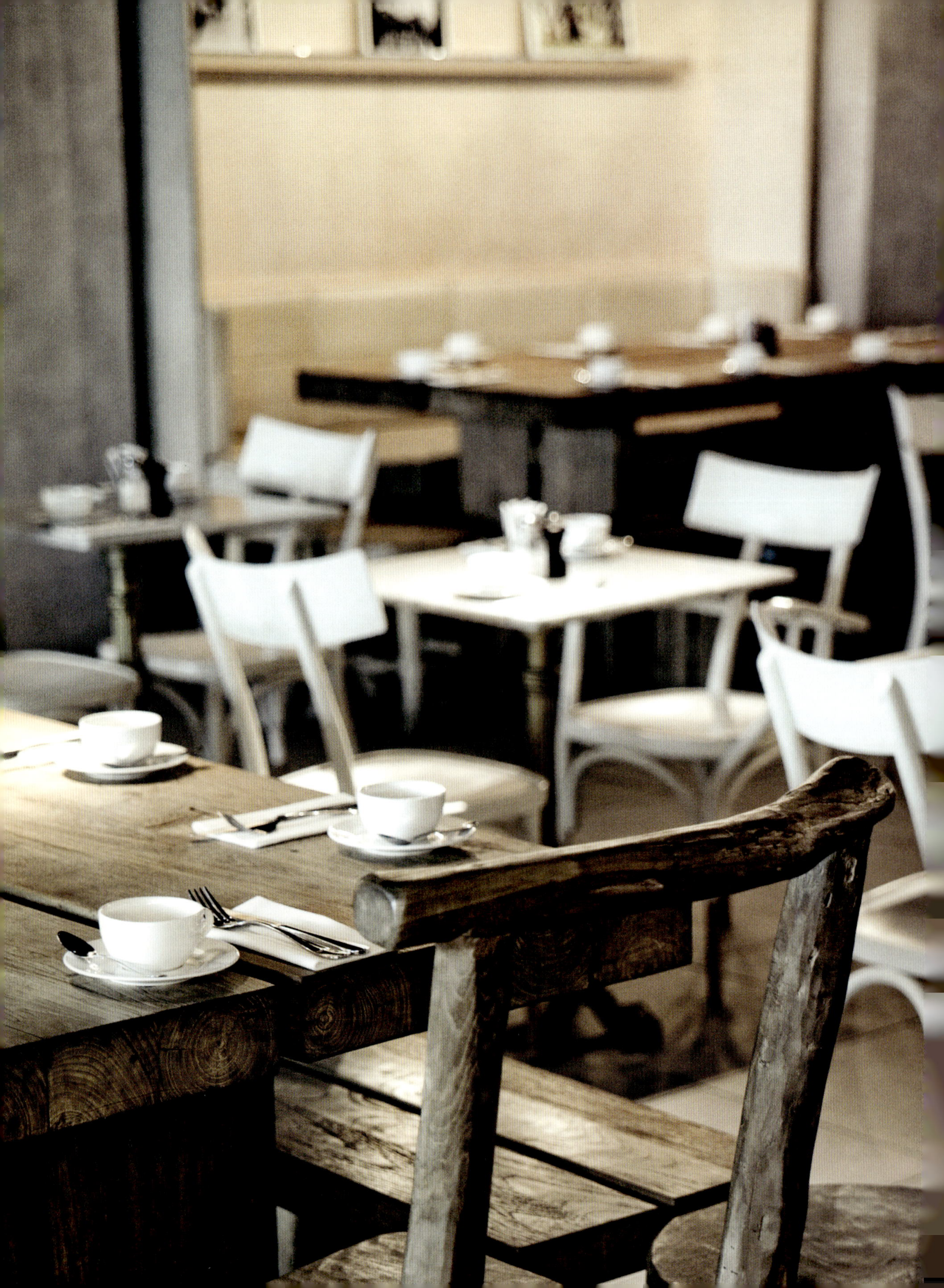

J'aime Paris

PARIS WILL ALWAYS BE PARIS

MAMA SHELTER / 109, rue de Bagnolet / Paris XXe

MAMA SHELTER

You can have a drink, a meal, a look around and even sleep at Mama Shelter! Sip your drink at the Philippe Starck designed bar. Lift your head and feast your eyes on the incredible slate ceiling covered in stylish graffiti. You can referee a fierce game of table football while placing your order, or why not have dinner with friends? The 'simple' menu prepared by Alain Senderens: warm, melt-in-your-mouth leeks served with a herb vinaigrette, salmon topped with a light horseradish crème and duck foie gras terrine. For dessert, be amazed by Mama's baba.

MAMA SHELTER / 109 rue de Bagnolet / Paris XXe

J'aime Paris

PARIS WILL ALWAYS BE PARIS

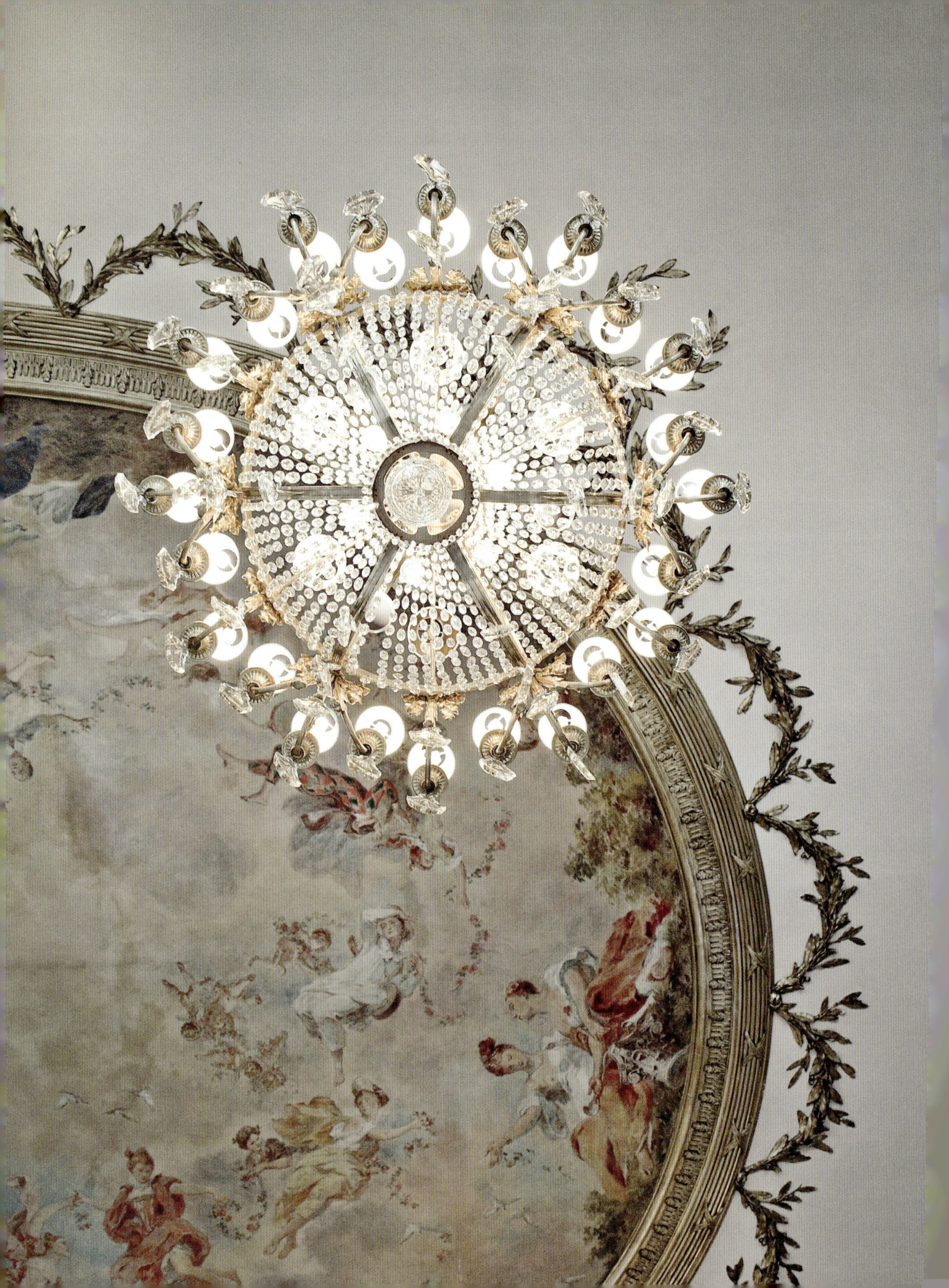

LE MEURICE / 228 rue de Rivoli / Paris Ier

MEU RICE

'I was born in Puteaux, and my parents managed bistros in Paris and its suburbs. Parisian cuisine has always been a part of my culture. Chefs from the different provinces often set up in Paris and bring the feel of their regions with them. I'm naturally drawn to combing the Paris region so that I can later enjoy myself with the produce I find. Today, Le Meurice is showcasing about 40 varieties of typically Parisian produce, such as Pontoise cabbage, Argenteuil asparagus, Houdan chicken and Paris petit pois.'

Yannick Alléno

J'aime Paris

PARIS WILL ALWAYS BE PARIS

LE MEURICE / 228 rue de Rivoli / Paris I er

- 213

MON VIEIL AMI / 69 rue Saint-Louis en l'île / Paris IVe

J'aime Paris

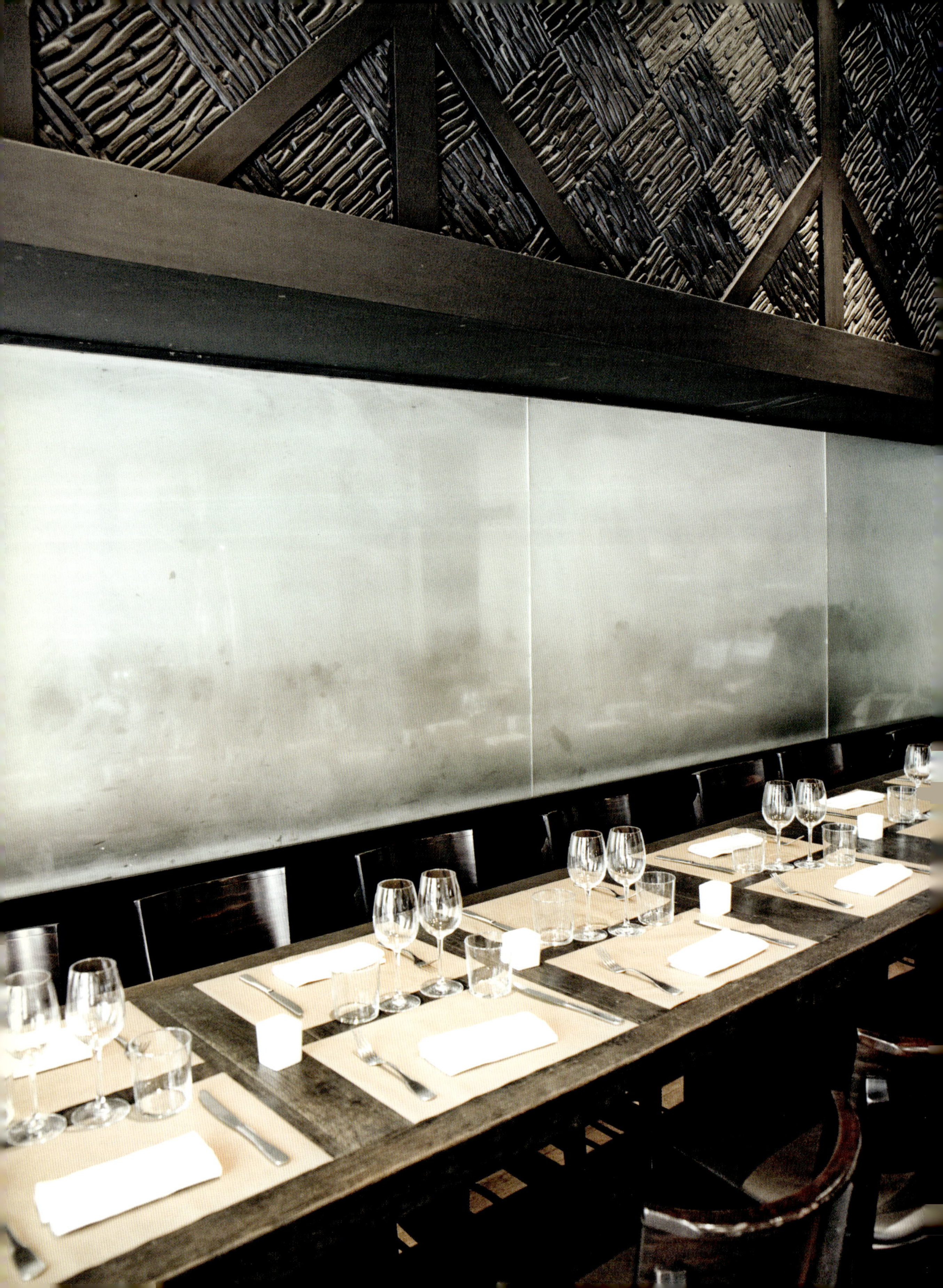

MON VIEIL AMI

'Remember, Alain, you were the one who encouraged me to visit this little bistro on the Île Saint-Louis seven years ago. What I wanted was simple: to welcome people here as friends, as one would at home. I pay tribute to my mother, who is the reason for my love of vegetables and could prepare them in 360 different ways — sautéed, in confit, stewed, raw... The cooking at Mon Vieil Ami is simple, the way I like it, and flavoursome and generous. My bistro is for friends.'

Antoine Westermann

MON VIEIL AMI / 69 rue Saint-Louis en l'île, Paris 4th

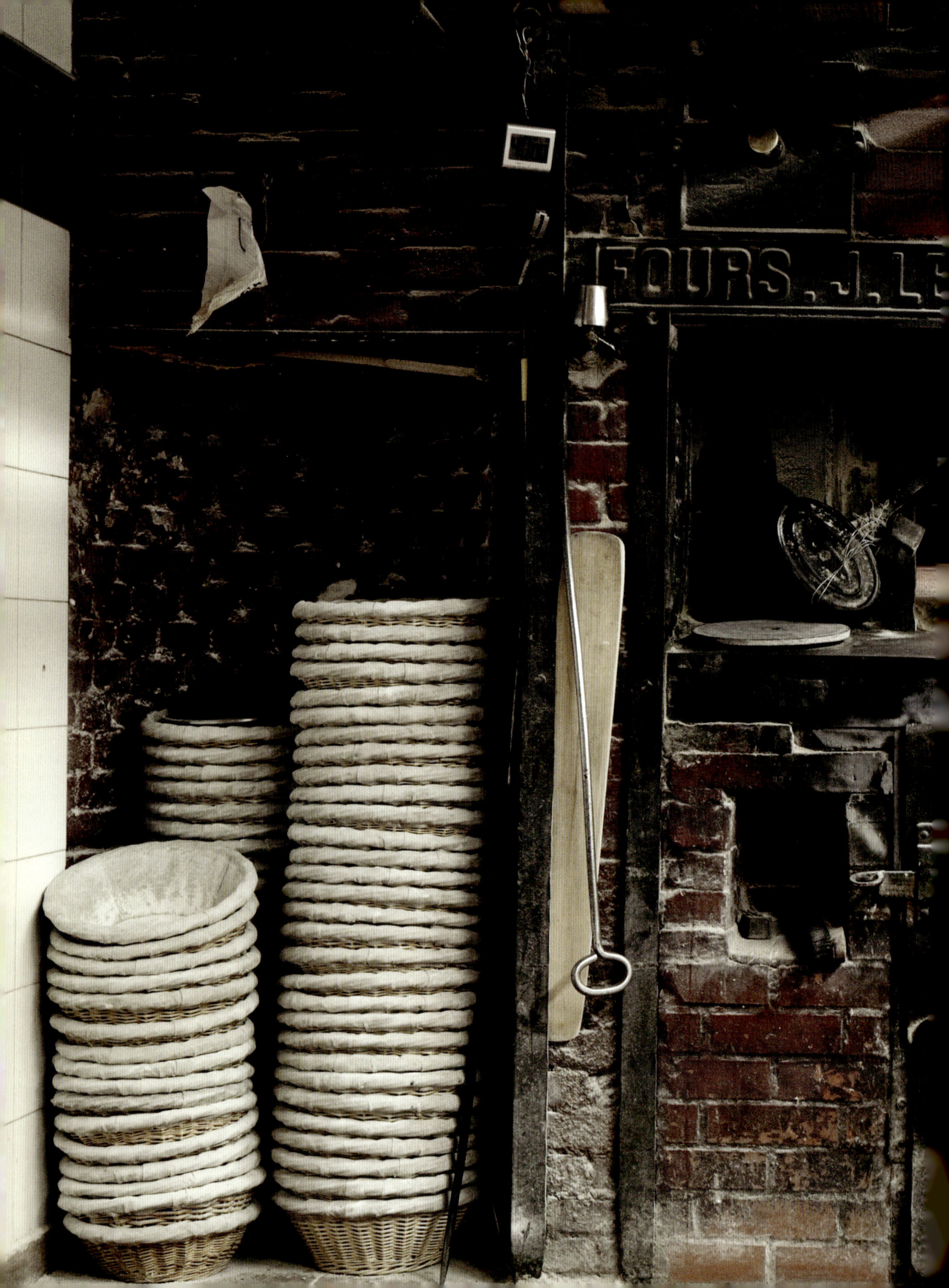
FOURS . J. LE

LE MOULIN DE LA VIERGE — 105 rue Vercingétorix / Paris XIV

219

MOU_{DE LA}LIN VIERGE

Flour: ecological and with natural leavening agents. Baking: in an old wood-fired oven, almost impossible to find in Paris. Mortal sin: '*Paresseuse*' (sloth), a delicious sourdough baguette. After that comes the famous *pain de campagne*, light on the inside with a crunchy crust, made by Alexandre Kamir, the greatest baker on God's earth. Venial sins: a light and wonderfully caramelised chantilly millefeuille, a formidable Tatin-style apple tart, a heavenly *flan pâtissier*, exquisite palmiers...

LE MOULIN DE LA VIERGE / 105 rue Vercingétorix / Paris XIV

- 221

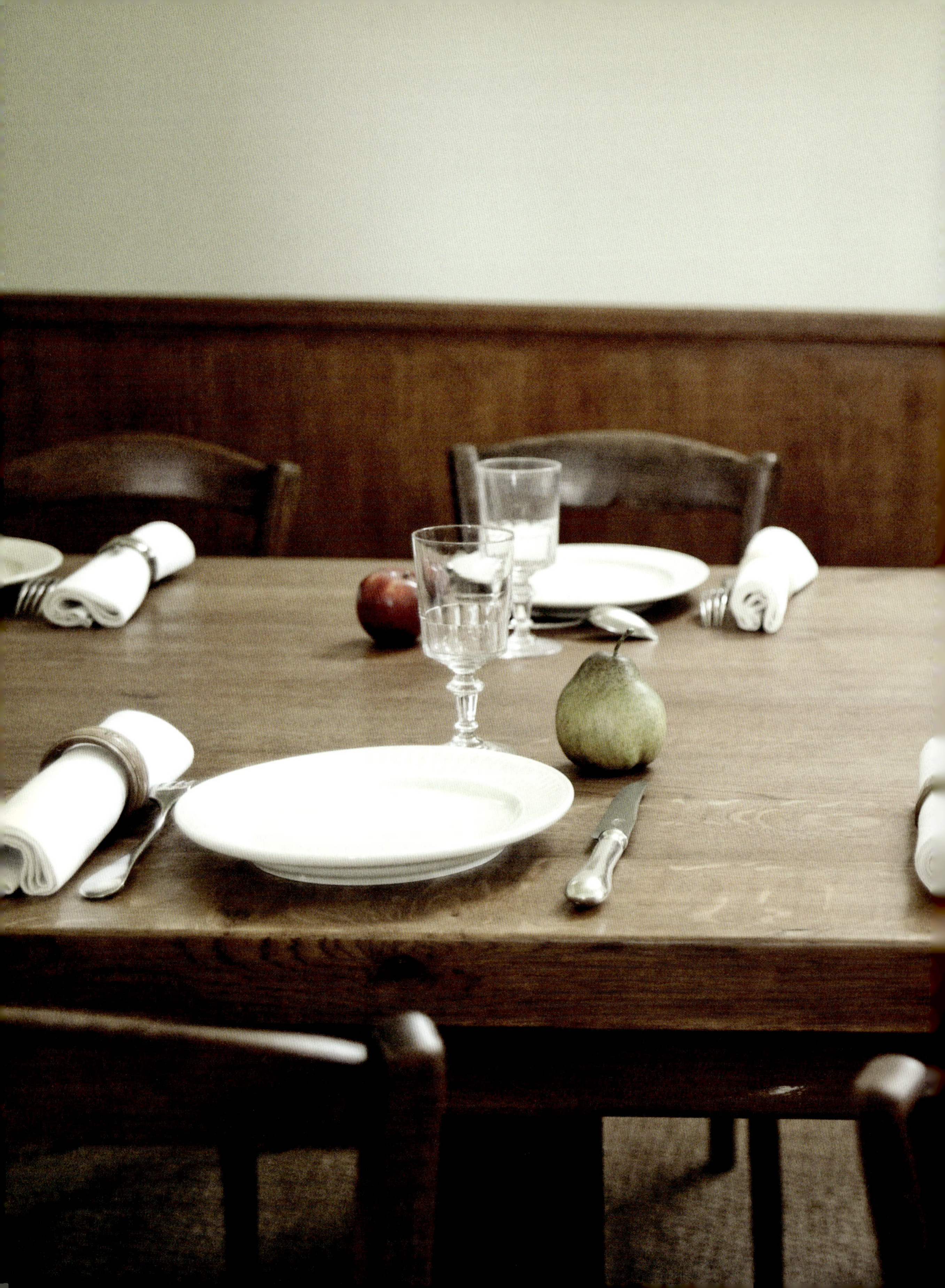

PARIS WILL ALWAYS BE PARIS — J'aime Paris

MUSÉE NISSIM DE CAMONDO / 63 rue de Monceau / Paris VIII

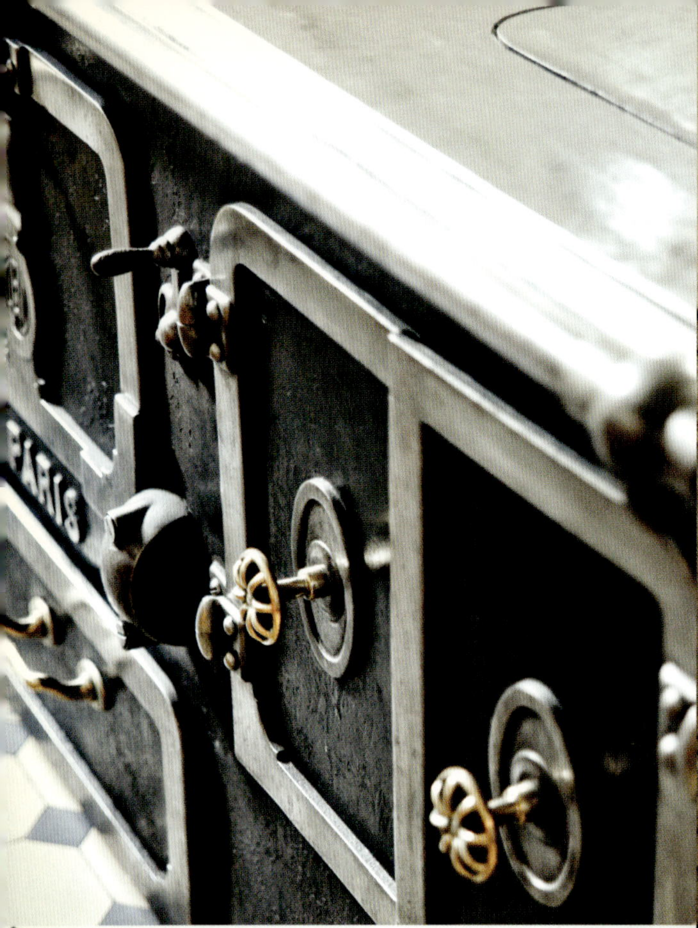
PARIS

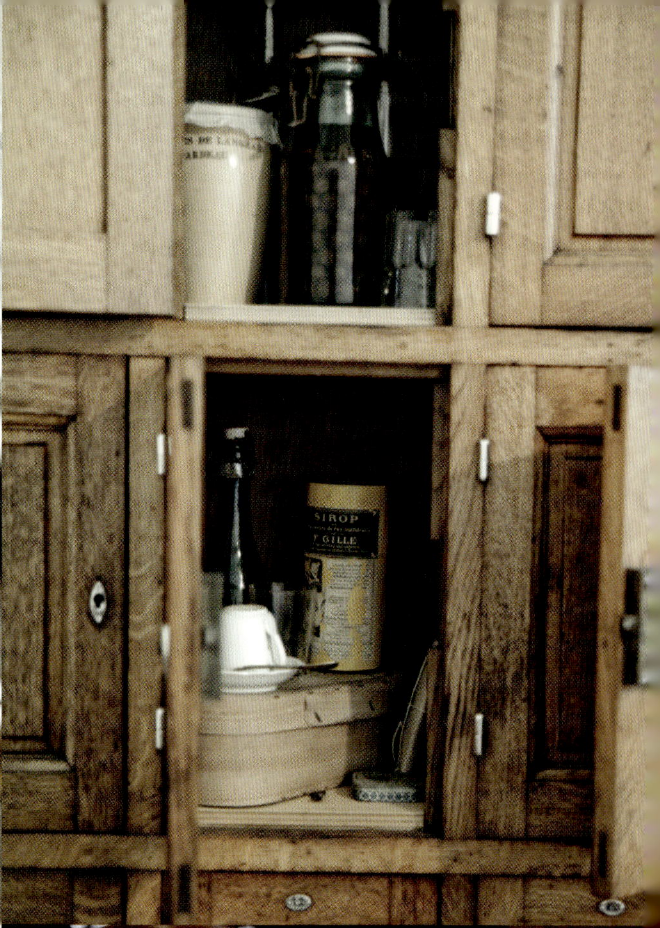
SIROP
GILLE

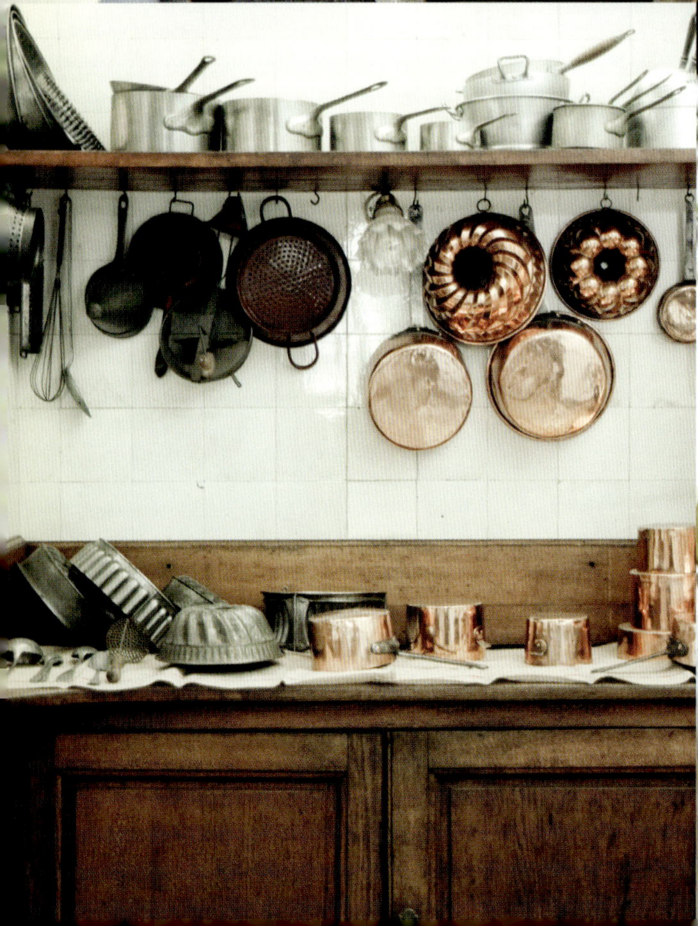

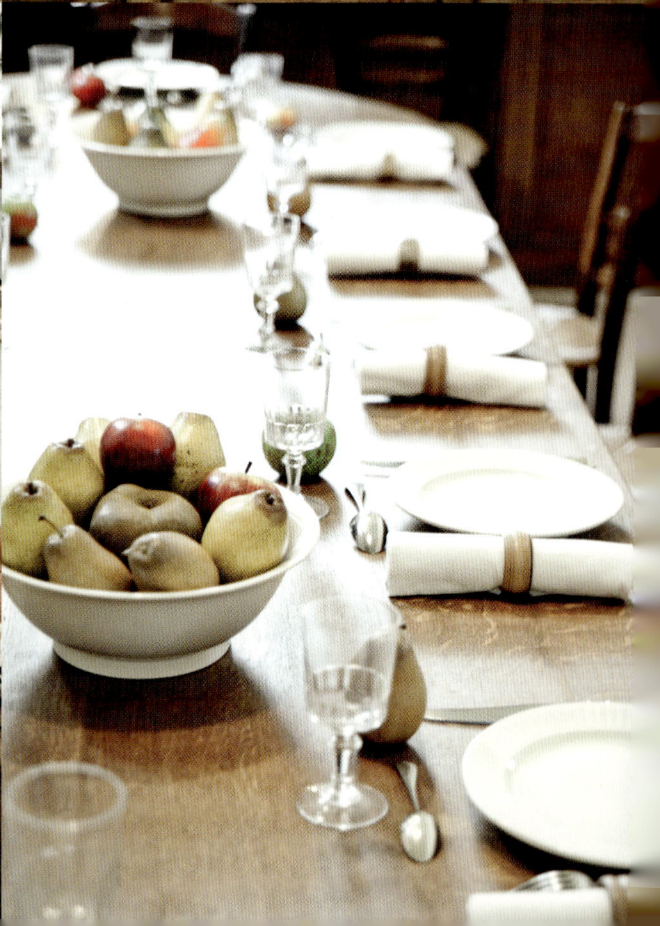

Let's dream. We take the service entrance and go directly to the kitchen, bypassing the office, which is reserved for the china. A majestic central stove and an impressive rotisserie, all in cast iron, await. Overlooking Monceau Park, the *salle des gens* — the staff dining room — is all wood panelling and damask napery, and perfect for a charming dinner. Both elegant and functional, the kitchen in the private home once belonging to Count Moïse de Camondo imposes its refinement even on the incredible collection of copper pots and pans. Today, it remains a tribute to the glory of French taste.

MUSÉE NISSIM DE CAMONDO

- 225

RIPOCHE Entrepreneur

HÔTEL DU PETIT MOULIN / 29-31 rue de Poitou, Paris IIIe

J'aime Paris

HÔTEL DU PETIT MOULIN

Outside is a bakery dating from 1900; inside... is a journey. There is something of Fellini in the red and lilac velvet that clashes with a leopard print cushion and a turquoise stool. There is music in these rooms, which either glitter at night like a Venetian mask or, on the contrary, are starkly rendered in a Provençal limewash. The moments you spend here, enclosed in this whimsical cocoon, are unique. The décor is by Christian Lacroix. It's up to you to find a costume...

HÔTEL DU PETIT MOULIN / 29 - 31 rue de Poitou

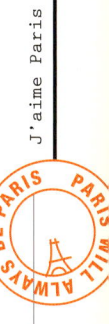

Paris IIIe

PARIS WILL ALWAYS BE PARIS

J'aime Paris

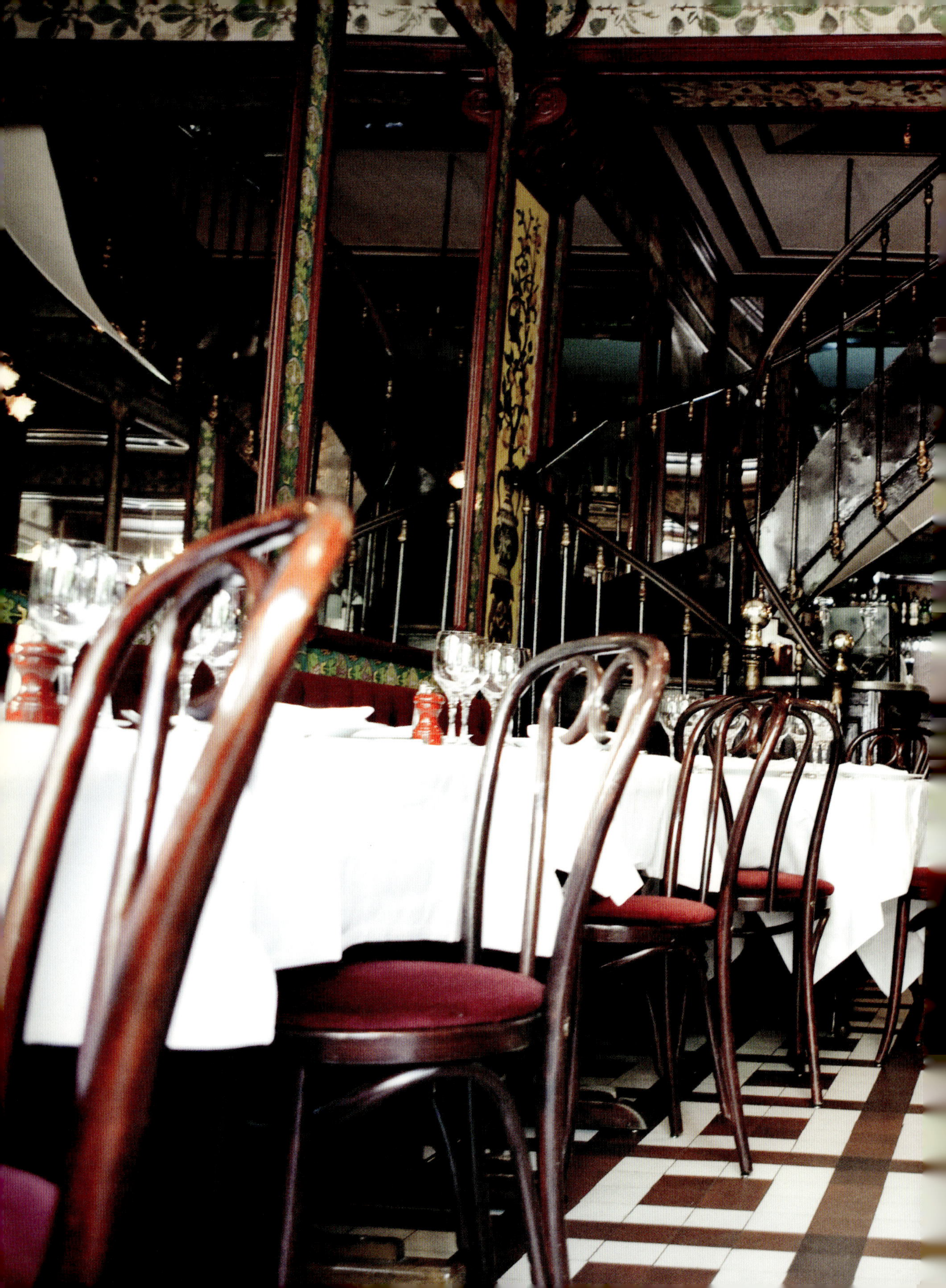

PHARAMOND / 24 rue de la Grande Truanderie / Paris Ier

PHARAMOND

Making your way among the restaurant terraces at Les Halles can be daunting. Suddenly, you find a little corner of Normandy in Paris that is as authentic as they come. The Caen-style tripe casserole has written the history of this establishment. Under the retro tiles and the copper mirrors, the lavish Norman veal rib appeals to mindless gluttony. Regulars gorge on magnificent escargots, stuffed with butter and garlic, and roasted to perfection. Figures Guests of a higher standing enjoy the private rooms on the first floor, where the ghost of Clemenceau crosses paths with the ghost of Coluche. That could be interesting...

PHARAMOND / 24 rue de la Grande Truanderie / Paris I

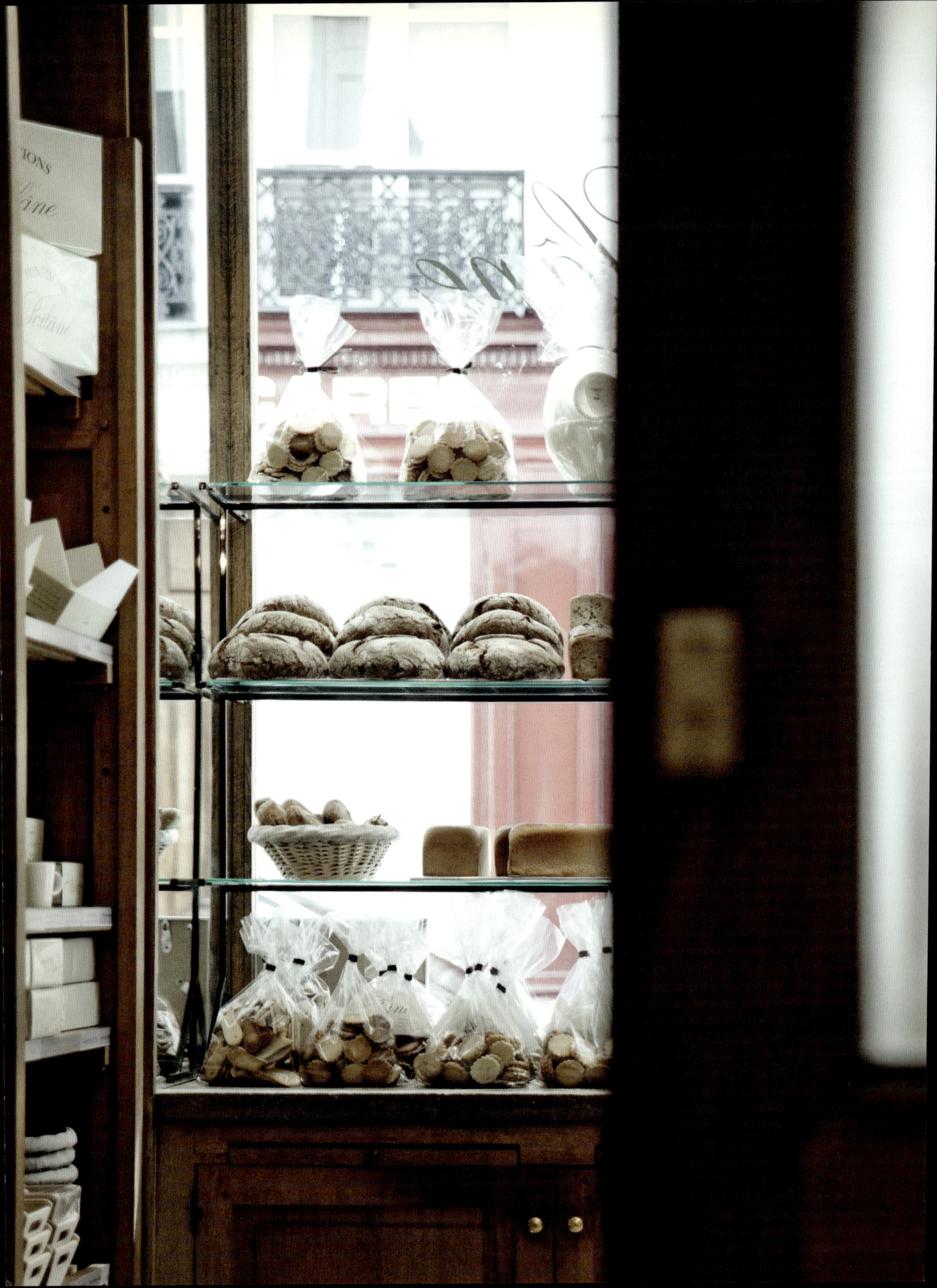

BOULANGERIE POILÂNE / 8 rue du Cherche-Midi / Paris VI

J'aime Paris

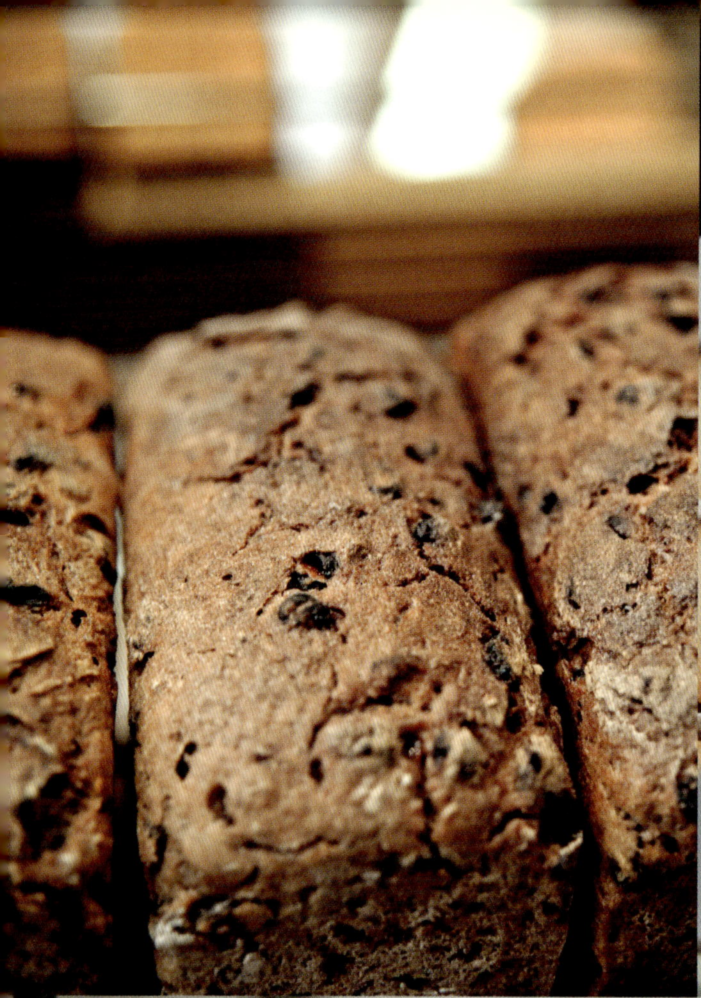

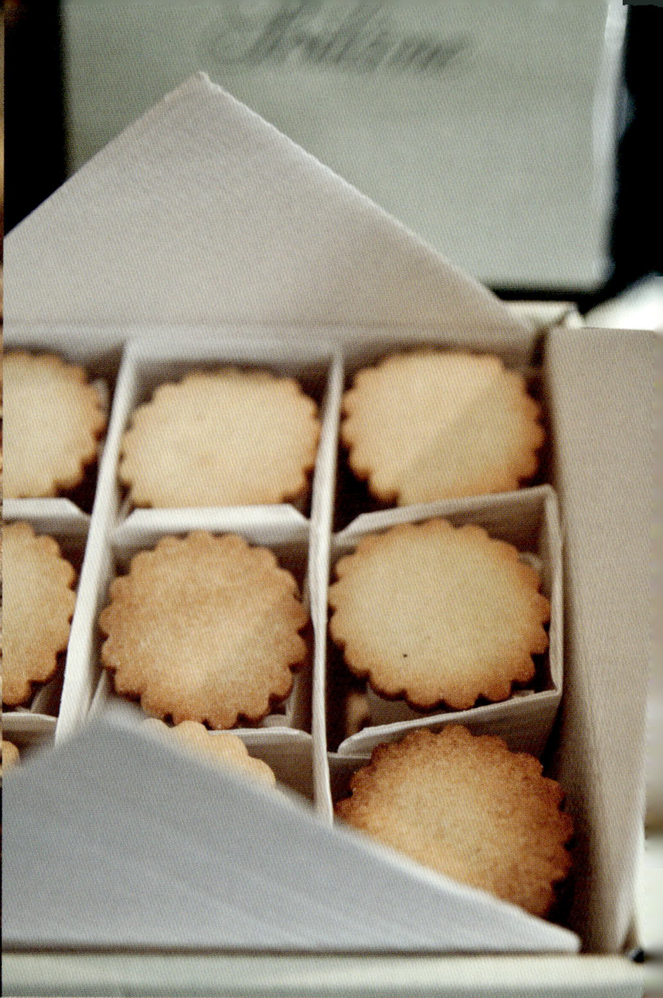

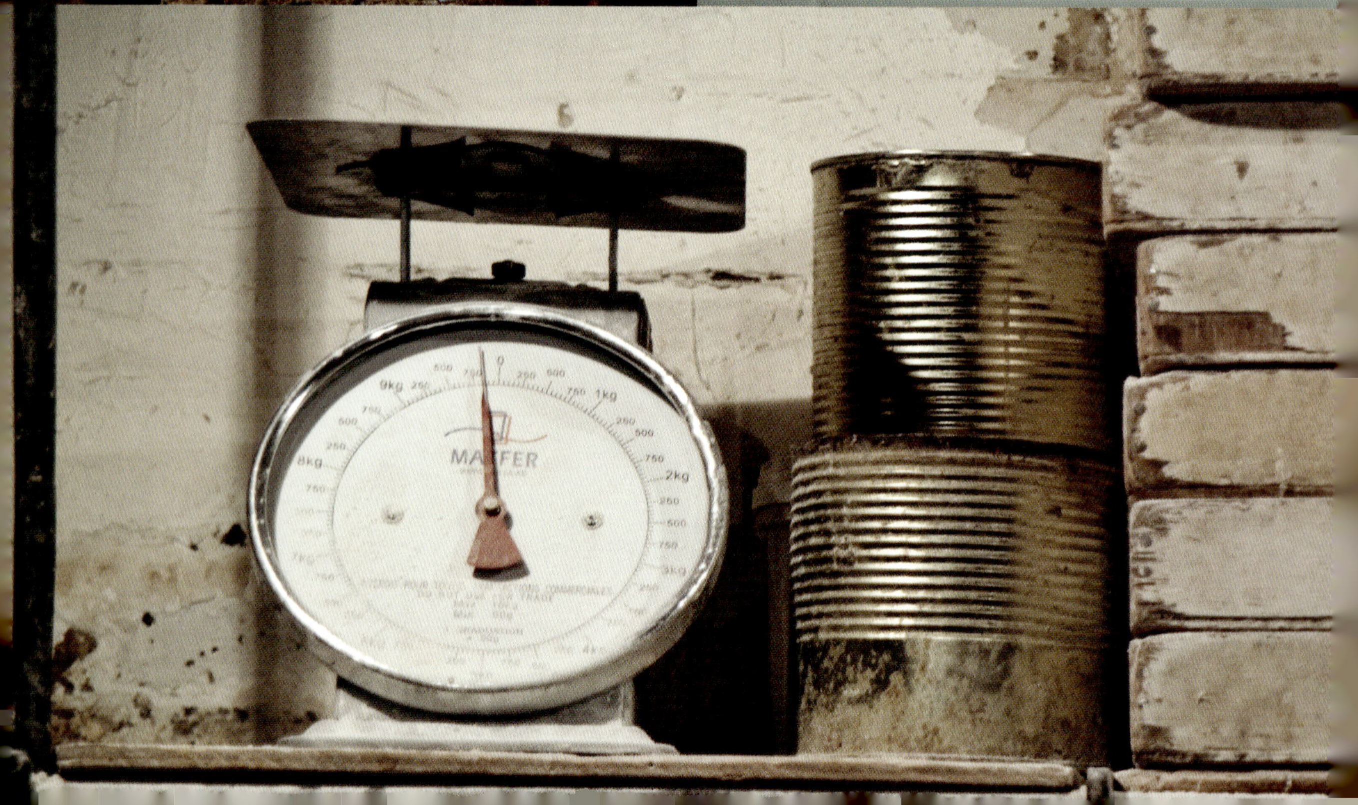
9kg
1kg
8kg
2kg

Apollonia Poilâne: The iconic Parisian baguette is white bread, originally bread for the rich. The success of our establishment came with people migrating from the provinces, who wanted *pain paysan*, country-style bread with rye.

Alain Ducasse: To eat with their rillettes, ham and sausage...

AP: Exactly. And the canvases you can see above me are by starving painters from the district who would trade their works for a loaf of bread. '*Une croûte contre une croûte*' ('a bad painting for a crust of bread') is what they would say.

AD: Is the bread still made by hand?

AP: Today there's a kneading machine. It's more hygienic than in the past when two or three bakers would lift the dough, giving it their muscle... and their sweat. All the bread is made at dawn in our 24 wood-fired ovens like the one in the basement. We deliver to Paris and the Paris area in the morning, and to the rest of France in the afternoon. That's 7000 loaves each day made in the traditional way; it takes six hours to make a large round loaf.

POILÂNE

BOULANGERIE POILÂNE / 8 rue du Cherche-Midi / Paris VIe

J'aime Paris

PARIS WILL ALWAYS BE PARIS

PRUNIER

PRUNIER

PRUNIER
RÉSERVATION - TÉL. 01 44 17 35 85

POUSSEZ

RESTAURANT PRUNIER / 16 avenue Victor Hugo / Paris XVIe

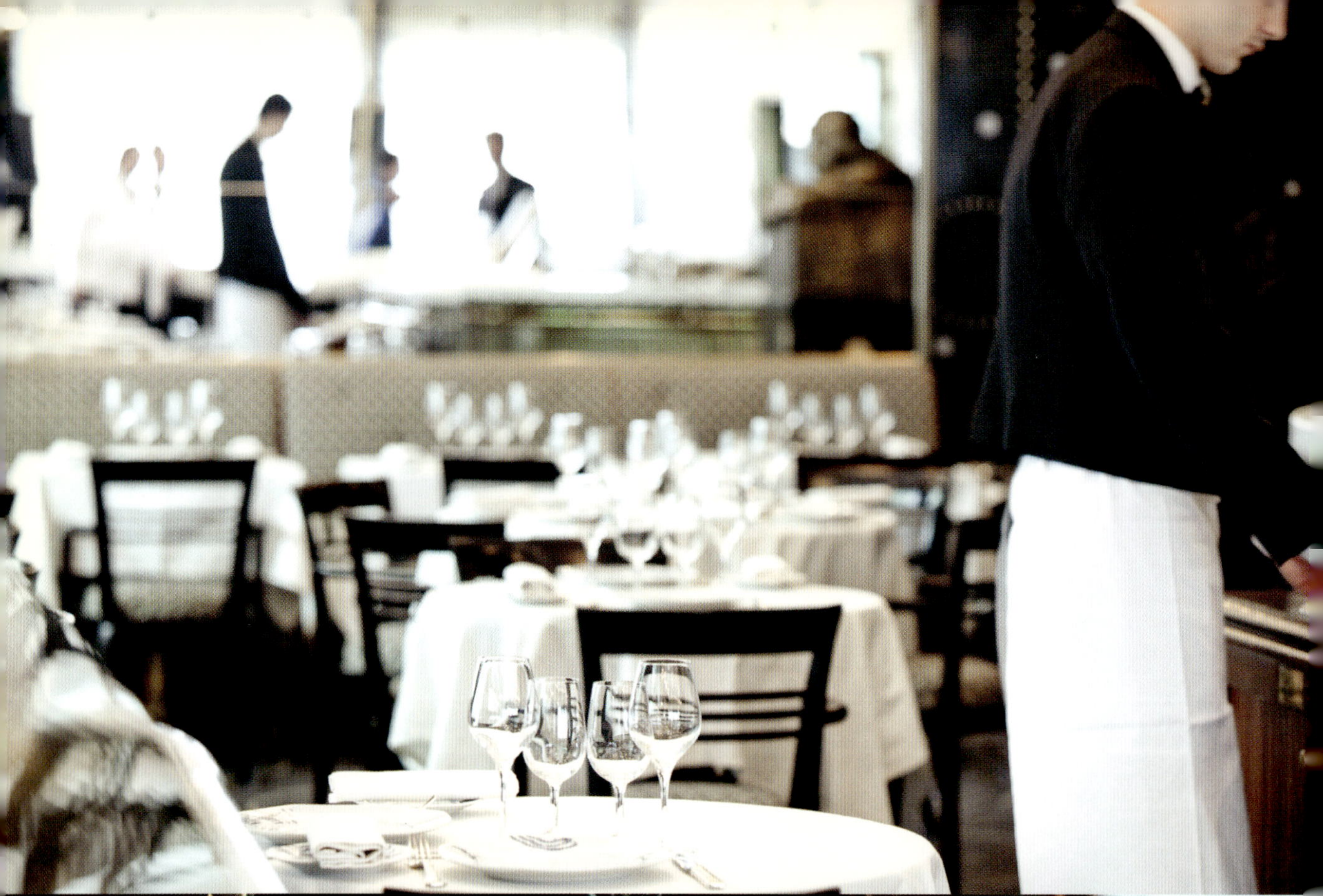

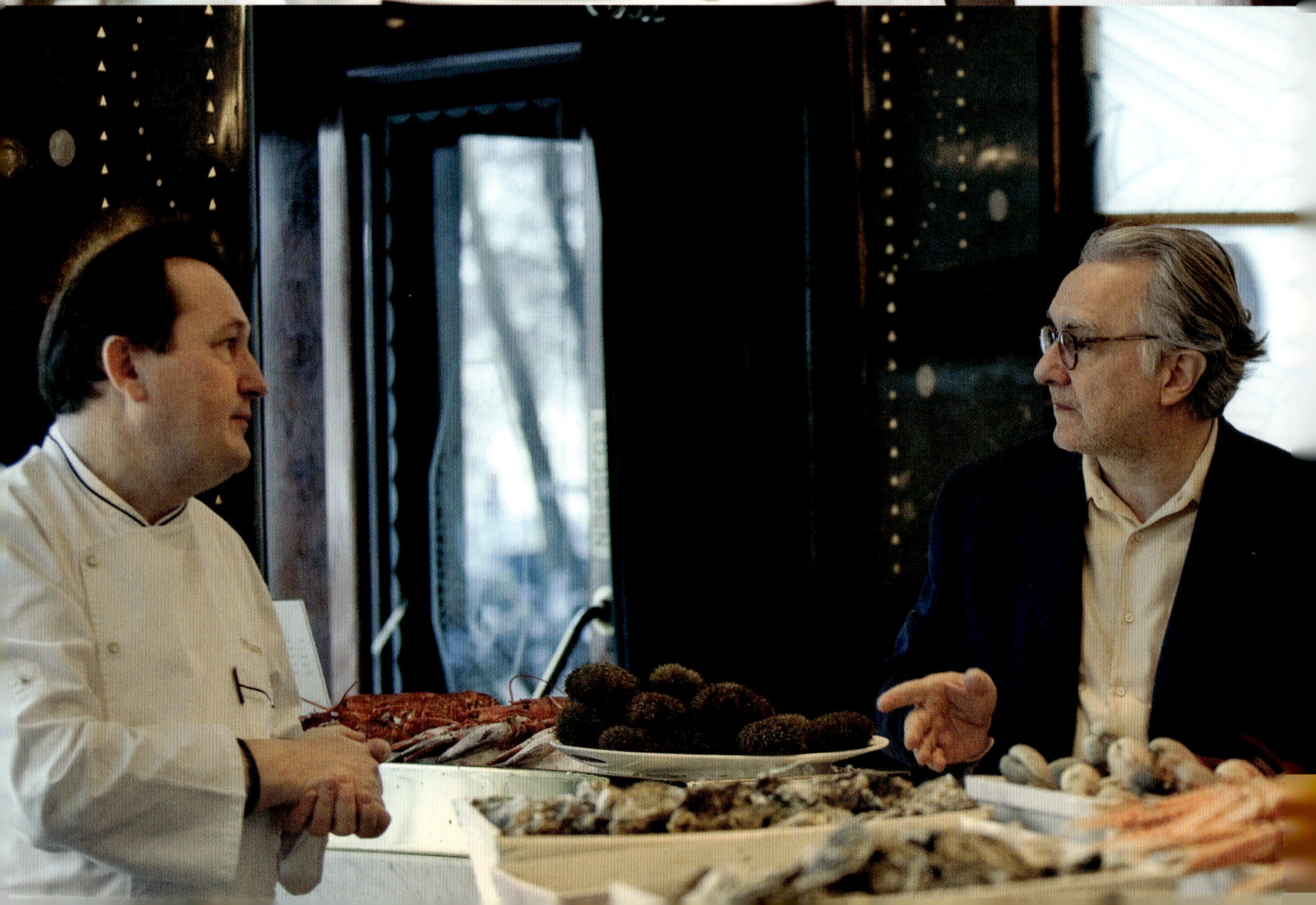

PRUNIER

The menu from 1932 reads: 'Smoked Fish and Caviars'. Even then, this long-standing purveyor of fine seafood was the toast of Paris and London with 'everything from the sea', reflected by fillets of sole Duglère, seared scallops and their famous fresh caviar. The menu has remained almost unchanged over the years, with its truffle *tartine*, hedgehog mushrooms in poulette sauce and the mature Stilton cut at your table. Here you will find timelessness in an Art Deco wrapping.

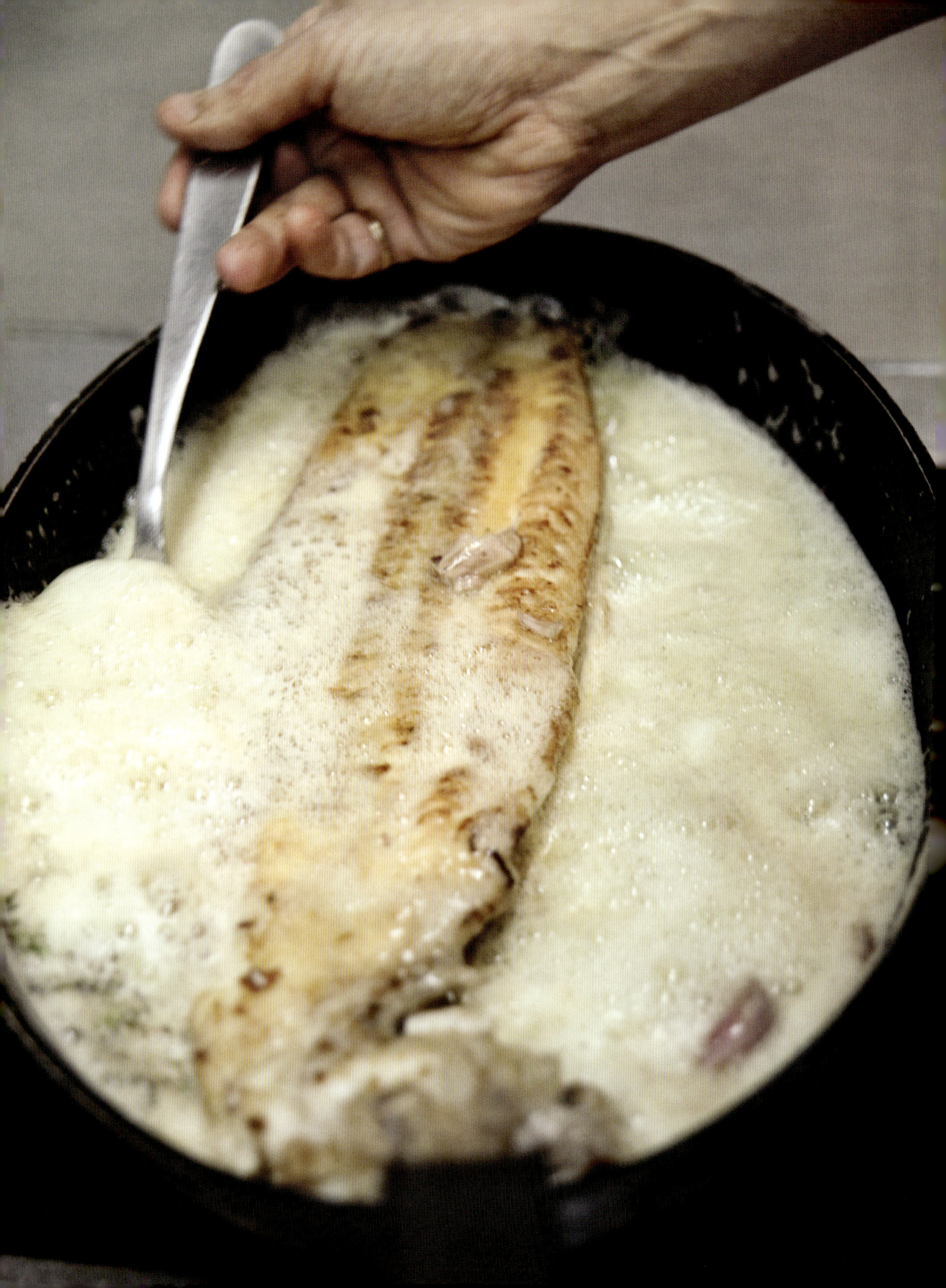

RECH / 62 avenue des Ternes / Paris XVIIe

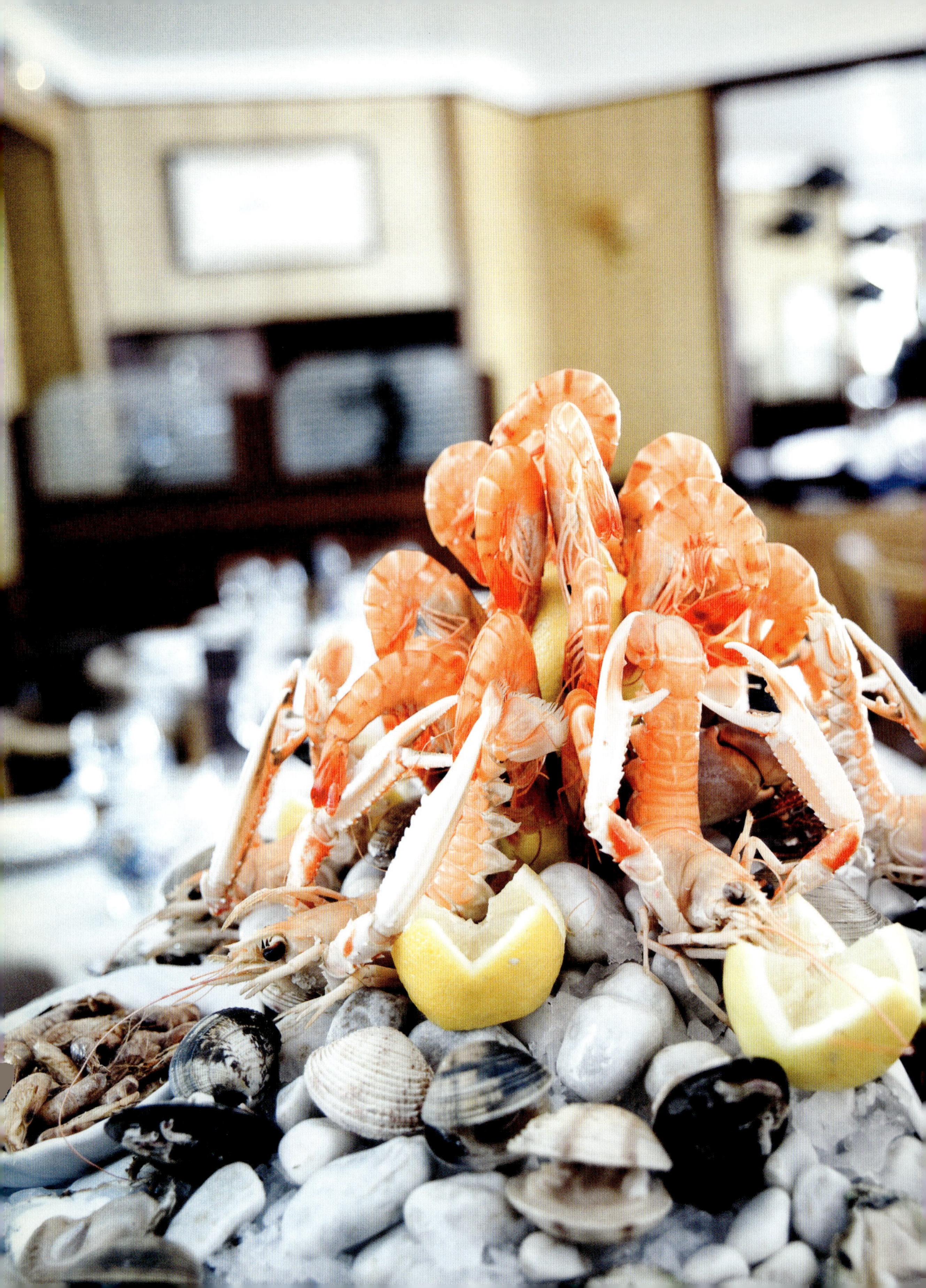

RECH / 62 avenue des Ternes / Paris XVIIe

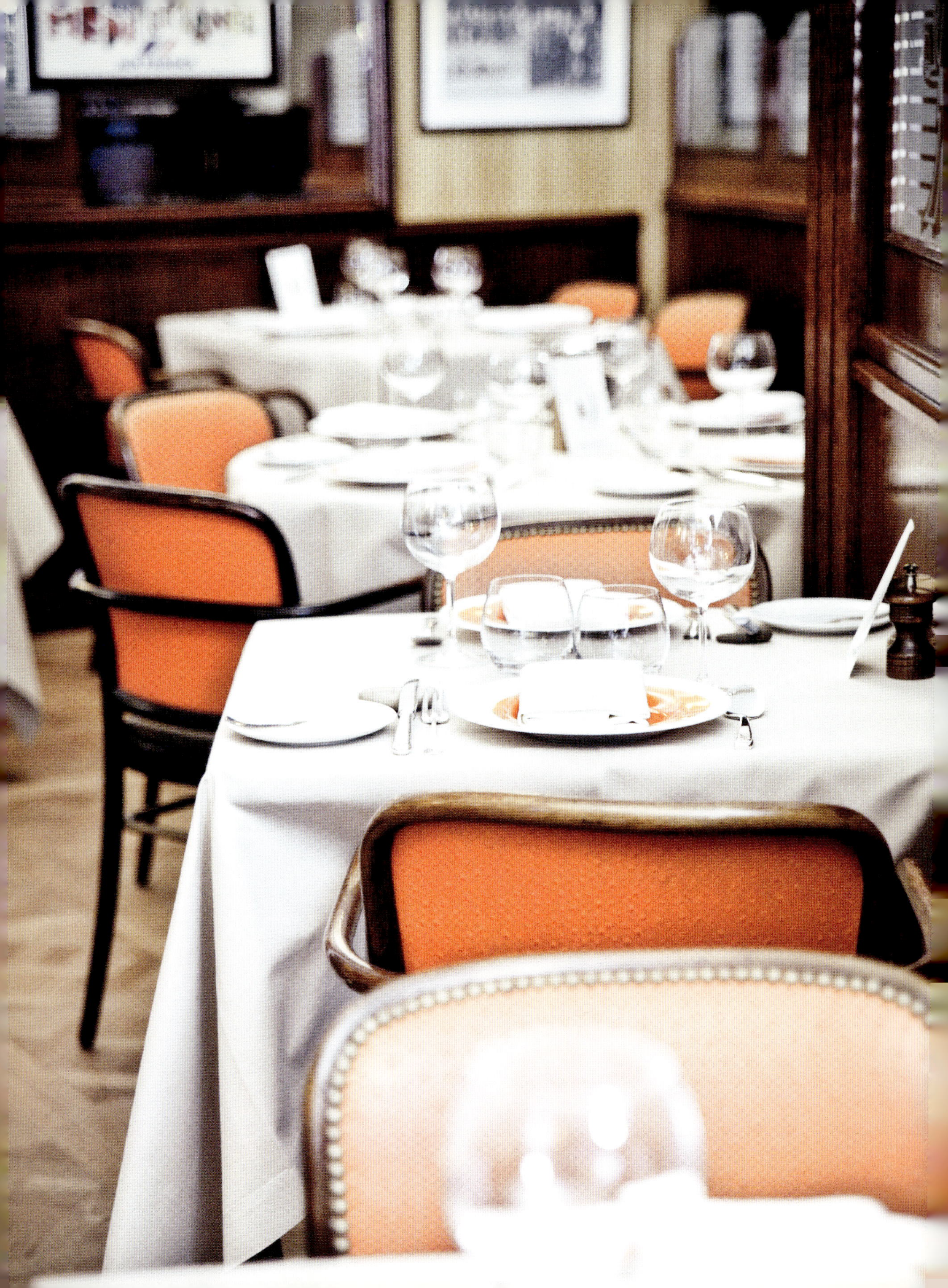

RECH

The sound of the surf, the cry of the seagulls, the smell of seaweed surround Malek, the oyster seller. You open the door and sense the richness of the Atlantic coast. Soft lighting and pale wood reveal the refined touches exemplified by the damask tablecloths and agate butter dishes. And when the sole meunière for two arrives, coppery on the outside and soft and silky on the palate, even the seagulls are silent. Under the creative leadership of Jacques Maximin, the menu changes with the tides. Julien Dumas prepares nothing but the freshest and most splendid products from the sea and rivers.

RECH / 62 avenue des Ternes / Paris XVIIe

- 247

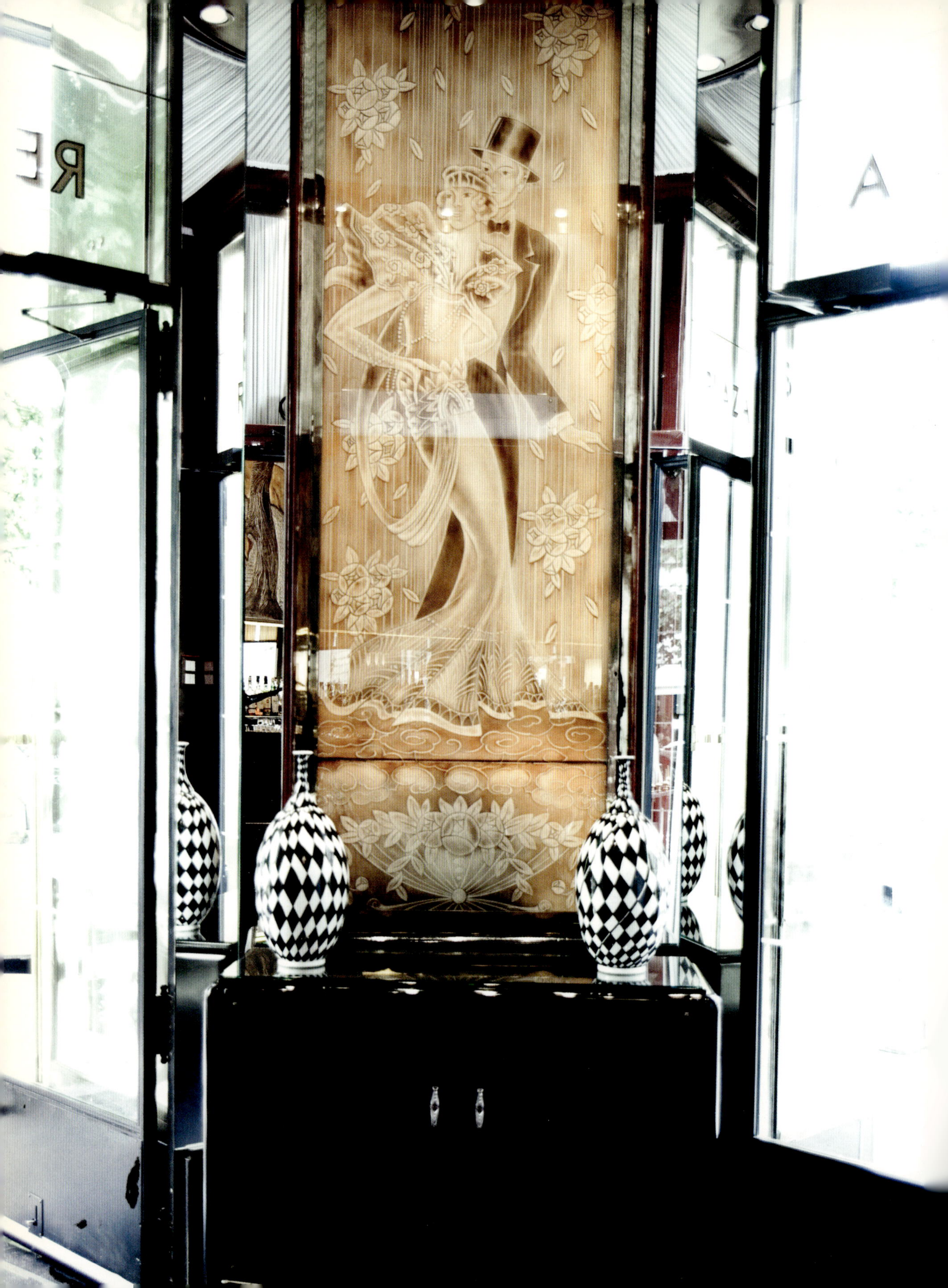

LE RELAIS PLAZA / 21 avenue Montaigne / Paris VIIIe

J'aime Paris

PARIS WILL ALWAYS BE PARIS

- 249

RELAIS PLAZA

Imagine the sophisticated dining room of the ocean liner the *SS Normandie* turned upside down by the heady madness of the Roaring Twenties. The Relais Plaza is just that: the height of elegance and exuberance. Under the great Lalique chandelier, the Russian pianist is having the time of his life while the district's beautiful people enjoy their dinner. The cuisine in Philippe Marc's brasserie brings together Wiener schnitzel, steak tartare with matchstick potatoes and skewered veal sweetbreads, sometimes venturing into green lasagne with mascarpone and chanterelle mushrooms or crayfish in roast juices. A rum baba brings the cruise to an end beautifully.

LE RELAIS PLAZA / 21 avenue Montaigne / Paris VIIIe

J'aime Paris

PARIS WILL ALWAYS BE PARIS

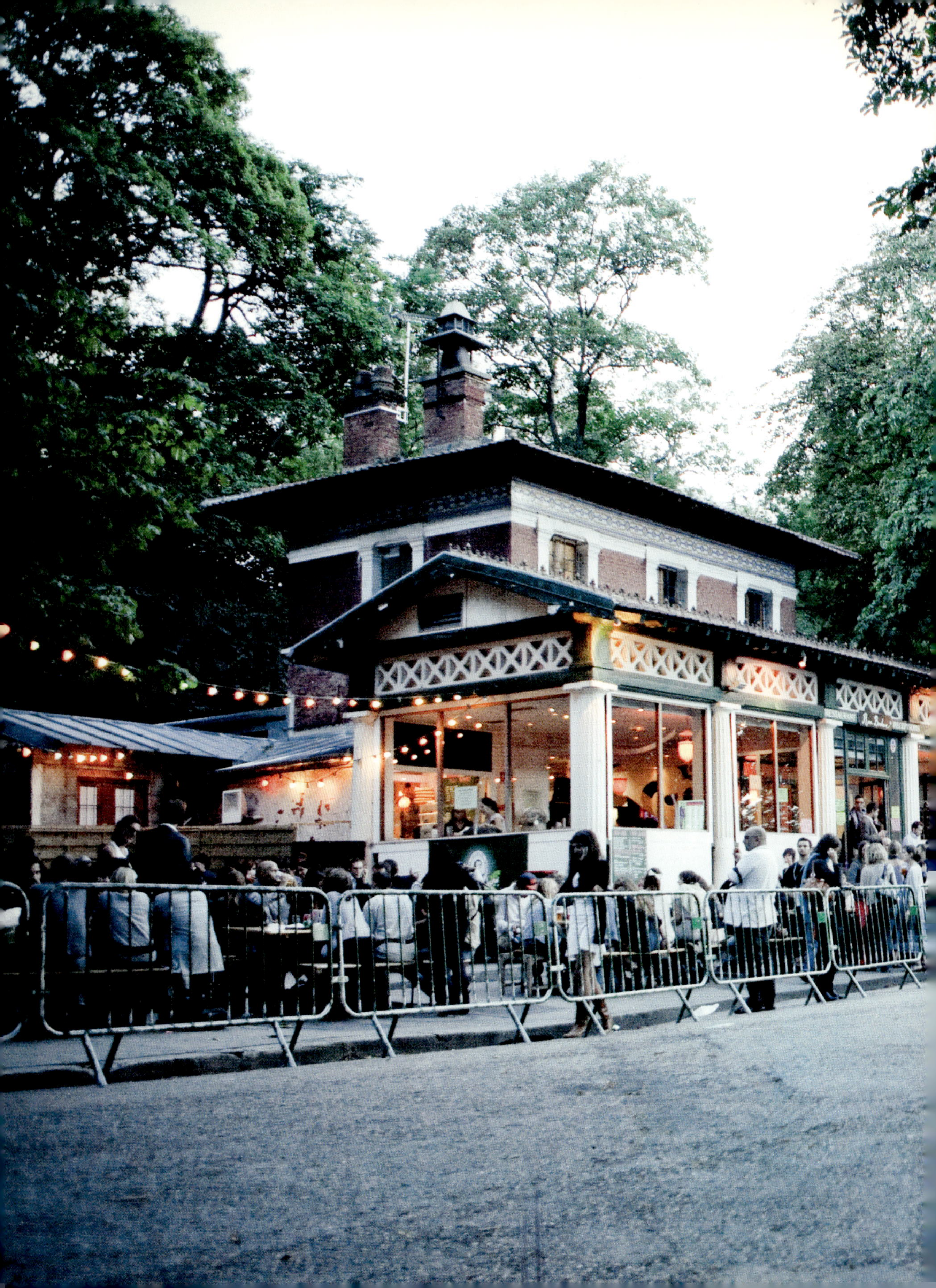

ROSA BONHEUR / 2 allée de la Cascade — Parc des Buttes-Chaumont / Paris XIX*

SANGRIA MAISON
LES BOISSONS DE ROSA
CARTE BLEUE MINIMUM 15 €
CHOCOLAT FROID 3,5 €
CARTE BLEUE MINIMUM 15 €
REDBULL
WEGA
PACIFIC
BIERE BLANCHE

ROSA BONHEUR

Here is a privileged spot for a terrace, laid out amid the trees in the heart of Buttes Chaumont Park. The *Ibérico* ham tapas, small salads and Basque pâté are perfect for a country-style brunch, perhaps taken on the lawn as a clandestine picnic with all of Paris at your feet. When the sun makes you feel as if you're in Spain, the mostly bio wines served on the terrace go perfectly with chorizo.

ROSA BONHEUR / 2 allée de la Cascade – Parc des Buttes-Chaumont – Paris XIX

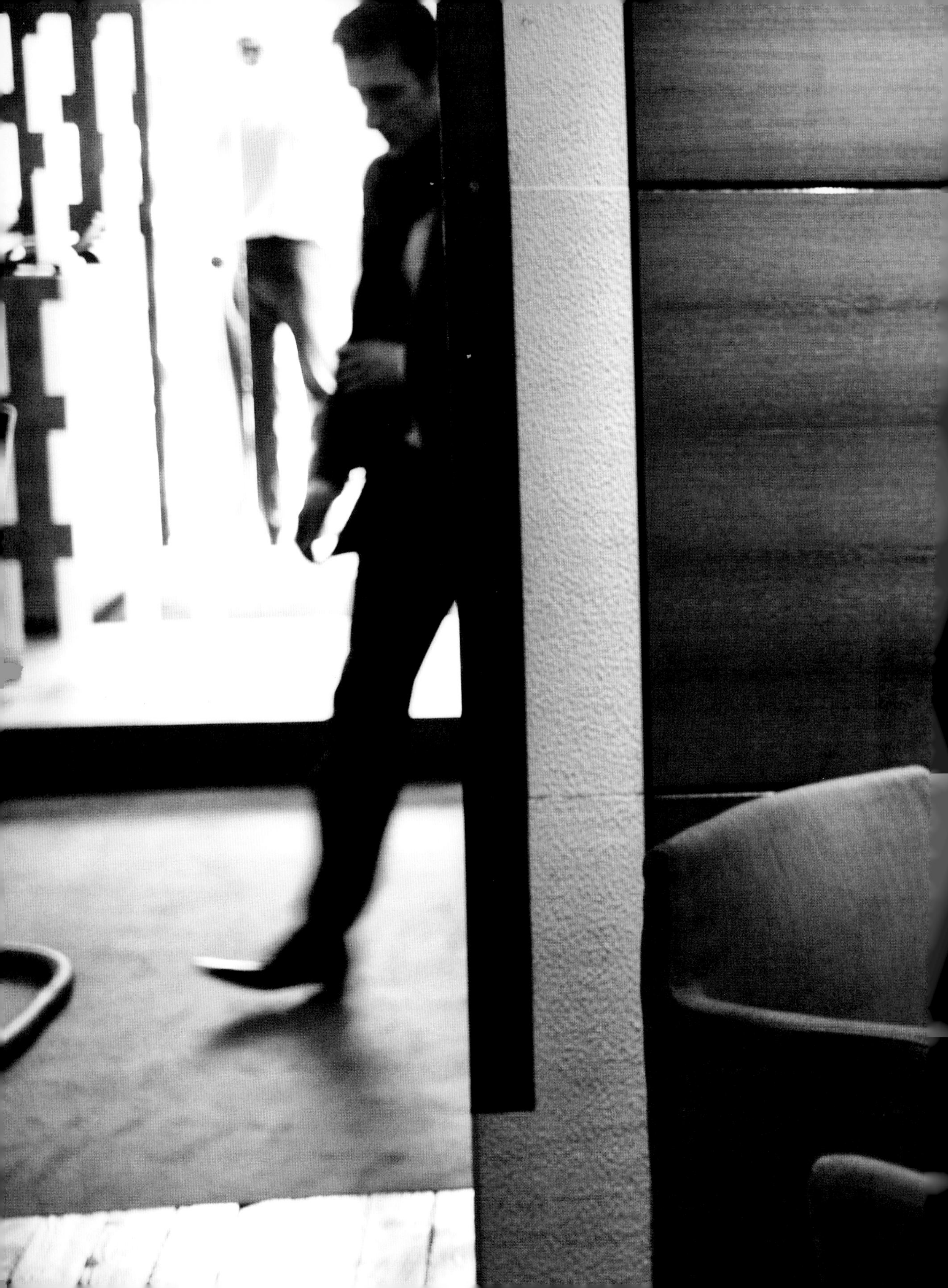

RESTAURANT GUY SAVOY. / 18 rue Troyon / Paris XVIIe

J'aime Paris

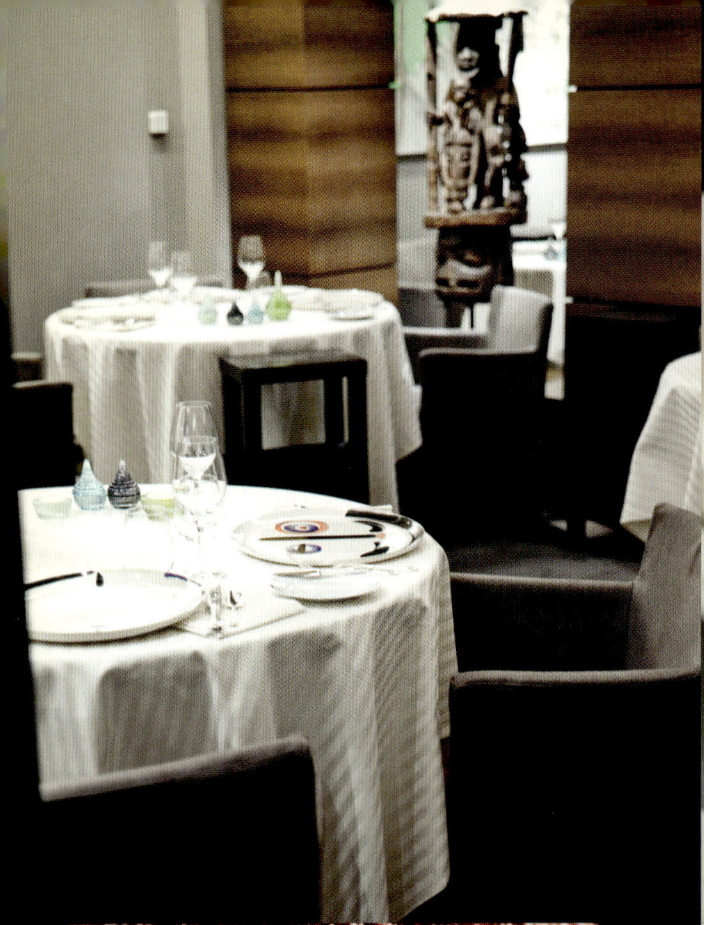
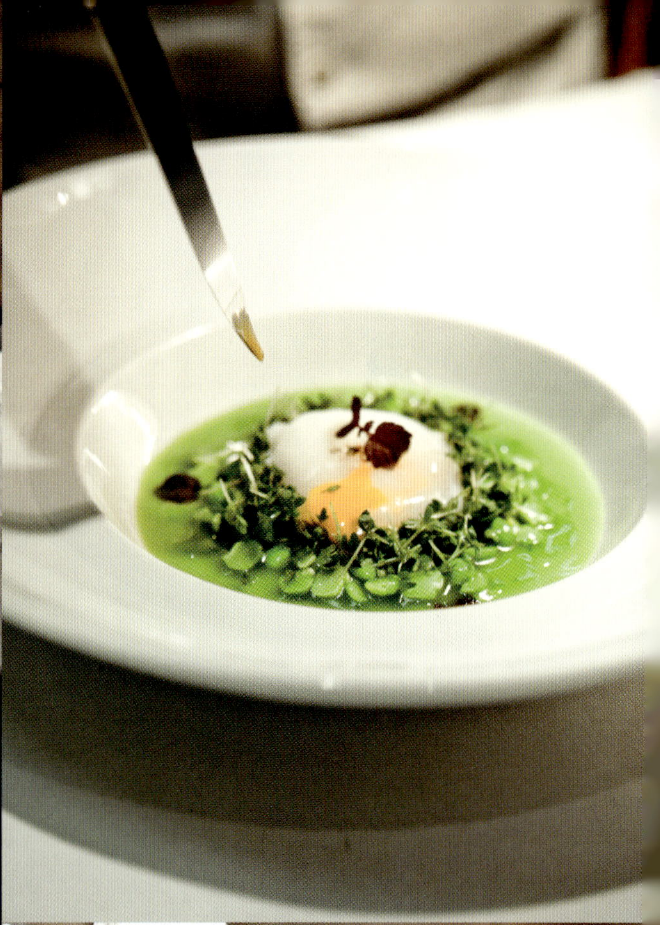
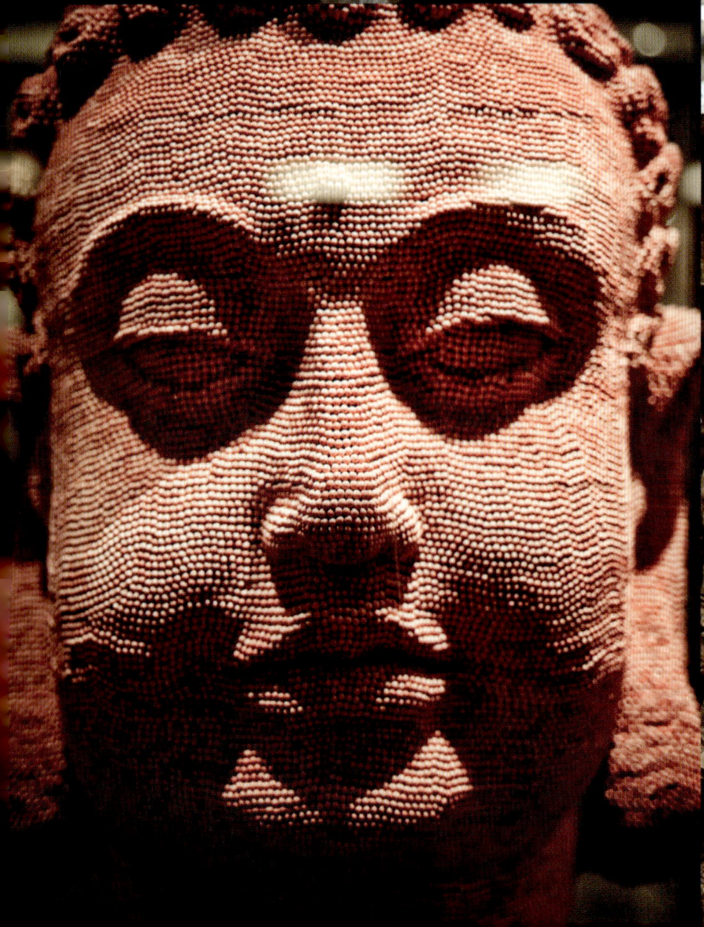
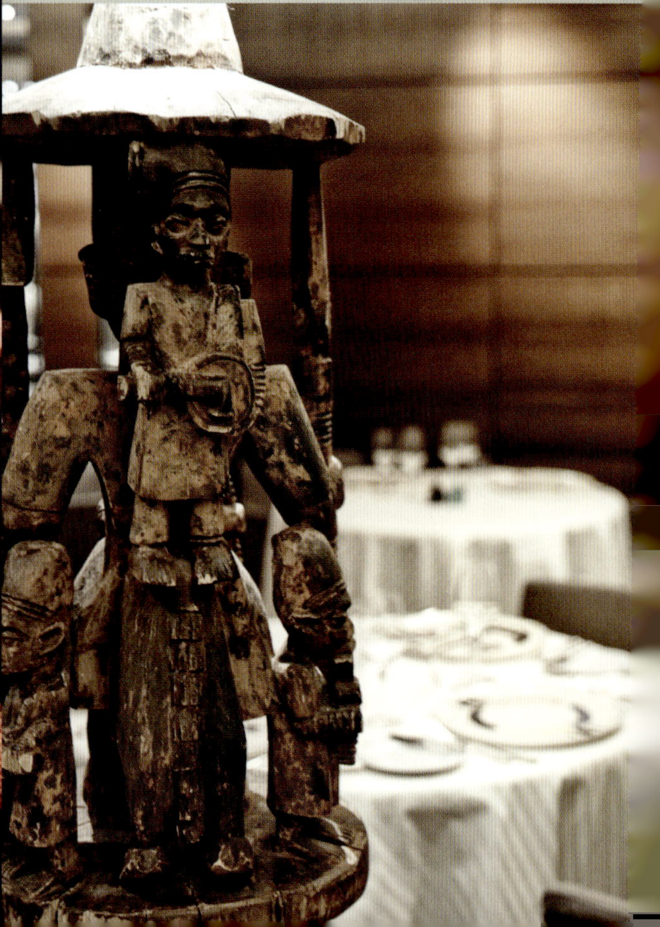

SA VOY

'If I hadn't been born in France, I wouldn't have considered becoming a chef! And as for Paris, discovering its monuments, museums and perspectives has been a source of fascination for me. Paris is a theatre, where I've been happy to perform for years; my dishes are my stage and my ingredients are my script. As of the end of 2011, I'll be acting out my role at the Hôtel de la Monnaie, a magnificent building on the Quai de Conti, which has been an integral part of the landscape of the Seine and the Louvre since 1775.'

Guy Savoy

RESTAURANT GUY SAVOY / 18 rue Troyon / Paris XVII° / J'aime Paris

Le

LE SELECT / 99 Boulevard du Montparnasse / Paris VIe

SELECT

Two round and proud pots, one large and one small, find their way to your table. First comes the rich, heady melted dark chocolate. Then the caress of frothing milk. This is the traditional hot chocolate served at Select, thick as a plush pile woollen carpet and as comforting as a roaring fire. A little of the Dadaist soul of Montparnasse still lingers at the bottom of the pot.

LE SELECT / 99 boulvard du Montparnas.e/ Paris VIe

PARIS WILL ALWAYS BE PARIS

J'aime Paris

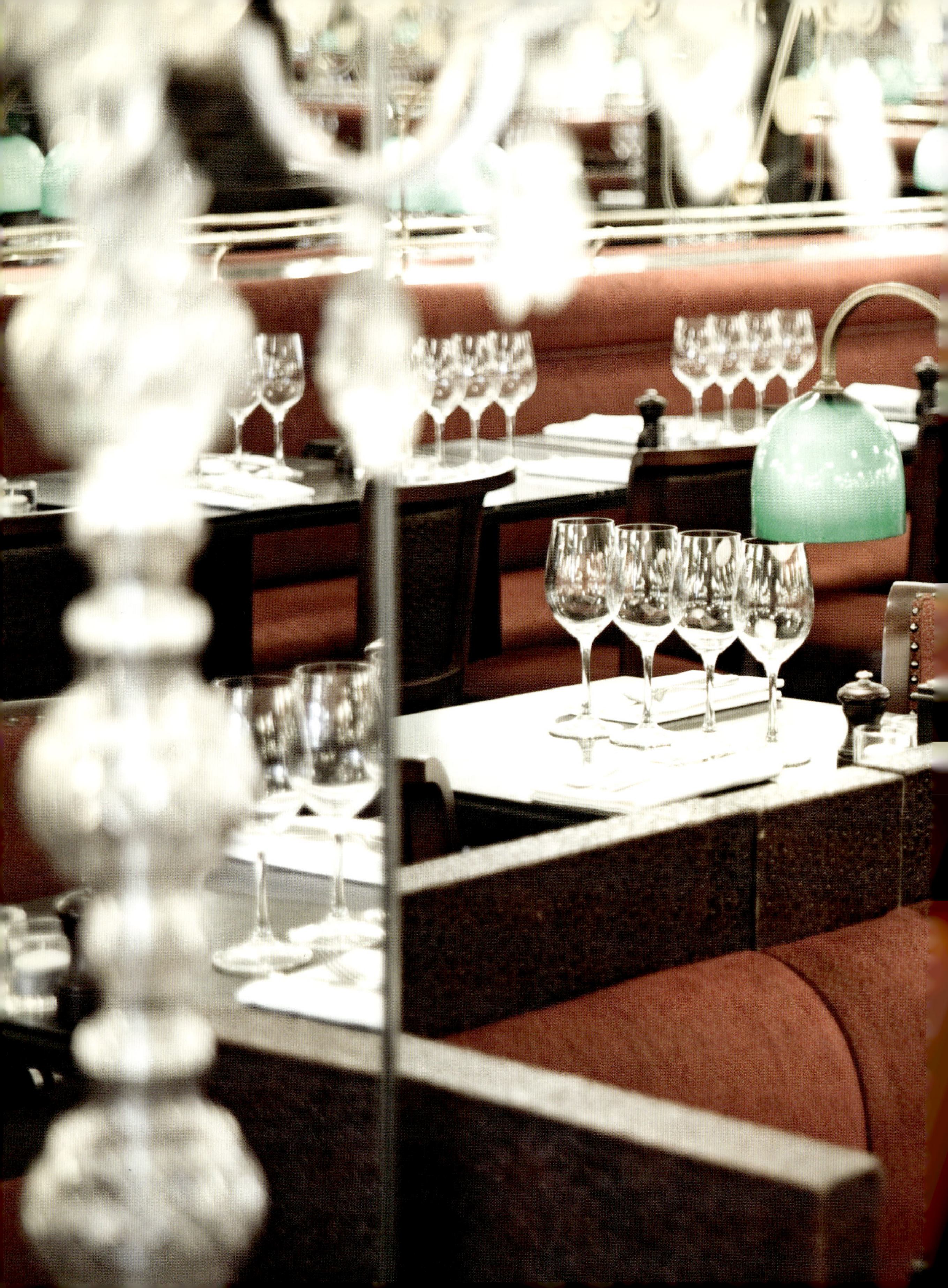

HÔTEL THOUMIEUX / 79 rue Saint-Dominique, Paris VIIe.

TH OU MIEUX

After five years at Les Ambassadeurs, the restaurant at the Hôtel de Crillon, Jean-François Piège has, together with Thierry Costes, taken over this hotel in the 7th arrondissement. He has also held on to his excellent suppliers from the hotel on the Place de la Concorde. The menu of the new Thoumieux has two parts: 'Room Service' for classic dishes such as squid carbonara and *lièvre* (hare) *à la royale*; and 'Ma Cuisine' for the chef's more audacious offerings, such as live langoustines with coconut and puffed pizza with tuna and rocket. The desserts are exquisite. Upstairs there is a small dining room for exclusive cuisine, and ten hotel rooms.

HÔTEL THOUMIEUX / 79 rue Saint-Dominique / Paris VIIe

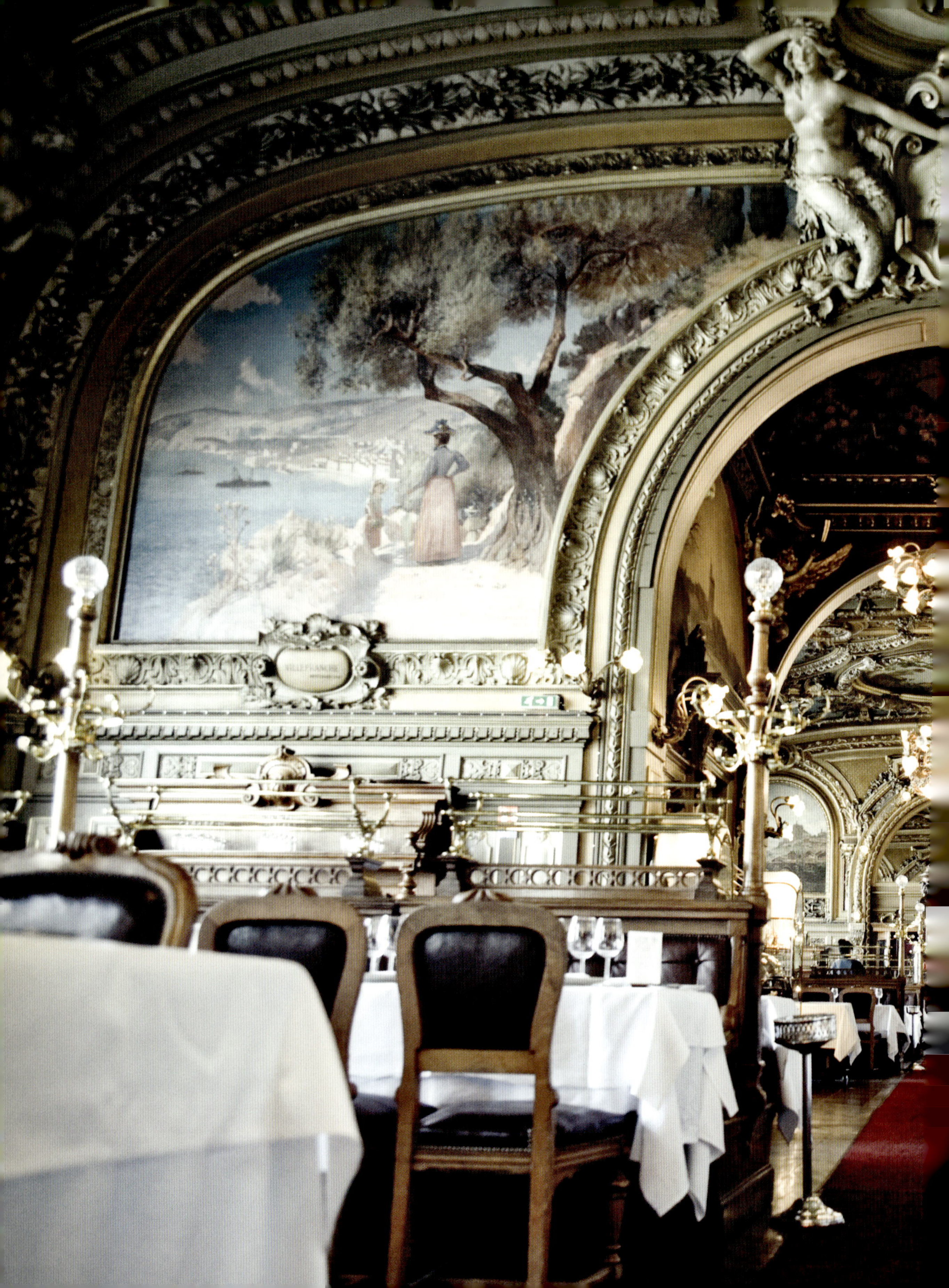

LE TRAIN BLEU / Place Louis Armand / Paris XII

TRAIN BLEU

Stationary travellers set off for a realm of gilt and frescos. When studying the ceiling, their imaginations wander the Île de France, sleepily cross the Rhône and awake at the seaside. The trains are outside, and there is noise and bustle, with people arriving, departing and staying behind. On the table, in the shadow of the huge booths, a *baba chantilly* glows.

LE TRAIN BLEU / Place Louis Armand / Paris XVe

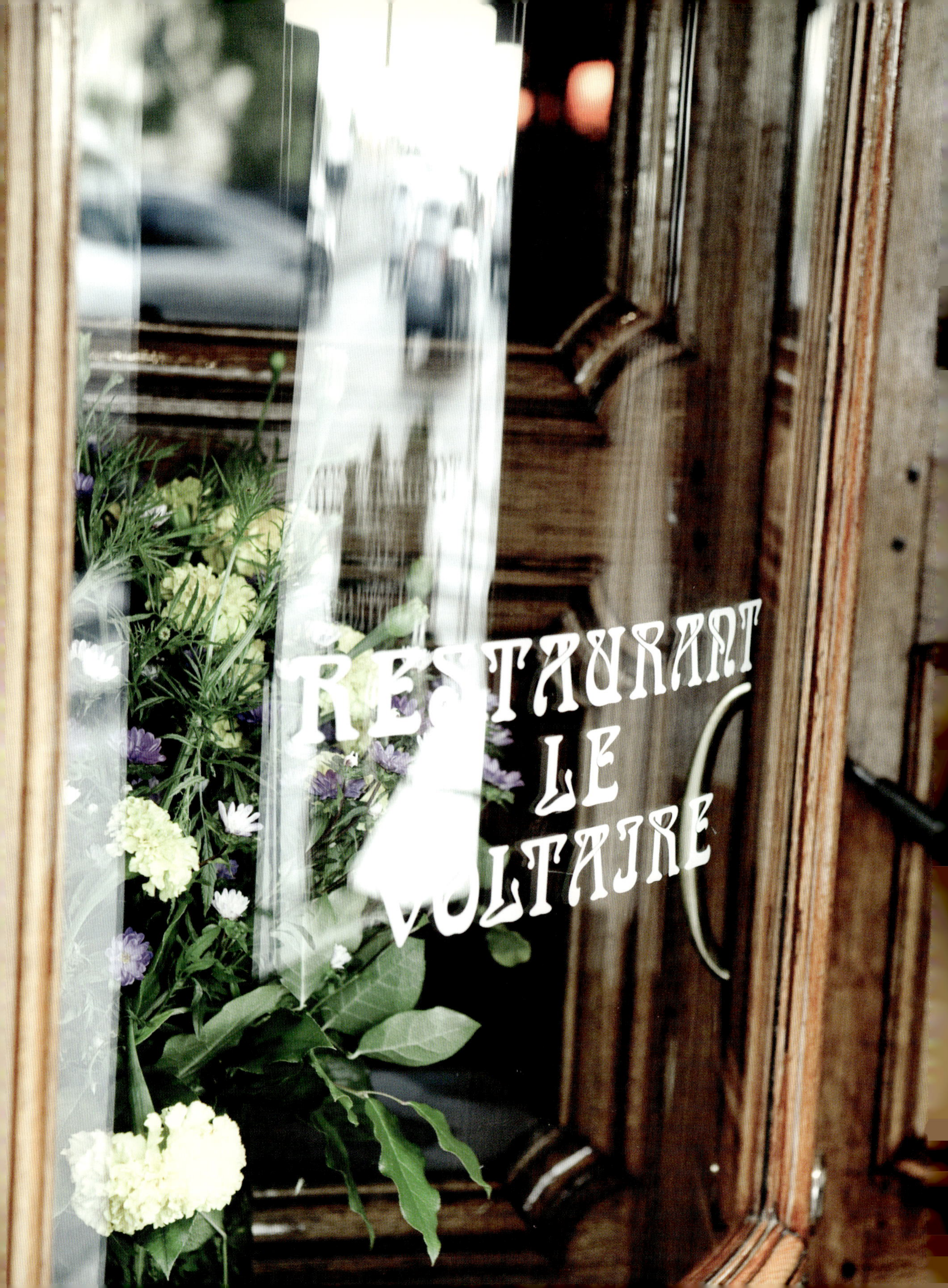
RESTAURANT
LE
VOLTAIRE

- 273

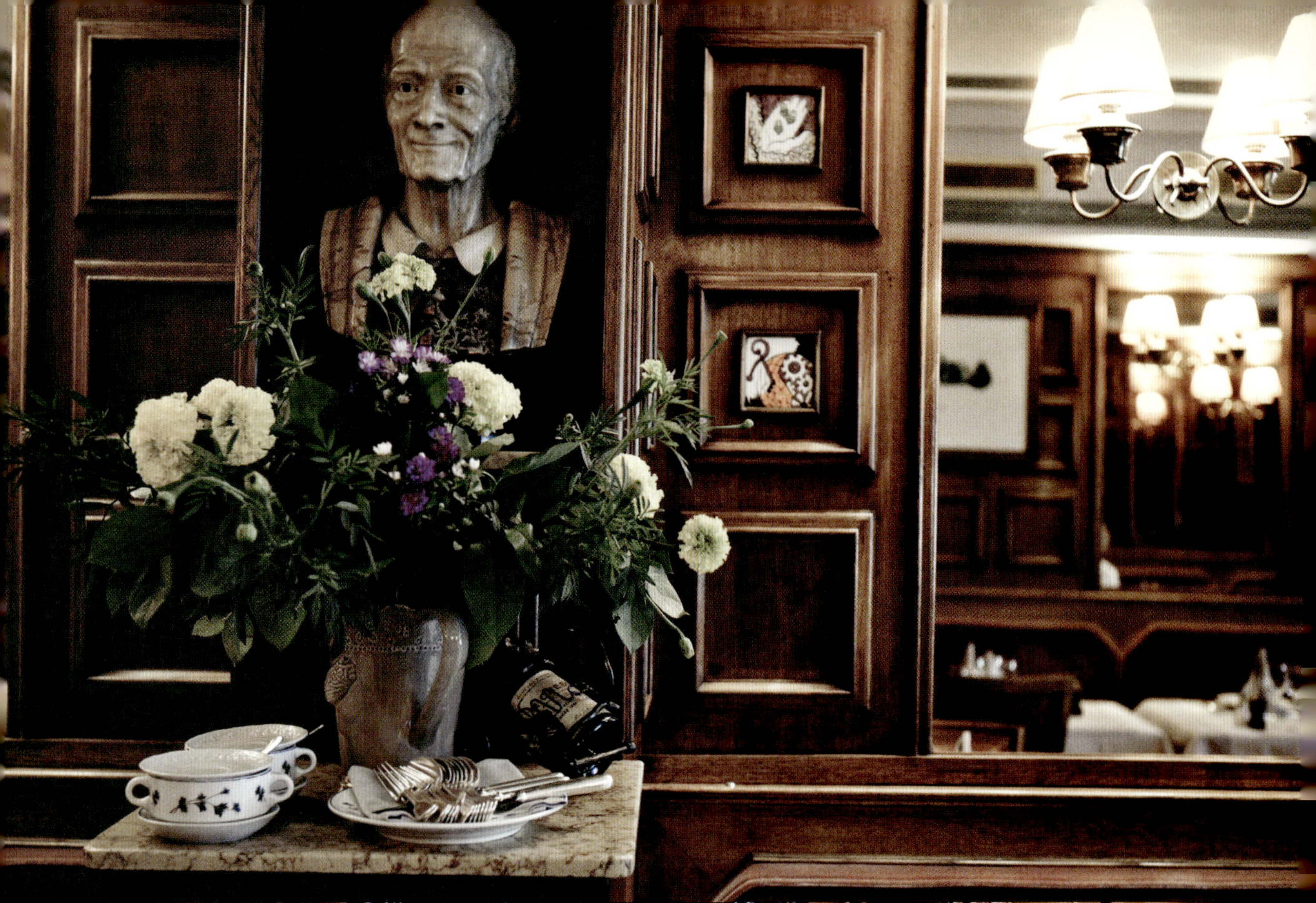
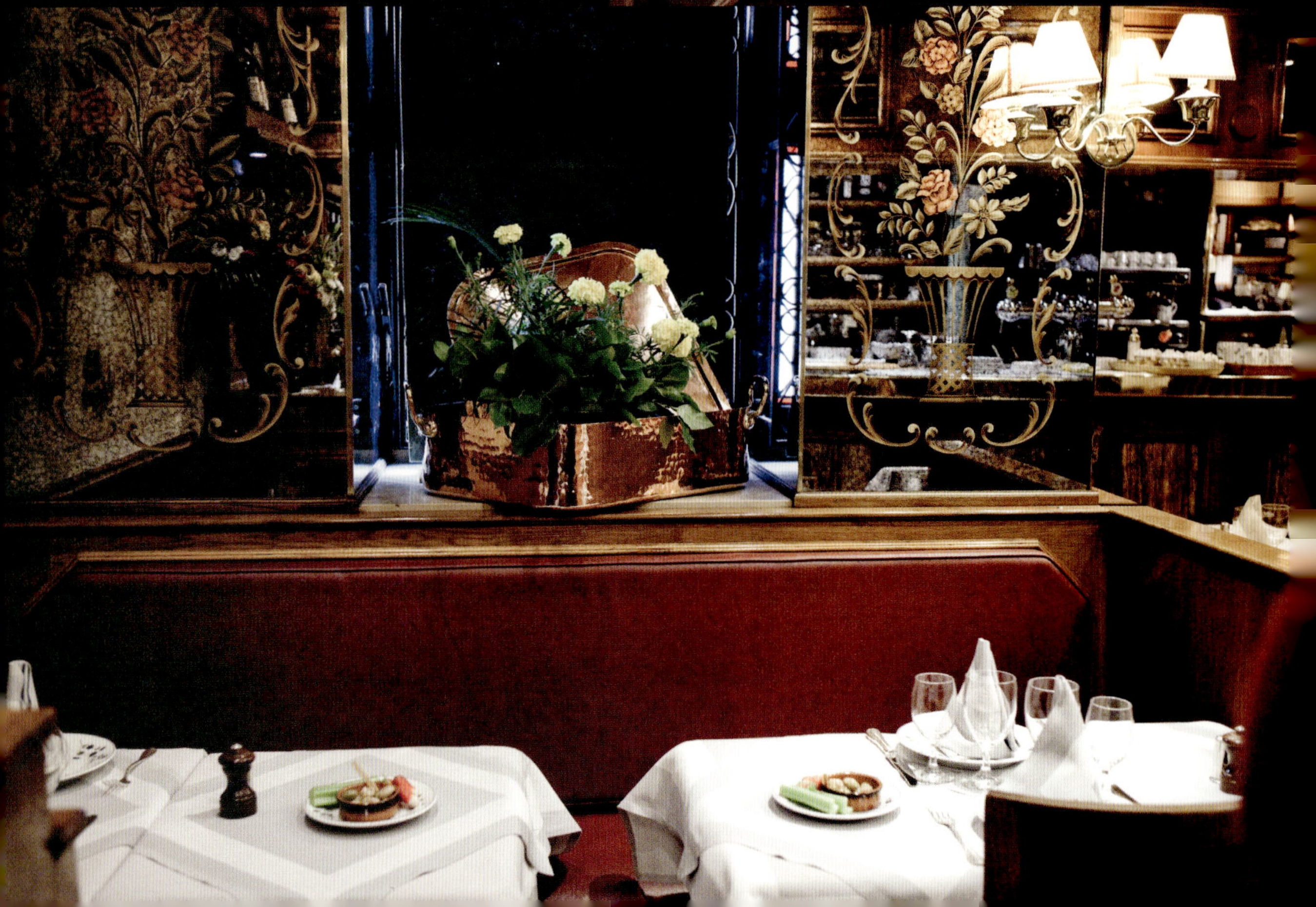

VOLT AIRE

An egg is cut in half. Then things become complicated. A few slices of radish, a small bunch of green beans and sliced fresh button mushrooms. Followed by a beautiful mayonnaise made with cream and mustard, coating the eggs with a new shell. A sprig of chervil forms an exclamation mark between two tomato smiles. This is how we like our egg with mayonnaise.

LE VOLTAIRE / 27 quai Voltaire / Paris VIIe

J'aime Paris

- 275

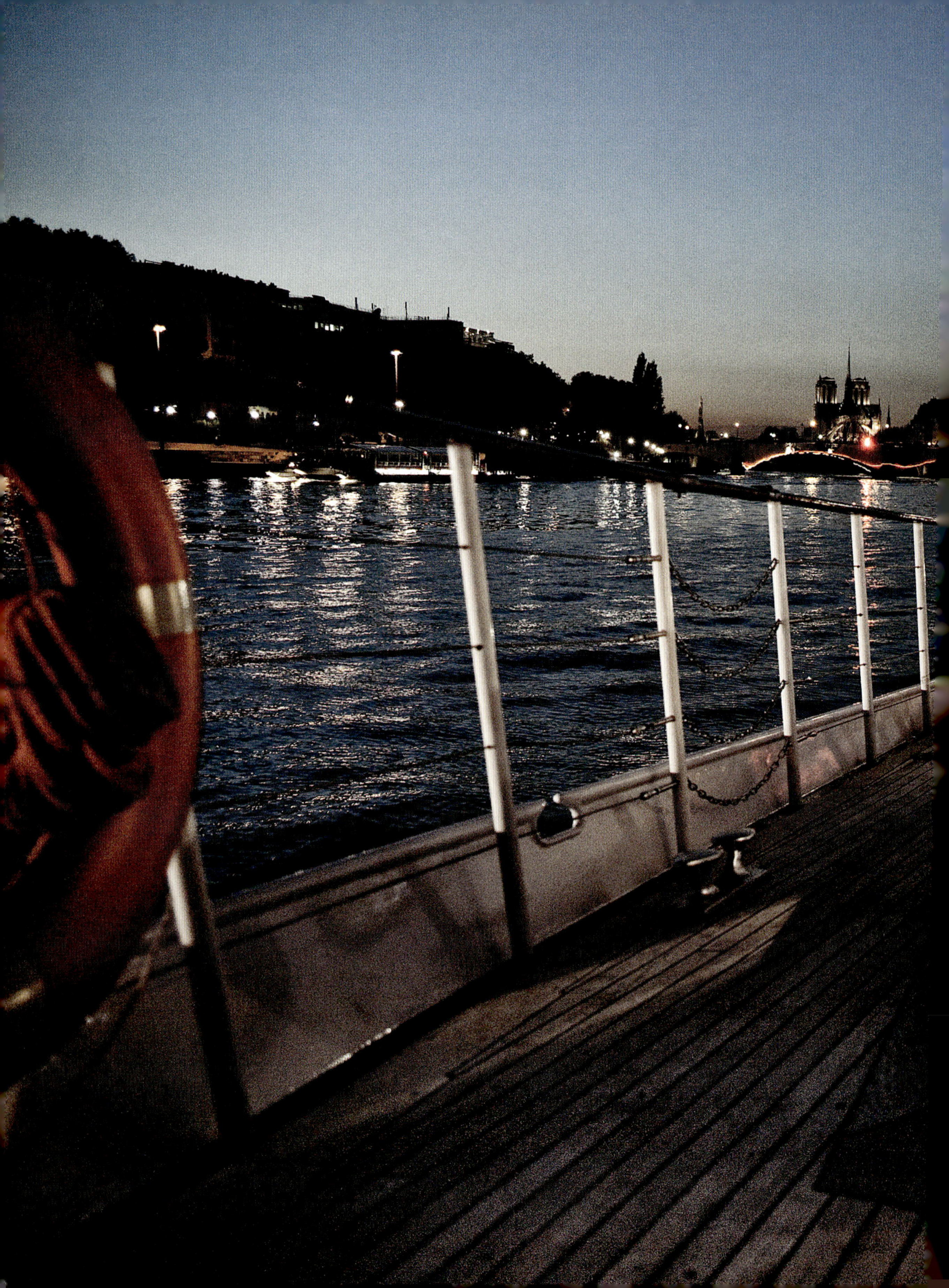

YACHTS DE PARIS / Port Henri IV / Paris IV°

J'aime Paris

PARIS WILL ALWAYS BE PARIS

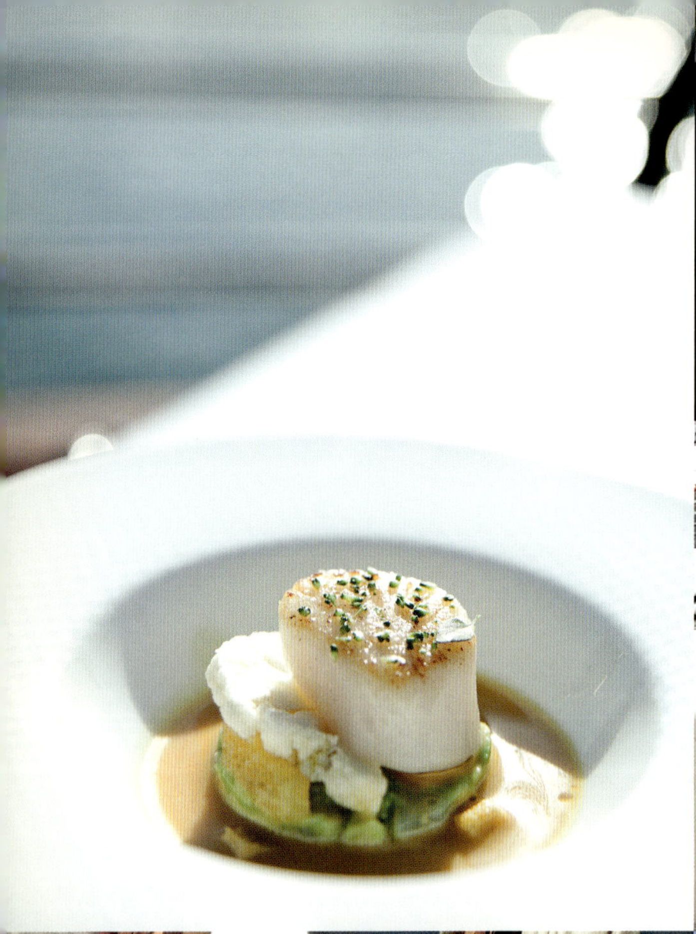
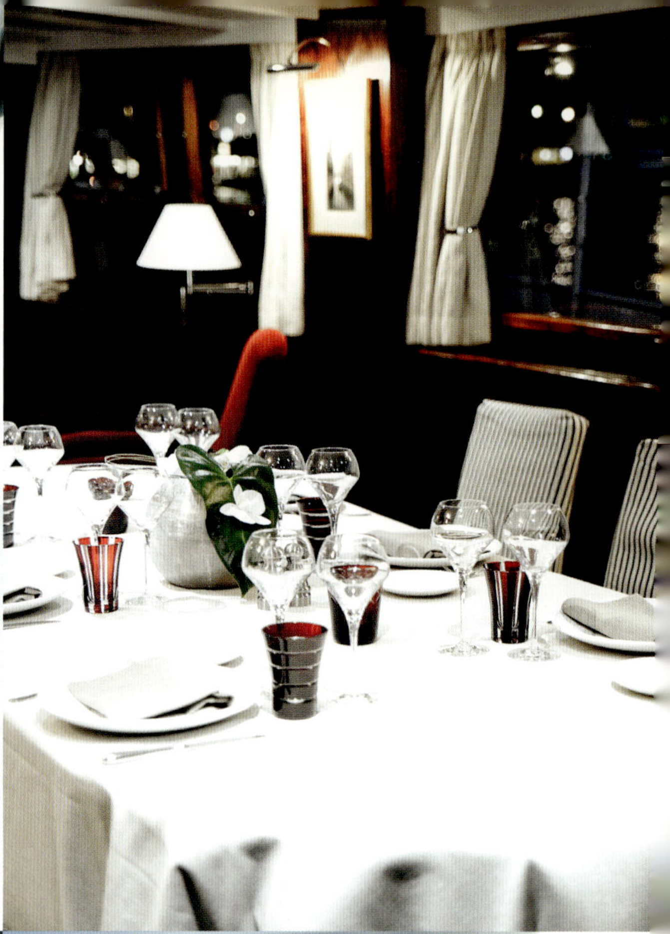
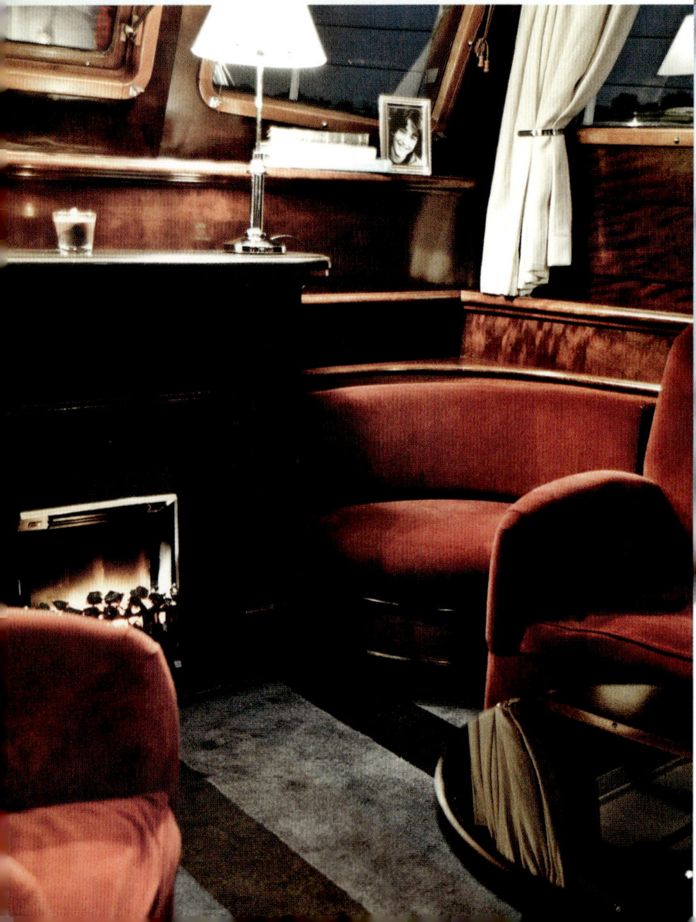
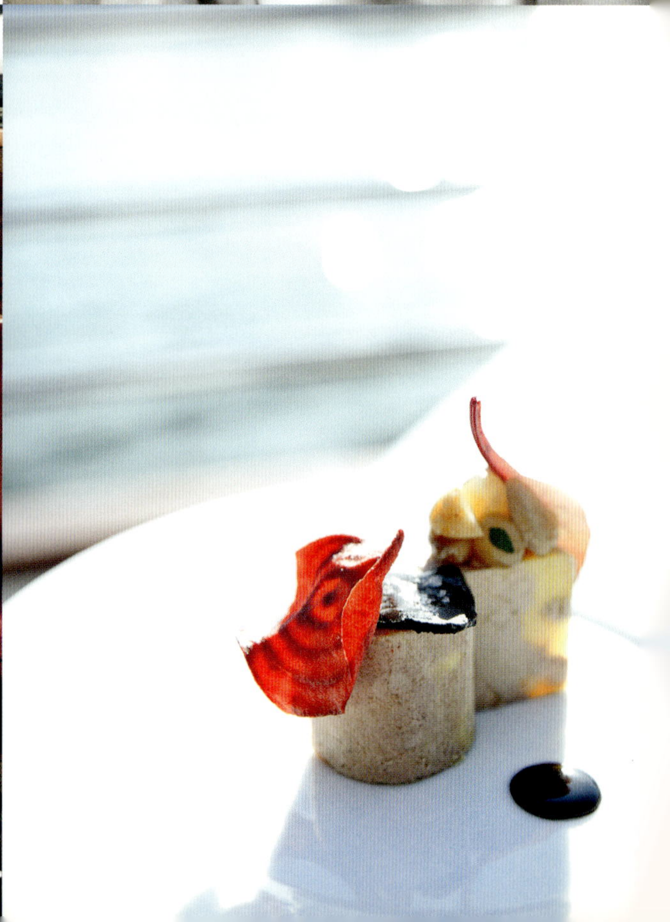

We embark on the privately booked *Cachemire* for an intimate gourmet cruise. Guy Krenzler, holder of the Meilleur Ouvrier de France award, is in charge of the food. Citrus-marinated scallops, avocado in suzette sauce, foie gras confit, peppered grapes and walnuts and black truffle emulsion are served. There is Baccarat crystal glassware and a marble fireplace, all of which makes this the sophisticated way to appreciate Paris and the Seine.

YACHTS DE PARIS

PARIS WILL ALWAYS BE PARIS

I ALSO LOVE...

L'ARÔME

3 rue Saint-Philippe du Roule / Paris VIIIe

The new décor of the restaurant features the tones of sienna, rosewood and ivory. It opens on to a beautiful kitchen. You want to try everything; but as the menu changes every day, your wish can never be granted. For example, depending on the season, you can choose a piece of veal sautéed with wild garlic, braised morels in Arbois wine and daikon with a marbled jus reduction. Its Michelin star is well deserved.

L'AUBERGE DU BONHEUR

Allée de Longchamp Bois de Boulogne / Paris XVIe

Tucked away behind La Grande Cascade, and owned by the Menut family, is a tranquil place graced by nature in the heart of the city, a place with beautiful trees, gravel that crunches under your heels and garden furniture... Under the starlit sky, the tantalising aroma of grilled meat fills the air as it wafts from the kitchen. It's summer in Paris.

HÔTEL LE BELLECHASSE

8 rue de Bellechasse / Paris VIIe

This new hotel designed by Christian Lacroix spreads its multicoloured wings. The décor oozes humour and elegance. Collages of old prints that have been enlarged and coloured are mixed together with a total disregard for convention. Your eye is first drawn to Elizabeth I, before you turn your attention to the bright scarlet faux Louis XIII wallpaper and become filled with wonder at the medieval geometries and take flight with the passing butterflies. You should experience this while having a really amazing breakfast in your room.

BATEAUX PARISIENS

Port de La Bourdonnais / Paris VIIe

You can hire one of these restaurant boats to take you down the Seine at twilight, or to enjoy any of their 'Prestige', 'Champagne', 'Jazz', 'Étoile' or 'Saveur' options for an intimate dinner just when the monuments begin to light up, the breeze is blowing and the imagination takes over... Green and white velouté cappuccino, duck breast in Port wine jus and iconic crêpes Suzette with orange butter bring out the magic of a supper under the lights. The extensive wine list is excellent. Whether you are from Paris or Tokyo, you will enjoy a special moment.

BRASSERIE LIPP

151 boulevard Saint-Germain / Paris VIe

This establishment is an historical monument. The 1900s interior and façade are listed. Even the menu has not changed in half a century! But don't be put off by this. Whatever the season, you must try the choucroute on your first visit. Like the unchanging plant motifs on the tiled walls, you will still be offered the choice of *blanquette de veau* (veal stew) or *boeuf gros sel* (boiled beef). Like some of the regulars, the millefeuilles are substantial.

LA CAVE DE JOËL ROBUCHON

3 rue Paul-Louis Courier / Paris VIIe

Even with 5000 different wines, the choice is perfect, and not without reason. Antoine Hernandez has been the sommelier with Joël Robuchon for over 20 years. Let yourself be guided to sound choices, such as 'La Marginale' Saumur-Champigny by Thierry Germain, bio Rieslings by Jean-Louis and Fabienne Mann or Champagnes by Bruno Paillard. Besides tastings, the house also offers to create and manage your own cellar.

LA CAVE DE L'OS A MOELLE

181 rue de Lourmel / Paris XV[e]

You have to work a little, as you do at home. You choose your wine from the shelf and pay the store price. You cut the still-warm bread to accompany your choice of starters: terrines, carrots, beetroot and a good mayonnaise. You get up and go to the back of the cellar where you serve yourself the day's still simmering special directly from the pot, or you choose the duck confit or stuffed vegetables. And you disturb other diners sharing your table. However, all your efforts are rewarded by an *île flottante* that is nigh-on perfect.

LA CAVE DES PAPILLES

35 rue Daguerre / Paris VI⁰

It's Sunday and the rue Daguerre feels like a cheese lovers' convention. You sympathise, but seek refuge in La Cave des Papilles. How about a French *vin nature* to go with couscous? After getting over your initial amazement, you are full of ideas. You choose a sparkling rosé, only slightly sweet, but cheerful and a little anarchic. It will be paella next time. You will be able to pick a wine from inside the cellar, where you can find a few hidden treasures, or just go for a cold bottle of bubbly.

CHAPEAU MELON

92 rue Rébeval / Paris XIX⁰

Hats off to Olivier Camus. Here's someone with a wonderful knowledge of how to drink and how to track down the highest quality labels of *vin nature*. He is a crusader for signature wines and an activist against unreliable appellations, a man on a quest for impeccable standards. He places his knowledge of French vineyards at the service of deluxe wine pairings.

CHEZ GEORGES

273 boulevard Pereire / Paris XVIIe

It's unavoidable: once through the door, you become a banker from a Balzac novel, or the editor-in-chief of *Le Figaro*, or the President of France. The two rows of white tablecloths form a guard of honour, but there's no need for you to greet the crowd when taking your seat. Here, the art of *cuisine bourgoise* is cultivated in all its glory: chicken liver terrine, lentil salad, veal sweetbreads with morels cooked to perfection, an elegant farm-raised veal rib and desserts *grand-mère* would make. The wine list features a number of select Bordeaux.

LES DEUX MAGOTS

6 place Saint-Germain-des-Prés / Paris VIe

The place to come to for the view and the cultural history of this district, which was partly written on these tables. Facing the Saint Germain church and the square where the Picasso statue stands, Les Deux Magots is one of the oldest Parisian cafés. It has always welcomed the inhabitants of Saint-Germain-des-Prés, celebrities and tourists, and has awarded a literary prize since 1933. Inside, certain drinks are still served by presenting customers with the bottle first. You must try a hot chocolate served the old-fashioned way.

LE DÔME

108 boulevard du Montparnasse / Paris XIVe

Aristocratic fish for a deluxe brasserie. They are sourced from the neighbouring Poissonnerie du Dôme and are beautiful, to match the Slavonic-style interior. The menu changes with the daily catch: darne of John Dory or bouillabaisse, grilled red mullet or a seafood platter. Regulars have included many notable figures, from Trotsky to Jean-Paul Sartre.

LES FINES GUEULES

43 rue Croix des Petits-Champs / Paris Ier

You allow yourself to be recommended a good wine to go with a sausage you are having at the bar. Then you discover the menu: meat from the exceptional butcher Desnoyer, sea bass with a vegetable garnish, line-caught black sea bream or asparagus from Le Blayais. All of the cold *charcuterie* products are cut on a vintage 1950 Berkel slicer, a red one for more authenticity. There is an impeccable selection of wines put together by Arnaud Bradol, the young owner. It's very difficult to decide between the *soupe de pêches* and the pear clafoutis. They like quality products here, and it shows.

LE FLAUBERT

10 rue Gustave Flaubert / Paris XVIIe

Elegant caramel-coloured woodwork effortlessly holds a beautiful collection of ceramic figurines. In the first of his 'bistros', Michel Rostang throws his weight behind simple cuisine. Featured dishes include Bresse chicken from suppliers Mieral, cooked in a rotisserie and served in two courses, or *penne au gratin* with lobster from the morning catch. The cheeses are from Fromagerie Laurent Dubois and the *escargots en brioche* are by Christine Ferber, known as *la fée des confitures* (the jam fairy).

FOUQUET'S

99 avenue des Champs-Elysées / Paris VIIIe

There are celebrities in the room, and on the plates, too. The Merlan Colbert whiting is done in the style preferred by Robert Hossein; and there is Lobster Jean Todt and a *palet au chocolat* in honour of the César Awards. For those worried about their health but not wanting to miss out on a taste experience, dietician Paule Neyrat helped to create a tuna ceviche with starfruit juice and a monkfish stew with coconut and tamarind.

G. DETOU

58 rue Tiquetonne / Paris IIe

Need something? Here's where you'll find it. One of the specialities of this establishment is patisserie supplies. Here you'll find the chocolate pellets professionals use, cream of tartar that you used to buy at the chemist's, dried cranberries to make cranberry biscuits, gelling agents, emulsifiers and a whole lot of other miscellaneous items. And that's without counting the pistachio and rose paste for making macaroons and the sparkles. As well as all that, you can seek advice from two lovely ladies on how to make your cakes a success.

LE GARDE MANGER

17 rue d'Aligre / Paris XIIe

A stone's throw away from the Aligre Market, Anne-Françoise Toussaint warmly welcomes you to Le Garde Manger, her Alsatian *delicatessen*. How about a glass of farm-fresh apple juice? It goes perfectly with the *flammekueche* cooked in a wood-fired oven. The traditional *baekeoffe*, the foie gras with turnips and the *spätzle* — noodles containing farm-fresh eggs — are all homemade. This grocery-eatery is filled with artisanal delicacies that come straight from Alsace: seasonal preserves by Christine Ferber, jars of choucroute and pork products, among others.

RESTAURANT JADIS

208 rue de la Croix-Nivert / Paris XVe

This is a bistro in an evening dress. The herring and potatoes is accompanied by a spinach and red orach velouté. The *gâteau de foie* comes with grilled langoustines and matching bisque. The rhubarb *panna cotta* is flavoured with hawthorn. It's daring and fresh, and a big hit.

LE PRÉ VERRE

8 rue Thénard / Paris V^e

There is cinnamon in the suckling pig, and other spices, too. After the surprise comes the pleasure. It radiates through the steaming and hearty dish with its typically French presentation; it climbs up through the fork, which pierces the creamy flesh; it teases the taste buds, evoking memories of Italian sausages with saffron and of Asian caramelised pork. Once it has taken hold, pleasure orders the brain to take another mouthful...

LES PAPILLES

30 rue Gay-Lussac / Paris V^e

The menu says it all: '*Retour du Marché*' (based on market availability), and below that: '*Marmite du Marché*' (market special). Nothing but fresh produce for this stylish bistro. The individual baking dishes come out of the oven and a bottle is taken from a shelf. The atmosphere is casual — there is a big screen in the basement room that is set up for customers on rugby nights — but the food is of a high standard.

LE PAVILLON DE LA REINE

28 place des Vosges / Paris IIIe

It's five o'clock, or thereabouts – time to flop into the soft armchairs in the bar. The warm hues, the books on the shelves and the creeper enveloping the building, creating effects with the sunlight, go to make a cosy atmosphere. Time seems to stand still... If you have time to spare, it would be a good idea to spend it in the Carita Spa, to let yourself be lulled by the soft lighting on the pebbles leading to the hammam.

LE PETIT VENDÔME

8 rue des Capucines / Paris IIe

If you manage to reach the bar, you will be able to try one of the best sandwiches in the capital. Cantal cheese, terrine, tripe, ham, cured ham or multicoloured sausages are piled high over and behind the counter. Wash it down with a glass of Saint-Pourçain wine accompanied by cocktail onions. With a little more time and a bigger appetite, you would be able to weave between the regulars to find a table where you would be forgiven for devouring a duck confit, a sausage with *aligot*, a good rib steak and some legendary *frites*.

PETROSSIAN

18 boulevard Latour-Maubourg / Paris VII[e]

Armen Petrossian watches over his little pearls. He has brought his famous pressed caviar back into fashion. This skilful blend of beluga, osetra and sevruga caviars had once fallen into obscurity. But Petrossian isn't only about caviar. A royal Kamchatka crab leg reaches out to visitors. The fine flesh comes off like that of a lobster. The delicate aromas are almost sweet. Your palate wants to enjoy the pleasure of its wondrously light texture to very the last morsel. This is crab at its finest.

LA POULE AU POT

9 rue Vauvilliers / Paris Ier

Take carrots, turnips, onions and cloves, and a chicken, of course. The place that has been known as 'Les Halles' best' has been offering King Henry IV's recipe for over 30 years. They do chicken in salad and in suprême sauce, too, for a change. The Ravaillacs of this world will take their revenge by ordering the salmon with saffron crème or the beef shin *pot-au-feu*. The atmosphere is as warm as the food.

LA RÉGALADE

49 avenue Jean Moulin / Paris XIVe

The concept is surprisingly simple: very good food and very good value. Clearly, the result of this is that the establishment run by Bruno Doucet, who has brilliantly reintroduced the formula created by Yves Camdeborde, is packed to the rafters. The caramelised farmhouse pork ribs and the squid pan fried elver-style in its own ink with rice are being devoured. It is a joy to see such a decidedly friendly wine list. The easy-going and attentive service makes the experience a relaxing one, so you can let yourself go with a little pot of vanilla cream with fresh raspberries. This place is worth its weight in gold.

LE RELAIS LOUIS XIII

8 rue des Grands Augustins / Paris VIe

The whole roast Challons duckling with spices and seasonal vegetables, and the duck confit parmentier, are obviously for two people, but the tone is set. Despite the overwhelming historical significance of this place — it is where Marie de Médicis had her son proclaimed King Louis XIII of France on hearing of the death of Henry IV — Manuel Martinez, holder of the Meilleur Ouvrier de France award, eschews refined products and elegant recipes. Spurning the distant gaze of the king in armour, it is impossible to resist the warm vanilla millefeuille.

LE REPAIRE DE CARTOUCHE

8 boulevard des Filles du Calvaire / Paris XIe

Rodolphe Paquin is Norman and he loves game. An example of this is his creamy game bird soup with chanterelle mushrooms. His pork chops, however, come from unstressed pigs raised on his family's farm. His *lièvre* (hare) *à la royale* is done like nobody else can, as is his veal chump chop in cider. And his terrines would make any of the regulars from the Verre Volé wine bar happy.

RESTAURANT JOSÉPHINE

« Chez Dumonet » / 117 rue du Cherche-Midi / Paris VI⁰

Come on! There's still a little room for a generous serving of millefeuille or the divine Grand Marnier soufflé... A guarantee of tradition, this is a family business that has been handed down to the next generation. With its worn leather and the patina on the silver, patterned mirrors and home cooking, 'Chez Dumonet' as the locals know it, is an authentic 1920s Parisian bistro. The terrines and foie gras are homemade and the steak tartare is prepared in the dining room. All is as it should be. Largesse is on the menu at Chez Dumonet; it's a matter of principle.

WEPLER

14 place Clichy / Paris XVIII⁰

What is there to see here? There's the atmosphere and the setting; this is a genuine Parisian brasserie. Everyone from Bonnard to Picasso, from Henry Miller to Blier and Truffaut, who filmed a scene from *Les Quatre Cent Coups* (The 400 Blows) here, were wild about the authenticity of the place. What is there to eat? Oysters — this establishment was the first to make them its speciality over a century ago — and choucroute, or Béarnaise grilled pig's trotters. It's authentic, we say.

PARIS: HOME TO THE REGIONS

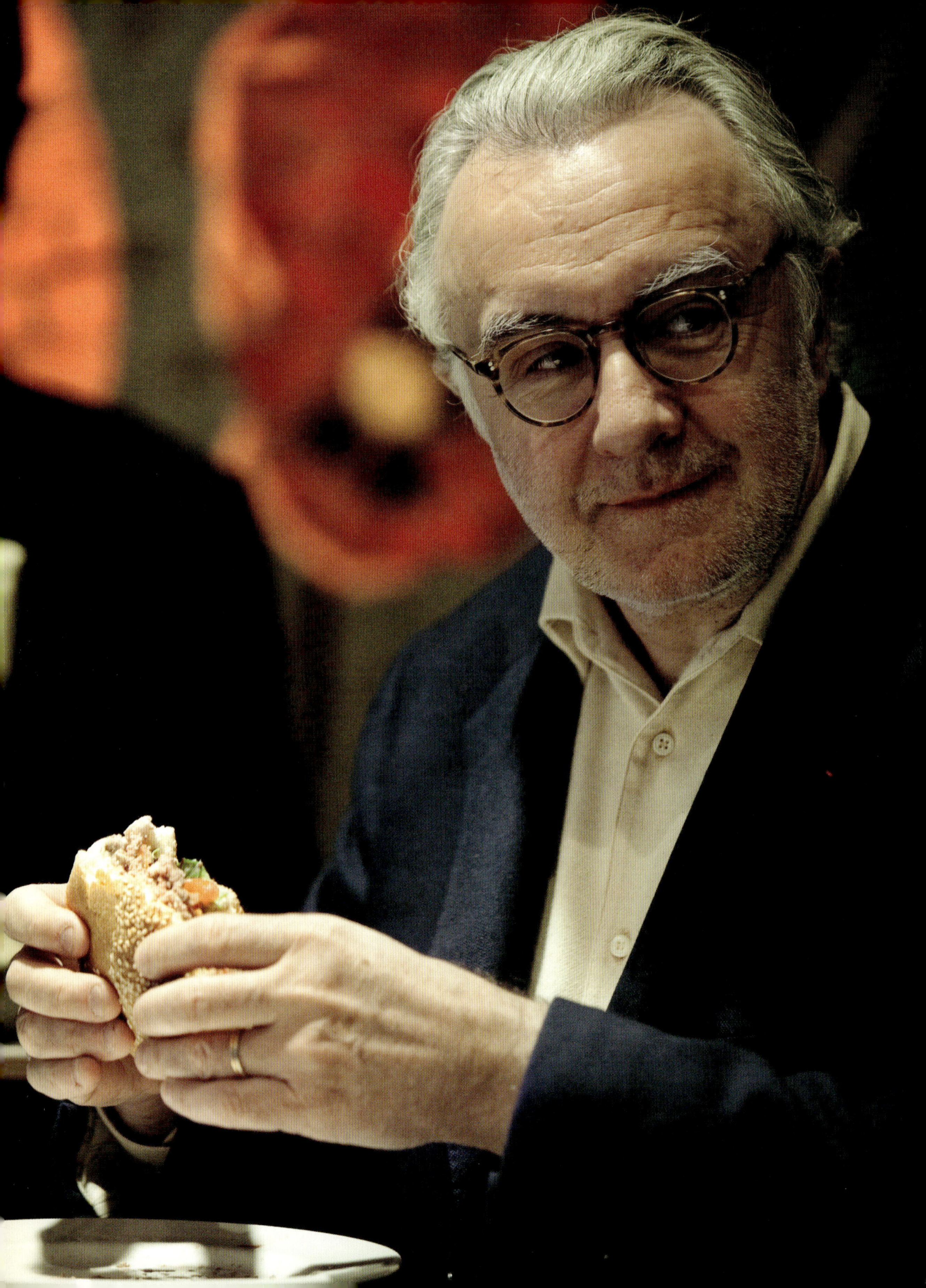

AU BRAC COR NER

'From farm to fork' is the fate of Christian Vallette's 320 cows. He makes them into hamburgers in his kitchen. Wait! Don't stop reading yet! This juicy and firm meat from Aubrac is mixed with wholegrain mustard mayonnaise. The bun, made from a combination of wheat and linseed, is as soft as white bread but with less sugar. There is just enough time for it to absorb the meat juices as you bite into the filling. You don't even need fries...

AUBRAC CORNER / 37 rue Marbeuf / Paris VIII°

RESTAURANT

32

E. QUINTON
KINÉSITHÉRAPEUTE

Laurence SIMONNET
PÉDICURE - PODOLOGUE

SÉVERINE CIRBA
MASSEUR KINÉSITHÉRAPEUTE

"AUX LYONNAIS"

AUX LYONNAIS / 32 rue Saint-Marc / Paris IIe

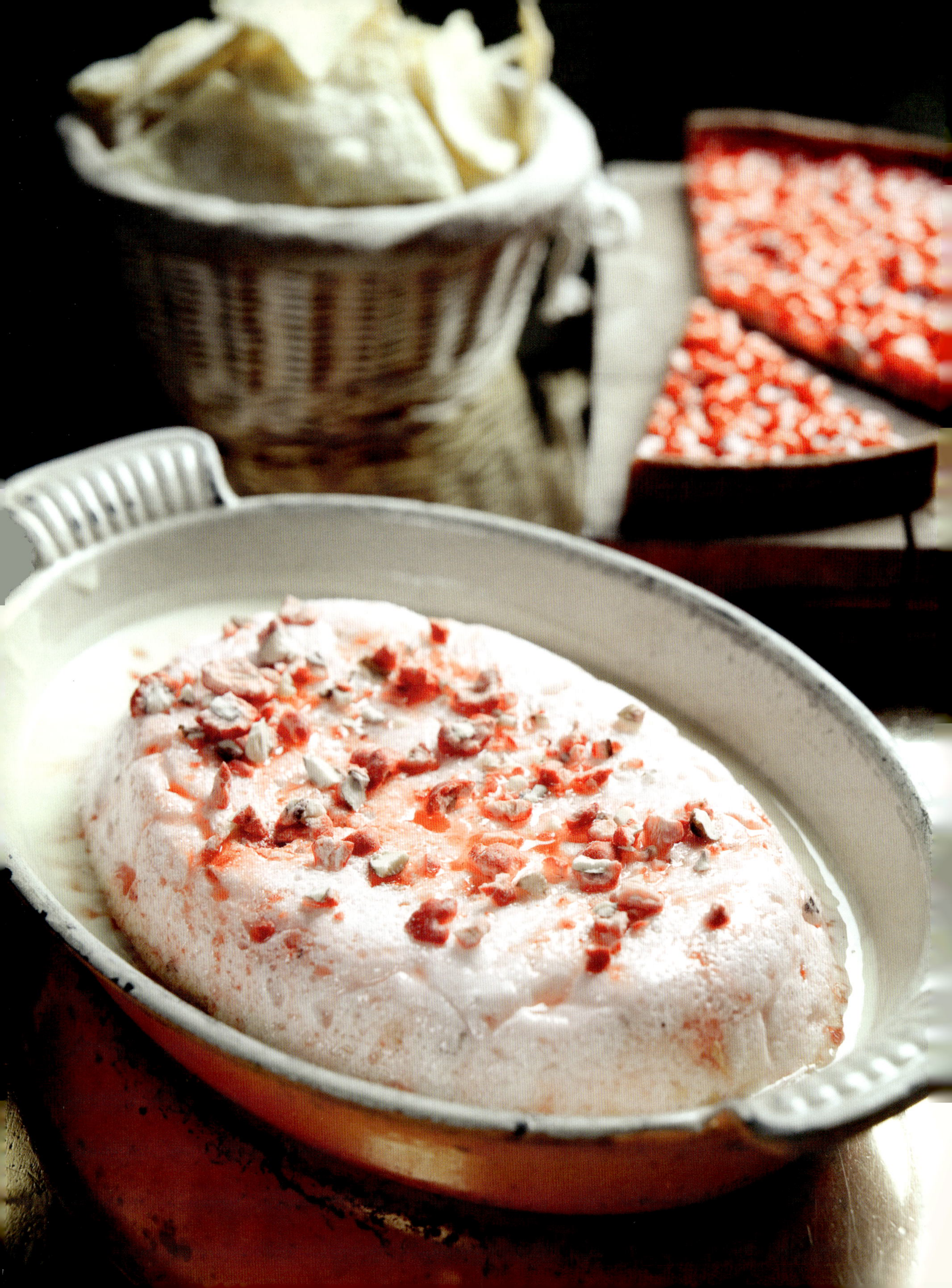

AUX LYONNAIS / 32 rue Saint-Marc / Paris II[e]

PARIS: HOME TO THE REGIONS

J'aime Paris

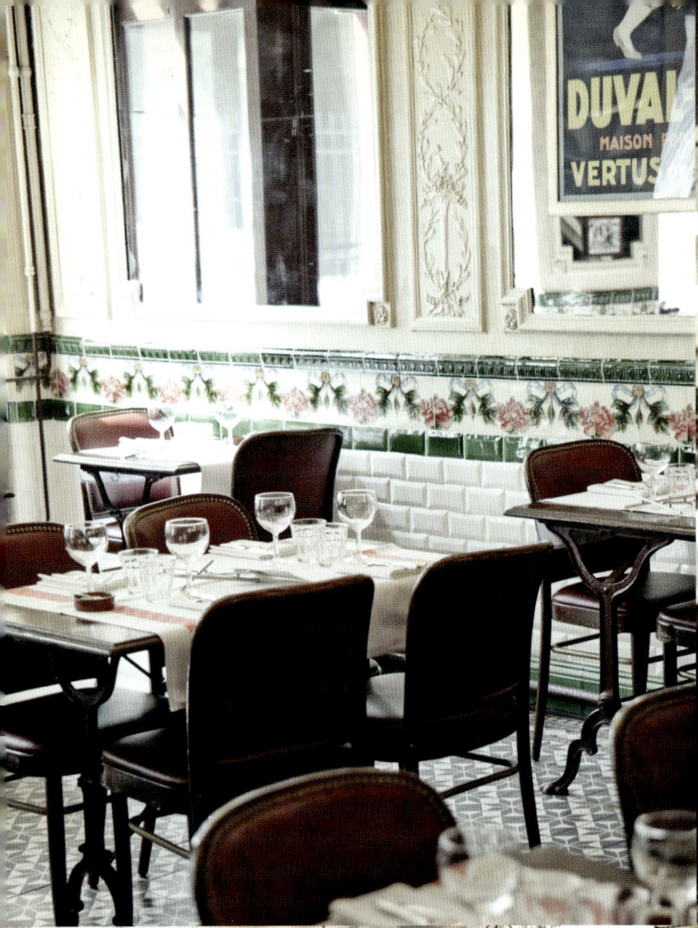
DUVAL
MAISON
VERTUS

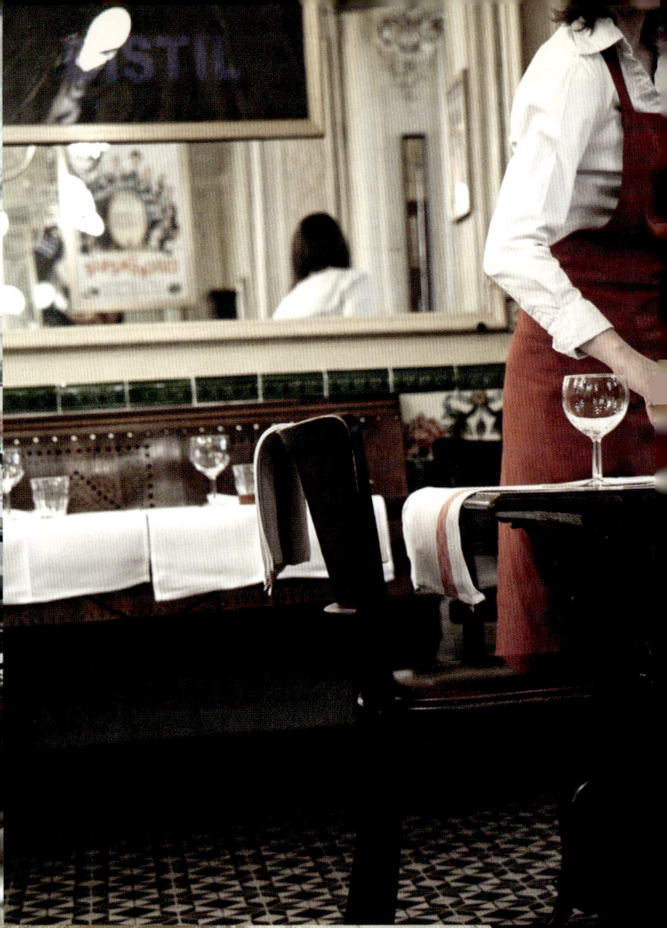

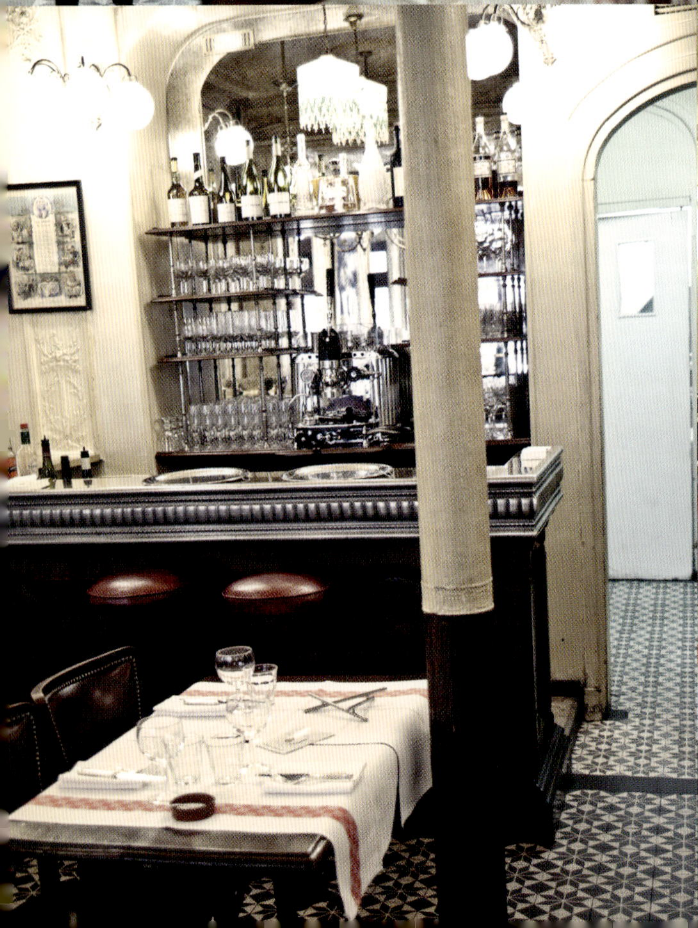

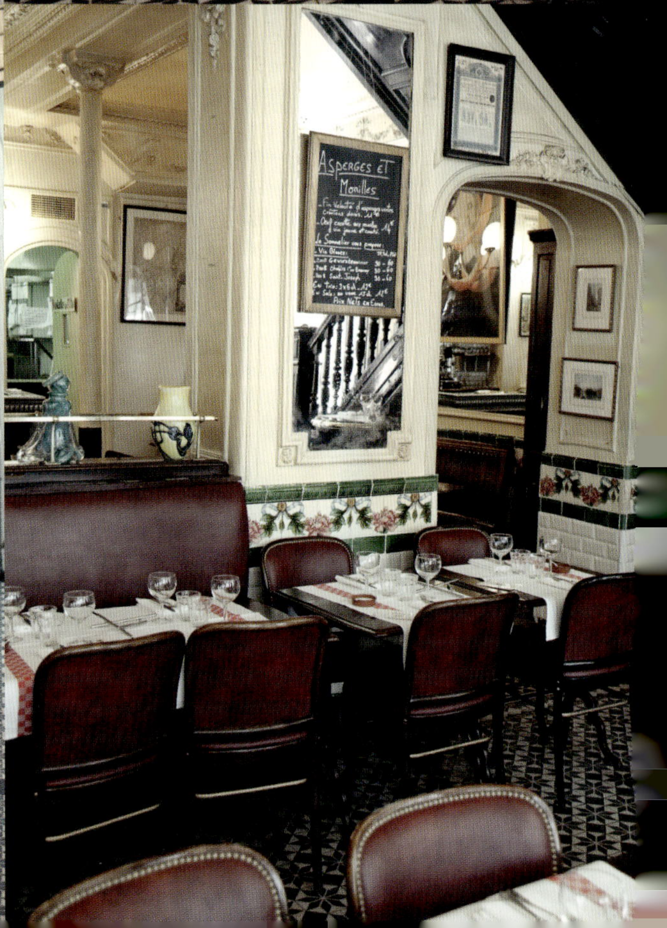
Asperges et
Morilles

AUX LYONNAIS

PARIS: HOME TO THE REGIONS · J'aime Paris

AUX LYONNAIS / 32 rue Saint-Marc / Paris IIe

The story of a legacy... There was once a typical Lyonnais *bouchon* (bistro) in the heart of Paris. There was no need to change anything, only to perpetuate its traditions and safeguard its culinary heritage. Each of the specialities prepared by Frédéric Thévenet, from the *pot de la cuisinière lyonnais* to the *île flottante* and pink praline tart, shines as brightly as the mirrors and Metro tiles. There is also a second, less-heralded legacy. There was once a young chef, Alain Ducasse, who discovered the wealth of Lyonnais cuisine working side by side with Alain Chapel in Mionnay. He grew fond of the noble region of Lyon and its iconic chefs Paul Bocuse and Michel Troigros. Aux Lyonnais is a *bouchon* deserving of praise.

- 305

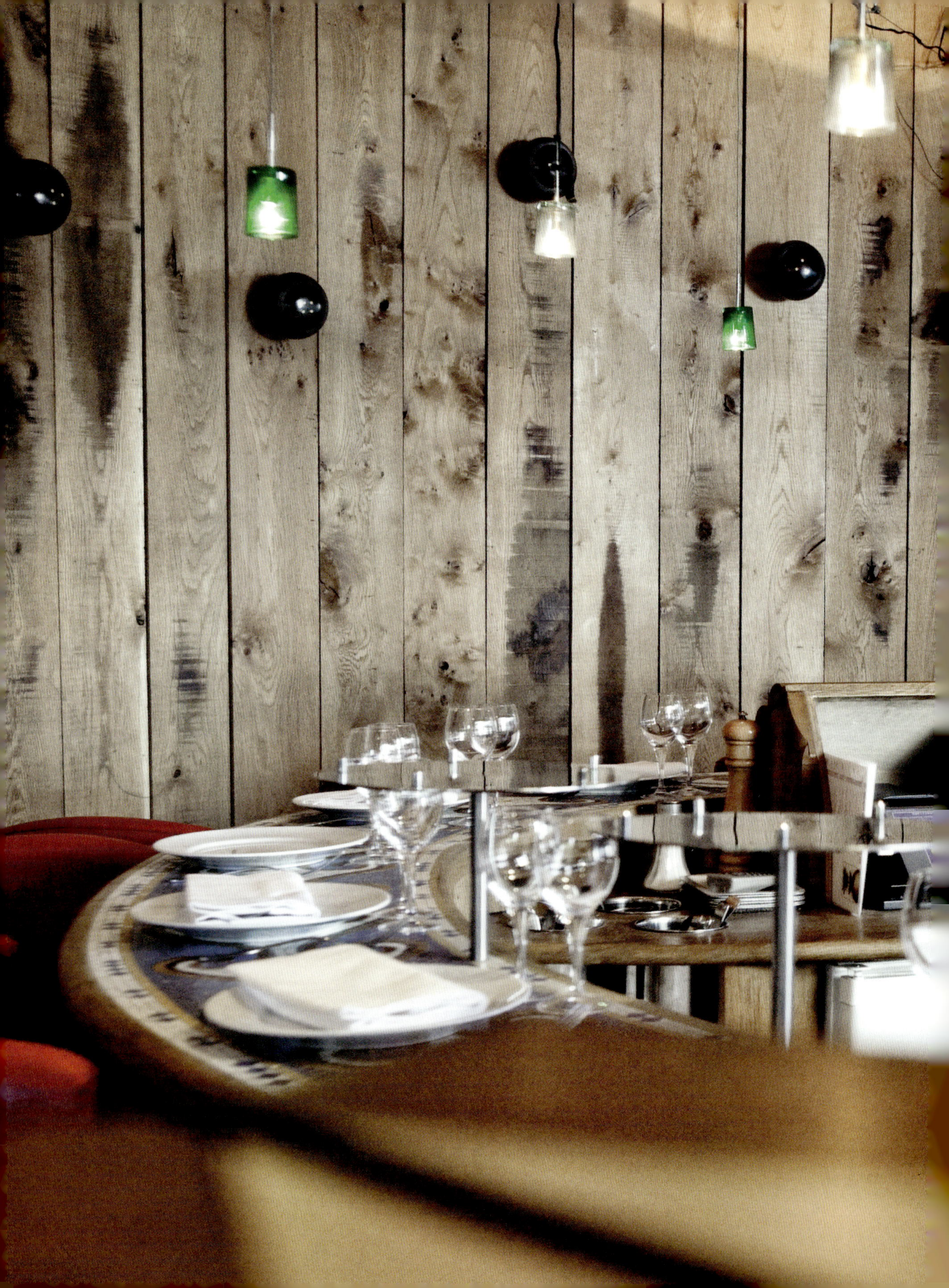

BALLON ET COQUILLAGES / 71 boulevard Gouvion Saint-Cyr / Paris XVII

- 307

BALLON ET COQUILLAGES

With its feel of a designer fishing cabin, the décor of this place takes you on holiday and to the moment you savour a seafood snack. The philosophy of this establishment belonging to the Menut group, also responsible for La Grande Cascade in the Bois de Boulogne, is clear: it's a seafood bar. Over the large round wooden bar, a plate of oysters is being prepared – what a good idea it was to serve them in threes. The seafood platters, individual or for two, consist of dog cockles, Indian prawns and beautiful crab claws.

BALLON ET COQUILLAGES / 71 boulevard Gouvion Saint-Cyr / Paris XVIIe

PARIS: HOME TO THE REGIONS

J'aime Paris

LAGUIOLE
DE TUNNEL
LE KILO 29.95€
SAINT-NECTAIRE
FROMAGE AU LAIT DE VACHE
TOMME DE SAVOIE
FERMIERE DE THONES
TOMME ABONDANCE
FROMAGE AU LAIT DE VACHE
FERMIER THONES 7423
LE KILO 32.80 €
Barthélemy
M.G 45%
FROMAGERIE BARTHÉLEMY
ARDI GASNA
BREBIS FERMIER DU PAYS BASQUE
ELIZAGARAIA - St-JEAN-PIED-DE-PORT
LE KILO 44.80 €
Barthélemy

BARTHÉLEMY, 51 rue de Grenelle, Paris VIIe.

BARTHELEMY

Madame Nicole is recommended for her Mont d'Or cheese, and also for her Époisse and vieux saler varieties. I fell in love immediately with her amazingly light Fontainebleau cream cheese, wrapped in gauze resembling a hat veil. It goes perfectly with the first raspberries and wild strawberries of the season. A little sugar in the whipped Fontainebleau crunches on my teeth, as it should.

J'aime Paris

REGIONS PARIS HOME TO THE REGIONS

BARTHÉLEMY / 51 rue de Grenelle / Paris VIIe,

- 313

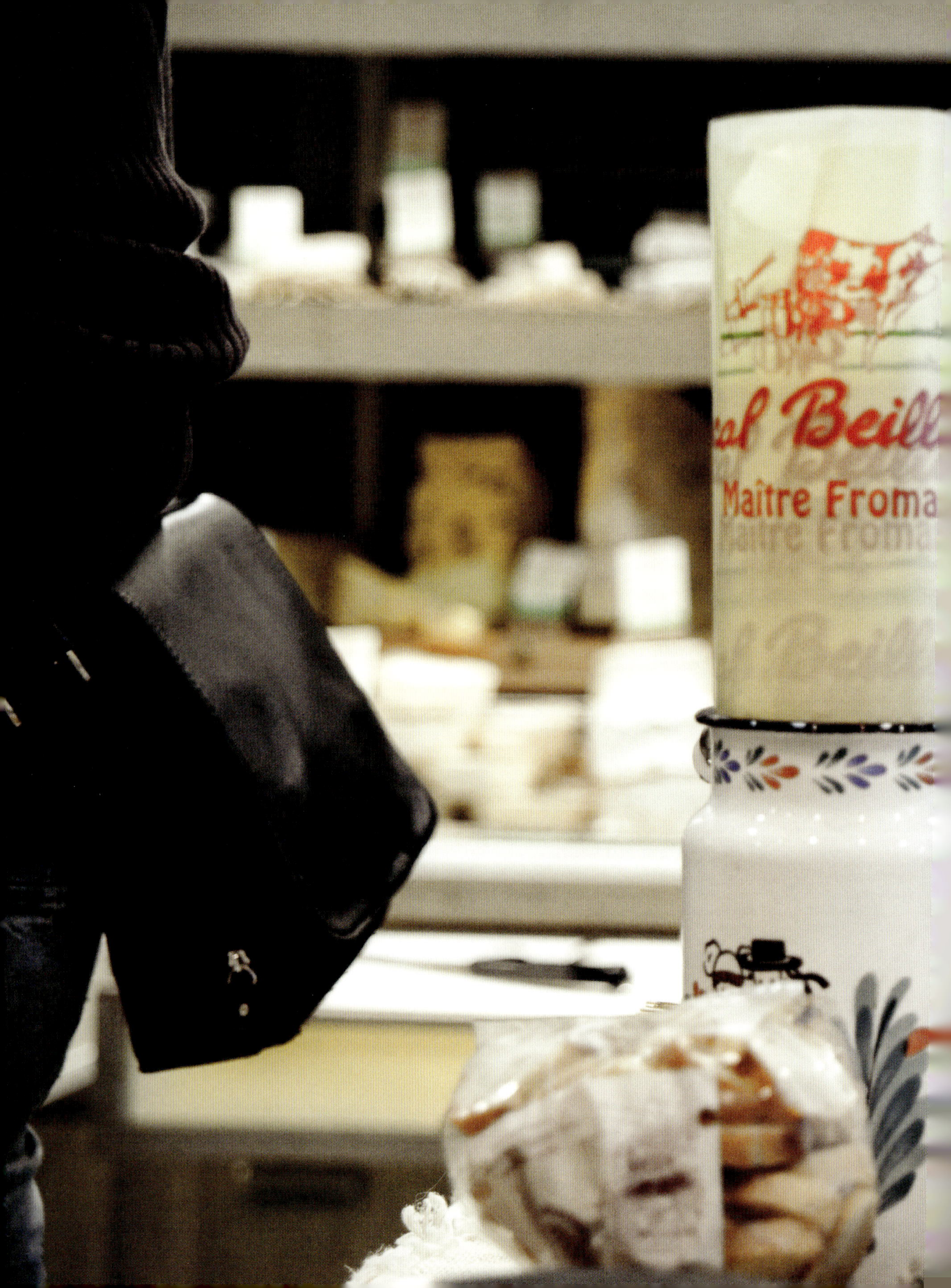
Maître Froma

FROMAGERIE BEILLEVAIRE / 140 rue de Belleville / Paris XX / PARIS - HOME TO THE REGIONS / J'aime Paris

Cœur de bœuf
Lait de Chèvre et de Vache - Bio
23 % Mat. grasses
2,80 € pièce

BRIE DE MEAU

BEILLE VAIRE

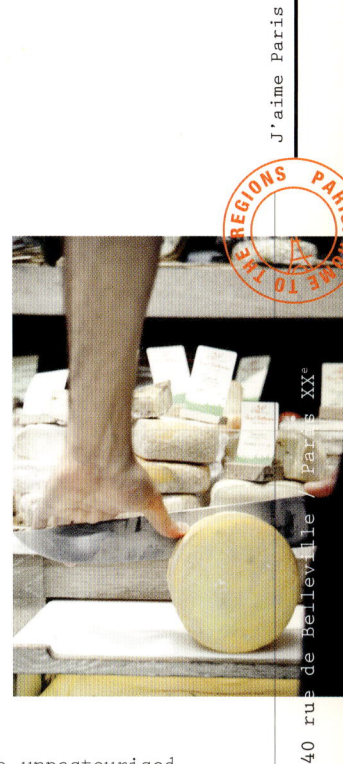

Ripe cheeses, homemade unpasteurised butter and *crémet nantais* cream cheese drive your taste buds wild at the Fromagerie Beillevaire. You receive such good advice there that you'll want to buy these high-quality products, which you'll dream about having on your plate.

FROMAGERIE BEILLEVAIRE / 140 rue de Belleville / Paris XXe

J'aime Paris

PARIS: REGIONS HOME TO THE

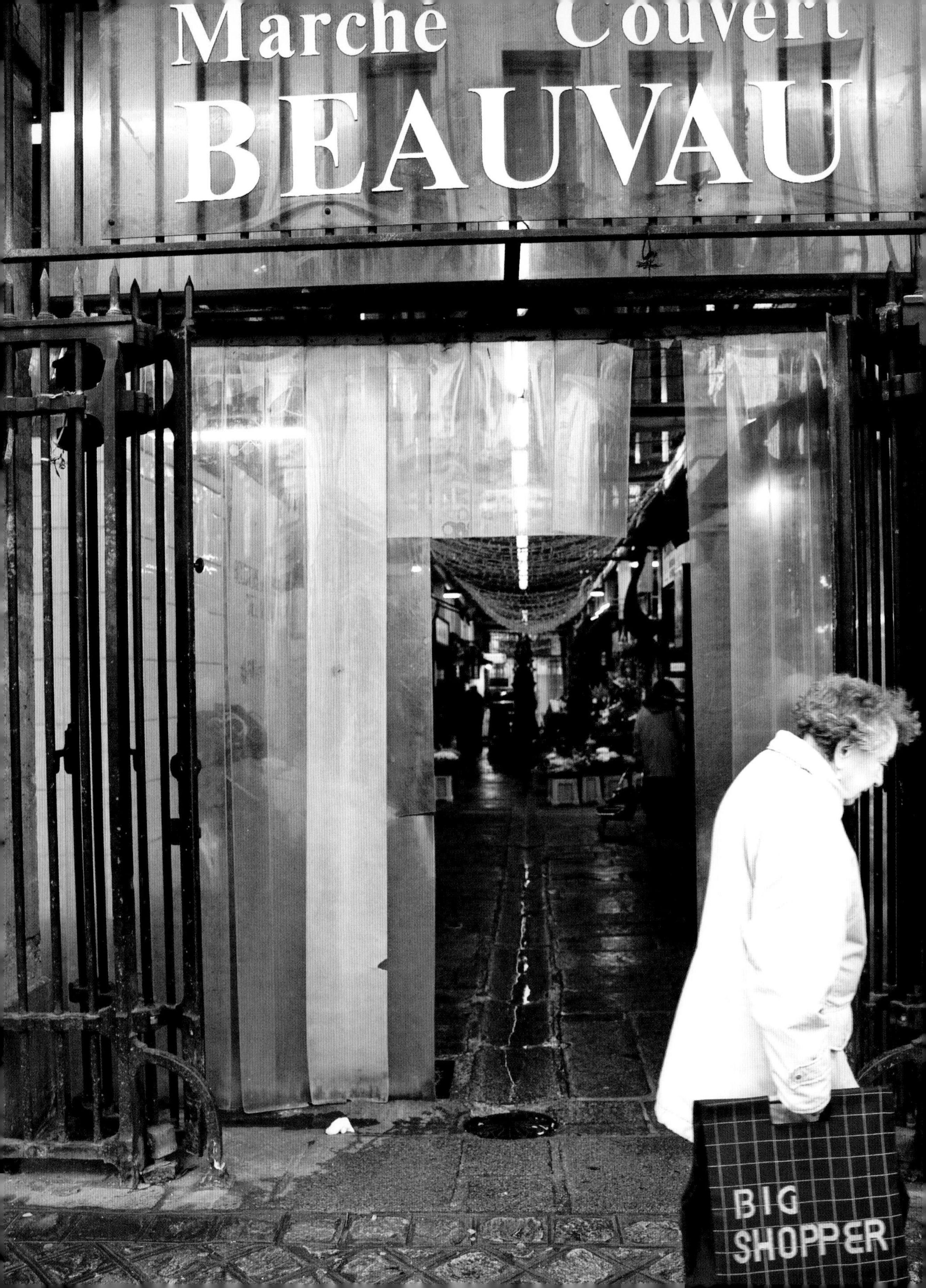
Marché Couvert
BEAUVAU
BIG
SHOPPER

BOUCHERIE MICHEL BRUNON / Marché couvert Beauvau / 12 place d'Aligre / Paris XII e

PARIS: HOME TO THE REGIONS

J'aime Paris

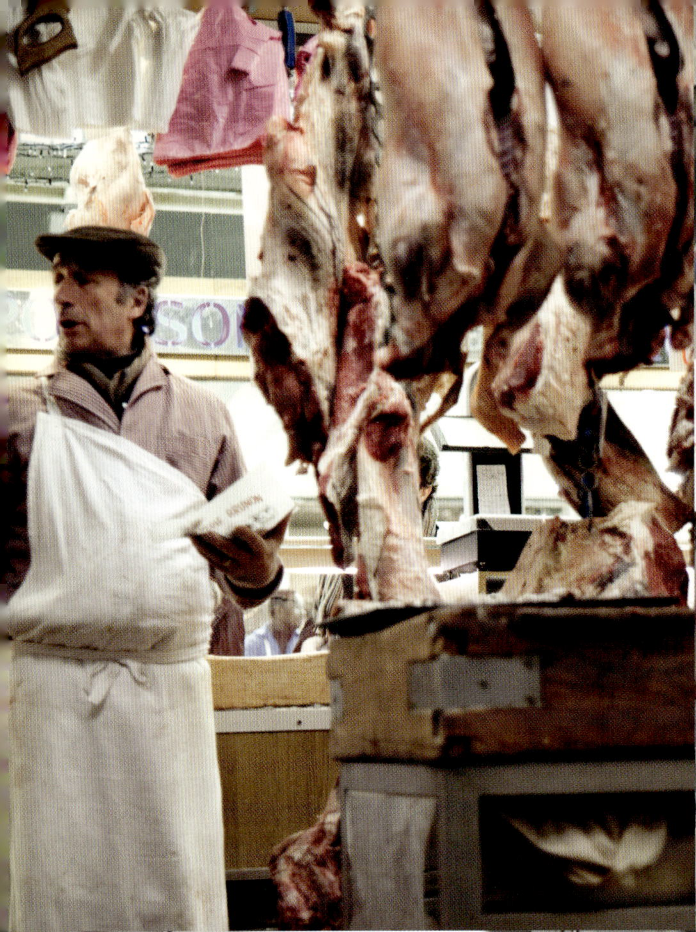

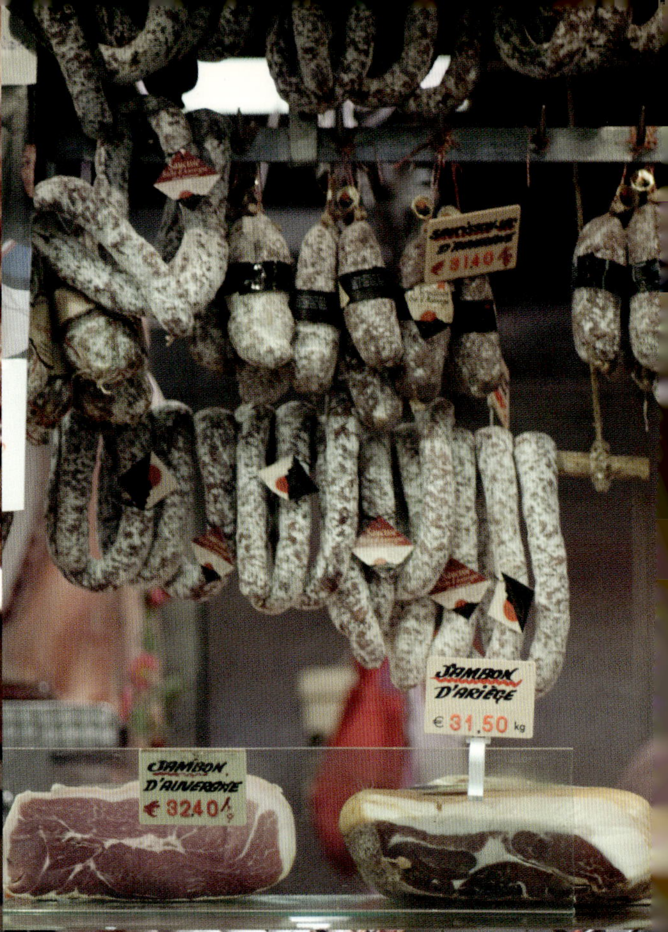
JAMBON D'ARIÈGE
€ 31,50 kg
JAMBON D'AUVERGNE
€ 3240

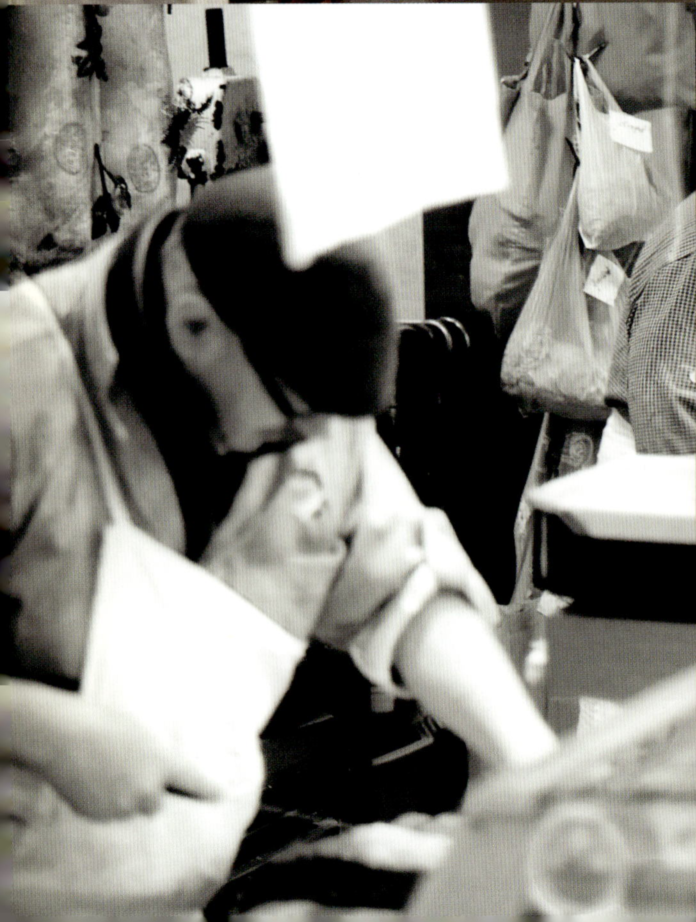

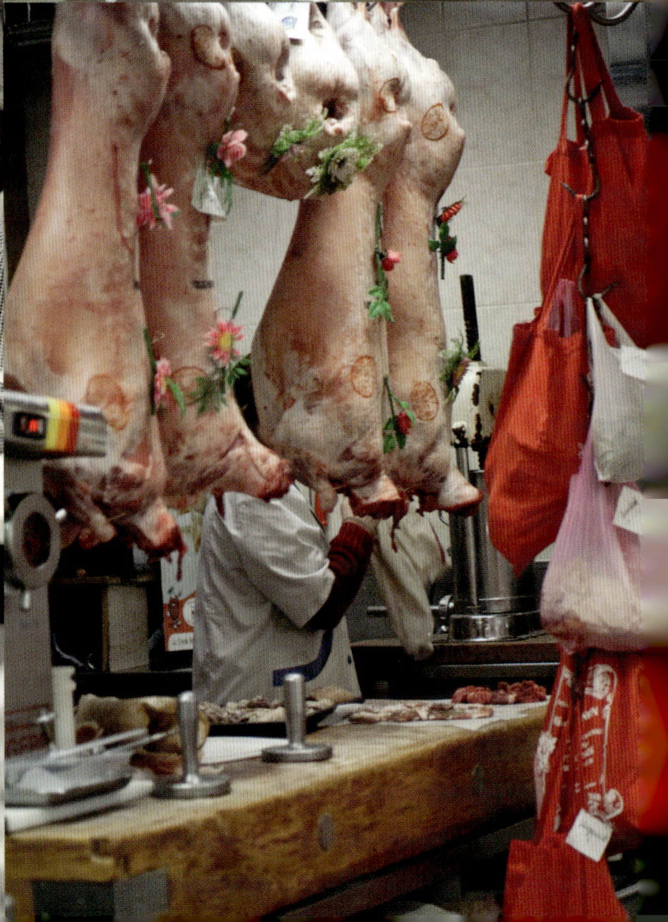

BRUNON

The carcass swings along a rail as if in a train crash, an inch away from the pretty brunette who is making chipolatas. There is a roar of sirloins, ribs and legs. 'This is a product for the initiated,' laughs Michel Brunon with a perfectly aged rib steak in his hand. It can be cut with a fork. 'I age all my meat myself, otherwise I won't eat it. And if I don't eat it, I won't sell it to my customers. I'm a butcher, not a meat seller.'

BOUCHERIE MICHEL BRUNON / Marché couvert Beauvau / 12 place d'Aligre / Paris XII

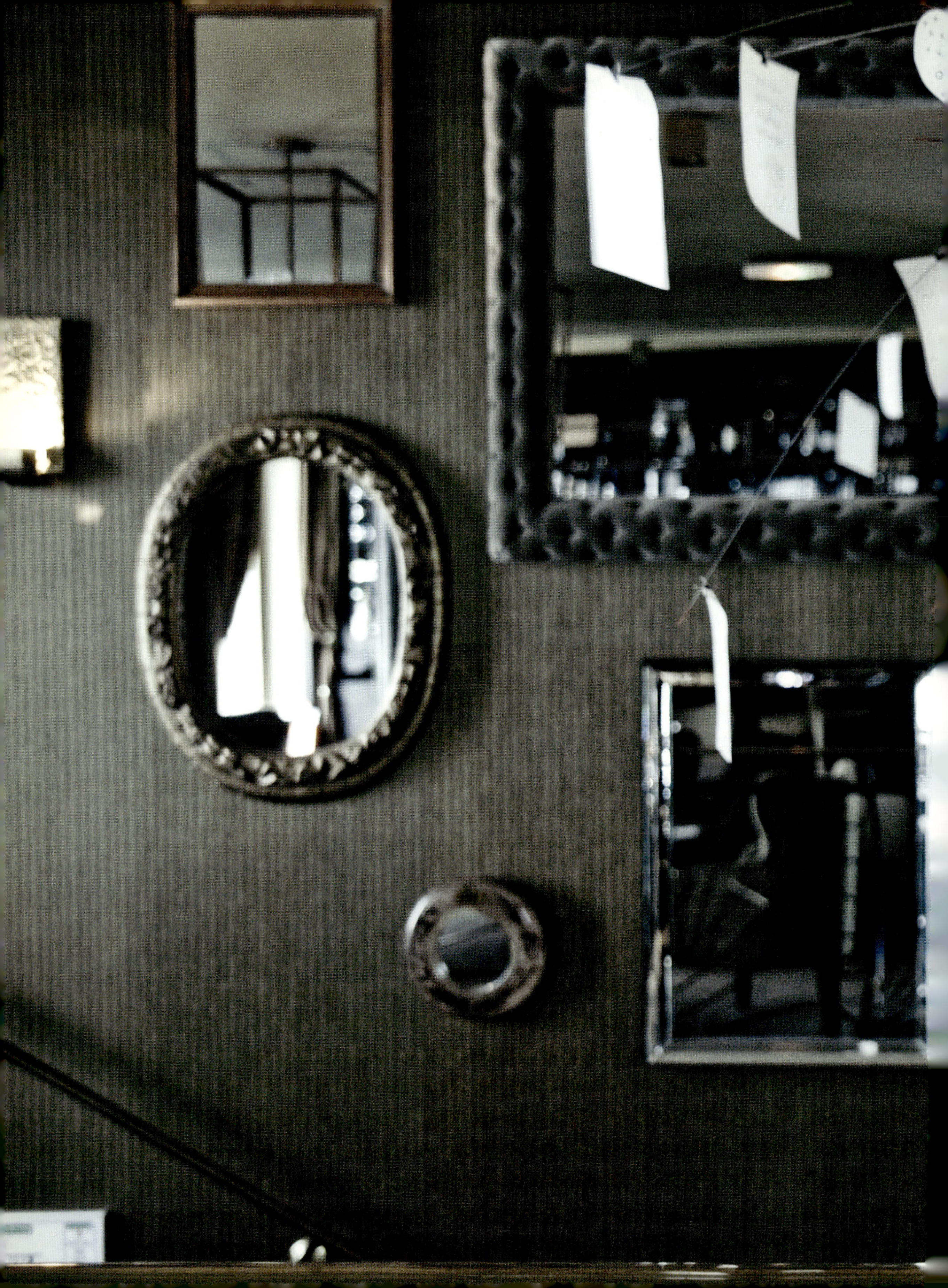

CHEZ FLOTTES / 2 rue Cambon / Paris Ier

PARIS. HOME TO THE REGIONS
J'aime Paris

CHEZ FLOTTES

Monsieur Gérard brandishes his big knife, the plump loaf pressed against his body. He slices the fresh Poilâne bread by hand. 'The secret is to slice it thinner than usual to enhance the flavour of the products. If you don't, you have nothing but bread in your mouth.' During his time feeding nocturnal Parisians, Gilbert Flottes, together with Lionel Poilâne, invented a simple but tasty gem: the Poilâne *croque-monsieur*. Today, his son Olivier manages the family brasserie.

PARIS: HOME TO THE REGIONS / J'aime Paris

CHEZ FLOTTES / 2 rue Cambon / Paris I er

- 325

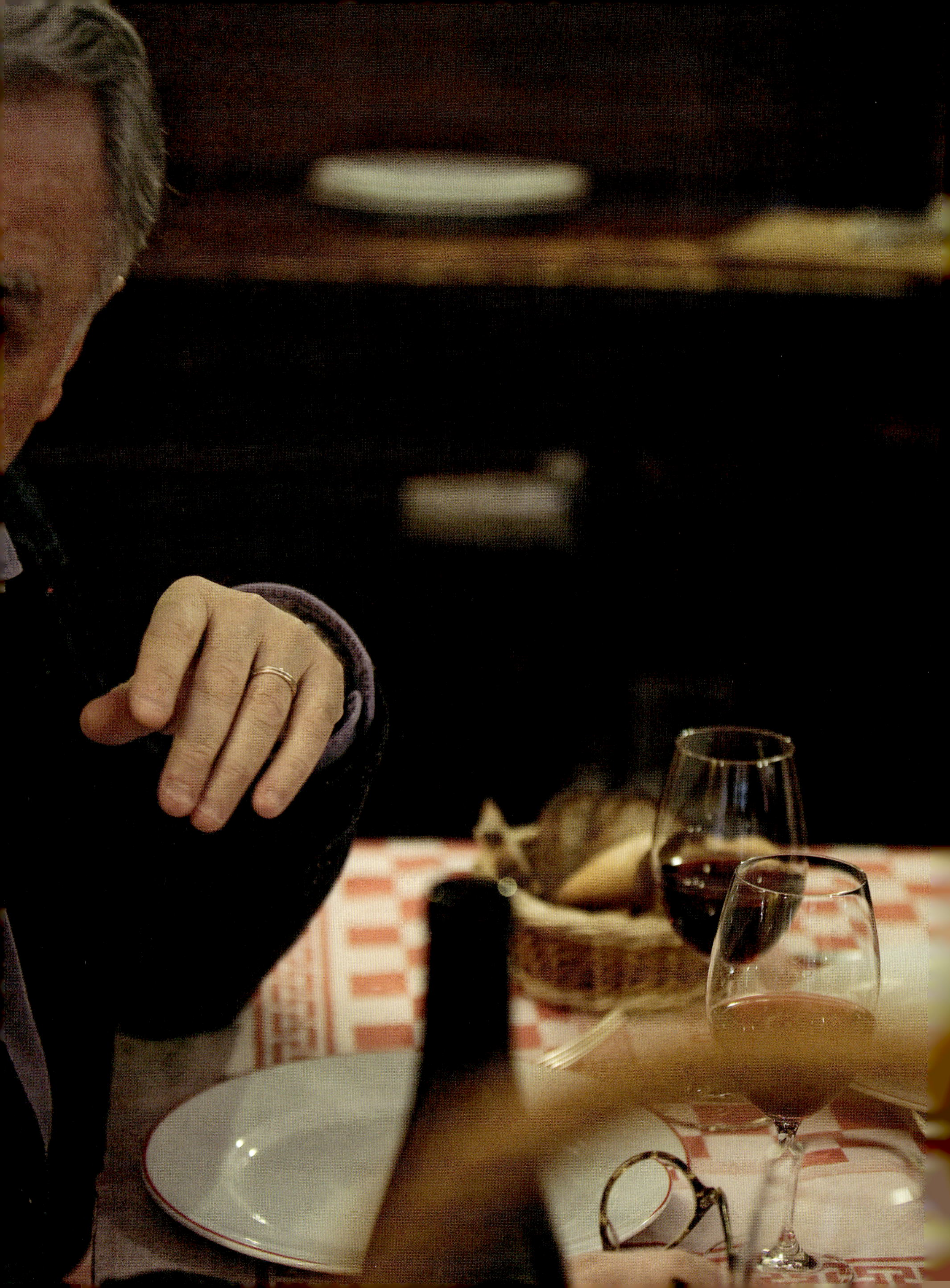

J'aime Paris

PARIS: HOME TO THE REGIONS

AUBERGE D'CHEZ EUX / 2 avenue de Lowendal / Paris VIIe

- 327

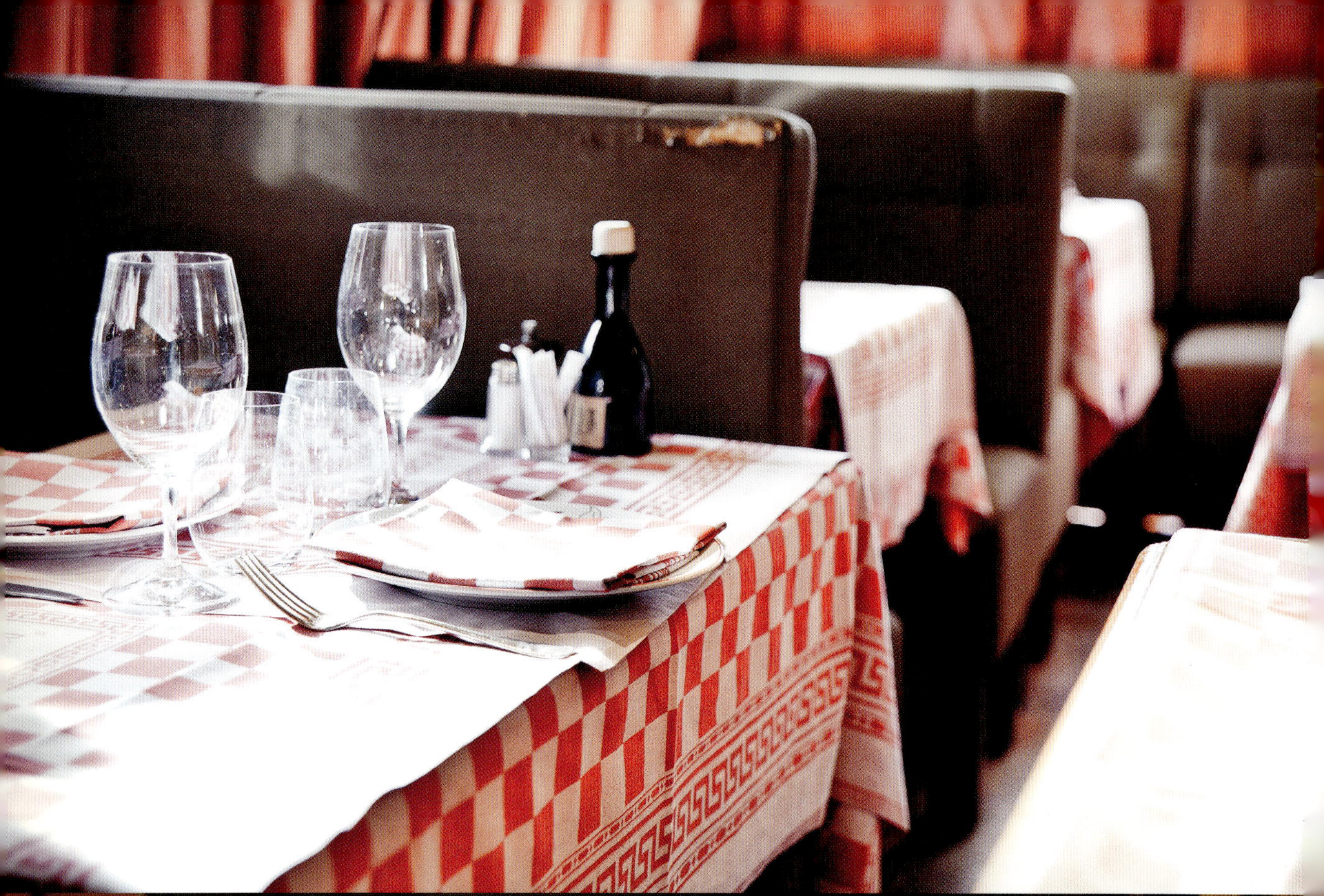

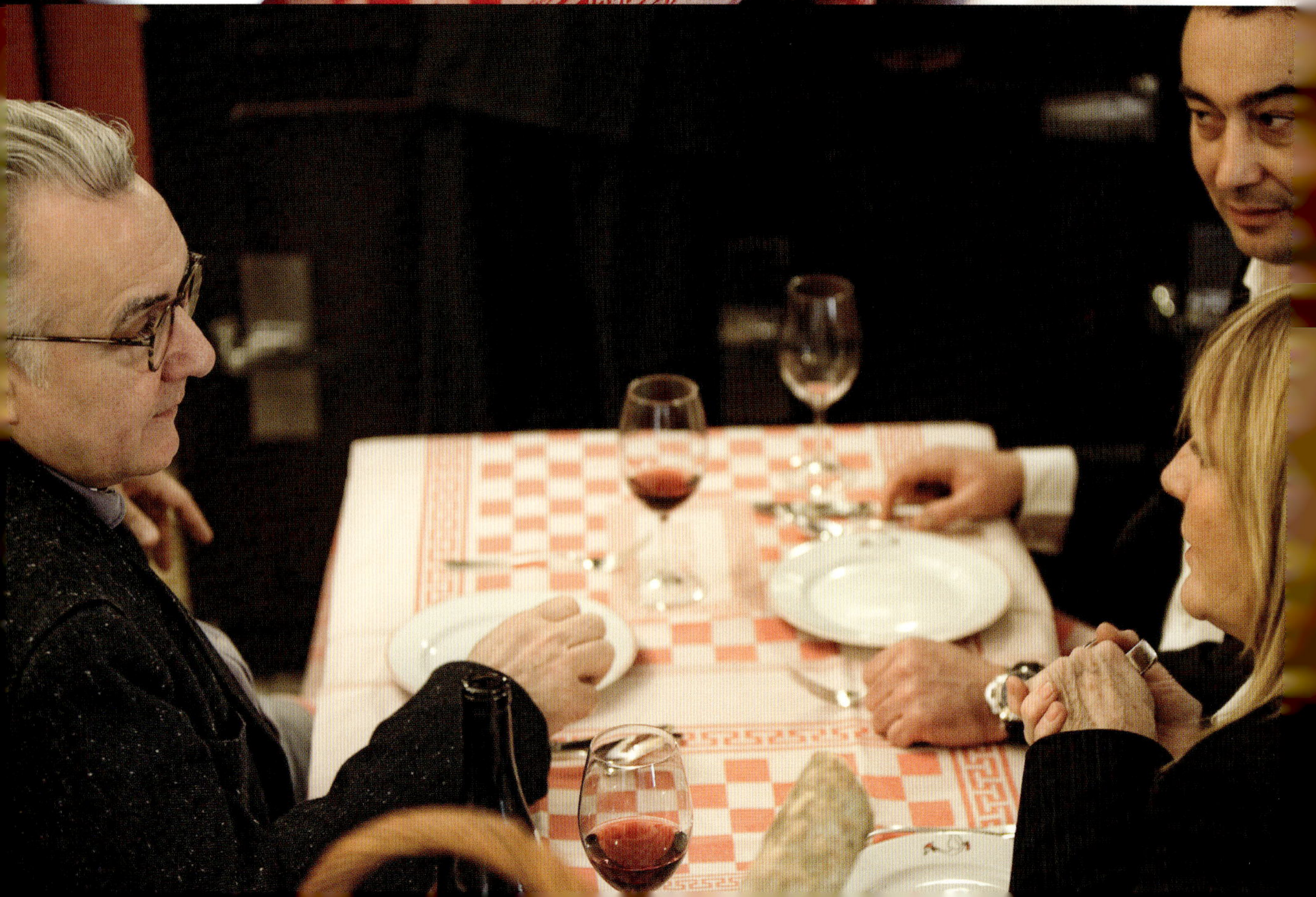

D' CHEZ EUX

J'aime Paris

PARIS: HOME TO THE REGIONS

AUBERGE D'CHEZ EUX / 2 avenue de Lowendal / Paris VIIe

Tableside carving? That *is* rare! The duck is served this way with its fig or pear accompaniment, depending on the season. Laurent and Catherine Brenta, from L'Évasion, manage this restaurant with its feel of the France of bygone days. Under the 1950 brine tub, diners attack the sausages, the starters trolley, the legendary cassoulet and the outstanding calf's head, but they surrender to the Paris-Brest.

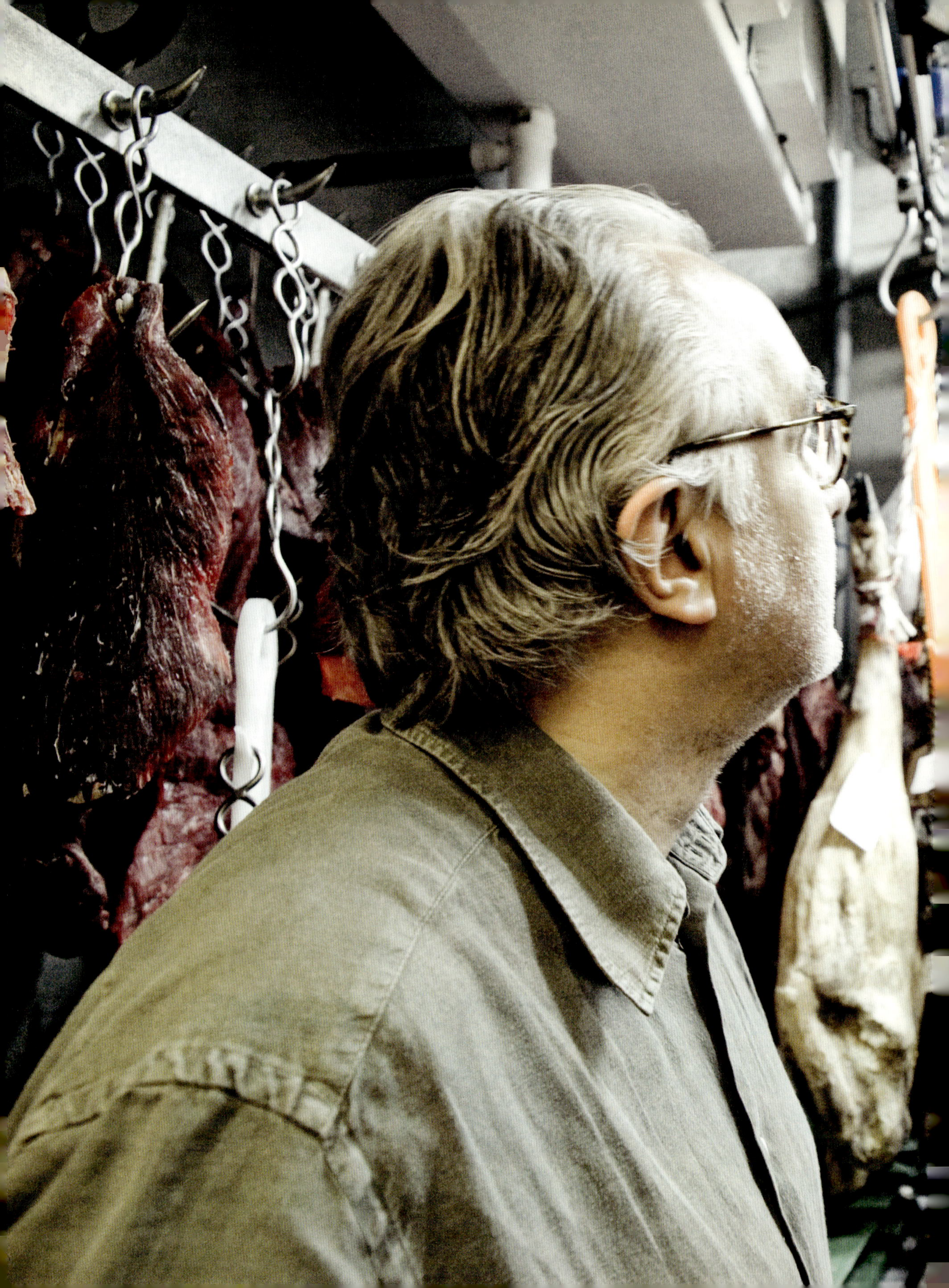

BOUCHERIE HUGO DESNOYER / 45 rue Boulard / Paris XIVe

PARIS: HOME TO THE REGIONS

J'aime Paris

- 331

DES
NOY
ER

'I left high school early and I didn't know what to do. Then my father put me in an apprenticeship with a butcher in Mayenne, my hometown. That was a revelation. It was just the thing. One thing led to another and here I am in rue Bolard, Paris. I travel 60,000 kilometres a year, crossing France from top to bottom to find lovely well-bred animals: lamb from Lozère, farmhouse pork from the Dordogne and prize-winning Corrèze calves. Today, breeders know what my customers — chefs and individuals — expect from them: the best.'

Hugo Desnoyer

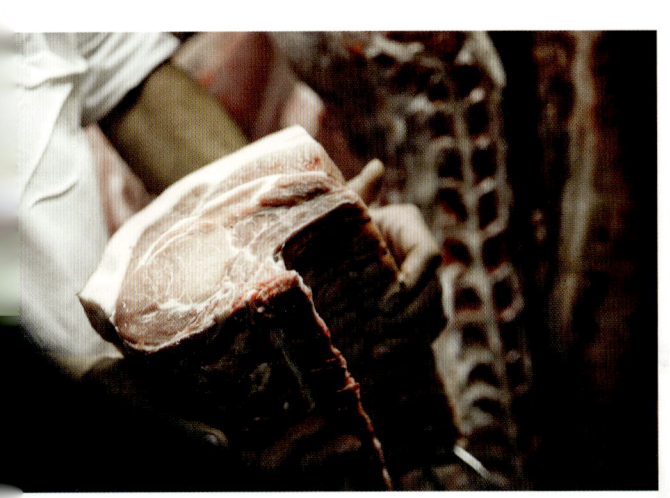

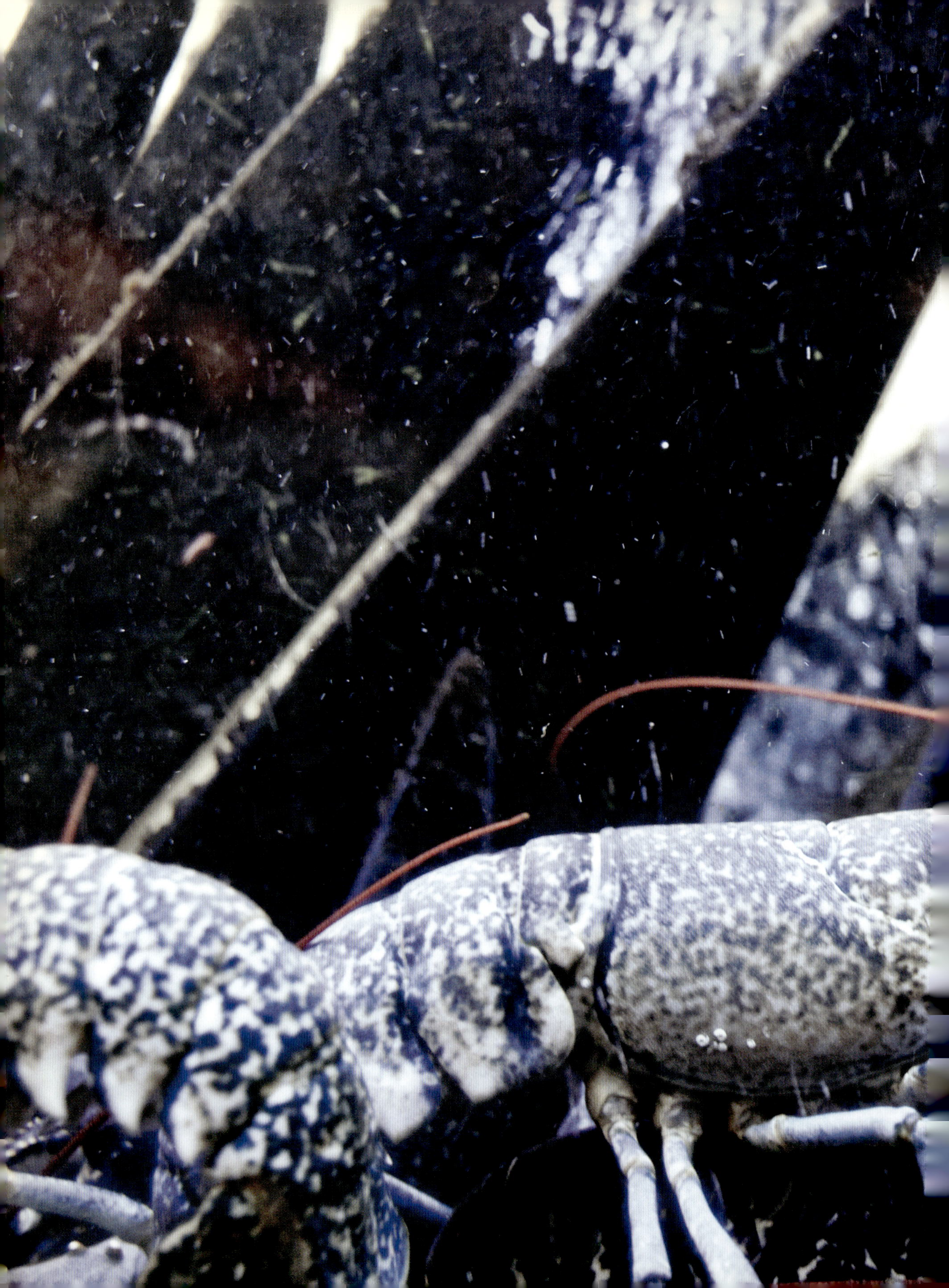

LA POISSONNERIE DU DÔME / 4 rue Delambre / Paris XIVe

J'aime Paris

PARIS: HOME TO THE REGIONS

- 335

DÔME

This is the equivalent of a five-star beauty salon for fish! Wild fish caught using artisanal techniques are pampered and delicately placed over waxed paper to prevent them from being burned by the ice. Chosen every night in small quantities from the best stalls, the fish barely have time to jump into the van before landing on your plate. This purveyor supplies the leading Parisian establishments with the finest catches: elvers, spider crabs and line-caught sea bass, among others.

LA POISSONNERIE DU DÔME / 4 rue Delambre / Paris XIVe

PARIS: HOME TO THE RÉGIONS — J'aime Paris

La grande baudroie

— 337

L'ÉC

L'ÉCUME SAINT-HONORÉ / 6 rue du Marché Saint-Honoré / Paris

ÉCUME SAINT-HONORÉ

You can hear the cry of seagulls in the distance. There is a notice on the blackboard: 'For dessert, raw scallops, soy sauce! Tender, tasty!' Opened and cut in front of you, the beauty reveals itself to be sweet and flowery, the ideal dessert to round off an outstanding tasting. Because here, the large selection of oysters, clams, mussels and shrimp comes with freshness and optimum flavour.

PARIS: HOME TO THE REGIONS

J'aime Paris

L'ÉCUME SAINT-HONORÉ / 6 rue du Marché Saint-Honoré / Paris Ier

- 341

PERE CLAUDE

01·47·34·04·04

ÉPICERIE DU PÈRE CLAUDE / 4 rue du Général de Castelnau / Paris XVe

ÉPICERIE DU PÈRE CLAUDE

Adjacent to his father's restaurant, Ludovic Perraudin has a grocery. His father had gone back to the Rungis markets that morning. While waiting, Ludovic, in charge of the grocery shop, prepared a sandwich for us.

Alain Ducasse: What boneless ham is this?

Ludovic Perraudin: 'Prince de Paris' — it's a ham from Brittany made in the traditional way. It isn't treated or chopped; the brine is injected into the ham, which is then rubbed in coarse salt. Only 250 hams are made this way each week, free from colouring, preservatives or gelatine.

AD: It has a fine, silky texture. Excellent. And it also smells like real ham. It's so unusual.

LP: How about a pickle?

AD: Of course not! That would ruin it.

ÉPICERIE DU PÈRE CLAUDE / 4 rue du Général de Castelnau / Paris XVe

J'aime Paris

PARIS: HOME TO THE REGIONS

MANZANAS
APPLES

*Cabas
. INDE .
12 €
12,00-*

GRAINETERIE DU MARCHÉ / 8 place d'Aligre / Paris XIIe

PARIS: HOME TO THE REGIONS

J'aime Paris

- 347

LES GRAINES
VENDUES AU
Lapro
1€50
Maïs
1€00
Tournesol
1€50

Rouges
Mogettes de Vendée

GRAI NE TERIE DU MARCHÉ

José watches over the seeds in his seed shop after hours... The shop's been in existence since 1895 and it's still going strong. Probably the most useful thing you can get there is advice on preparing and cooking their produce. You are overcome by the urge to buy everything. They have an amazing selection of pulses: *haricots tarbais*, tiny tender green flageolet beans, Soissons beans with taut skins and bulk pasta and rice in wooden crates — it's so hard to resist. There is durum wheat semolina for preparing couscous any which way: the fine variety is for more delicate dishes, while the medium size is for heartier, country-style cooking. It's all sold in the old-fashioned way, in brown paper packets. And don't miss the gardening section at the back of the shop. There's all kinds of bird feed, just like in the good old days.

J'aime Paris

PARIS: HOME TO THE REGIONS

GRAINETERIE DU MARCHÉ / 8 place d'Aligre / Paris XIIe

MARCHÉ GROS LA FONTAINE

A little market that doesn't seem like much at all. But an elegant quarter calls for a sophisticated market, and the attractive stalls supply Alain Ducasse's cooking school. Joël Thiébault can be found here, with his bunches of multicoloured radishes and his slightly more familiar herbs.

MARCHÉ GROS-LA FONTAINE / Rue Gros, rue Jean de La Fontaine Paris XVIe J'aime Paris

- 351

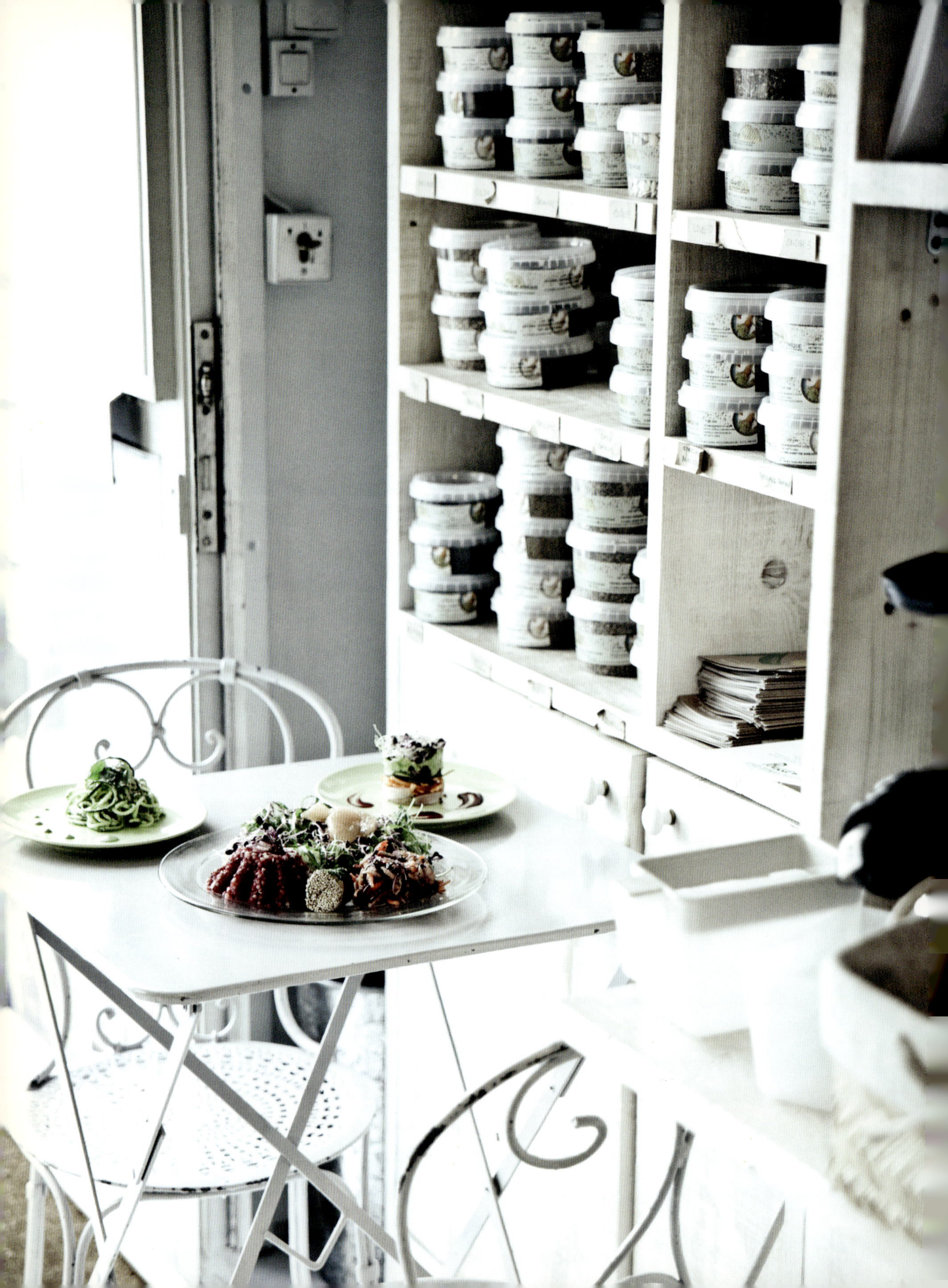

PARIS: HOME TO THE REGIONS

J'aime Paris

POUSSE POUSSE / 7 rue Notre-Dame de Lorette / Paris IXe

- 353

POUSSE POUSSE

A whole-living-foods specialist, Lawrence Aboucaya owns a small deli-restaurant. Using sprouts, young shoots and wheatgrass, juice is made with a special extractor so as not to 'break up the molecules'. The same principle is applied to quiches, salads, vegetable or fresh fruit juices, all presented in an ornate, warm and cosy ambiance.

PARIS: HOME TO THE REGIONS

J'aime Paris

POUSSE POUSSE / 7 rue Notre-Dame de Lorette / Paris IX

355

Le QUINCY

LE QUINCY / 28 avenue Ledru Rollin / Paris XIIe

PARIS: HOME TO THE REGIONS

J'aime Paris

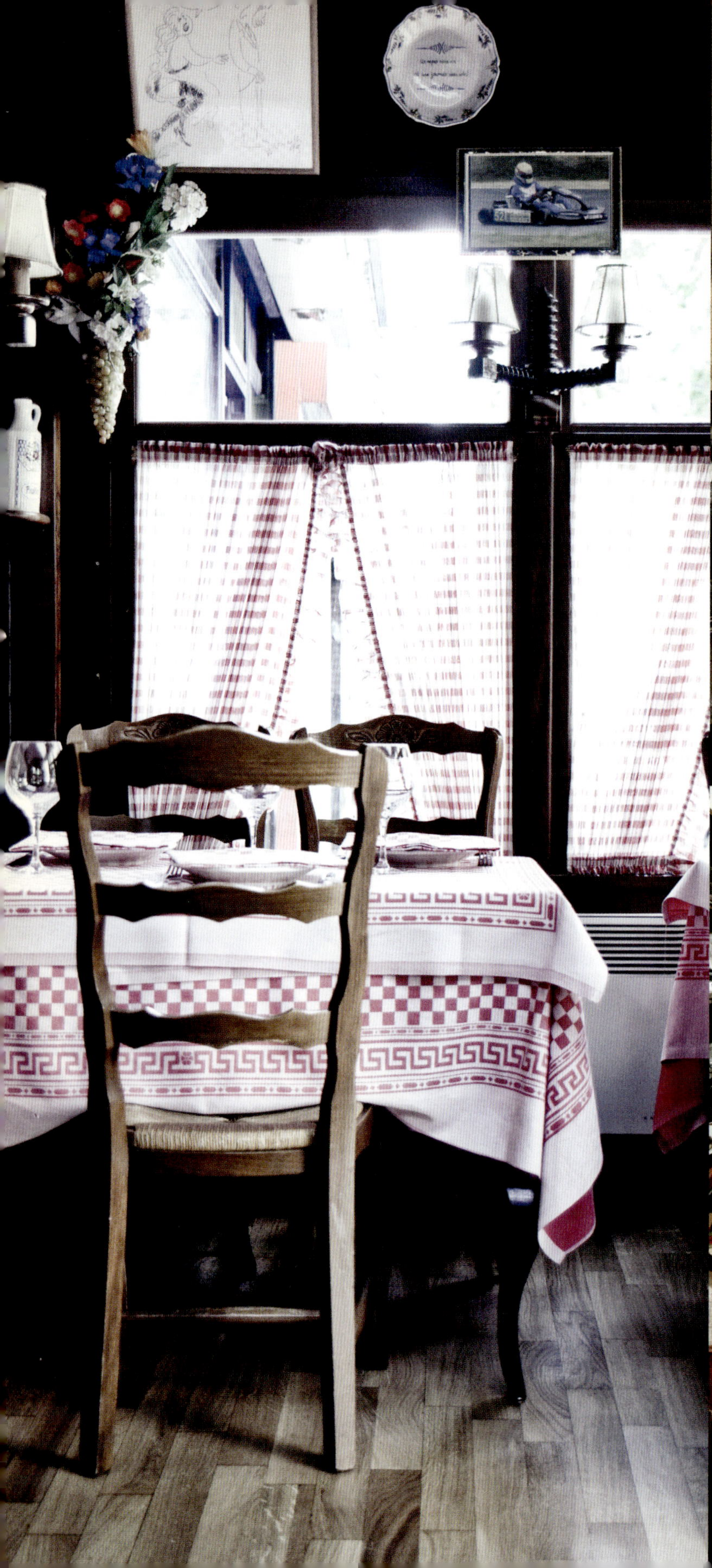

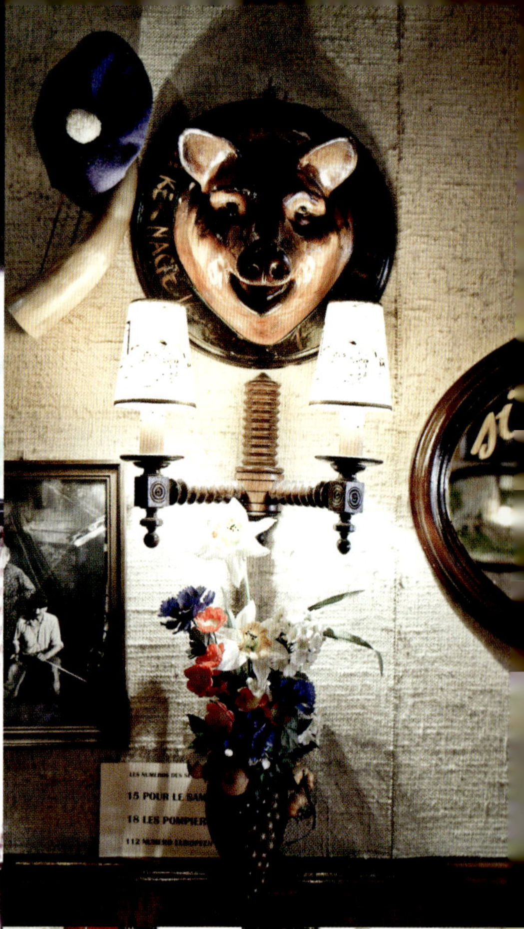
18 LES POMPIERS

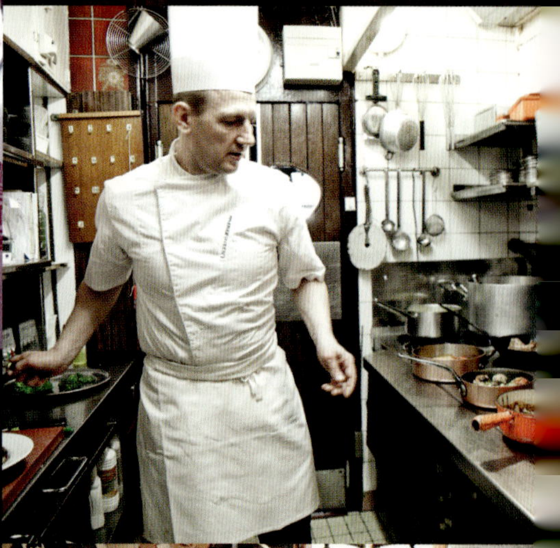

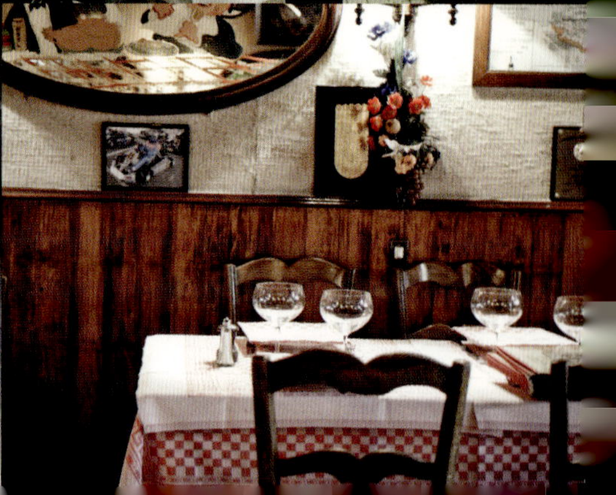

QUINCY

Come rain, hail or shine, you'll find a bow tie on the menu. Appearing just above is Bobosse, the down-to-earth owner of a mountain inn right in the middle of Paris. Enormous plates, fresh produce, French recipes. It's crayfish season, real 'red claws'. As the innkeeper would say: 'You just have to peel them apart for yourself'!

J'aime Paris / PARIS: HOME TO THE REGIONS / 28 avenue Ledru-Rollin / Paris XIIe / LE QUINCY

- 359

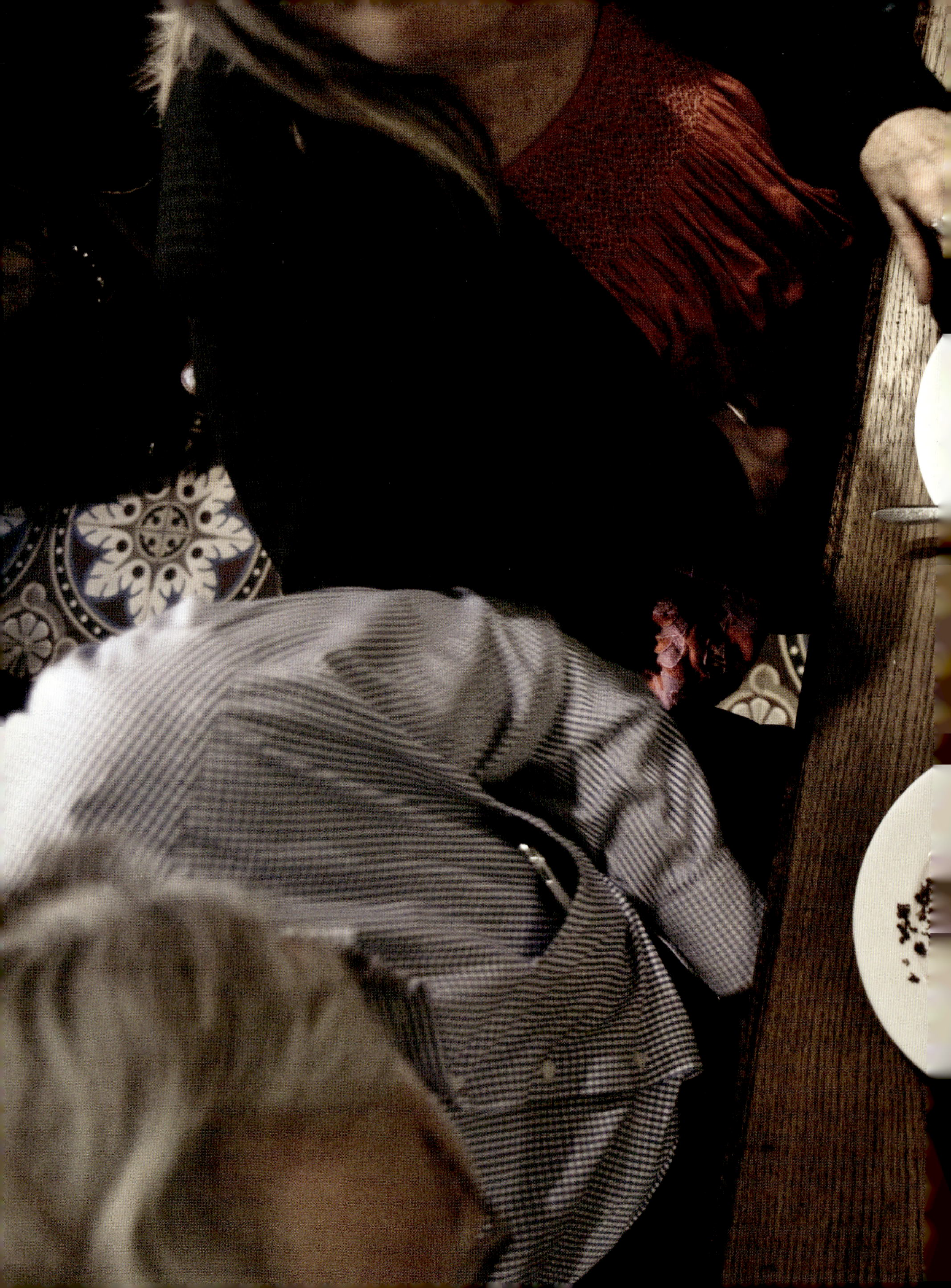

- 361

RACINES / 8 passage des Panoramas / Paris II

J'aime Paris

PARIS: HOME TO THE REGIONS

RACINES

A smart eatery in the style of a Jean Prouvé design, with the option of buying wines — where would you find that? In the oldest arcade in Paris' Grands Boulevards district: the Passage des Panoramas, where the first moving images were taken, the precursor of cinema. Formerly from L'Arpège, Restaurant Laurent and Le Divellec, Nicolas Gauduin prepares his produce with talent and simplicity, under the watchful eye of owner David Lanher, a man with exacting standards. Fattened chickens and ducks, completely plucked, cooked whole in their skin, accompanied by fabulous crunchy seasonal vegetables from Alain Passard's kitchen garden. There is a good selection of 'natural' wines, now also including other varieties.

PARIS: HOME TO THE REGIONS · J'aime Paris

RACINES / 8 passage des Panoramas / Paris IIe

- 363

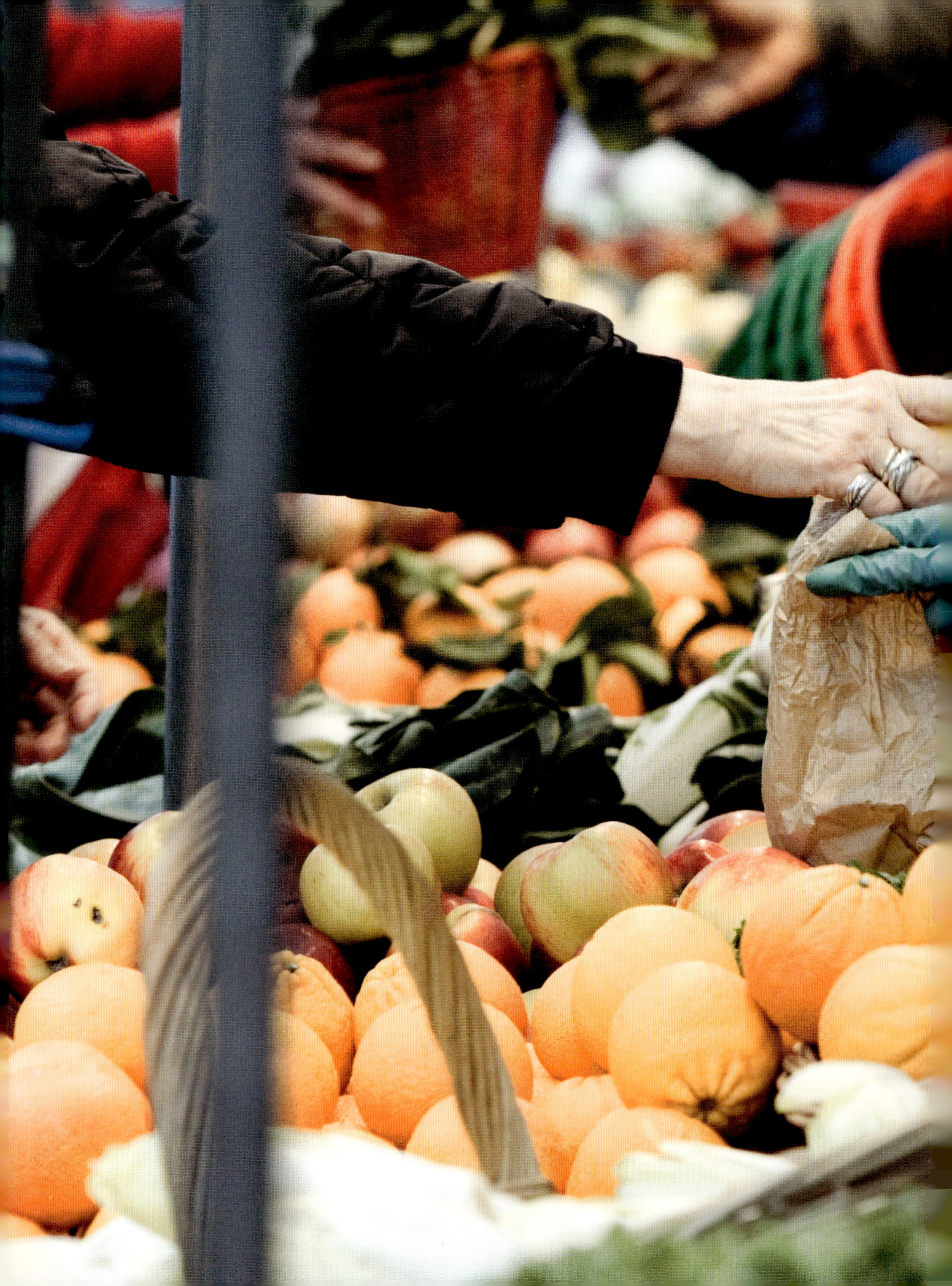

MARCHÉ RASPAIL / Boulevard Raspail / Paris VIe

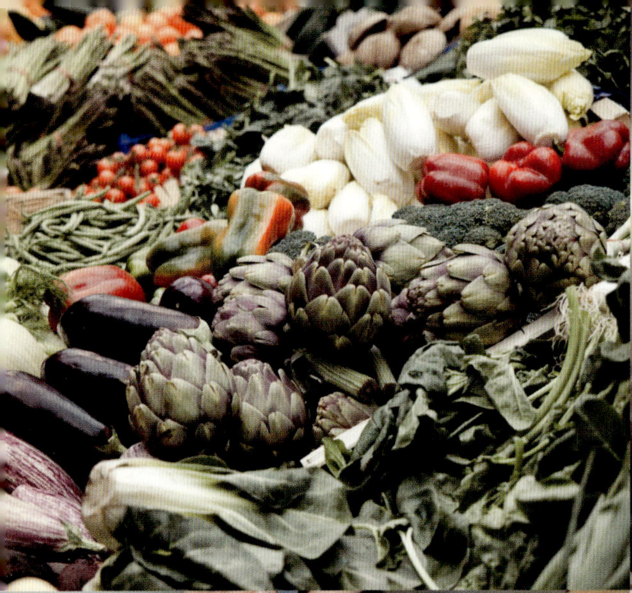
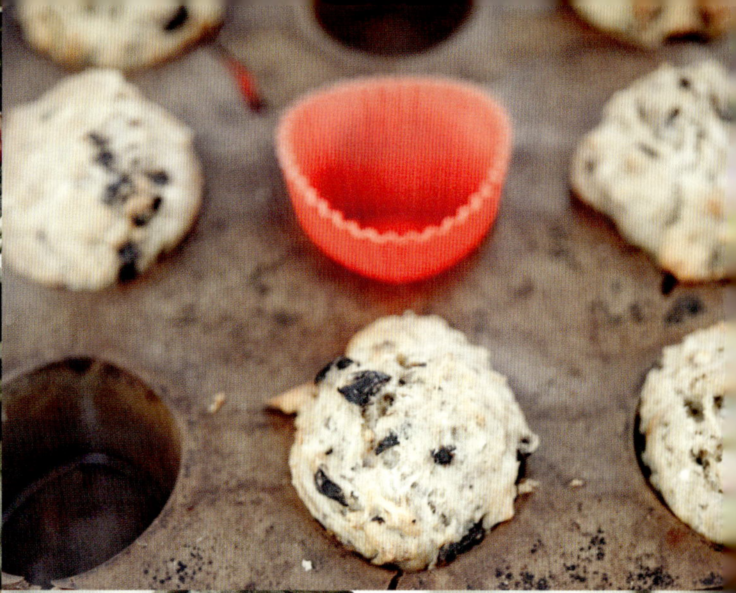
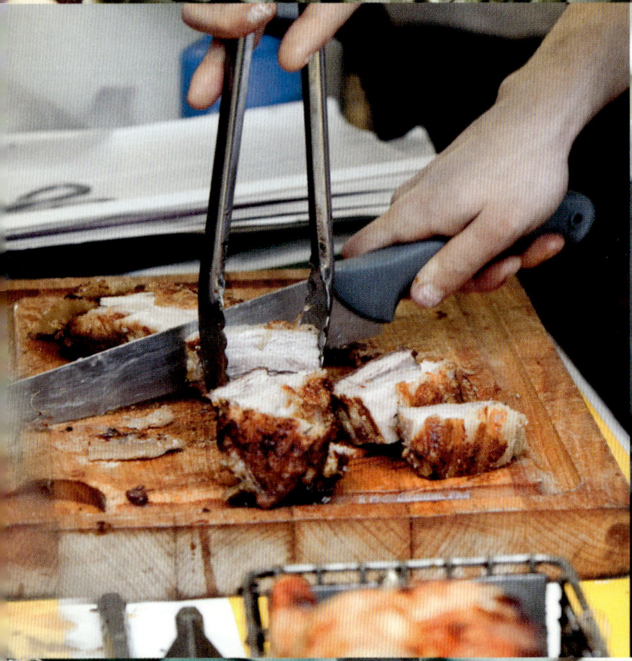
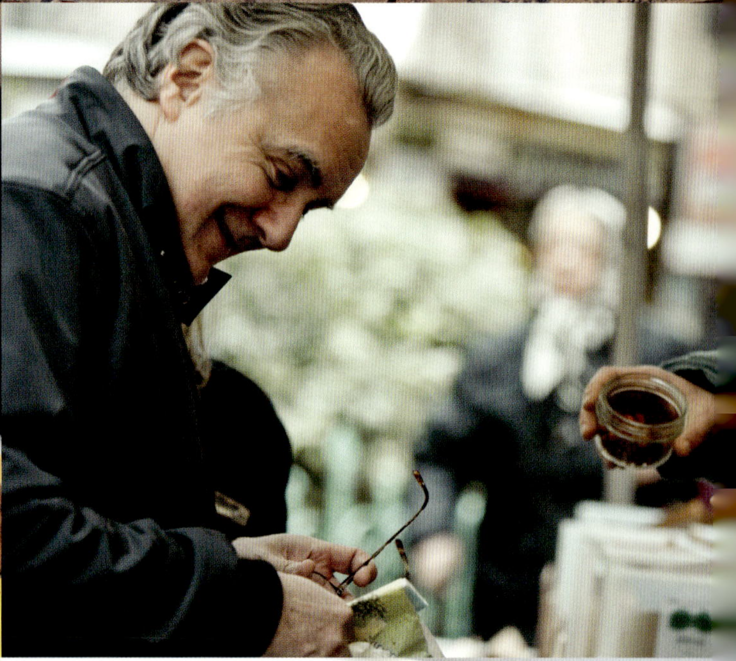
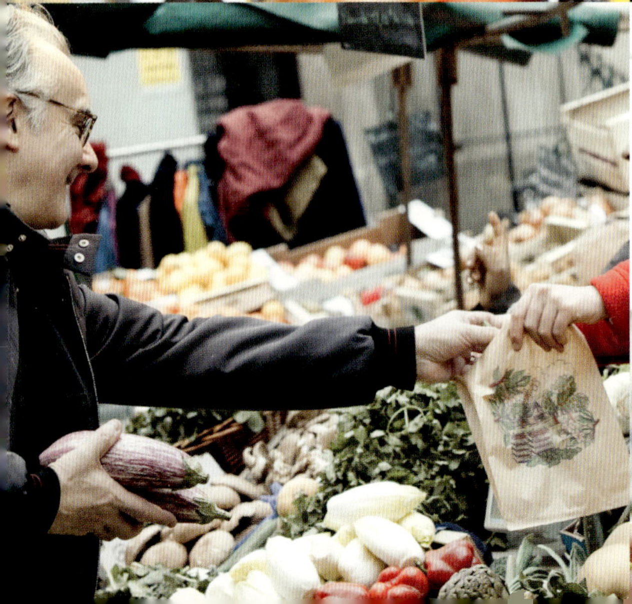
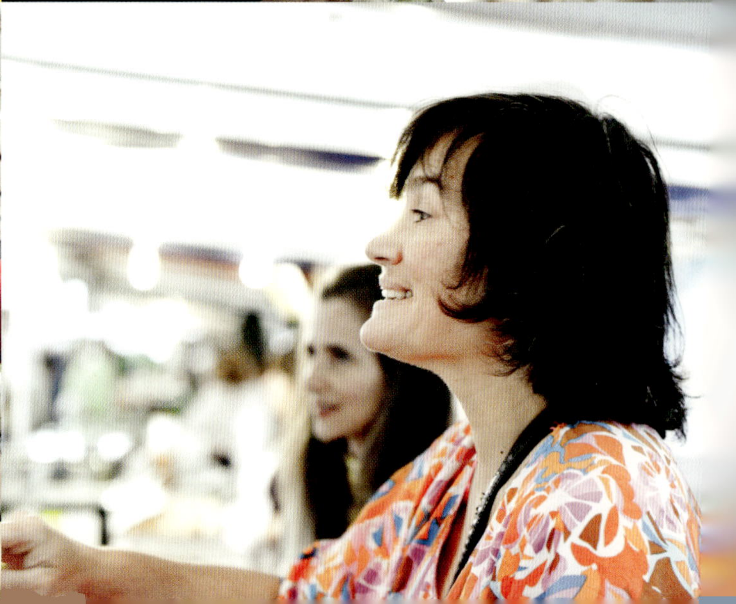

MARCHÉ RASPAIL

A market that offers three full meals: the all-day menu stretches the length of Boulevard Raspail. For breakfast: English muffins, home-baked with a smile, and poached eggs. At lunch, it's very tempting to send the entire array of organic vegetables to the roasting pan. And for dinner, roast suckling pig, very good farm cheeses, citrus salad. If we could, we'd cook this way all year round.

MARCHÉ RASPAIL / Boulevard Raspail / Paris VIe

PARIS: HOME TO THE REGIONS

J'aime Paris

- 367

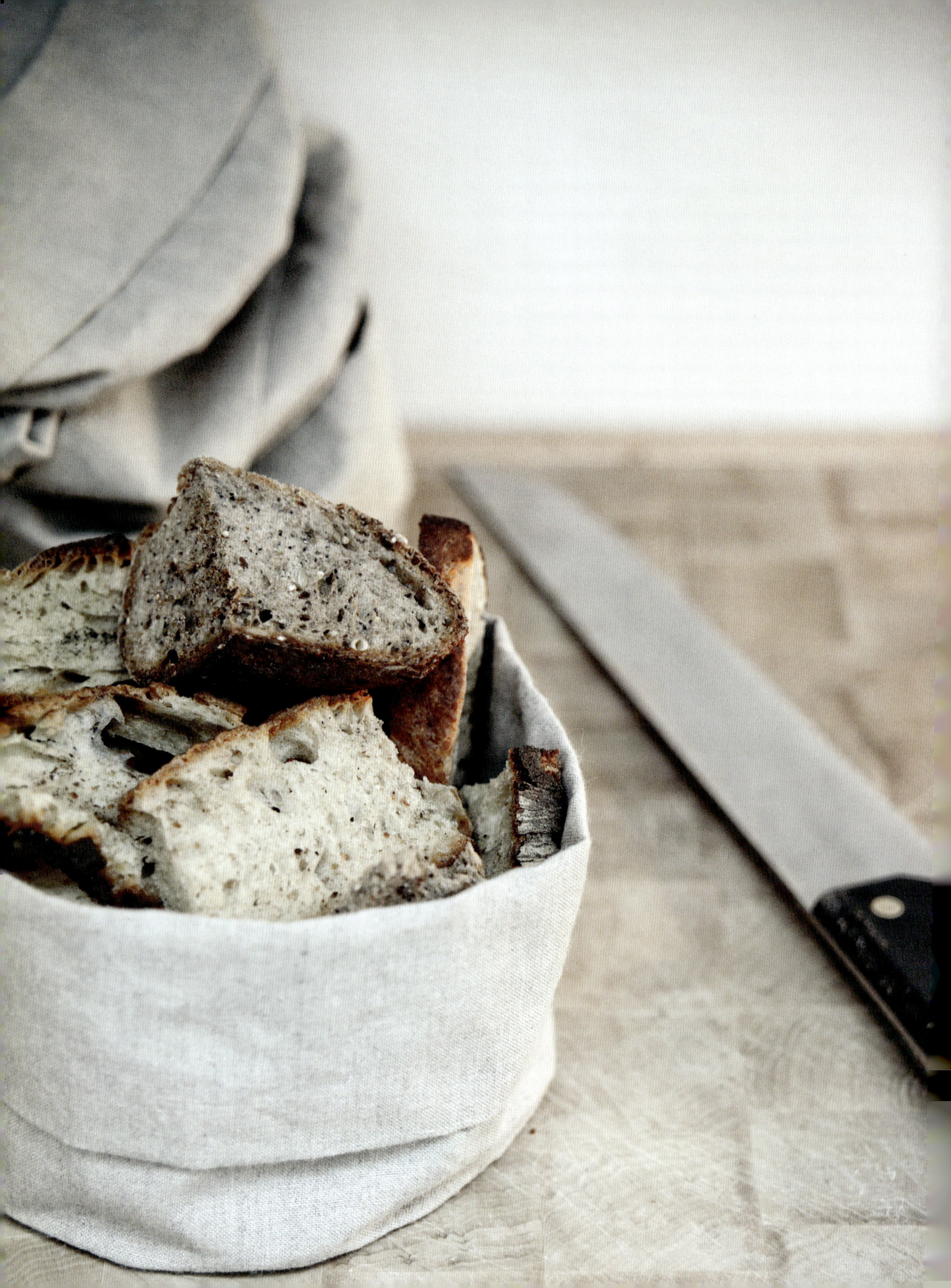

SATURNE / 17 rue Notre-Dame des Victoires / Paris IIe

J'aime Paris

PARIS: HOME TO THE REGIONS

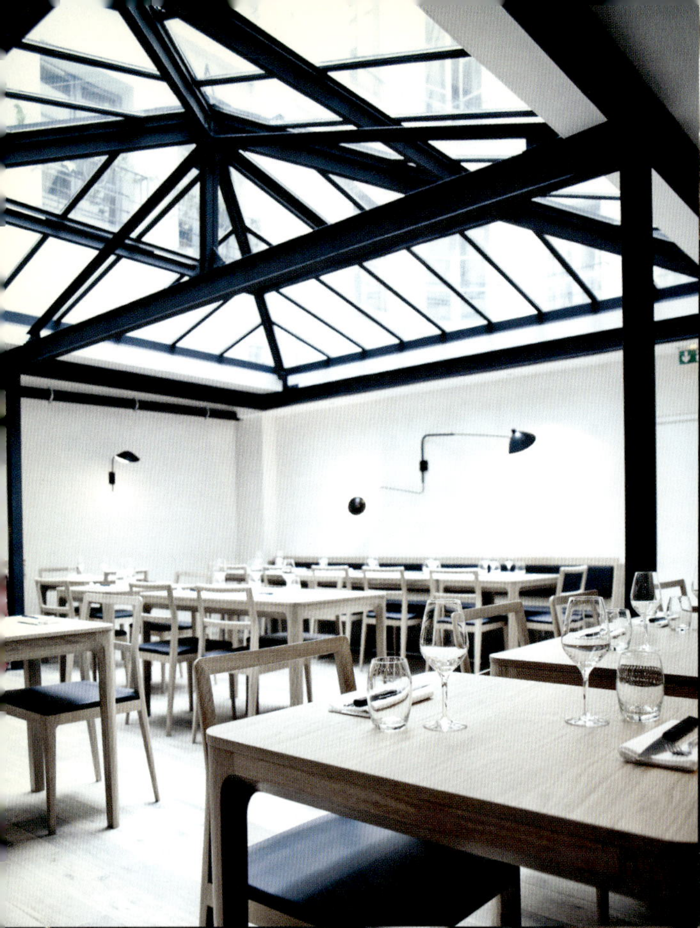

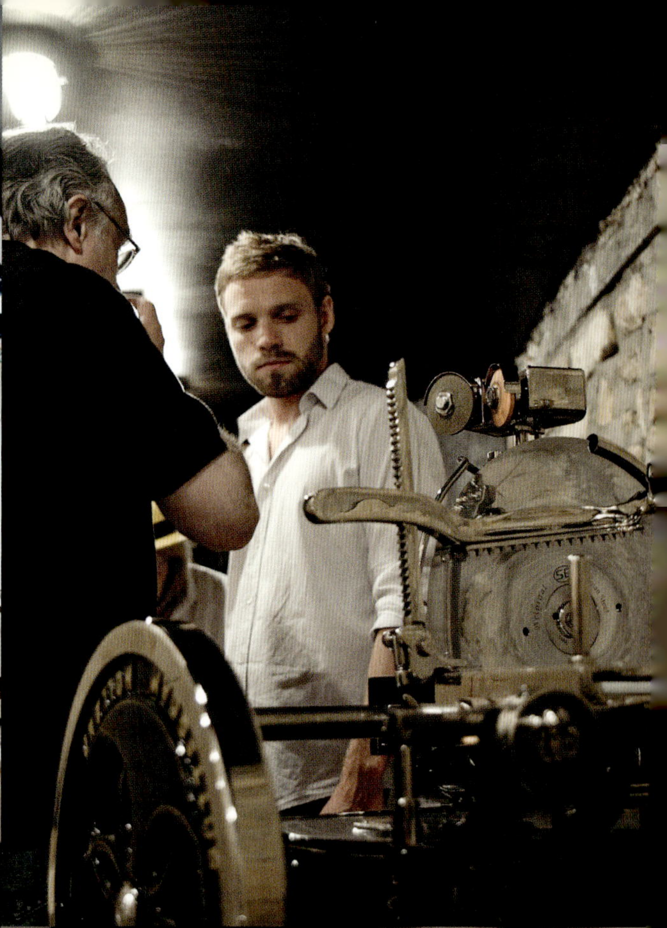

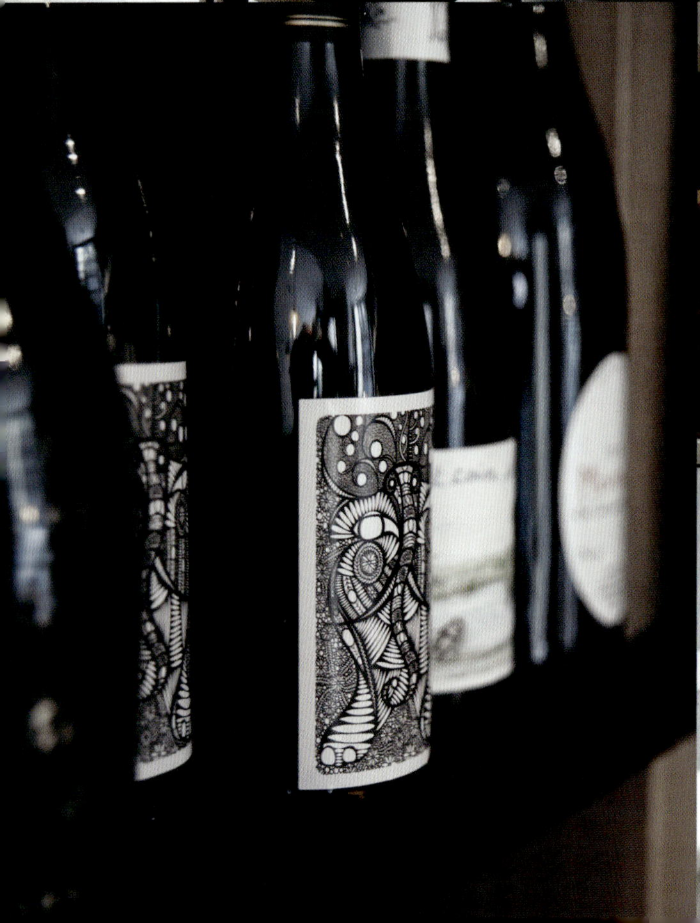

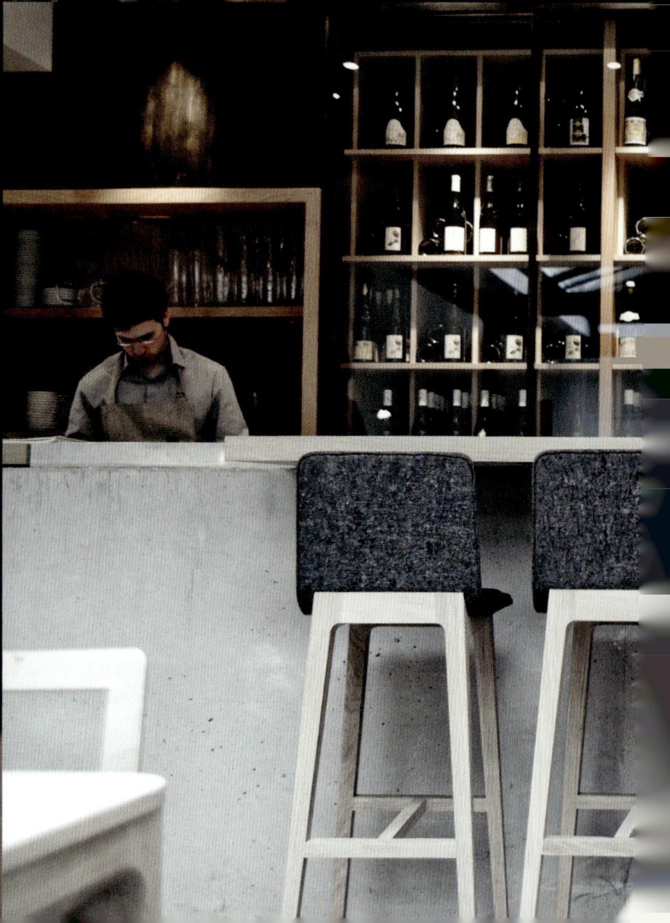

SATURNE

It's good to go down into the cellar, where the air is quite crisp and charged with emotion. There you will find Ewen Lemoigne, who is in charge of the altar wine. But it isn't just any wine; it's the wine used to pay tribute to Saturn, the god of seeds and farmers. For their new chapel, Ewen trusts only artisan winemakers - men who make wine on a human scale, men who work the ground and their land in tune with the living world. And Sven Chartier cooks with extreme roughness, similar to wine production; the best produce handled only in large quantities and served with just a touch of seasoning — nothing more!

SATURNE / 17 rue Notre-Dame des Victoires / Paris IIᵉ

- 371

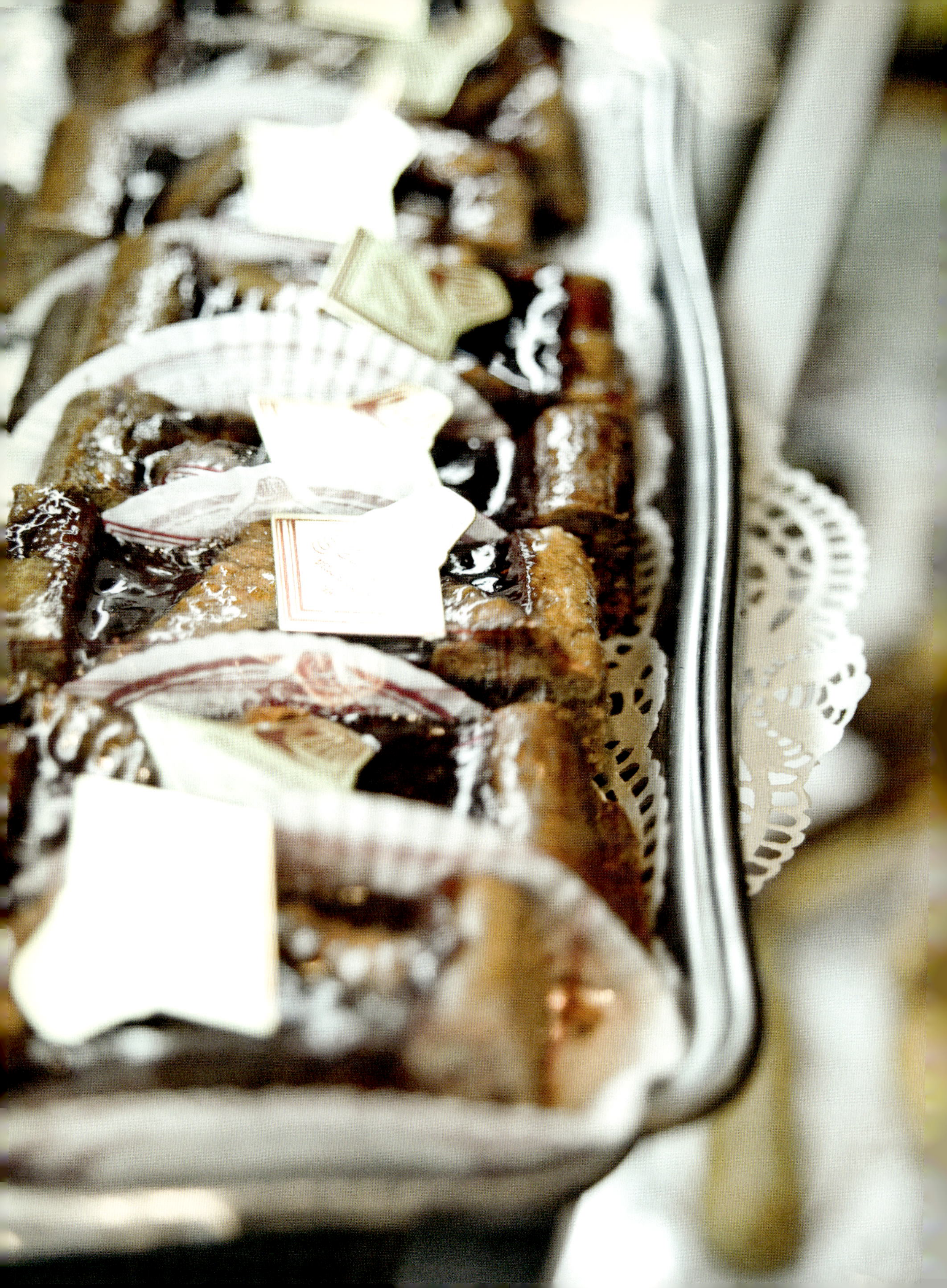

SCHMID

J'aime Paris

PARIS: HOME TO THE REGIONS

SCHMID TRAITEUR / 76 boulevard de Strasbourg / Paris X^e

When they say the whole of Alsace, they really mean the whole of Alsace. From horseradish to Black Forest cake, you pass through an ocean of cooked-meat cuts. There is turnip pickled in brine, which can be served just as you would sauerkraut, and both plain liver sausages and truffled ones that can be used as a spread. You can chew on a pretzel while awaiting your turn. It's Christmas under a cloud of icing sugar, and this has lasted for a full century.

Banana Bread
2€ pièce avec Noix
8€ demi
15€ entier

...ND
...MAGE
ET
...HARCUTERIE

SPRING / 6 rue Bailleul / Paris Ier

SPRING

Daniel Rose, a native of Chicago, is an atypical chef, a self-taught man dedicated to gastronomy. After training with Paul — Bocuse to you — he pursued his dream of creating a new, more personal and more filtered space, one that is half light and half shade. His open professional kitchen is located on the ground floor of the courtyard, serving approximately 20 covers. In the basement, an arched room — pure 18th century style — with a bar serving snacks. Underground, a cellar storing bottles of the day with a selection displaying more than just natural wines. An absolute must-see right next door, Spring Boutique: it offers 100 per cent organic artisan wines for sale, a deli, a few cured meats — Laborie sausages and San Daniele prosciutto bearing the mark of Levi Gregoris — and seasonal cheeses.

SPRING / 6 rue Bailleul / Paris Ier

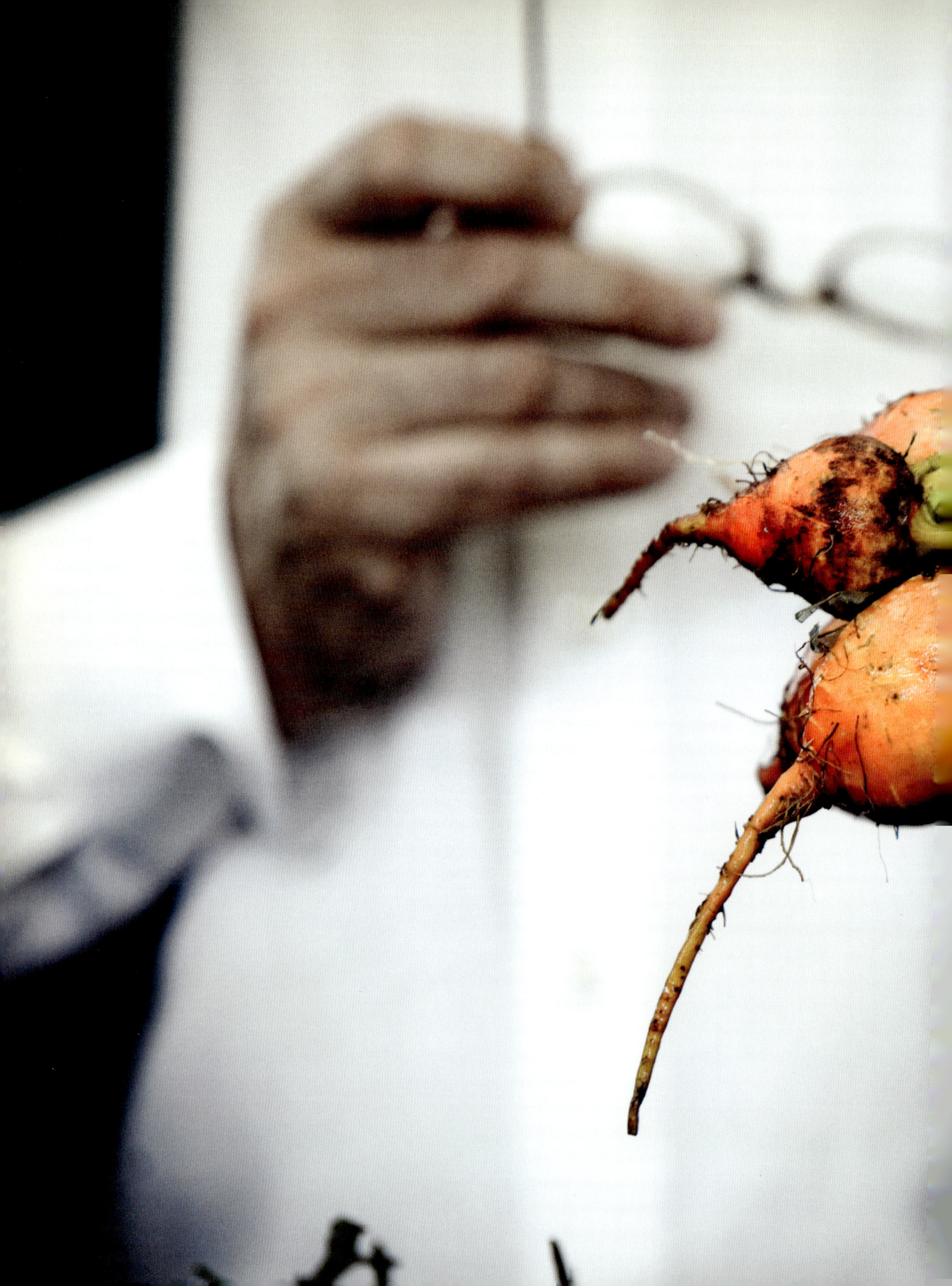

JOËL THIÉBAULT MARAÎCHER / Marché de l'Alma, Avenue du Président Wilson / Paris XVIe

THIÉBAULT

Unbeatable for roots, the man lays out a vast vegetable rainbow. Heritage carrots, green, yellow and purple radishes, multicoloured Swiss chard exuding the celebratory spirit of a Tuscan pie. An amazing aromatic selection, including sage-tarragon which gives off a certain astringency that lasts through the cooking process. Joël Thiébault is one of the very first to have offered Vitelotte potatoes, and provides long-forgotten vegetables to starred chefs.

J'aime Paris

PARIS: HOME TO THE REGIONS

JOËL THIÉBAULT MARAÎCHER / Marché de l'Alma, Avenue du Président Wilson / Paris XVIe

381

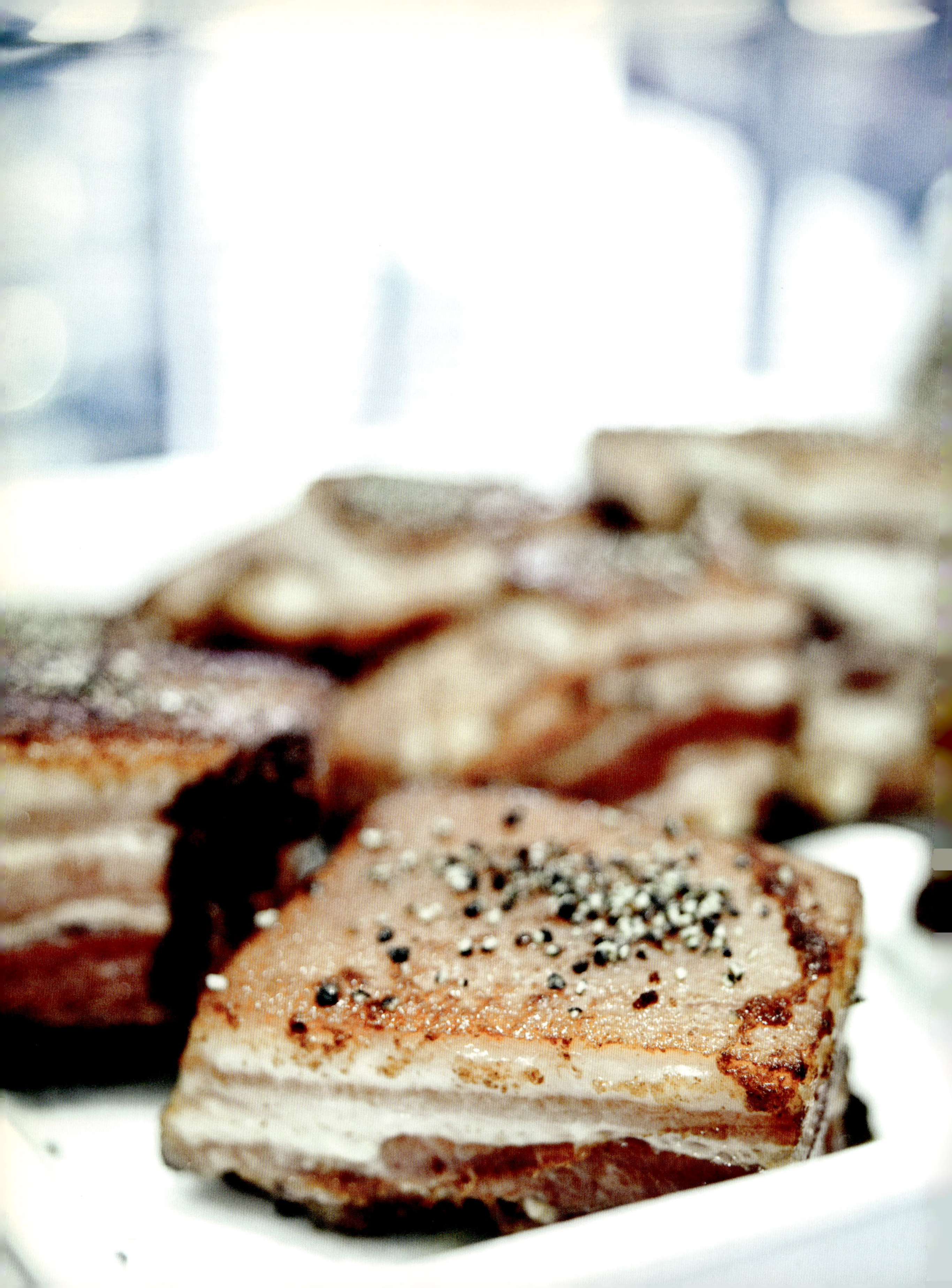

GILLES VÉROT – CHARCUTIER / 3 rue Notre-Dame des Champs / Paris VIe

J'aime Paris

PARIS: HOME TO THE REGIONS

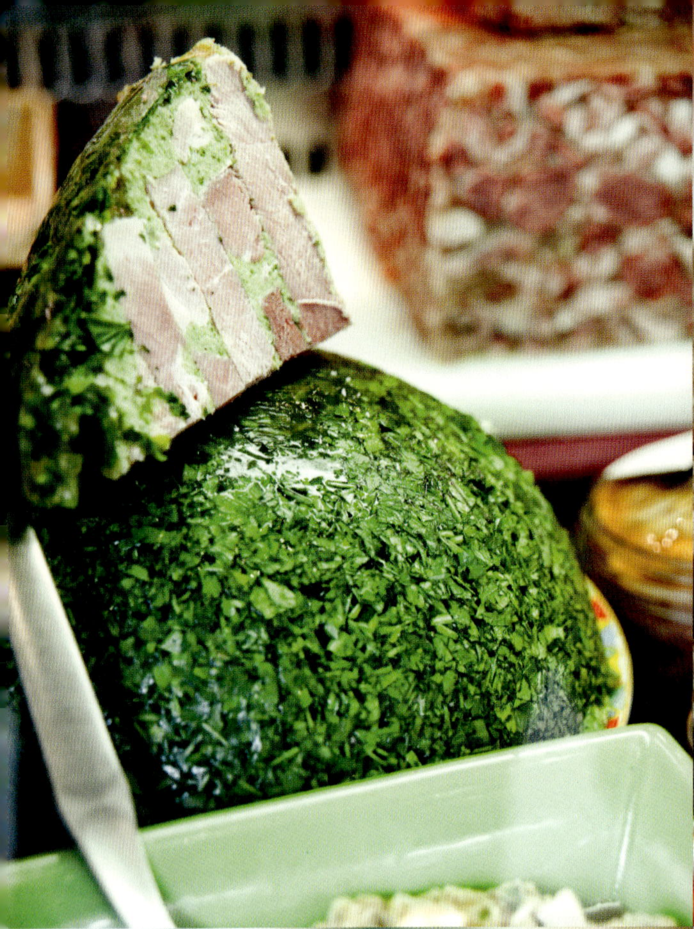
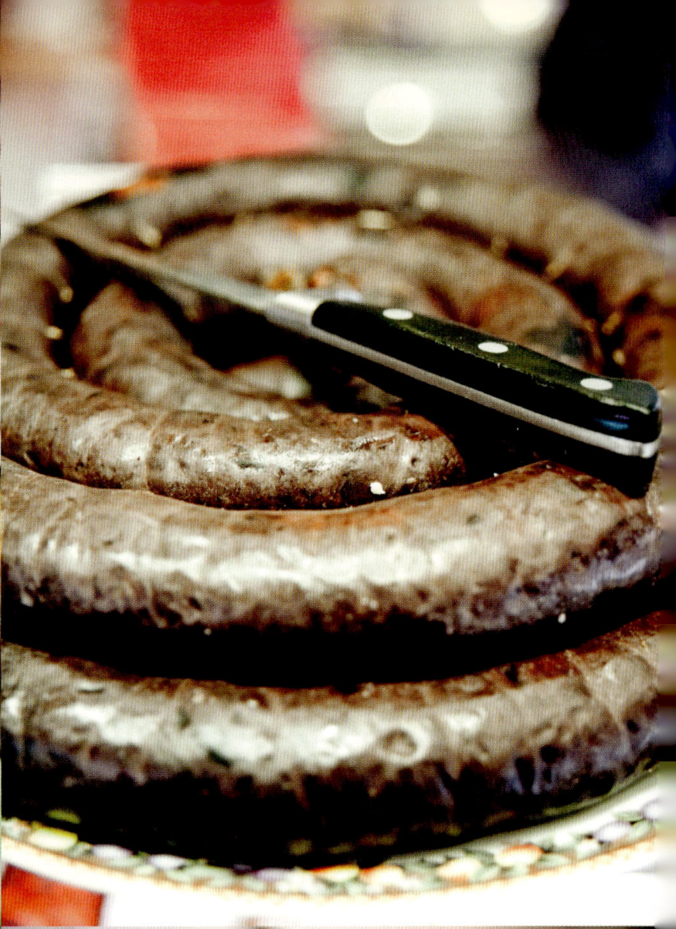
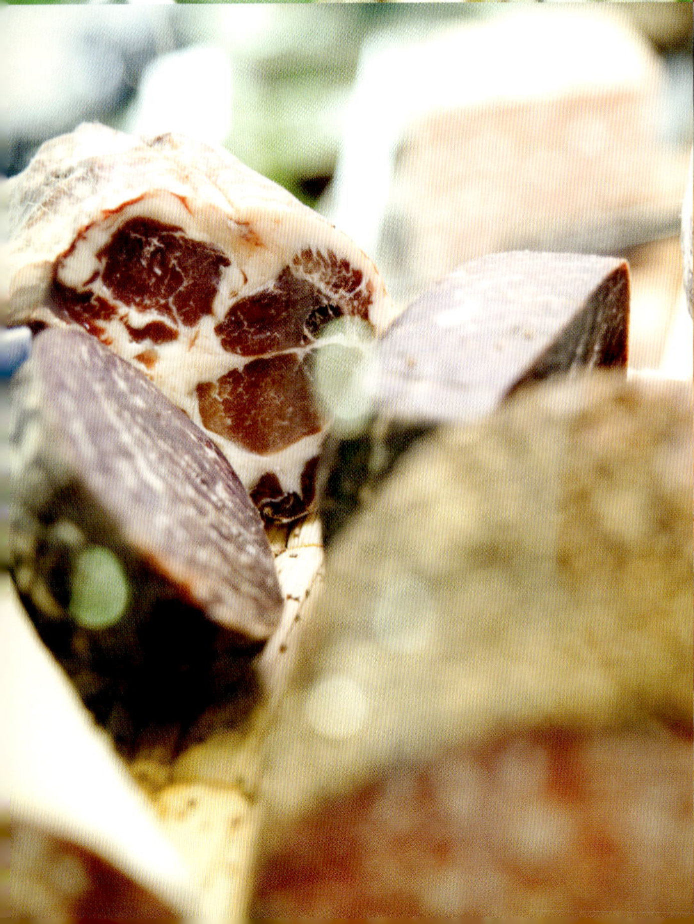
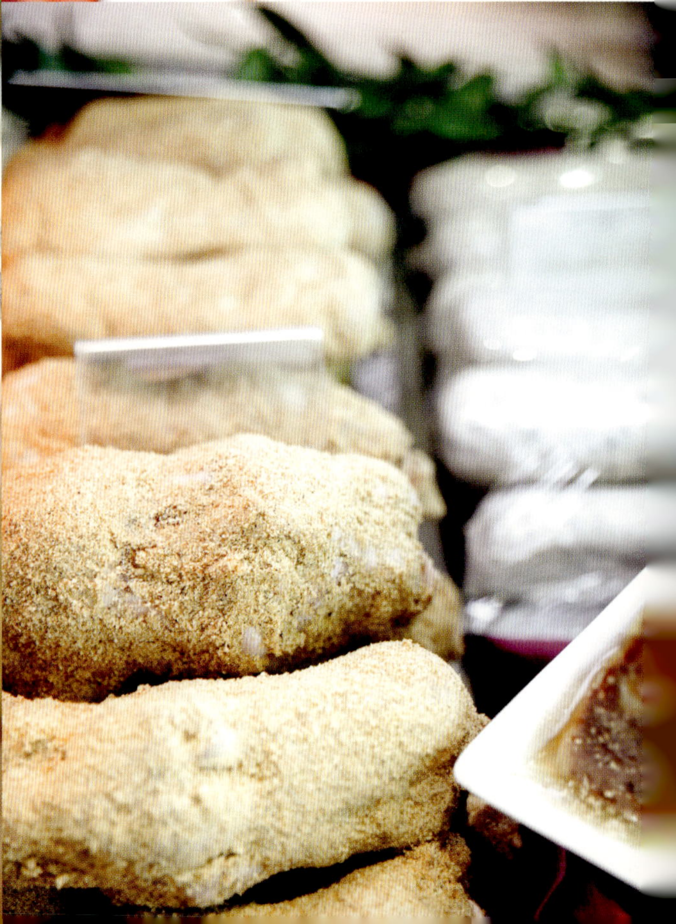

VÉ ROT

Champion of France for his brawn; an award for best liver pâté – the list goes on: Gilles Vérot is doing justice to his pigs. We really like his ham pasties and his pistachio meat pie intended 'for the purists'. Excellent quality of parsley-garnished jellied hams and sausages. A very good pork butcher – just the way we like them – who is also winning over New Yorkers with Daniel Boulud.

GILLES VÉROT – CHARCUTIER / 3 rue Notre-Dame des Champs / Paris VIe

J'aime Paris

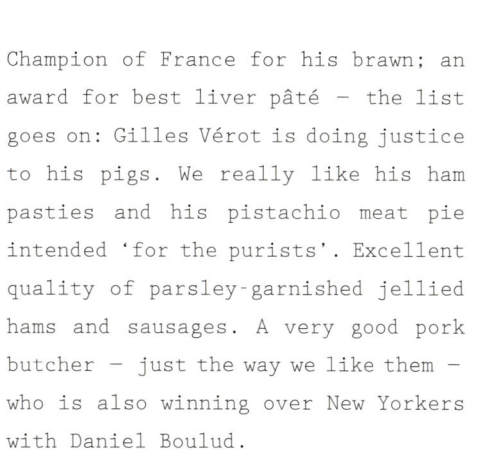

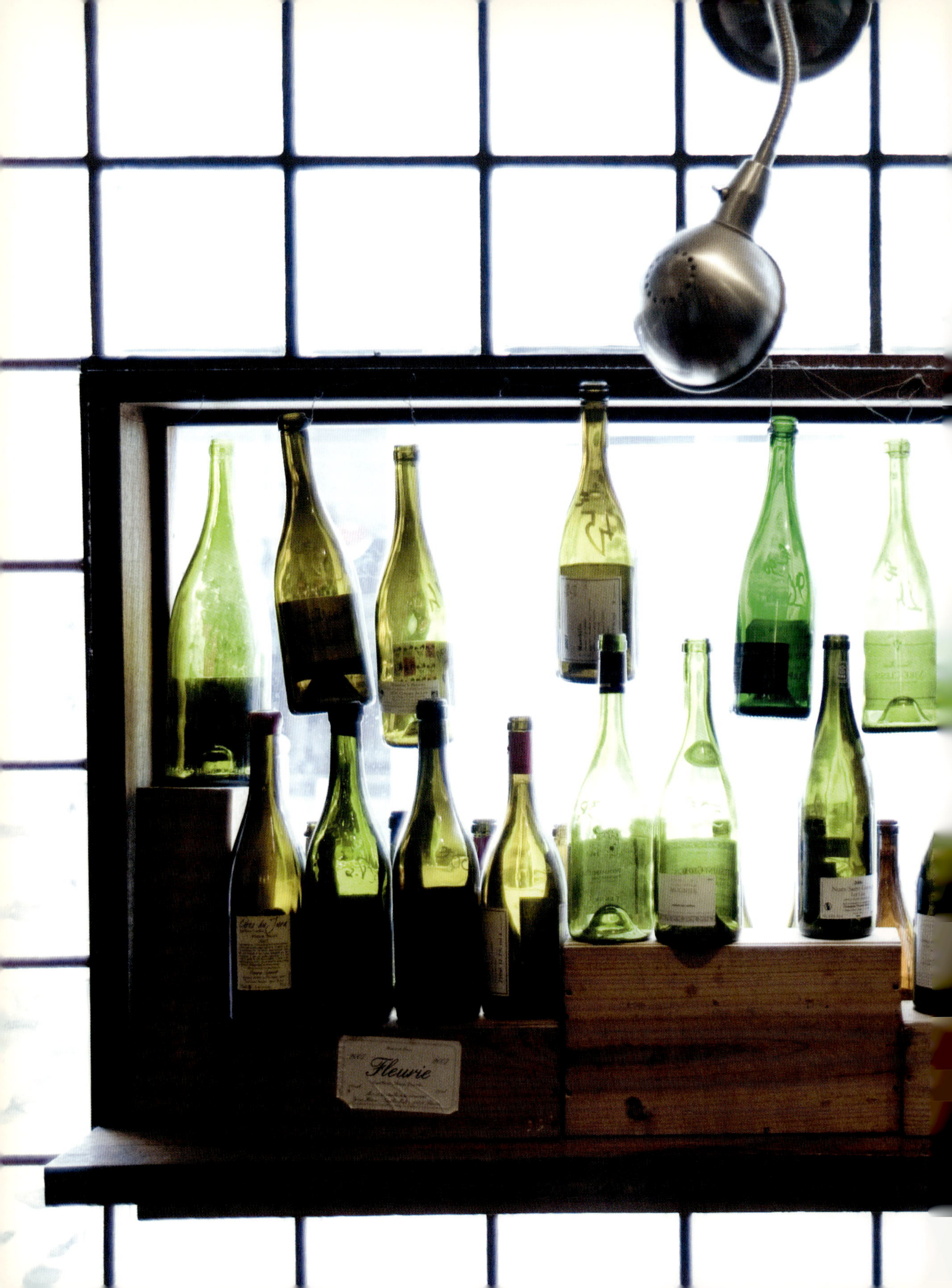
Fleurie

LES AUTHENTIQUES

Les Entrées et Amuse Bouches

- Le P'tit Creux (Fromages ou Charcuteries)
- La Terrine de Campagne
- La Terrine de Volaille aux Abricots Secs
- La Galantine de Lapin au Foie Gras
- Le Pâté en Croûte Traditionnel de Volaille aux Pistaches
- Cuisses de Cailles Fumées, Choukroute Crue au Curry
- Salade de Museau et Oreilles de Goret aux Cèpes Secs
- Fines Tranches de Bresaola, Salade d'Endives "Pleine Terre"
- Anguille Fumée Laquée, Mini-Poireaux Nouveaux
- Rémoulade de Chair de Tourteaux au Céleri Rave
- Poêlée de Gambas Chesapeake Bay au Houmous
- Salade de Pissenlit des Familles, Oeuf Rollet, Guanciale di Colonnata
- Carpaccio de Loup de Mer, Râpé de Choux-Fleurs, Huile d'Olive Citronnée
- Harengs Fumés de Hollande "Au Soleil"

Les Plats du Verre Volé

- L'Assiette de Fromages, de Charcuteries, La Mixte
- La Saucisse de Toulouse Coupée au Couteau
- L'Andouillette Tirée à la Ficelle
- Le Boudin Noir, Confiture d'Oignons
- Le Véritable Jambon Blanc de Paris

LE VERRE VOLÉ / 67 rue Lancry / Paris Xe

PARIS: HOME TO THE REGIONS

J'aime Paris

VERRE VOLÉ

Alain Ducasse: Is there a real kitchen now?

Cyril Bordarier: Yes, a real one with a piano hob, and Delphine, Ryo and Kelly alternating during the week.

AD: So, what are we eating today?

CB: A rib steak from Desnoyer, or sea bass that comes directly from an auction in the Channel. The cauliflower is Annie Bertin's. The capers come from La Tête dans les Olives and dessert is from Desmoulins, in Boulevard Voltaire. Do you want to try it?

AD: Of course.

CB: Enjoy, it's today's menu. It'll change tomorrow.

LE VERRE VOLÉ / 67 rue Lancry / Paris X^e

PARIS: HOME TO THE REGIONS

I ALSO LOVE...

MARCHÉ D'ALIGRE

Rue d'Aligre / Paris XII⁰

This is one of the oldest markets in Paris — the market building dates from 1779 — and also one of the most popular. Open every day except Monday, it is home to Michel Brunon, a butcher selling aged and marbled meats. Nearby is Sur les Quais, a delicatessen selling products from around the world and an absolute treasure trove. The other side of the square is like being on another planet. Here you will find the oldest seed shop in Paris, with its selection of pulses and herbal teas, country tableware, and a cat that has to be gently nudged aside in order to reach the verbena.

FROMAGERIE ALLEOSSE

13 rue Poncelet / Paris XVII⁰

Under the shop there is a cellar; actually, there are four cellars, one each for storing bloomy rind cheese, washed rind cheese, goat's cheese and tomme cheeses. This establishment is unique in Paris, as is the know-how of its master cheesemaker. There is a host of specialities from everywhere, with a preference for goat's cheese, and extra-fresh *burrata* at weekends

AUBERGE PYRÉNEES-CÉVENNES

106 rue de la Folie-Méricourt / Paris XIe

Gargantuan feasts take place under a ceiling hung with cold meat products. On the brown checked tablecloth, the cassoulet is XXL, the pork trotter is breaded and the veal liver is legendary. Round off your meal with a baba or profiterole, if you have room. Like being between Lyon and the south-west, here you will soon find yourself among friends. The welcome you will receive is warm and light-hearted.

BAR À PATATES

Marché de l'Alma, Avenue du Président Wilson / Paris XVIe

Alain Ducasse: What is your advice for making a good Parisian frite?
Carine Bars: Actually, I recommend a Sicilian potato: the Spunta. For sautéed potatoes, the very thin and very tasty Île de Ré variety is better. Otherwise... we also have Rubis potatoes this morning. You don't normally peel them.

MARCHÉ BASTILLE

Boulevard Richard Lenoir / Paris XI°

This is one of the largest markets in Paris, bringing together around 100 stallholders. You are spoilt for choice with such reasonable prices. The products sold here are often of good quality, like the fish at the stall run by Jacky Lorenzo, a popular figure at the market. Tourists come to admire the regional produce, while we appreciate the lively atmosphere in this genuine neighbourhood market.

FROMAGERIE MARIE-ANNE CANTIN

12 rue du Champs de Mars / Paris VII°

Daughter of Christian Cantin, founder of the Cheesemakers' Guild, Marie-Anne runs this business with her daughter and her husband Antoine. Holder of the Meilleur Ouvrier de France award, she is leading the fight against the standardisation of taste. Her cheeses are carefully chosen, having been produced in limited quantities by small-scale operations. Marie-Anne matures them in her own cellar, for several months in the case of the Beaufort and Comté cheeses. If you're passionate about cheese, you can arrange a tasting, which will be tailored to suit your palate.

CHEZ GEORGES

1 rue du Mail / Paris II⁰

This establishment has been popular since 1926. It's a real brasserie with classic brasserie fare, taken over by the owners of La Grande Cascade and L'Auberge du Bonheur. A trolley displays the daily specials, the quintessential dishes: artfully carved leg of lamb with beans and steaming *pot-au-feu* with amazing vegetables. A warm welcome and a good wine list await you. This is a place to enjoy a memorable experience. Good old Menut!

CRÊPES & GALETTES

37 rue Linné / Paris V⁰

There's a queue here even when it rains. In front of us, a couple of students order a caramel crêpe with salted butter and Speculoos cream. Behind, a grandfather has come to treat his grandchildren to the compote and cinnamon crêpe. An Emmenthal and hazelnut galette (buckwheat flour pancake) gets underway. The neighbourhood has a foster mother in Christiane Hérouard, who for 25 years has been spoiling the locals in Place Jussieu with fresh ingredients and gourmet recipes. She even thickened her homemade batter a little to satisfy 'her' students.

MARCHÉ DES ENFANTS ROUGES

39 rue de Bretagne / Paris IIIe

The orphanage founded here by Queen Margot and the red uniforms of its occupants have given way to a neighbourhood market. When it opened in 1777, there was even a well and a cowshed. Today, the little market is housed in a glazed hall. It is like a village square and has the same charm. It's peaceful during the week, but bustling on Sundays. You can have a light snack at one of the stallholders' tables or in the pretty square surrounding the market.

ITINÉRAIRES

5 rue de Pontoise / Paris V^e

It's a fitting name, evoking a bistro that has toured the world. In the frying pan, together with the artichokes and chanterelles, are soya bean flowers and toasted hazelnuts. You can taste chef Sylvain Sendra's marvellous creations, such as his green asparagus with foie gras and dried tuna dressing. The place is absolutely packed — we wonder why!

- 395

MARCHÉ PASSY
Angle des rues Duban et Bois-le-Vent / Paris XVIᵉ

Behind the white facade and glass bricks, the tall retro building houses a good neighbourhood market. Classic quality: greengrocers, butchers, fishmongers. The advantage for residents is that it's open until evening. You can pass by on your way home from work to pick out the makings of a super-fresh dinner.

LE PÈRE CLAUDE
51 avenue de la Motte Piquet / Paris XVᵉ

Now this is a true rotisserie. Which do you prefer: roast free-range chicken — plump with crispy skin — rotating before your very eyes, or its heavenly homemade purée? Red and white meat of noble origin, Burgundy snails, mushrooms *a la plancha* are selected and prepared for the gourmet elite with the precision of a Swiss watchmaker. Carnivore friends, don't miss the roast meat platter: lamb, beef, sausage, pork tripe sausage, black pudding. Unforgettable foie gras.

FROMAGERIE QUATREHOMME
62 rue de Sèvres / Paris VIIᵉ

In the business for 25 years, Meilleur Ouvrier de France Marie Quatrehomme family-manages three Parisian boutiques. She also supplies the hotel Le Meurice, Pierre Gagnaire and Guy Savoy. We are well aware, too, that as early as 20 years ago the team had no qualms in unveiling Roquefort Carles, less popular, less expensive and less salty than its well-known rivals. The range of refined cheeses satisfies almost every palate.

RIBOULDINGUE

10 rue Saint-Julien le Pauvre / Paris V⁰

The menu is all-consuming: whole kidneys with *gratin dauphinois*, sweetbreads, brains, oxtail and *sabodet* just like you'd find in Lyon. Even snout, and cow's teats... The restaurant is welcoming, the team young and totally involved in this respectful, modern cuisine. Nadège, the owner, trained at La Régalade in the Yves Camdeborde era, and selects her bottles with precision.

WINE BY ONE

9 rue des Capucines / Paris I⁰ʳ

That's it. You're no longer lost in a sea of labels. You slot your smart card into a machine, you choose the size of your glass — 30, 60 or 120 ml — and let the computer tell you about the grape variety, pull up the tasting cards, suggest food-wine pairings. You can choose from over 100 references, to be savoured in a space-shuttle setting designed by the Nespresso space designers. The wine merchant's section sells the same bottles, which you can sample before buying.

PARIS: WHERE THE WORLD MEETS

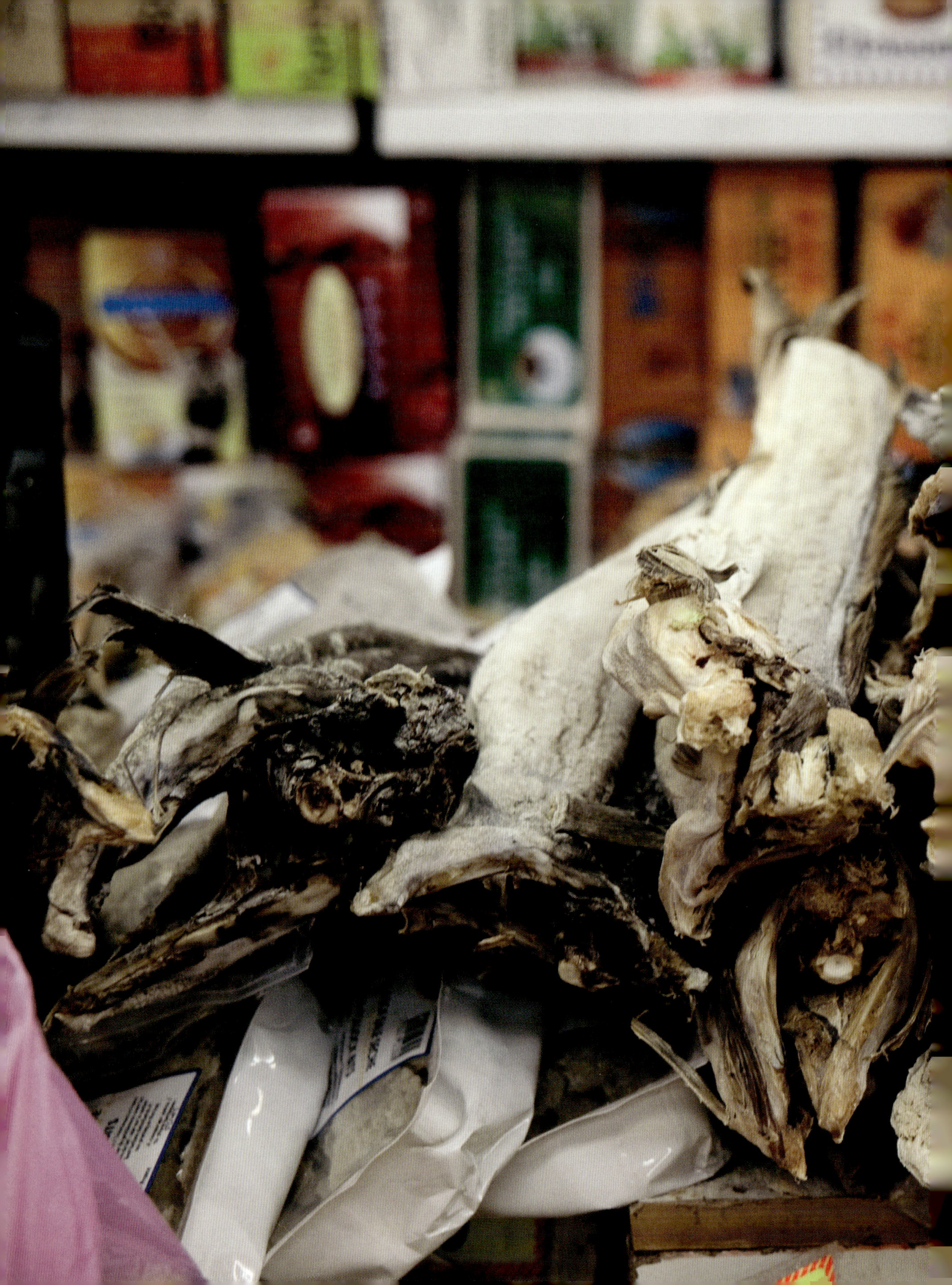

ASIE ANTILLES AFRIQUE / 88bis–90 rue du Faubourg du Temple / Paris XIe

J'aime Paris

THE WORLD MEETS PARIS: WHERE

oeufes FRAISE
3 €50

A.
A.
A.

The whole world contained in a hessian bag. One slaloms between the mountains of rice from all continents, legumes, yams, sweet potatoes in a variety of colours. It's packed with African mamas and Chinese papas. A West Indian man has come to choose his pork in vinegar and his 'bonda Man Jacques' or 'the behind of mother Jacques' peppers, in Creole. Fans of the exotic, and taste adventurers, leave with two different types of plantain bananas to sample.

J'aime Paris

THE WORLD MEETS PARIS: WHERE

ASIE ANTILES AFRIQUE / 88bis–90 rue du Faubourg du Temple / Paris XIe

- 403

SAN FERMIN
PAMPLONA

Jambon
IBAÏONA
millesime
juin 2008
Affinage naturel
PAYS BASQUE
A FARIA
PARIS 15

AFARIA / 15 rue Desnouettes / Paris XVe

WHERE THE WORLD MEETS PARIS: J'aime Paris

- 405

TAPAS
servis au bar et table d'hôtes

Tortilla de P. de Terre	8 €
Pot de Boudin au Piment d'Espelette	6 €
Sabot de Jambon Ibaiona	7 €
Brochettes de Porc façon Lomo	8 €
Sucrines, Pan con Tomate	8 €
Chipirons frits au Piment doux	11 €
Pieds de Cochon en Escabèche	8 €
Fraîcheur de Saumon	2 €/pièce
Gambas en crémeux d'épices	11 €
Panis au chorizo	9 €
Humus de Tarbais et croutons	8 €
Accras de Morue au Piment	7 €
Coeurs de Canard en Persillade	9 €
Bocal de Foie Gras	19 €

AFARIA

The cuisine of the Pyrenees — chef Julien Duboué is of Basque origin — surfs on the fusion wave. Seasonal produce, themed menus, a sought-after offering. Rockfish roasted with chorizo, foie gras pan fried with raisins, apple black pudding in mustard pastry, or small pasta shell paella. Book the communal table with a group of friends to fully enjoy the heady atmosphere.

AFARIA / 15 rue Desnouettes / Paris XVe

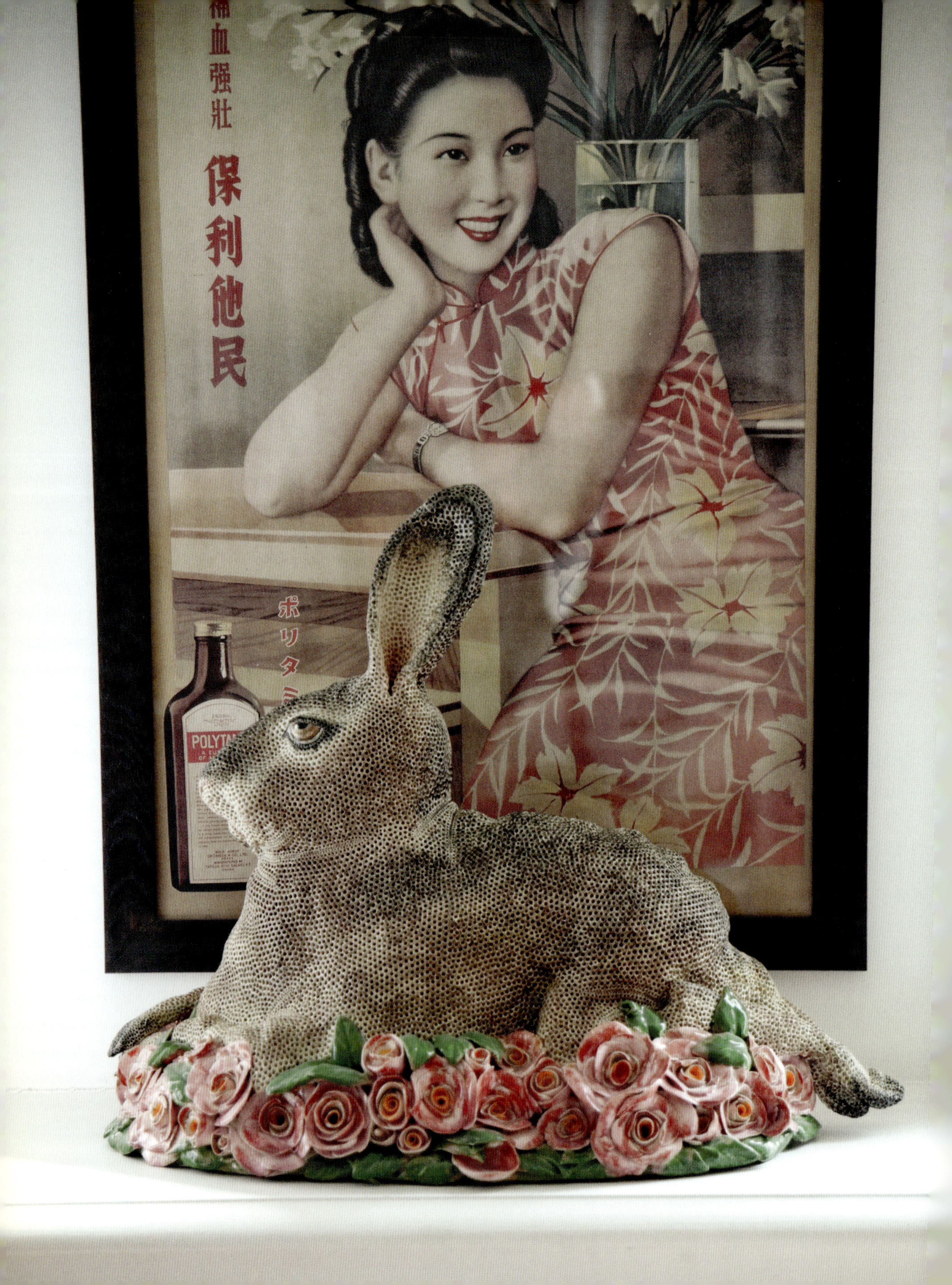
保利他民

Betsy Bernardaud / Paris VIIᵉ

J'aime Paris

- 409

BETSY BERNARDAUD

Betsy Bernardaud shops in the Jewish quarter. In her warm kitchen, perched on the countertop, you share a special moment among friends. A sandwich, quite simply. But not just any. It's called a 'Reuben', originating in Eastern Europe, with a detour via New York. *Yiddish broït*, a white bread with cumin, lightly browned in butter in the pan; very good, thinly sliced pastrami with a Panzer sauerkraut. It's crisp, juicy and tender, and melts in your mouth. The savoury, sour and sweet flavours come through without the fuss. Simple and delicious. Moments of friendship need nothing more.

BETSY BERNARDAUD / Paris VIIe

J'aime Paris

WHERE THE WORLD MEETS PARIS

- 411

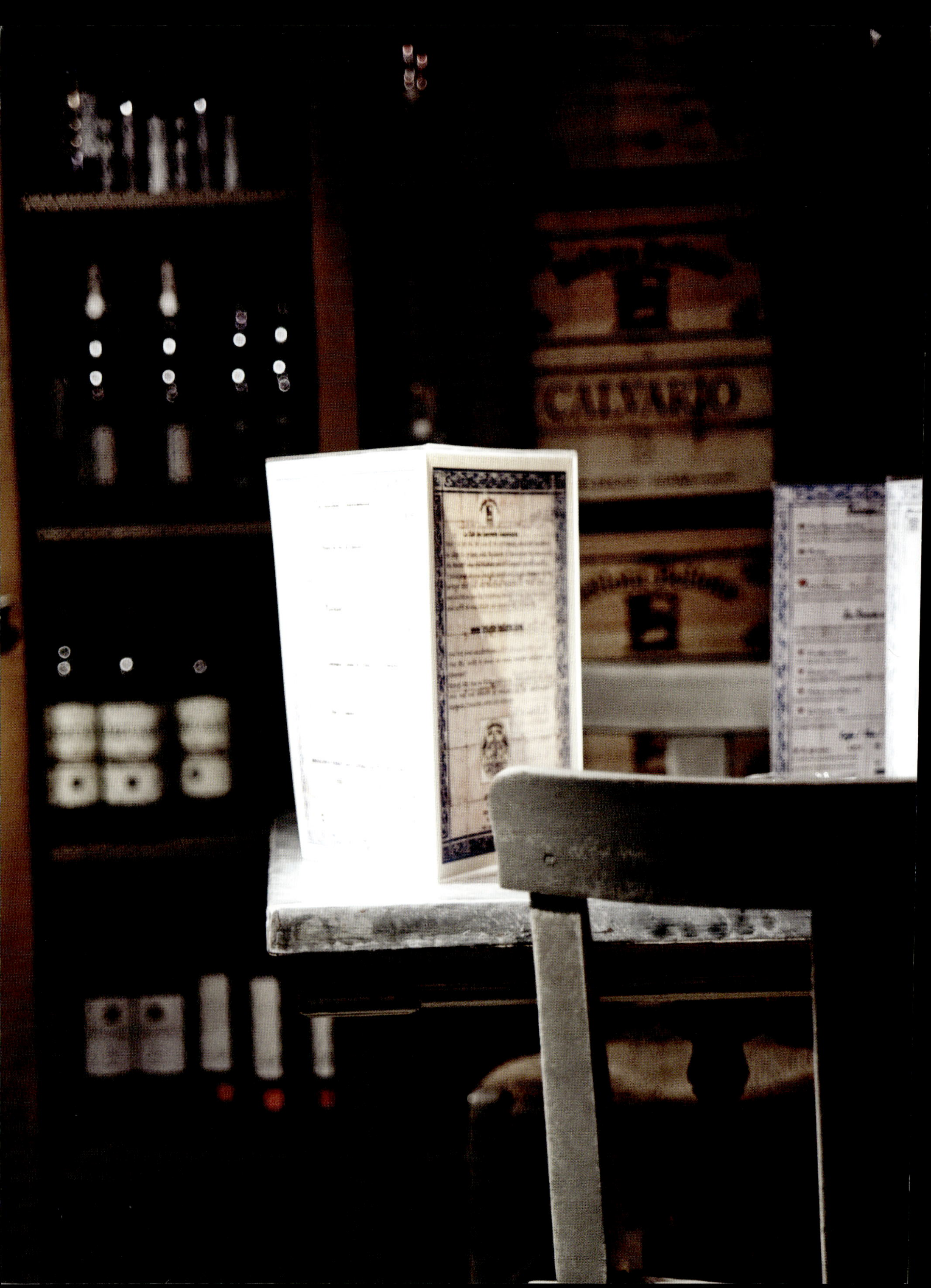
CALVARIO

BYZANCE CHAMPS-ÉLYSÉES BELLOTA / BELLOTA RIVE DROITE / 11 rue Clément Marot / Paris VIII

WHERE THE WORLD MEETS PARIS:

J'aime Paris

413

BYZANCE
CHAMPS-ÉLYSÉES

Philippe Poulachon: Alain, you were one of my very first clients to have my Ibérico Spanish ham, in May 1995. When I offered you my very best Bellota hams, I almost needed to know the pig's first name! I found that very stimulating, and so I travelled extensively around Spain, looking to understand, in a scientific way, why these hams were the best, how one chooses them, when, with whom...

Alain Ducasse: But there aren't only hams in your shop. Tell us about the rest!

PP: As you know, I started out with salmon and caviar. Then, as I was going to Spain between 10 and 15 times a year, I met enthusiasts like myself, which allowed me to build up my selection of products. There are Cantabrian anchovies, olive oils, Spanish wines and here, this *Torta de Salamanca*, a fabulous ewe's milk cheese that is made using thistle rennet. It's one of a kind!

BYZANCE CHAMPS-ÉLYSÉES BELLOTA / BELLOTA RIVE DROITE / 11 rue Clément Marot / Paris VIIIe

J'aime Paris

- 415

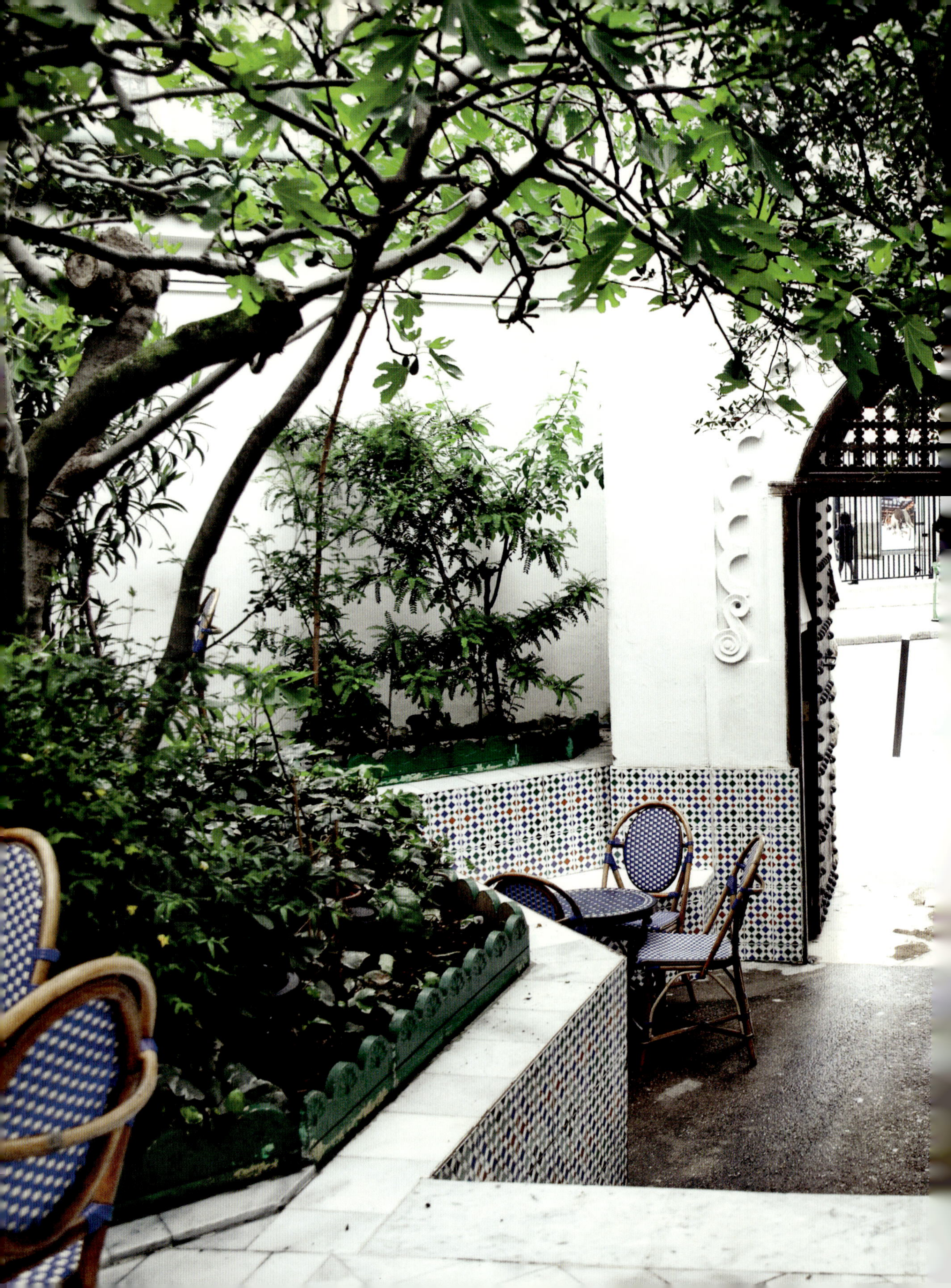

CAFÉ MAURE DE LA MOSQUÉE DE PARIS // 2 rue Geoffroy Saint Hilaire, Paris V⁽ᵉ⁾

417

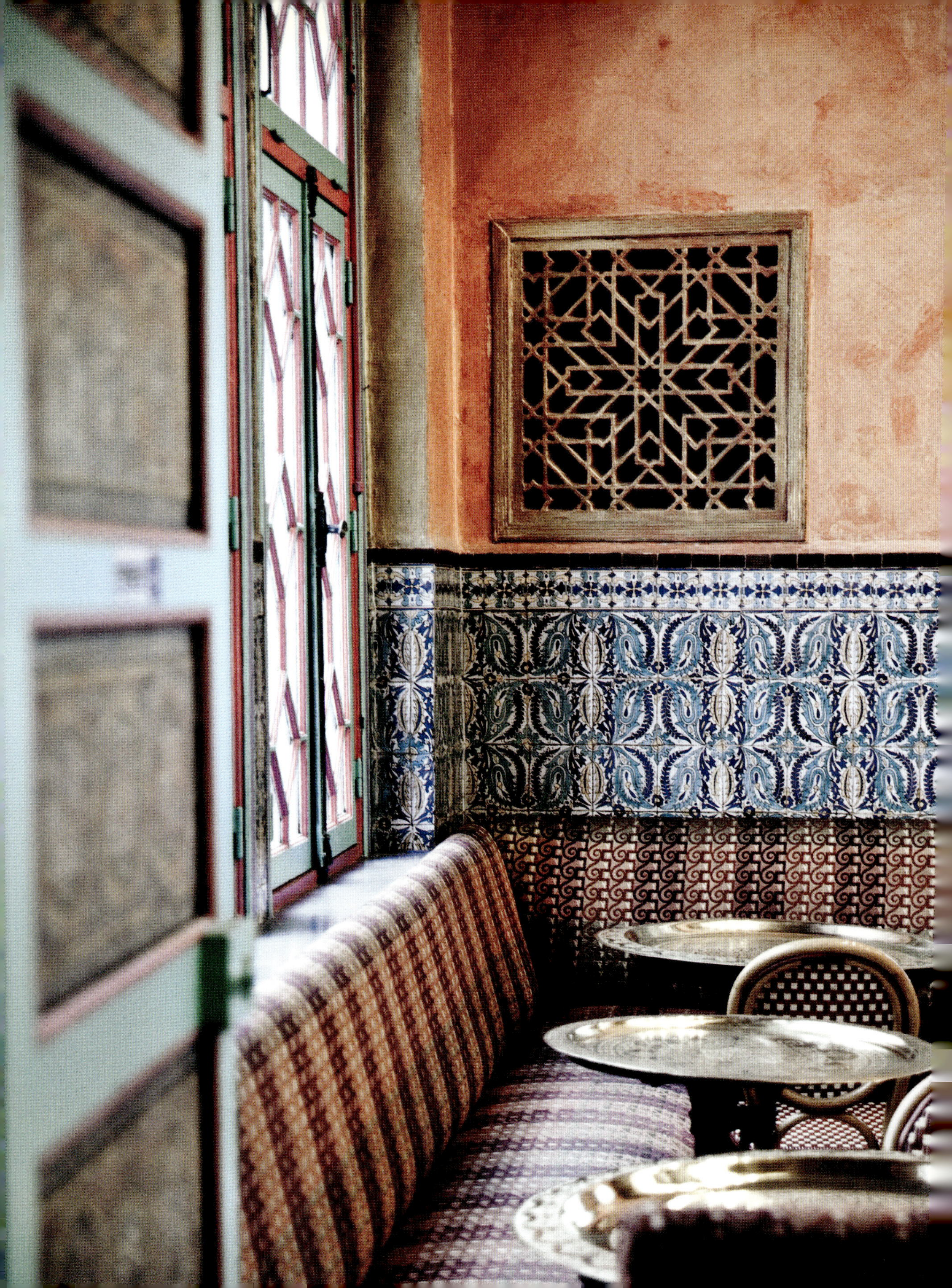

CAFÉ MAURE

The sun warms the fig trees, with the sweetish aroma drifting through the courtyard. Much self-control is needed to walk past the pastries counter. Behind the door lies the Orient. You glide under the trellis archway for a mint tea, or a Turkish coffee on its hammered-copper tray. It's an oasis, a Mediterranean microcosm, an endless summer, perfumed with honey and almonds.

CAFÉ MAURE DE LA MOSQUÉE DE PARIS / 9 rue Geoffroy Saint Hilaire / Paris V^e

- 419

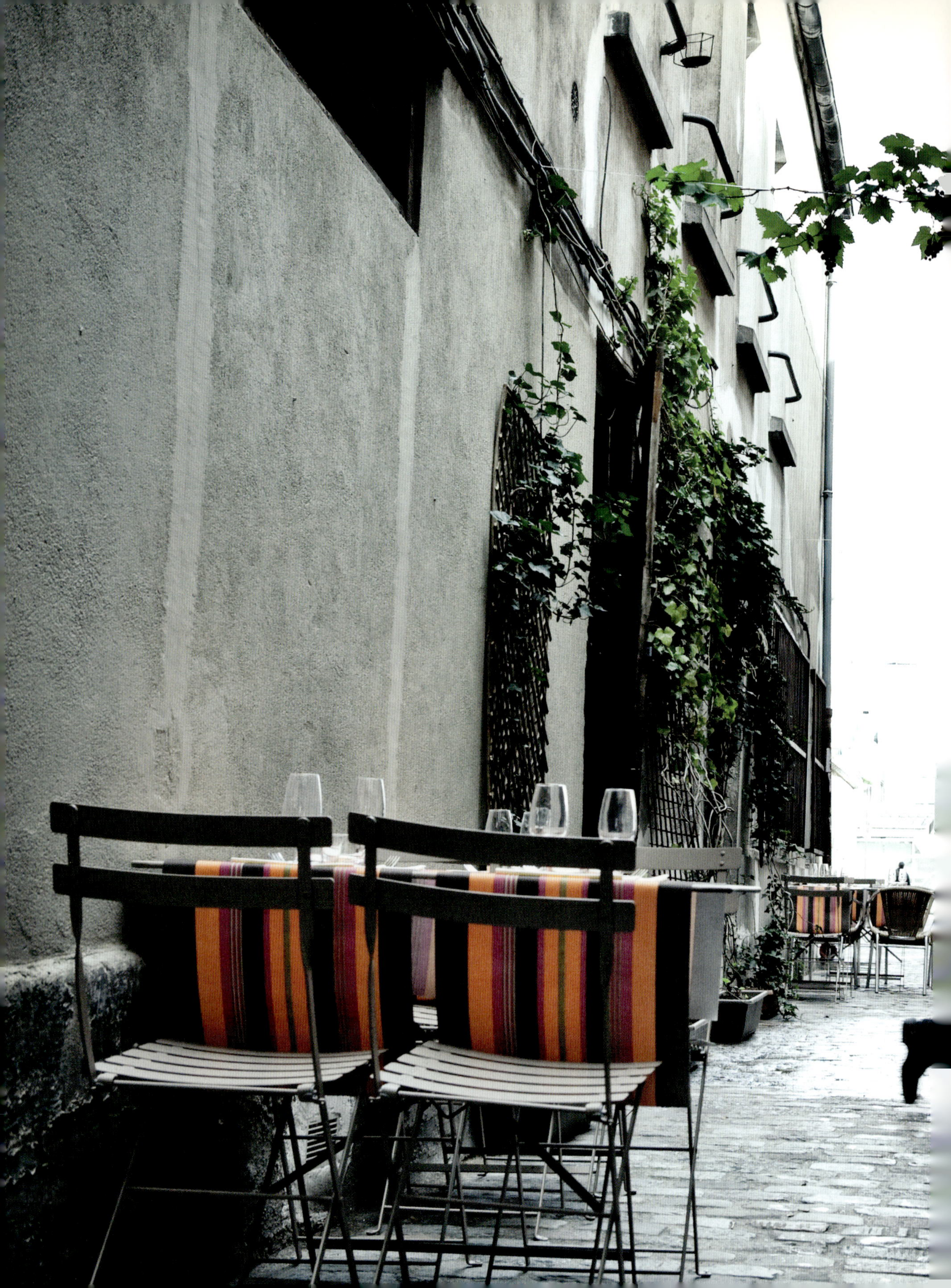

CAFFÈ DEI COPPI / 159 rue du Faubourg Saint-Antoine / Paris XI

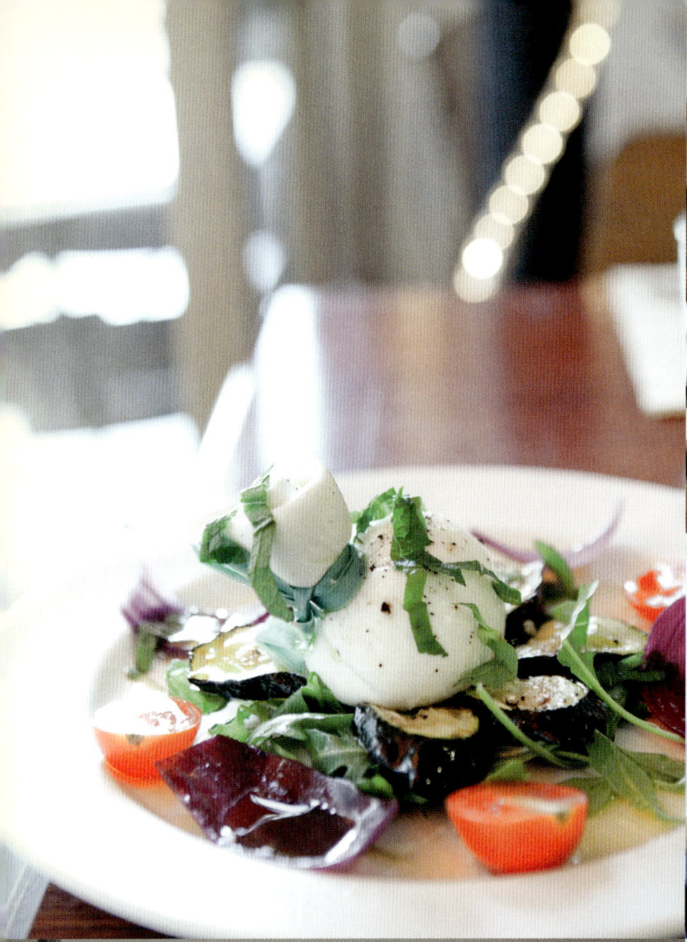
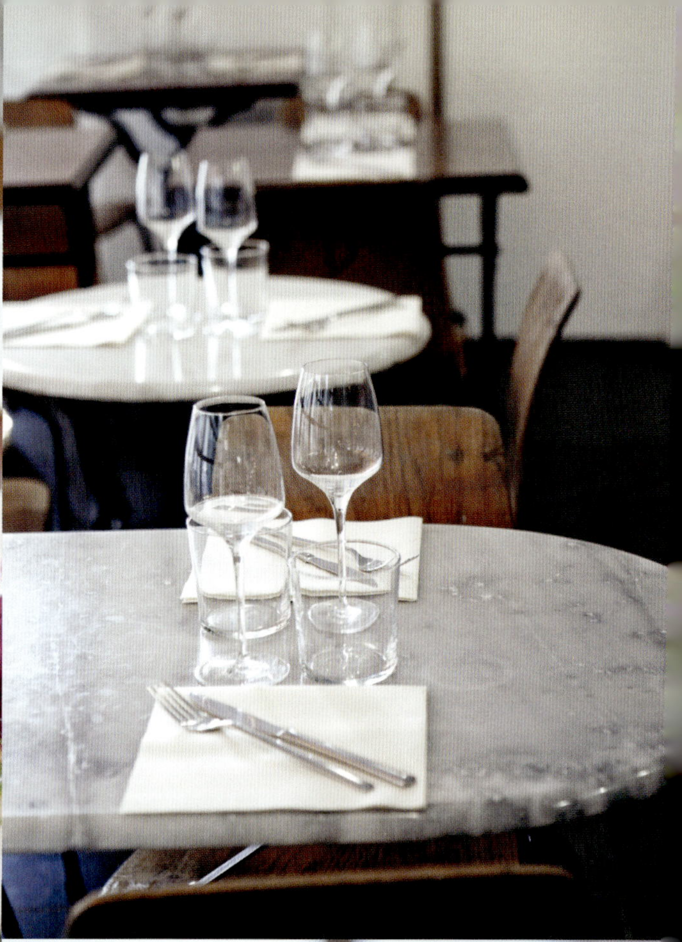
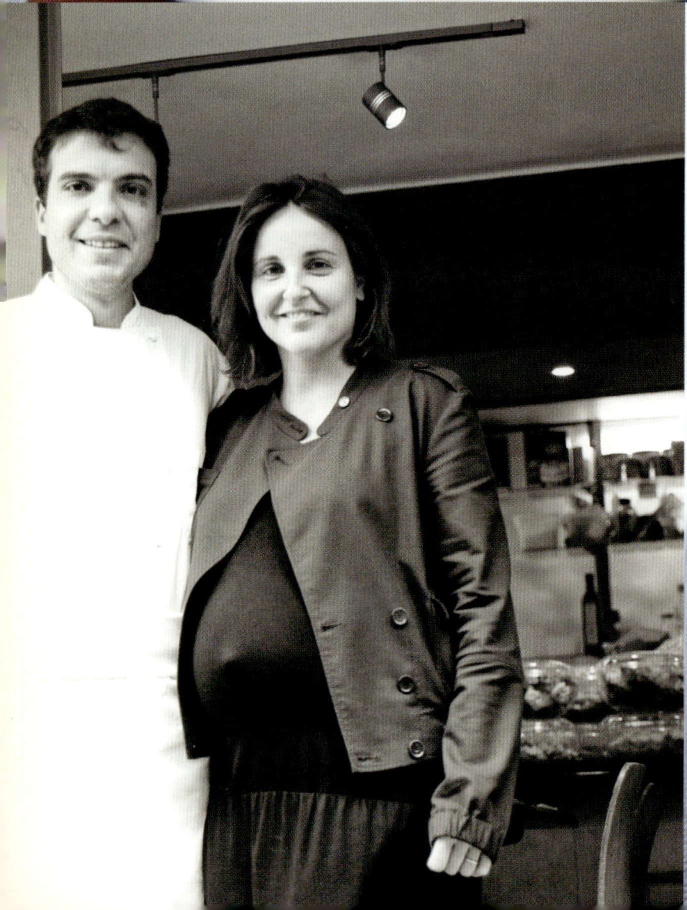
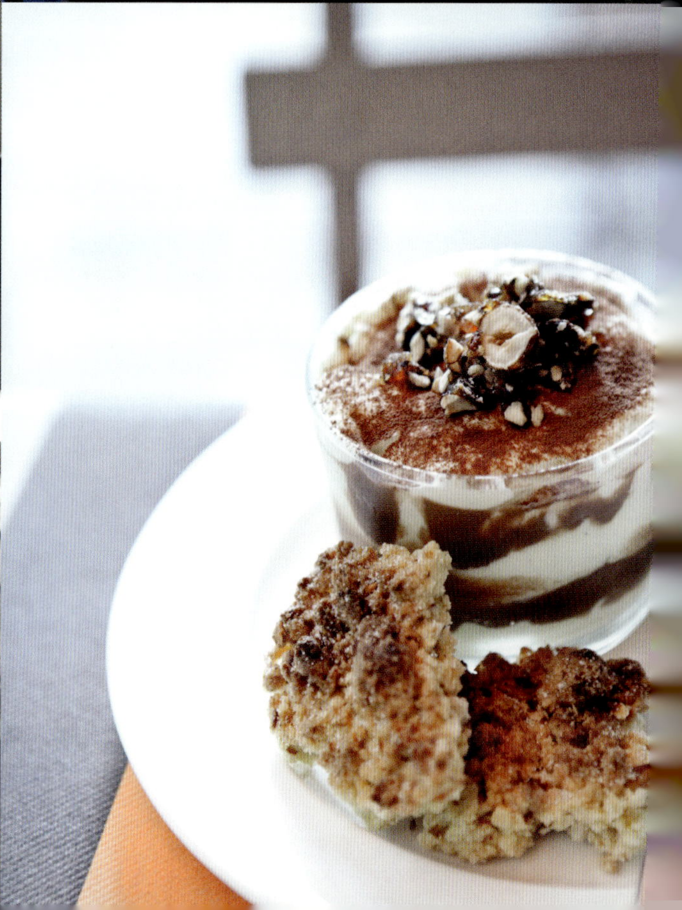

CAFFÈ DEI CIOPPI

J'aime Paris — THE WORLD MEETS PARIS: WHERE THE WORLD MEETS PARIS / 159 rue du Faubourg Saint-Antoine / Paris XIe

Delicacy, your name is *sbrisolona*. A little dry biscuit that doesn't look like much, really, or maybe just like a biscuit! Powdered almonds, cornflour. Sink your teeth into it, though, and it's just like Verdi at La Scala, or a dive into the Trevi Fountain — in this case, into a little mascarpone cream pot. Fabrizio and Federica don't stop at the sweets, of course. They prepare pure, simple trattoria cuisine with great panache.

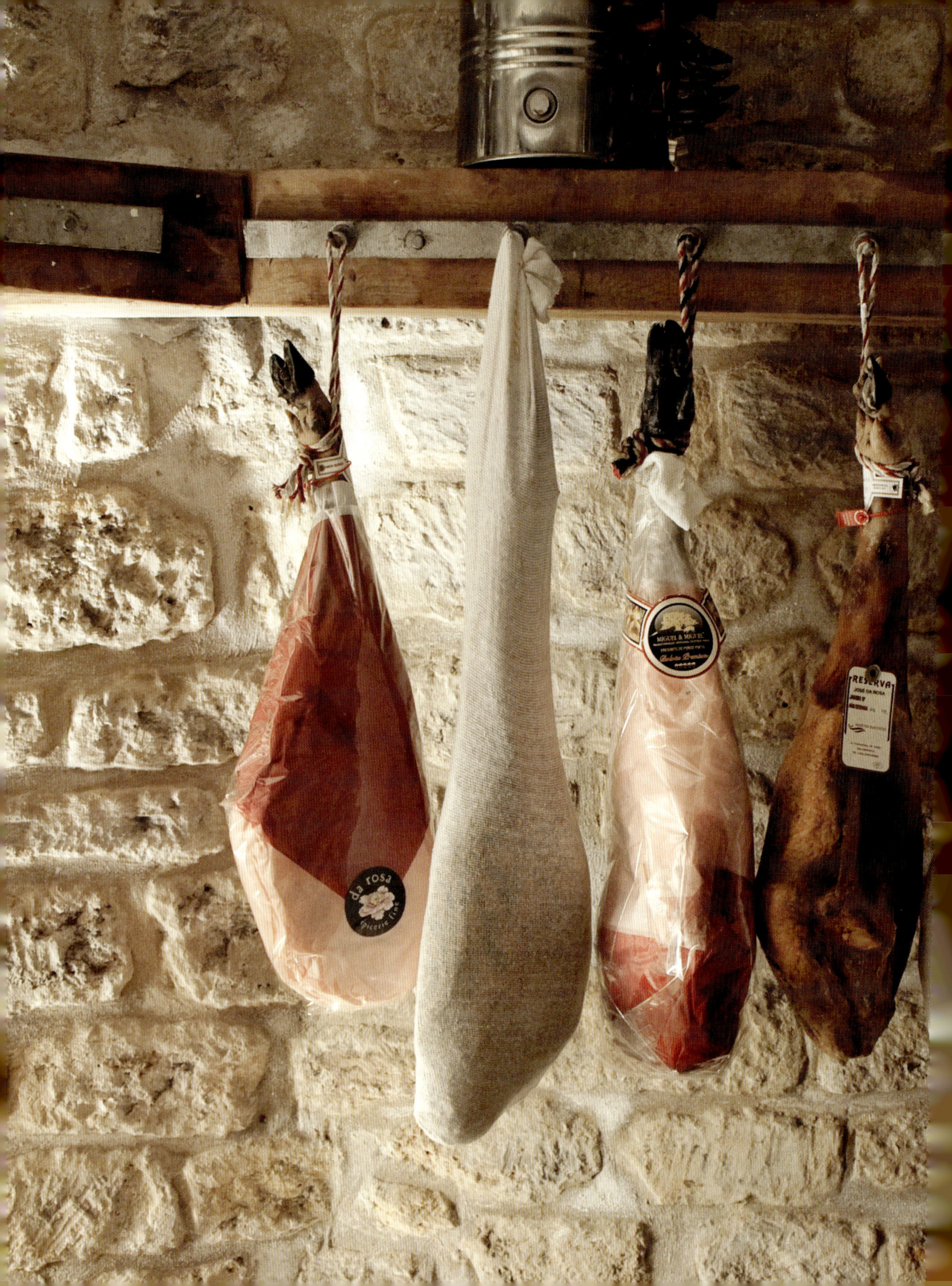
da rosa
RESERVA

DA ROSA ÉPICERIE FINE / 62 rue de Seine / Paris VIe

J'aime Paris

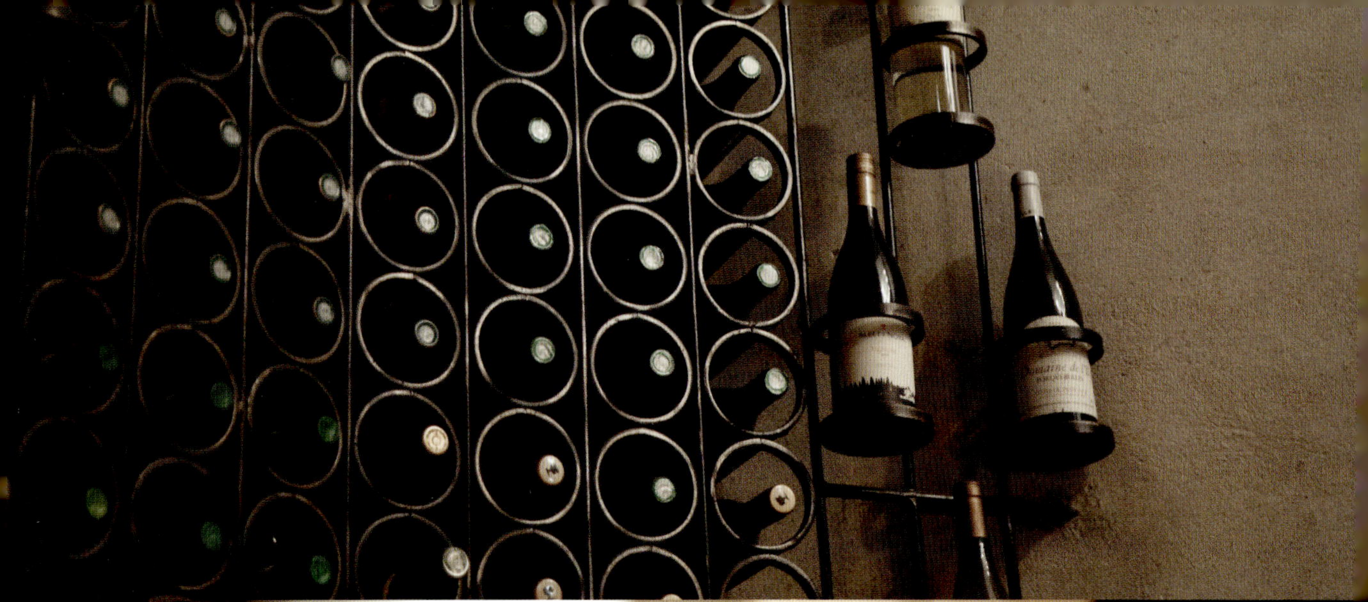

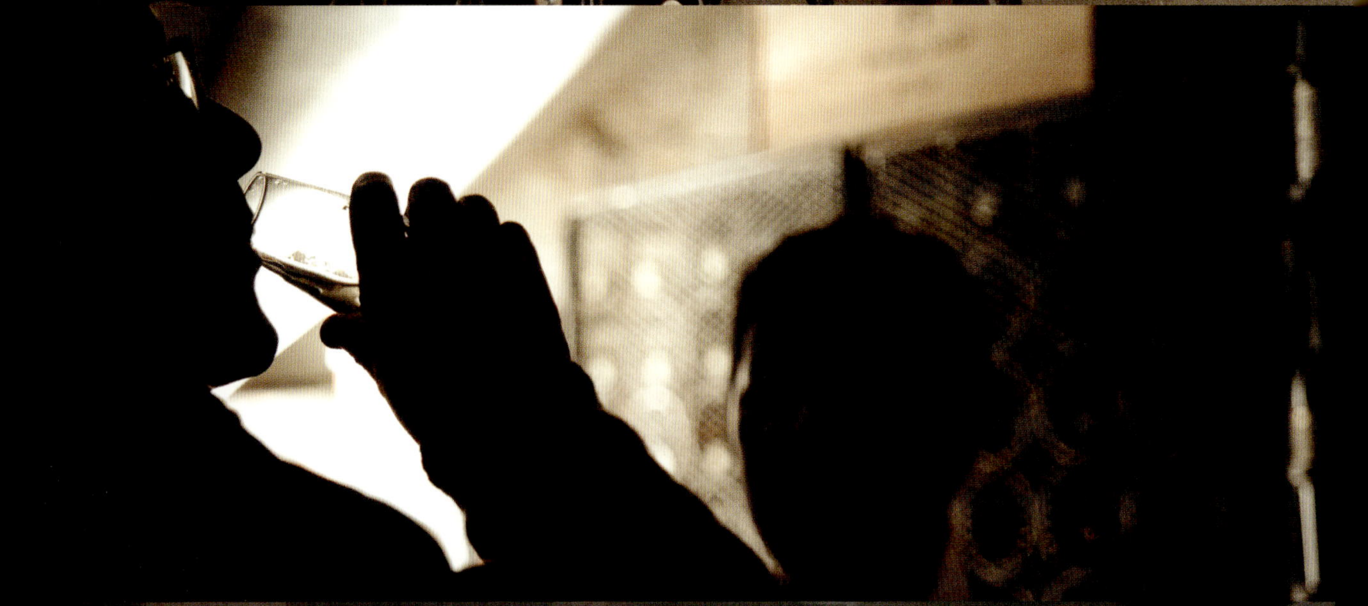

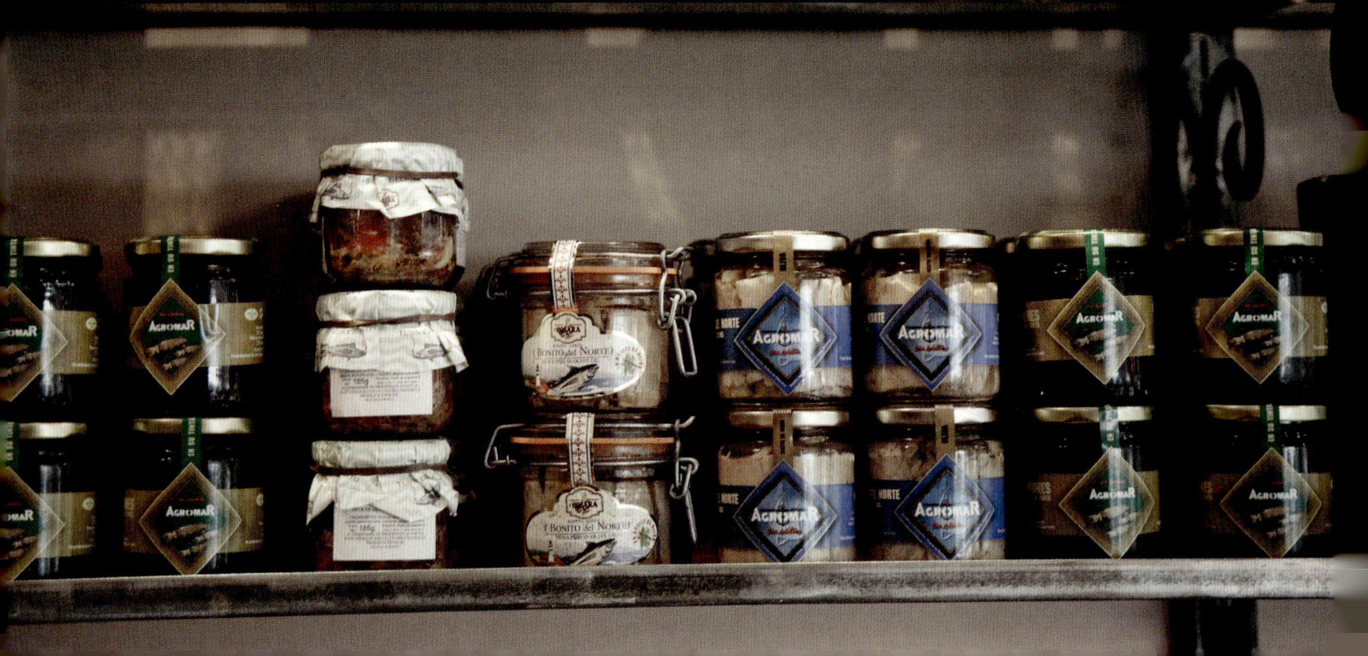
AGROMAR
Bonito del Norte

DA RO SA

The roughness of the natural stone walls. The rasping of a Portuguese accent burning up in the summer, icy in winter. The pungent and intoxicating aromas of Iberian hams curing along the ceiling. But, under the surface, the complex fruitiness of the *bellota*, which lasts in the mouth as long as a juicy tomato on some hot bread, the pepperiness of a cheese. In this deli-canteen that looks like none other, we settle in, as if in the Mediterranean...

DA ROSA, ÉPICERIE FINE / 62 rue de Seine / Paris VI

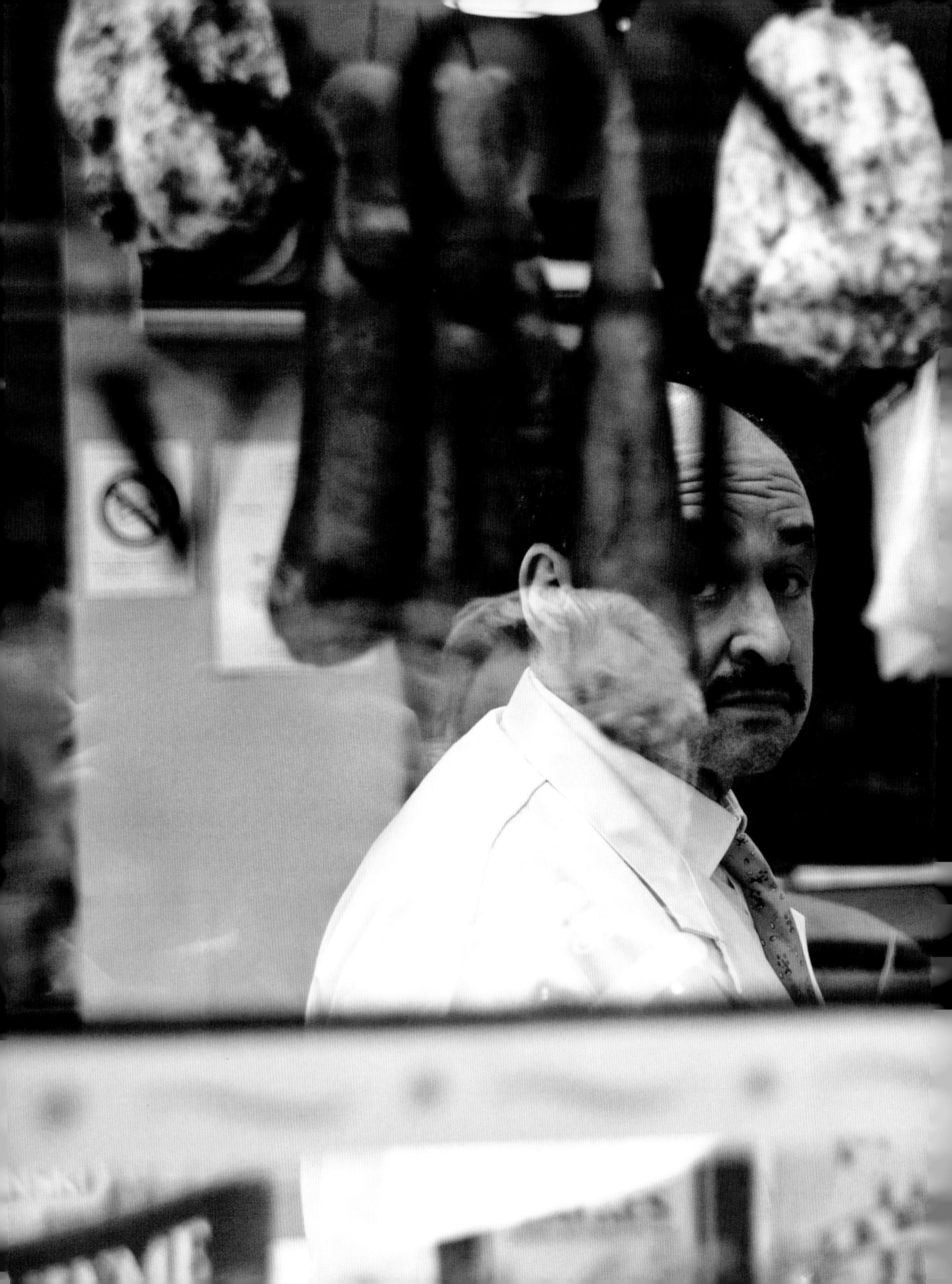

BOUCHERIE DAVID / 6 rue des Ecouffes / Paris IVe

J'aime Paris

DAVID

Brooklyn delicatessens may as well go back to where they came from. In variety and quality, David's place has few rivals. This is where people come for the *pastrami* to make the fabulous 'Reuben Sandwich'. But Michel Khalifa doesn't let us off so easily. He offers us tastes of his take on chicken liver with onions, as silky as a foie gras. He thinly slices his Podze calf's tongue, complex and delicate. Next to traditional fare lie the house dishes: duck pastrami, hazelnut sausages. Carried along by the enthusiasm and generosity of its owner, we'd happily taste the whole shop.

BOUCHERIE DAVID / 6 rue des Ecouffes / Paris IVe

J'aime Paris

WHERE THE WORLD MEETS PARIS

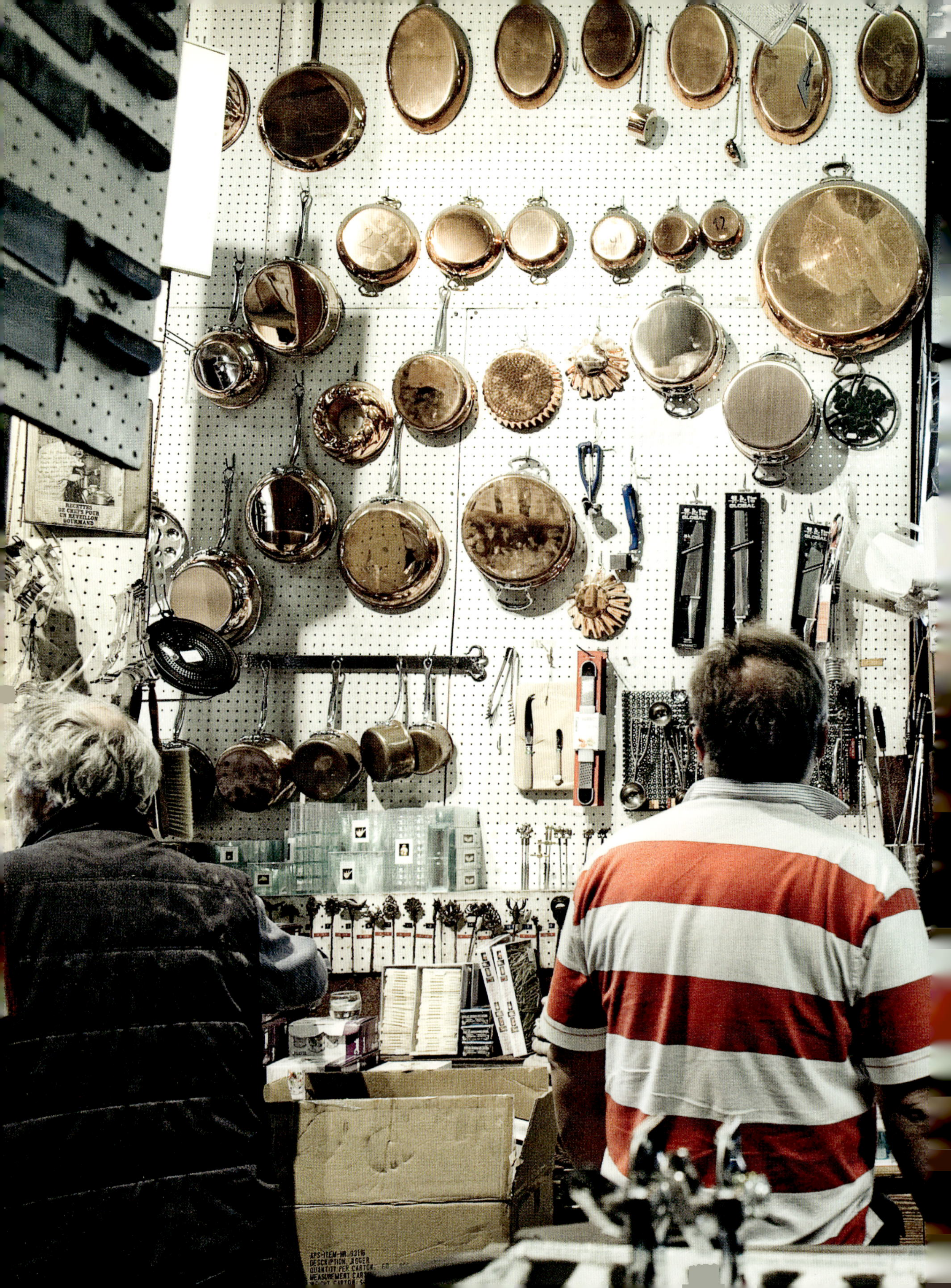
RECETTES
DE CHEFS POUR
UN REVEILLON
GOURMAND
GLOBAL

- 433

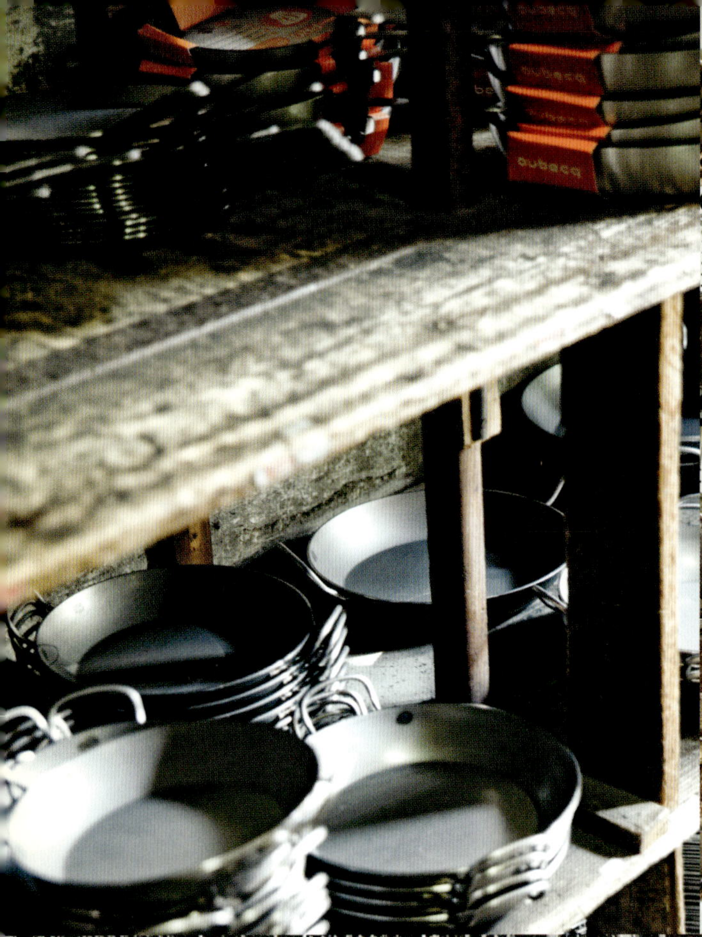
aubecq
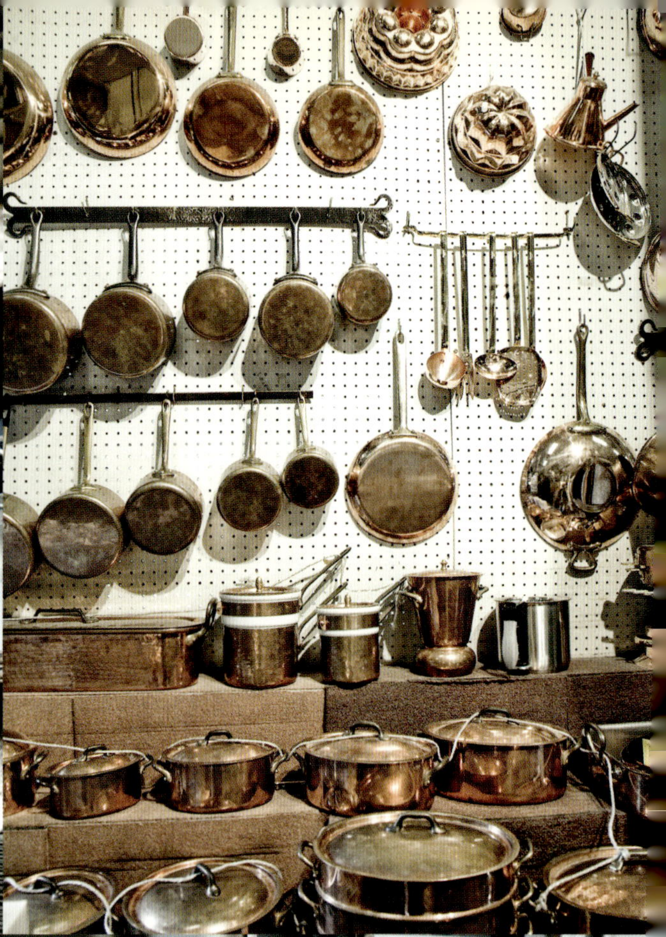
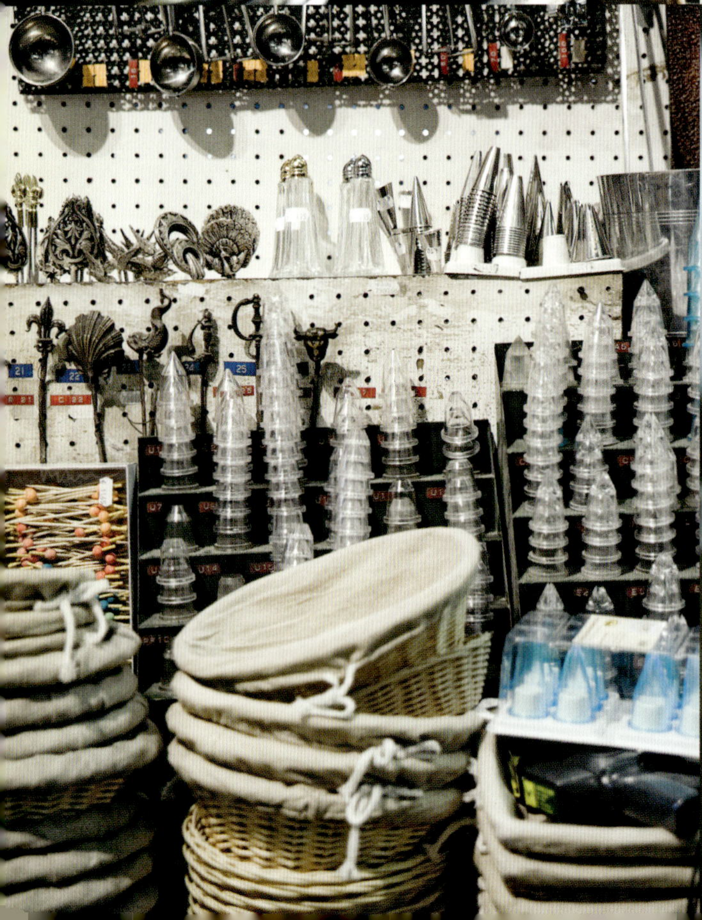
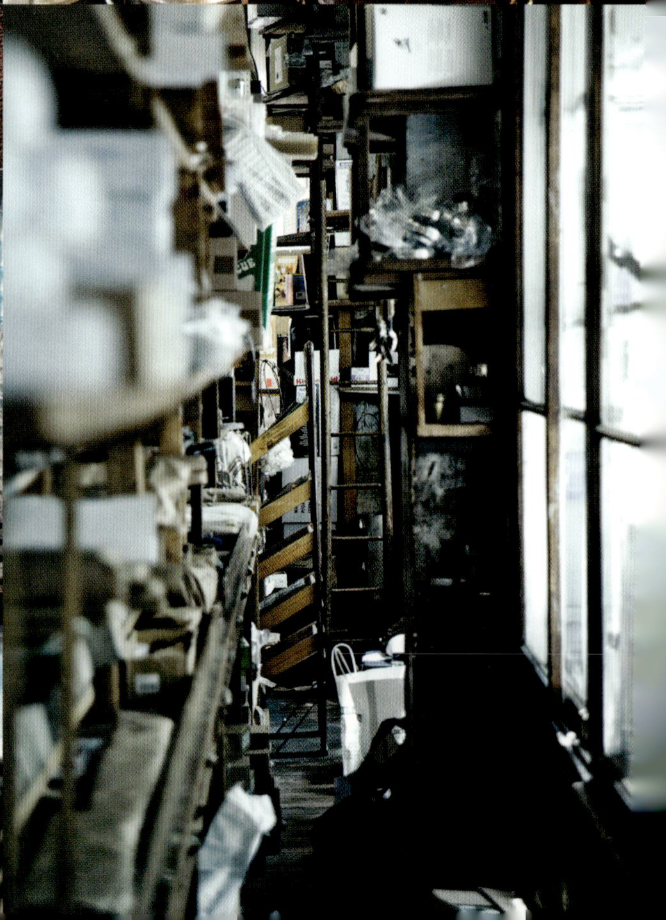

The old washed parquet floor squeaks under our feet. Entering behind us, a ray of sun bounces off the copper, stainless steel and tin saucepans. Floors above, floors below, kitchen utensils everywhere, for the kitchen and patisserie, couscous sieves stacked up so high up you need a mountaineering permit. The house is almost 200 years old; you can feel it in the care that has gone into the duck press and hâtelets, into the schoolchildren's grey pinafores, in the traditional style of domestic staff. For a beautiful copper preserving pan, this is the place to come.

DEHIL LERIN

J'aime Paris — WHERE THE WORLD MEETS PARIS

E. DEHILLERIN / 18 – 20 rue Coquillière / Paris I er

- 435

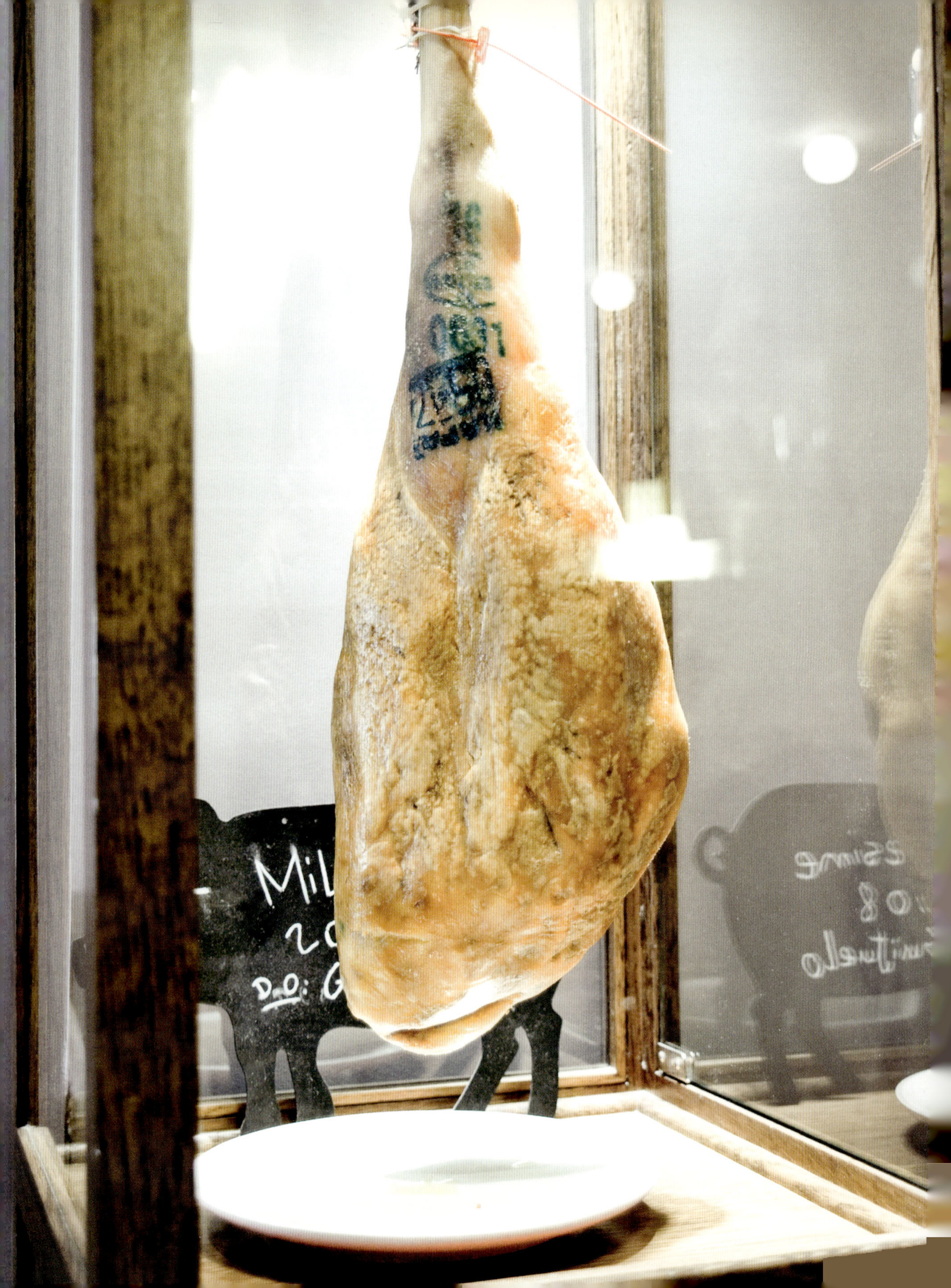

EL FOGÓN / 45 quai des Grands Augustins / Paris VIe

J'aime Paris

dictionnaire
Fogón-Français

EL FOGÓN

'El Temperador' is the name of the glass-fronted counter displaying hams. It is visible from every corner of the room. Your mouth begins to water even before the arrival of the garlic-almond gazpacho. Followed by 'a *banda sin banda*' rice, a gastronomic *pièce de résistance*. Alberto Herráiz has earned a star from the Red Guide. His cuisine, like his tables, holds many secrets.

J'aime Paris

WHERE THE WORLD MEETS PARIS

EL FOGÓN / 45 quai des Grands Augustins / Paris VIe

- 439

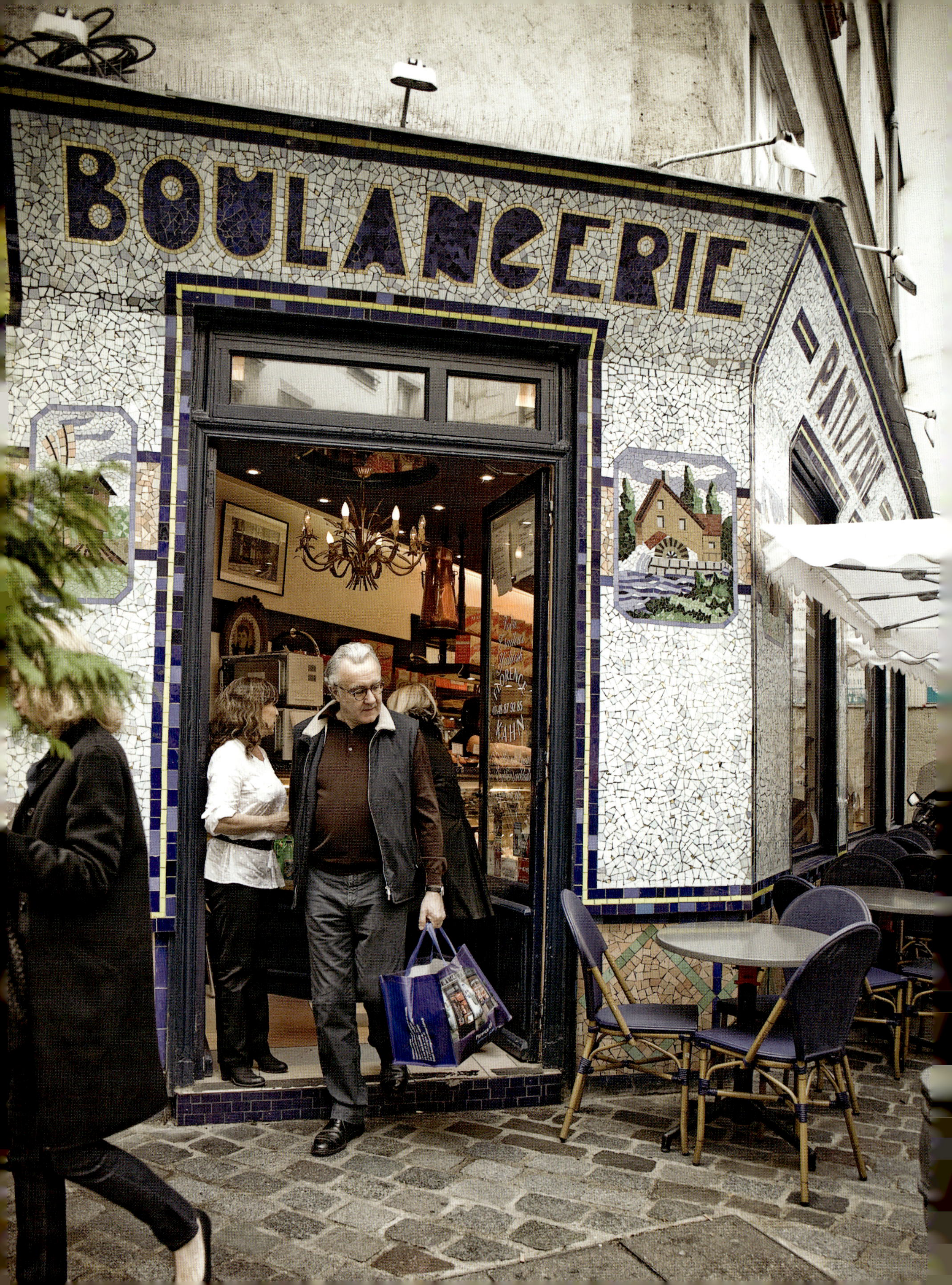
BOULANGERIE

FLORENCE KAHN / 24 rue des Ecouffes / Paris IVe

J'aime Paris

FLORENCE KAHN

With its blue and white mosaic tiles, this is one of the prettiest shop fronts in the Marais, or perhaps in the whole of Paris. Inside, Florence Kahn's delicatessen keeps the promises made by the facade, and more. Creative variations on chicken liver mousse and smoked fish, fine cooked meats. Succulent cheesecake, little onion breads still warm from the oven, just waiting to be stuffed. Generous sandwiches as an alternative to falafels. Of course, this is all homemade, prepared on the day, flavoursome. On the shelves, we find a packet of *ferfels*: handcrafted pasta twice-baked in the oven, which gives it its characteristic flavour; we'll try it that very night.

J'aime Paris

WHERE THE WORLD MEETS PARIS

FLORENCE KAHN / 24 rue des Ecouffes / Paris IVe

- 443

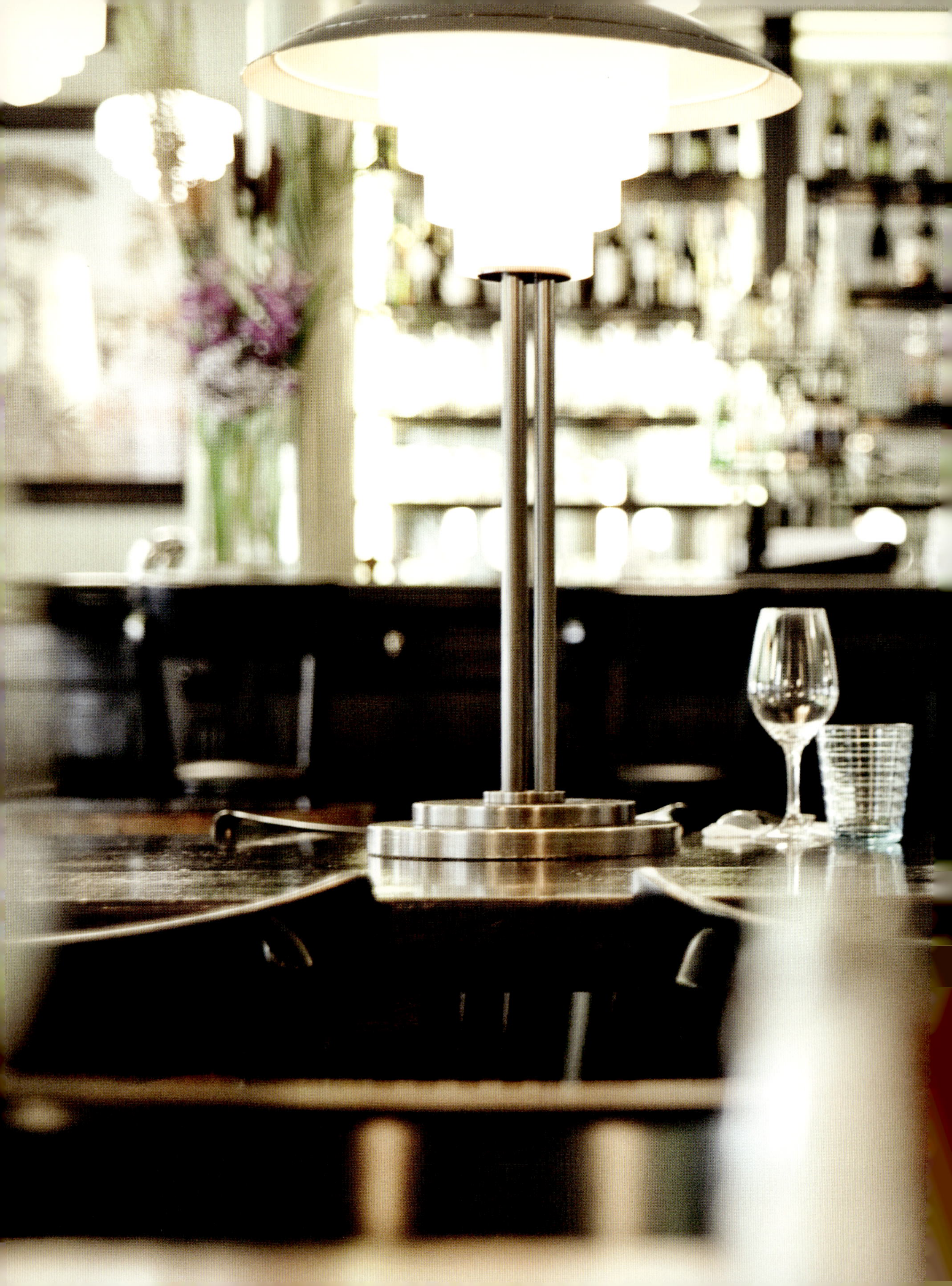

LA GAZZETTA / 29 rue de Cotte / Paris XII°

J'aime Paris

WHERE THE WORLD MEETS PARIS

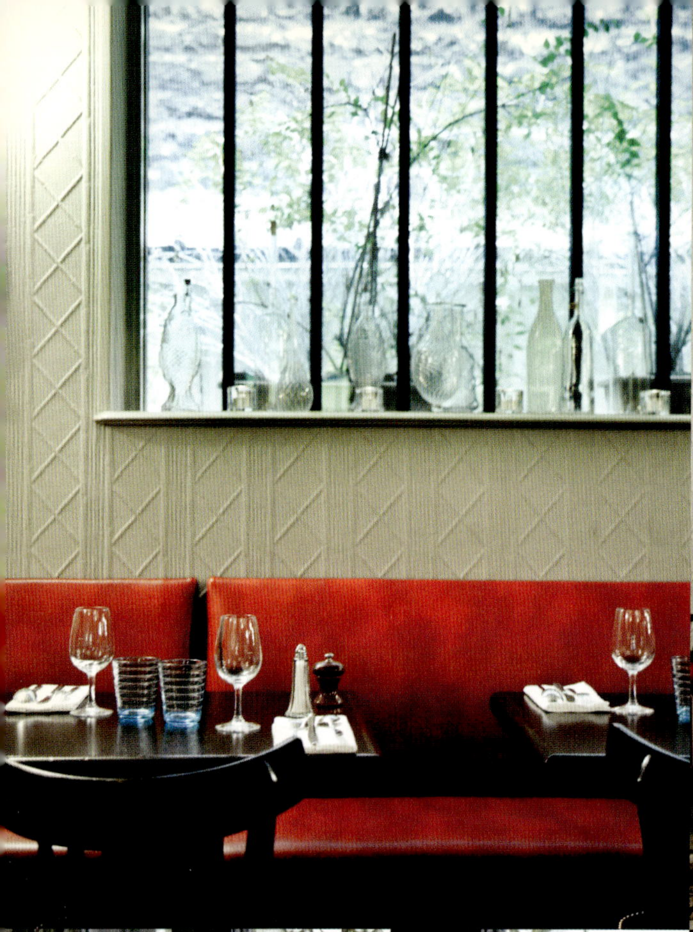
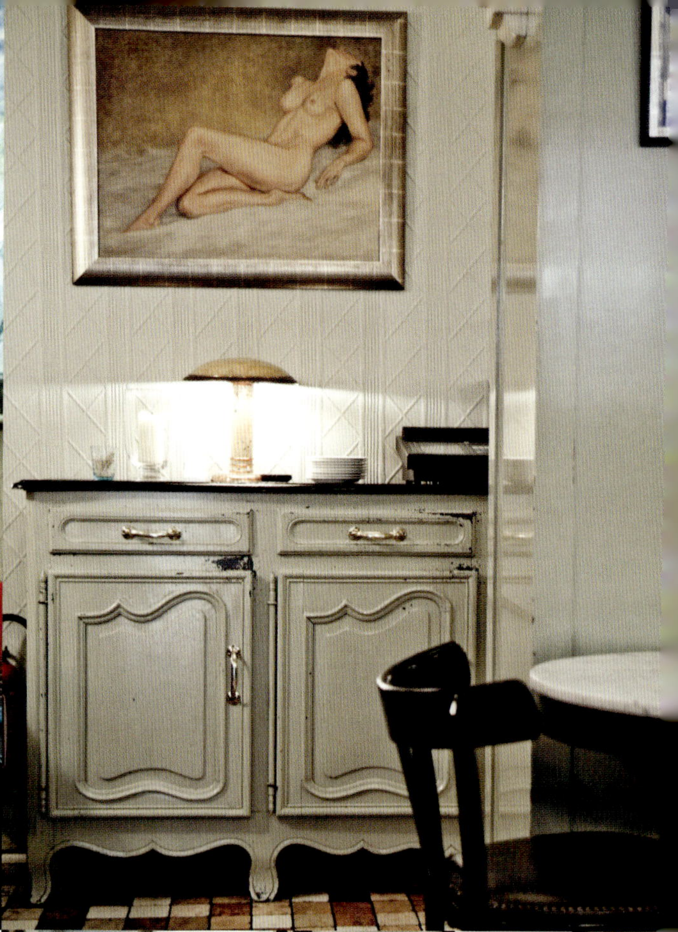
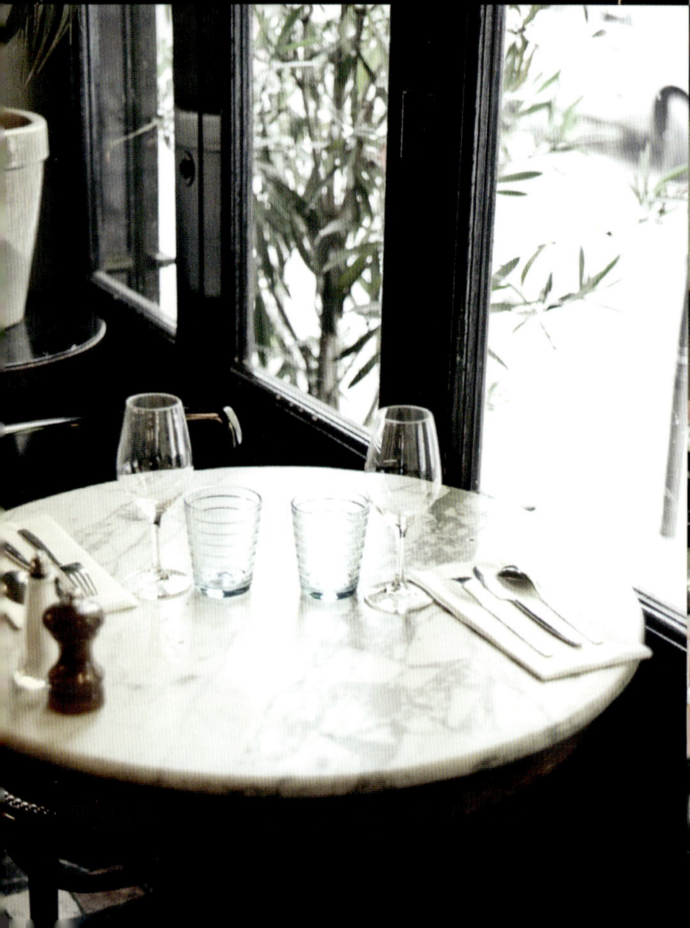
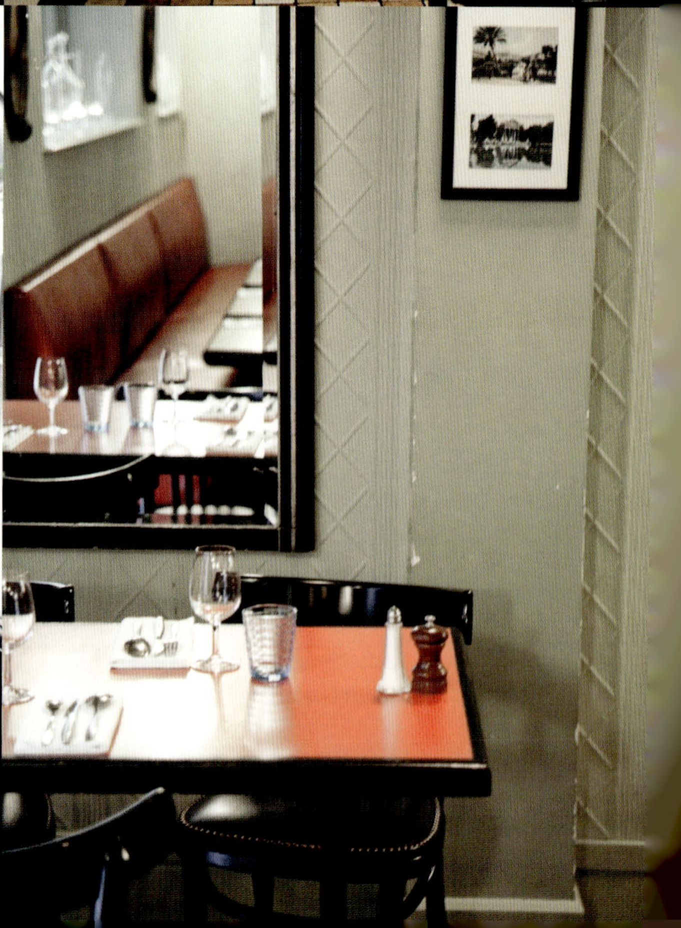

WHERE THE WORLD MEETS PARIS: J'aime Paris

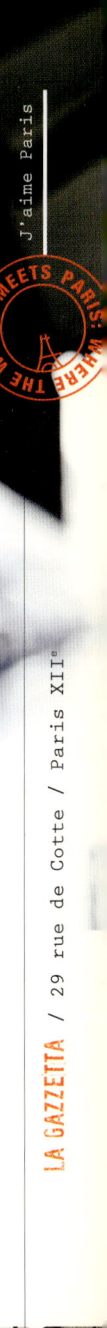

LA GAZZETTA / 29 rue de Cotte / Paris XIIe

GAZZETTA

This place is cosy-cosmopolitan, ideal for a lunch after returning from the market. Established and managed by the team of Le Fumoir, the restaurant has given chef Petter Nilsson, a Viking super-brilliant in heritage vegetables, carte blanche. Petter is an author, his universe unforgiving: *bonito tartare* and barbecued leeks, radishes and horseradish, celery braised with bay leaves, green tomato preserve, watercress and chanterelles...

PINOT NERO
PLOZNER
SAUVIGNON
CHARDONNAY
VISTORTA
Conte Brandolini D'ADDA
TREANNI
PINOT GRIGIO
Speri
SANT'URBANO

IDEA VINO / 88 avenue Parmentier / Paris XIe

IDEA VINO

'My mother doesn't like pasta. That's really unusual for an Italian.' Now Rita Pinna makes up for this. 'Italians always have a pot of pasta with tomato and basil on the stove. After that, you can invent and enrich.' And you can do so with exceptional products: capers from Pantelleria in Sicily, balsamic vinegar as good as a love potion, citrus oils. 'We always aim to find entertaining recipes for our guests. In summer, I use saffron-infused tagliatelle, garnished with scampi and orange zest, with a touch of *piment d'Espelette*,' explains Rita. This dish should be accompanied by a glass of white wine from the slopes of Etna, selected in a cellar that single-handedly succeeds in embodying Italian unity.

IDEA VINO / 88 avenue Parmentier / Paris XIe

IL CAMPIONISSIMO

Suggestions

× Pizza Alla Saerle 22€ : fond Pissaladière, lit de Roquette, sardines en filets marinées à la vénitienne.

× Pizza Stromboli 26€ : fond Comté & saumuré de fenouil, sardines en filets marinées à la vénitienne, et écorces d'oranges confites, baie Rose.

× Pizza Torino 22€ : fond mascarpone et gorgonzola, lit pomme fruit, Roquette, jambon de Parme.

× Pizza Trieste 11€ : Sauce tomate, Mozzarella, Roquette, jambon de Parme, copeaux de parmesan.

× Pizza Capri 15€ : huile d'olive, parmesan, Mozzarella, Ricotta et Épinard.

• Dessert 4,50€ Coupe de fraise, chantilly aux Agrumes (Maison)

'We could spend two months in search of the perfect balance of colour, crunchiness and softness for a pizza — sheer perfection! On top of that, our thing is the cooked and the raw. We often add raw ingredients to the pizza as soon as it comes out of the oven to add freshness, without spoiling the flavour. For example, we no longer cook the ham. But the pizza base depends on the quality of the dough, which means the ingredients and time. When I go into my lab to make a dough, I come out six hours later. There isn't just one recipe, there are a hundred. I am constantly in search of the perfect recipe. Even my wife tells me to stop, but our guests are happy, and that's my aim.'

Gino Jaskula Toniolo

WHERE THE WORLD MEETS PARIS: J'aime Paris

IL CAMPIONISSIMO / 98 rue de Montmartre / Paris IIe

SPECIALITES
AGGI
ENT A TOUT MENAGE
LU
BISCUITS
EFEVRE-UTILE
SUCHA

ISRAËL / 30 rue François Miron / Paris IV€

IZRAËL

Alain Ducasse: What is the product that is unique to your place?

Françoise Izraël: Well, just one of them is cumin... there is cumin and cumin. If you take mine... come, give me your hand, sniff and see. We have everything and nothing, if you want, you must come, smell, see! The curry, you know, is our own recipe. People are happy with it. Smell this pepper; it's wild! So is the vanilla — we are the only ones who bring it in from Tahiti.

AD: I see you also have fresh produce and cooked meats as well?

FI: Yes, of course. If it's good, it fits in here. That's our condition.

IZRAEL / 30 rue François Miron / Paris IVe

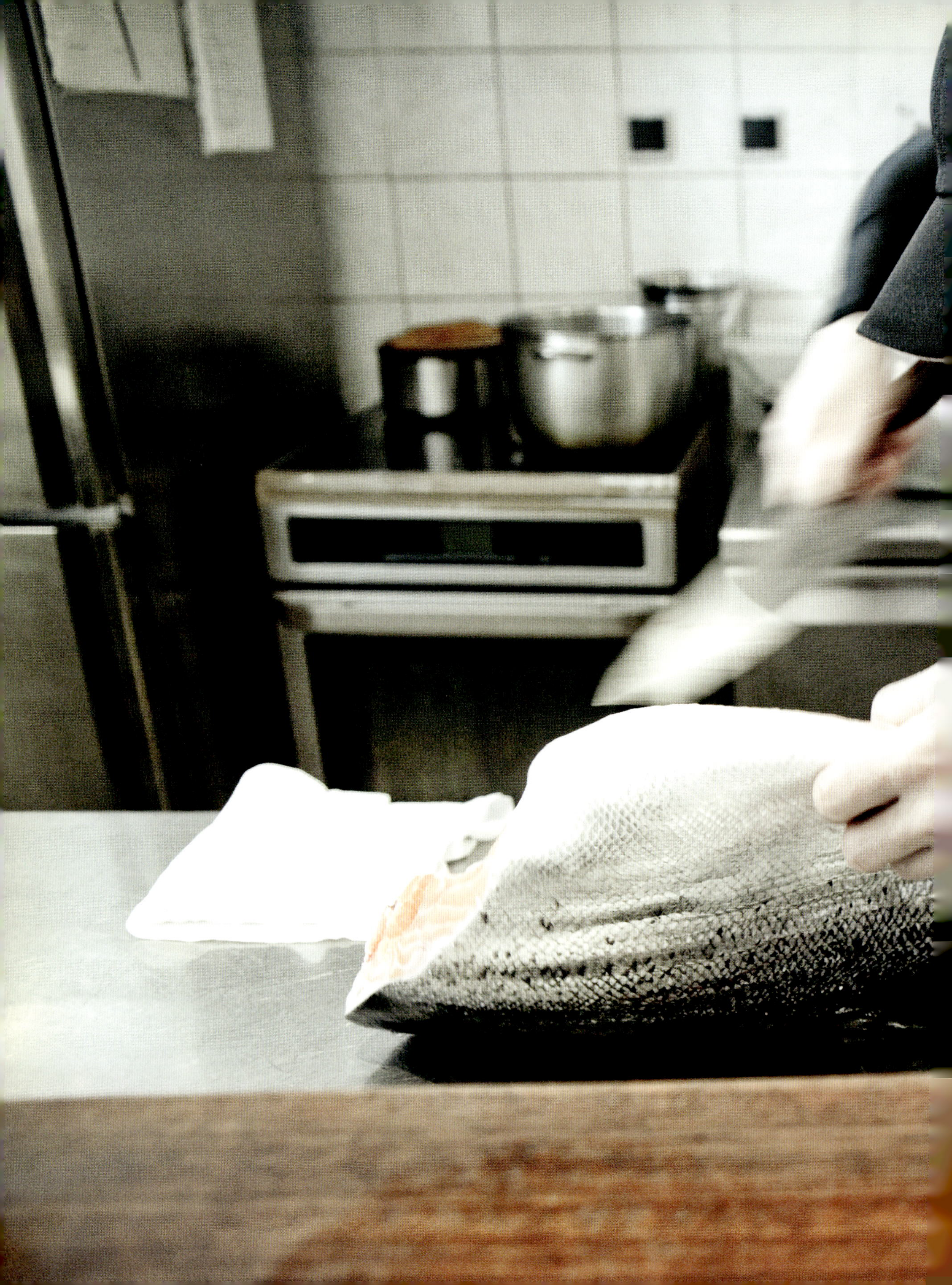

KAISEKI / 7 bis rue André Lefebvre / Paris XVᵉ

J'aime Paris

WHERE THE WORLD MEETS PARIS

KAI SE KI

'Takeuchi sensei' holds his breath. He gathers impetus. He throws himself on the salmon. Filleted in a few precise attacks. The knife flies and lands suddenly in a block of polystyrene. A fresh strawberry is puréed with the knife blade. Then a mango, an avocado, pineapple... Dye on his knife; a red, yellow and then green line appears on the mauve rice. He comes to a halt. We breathe and admire the unusual work of Hissa Takeuchi, master of 'dripping': beetroot juice coulis, the tinted lines of squid ink, trails of Matcha tea, cherry juice droplets, raw scallops in their shell, drizzled with olive oil and passion fruit pulp. This is just the beginning.

THE WORLD MEETS PARIS: WHERE J'aime Paris

KAISEKI / 7bis rue André Lefèbvre / Paris XVe

- 461

SPATULE HETRE
BOIS 350
Code article
MATFER
114114

004265
CUILLERE SILICONE 320MM
7,65 € HT

004152
SPATULE RACLETTE HETRE
300MM
2,30 € HT

MORA / 13 rue Montmartre / Paris Ier

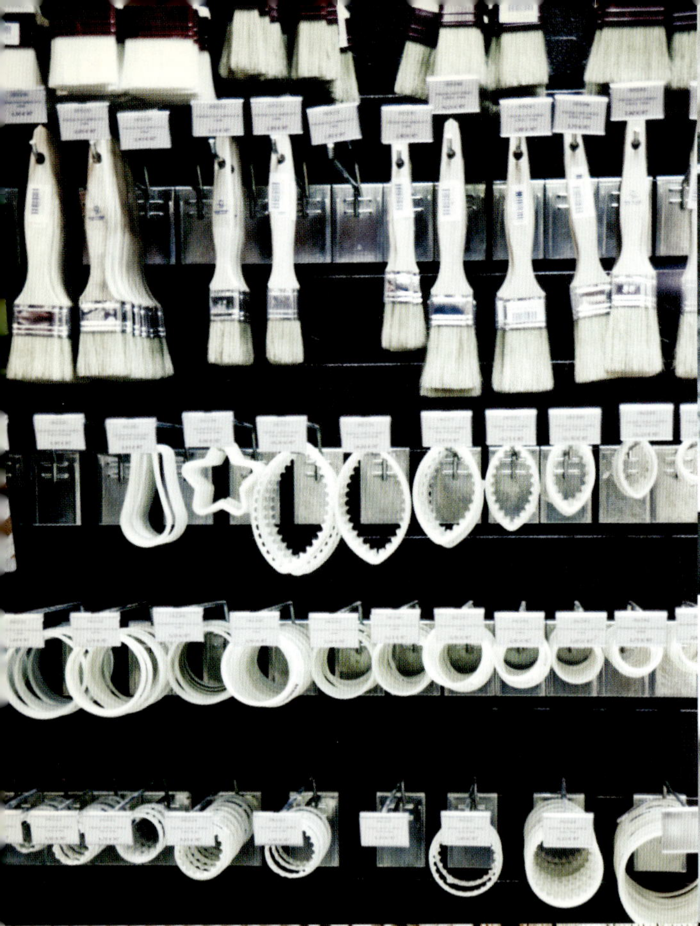
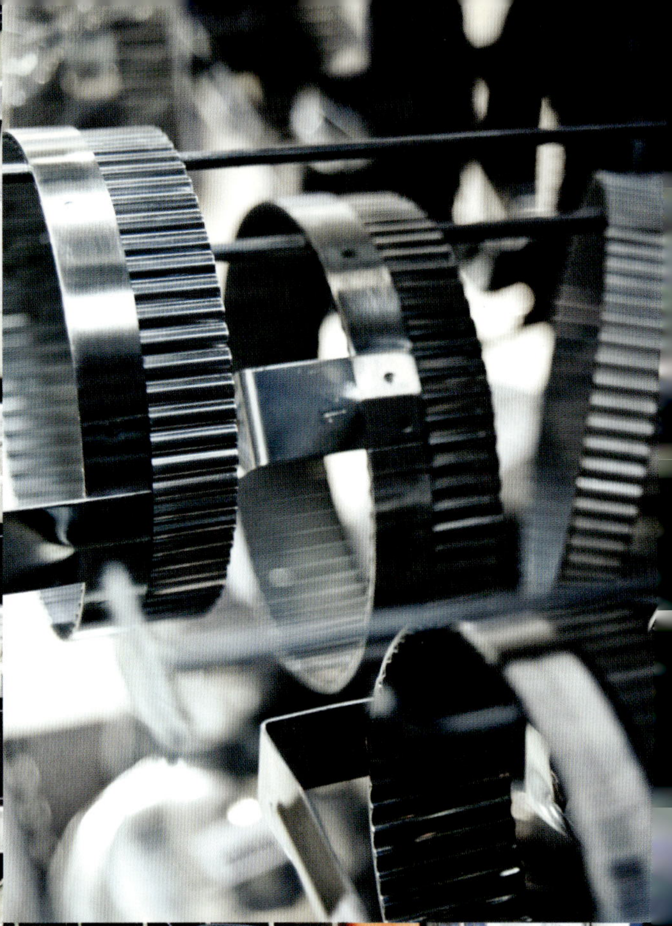
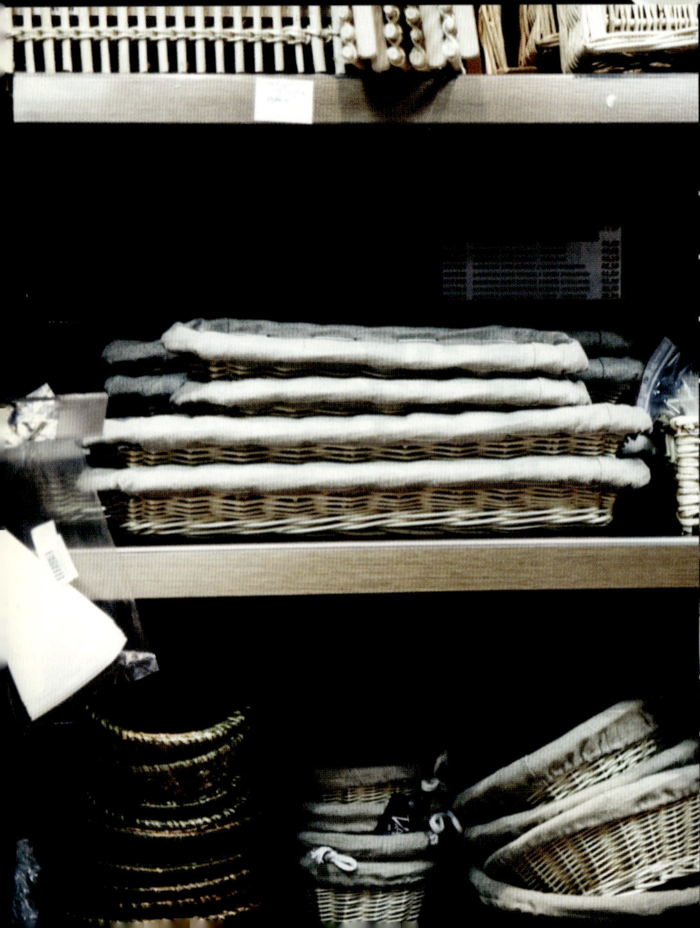
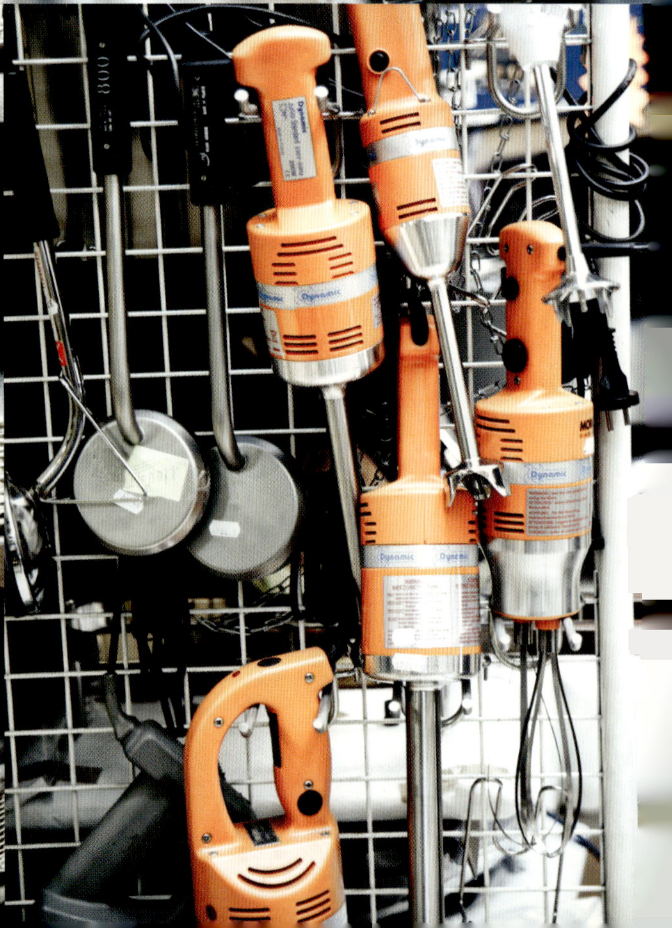
Dynamic

From Constantinople to St Petersburg, for just under two centuries Mora house has been supplying the world's top cooks and pastry chefs. It's simple: they have everything. From pink eggcups to the 'K5 Super' mixer with earth-shattering movement, valve-funnels, refractometers and the 'Sultan' decorating tube. For the impossible, they would probably ask for a few days' grace.

MORA / 13 rue Montmartre / Paris 1er

- 465

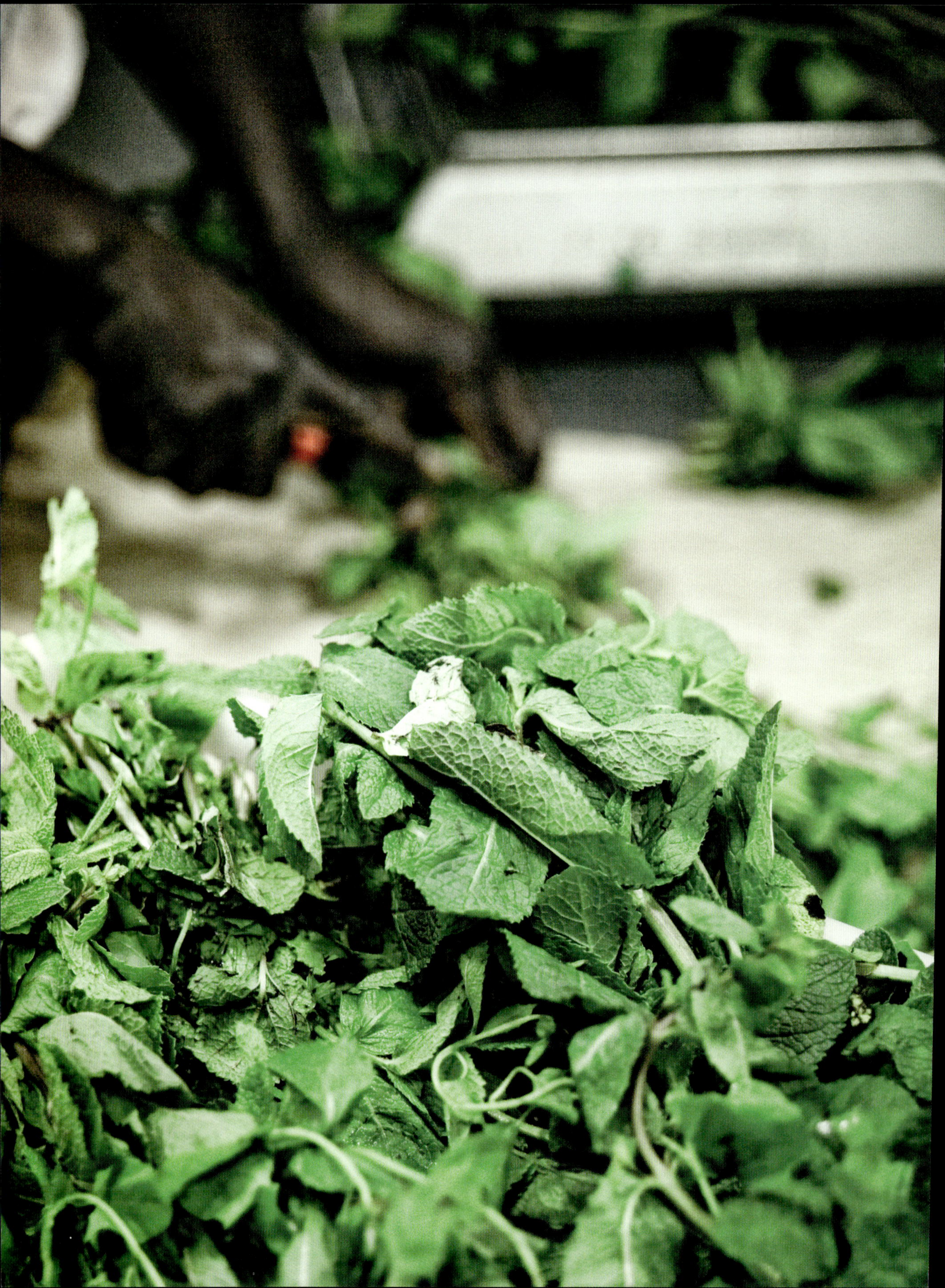

SOU QUAN / 35 place Maubert / Paris V^e

Mademoiselle

GOLDEN BUTTERFLY
RIZ LONG PARFUME
PRODUIT D'IMPORTATIO
EXTRA SUPER
POIDS NET 5

RED CHILLI
LONG TERM
THAILAND

SOU QUAN

You go down the little steps at Place Maubert. Lam will take you under his wing. He knows how to choose imported mangoes, ultra-fresh vegetables, lychees that are to perfume Pierre Hermé's *Ispahan*. Amid a wide variety of produce, you can sometimes find spicy soft fish roe (*maitenko*), so take advantage.

SUR LES QUAIS

The wooden shelves show off the little things that make us love to go 'to the quay'. A counter of sweets displayed in front of you, another a little further away also offering treasures... how can you resist? Let yourself go; there are no limits here. Start by trying a dried mandarin rind dusted in sugar. Nothing escapes the attention of Paul Vautrain, an aesthete who knows how to awaken your senses. Over here, an unbeatable quince paste cooked to perfection to accompany a flavoursome Manchego cheese. Over there, a pleiad of olive oils in cruets, sold by the litre self-service-style, providing delicate seasonings.

J'aime Paris

J'AIME PARIS: WHERE THE WORLD MEETS PARIS

SUR LES QUAIS / 7 place d'Aligre / Paris XIIe

la tête da

LA TÊTE DANS LES OLIVES / 2 rue Sainte Marthe / Paris Xe

LA TÊTE DANS LES OLIVES

Cédric Casanova: So, chef, what are you going to make from my olives?

Alain Ducasse: *Mamma mia*, they're very salty! I'll start by soaking them for 48 hours in fresh water. Afterwards, I'll add olive oil — but which one?

CC: Preferably the Bianca one. It's light and refined, with lemon aromas. In the large tin cruet.

AD: Good idea. Pass me the fennel seeds, in the basket over there, and the pink pepper.

CC: *Buon appetito!*

J'aime Paris

WHERE THE WORLD MEETS PARIS:

LA TÊTE DANS LES OLIVES / 2 rue Sainte Marthe / Paris Xᵉ

— 475

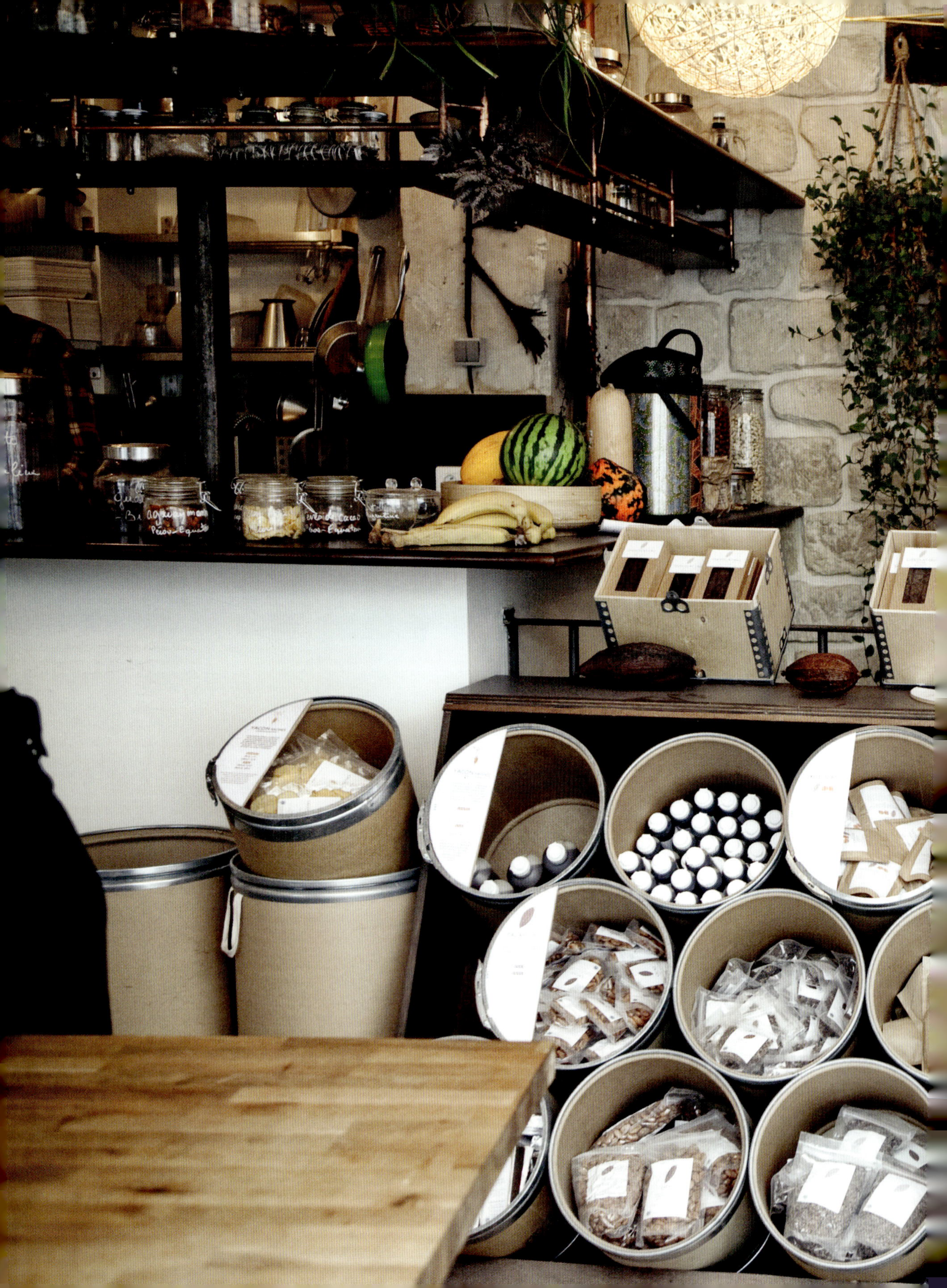

VOY, ALIMENTO AU BAR DES ARTISANS / 23 rue des Vinaigriers / Paris Xᵉ

J'aime Paris

THE WORLD MEETS PARIS

477

VOY ALI MEN TO

On the vegan Sunday brunch menu: blinis with almond purée and alfalfa bean sprouts, half-cooked, half-raw soup, banana-milk rice-lacuma-maca milkshake, the traditional *xocolatl* of the Aztecs, with cinnamon. Pascal, a dietician and druid from time to time, willingly introduces 'superfoods': Klamath seaweed to stimulate the brain, achiote as an antioxidant, aloe vera sliced from the leaf, and stevia and yacon syrup as sweeteners instead of sugar... At the same time, Jean-François goes to meet Parisians at the organic markets. You can shop there, eat on the premises and leave armed with the day's menu.

VOY. ALIMENTO AU BAR DES ARTISANS / 23 rue des Vinaigriers / Paris Xᵉ

J'aime Paris

THE WORLD MEETS PARIS: WHERE

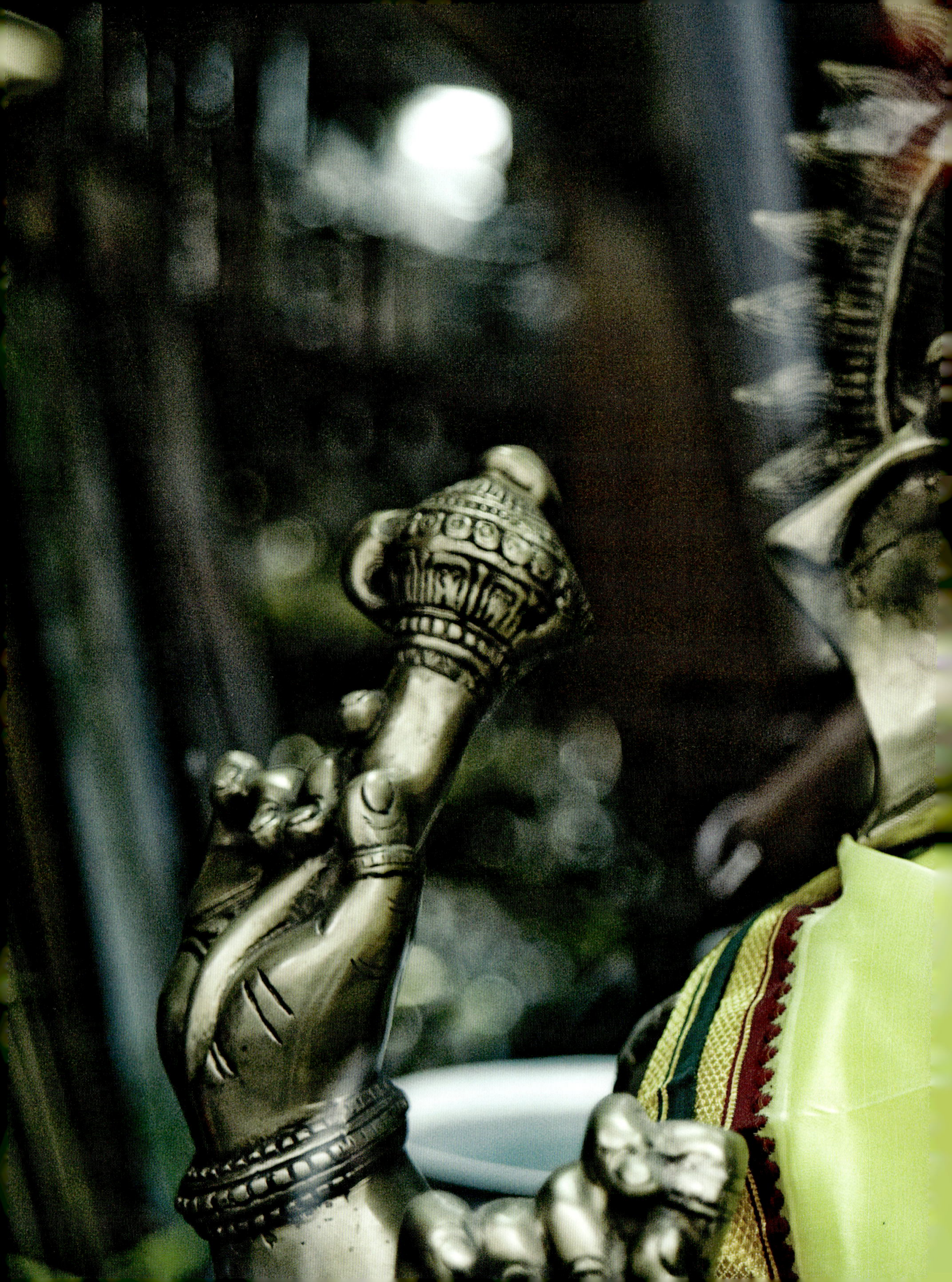

VT CASH & CARRY / 11–15 rue Cail / Paris X^e

J'aime Paris

WHERE THE WORLD MEETS PARIS

– 481

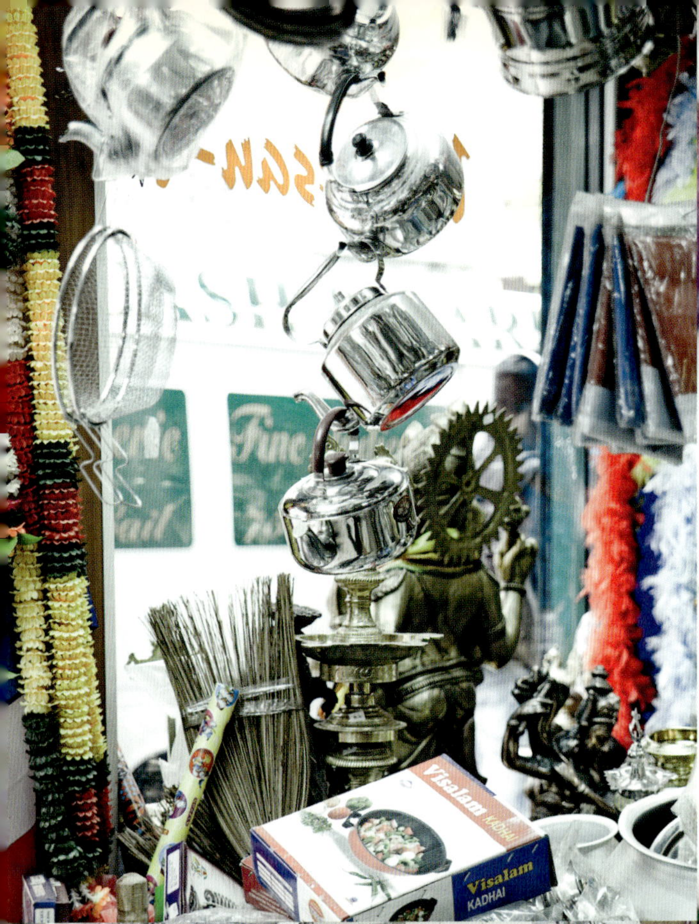
Visalam
Visalam
KADHAI

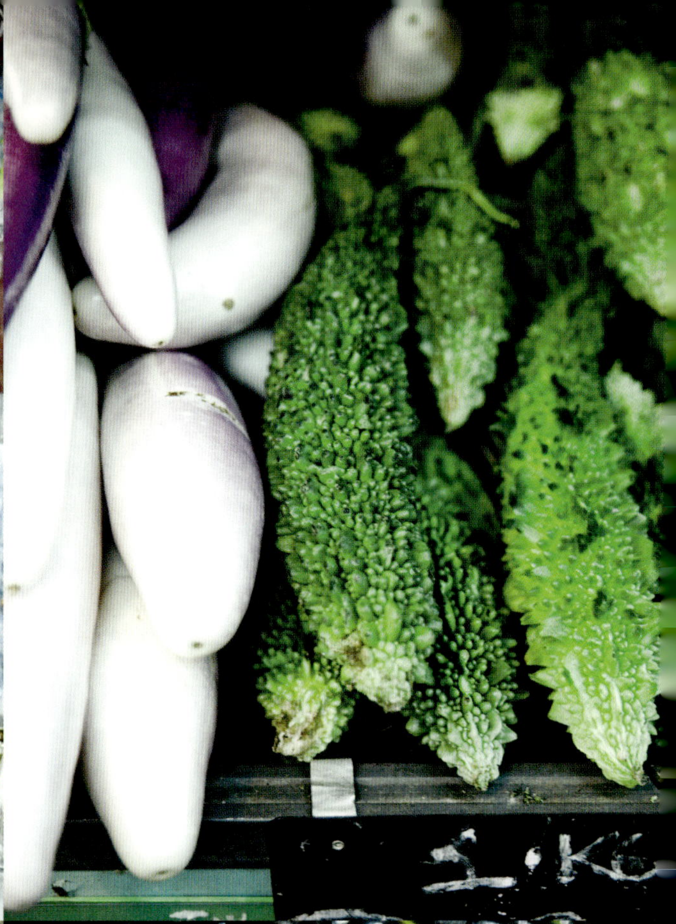

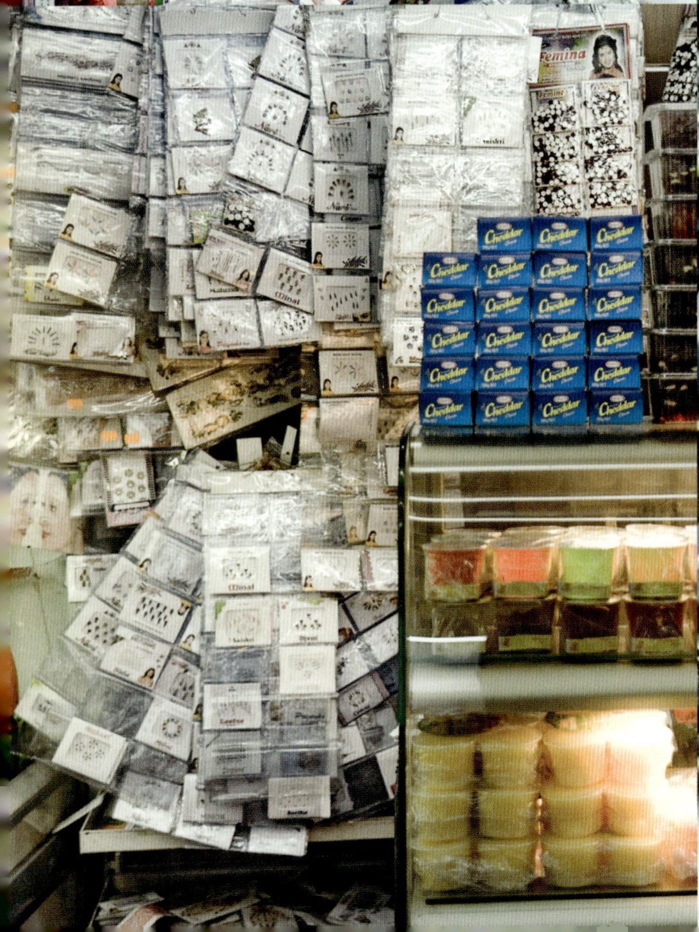
Femina
Cheddar

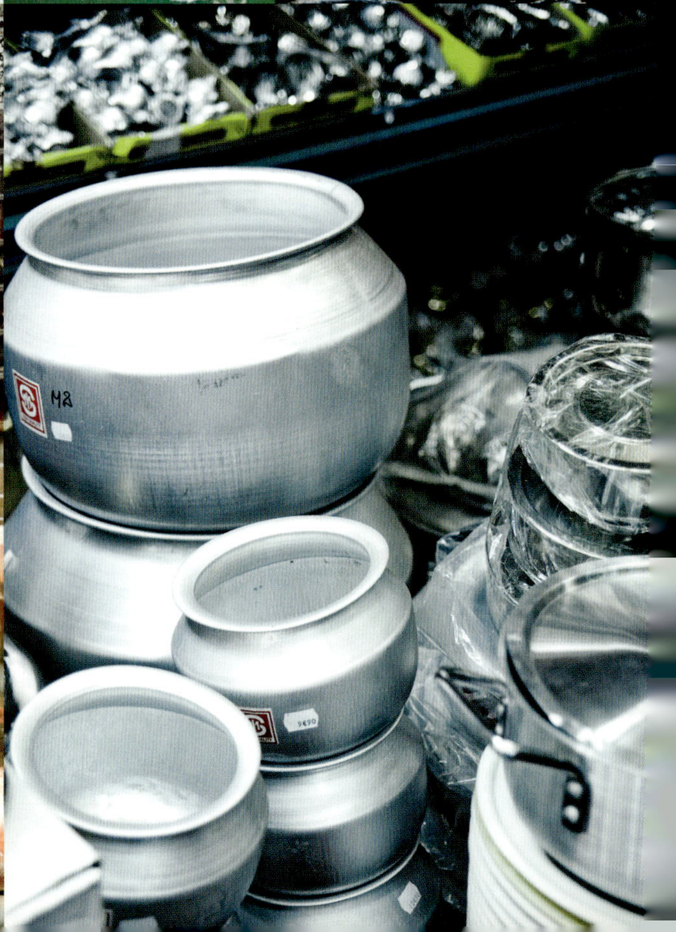

VT CASH & CARRY

To get your hands on cardamom, mustard seeds or green lentil flour essential for poppadoms, this Little India address is the place to go. Connoisseurs will fill their pockets with custard powder, packets of agar-agar and textured soy protein. Also offering a variety of spices — positively 'Bollyfoodian'!

J'aime Paris

THE WORLD MEETS PARIS:

VT CASH & CARRY, 11–15 Rue Cail, Paris

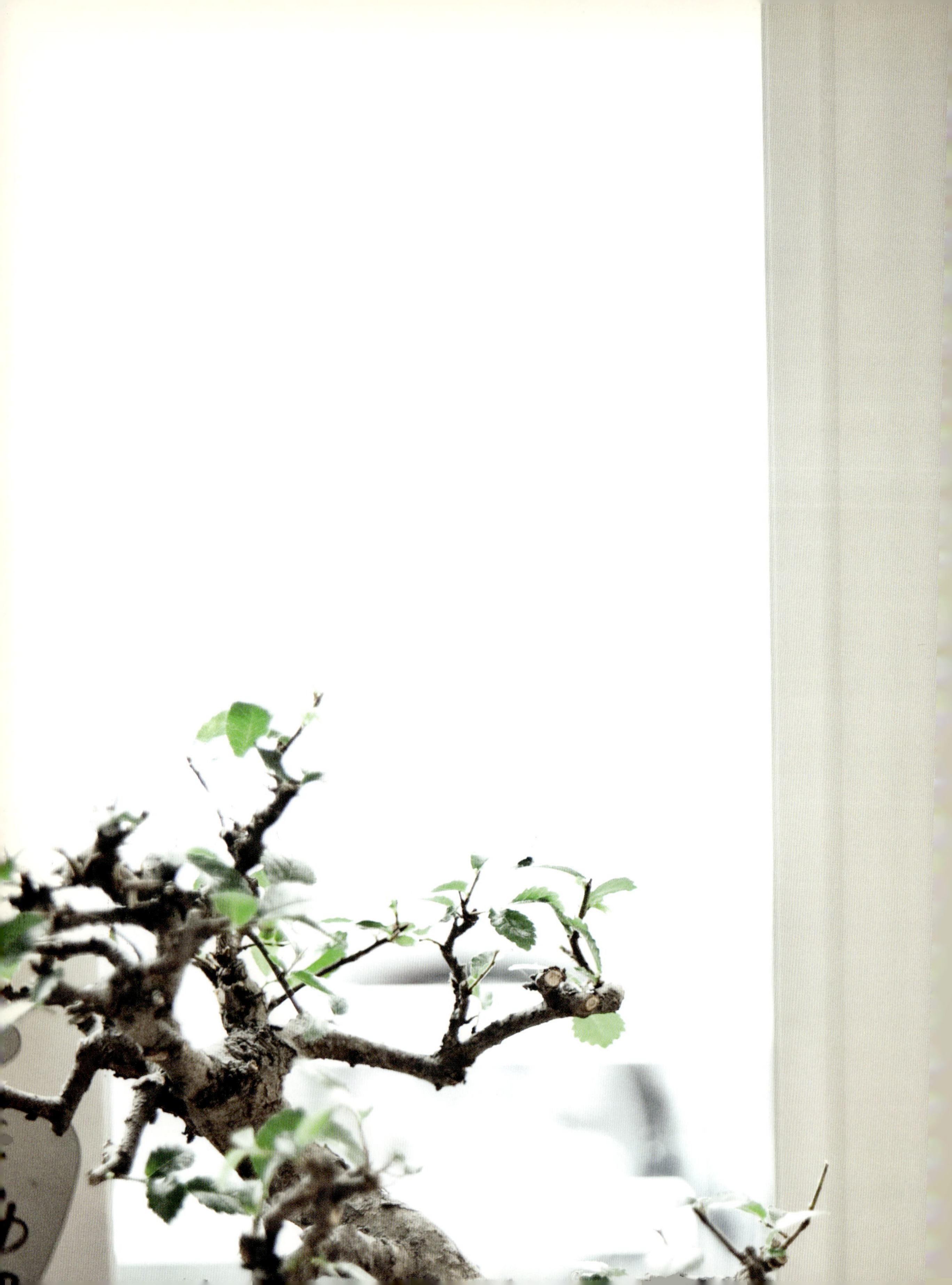

WORKSHOP ISSÉ / 11 rue Saint-Augustin / Paris IIe

WHERE THE WORLD MEETS PARIS

J'aime Paris

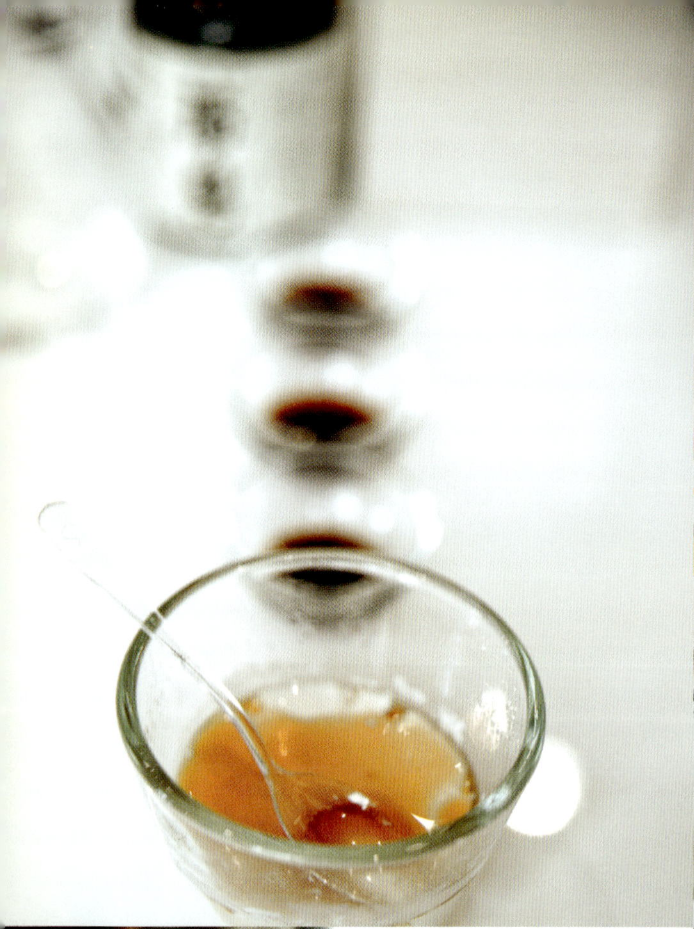

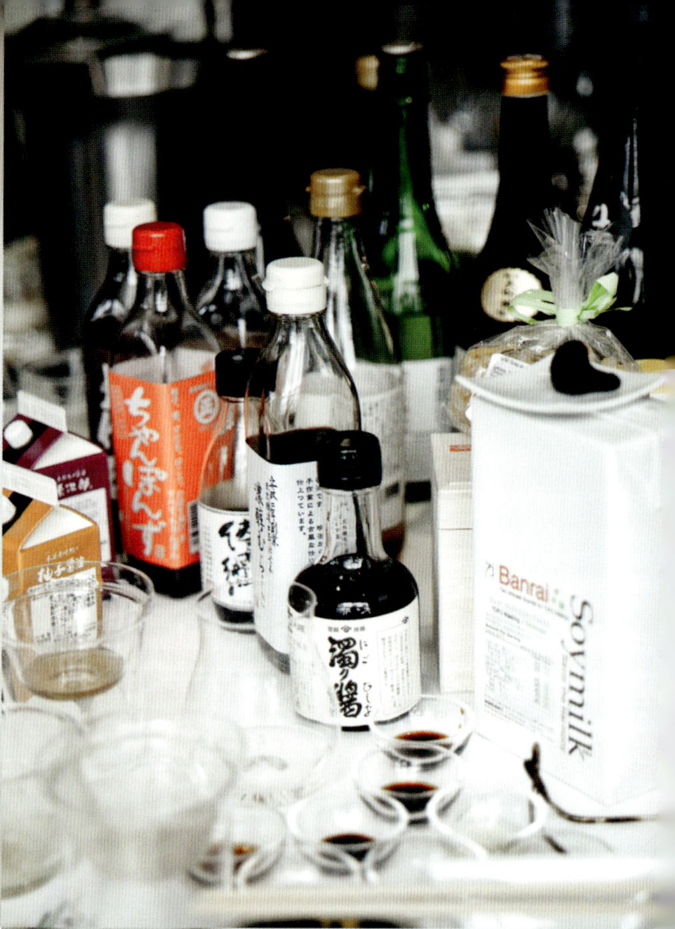
ちゃんぽんず
濁り醤
Banrai
Soymilk

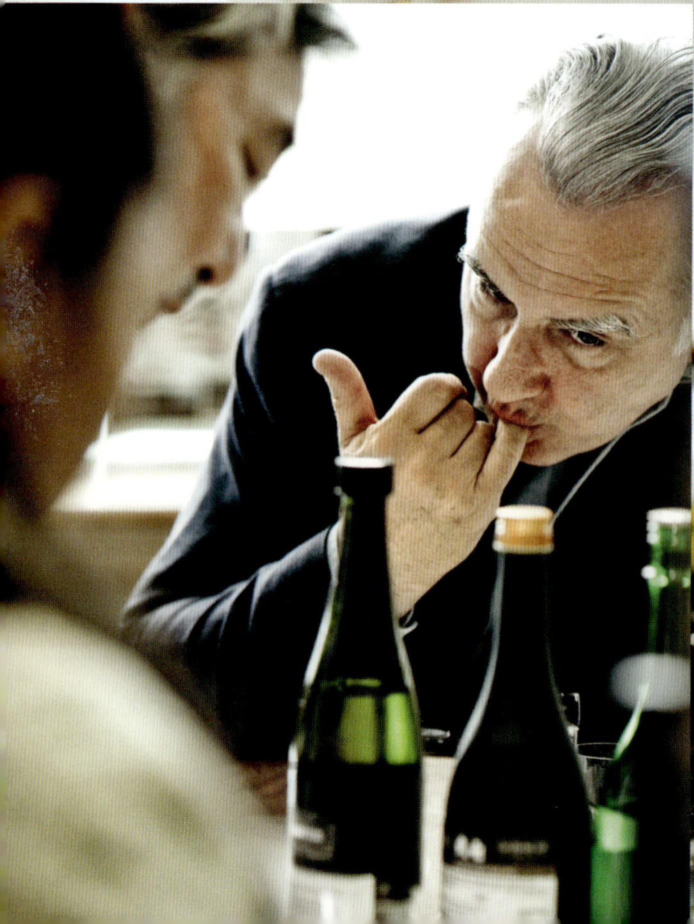

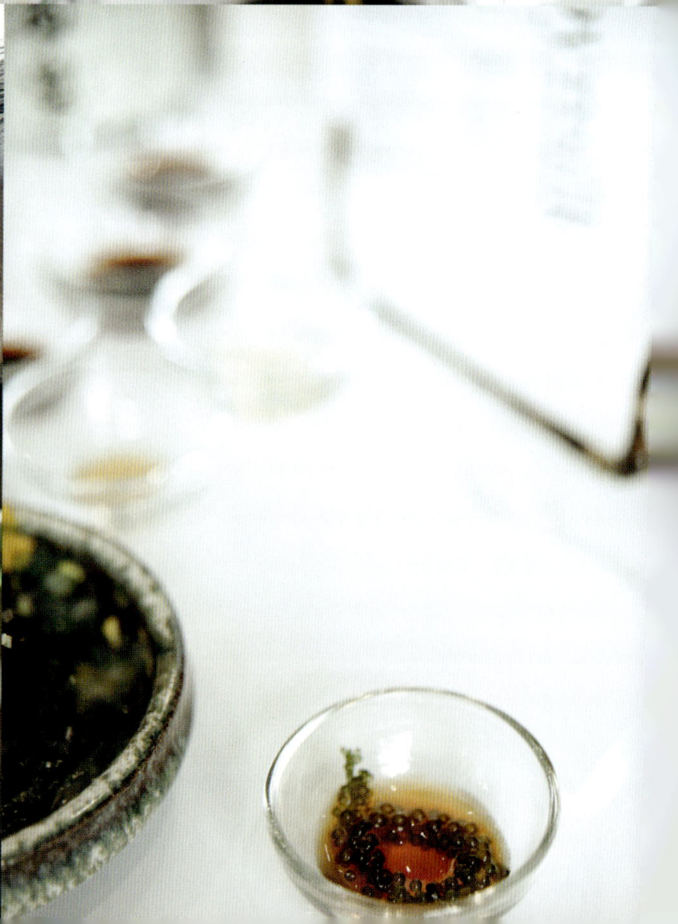

WORKSHOP ISSÉ

WORKSHOP ISSÉ / 11 rue Saint-Augustin // Paris IIe // J'aime Paris

Japanese sensations. Opalescent konnyaku spaghetti, lifted with a touch of super-fresh wasabi and light soy sauce. The delicacy of soya tofu, the explosive intensity of a mirin that's consumed like a liqueur. Magical miso, yuzu juice, incomparable soya milks. Master Toshiro Kuroda instructs on the top bouillons, everything about kombus, the complexity of soya. Even the dog, the temple's guardian, has a place among the porcelain and Senchô pepper tree bonsais.

- 487

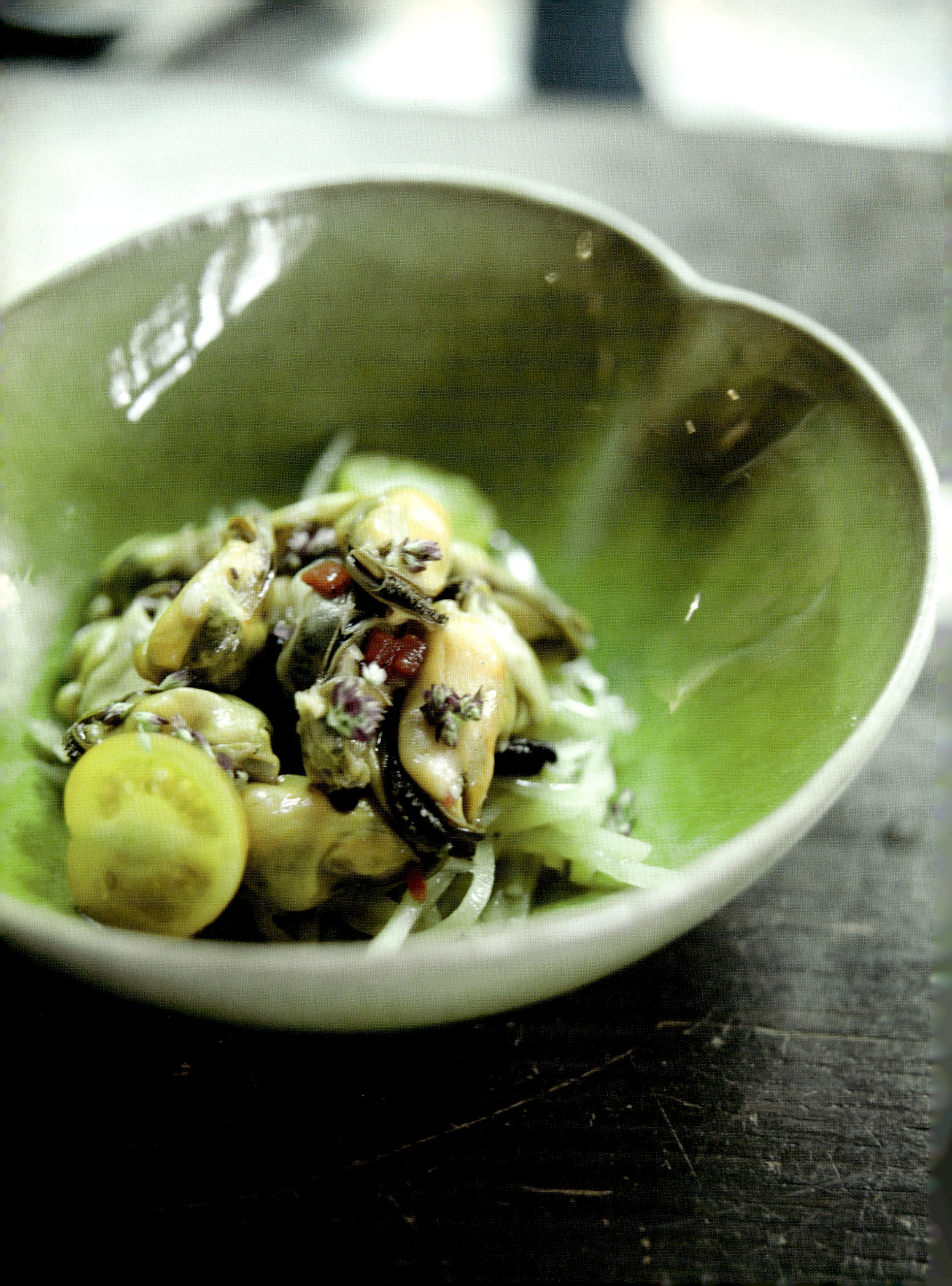

YAM'TCHA / 4 rue Sauval / Paris 1ᵉʳ

YAM' TCHA

Potatoes? Just like that, in the wok, 45 seconds, almost raw? The high priestess of the flame officiates, and the spud, prepared like green mango, is ennobled. Also transformed: steamed aubergines enhanced with fermented black beans, wedge clams in the wok, duck in all its guises. Sit at the bar for a bird's-eye view over the clever and skilful work of Adeline Grattard.

YAM'TCHA / 4 rue Sauval / Paris I[er]

J'aime Paris

WHERE THE WORLD MEETS PARIS:

- 491

ze kitchen
galerie
restauran

ZE KITCHEN GALERIE / 4 rue des Grands Augustins / Paris VIe

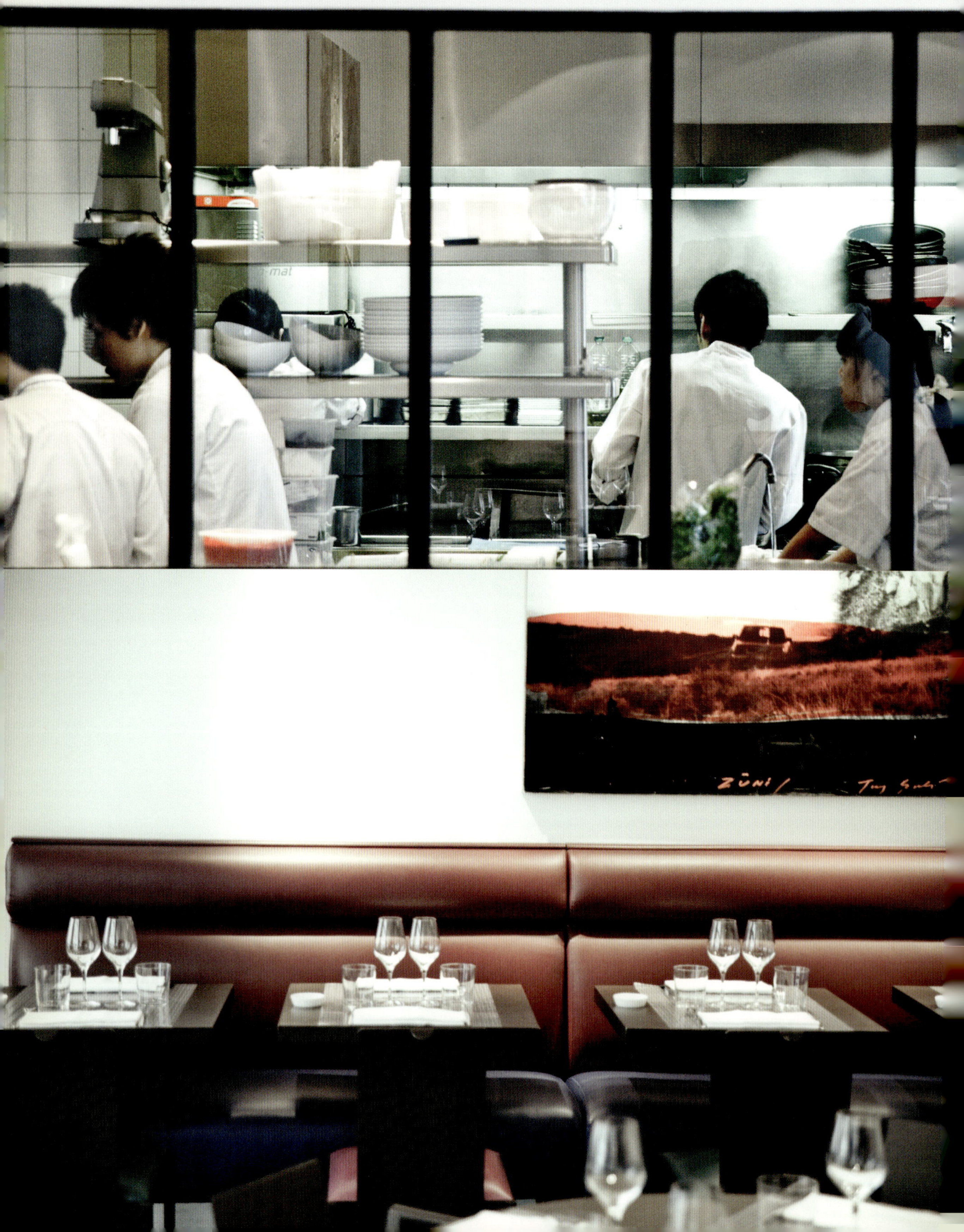
ZÜNI /

ZE KITCHEN GALERIE

'My definition of cuisine: freedom of expression. I function between different desires, moods, passions, discoveries, travels. My inquisitiveness is the source of the cuisine I prepare today, which is a reinterpretation of classic French dishes but one that is open to foreign influences. I am also privileged to work with fabulous market gardeners – Joël Thiébault and Asafumi Yamashita – my goldsmith market gardeners, each of whom, with their own sensibility, brings me vegetables of incredible freshness and taste. Both of them are located in the Parisian Basin. What they harvest in the morning is delivered to me at midday! I get on well with them: in fact, they're just like me, they feel and explore.'

William Ledeuil

ZE KITCHEN GALERIE / 4 rue des Grands Augustins / Paris VIe

J'aime Paris

Traiteur
Tél: 01 42 00 25 15
Formule
entrée plat
ou
plat dessert
17€90
entrée plat
dessert
21€90
Formule
midi
merci
Ticket

ZERDA CAFÉ / 15 rue René Boulanger / Paris X*

ZERDA CAFÉ

Jaffar Achour: Here's the sweet couscous, a recipe from Tlemcen, in the west of Algeria. It has the famous skinless and seedless dates. The crunchy inside is provided by Speculoos biscuits. And there's spice, cinnamon...

Alain Ducasse: I love distinguishing a hint of cinnamon, but I don't like to overly notice it. This is really delicately prepared.

JA: Here is the vegetable Berber couscous. You must oil the semolina as soon as it comes out of the steam — burning your hands in the process — otherwise it becomes oily. It's a spring couscous. On the side are finely sliced, crunchy onions.

AD: In fact, there is a whole range of different types of couscous...

JA: As far as we know, almost 450... We also prepare *berkoukes*, with larger rolled grains. It's prepared with or without meat. Here, we also serve it with shellfish.

AD: What a good idea!

ZERDA CÁFÉ / 15 rue René Boulanger / Paris Xe

PARIS: WHERE THE WORLD MEETS

I ALSO LOVE...

AMICI MIEI

44 rue Saint Sabin / Paris XIe

People don't go there only for the owner, an authentic Sardinian, but rather for the pizzas. The *à la rucola* option delights the regulars, some of whom are food critics whose offices are right next door. We also love their *pizza bianca* (thin, crispy base, drizzled with spicy olive oil and *fleur de sel*), to be shared with companions while you wait, as well as the *radicchio* (Treviso) option. And if you're not in the mood for pizza, sashay over to the seaside: the small fried fish are divine and the baby squid are to die for.

L'AS DU FALAFEL

34 rue des Rosiers / Paris IVe

Are they giving their falafels away? You'd almost think so, considering the queue that forms when it's close to eating time. Polite customers abound, even with staff seemingly detached from this world. Not a very exotic look - judging by the red canteen tray — but for nothing in this world would we go anywhere else. The crispness of their herb balls creates, for a minute, the illusion that we all have an Israeli grandmother. With a glass of lemonade — incredibly sweet, incredibly acidic — we're on holiday.

- 501

AUX COMPTOIRS DES INDES

50 rue de la Fontaine au Roi / Paris XIe

Even the little sauces — the minted green one, the strong yet delicate red one — are homemade. They showcase the care the chef takes in preparing his South Indian cuisine. The tenderness of lamb with almond and cashew nut cream steeped in its 45 different spices. The milky smoothness of a *kulfi*, a pistachio ice-cream with a hint of salt.

LE CHERCHE-MIDI

22 rue du Cherche Midi / Paris VIe

The antipasti of the house, fish of the day and carpaccios are of unquestionable freshness. They go hand in hand with remarkable olive oil and very good mozzarella. No pizzas, nor any combination of unusual products, just the produce prepared in a traditional way, with simplicity. You'll find a warm atmosphere in the small, tightly packed room, as well as a terrace, which is chock-full in good weather.

MARCHÉ DEJEAN

Rue Dejean / Paris XVIII°

Tilapia, thiof and capitaine — or even sinking your teeth into a barracuda? A live chicken or an agouti? Chewing on a golden cob — hot, corn, hot! — we let ourselves get carried away by the wafts of amazing aromas, the vibrant colours of the pepper stalls, the almost unimaginable look of a zebra-striped kettle. You bounce from one stall to the next — 'Dabou's market', 'Exotic Ivory', 'Abidjan is Great' — under the beams of the elevated section of the underground, you feel the urge to crack open a ginger beer.

FOYER VIETNAM

80 rue Monge / Paris V°

Fans of peace and quiet, sophistication and elegance might prefer to go somewhere else. In the Vietnamese Student Association's canteen, vegetables are eaten in deafening noise on outdated Formica tops. The cuisine is typically Vietnamese: beef *tung choy* salad or chicken salad with banana flowers, *pho* soup in stainless steel bowls, and famous *balut* (with a chick inside) — this, at least as much as the modest prices, ensures that word of the place spreads between generations of students.

- 503

GOUMANYAT

3 rue Charles François Dupuis / Paris IIIe

In 1809, the Thiercelin family established the first saffron-processing company in the world, at Pithiviers-en-Gâtinais, in an enceinte tower dating to the Middle Ages. Goumanyat is their Parisian outlet and Jean Thiercelin, master craftsman, represents the seventh generation. Ancient cabinets and jars contain a whole range of spices, among which the house blends of the Sultan and the Pharaoh. Oils and syrups are also found here, as well as Ayurvedic teas and granules for molecular gastronomy.

I GOLOSI

6 rue de la Grange Batelière / Paris IXe

The chef is Venetian, but not sectarian. His fish from Laguna and his risottos go hand in hand with Tuscan game and oxtail *à la romaine*. Wine by the glass is selected from a very sophisticated menu which gives the house its reputation, to accompany the dishes that change each week. All of the restaurant's products can be found at the deli next door. A place one never grows tired of.

IL VINO

13 boulevard de la Tour Maubourg / Paris VII⁰

On the menu, wines, nothing but wines! Choose your bottle, and Enrico Bernardo, top sommelier in the world, will serve you the food that best accompanies it. The maestro is a purist who has designed his own line of Schott Zwiesel glasses, and his Laguiole corkscrew. You will be guided through the 1500 labels from all corners of the world.

MICHELANGELO

3 rue André Barsacq / Paris XVIII⁰

Every morning, under the shade of the Montmartre cable car, Michelangelo Riina, a straightforward Sicilian, goes to the market and composes the menu. Every evening, he — alone — paces up and down the few centimetres that separate the open kitchen from his 15 or so guests. Between his hands, Sicilian cuisine bursts with flavours and colours, like his Gorgonzola *arancini*. Imagination, too, such as his giant prawn and pistachio tagliatelle. A well-mastered and modern Mediterranean experience.

MOUSSA L'AFRICAIN

25—27 avenue Corentin Cariou/ Paris XIX⁰

For some, Paris-Dakar means jeeps roaring through the dunes. For gourmets, it's more likely a *yassa* chicken. Or a *tiep*, a traditional Senegalese dish, or an *ndolé*, a Cameroonian bitterleaf stew — the heart wavers. Alexandre Bella Ola, Cameroonian chef-cook, invites you on a trip through darkest Africa. To start off, Malian, Ivorian, Senegalese and Cameroonian specialities, accompanied by delicious piping-hot plantain banana fritters.

BOULANGERIE MURCIANO

14 rue des Rosiers / Paris IV⁰

The Murciano bakery—patisserie lies in rue des Rosiers, in the heart of the traditional Jewish quarter of Paris. People go there to buy *challah*, the famous plaited bread, made with poppy seeds or raisins. The 'plain' one is ideal for endlessly soaking up *molokheya*, a type of ragout made from Kerria powder, an aromatic herb with a spinach-like taste. The apple strudel is delicately flavoured with cinnamon; it makes you want to sink your teeth into it. Everything here is kosher.

NON SOLO CUCINA

135 rue du Ranelagh / Paris XVIe

You imagine yourself in Sicily here, with the chef as guide. Today, it's sautéed mussels and clam chowder, followed by spaghetti with sardines and wild fennel, the whole dish washed down with a full-bodied Sicilian wine. For dessert, you indulge in the amazing sweet courgette tart or the delicious cannoli with sweetened ricotta. Everything begs to be tasted and you return without any arm-twisting. It's hearty, it's cheerful, it's good.

NON SOLO PASTA

50 rue du Ruisseau / Paris XVIII[e]

You'll find a family ambiance at this quarter's canteen-dinette-caterer. Light wood tabletops, a welcoming smile, lunch during the week, dinner at the weekend. Francesco offers authentic Italian cuisine: *penne all'arrabbiata* and *fusilli alla matriciana*, tuna and tomato *galletti* that melt in the mouth, delicately flavoured with lightly spiced virgin olive oil. Try the *panna cotta* served with caramel. The Nutella mousse is just the thing to accompany a *ristretto*.

LA NOUVELLE MER DE CHINE

159 rue du Château des Rentiers / Paris XIII⁰

Brave the less than attractive street and the wind that gusts in. As if on the shores of the China Sea, a light, subtle cuisine is being prepared. Melting prawn fritters, crunchy at first, then juicy, with a delicate lemon-garlic-salt-pepper sauce in perfect harmony; green apple salad prepared in julienne strips like a papaya; duck's tongue, salted and peppered; chicken cooked at low temperature or lemon duck. The large, calm plates are at the mercy of a gentle breeze.

PAKKAI

71 avenue d'Ivry / Paris XIII⁰

Absolutely... frozen foods! This most demanding Asian mama is not afraid to make use of them herself, because it's not always possible to go to Singapore in search of soft-shell crab during the three weeks of its moulting. At Pakkai, you'll find a wide range of fish and shellfish, as well as steamy mouthfuls as good as any you'd get from the quarter's main rivals. A variety of Thai dishes which are a dream come true for every single time-pressed person. Free tastings on Sundays.

CHARCUTERIE PANZER

26 rue des Rosiers / Paris IV⁰

The shop window greets us with the sight of famous Cracow sausages. They have the same smile as Mr Panzer junior. Obviously, everything is kosher, from the Tunisian salami to the duck foie gras and cured saucisson. Self-restraint is needed not to plunge a hand into the barrel of dill gherkins. You'll find yourself inspired by the beef jerky carpaccio, calf's shoulder in herbs and spices, pickled pork tongue and paprika turkey, making up an English platter with an Ashkenazi influence.

PARIS STORE

44 avenue d'Ivry / Paris XIII⁰

One of the largest Asian supermarkets in the capital. Here you'll discover what delights the connoisseurs and takes the aspirant novice by surprise: century eggs, lemongrass sausages, banana leaves, liquorice-infused prunes... a large fresh-food department, dragon- and sugar-apple fruit, Thai basil and bitter gourds. Amusing legumes and cereals, such as brown rice that turns to a lilac colour on cooking. Modest prices, but sometimes an unnerving choice — it's wise to know what you've come to seek out.

PHO DŌNG HUŌNG

14 rue Louis Bonnet / Paris XIe

The ideal would be to have a huge paper serviette for a more comfortable tasting experience. As soon as you're seated, the waiter brings a mysterious-looking brown and creamy sauce to the table, with a plate of extremely fresh herbs and spices. If you're a beginner, do what the person sitting next to you does — dip the crunchy soya bean sprouts in the sauce. As simple as that! Pho Dong Huong is a legendary family-run Vietnamese temple. Special mention goes to the frittered crêpe and the *bo bun cha gio*.

PHO TAI

13 rue Philibert Lucot / Paris XIIIe

The goddess of delicacy, who has descended to earth to seduce men, knows where to get her supply of ammunition. Divine spring rolls with slightly warmed beef, melt-in-the-mouth grilled chicken just like in Hanoi — huge portions and subtle flavourings are served with a crafty smile. In his previous establishment in rue de Longchamp, chef Te Ve Pin, the man who made the very first *pho* soup in Paris, earned himself the nickname 'the Chinese Robuchon'. Today, his menu offers the same prices as the neighbouring greasy spoons. The bargain of the century.

PICCOLA TOSCANA

10 rue Rochambeau / Paris IX°

You push open the deli's door and, just like in Florence, you order a *tramezzino alla porchetta* — a roast suckling pig sandwich. While it's being prepared, immerse yourself in the refined pecorinos or the Margherita *panforte*, a Siennese nougat with candied citrus fruit. Let yourself be tempted by the communal table for dining guests and the little terrace, for a plate of truffled pasta.

LA RÉGINETTE

Galerie 66 / 49 rue de Ponthieu / Paris VIII°

A jam-packed canteen at Régine's — it closes when Paris starts waking up and is run by Nathalie Bénézeth and her younger brother Alexis. Inside, it's like a Streamline yacht. What light, crispy dough! The pizza man is a master craftsman, putting on a show; throwing the dough up towards the ceiling and catching it in midair, just centimetres above your head! There's even a mini Nutella pizzetta — don't even think about denying yourself dessert.

RINO

46 rue Trousseau / Paris XIe

Giovanni Passerini was Petter Nilsson's sous-chef at La Gazzetta. Prior to that, he dabbled at L'Arpège and was Chateaubriand's meat slicer. He spread his wings in a micro bistro where you only see the kitchen — tomato red — and plates. Italian influences are evident in the pearl barley risotto with orange preserve or the pear *baba* with ricotta; instinct and market freshness in the yellow pollock with green cabbage and hazelnuts or hake with Swiss chard and olive oil. It's what we call an authentic kitchen.

SARDEGNA A TAVÓLA

1 rue de Cotte / Paris XII⁰

We're sort of looking out for the pickpockets and the idyllic beach. That's the only thing missing, otherwise we'd be in Sardinia. Dionysian pastas, shellfish prepared with precision, a fresh take on classics such as tripe with beans, and a semi-tyrannical, semi-benevolent host. King crab claws served on a board with rocket — we'd even eat them off the bald head of a mafioso! Everything takes place in the shade of melancholic hams — we're captivated by the experience.

LE STRESA

7 rue Chambiges / Paris VIII⁰

Cuisine originating from all corners of Italy: Roman artichokes, truffles from Alba, Venetian veal with onions, *parmigiana* asparagus. The mini pizzas are enjoyed by the mini mafiosi who find themselves among connoisseurs. People also come to the Stresa's pretty terrace for the three sculptures of Cesar and the hope of dining in the shadow of some celebrity, surrounded by a décor of red velour which has retained its 1950s charm.

PARIS, SWEET PARIS

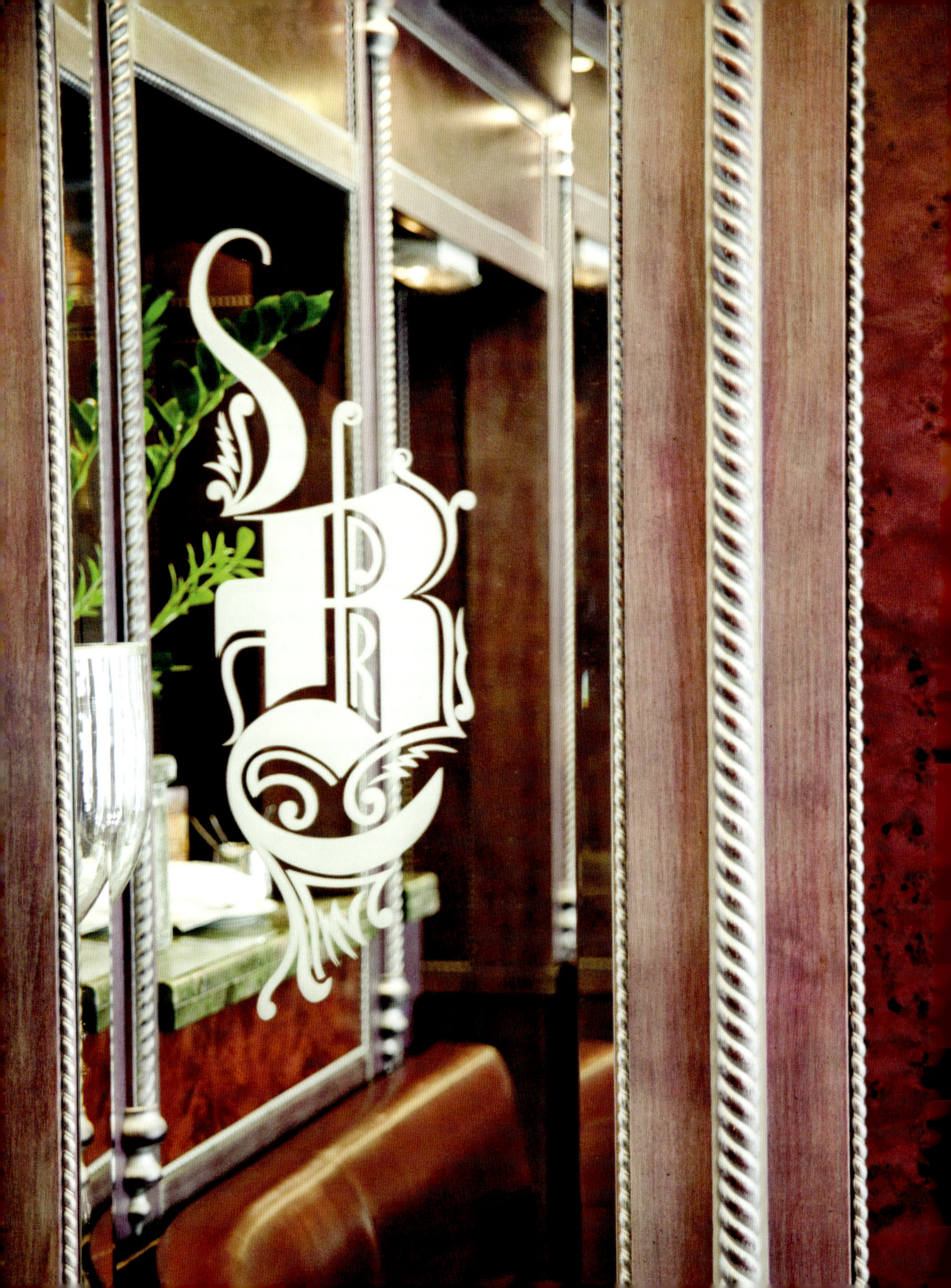

PARIS, SWEET PARIS

J'aime Paris

GLACIER BERTHILLON / 29-31 rue Saint-Louis en l'île / Paris IVe

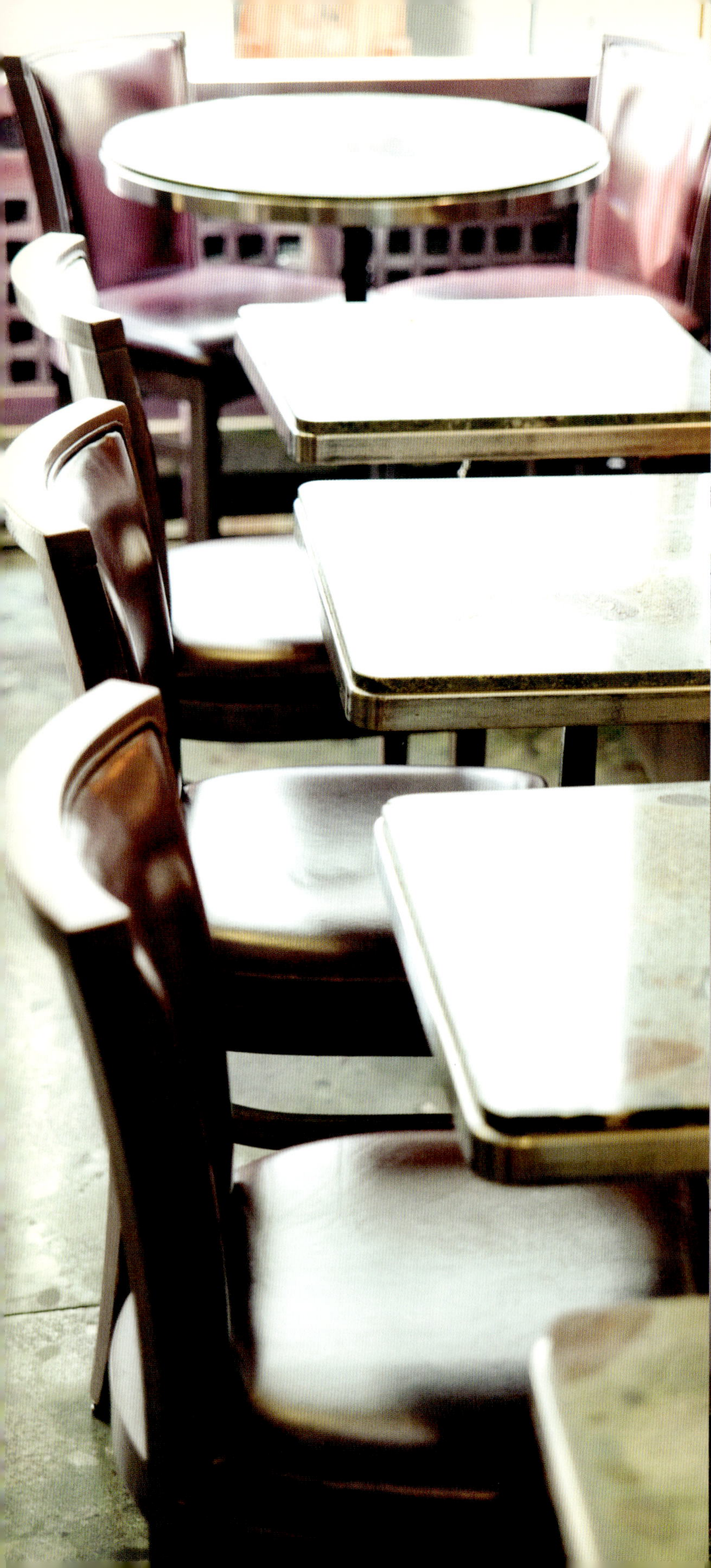

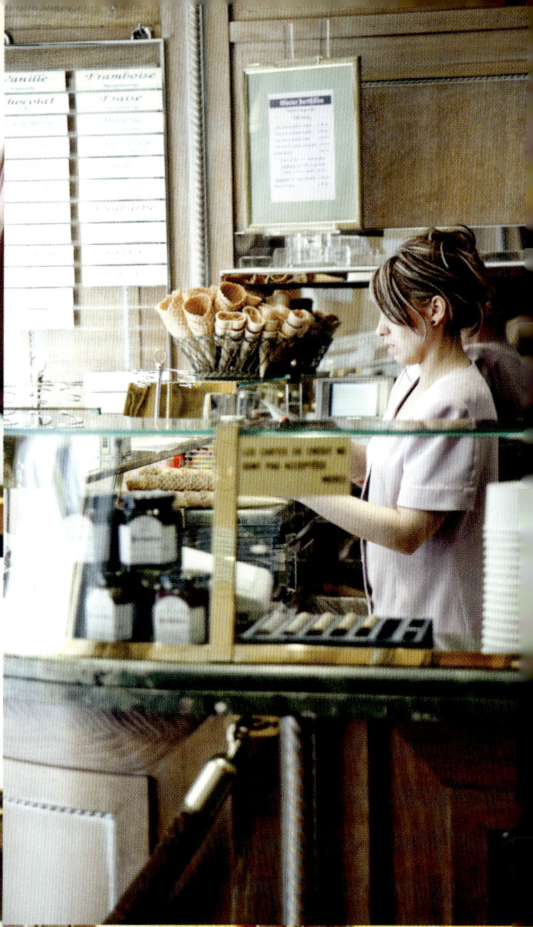
Framboise
Fraise

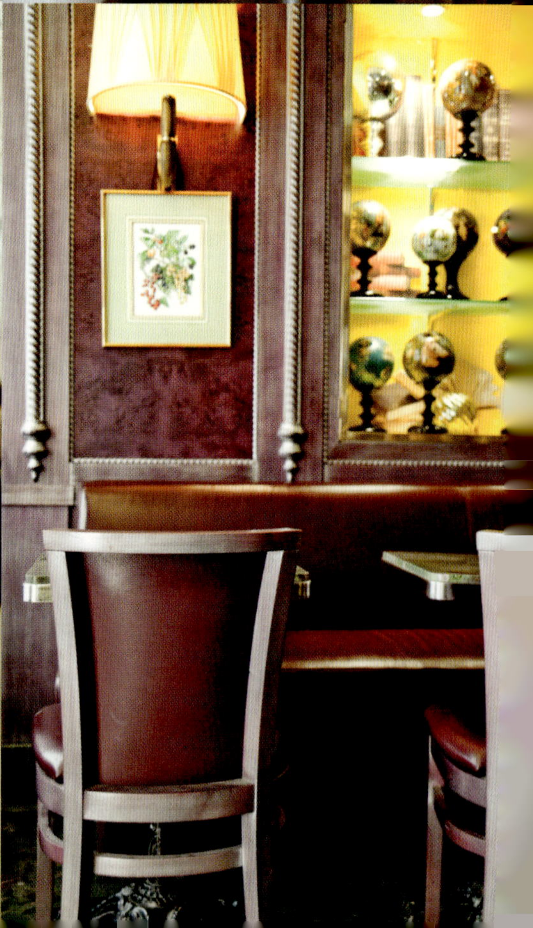

BERTHILLON

PARIS, SWEET PARIS / J'aime Paris

GLACIER BERTHILLON / 29-31 rue Saint-Louis en l'île / Paris IVe

A biting-cold winter has hit Paris. In an empty tearoom, the entire Berthillon team, huddled together as if round a fireplace, is carefully crumbling a glistening mountain of candied chestnuts. Who eats ice-cream in this weather? The Parisians, it seems. They patiently await their turn, captivated by candied chestnut with a Christmas Eve scent. In summer, the chestnut gives way to wild strawberries, and the Parisians are joined by gourmets from around the world. We can understand why!

- 519

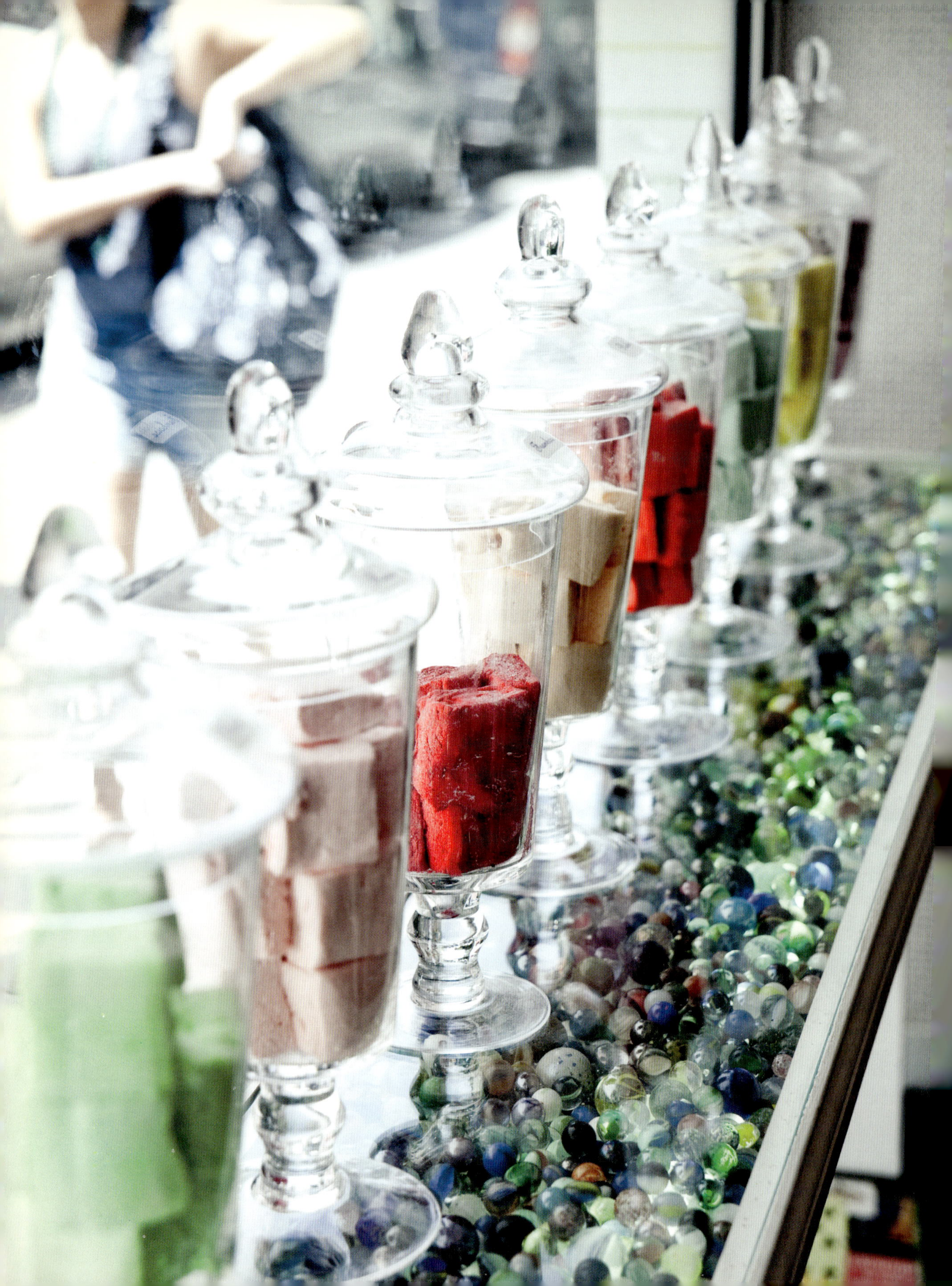

J'aime Paris

PARIS, SWEET PARIS

LE BONBON AU PALAIS / 19 rue Monge / Paris V^e

Guimauve fantaisie
1,30€ pièce

bien plus belle
Bonbons...
réuni les meilleurs
artisanaux de France
GEORGES

BON BON AU PALAIS

The taste of a memory nestles in gleaming glass jars. The sweet slips from the tongue at the Palace – a 'Sucre de pomme', a multicoloured 'Froufrou', a 'Negus', a caramelised nut – and childhood sets off on its magic carpet ride. Each jeweller's marvel comes from the artisan who created it, sometimes a few centuries ago, sometimes according to a secret recipe still fiercely guarded by protective nuns. While we listen attentively to the story behind liquorice and fruit jellies, the marshmallow tasting of freshly blooming orange flowers melts silently in my mouth.

LE BONBON AU PALAIS / 19 rue Monge / Paris V

J'aime Paris

PARIS, SWEET PARIS

GENUINE ANTIGUA
NOT FOR SALE
CLEAN COFFEE
PRODUCT OF GUATEMALA
PRODUCT OF GUATEMALA

LA CAFÉOTHÈQUE / 52 rue de l'Hôtel de Ville / Paris IVᵉ

CAFÉOTHEQUE

Here, we talk about Grand Crus. Terroirs. Fruit and floral notes, honey and spicy aromas. Soil acidity and pluviometry. Here, we turn up our noses at all types of blends, even if they're from the region. We are purists and proud of it. This is a coffee house. A house of stories. Once upon a time, there was a coffee bean that was picked up after it had been digested by the Jacu bird, somewhere in the Amazonian rainforest. Here, we begin our initiation.

J'aime Paris

PARIS, SWEET PARIS

LA CAFÉOTHÈQUE / 52 rue de l'Hôtel de Ville / Paris IVe

- 527

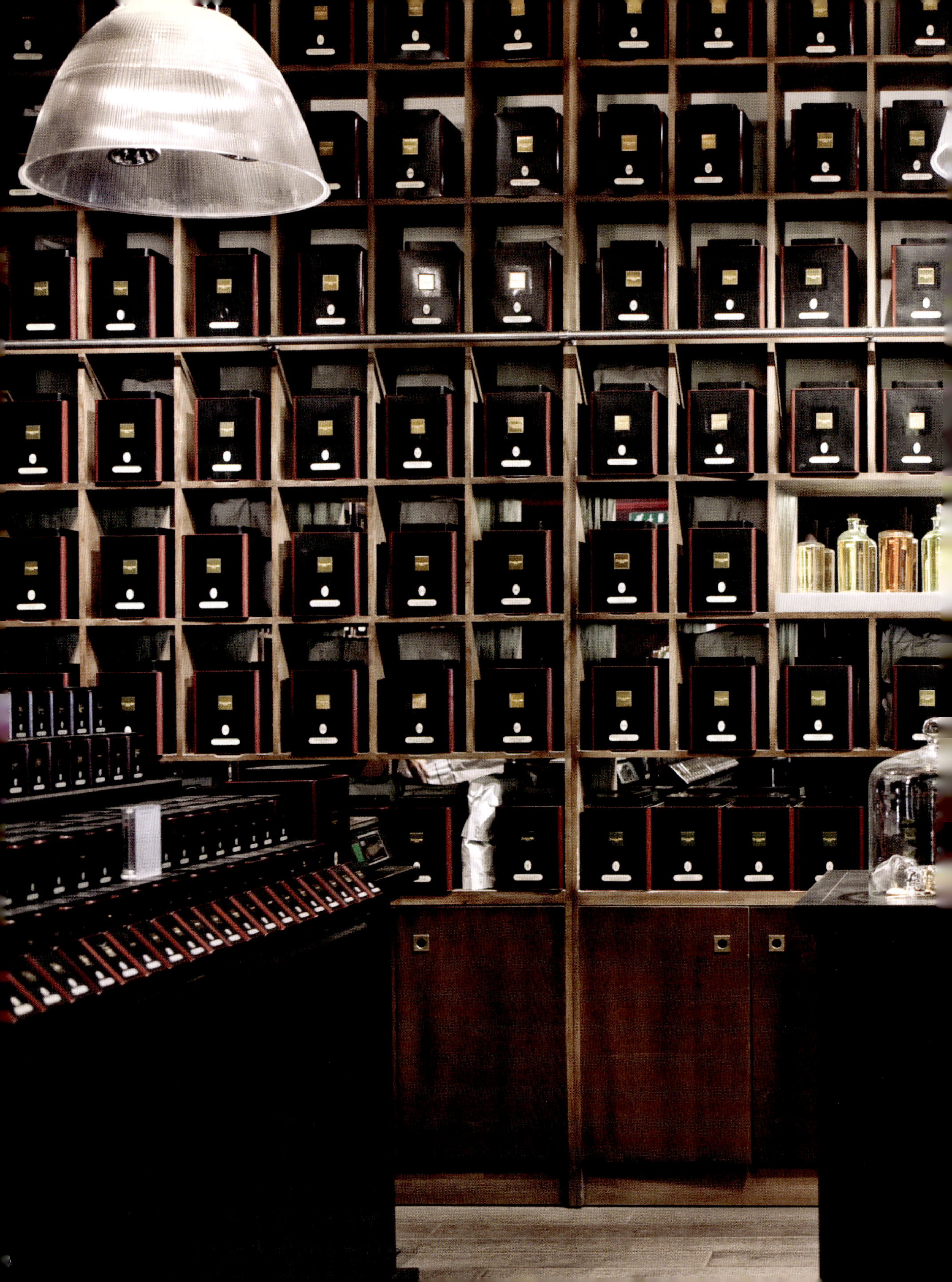

J'aime Paris

PARIS SWEET PARIS

DAMMANN FRÈRES / 15 place des Vosges / Paris IVᵉ

DAMMANN

In the shade of the archways of the elegant Place des Vosges, the Dammann Frères tea house is a haven of peace. From selecting to importing teas, as well as creating new blends, this family business has been perpetuating its know-how for the past three generations. The 'Lumières' box — a stylish leather case containing tins of tea and an infusing spoon — and the 'Safari' chest — a marvellous tea set that is perfect for a tête-à-tête — are the epitome of refinement. Besides original teas sold loose, in sachets or in balls - the white tea with nasturtium is exquisite — cold-infused teas and herbal infusions, such as the '*Tisane au 40 sous*' with rosehip, orange leaf, bitter orange, liquorice, verbena and thyme, make you forget the goings-on in the Marais quarter and beckon you to distant travels.

PARIS, SWEET PARIS

J'aime Paris

DAMMANN FRÈRES / 15 place des Vosges / Paris IVe

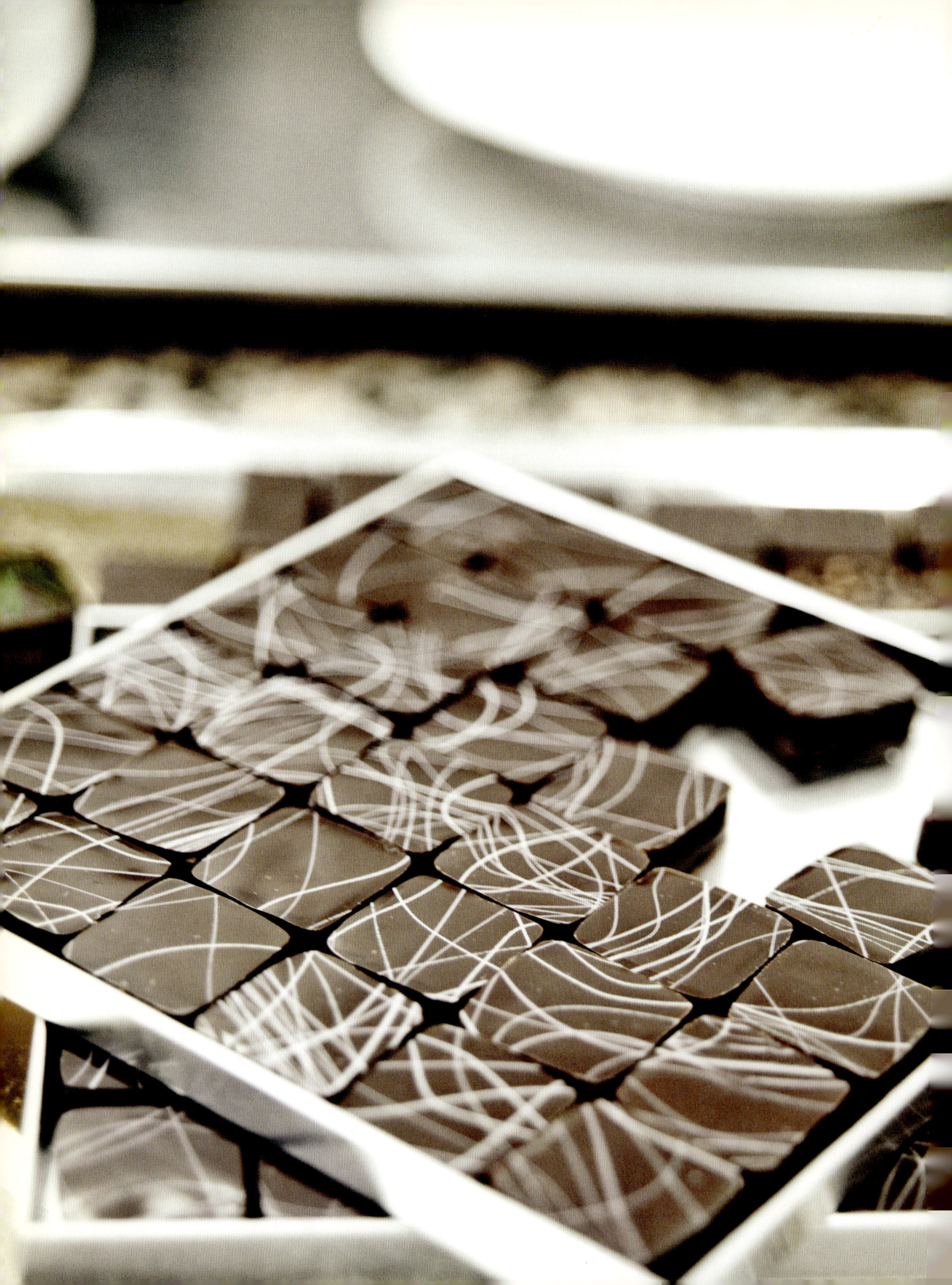

CHOCOLATERIE JACQUES GÉNIN / 18 rue Saint-Charles / Paris XV

PARIS, SWEET PARIS

J'aime Paris

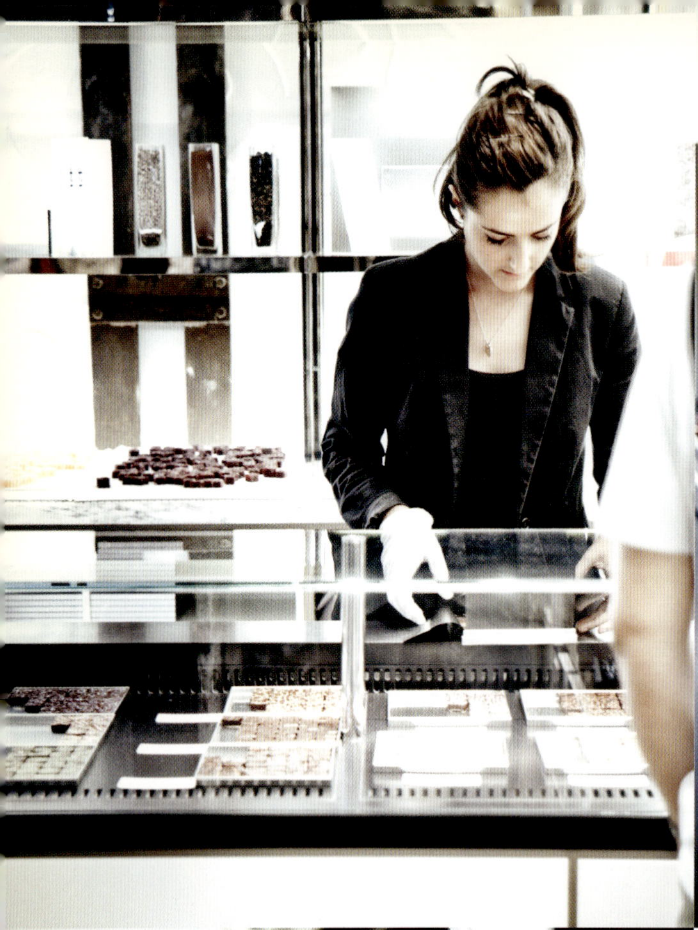
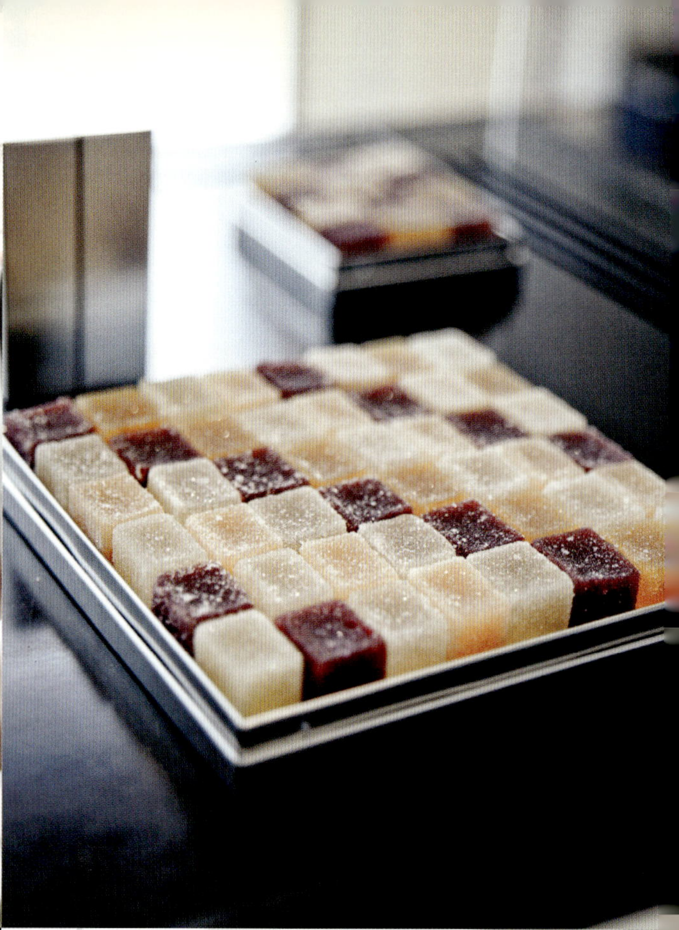
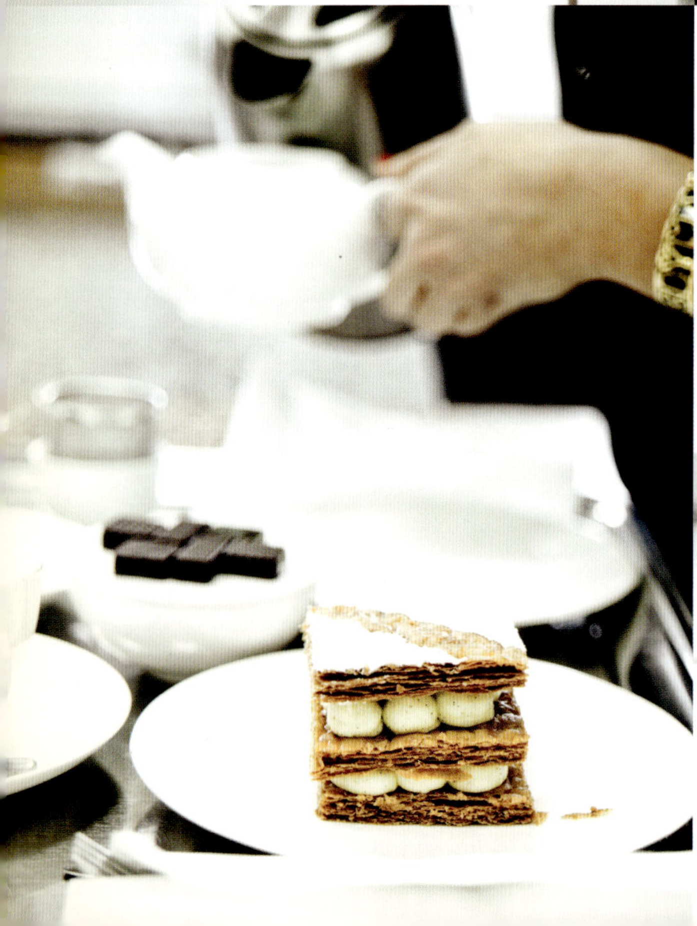
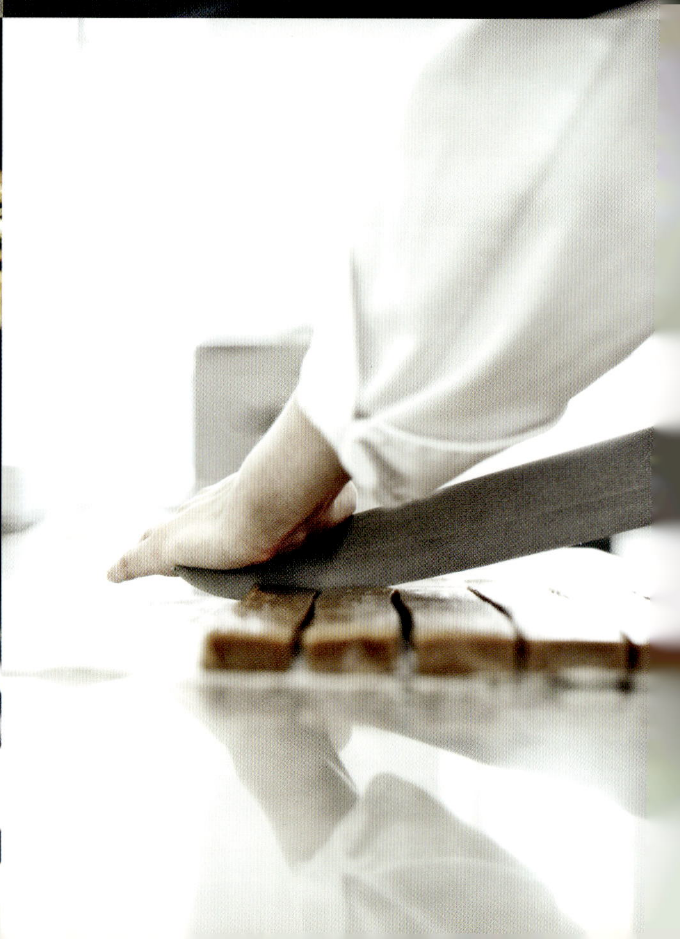

GÉNIN

Caramel. Or chocolate. A chocolate éclair with a plain caramel, or a caramel éclair with a chocolate toffee? Or maybe a hot chocolate, with some nougat... In the end, it's a tiny millefeuille. It's out of the question to even think about passing by the rainbow of fruit jellies, offering a splashing dive into the texture and scent of fruit. Come on, let's keep it simple: a toffee, made with salted butter and sprinkled with nuts.

CHOCOLATERIE JACQUES GÉNIN / 18 rue Saint-Charles / Paris XV

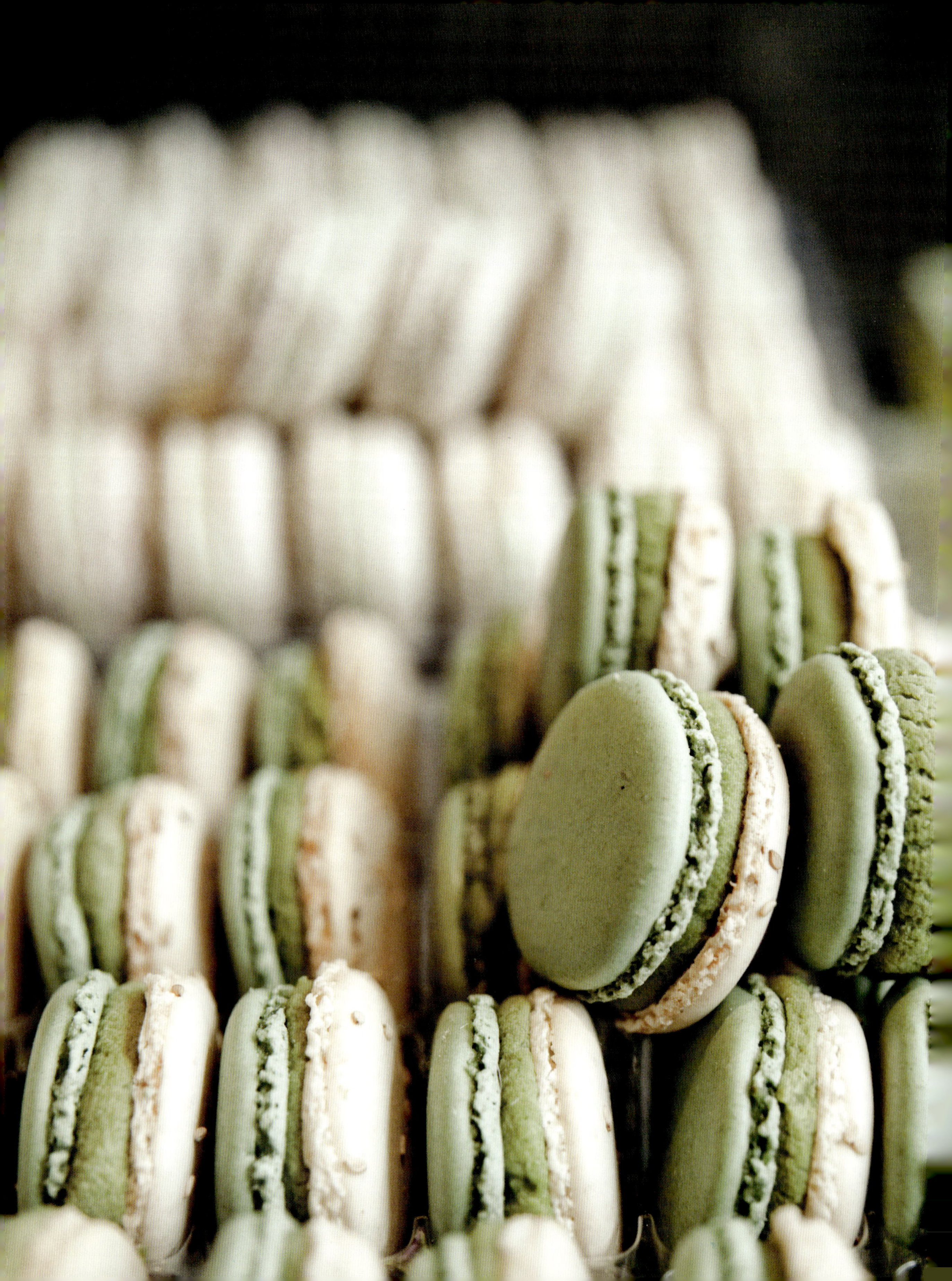

J'aime Paris

PARIS, SWEET PARIS

PIERRE HERMÉ PARIS / 72 rue Bonaparte / Paris VIe

- 537

HERMÉ

Pierre Hermé: So, would you like to taste a macaroon? This one is jasmine-flavoured. There's also cinnamon-cherry-pistachio, rose, chocolate, caramel, wasabi-strawberry, apricot-pistachio and milk chocolate-passion fruit, among many others...

Alain Ducasse: You know that I like them hard, without fillings!

PH: Personally, I like them soft, creamy, smooth as can be, with just a light crunchy crust. There are many different palates!

AD: So why did you leave your beloved Alsace and the family patisserie?

PH: To learn. I came to Paris at the age of 14, and I never went back. One thing led to another. I wanted to open my own place and to work as I wanted, which was to give my patisserie a contemporary look: going back to basics; not decorating with chocolate when there's no need. Everything going into a cake or a macaroon or a chocolate must contribute to its taste and balance.

PARIS, SWEET PARIS

J'aime Paris

PIERRE HERMÉ PARIS / 72 rue Bonaparte / Paris VIe

539

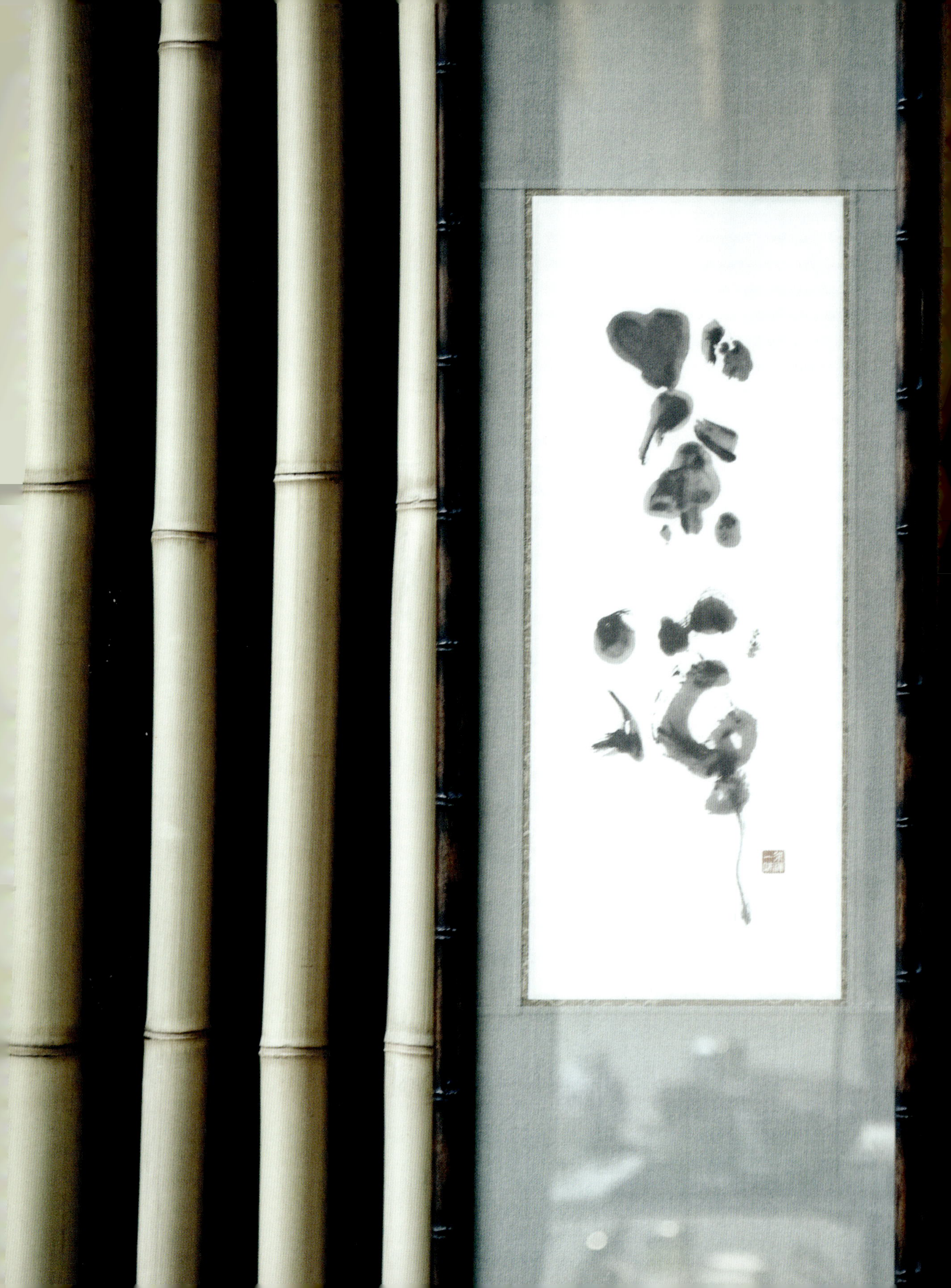

JUGETSUDO / 95 rue de Seine / Paris VIe

J'aime Paris

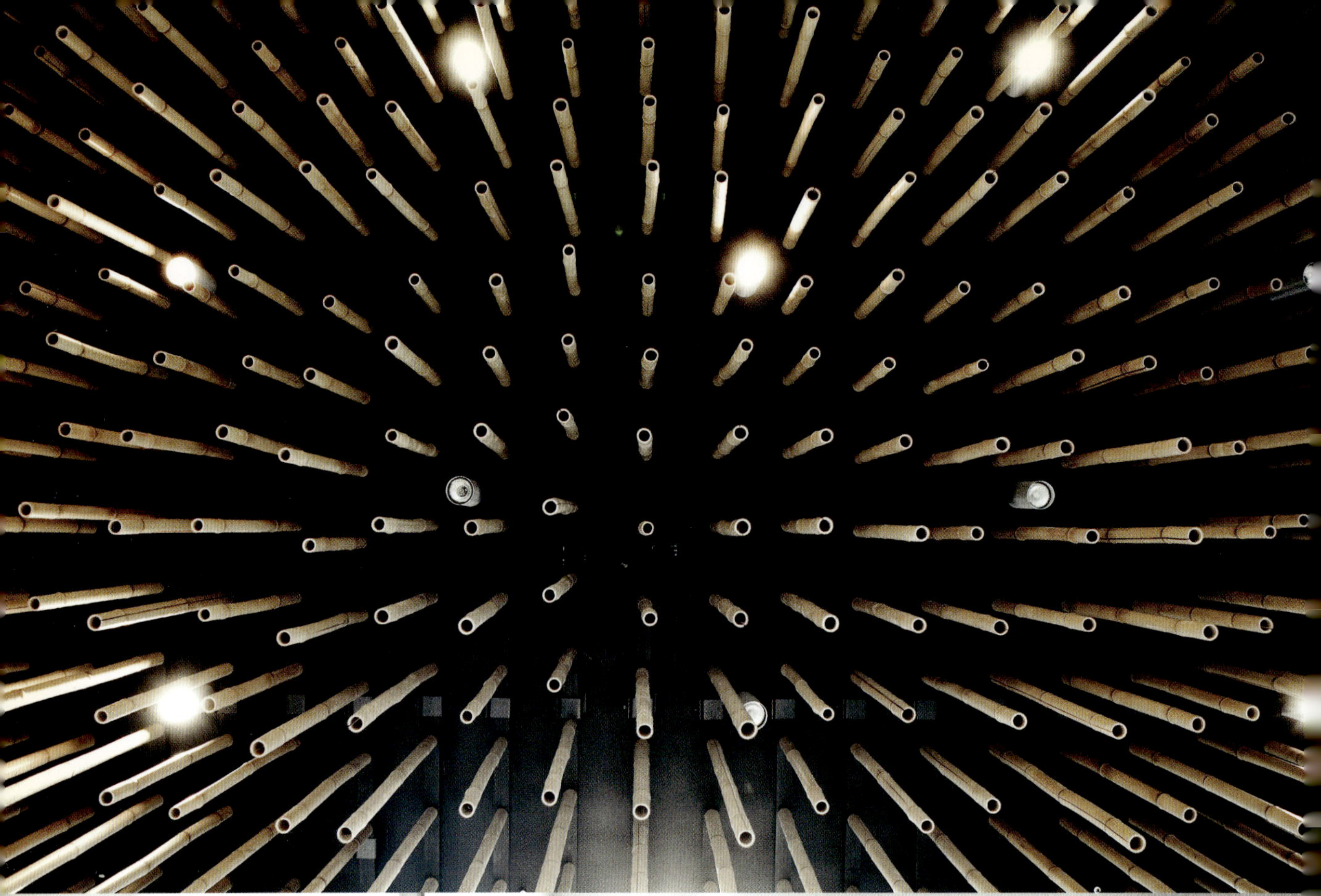

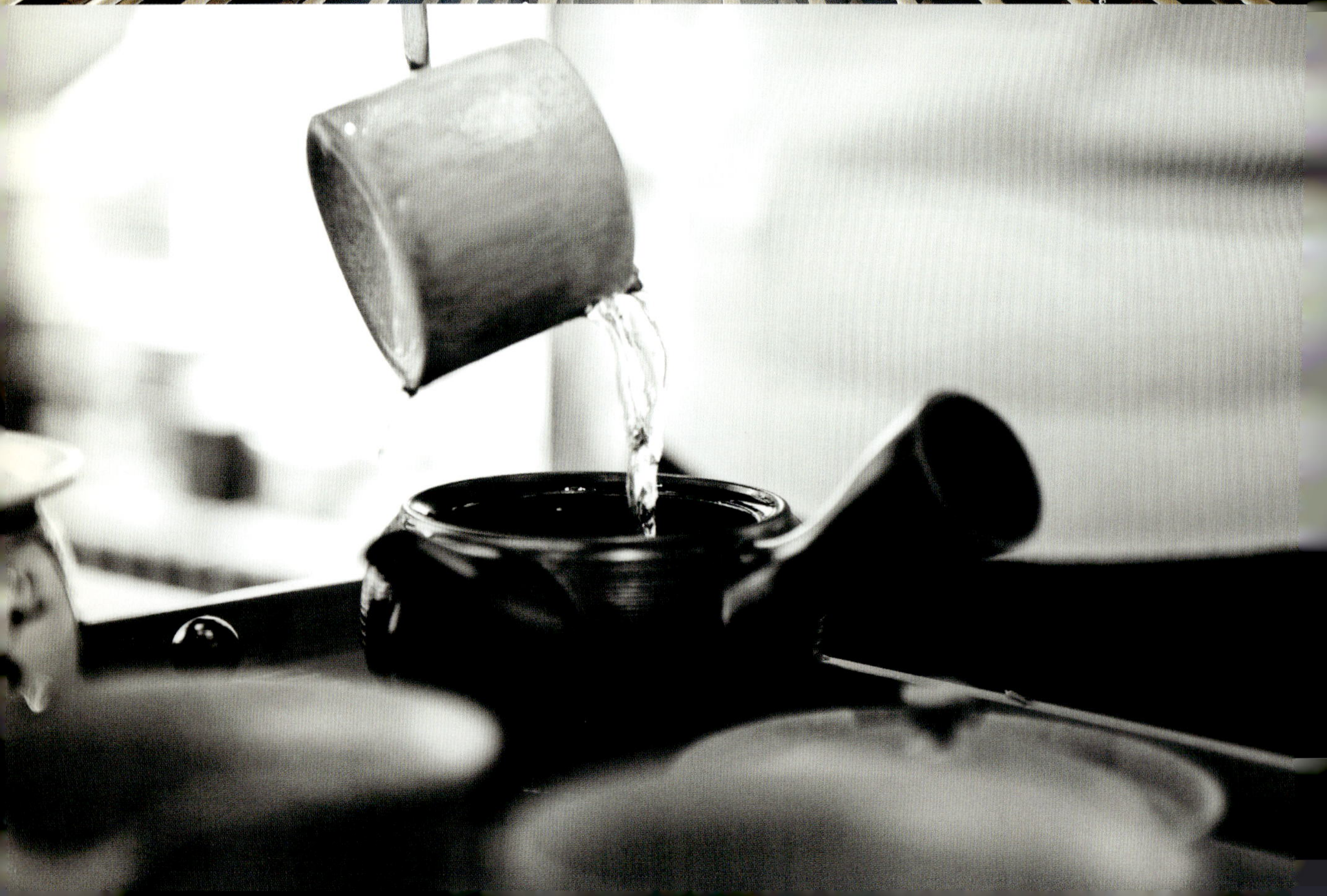

JU GET SU DO

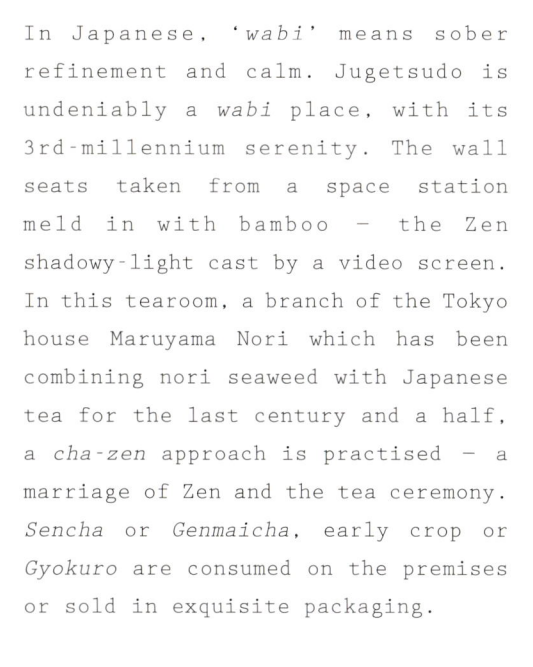

In Japanese, 'wabi' means sober refinement and calm. Jugetsudo is undeniably a wabi place, with its 3rd-millennium serenity. The wall seats taken from a space station meld in with bamboo — the Zen shadowy-light cast by a video screen. In this tearoom, a branch of the Tokyo house Maruyama Nori which has been combining nori seaweed with Japanese tea for the last century and a half, a *cha-zen* approach is practised — a marriage of Zen and the tea ceremony. *Sencha* or *Genmaicha*, early crop or *Gyokuro* are consumed on the premises or sold in exquisite packaging.

JUGETSUDO / 95 rue de Seine / Paris VIe

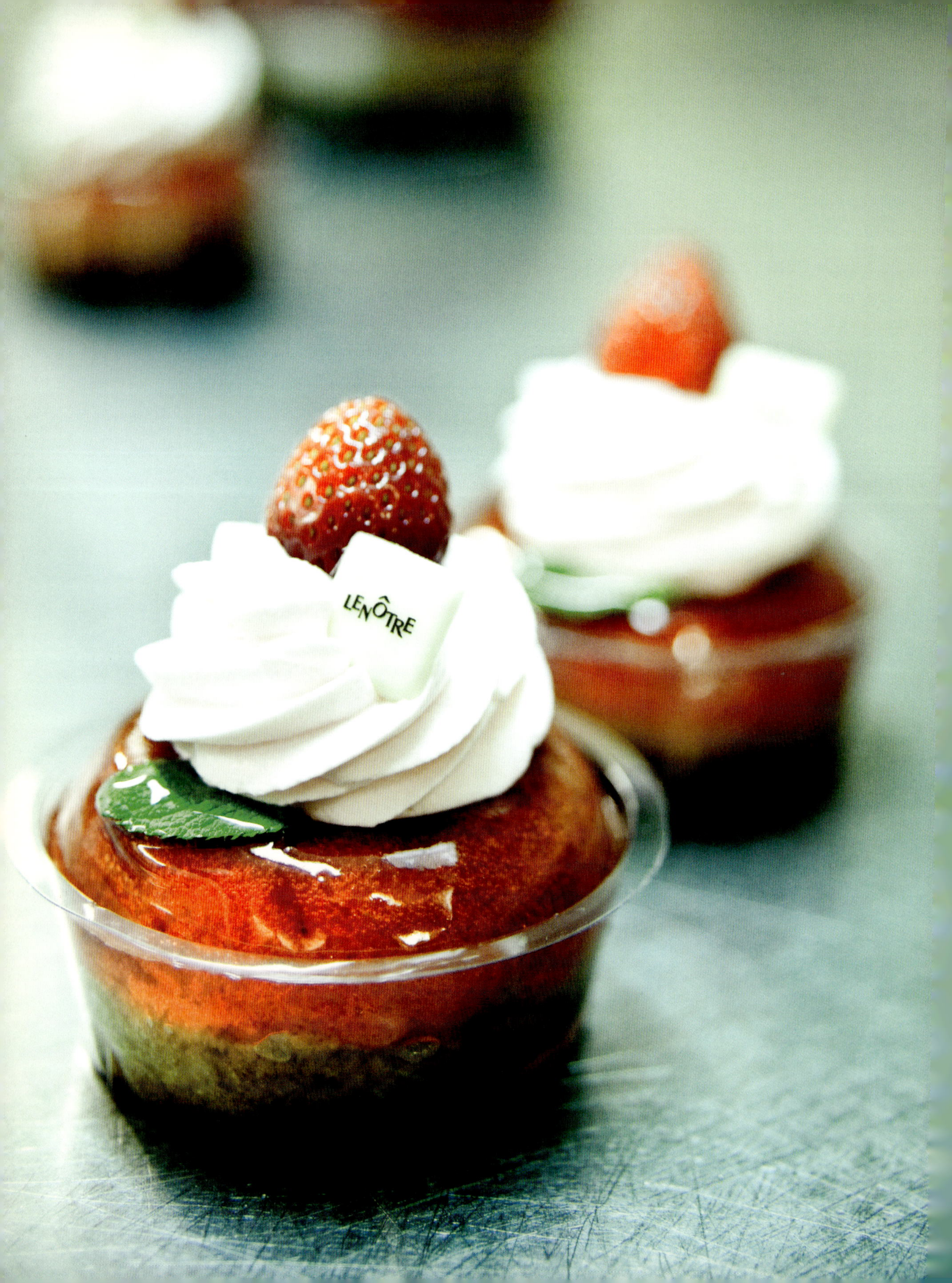
LENÔTRE

LENÔTRE / avenue Victor Hugo / Paris XVIe

PARIS, J'AIME PARIS

J'aime Paris

LENOTRE Gaston Lenôtre, a true leading chef of his generation and creative genius, knew how to break the traditional mould of patisserie-making. Over 40 years ago, this tasteful ambassador opened the first school for gastronomic training and improvement in France. Know-how that today is upheld by the Lenôtre house which continues to promote the French culinary heritage.

PARIS, SWEET PARIS

J'aime Paris

LENÔTRE / 48 avenue Victor Hugo / Paris XVIe

- 547

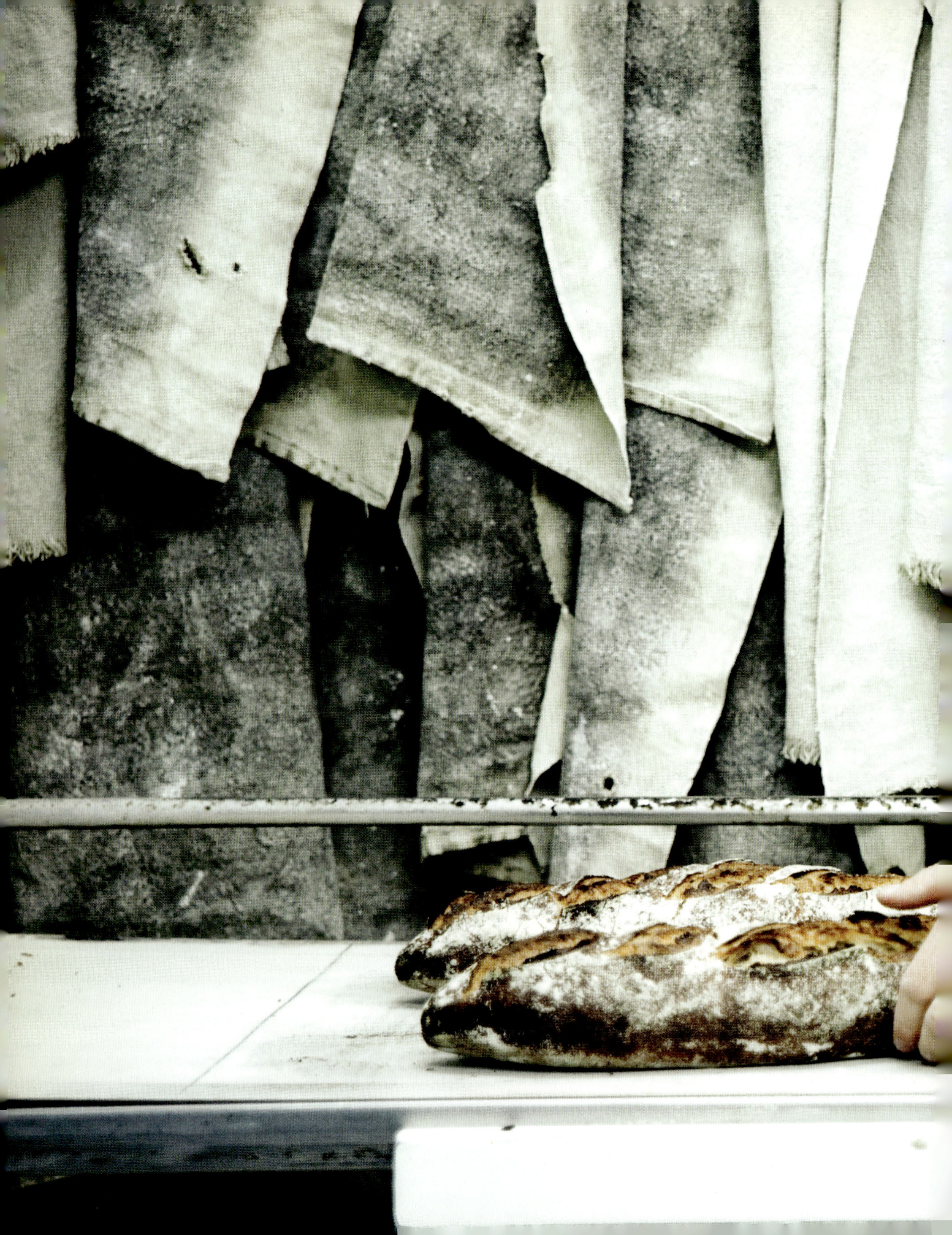

PATISSERIE RAOUL MAEDER / 158 boulevard Berthier / Paris XVIII

MAEDER

Apricot bread for white meats. Truffle bread to delight two scrambled eggs. Aniseed and orange-flavoured bread for teatime. Black hazelnut bread as a cake. And if you manage to escape from the fascination of breads, it's only to fall under the spell of a savoury *kugelhopf* with morsels of bacon, almonds and pistachios. Maybe even a pretzel, from pure Alsace stock. It's an absolute must to return in the really cold season for the delicious hot chocolate.

PATISSERIE RAOUL MAEDER / 158 Boulevard Berthier / Paris XVIII

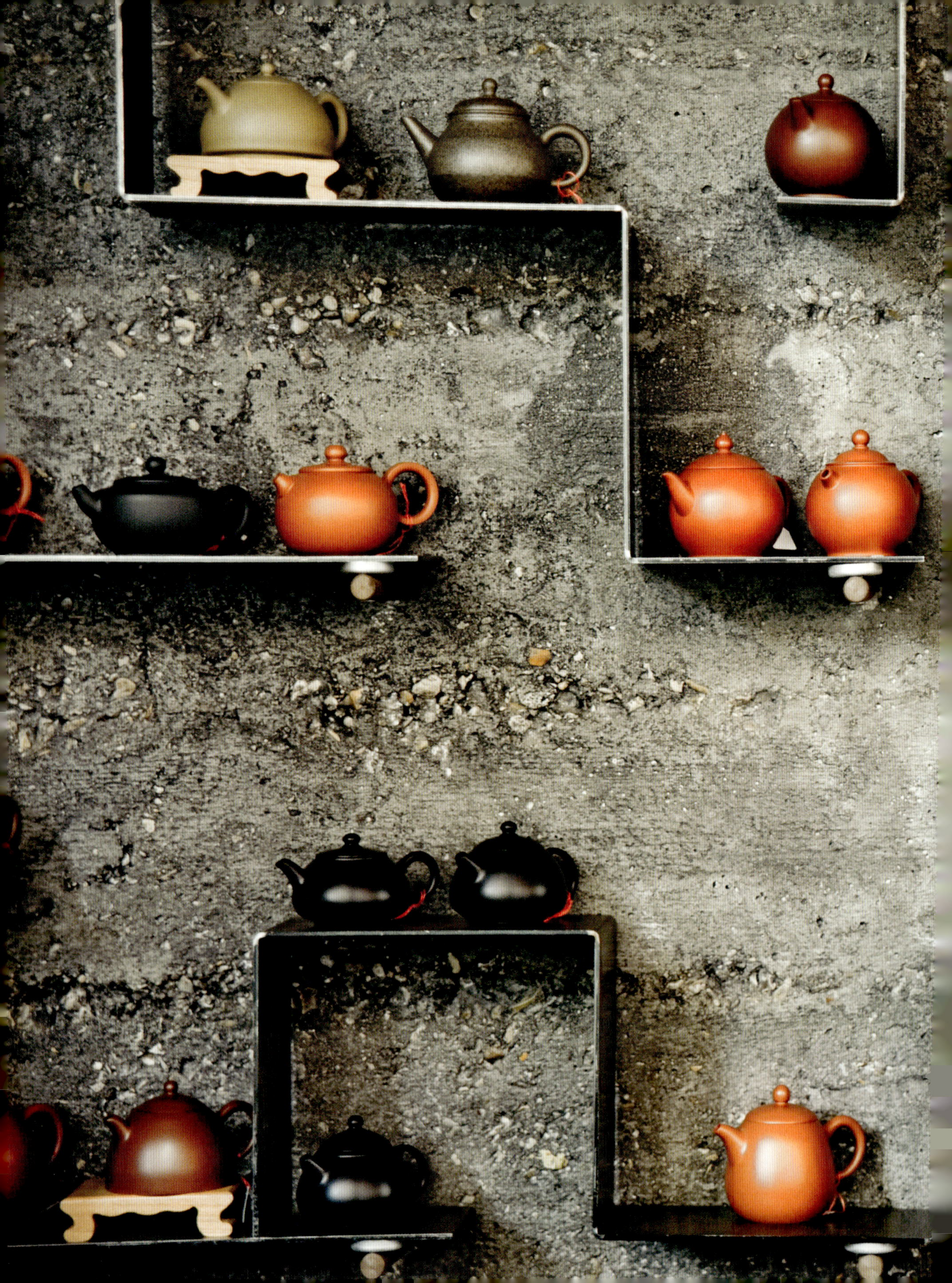

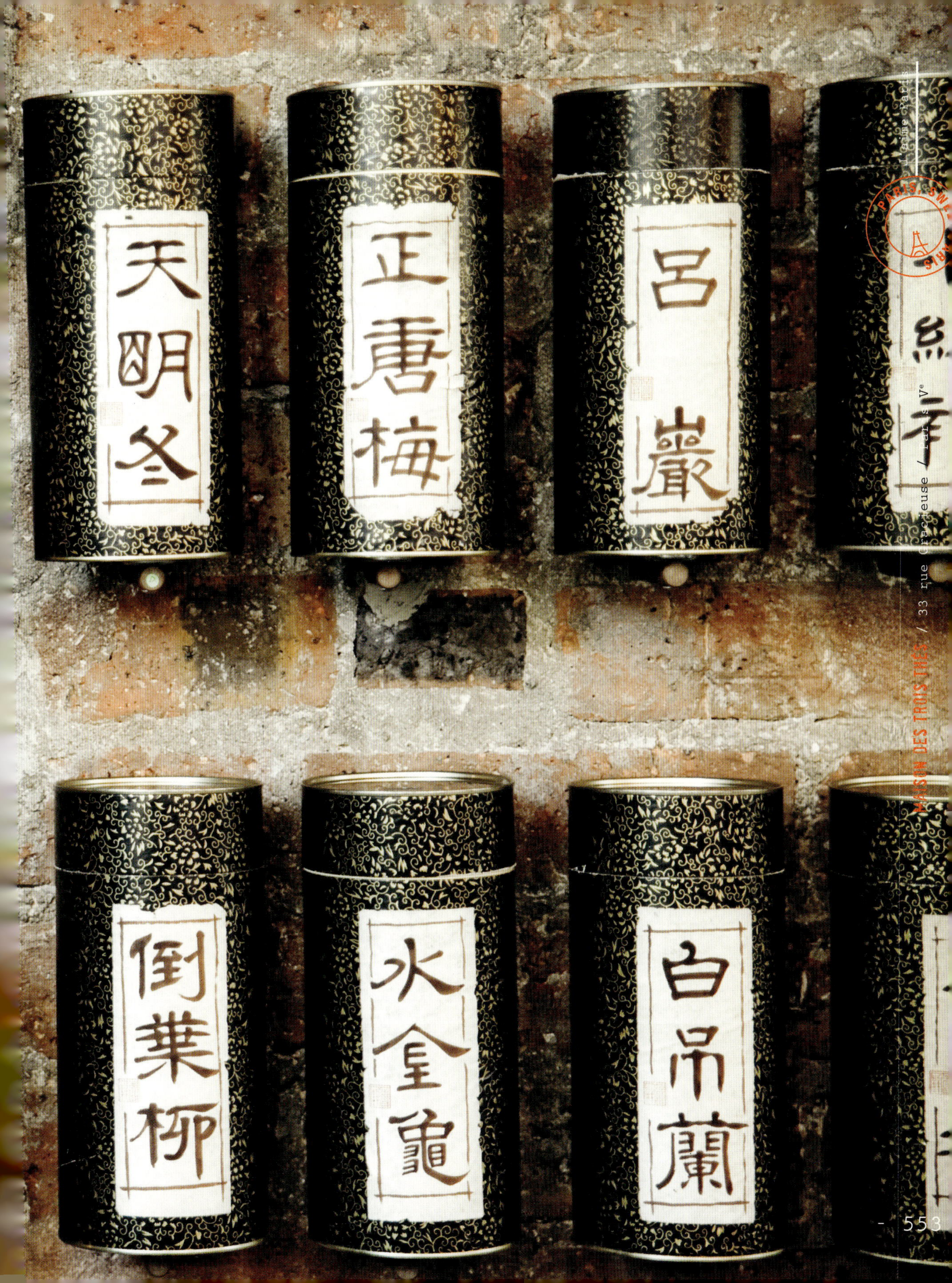

MAISON DES TROIS THÉS / 33 rue Gracieuse / Paris V^e

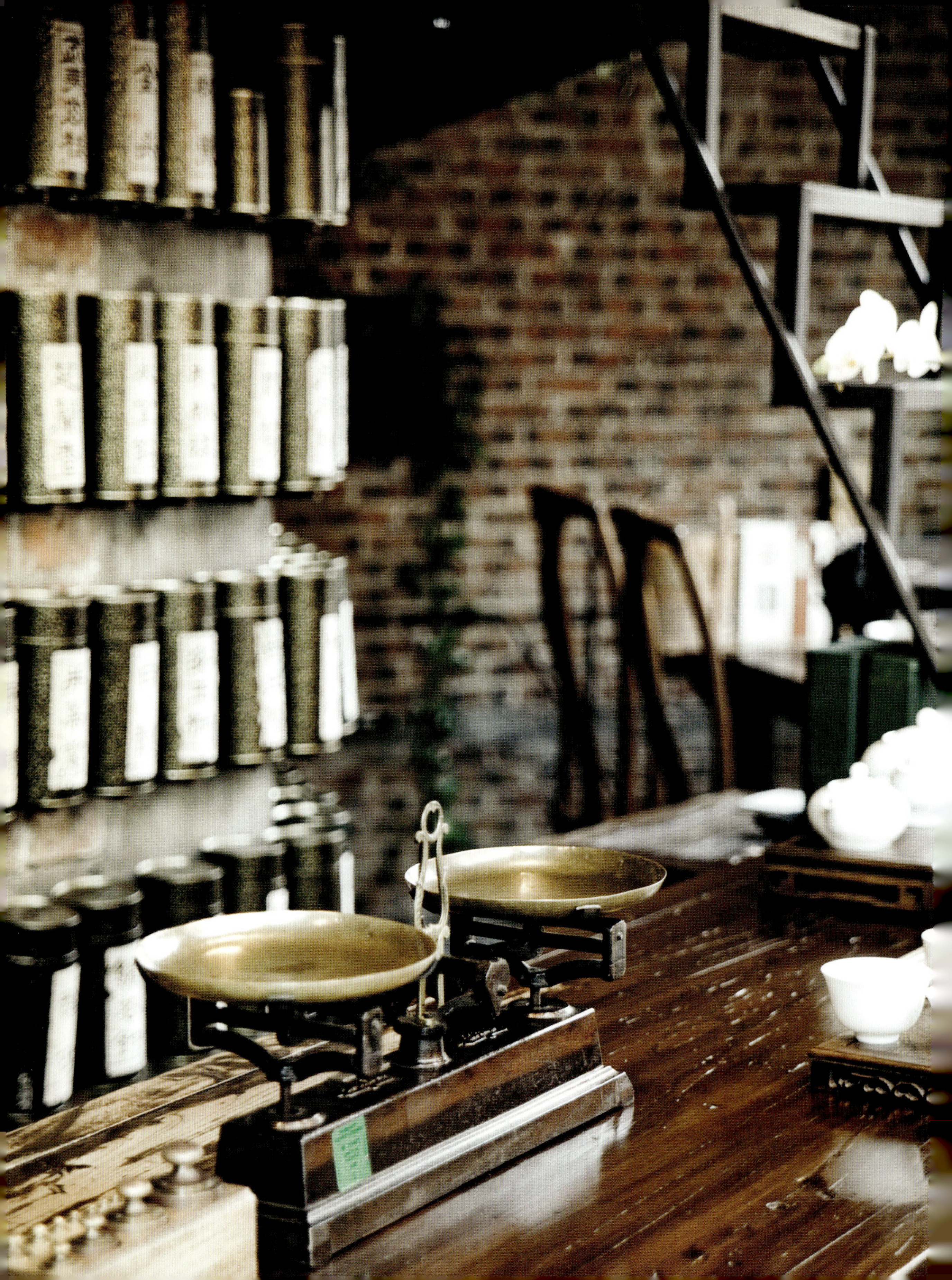

MAISON DES TROIS THÉS

You ring the bell, and wait for the door to open. In the Chinese tea temple, enveloped in silence, the ritual is already underway. You discover the infinite universe of the magic leaf, the green teas of spring, just picked, *Pu-Erh* on tap for large pots. Shoes are removed before taking a place in the tearoom where you taste the precious water as part of the *zhong* (simple Chinese ceremony) or the *gong fu cha* (sophisticated ceremony), thanks to Master Tseng's infinite knowledge.

MAISON DES TROIS THÉS / 33 rue Gracieuse / Paris V᷉

PARIS, SWEET PARIS

J'aime Paris

MAR IAGE FRE RES

The tea I sample responds to the gentle name of number 419. Strange, this administrative numbering system, here, among this dark wood panelling, in this chocolate-box setting. But then again, 'Tamaryokucha' is rather unpronounceable. However, its pretty dark green twisted leaves, its extremely delicate keynotes, its silky texture and *umami* taste make for a brilliant brew. And as a wrapped parcel, accompanying a fillet of white fish, it's an aromatic revelation.

J'aime Paris

PARIS, SWEET PARIS

MARIAGE FRÈRES / 30, rue du Bourg-Tibourg / Paris IV*

- 557

MAISON
d'Iran
20 €

PAIN DE SUCRE / 14 rue Rambuteau / Paris III

- 559

Pralines roses
ou caramel
7.00 €

PAIN de SUCRE

This patisserie has it all. It's run by Nathalie Robert and Didier Mathray, the master of the house — a former pastry chef for Pierre Gagnaire — who greets us. He doesn't lack humour or imagination. Their '*Pain de sel*' exudes spirit and their buckwheat dough with foie gras is an irresistible specimen. Don't miss the '*Pirouette Pomme*', a caramelised apple tart with rosemary and almond, pistachio and lime cream — a dazzling combination. All the scents of the scrubland find their way into your mouth. Only one desire remains: to return.

Sablé au beurre des Charentes

2.5 €

PAIN DE SUCRE / 14 rue Rambuteau / Paris IIIe

J'aime Paris

PARIS, SWEET PARIS

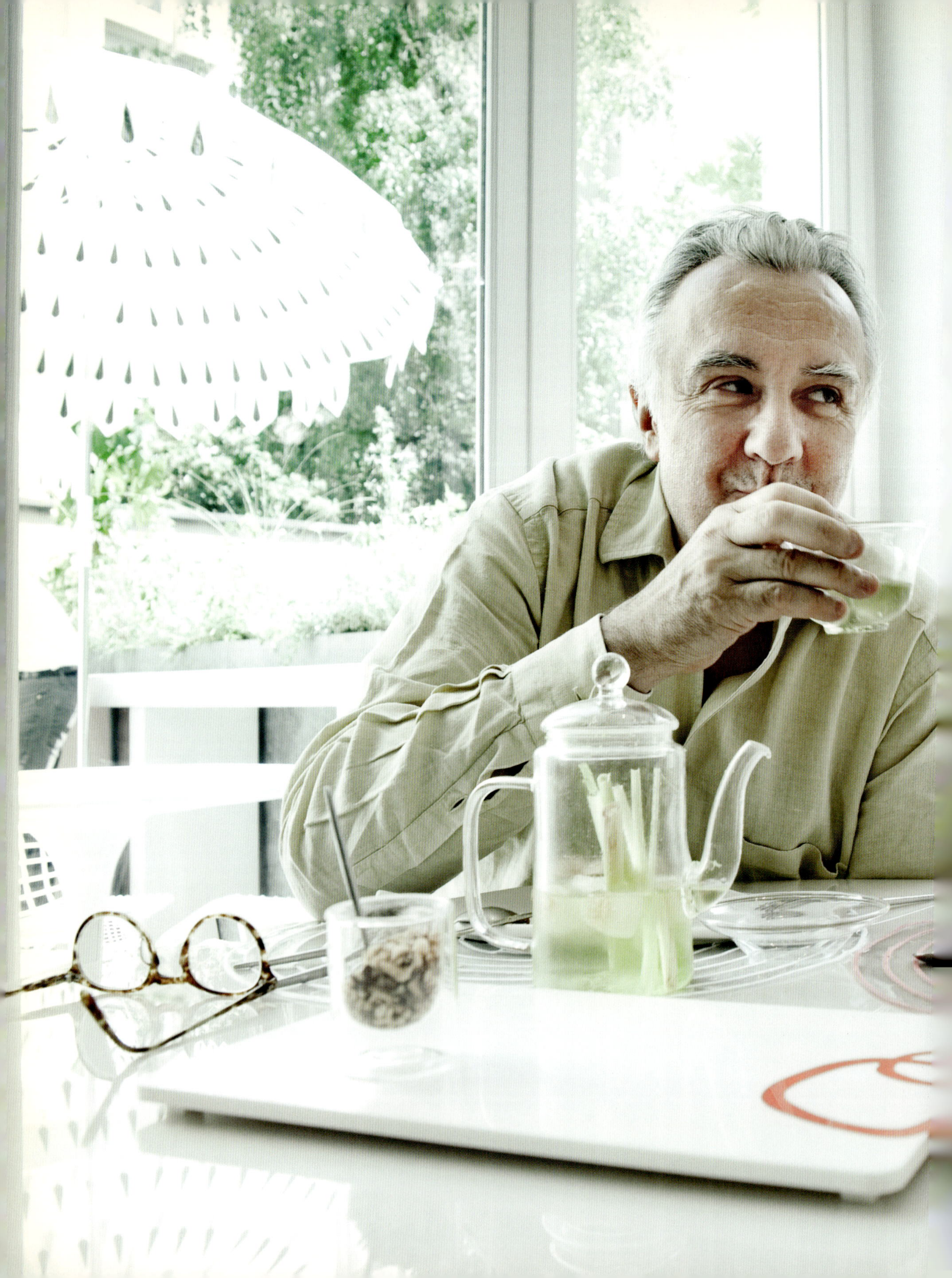

J'aime Paris

PARIS, SWEET PARIS

LA PÂTISSERIE DES RÊVES / 93 rue du Bac / Paris VIe

- 563

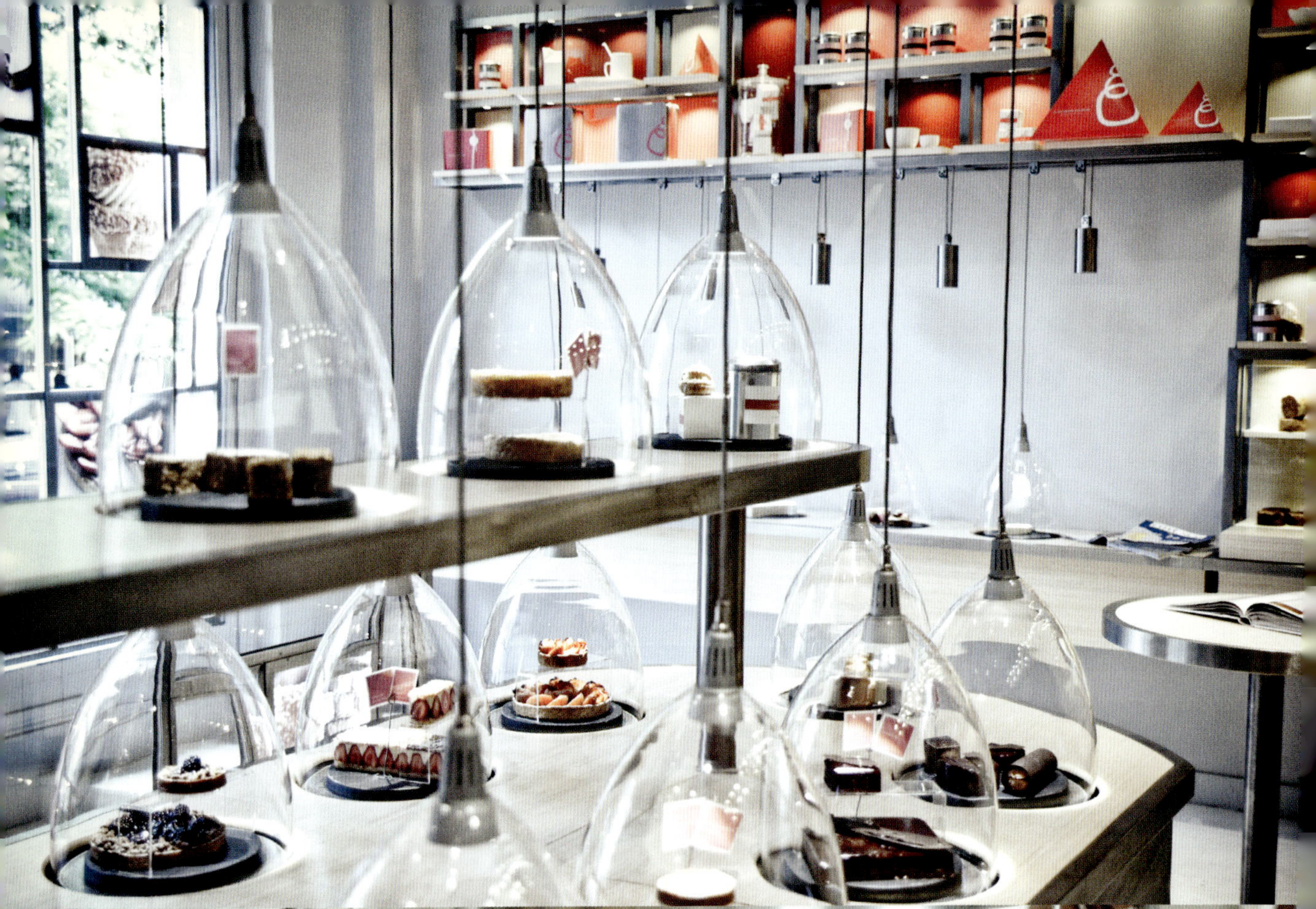
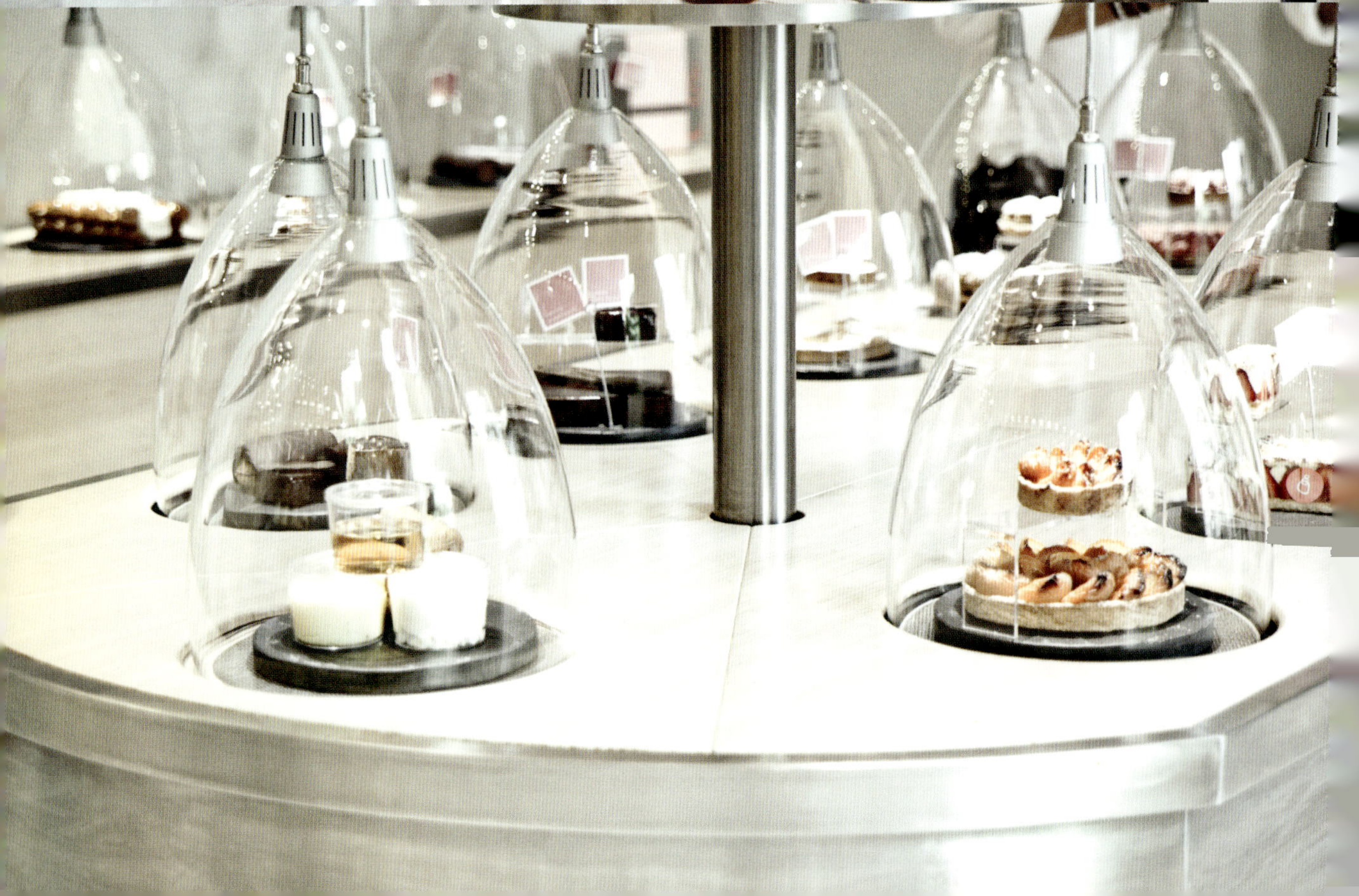

PÂTISSERIE DES RÊVES

A millefeuille, theoretically, is crispy. On the other hand, no it's not. This one melts in your mouth. It fades away like an aristocrat, in a rustle of vanilla-flavoured cream, which lasts until the last puff, thanks to the pastry chef's unrelenting technique in corsetry. Only on Sundays, otherwise people would no longer go to work. And another thing! Following the rue du Bac, Philippe Conticini, one of the greatest pastry chefs of his generation, invested in rue de Longchamp. Finally! Come and rediscover his classics: Paris-Brest, tarte tatin with lime Chantilly cream, éclairs filled with chocolate or tasting of strong coffee — or try the cakes of the day.

J'aime Paris

PARIS, SWEET PARIS

LA PÂTISSERIE DES RÊVES / 93 rue du Bac / Paris VIe

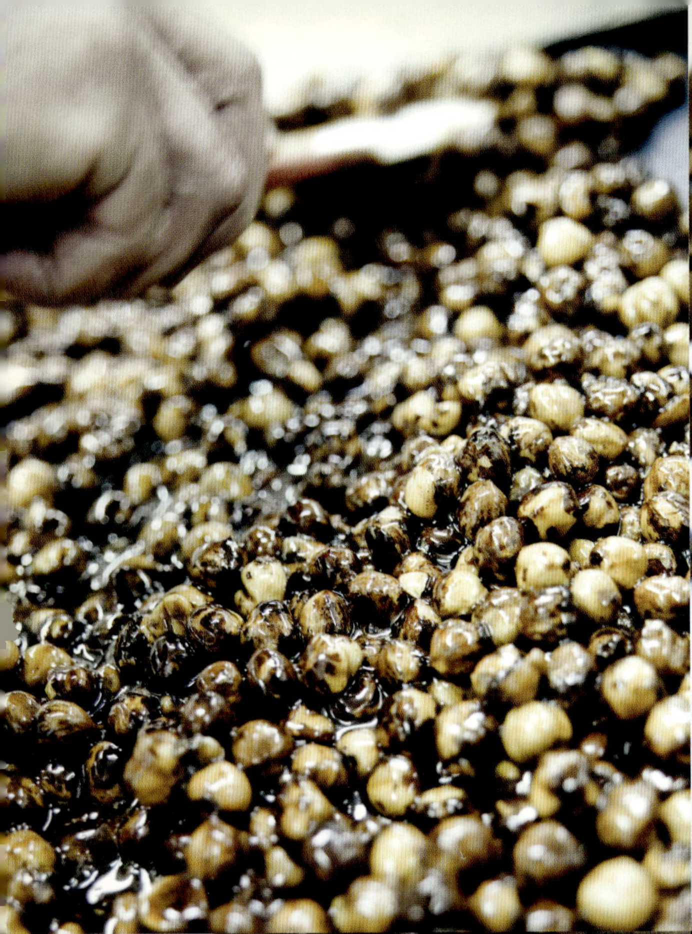
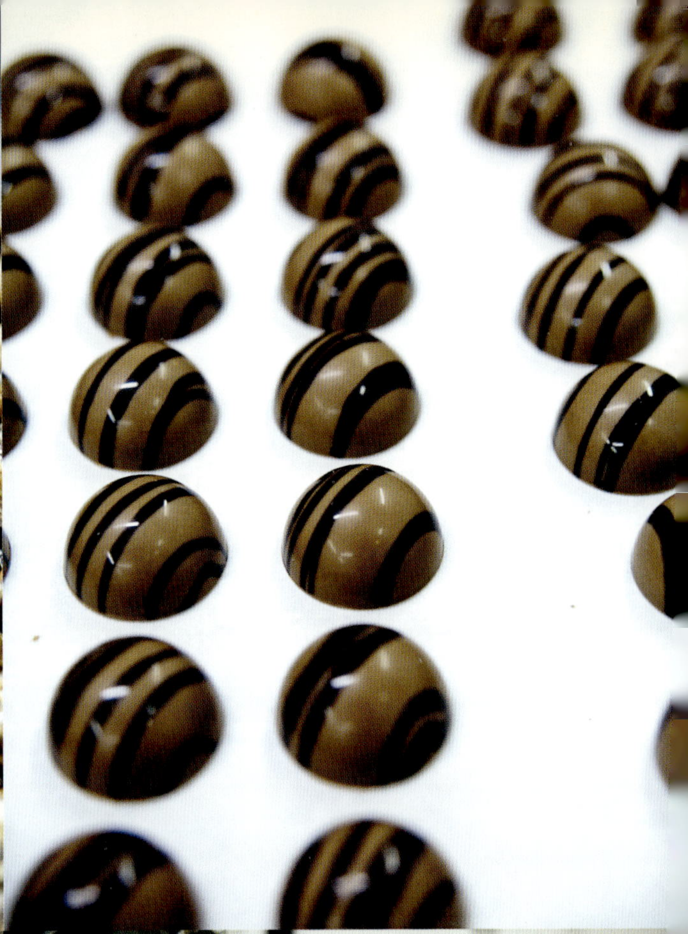
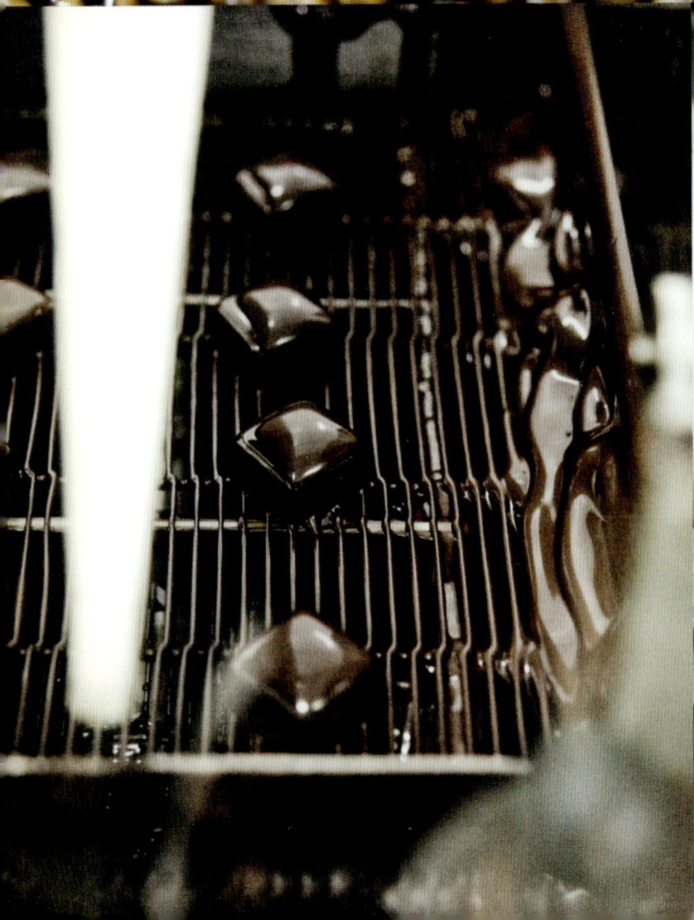
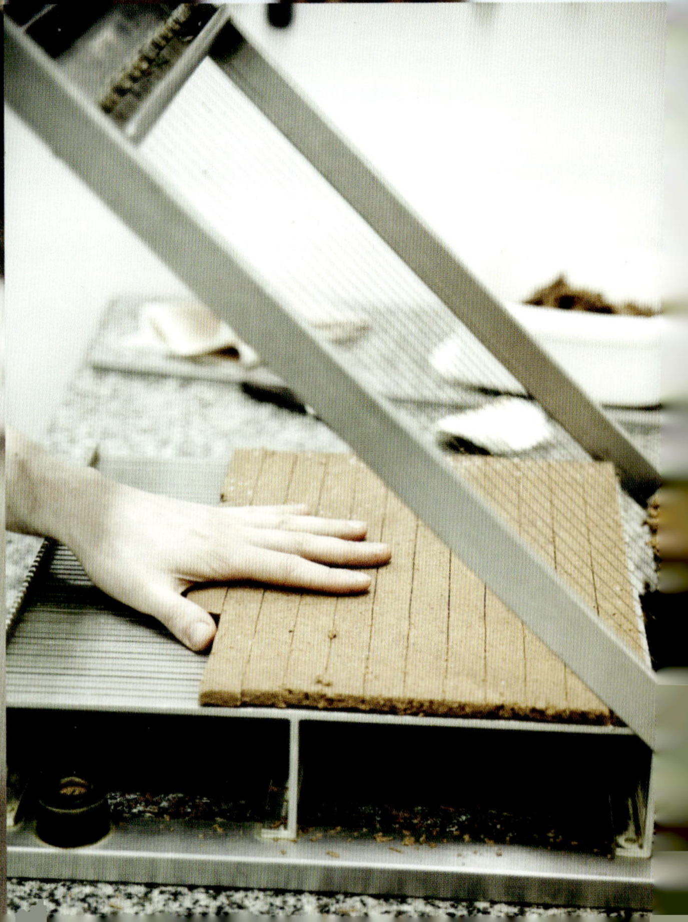

RÉ GIS

The fruit jellies border on the sublime. Sophisticated artisan preparation, with a recipe containing up to 80 per cent fruit pulp. The *marron glacé* is imperial, the transalpine chestnut preserved and lacquered, hiding a hint of sugar syrup at its centre, the jewel at the heart of the lotus. As for the chocolates, they are prepared each day with infinite care. A good destination, for the last half a century.

RÉGIS CHOCOLATIER / 89 rue de Passy / Paris XVI

J'aime Paris

- 567

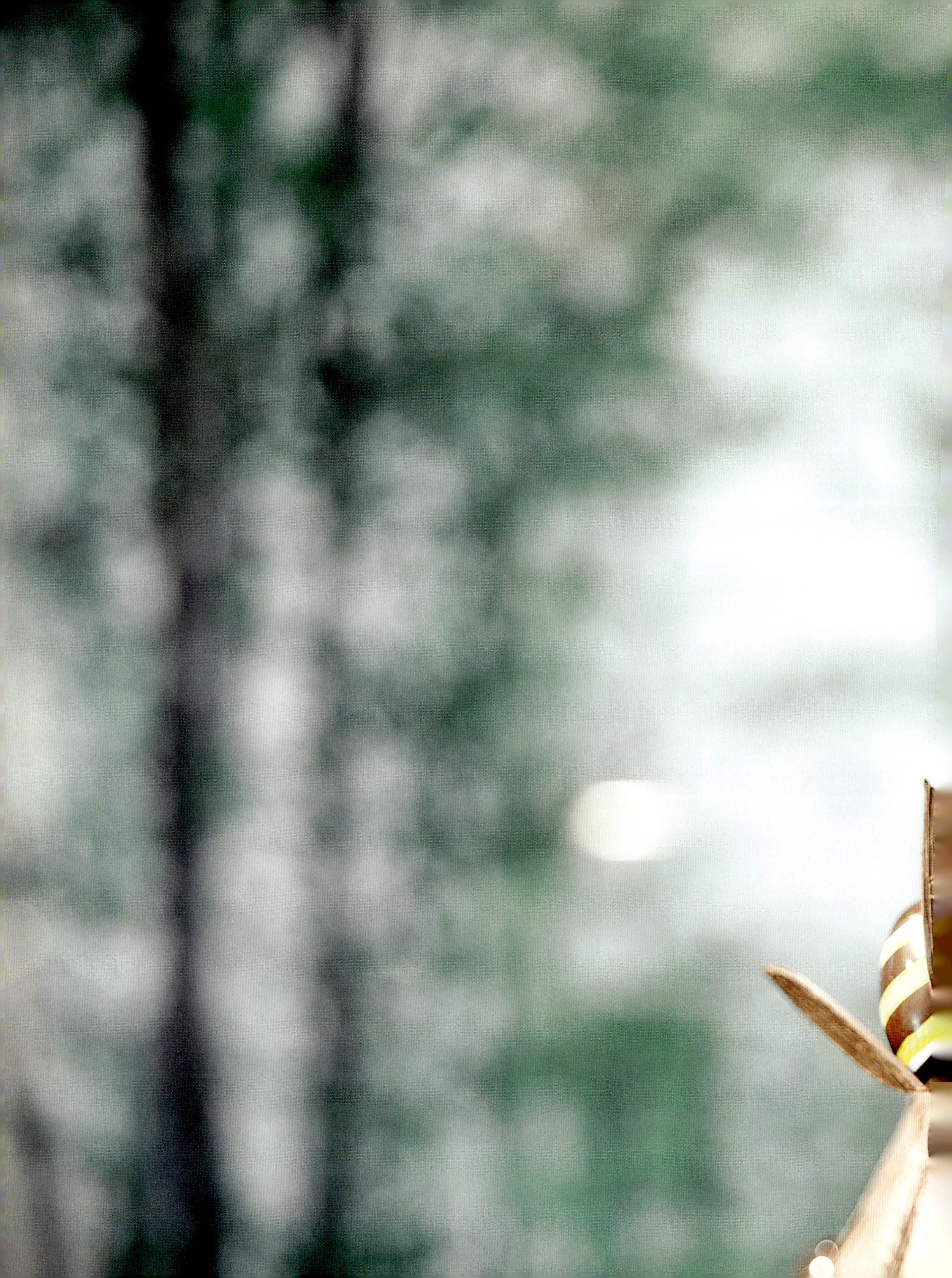

PIERRE HERMÉ / 108 Boulevard Saint-Germain / Paris VI⁰

4.06.-

Patrick Roger

ROGER

J'aime Paris

PARIS, SWEET PARIS

PATRICK ROGER — 108, boulevard Saint-Germain / Paris VIe

A grand master chocolate-maker, nothing scares Patrick Roger. This Meilleur Ouvrier de France is an eccentric and highly inspired artist. In his search for excellence, he makes no concessions. The wildflower honey he uses in his caramels comes from hives on the roof of the chocolate factory. His 'Coloured' chocolate sweets offer delicate combinations: creamy toffee, verbena and yuzu for the 'Wild' slate colour, or caramel, vinegar and raisin for the 'Rafale' golden button. Unless you succumb instead to the chocolate morsels that answer to evocative names such as 'Jealousy', 'Insolence', 'Fantasme' or 'Marie Galante'.

- 571

écoledecuisine
alain ducasse

ÉCOLE DE CUISINE ALAIN DUCASSE / 64 rue du ranelagh / Paris XVIe

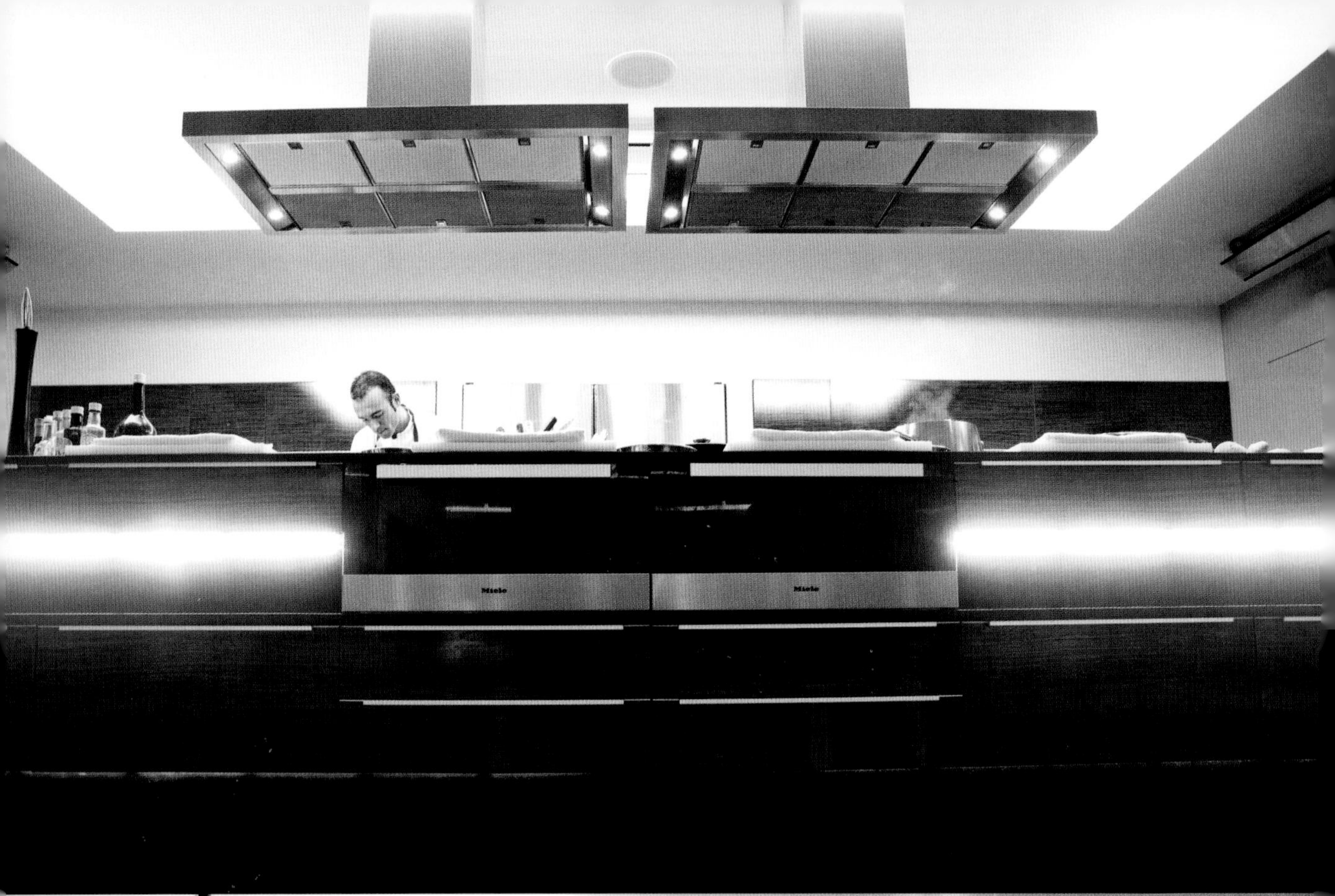

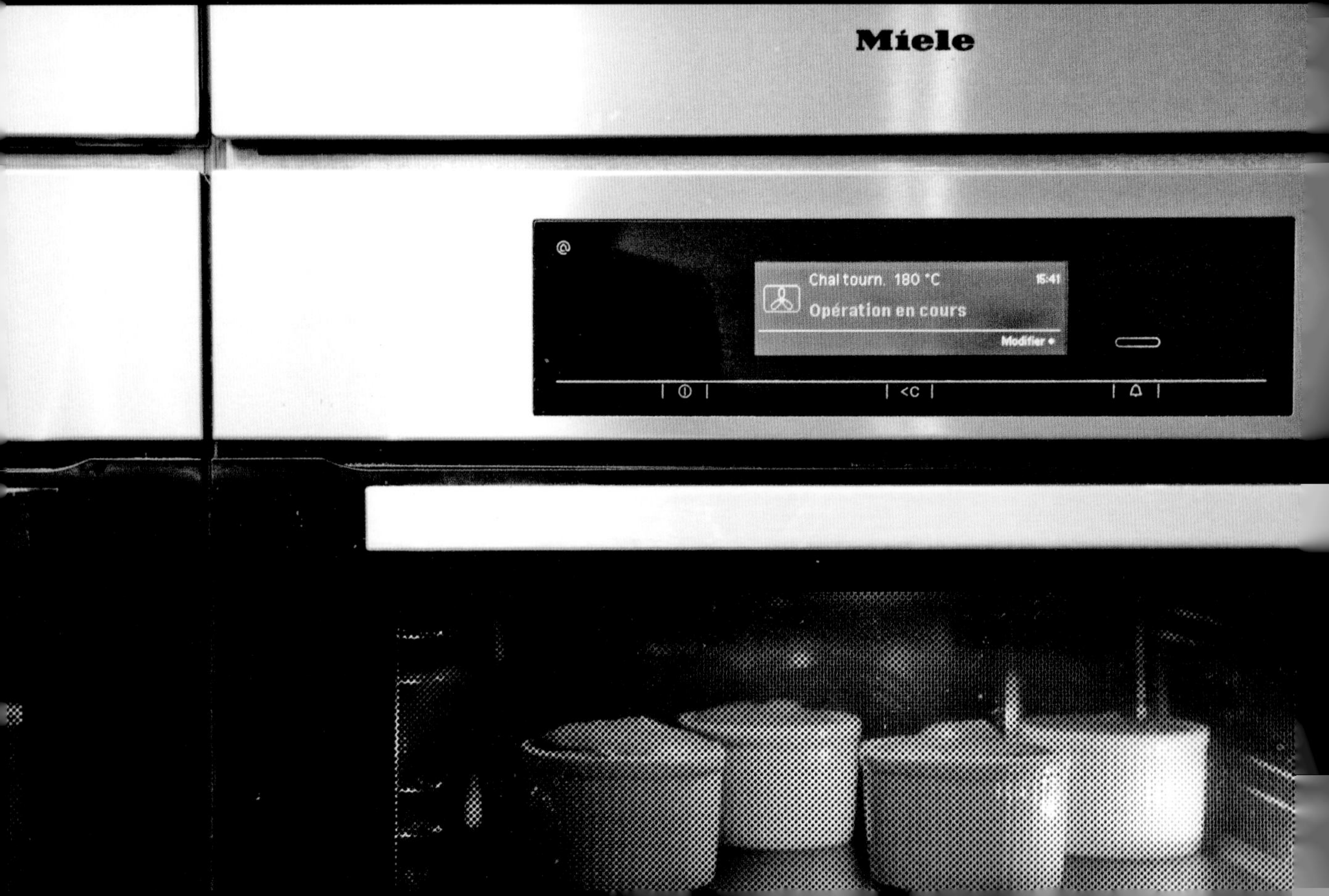
Miele
Chal tourn. 180 °C
15:41
Opération en cours
Modifier

MIE
LE

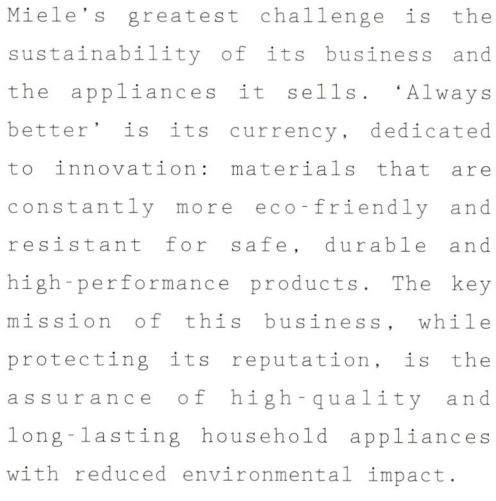

Miele's greatest challenge is the sustainability of its business and the appliances it sells. 'Always better' is its currency, dedicated to innovation: materials that are constantly more eco-friendly and resistant for safe, durable and high-performance products. The key mission of this business, while protecting its reputation, is the assurance of high-quality and long-lasting household appliances with reduced environmental impact.

MIELE / 55 boulevard Malesherbes / Paris VIIIe

PERENE The kitchen is a living space where people like to come together to share happy moments. Deeply emotional moments, in a fitting environment. At the cooking school, Perene and his talented staff have dedicated their expertise to meeting expectations both in terms of taste and requirements. Experienced artisans, they know how to translate this excellence into kitchen-studios dedicated to sensory pleasure, and aligned as closely as possible to domestic needs, ensuring they remain true to the home environment. This is the fruit of valuable interaction.

cuisine OLIVE

PERENE / 16 avenue Mozart / Paris XVI

PARIS, SWEET PARIS

J'aime Paris

PARIS, SWEET PARIS

I ALSO LOVE...

LE CHALET DES ÎLES

Lac Inférieur du Bois de Boulogne / Paris XVIe

Travelling to a restaurant by boat does not happen every day in Paris. It's a short trip, but the passengers are already enjoying these moments of escape from Parisian life. At the edge of the lake, the weeping willows form a shield, impenetrable and gentle. In this soothing setting, orangeade suddenly takes on a totally different taste.

HARRY'S NEW YORK BAR

5 rue Daunou / Paris IIe

It's in the crowded red velour basement, on the very same piano, that *Gershwin* composed *An American in Paris*. The partitioning was burnt during the war, to light the stove... Americans in Paris still come here to delight in the legendary Irish coffee. Vibrant evenings are held here when the American presidential elections are drawing near.

JEAN-PAUL HÉVIN CHOCOLATIER

231 rue Saint-Honoré / Paris Ier

Jean-Paul Hévin's chocolates are unique. His extra-dark chocolate cream fillings, his Grand Cru beans, his not overly sweet creations, could make you fear a slightly dry approach. But this doesn't emanate from coolness. It's elegance. He plays on chocolate-cheese-herb and spice combinations, such as Époisses cheese-cumin, Pont-l'Évêque with thyme, goat's cheese-hazelnut and Roquefort-nut. Pure fine art.

LADURÉE
21 rue Bonaparte / Paris VIe

The Ladurée house remains true to its name. For almost 500 years, 16 rue Royale — one of the capital's very first tearooms — has been welcoming gourmets, regulars and tourists. In the heart of Saint-Germain-des-Prés, a special mention goes to the boutique on rue Bonaparte. Capturing the art of living the French way, Ladurée perpetuates the great patisserie tradition, while at the same time innovating through the blackcurrant-violet macaroon and the divine rose éclair.

PÂTISSERIE ARNAUD LARHER
53 rue Caulaincourt / Paris XVIIIe

Trained at Fauchon and Pierre Hermé, this man did not wait for his tricolour stripe, achieved in 2007, to write his name in gold dust in the world of delicacies. His creations - such as his chocolate marshmallow or his 'Frisson', lime-pulp ganache — remain both in mouth and memory for a long time. Arnaud Larher creates a pink poppy éclair, and revisits the pistachio macaroon. Ices in summer; hot chocolate, old-style, in winter ends up drowning its taster in sinfulness. Too cute.

MULOT

76 rue de Seine / Paris VI°

Seasonal fruit tarts, clafoutis, desserts, sumptuous melting tarts — nothing has been left out. Right in front of you, a variety of generously filled sandwiches make your mouth water. On your right, amid the delicious scents, choose from among the collection of refined chocolates and heaps of macaroons. Unless you prefer to have a bite to eat on the premises. It's not by chance that Mulot patisserie has been operating in the heart of Saint-Germain-des-Prés for 25 years.

NANI

102 boulevard de Belleville / Paris XX°

At first sight, it's a Maghreb patisserie just like the many others the area houses. In reality, Nani is Paris' first kosher patisserie. This is where it's a must to be tempted by a Tunisian millefeuille, an 'Idéal' or an almond 'Boulou'. However, the best of the best — the Holy Grail — are the opalescent glass jars lining the shop window. Since 1962, the establishment has been making its own almond-flavoured *orgeat* syrup, as creamy as the Milky Way on a starry evening.

LE PALAIS DES THÉS

64 rue Vieille du Temple / Paris III

At the centre of the light-wood boutique, a large samovar is on the boil. Help yourself: the tasting of the day encourages finding a favourite. A well-considered selection of Asian Grand Crus, discoveries from the ends of the earth, light and floral blends. Patience is advised: if it takes an hour to find the perfect tea, so much the better!

THE TEA CADDY

14 rue Saint-Julien le Pauvre / Paris V

The street has an air of spring about it, the cosy tearoom having won over English gourmets. Beside a tea flower served in a 'Blue Willow' cup, Olivier Langois offers scones with whipped cream and homemade strawberry jam, or a divine apple pie. For the incurable eggs and bacon brigade, an English breakfast can also be ordered.

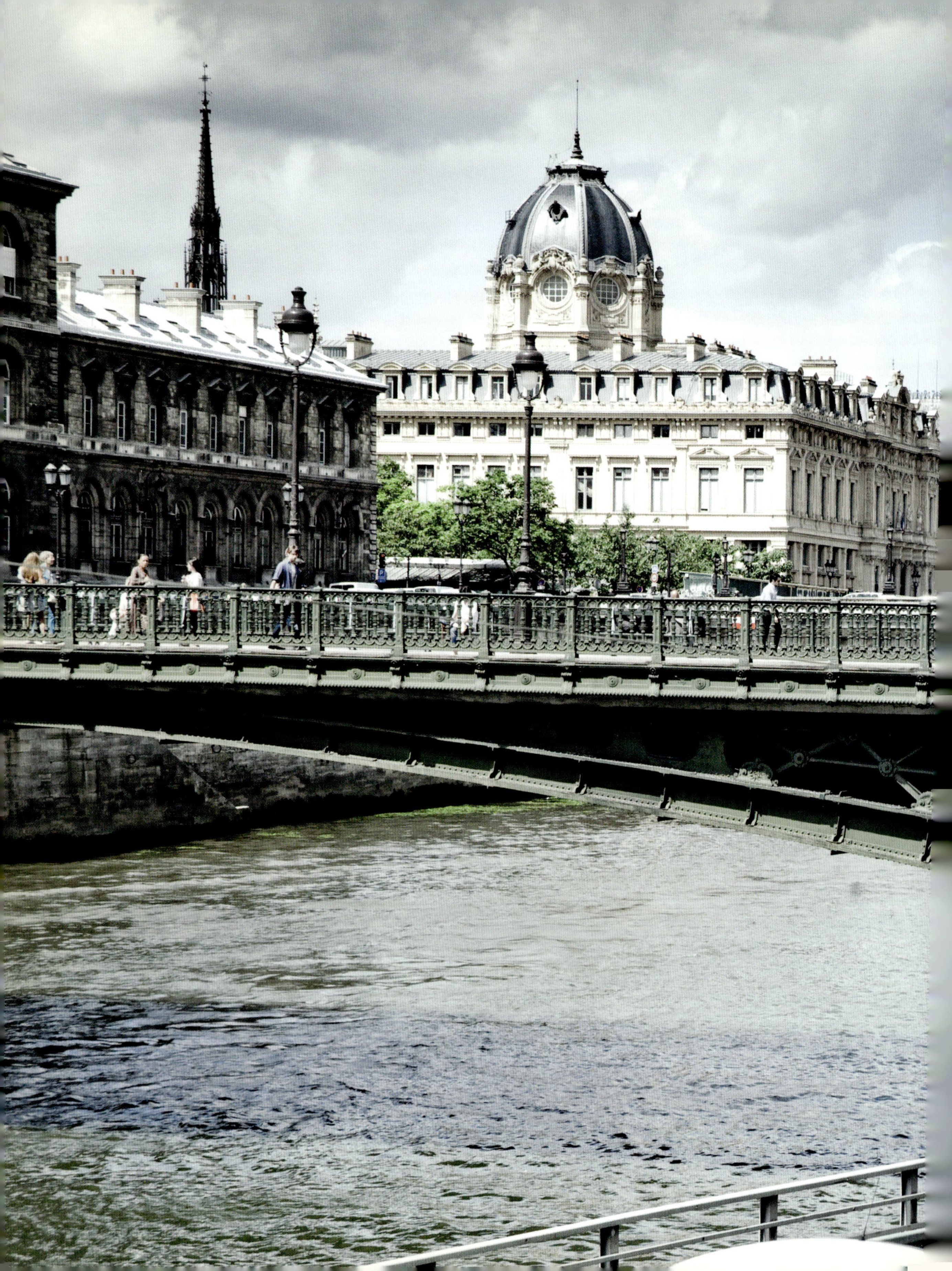

J'aime Paris

ALPHABETICAL INDEX

B/ Book	D/ Directory		A/ Area	E/ Establishment type
B/	D/		A/	E/
21	4	1728	VIIIe	RESTAURANT
13	4	21	VIe	RESTAURANT
17	4	39 V	VIIIe	RESTAURANT
25	4	58 Tour Eiffel	VIIe	RESTAURANT

A

401	32	A.A.A. Asie Antilles Afrique	XIe	DELICATESSEN
405	32	Afaria	XVe	RESTAURANT
29	4	Alain Ducasse au Plaza Athénée	VIIIe	RESTAURANT
37	4	Alfred	Ier	RESTAURANT
391	22	Aligre (Marché d')	XIIe	MARKET
291	22	Alleosse (Fromagerie)	XVIIe	FROMAGERIE
501	32	Amici Miei	XIe	RESTAURANT
281	5	Arôme (L')	VIIIe	RESTAURANT
501	32	As du Falafel (L')	IVe	DELICATESSEN
39	5	Assiette (L')	XIVe	RESTAURANT
43	5	Atelier de Joël Robuchon (L')	VIIe	RESTAURANT
281	5	Auberge du Bonheur (L')	XVIe	RESTAURANT
392	22	Auberge Pyrénnées-Cévennes	XIe	RESTAURANT
299	22	Aubrac Corner	VIIIe	RESTAURANT
502	32	Aux comptoirs des Indes	XIe	RESTAURANT
47	5	Aux Deux Amis	XIe	BRASSERIE
301	22	Aux Lyonnais	IIe	RESTAURANT

B

51	5	Bain Marie (Au)	VIIe	KITCHEN SUPPLIES
307	22	Ballon et Coquillages	XVIIe	FISH MONGER
55	6	Balzar	Ve	BRASSERIE
392	23	Bar à Patates	XVIe	MARKET
59	6	Bar aux Folies	XXe	CAFÉ
63	6	Baratin (Le)	XXe	RESTAURANT
311	23	Barthélemy	VIIe	FROMAGERIE
393	23	Bastille (Marché)	XIe	MARKET
283	6	Bateaux Parisiens	VIIe	RESTAURANT
67	6	BE	VIIIe	BAKERY
315	23	Beillevaire (Fromagerie)	XXe	FROMAGERIE
282	6	Bellechasse (Hôtel le)	VIIe	HOTEL
71	7	Benoit	IVe	RESTAURANT
517	44	Berthillon (Glacier)	IVe	ICE CREAM PARLOUR
409	32	Betsy Bernardaud	VIIe	DELICATESSEN
77	7	Bidou bar	XVIIe	BAR
81	7	Bistrot Paul Bert	XIe	RESTAURANT
521	44	Bonbon au Palais (Le)	Ve	CONFECTIONER
283	7	Brasserie Lipp	VIe	RESTAURANT
319	23	Boucherie Michel Brunon	XIIe	BUTCHER
413	33	Byzance Champs Élysées Bellota / Bellota Rive Droite	VIIIe	DELICATESSEN

C

85	7	Café Constant	VIIe	CAFÉ
89	7	Café de Flore	VIe	CAFÉ
93	8	Café de la Nouvelle Mairie	Ve	CAFÉ
417	33	Café Maure de la Mosquée de Paris	Ve	CAFÉ
525	44	Caféothèque (La)	IVe	TEA/CAFÉ
421	33	Caffè dei Cioppi	XIe	RESTAURANT
223	15	Camondo (Musée Nissim de)	VIIIe	KITCHEN SUPPLIES
393	24	Cantin (Fromagerie Marie-Anne)	VIIe	FROMAGERIE
95	8	Carré des Feuillants (Le)	Ier	RESTAURANT
284	8	Cave de Joël Robuchon (La)	VIIe	RESTAURANT
284	8	Cave de l'Os à Moelle (La)	XVe	BAR
285	8	Cave des Papilles (La)	XIVe	WINE MERCHANTS
99	8	Caves Augé (Les)	VIIIe	WINE MERCHANTS
579	44	Chalet des Îles (Le)	XVIe	RESTAURANT
285	9	Chapeau Melon	XIXe	BAR

| B/ Book | D/ Directory | A/ Area | E/ Establishment type |

B/	D/		A/	E/
3	9	Chardenoux (Le)	XIe	RESTAURANT
107	9	Chartier (Restaurant)	IXe	RESTAURANT
111	9	Chateaubriand (Le)	XIe	RESTAURANT
502	33	Cherche Midi (Le)	VIe	RESTAURANT
323	25	Chez Flottes	Ier	RESTAURANT
286	9	Chez Georges	XVIIe	RESTAURANT
394	25	Chez Georges	IIe	RESTAURANT
115	9	Chez l'Ami Jean	VIIe	RESTAURANT
119	10	Chez l'Ami Louis	IIIe	RESTAURANT
123	10	Citrus Étoilé	VIIIe	RESTAURANT
127	10	Closerie des Lilas (La)	VIe	RESTAURANT
131	10	Costes (Hôtel)	Ier	RESTAURANT
135	10	Cour Jardin (La)	VIIIe	RESTAURANT
139	10	Crémerie (La)	VIe	RESTAURANT
394	25	Crêpes et Galettes	Ve	DELICATESSEN

D

327	25	D'Chez Eux (Auberge)	VIIe	RESTAURANT
425	33	Da Rosa épicerie fine	VIe	DELICATESSEN
529	44	Dammann Frères	IVe	TEA/CAFÉ
429	33	David (Boucherie)	IVe	BUTCHER
433	34	Dehillerin	Ier	KITCHEN SUPPLIES
503	34	Dejean (Marché)	XVIIIe	MARKET
331	25	Desnoyer (Boucherie Hugo)	XIVe	BUTCHER
286	11	Deux Magots (Les)	VIe	CAFÉ
143	11	Divellec (Le)	VIIe	RESTAURANT
335	25	Dôme (La Poissonnerie du)	XIVe	FISH MONGER
287	11	Dôme (Le)	XIVe	RESTAURANT
147	11	Drouant	IIe	RESTAURANT
151	11	Du Pain et des Idées	Xe	BAKERY

E

155	11	Écailler du bistrot (L')	XIe	RESTAURANT
339	26	Écume Saint-Honoré (L')	Ier	FISH MONGER
437	34	El Fogón	VIe	RESTAURANT
395	26	Enfants Rouges (Marché des)	XVe	MARKET
343	26	Épicerie du Père Claude (L')	IIIe	DELICATESSEN

F

287	12	Fines Gueules (Les)	Ier	RESTAURANT
288	12	Flaubert (Le)	XVIIe	RESTAURANT
441	34	Florence Kahn	IVe	DELICATESSEN
157	12	Fontaine de Mars (La)	VIIe	RESTAURANT
161	12	Forum (Le)	VIIIe	BAR
165	12	Fougères (Les)	XVIIe	RESTAURANT
288	12	Fouquet's	VIIIe	DELICATESSEN
503	34	Foyer Vietnam	Ve	RESTAURANT
169	13	Frenchie	IIe	RESTAURANT

G

289	13	G. Detou	IIe	KITCHEN SUPPLIES
289	13	Garde Manger (Le)	XIIe	DELICATESSEN
445	34	Gazzetta (La)	XIIe	RESTAURANT
533	44	Génin (Chocolaterie Jacques)	XVe	CONFECTIONER
504	35	Goumanyat	IIIe	DELICATESSEN
173	13	Gourmets des Ternes (Les)	VIIIe	RESTAURANT
347	26	Graineterie du marché (La)	XIIe	DELICATESSEN
177	13	Grande cascade (La)	XVIe	RESTAURANT
351	26	Gros-La Fontaine (Marché)	XVIe	MARKET

H

579	45	Harry's New York Bar	IIe	BAR
537	45	Hermé Paris (Pierre)	Ier	PATISSERIE
590	45	Hévin Chocolatier (Jean-Paul)	VIe	CONFECTIONER

J'aime Paris

ALPHABETICAL INDEX

- 587

B/	D/		A/	E/

I

B/	D/		A/	E/
504	35	I Golosi	IXe	RESTAURANT
449	35	Idea Vino	XIe	DELICATESSEN
453	35	Il Campionissimo	IIe	RESTAURANT
505	35	Il Vino	VIIe	RESTAURANT
395	26	Itinéraires	Ve	RESTAURANT
455	35	Izraël	IVe	DELICATESSEN

J

B/	D/		A/	E/
290	13	Jadis (Restaurant)	XVe	RESTAURANT
181	14	Jeu de Quilles (Le)	XIVe	RESTAURANT
541	45	Jugetsudo	VIe	TEA/CAFÉ
189	14	Jules Verne (Le)	VIIe	RESTAURANT

K

B/	D/		A/	E/
459	37	Kaiseki	XVe	RESTAURANT
185	14	Kei	IIe	RESTAURANT

L

B/	D/		A/	E/
581	45	Ladurée	VIe	PATISSERIE
581	45	Larher (Pâtisserie Arnaud)	XVIIIe	PATISSERIE
195	14	Lasserre	VIIIe	RESTAURANT
199	14	Laurent (Le)	VIIIe	RESTAURANT
203	15	Ledoyen	VIIIe	RESTAURANT
545	47	Lenôtre	XVIe	PATISSERIE

M

B/	D/		A/	E/
549	47	Maeder (Pâtisserie Raoul)	XVIIe	PATISSERIE
553	47	Maison des Trois Thés	Ve	TEA/CAFÉ
207	15	Mama Shelter	XXe	RESTAURANT
557	47	Mariage Frères	IVe	TEA/CAFÉ
211	15	Meurice (Le)	Ier	RESTAURANT
505	37	Michelangelo	XVIIIe	RESTAURANT
575	47	Miele	VIIIe	KITCHEN SUPPLIES
215	15	Mon Vieil Ami	IVe	RESTAURANT
463	37	Mora	Ier	KITCHEN SUPPLIES
219	15	Moulin de la Vierge (Le)	XIVe	BAKERY
506	37	Moussa l'Africain	XIXe	RESTAURANT
582	47	Mulot	VIe	PATISSERIE
506	37	Murciano (Boulangerie)	IVe	BAKERY

N

B/	D/		A/	E/
582	48	Nani	XXe	PATISSERIE
507	37	Non Solo Cucina	XVIe	RESTAURANT
507	38	Non solo pasta	XVIIIe	RESTAURANT
508	38	Nouvelle Mer de Chine (La)	XIIIe	RESTAURANT

P

B/	D/		A/	E/
559	48	Pain de Sucre	IIIe	PATISSERIE
508	38	Pakkai	XIIIe	DELICATESSEN
583	48	Palais des Thés (Le)	IIIe	TEA/CAFÉ
509	38	Panzer (Charcuterie)	IVe	BUTCHERY
291	16	Papilles (Les)	Ve	DELICATESSEN
509	38	Paris Store	XIIIe	DELICATESSEN
396	27	Passy (Marché)	XVIe	MARKET
563	48	Pâtisserie des Rêves (La)	VIe	PATISSERIE
292	16	Pavillon de la Reine (Le)	IIIe	HOTEL
396	27	Père Claude (Le)	XVe	RESTAURANT
577	48	Pérène	XVIe	KITCHEN SUPPLIES
227	16	Petit Moulin (Hôtel du)	IIIe	HOTEL
292	16	Petit Vendôme (Le)	IIe	RESTAURANT
292	16	Petrossian	VIIe	RESTAURANT
231	16	Pharamond	Ier	RESTAURANT
510	38	Pho Dong Huong	XIe	CONFECTIONER

B/	D/		A/	E/
510	39	Pho Tai	XIIIe	RESTAURANT
511	39	Piccola Toscana	IXe	DELICATESSEN
235	17	Poilâne (Boulangerie)	VIe	BAKERY
293	17	Poule au pot (La)	Ier	RESTAURANT
353	27	Pousse Pousse	IXe	CONFECTIONER
290	14	Pré Verre (Le)	Ve	RESTAURANT
239	17	Prunier (Restaurant)	XVIe	RESTAURANT

Q

396	27	Quatrehomme (Fromagerie)	VIIe	FROMAGERIE
357	27	Quincy (Le)	XIIe	RESTAURANT

R

361	27	Racines	IIe	RESTAURANT
365	28	Raspail (Marché)	VIe	MARKET
243	17	Rech	XVIIe	RESTAURANT
293	17	Régalade (La)	XIVe	RESTAURANT
511	39	Réginette (La)	VIIIe	RESTAURANT
567	48	Régis Chocolatier	XVIe	CONFECTIONER
294	17	Relais Louis XIII (Le)	VIe	RESTAURANT
249	18	Relais Plaza (Le)	VIIIe	RESTAURANT
294	18	Repaire de Cartouche (Le)	XIe	RESTAURANT
295	18	Rest. Joséphine 'Chez Dumonet'	VIe	DELICATESSEN
397	28	Ribouldingue	Ve	RESTAURANT
512	39	Rino	XIe	RESTAURANT
569	49	Roger (Patrick)	VIe	CONFECTIONER
253	18	Rosa Bonheur	XIXe	RESTAURANT

S

513	39	Sardegna a Tavola	XIIe	RESTAURANT
369	28	Saturne	IIe	RESTAURANT
257	18	Savoy (Restaurant Guy)	XVIIe	RESTAURANT
373	28	Schmid Traiteur	Xe	BUTCHERY
261	18	Select (Le)	VIe	CAFÉ
467	39	Sou Quan	Ve	DELICATESSEN
375	28	Spring	Ier	RESTAURANT
513	40	Stresa (Le)	VIIIe	RESTAURANT
471	40	Sur les Quais	XIIe	DELICATESSEN

T

473	40	Tête dans les olives (La)	Xe	DELICATESSEN
583	49	The Tea Caddy	Ve	TEA/CAFÉ
379	28	Joël Thiébault maraîcher	XVIe	MARKET
265	19	Thoumieux (Hôtel)	VIIe	RESTAURANT
269	19	Train bleu (Le)	XIIe	RESTAURANT

V

383	29	Vérot - Charcutier (Gilles)	VIe	BUTCHERY
387	29	Verre volé (Le)	Xe	WINE MERCHANTS
273	19	Voltaire (Le)	VIIe	BAR
477	40	Voy Alimento (au Bar des Artisans)	Xe	BAR
481	40	VT Cash and Carry	Xe	DELICATESSEN

W

295	19	Wepler	XVIIIe	RESTAURANT
397	29	Wine by One	Ier	WINE MERCHANTS
485	40	Workshop Issé	IIe	RESTAURANT

Y

277	19	Yachts de Paris	IVe	RESTAURANT
489	41	Yam'Tcha	Ier	RESTAURANT

Z

493	41	Ze Kitchen galerie	VIe	RESTAURANT
497	41	Zerda Café	Xe	RESTAURANT

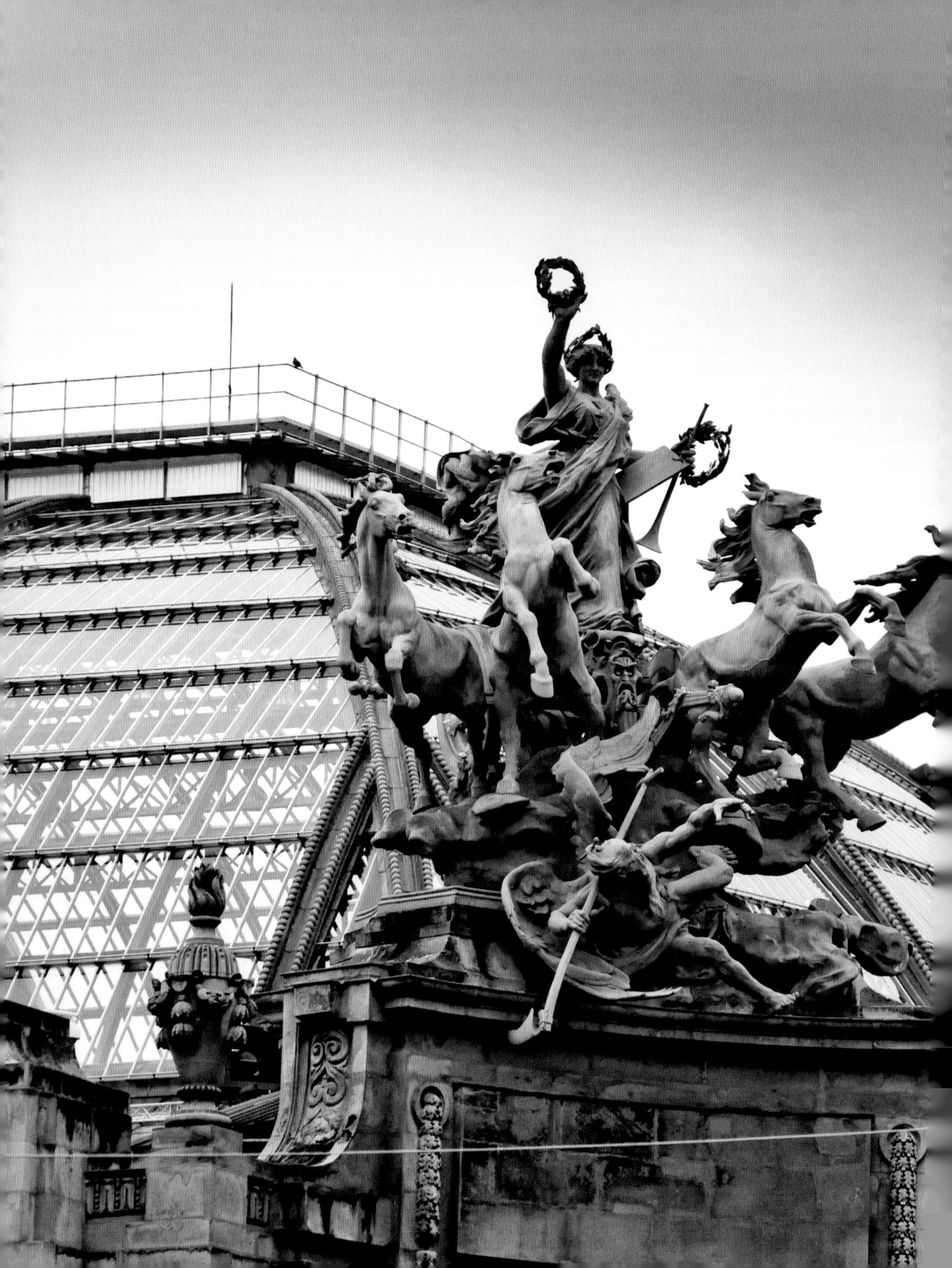

J'aime Paris

This book is a story of taste, good food, personal favourites and high adrenaline! But, above all, it has been an incredible human adventure, for which I must thank all the people involved. I would first like to thank all those who shared their profession and their passion with us: artisans, artists, butchers, chefs, confectioners, kitchen designers, grocers, suppliers, cheese-makers, market gardeners, pastry cooks, fishmongers, restaurateurs and everyone who has helped us along this journey.

Thank you to Frédérick e. Grasser Hermé, author of *La cuisinière du cuisinier*, who has guided us through this adventure. Her curiosity, discoveries and intuition have been an endless source of inspiration. Thank you to those who sat down with us to share a meal, a drink and a moment of friendship. Special thanks go to Betsy Bernardaud, who welcomed us into her home for a delicious Reuben sandwich after the market.

I would like to thank all those who have helped to create this book and made this adventure possible.
Thanks to:
-Pierre Monetta, photographer, who sensitively translated into images the soul of these places and the people who give life to them;
-Pierre Tachon, art director, who has given this work the harmony, balance and modernity I was looking for;
-Claire Dixsaut, writer, for her excellent work;
-Christophe Saintagne, executive chef and close collaborator, for his invaluable advice;
-The École de Cuisine, which welcomed us in for a truly unforgettable pastry making course!
Also Emmanuel Jirou-Najou, publishing director; Alice Vasseur, head of marketing and multimedia production; Aurélie Legay, editor; and the editorial staff: Laëtitia Teil, Bénédicte de Bary and Caroline Briens.

Lastly I thank my family for their unwavering support.
I'm passing the baton to you now. Enjoy and have seconds! Discover or rediscover Paris and make it your own!

J'aime Paris

ACKNOWLEDGEMENTS

- 593

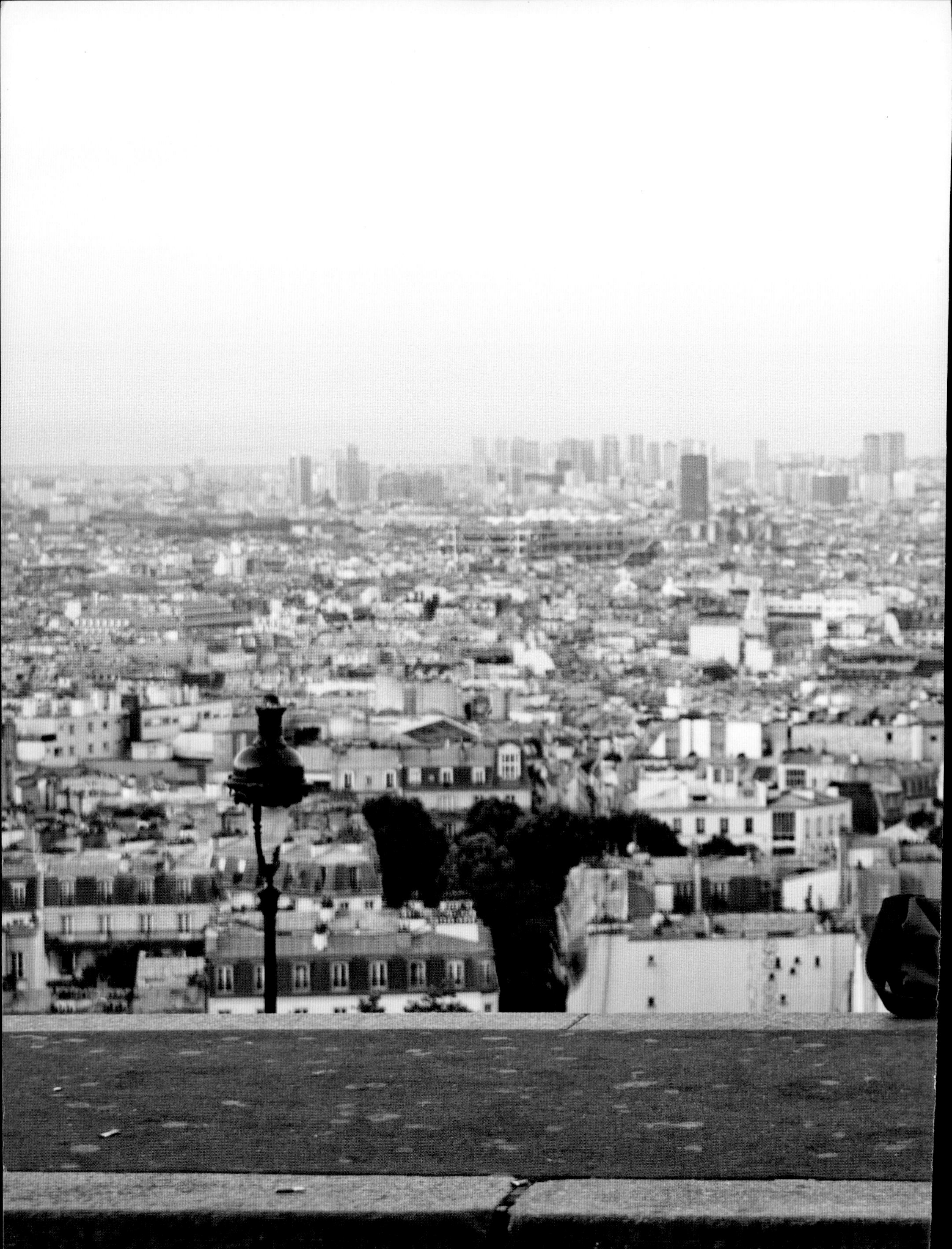

J'aime Paris

COLLECTION DIRECTOR
Emmanuel Jirou-Najou

PROJECT AND MARKETING MANAGER
Alice Vasseur

EDITOR
Aurélie Legay
thanks to Axelle and Julie

PHOTOGRAPHY
Pierre Monetta

ART DIRECTION / GRAPHIC DESIGN
Pierre Tachon / Soins graphiques

TEXTS
Claire Dixsaut,
Frédérick e. Grasser Hermé,
Christophe Saintagne

PROOFREADING
Catherine Pétrini

PHOTO-ENGRAVING
Key Graphic,
Maury Imprimeur

Printed in China
Legal deposit : 4th quarter 2011
ISBN : 9781742701875

© Alain Ducasse Édition 2011
© Hardie Grant Books 2011

A TASTE OF PARIS IN
200 CULINARY DESTINATIONS

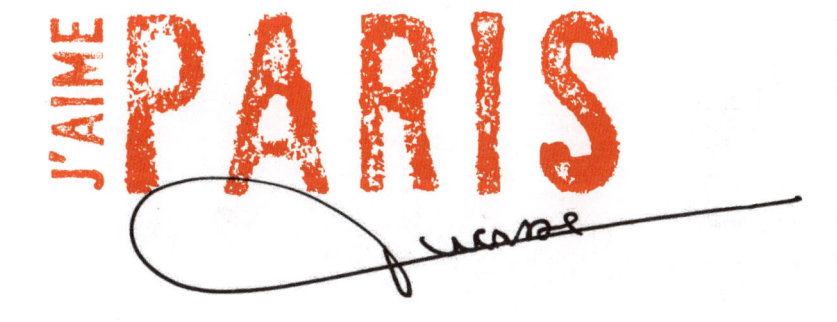

J'AIME PARIS

Ducasse

hardie grant books
MELBOURNE · LONDON

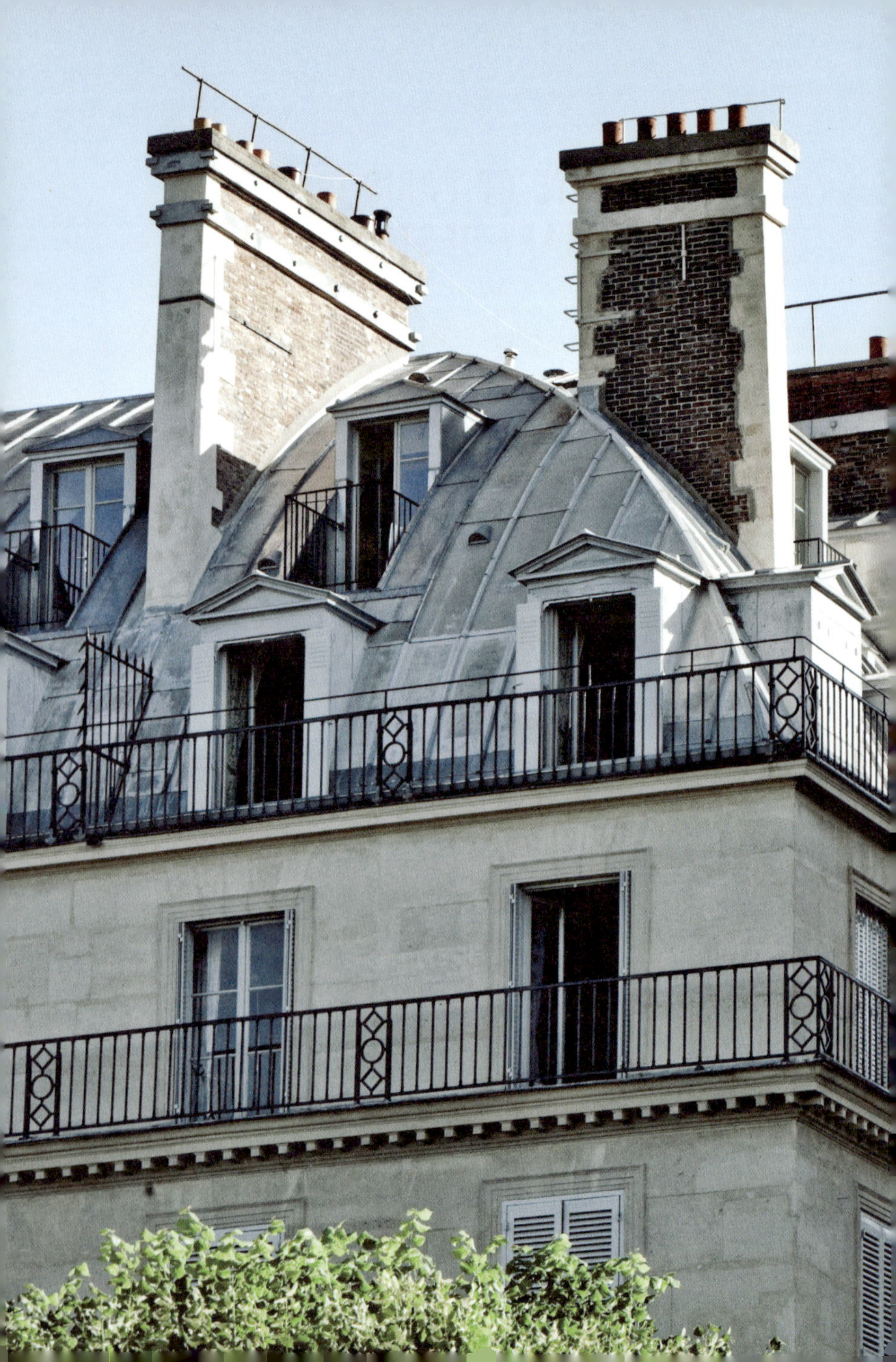

PARIS WILL ALWAYS BE PARIS

PARIS VI°
21
TUESDAY – SATURDAY
21 rue Mazarine
01 46 33 76 90
-

This restaurant is run by Paul Michelli, who is truly inventive with fish. On the menu that day were mogette beans with bottarga, sea bass and salmon tartare and *main cousu* ('hand-stitched') herring, followed by fish and chips with bacon and egg, pasta with small cuttlefish in its ink, monkfish cheek goujonettes and saffron curry. On the table was a copy of *Le Phare de Ré*, the newspaper 'of local interest with advertisements and miscellaneous notices', a souvenir from the island where the chef opened his first restaurant.

PARIS VIII°
1728
EVERY DAY; TEAROOM OPEN SATURDAY ONLY
8 rue d'Anjou
01 40 17 04 77
www.restaurant-1728.com

Lafayette lived in this house and Madame de Pompadour held court here. The Asian-inspired cuisine served in the small and adorably quaint Trois Ors room is somewhat unusual but refreshingly different. More classic is the elegant tea menu, with pastries by Arnaud Larher, a disciple of Pierre Hermé.

PARIS VIII°
39 V
MONDAY – FRIDAY
39 avenue George V
01 56 62 39 05
www.le39v.com

'Above all, 39V is a wonderful story of harmony. I wanted to gather together in this place the ingredients to make my recipe for happiness: love, involvement, humanity, good humour, conversation, sharing, discipline, beauty, sensuality, respect... and to put hospitality back into the heart of our daily preoccupations, both in the dining room and the kitchen. Located at the centre of the triangle d'or and hidden away under the rooftops of Paris, 39V is a haven of peace that offers genuine and simple cuisine.'
Frédéric Vardon

PARIS VII°
58 TOUR EIFFEL
EVERY DAY
6 avenue Gustave Eiffel
01 45 55 99 87
www.restaurants-toureiffel.com

The giant sundial on the Champs de Mars tells you it's midday – time for a picnic on level one of the Eiffel Tower. Start with a cool drink in the sunny open-air bar and enjoy the view over the Chaillot Hill. Then head for the kitchen – your picnic basket awaits. When evening falls, feast on iced pea velouté or *marbré de canard* or beef fillet, and *vacherin du jour* or profiteroles. A gastronomic experience 95 metres above the ground.

PARIS VIII°
ALAIN DUCASSE
AU PLAZA ATHÉNÉE
MONDAY – FRIDAY
25 avenue Montaigne
01 53 67 65 00
www.alain-ducasse.com

'Here I wanted to go back to basics, to start afresh with real flavours and original aromas that could express their strength and subtlety. I wanted to give technique its proper and only role, which is to reveal natural flavour. It's a radical approach – daring to create an unrefined cuisine, in the sense that it works with simplicity. The preparation is pared away – one product, one garnish – to leave the strength of the flavour in its place.'
Alain Ducasse

PARIS I“
ALFRED
TUESDAY – SATURDAY
52 rue de Richelieu
01 42 97 54 40
-

A few steps down from the Palais Royal gardens is the establishment run by William Abitbol. You are suspended, as if seated in the dress circle at the Opéra. The golden light shining through an old lampshade gives a soft glaze to the Gauloise chicken and the gilthead bream tartare with purslane. Though simple in appearance, each vegetable on the large plate is prepared differently to respect its individual flavour. The food is market-fresh every day, but the chocolate mousse is timeless.

PARIS VIII
L'ARÔME
MONDAY – FRIDAY
3 rue Saint-Philippe du Roule
01 42 25 55 98
www.larome.fr

The new décor of the restaurant features the tones of sienna, rosewood and ivory. It opens on to a beautiful kitchen. You'll want to try everything, but as the menu changes every day, your wish can never be granted. For example, depending on the season, you can choose a piece of veal sautéed with wild garlic, braised morels in Arbois wine and daikon with a marbled jus reduction. Its Michelin star is well deserved.

PARIS XIV
L'ASSIETTE
WEDNESDAY LUNCHTIME – SUNDAY LUNCHTIME
181 rue du Château
01 43 22 64 86
www.restaurant-lassiette.com

Alain Ducasse: What are you going to let us try today?
David Rathgeber: My *sauté gourmand*: veal sweetbreads, crayfish, wild mushrooms and warm foie gras. I do large sweetbread escalopes in a *beurre mousseux*. I add the crayfish, the Saint George's mushrooms and a few asparagus tips. Then I deglaze with cognac. I cover lightly with the Nantua sauce before adding the foie gras escalopes, the *fleur de sel* and a good sprinkling of pepper... *À table!*

PARIS VII
L'ATELIER DE JOËL ROBUCHON
EVERY DAY
5 rue de Montalembert
01 42 22 56 56
www.joel-robuchon.com

'When Robuchon wanted to create a new restaurant concept in 2003, he naturally joined forces with his main associates. We didn't want to work under pressure, and, above all, we wanted to be physically closer to our patrons, which is why we have this open kitchen. The way the kitchen works has also evolved. We always use quality produce, reared or harvested directly by our suppliers, and prepared with great simplicity. Today we welcome our guests as friends; it's our finest reward.'
Éric Lecerf

PARIS XVI
L'AUBERGE DU BONHEUR
EVERY DAY
Allée de Longchamp, Bois de Boulogne
01 42 24 10 17
www.aubergedubonheur.fr

Tucked away behind La Grande Cascade, and owned by the Menut family, is a tranquil place graced by nature in the heart of the city; a place with beautiful trees, gravel that crunches under your heels and garden furniture... Under the starlit sky, the tantalising aroma of grilled meat fills the air as it wafts from the kitchen. It's summer in Paris.

PARIS XI
AUX DEUX AMIS
TUESDAY – SATURDAY
45 rue Oberkampf
01 58 30 38 13
-

Aux Deux Amis has been rejuvenated. While the décor hasn't changed, the menu has been updated. Quench your thirst with a glass of *vin nature* before sitting under the neon lights to enjoy the daily specials. There is no need to make things complex for them to be good; just enjoy the moment. Don't forget to have your last drink outside on the terrace and take in the buzzing street atmosphere!

PARIS VII
AU BAIN MARIE
MONDAY – SATURDAY
56 rue de l'Université
01 42 71 08 69
-

An English duck press, the fine detail of a 1920s picnic case, a series of late 19th-century lemon-shaped bar citrus squeezers, an unusual ivory truffle grater... We're in the establishment run by Aude Clément, actually resembling the attic of a collector and traveller, where she has opened her chest full of extraordinary objects. With a flash of cloth, a genie is released from a soup tureen.

PARIS Vᵉ
BALZAR
EVERY DAY
49 rue des Écoles
01 43 54 13 67
www.brasseriebalzar.com

The terrace seems to have been set up for Smurfs! With your knees firmly wedged under your chin, you wonder if there might be other, less cramped, tables around the Sorbonne. But you go there for Sartre and Camus, or to wait until it's time for the cinema – where your seats will be even worse – and to be teased by the waiters. You also go there to enjoy such classic bistro fare as celery remoulade and leeks vinaigrette. It's an institution.

PARIS XXᵉ
BAR AUX FOLIES
EVERY DAY
8 rue de Belleville
01 46 36 65 98
-

This place was once a cabaret where Piaf and Maurice Chevalier sang. It has retained the feel of a Parisian *café théâtre* with its columns and mosaic floor. You can have your coffee while standing at the counter like in the old days, avoiding the reflection of the coloured neon lights in the large mirror that runs along the bar. Or indulge in the pleasure of a beer on the terrace while watching the world stroll by. You'll suddenly feel completely at ease there, in the true Parisian spirit.

PARIS XXᵉ
LE BARATIN
TUESDAY – SATURDAY
3 rue Jouye-Rouve
01 43 49 39 70
-

Raquel doesn't speak. She has no time, because time is of the essence. Simplicity is simmering gently in the serenity of her large shiny aluminium pans and the intimacy of her tiny kitchen. The delicate monkfish liver terrine, mackerel sashimi, horseradish and fresh raspberries display the colours of her personal and perfectly disciplined cuisine. The list of *vins nature* chosen by Philippe Pinoteau, 'Pinuche' to his friends, are a real talking point, and will no doubt take care of conversation.

PARIS VIIᵉ
BATEAUX PARISIENS
EVERY DAY
Port de La Bourdonnais
08 25 01 01 01
www.bateauxparisiens.com

You can hire one of these restaurant boats to take you down the Seine at twilight, or to enjoy any of their 'Prestige', 'Champagne', 'Jazz', 'Étoile' or 'Saveur' options for an intimate dinner. As the monuments begin to light up, the breeze is blowing and the imagination takes over. Green and white velouté cappuccino, duck breast in Port wine jus and iconic crêpes Suzette with orange butter bring out the magic of a supper under the lights. The extensive wine list is excellent. Whether you are from Paris or Tokyo, you will enjoy a special moment.

PARIS VIIIᵉ
BE
TUESDAY – SUNDAY
73 boulevard de Courcelles
01 46 22 20 20
www.boulangepicier.com

Just because you lead a hectic life doesn't mean you have to eat badly. The bread here is made from scratch and baked in the oven that is the central fixture of this bakery-cum-grocery store. The sandwiches are made with the best fillings: tuna belly, sardines in oil, tomato confit, cured ham and rocket, among others. In five minutes your *be box®* is ready to take away. For your evening meal, have a blood sausage, a packet of good pasta and olive oil, which you'll find on the shelves. Just follow the instructions on the label. You will also find superb pastries and chocolate pizza.

PARIS VIIᵉ
HÔTEL LE BELLECHASSE
EVERY DAY
8 rue de Bellechasse
01 45 50 22 31
www.lebellechasse.com

This new hotel designed by Christian Lacroix spreads its multicoloured wings. The décor oozes humour and elegance. Collages of old prints that have been enlarged and coloured are mixed together with a total disregard for convention. Your eye is first drawn to Elizabeth I, before you turn your attention to the bright scarlet faux Louis XIII wallpaper and become filled with wonder at the medieval geometries, taking flight with the passing butterflies. You should experience this while having a really amazing breakfast in your room.

PARIS IVe
BENOIT
EVERY DAY
20 rue Saint-Martin
01 42 72 25 76
www.esprit-bistrot.com

A landmark to the Parisian appetite for indulgence, Benoit has been treating the taste buds of the French capital since 1912. But with a modern twist – true Parisian cuisine. Depending on the season, enjoy stuffed tomatoes or asparagus in mousseline sauce, followed by sole à la Nantua or Lucullus-style veal tongue. Then there is the rare pleasure of authentic profiteroles.

PARIS XVIIe
BIDOU BAR
MONDAY – SATURDAY
12 rue Anatole de la Forge
01 43 80 09 18 / 06 09 97 53 67
-

Piaf is there, two stools away. She must have felt at home in this now legendary bar, among the carefully lined up bottles, the dark woodwork with rounded corners and the sleek leather banquettes. The atmosphere is laid-back. A portrait of *Les Tontons Flingueurs* watches over from the back wall between two old radios. Even today, the cuisine served here is in the typical *Parigot/tête de veau* (down-to-earth Parisian) style. Blackboard specials from 11 a.m. to 2 p.m. Good wine list. Champagne!

PARIS XIe
BISTROT PAUL BERT
TUESDAY – SATURDAY
18 rue Paul Bert
01 43 72 24 01
-

Jean Gabin is having problems with his son, a lad named Claude Brasseur, and with his daughter, Jeanne Moreau. Gabin is from the country, Brasseur is a racing cyclist and Jeanne Moreau is infatuated with an old beau. When you sit down in Bistrot Paul Bert, what you see is *Gas-oil (Hi-Jack Highway)*, Gabin's great films, Moreau's smile and Paris in black and white.

PARIS VIe
BRASSERIE LIPP
EVERY DAY
151 boulevard Saint-Germain
01 45 48 53 91
-

This establishment is an historical monument. The 1900s interior and façade are listed and even the menu has not changed in half a century. But don't be put off by this. Whatever the season, you must try the choucroute on your first visit. Like the unchanging plant motifs on the tiled walls, you will still be offered the choice of *blanquette de veau* (veal stew) or *boeuf gros sel* (boiled beef). Like some of the regulars, the millefeuilles are substantial.

PARIS VIIe
CAFÉ CONSTANT
EVERY DAY
139 rue Saint-Dominique
01 47 53 73 34
www.cafeconstant.com

Christian Constant has entrusted the reins of this establishment to the former head chef of his Les Fables de La Fontaine restaurant. The brasserie food is inspired by Constant's mother and revisited by one who knows what he's doing. You are transported back to his childhood with roast berry chicken within herb butter and vanilla rice pudding. There are also forays into more modern dishes such as saddle of rabbit ballotine with artichoke carpaccio, or crisp pastry-wrapped shrimp with basil. Come back the next morning for a chocolate croissant at the bar.

PARIS VIe
CAFÉ DE FLORE
EVERY DAY
172 boulevard Saint-Germain
01 45 44 33 40
www.cafedeflore.fr

The dish arrives boiling hot and golden. The regular customer barely looks at his Welsh rarebit, a melted Cheddar treat. It consists of tasty morsels of bread under a creamy, beer-flavoured coating *au gratin*. On the terrace, in the shadow of Sartre and his 'Beaver', you trace the back of your spoon over the green writing on the saucer while enjoying life. A cappuccino with the froth rising like a soufflé and a buttered slice of Parisian baguette are just the thing to start the day.

PARIS V⁰
CAFÉ DE LA NOUVELLE MAIRIE
MONDAY – FRIDAY
19–21 rue des Fossés Saint-Jacques
01 44 07 04 41
-

A stone's throw from the Panthéon, lunch is being served in a small shady square. The students have come from the Lycée Henri IV on the rue d'Ulm. They take their time, sporting moustaches from their almost solid hot chocolates. A pretty blonde girl flicks through the newspaper under a blackboard that reads 'Fine wines, *vins nature*'. After rabbit terrine and a glass of Anjou, it's back to school.

PARIS I⁰ʳ
LE CARRÉ DES FEUILLANTS
MONDAY – FRIDAY, SATURDAY EVENING
14 rue de Castiglione
01 42 86 82 82
www.carredesfeuillants.fr

At the end of a passageway, a box-like building stands on the site of the former Feuillant monastery built in the time of Henri IV. Alain Dutournier has a keen sense of beauty, and he treats us to elegant and contemporary dishes influenced by the food of south-west France. People come here to sample its generous, characterful cuisine: foie gras, langoustines with sweet garlic nougatine, veal sweetbreads with fresh morels, and wild strawberry, rose and lychee macaroons. Place Vendôme is nearby, yet we could almost be in the south.

PARIS VII⁰
LA CAVE DE JOËL ROBUCHON
MONDAY – SATURDAY
3 rue Paul-Louis Courier
01 42 22 11 02
www.joel-robuchon.com

Even with 5,000 different wines, the choice is perfect, and not without reason. Antoine Hernandez has been the sommelier with Joël Robuchon for over 20 years. Let yourself be guided to sound choices, such as 'La Marginale' Saumur-Champigny by Thierry Germain, bio Rieslings by Jean-Louis and Fabienne Mann or Champagnes by Bruno Paillard. Besides tastings, the house also offers to create and manage your own cellar.

PARIS XV⁰
LA CAVE DE L'OS À MOELLE
TUESDAY – SUNDAY
181 rue de Lourmel
01 45 57 28 28
-

You have to work a little, as you do at home. You choose your wine from the shelf and pay the store price. You cut the still-warm bread to accompany your choice of starters: terrines, carrots, beetroot and a good mayonnaise. You get up and go to the back of the cellar where you serve yourself the day's still simmering special directly from the pot, or you choose the duck confit or stuffed vegetables. And you disturb other diners sharing your table. However, all your efforts are rewarded by an *île flottante* that is nigh-on perfect.

PARIS XIV⁰
LA CAVE DES PAPILLES
TUESDAY – SUNDAY
35 rue Daguerre
01 43 20 05 74
www.lacavedespapilles.blogspot.com

It's Sunday and the rue Daguerre feels like a cheese lovers' convention. You sympathise, but seek refuge in La Cave des Papilles. How about a French *vin nature* to go with couscous? After getting over your initial amazement, you are full of ideas. You choose a sparkling rosé, only slightly sweet, but cheerful and a little anarchic. It will be paella next time. You will be able to pick a wine from inside the cellar, where you can find a few hidden treasures, or just go for a cold bottle of bubbly.

PARIS VIII⁰
LES CAVES AUGÉ
MONDAY – SATURDAY
116 boulevard Haussmann
01 45 22 16 97
www.cavesauge.com

The apostles of *vin nature* have been preaching here for over 20 years. The establishment's chirpy owner Marc Sibard, former head sommelier at Fouquet's, makes a stand in defence of the honour of small-scale producers. Inside his Ali Baba's cave, the goods lift comes to the surface with some very pretty bottles, uncompromisingly guaranteed from their *terroir* and free from chemical additives.

PARIS XIXᵉ
CHAPEAU MELON
WEDNESDAY – SUNDAY
92 rue Rébeval
01 42 02 68 60
-

Hats off to Olivier Camus. Here's someone with a wonderful knowledge of how to drink and how to track down the highest quality labels of *vin nature*. He is a crusader for signature wines and an activist against unreliable appellations, a man on a quest for impeccable standards. He places his knowledge of French vineyards at the service of deluxe wine pairings.

PARIS XIᵉ
LE CHARDENOUX
EVERY DAY
1 rue Jules Valles
01 43 71 49 52
www.restaurantlechardenoux.com

'I was looking for a very Parisian location, where I could create an easy and uncomplicated cuisine. A bistro is associated with the idea of a chef – timeless, charming, authentic, gourmet... I pushed open the door at Le Chardenoux and I said to myself: this is the place. We've been interpreting the great Parisian classics ever since: beef tartare, Landes asparagus with mimosa sauce, saddle of lamb cooked in a clay crust, chicken cooked in hay, French toast, waffles. But this doesn't mean we can't do other more exotic things, like curried clams, for instance.' Cyril Lignac

PARIS IXᵉ
RESTAURANT CHARTIER
EVERY DAY
7 rue du Faubourg Montmartre
01 47 70 86 29
www.restaurant-chartier.com

This reasonably priced restaurant has always had *bouillon* as its signature dish, a broth made from meat and vegetables served directly at the table. Chartier is popular for its unusual mix of simple bistro cooking and opulent theatrical décor. As if seated in a velvet-lined box, you can appreciate this quality simply by biting into an egg with mayonnaise. Canteen-style dishes are the order of the day, with grated carrots and cucumbers in cream. The menu scrawled on the paper tablecloth is almost worth framing.

PARIS XIᵉ
LE CHATEAUBRIAND
TUESDAY – SATURDAY
129 avenue Parmentier
01 43 57 45 95
-

Warning, cuisine on the move – frequent turbulence; chance of dizziness; unexpected encounters with shellfish and dashi; anchovies or mango coming aground on a carpaccio. At the helm, Inaki Aizpitarte smiles behind his beard. Drawing on his Basque roots, he creates a soft fruit piperade and a rose-flavoured fromage frais. For dessert, he is bold enough to serve his already famous *banane ecrasée* (mashed banana). You come back to land a little shaken after having discovered new horizons; it's as if you have just gone for a spin in a flying saucer.

PARIS XVIIᵉ
CHEZ GEORGES
EVERY DAY
273 boulevard Pereire
01 45 74 31 00
www.restaurant-chezgeorges.fr

It's unavoidable: once through the door, you become a banker from a Balzac novel, or the editor-in-chief of *Le Figaro*, or the President of France. The two rows of white tablecloths form a guard of honour, but there's no need for you to greet the crowd when taking your seat. Here, the art of *cuisine bourgoise* is cultivated in all its glory: chicken liver terrine, lentil salad, veal sweetbreads with morels cooked to perfection, an elegant farm-raised veal rib and desserts *grand-mère* would make. The wine list features a number of select Bordeaux.

PARIS VIIᵉ
CHEZ L'AMI JEAN
TUESDAY – SATURDAY
27 rue Malar
01 47 05 86 89
www.amijean.eu

'The philosophy behind my kitchen and cooking is simple: no partitions; no barriers; inspiration from tradition; being free... do you know what I mean? In fact just cooking! My strategy is to find the best produce, sourced from all over France, and then to do everything from A to Z, something different every day. Today I've made this: octopus terrine with foie gras and smoked salt. That's for today, but I don't know about tomorrow. The easy thing would be to make it again, but that wouldn't be any fun... Freedom is what counts here!' Stéphane Jego

PARIS IIIe
CHEZ L'AMI LOUIS
WEDNESDAY – SUNDAY
32 rue du Vertbois
01 48 87 77 48
-

In 1924, this establishment, which served *bouillon* and fried dishes, was owned by Louis Pedebosq. Antoine Magnin bought the business in 1936 and continued to offer traditional cuisine. Several generations of customers frequent the restaurant today, each of whom has a particular emotional attachment to it. Its last owner, Thierry de La Brosse, perfectly preserved the spirit of the place. Now that he has joined the angels, it is certain that his successors will, under the benevolent supervision of Monsieur Louis, be able to carry on his legacy.

PARIS VIIIe
CITRUS ÉTOILE
MONDAY – FRIDAY
6 rue Arsène Houssaye
01 42 89 15 51
www.citrusetoile.fr

During his ten years in Hollywood, Gilles Epié learned the lessons of lively and light cuisine. Steaming and lemon juice are enough to bring out the best in food: duck foie gras ravioli with truffles and morels or steamed calf's liver with chanterelle mushrooms. The chic décor features a palette of electrifying citrus colours. Epié's wife Élizabeth, a former model he met in Los Angeles, supervises the front of house with enthusiasm and energy. She offers an extremely warm welcome to all guests.

PARIS VIe
LA CLOSERIE DES LILAS
EVERY DAY
171 boulevard du Montparnasse
01 40 51 34 50
www.closeriedeslilas.fr

You automatically look under the banquette in case Picasso left behind a splash of paint, Hemingway a page of one of his manuscripts or Rimbaud a free verse. Regulars who come here – even in Aragon's day – are in the know: you have to go to the brasserie, the restaurant is for the *bourgeois*. What matters is that you enjoy the arbour and its famous lilac trees, while letting the legendary hand-cut steak tartare or haddock *à la crème* melt in your mouth and tantalise your taste buds.

PARIS Ier
HÔTEL COSTES
EVERY DAY
239 rue Saint-Honoré
01 42 44 50 25
www.hotelcostes.com

Here is Costes, in the style of Jean-Louis. People go there to check out the scene and to be treated badly. Jacques García's neo-Napoleon III décor, with its cardinal red draperies and velvet, is worth seeing – and so are the clientele. But if you come back, it won't be by chance. The quality of the food is exacting and constant, almost obsessively so. The menu doesn't change often, but why alter something that works? Signature dishes include the famous 'Crying Tiger', a reworking of the Thai classic.

PARIS VIIIe
LA COUR JARDIN
EVERY DAY
25 avenue Montaigne
01 53 67 66 02
www.plaza-athenee-paris.fr

From May to September, the Hotel Plaza Athénée opens its courtyard and sets up a summer restaurant. Sheltered from view in the cool garden, you can enjoy a special moment with a Mediterranean feel. Heritage tomatoes, fava beans, artichokes, fennel, courgette flowers. Vegetables dominate the menu. Enjoy listening to the birds in a chic rustic atmosphere.

PARIS VIe
LA CRÉMERIE
EVERY DAY
9 rue des Quatre-Vents
01 43 54 99 30
www.lacremerie.fr

It's always a magical moment when the scissor tip cuts the pouch, which opens like petals. Inside, happiness takes on the form of *burrata cremossissima*. A drizzle of olive oil, a few cherry tomatoes and a scant sprinkling of herbs are added. A spoon sinks into it and would like to stay there forever. While Serge cuts *prosciutto* on the Berkel slicer, Hélène prepares a vegetable tian. We're ready for the ripe Camembert, handsome Serge's pride and joy.

PARIS VI⁰
LES DEUX MAGOTS
EVERY DAY
6 place Saint-Germain-des-Prés
01 45 48 55 25
www.lesdeuxmagots.fr

The place to come to for the view and the cultural history of this district, which was partly written on these tables. Facing the Saint Germain church and the square where the Picasso statue stands, Les Deux Magots is one of the oldest Parisian cafés. It has always welcomed the inhabitants of Saint-Germain-des-Prés, celebrities and tourists, and has awarded a literary prize since 1933. Inside, certain drinks are still served by presenting customers with the bottle first. You must try a hot chocolate served the old-fashioned way.

PARIS VII⁰
LE DIVELLEC
MONDAY – FRIDAY
107 rue de l'Université
01 45 51 91 96
www.le-divellec.com

'Paris? I was born there. But my parents moved to La Rochelle when I was young. I returned to Paris in 1983, and I brought back coastal cuisine with me – fish, crustaceans and shellfish... This morning I received these seven-kilo turbots, some wedge sole and mullets as wide as your arm from my wholesalers in Brittany. I taught my waiters to handle and bone fish in front of customers. This means a lot to me; it's the identity of the house.'   Jacques Le Divellec

PARIS XIV⁰
LE DÔME
EVERY DAY
108 boulevard du Montparnasse
01 43 35 25 81
-

Aristocratic fish for a deluxe brasserie. They are sourced from the neighbouring Poissonnerie du Dôme and are beautiful, to match the Slavonic-style interior. The menu changes with the daily catch: darne of John Dory or bouillabaisse, grilled red mullet or a seafood platter. Regulars have included many notable figures, from Trotsky to Jean-Paul Sartre.

PARIS II⁰
DROUANT
TUESDAY – SUNDAY
16–18 place Gaillon
01 42 65 15 16
www.drouant.com

'One day during my life as a chef, I told myself that I had to grow further in the art of cooking. So I gave back my three Michelin stars and I simplified my cuisine by removing it from the gastronomy scene. But there are certain pillars that are untouchable when cooking: pleasure, indulgence, warmth and generosity. Since 2006, Drouant, this monument in Parisian restaurant culture and literature, has allowed me to express myself and to spread my wings...'
Antoine Westermann

PARIS X⁰
DU PAIN ET DES IDÉES
MONDAY – FRIDAY
34 rue Yves Toudic
01 42 40 44 52
www.dupainetdesidees.com

'Time makes the difference – time and the number of stages. Working slowly keeps the leavening wilder. But it's also more fragile. It's like wine. Certain types of leavening will express themselves if you aren't too aggressive with them. It's living beings that are transformed; you can only adapt to the material.'   Christophe Vasseur, baker

PARIS XI⁰
L'ÉCAILLER DU BISTROT
TUESDAY – SATURDAY
22 rue Paul Bert
01 43 72 76 77
-

This is the seafood restaurant belonging to Bistrot Paul Bert, Edith Piaf's haunt that we liked so much. On the style side, it's definitely a notch above the other. On the food side, it's also good, and not without reason: the chef's father-in-law is a fisherman. There are a dozen seafood dishes on the blackboard featuring fish, shellfish and shelled crab. There's also a good-value lobster menu.

PARIS Ier
LES FINES GUEULES
EVERY DAY
43 rue Croix des Petits-Champs
01 42 61 35 41
www.lesfinesgueules.fr

You allow yourself to be recommended a good wine to go with a sausage you are having at the bar. Then you discover the menu: meat from the exceptional butcher Desnoyer, sea bass with a vegetable garnish, line-caught black sea bream or asparagus from Le Blayais. There is an impeccable selection of wines put together by Arnaud Bradol, the young owner. It's very difficult to decide between the *soupe de pêches* and the pear clafoutis. They like quality products here, and it shows.

PARIS XVIIe
LE FLAUBERT
MONDAY EVENING – FRIDAY, SATURDAY EVENING
10 rue Gustave Flaubert
01 42 67 05 81
www.michelrostang.com

Elegant caramel-coloured woodwork effortlessly holds a beautiful collection of ceramic figurines. In the first of his 'bistros', Michel Rostang throws his weight behind simple cuisine. Featured dishes include Bresse chicken from suppliers Mieral, cooked in a rotisserie and served in two courses, or *penne au gratin* with lobster from the morning catch. The cheeses are from Fromagerie Laurent Dubois and the *escargots en brioche* are by Christine Ferber, known as la *fée des confitures* (the jam fairy).

PARIS VIIe
LA FONTAINE DE MARS
EVERY DAY
129 rue Saint-Dominique
01 47 05 46 44
www.fontainedemars.com

In this traditional bistro – complete with checked tablecloths, moleskin banquettes and straw-bottom chairs – Christiane and Jacques Boudon showcase products from the south-west of France: cassoulet with Tarbes beans, Basque country blood sausage by Christian Parra and *tourtière landaise* prune pie, among others. However they don't neglect the rest of the country, with their charcuterie products coming from Mainon Laborie in the Auvergne region, and Duval andouillette sausages. The eggs poached in Madiran wine are a highlight.

PARIS VIIIe
LE FORUM
MONDAY – SATURDAY
4 boulevard Malesherbes
01 42 65 37 86
www.bar-le-forum.com

Why on earth is this so good? The spirits come in all colours with the most fashionable labels. There are more than 25 cocktail recipes and a third-millennium London ambience. The cocktails in this institution of Parisian nightlife, stirred not shaken by Josaine Biolatto, are true culinary concoctions. They radiate quality, inventiveness and humour. You could while the night away just enjoying them.

PARIS XVIIe
LES FOUGÈRES
MONDAY – FRIDAY
10 rue Villebois Mareuil
01 40 68 78 66
www.restaurant-les-fougeres.com

'My favourite ingredient is mackerel. I like to start with a simple product that is available to everybody and reveal all its complexity in a dish that will surprise my guests. My favourite recipe is cuttlefish fillets with seasonal vegetables. Shiitake mushrooms are perfect in May, with their marked aroma of black truffles. I like to use unexpected ingredients like *écume de mer* sauce, *Juliette des Sables* potatoes and lemongrass to enhance regional produce like this sublime farmhouse pork.'
Stéphane Duchiron

PARIS VIIIe
FOUQUET'S
EVERY DAY
99 avenue des Champs-Elysées
01 40 69 60 50
www.fouquetsbarriere.com

There are celebrities in the room, and on the plates, too. The Merlan Colbert whiting is done in the style preferred by Robert Hossein; and there is Lobster Jean Todt and a *palet au chocolat* in honour of the César Awards. For those worried about their health but not wanting to miss out on a taste experience, dietician Paule Neyrat helped to create a tuna ceviche with starfruit juice and a monkfish stew with coconut and tamarind.

PARIS IIe
FRENCHIE
TUESDAY EVENING – SATURDAY EVENING
5 rue du Nil
01 40 39 96 19
www.frenchie-restaurant.com

'I went abroad at a very young age. I worked in New York and London. From what I learned during those years of training, I've tried to retain a spontaneous and honest way of cooking, and to use flavours that are considered unusual in France: pickles, chutneys and citrus condiments. As I work alone in the kitchen, I have to get down to the essentials, to the flavour. Afterwards, for the garnish, you know there is a French school of classical garden... I'm more the English garden type; I go for an organised chaos, but one that's always harmonious!' **Grégory Marchand**

PARIS IIe
G. DETOU
MONDAY – SATURDAY
58 rue Tiquetonne
01 42 36 54 67
www.gdetou.com

Need something? Here's where you'll find it. One of the specialities of this establishment, is patisserie supplies. Here you'll find the chocolate pellets professionals use, cream of tartar that you used to buy at the chemist's, dried cranberries to make cranberry biscuits, gelling agents, emulsifiers and a whole lot of other miscellaneous items. And that's without counting the pistachio and rose paste for making macaroons and the sparkles. As well as all that, you can seek advice from two lovely ladies on how to make your cakes a success.

PARIS XIIe
LE GARDE MANGER
MONDAY – SATURDAY
17 rue d'Aligre
01 40 01 02 31
-

A stone's throw away from the Aligre Market, Anne-Françoise Toussaint warmly welcomes you to Le Garde Manger, her Alsatian *delicatessen*. How about a glass of farm-fresh apple juice? It goes perfectly with the *flammekueche* cooked in a wood-fired oven. The traditional *baekeoffe*, the foie gras with turnips and the *spätzle* – noodles containing farm-fresh eggs – are all homemade. This grocery–eatery is filled with artisanal delicacies that come straight from Alsace: seasonal preserves by Christine Ferber, jars of choucroute and pork products, among others.

PARIS VIIIe
LES GOURMETS DES TERNES
MONDAY – FRIDAY
87 boulevard de Courcelles
01 42 27 43 04
www.lesgourmetsdesternes.com

If you're a lover of straightforward cuisine and big servings, this is a really good bistro. You'll appreciate the brawn, the andouillette sausage and leeks vinaigrette. And you'll especially love the enormous 'special' steak with marrow. And you can't leave without having the *baba chantilly* dessert, which rhymes with yippee and arouses passions. Booking is recommended.

PARIS XVIe
LA GRANDE CASCADE
EVERY DAY
Bois de Boulogne
01 45 27 33 51
www.grandecascade.com

At midday, you are charmed by the décor, the Second Empire pavilion and the cool murmuring of the waterfall. At night, away from Paris and the notion of time, you enjoy the elegant cuisine at this, the Menut family's flagship restaurant. Here the classics are treated with a good dose of inventiveness: escargots with verbena butter, baked cod steak with butternut *mousseline*, or horseradish *espuma* and toasted *kouglof* to go with duck foie gras. As impressionist as a Sunday in the country.

PARIS XVe
RESTAURANT JADIS
MONDAY – SATURDAY
208 rue de la Croix-Nivert
01 45 57 73 20
www.bistrot-jadis.com

This is a bistro in evening dress. The herring and potatoes are accompanied by a spinach and red orach velouté. The *gâteau de foie* comes with grilled langoustines and matching bisque. The rhubarb *panna cotta* is flavoured with hawthorn. It's daring and fresh, and a big hit.

PARIS XIVe
LE JEU DE QUILLES
WEDNESDAY – SATURDAY
45 rue Boulard
01 53 90 76 22
-

A superb selection of unprocessed products is served generously by Benoît Reix, who presides over the place from behind the bar. For our tasting pleasure that day: a *burrata* from Puglia, a soft mixture of cow's milk and creamy mozzarella, to be eaten with a teaspoon. It was matched to great effect. A freshly picked ripe tomato drizzled with a mild olive oil... *fleur de sel* would have been too much! Behind the bar, Benoît proposed good bio wines in classic styles.

PARIS VIIe
LE JULES VERNE
EVERY DAY
Altima – 6 avenue Gustave Eiffel
01 45 55 61 44
www.lejulesverne-paris.com

The Eiffel Tower – no Parisian can ever be indifferent about it. When it starts to sparkle the moment you look at it, and when you discover the lights of the city through the bay window, the Eiffel Tower offers you the magic of Paris as a gift. In this unique place, iconic landmark of France, the cuisine Pascal Féraud serves is 100 per cent French. From olive oil to morel mushrooms, it is a tricolour rainbow of the best products from the country's regions. Down-to-earth cooking to accompany a moment of weightlessness.

PARIS Ier
KEI
TUESDAY – SATURDAY
5 rue Coq-Héron
01 42 33 14 74
www.restaurant-kei.com

Kei Kobayashi is a very Japanese chef who is actually French! His influences are therefore mixed: the aestheticism, the verticality of his constructions, poetic harmony of colours and delicate flavours are inspired by Japan; while France has taught him the precision of actions and cooking times, meticulous finishing touches and respect for ingredients. The result is a rich and creative palette of subtle combinations where defined flavours culminate in a unique and perfectly executed cuisine.

PARIS VIIIe
LASSERRE
DINNER TUESDAY – SATURDAY; LUNCH THURSDAY AND FRIDAY
17 avenue Franklin Roosevelt
01 43 59 53 43
www.restaurant-lasserre.com

After the war, the modest bistro he founded moved into the adjacent mansion, which had been restored. This legendary restaurant is the fruit of the labours and passion of this man. Over the years, it earned him international renown and breathed life into a classic, delicate French cuisine. Today, Restaurant Lasserre has taken on a new impetus with the arrival of Christophe Moret. The opportunity was also taken to refresh the décor of the main dining room, where the retractable roof opens for dinner under the stars.

PARIS VIIIe
LE LAURENT
EVERY DAY
41 avenue Gabriel
01 42 25 00 39
www.le-laurent.com

'First of all we had to soak up the history of this place, to listen to it and feel it. Then we had to offer dishes suited to the sensitivity of Philippe Bourguignon, who has managed this establishment since 1976. The benchmarks we set were subtlety, elegance and respect for the products we use. Today, the spider crab in lobster jelly and fennel crème, the winter vegetable *palette de couleurs*, the turbot in a salt crust and the milk-fed veal confit are part of the history of this house. We are very proud of that.' **Alain Pégouret**

PARIS V^e
LE PRÉ VERRE
TUESDAY – SATURDAY
8 rue Thénard
01 43 54 59 47
www.lepreverre.com

There is cinnamon in the suckling pig, and other spices, too. After the surprise comes the pleasure. It radiates through the steaming and hearty dish with its typically French presentation; it climbs up through the fork, which pierces the creamy flesh; it teases the taste buds, evoking memories of Italian sausages with saffron and of Asian caramelised pork. Once it has taken hold, pleasure orders the brain to take another mouthful...

PARIS VIII⁰
LEDOYEN
MONDAY EVENING – FRIDAY EVENING
1 avenue Dutuit
01 53 05 10 01
www.ledoyen.com

'What cuisine do I create today? One that combines visual simplicity with complex flavours, while at the same time being elegant and full of freshness. Among the highlights are the veal sweetbreads with lemongrass, the turbot with truffle emulsion and the langoustines with citrus. It's always a pleasure to discover in the Carré des Champs Elysées district a legendary place in the midst of an oasis of greenery. This is Paris at its most magical!' **Christian Le Squer**

PARIS XX⁰
MAMA SHELTER
EVERY DAY
109 rue de Bagnolet
01 43 48 45 45
www.mamashelter.com

Sip your drink at the Philippe Starck designed bar. Lift your head and feast your eyes on the incredible slate ceiling covered in stylish graffiti. You can referee a fierce game of table football while placing your order, or why not have dinner with friends? The 'simple' menu prepared by Alain Senderens offers warm, melt-in-your-mouth leeks served with a herb vinaigrette, salmon topped with a light horseradish crème and duck foie gras terrine. For dessert, be amazed by Mama's *baba*.

PARIS I⁰ʳ
LE MEURICE
MONDAY – FRIDAY
228 rue de Rivoli
01 44 58 10 55
www.meuricehotel.fr/restaurant-le-meurice

'I was born in Puteaux, and my parents managed bistros in Paris and its suburbs. Parisian cuisine has always been a part of my culture. I'm naturally drawn to combing the Paris region so that I can later enjoy myself with the produce I find. Today, Le Meurice is showcasing about 40 varieties of typically Parisian produce, such as Pontoise cabbage, Argenteuil asparagus, Houdan chicken and Paris petit pois.'

Yannick Alléno

PARIS IV⁰
MON VIEIL AMI
WEDNESDAY – SUNDAY
69 rue Saint-Louis en l'Île
01 40 46 01 35
www.mon-vieil-ami.com

'Remember, Alain, you were the one who encouraged me to visit this little bistro on the Île Saint-Louis seven years ago. What I wanted was simple: to welcome people here as friends, as one would at home. I pay tribute to my mother, who is the reason for my love of vegetables and could prepare them in 360 different ways – sautéed, in confit, stewed, raw... The cooking at Mon Vieil Ami is simple, the way I like it, and flavoursome and generous. My bistro is for friends.' **Antoine Westermann**

PARIS XIV⁰
LE MOULIN DE LA VIERGE
MONDAY – SATURDAY
105 rue Vercingétorix
01 45 43 09 84
www.lemoulindelavierge.com

Flour: ecological and with natural leavening agents. Baking: in an old wood-fired oven, almost impossible to find in Paris. Mortal sin: '*Paresseuse*' (sloth), a sourdough baguette. After that comes the famous *pain de campagne*, light on the inside with a crunchy crust, made by Alexandre Kamir, the greatest baker on God's earth. Venial sins: a light and wonderfully caramelised chantilly millefeuille, a formidable Tatin-style apple tart, a heavenly *flan pâtissier*...

PARIS VIII⁰
MUSÉE NISSIM DE CAMONDO
WEDNESDAY – SUNDAY
63 rue de Monceau
01 53 89 06 50
www.lesartsdecoratifs.fr

Let's dream. We take the service entrance and go directly to the kitchen, bypassing the office, which is reserved for the china. A majestic central stove and an impressive rotisserie, all in cast iron, await. Both elegant and functional, the kitchen in the private home once belonging to Count Moïse de Camondo imposes its refinement even on the incredible collection of copper pots and pans. Today, it remains a tribute to the glory of French taste.

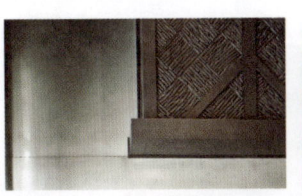

PARIS Vᵉ
LES PAPILLES
MONDAY – SATURDAY
30 rue Gay-Lussac
01 43 25 20 79
www.lespapillesparis.fr
-

The menu says it all: '*Retour du Marché*' (based on market availability), and below that: '*Marmite du Marché*' (market special). Nothing but fresh produce for this stylish bistro. The individual baking dishes come out of the oven and a bottle is taken from a shelf. The atmosphere is casual – there is a big screen in the basement room that is set up for customers on rugby nights – but the food is of a high standard.

PARIS IIIᵉ
LE PAVILLON DE LA REINE
EVERY DAY
28 place des Vosges
01 40 29 19 19
-

It's five o'clock, or thereabouts. It's time to flop into the soft armchairs in the bar. The warm hues, the books on the shelves and the creeper enveloping the building, creating effects with the sunlight, go to make a cosy atmosphere. Time seems to stand still. If you have time to spare, it would be a good idea to spend it in the Carita Spa, to let yourself be lulled by the soft lighting on the pebbles leading to the hammam.

PARIS IIIᵉ
HÔTEL DU PETIT MOULIN
EVERY DAY
29–31 rue de Poitou
01 42 74 10 10
-

Outside is a bakery dating from 1900; inside. is a journey. There is something of Fellini in the red and lilac velvet which clashes with a leopard print cushion and a turquoise stool. There is music in these rooms, which either glitter at night like a Venetian mask or, on the contrary, are starkly rendered in a Provençal limewash. The moments you spend here, enclosed in this whimsical cocoon, are unique. The décor is by Christian Lacroix. It's up to you to find a costume...

PARIS IIᵉ
LE PETIT VENDÔME
MONDAY – FRIDAY
8 rue des Capucines
01 42 61 05 88
www.pavillon-de-la-reine.fr

If you manage to reach the bar, you will be able to try one of the best sandwiches in the capital. Cantal cheese, terrine, tripe, ham, cured ham or multicoloured sausages are piled high over and behind the counter. Wash it down with a glass of Saint-Pourçain wine accompanied by cocktail onions. With a little more time and a bigger appetite, you would be able to weave between the regulars to find a table where you would be forgiven for devouring a duck confit, a sausage with *aligot*, a good rib steak and some legendary *frites*.

PARIS VIIᵉ
PETROSSIAN
TUESDAY – SATURDAY
18 boulevard de la Tour-Maubourg
01 44 11 32 22
www.petrossian.fr

Armen Petrossian watches over his little pearls. He has brought his famous pressed caviar back into fashion. This skilful blend of beluga, osetra and sevruga caviars had once fallen into obscurity. But Petrossian isn't only about caviar. A royal Kamchatka crab leg reaches out to visitors. The fine flesh comes off like that of a lobster. The delicate aromas are almost sweet. Your palate wants to enjoy the pleasure of its wondrously light texture to very the last morsel. This is crab at its finest.

PARIS Iᵉʳ
PHARAMOND
TUESDAY – SUNDAY
24 rue de la Grande Truanderie
01 40 28 45 18
www.pharamond.fr

The Caen-style tripe casserole has written the history of this establishment. Under the retro tiles and the copper mirrors, the lavish Norman veal rib appeals to mindless gluttony. Regulars gorge on magnificent escargots, stuffed with butter and garlic, and roasted to perfection. Figures Guests of a higher standing enjoy the private rooms on the first floor, where the ghost of Clemenceau crosses paths with the ghost of Coluche. That could be interesting...

PARIS VI⁰
BOULANGERIE POILÂNE
MONDAY – SATURDAY
8 rue du Cherche-Midi
01 45 48 42 59
www.poilane.fr

Apollonia Poilâne: The iconic Parisian baguette is white bread, originally for the rich. Our establishment became successful when people migrated from the provinces and wanted *pain paysan*, country-style bread with rye.

Alain Ducasse: To eat with their rillettes, ham and sausage...

AP: Exactly. And the canvases you can see above me are by starving painters from the district who would trade their works for a loaf of bread. '*Une croûte contre une croûte*' ('a bad painting for a crust of bread') is what they would say.

PARIS I ᵉʳ
LA POULE AU POT
TUESDAY – SUNDAY
9 rue Vauvilliers
01 42 36 32 96
www.lapouleaupot.fr

Take carrots, turnips, onions and cloves, and a chicken, of course. The place that has been known as 'Les Halles' best' has been offering King Henry IV's recipe for over 30 years. They do chicken in salad and in suprême sauce, too, for a change. The Ravaillacs of this world will take their revenge by ordering the salmon with saffron crème or the beef shin *pot-au-feu*. The atmosphere is as warm as the food.

PARIS XVI⁰
RESTAURANT PRUNIER
MONDAY – SATURDAY
16 avenue Victor Hugo
01 44 17 35 85
www.prunier.com

The menu from 1932 reads: 'Smoked Fish and Caviars'. Even then, this long-standing purveyor of fine seafood was the toast of Paris and London with 'everything from the sea', reflected by fillets of sole Duglère, seared scallops and their famous fresh caviar. The menu has remained almost unchanged over the years, with its truffle *tartine*, hedgehog mushrooms in poulette sauce and the mature Stilton cut at your table. Here you will find timelessness in an Art Deco wrapping.

PARIS XVII⁰
RECH
TUESDAY – SATURDAY
62 avenue des Ternes
01 45 72 29 47
www.restaurant-rech.fr

You open the door and sense the richness of the Atlantic coast. Soft lighting and pale wood reveal the refined touches exemplified by the damask tablecloths and agate butter dishes. And when the sole meunière for two arrives, coppery on the outside and soft and silky on the palate, even the seagulls are silent. Under the creative leadership of Jacques Maximin, the menu changes with the tides. Julien Dumas prepares nothing but the freshest and most splendid products from the sea and rivers.

PARIS XIV⁰
LA RÉGALADE
MONDAY – FRIDAY
49 avenue Jean Moulin
01 45 45 68 58
-

The concept is surprisingly simple: very good food and very good value. Clearly, the result of this is that the establishment run by Bruno Doucet, who has brilliantly reintroduced the formula created by Yves Camdeborde, is packed to the rafters. The caramelised farmhouse pork ribs and the squid pan fried elver-style in its own ink with rice are being devoured. It is a joy to see such a decidedly friendly wine list. The easy-going and attentive service makes the experience a relaxing one. This place is worth its weight in gold.

PARIS VI⁰
LE RELAIS LOUIS XIII
TUESDAY – SATURDAY
8 rue des Grands Augustins
01 43 26 75 96
www.relaislouis13.com

The whole roast Challons duckling with spices and seasonal vegetables, and the duck confit parmentier, are obviously for two people, but the tone is set. Despite the overwhelming historical significance of this place – it is where Marie de Médicis had her son proclaimed King Louis XIII of France on hearing of the death of Henry IV – Manuel Martinez, holder of the Meilleur Ouvrier de France award, eschews refined products and elegant recipes. Spurning the distant gaze of the king in armour, it is impossible to resist the warm vanilla millefeuille.

PARIS VIII⁰
LE RELAIS PLAZA
EVERY DAY
21 avenue Montaigne
01 53 67 66 65
www.plaza-athenee-paris.com

Imagine the sophisticated dining room of the ocean liner the *SS Normandie* turned upside down by the heady madness of the Roaring Twenties. The Relais Plaza is just that: the height of elegance and exuberance. The cuisine in Philippe Marc's brasserie brings together Wiener schnitzel, steak tartare with matchstick potatoes and skewered veal sweetbreads, sometimes venturing into green lasagne with mascarpone and chanterelle mushrooms or crayfish in roast juices. A rum baba brings the cruise to an end beautifully.

PARIS XI⁰
LE REPAIRE DE CARTOUCHE
TUESDAY – SATURDAY
8 boulevard des Filles du Calvaire
01 47 00 25 86
-

Rodolphe Paquin is Norman and he loves game. An example of this is his creamy game bird soup with chanterelle mushrooms. His pork chops, however, come from unstressed pigs raised on his family's farm. His *lièvre* (hare) *à la royale* is done like nobody else can, as is his veal chump chop in cider. And his terrines would make any of the regulars from the Verre Volé wine bar happy.

PARIS VI⁰
RESTAURANT JOSÉPHINE
« CHEZ DUMONET »
MONDAY – FRIDAY
117 rue du Cherche-Midi
01 45 48 52 40
-

Come on! There's still a little room for a generous serving of millefeuille or the divine Grand Marnier soufflé... A guarantee of tradition, this is a family business that has been handed down to the next generation. With its worn leather and the patina on the silver, patterned mirrors and home cooking, 'Chez Dumonet' as the locals know it, is an authentic 1920s Parisian bistro. The terrines and foie gras are homemade and the steak tartare is prepared in the dining room. All is as it should be. Largesse is on the menu at Chez Dumonet; it's a matter of principle.

PARIS XIX⁰
ROSA BONHEUR
EVERY DAY
2 allée de la Cascade
Parc des Buttes-Chaumont
01 42 00 00 45
www.rosabonheur.fr

Here is a privileged spot for a terrace, laid out amid the trees in the heart of Buttes Chaumont Park. The *Ibérico* ham tapas, small salads and Basque pâté are perfect for a country-style brunch, perhaps taken on the lawn as a clandestine picnic with all of Paris at your feet. When the sun makes you feel as if you're in Spain, the mostly bio wines served on the terrace go perfectly with chorizo.

PARIS XVII⁰
RESTAURANT GUY SAVOY
TUESDAY – SATURDAY
18 rue Troyon
01 43 80 40 61
www.guysavoy.com

'If I hadn't been born in France, I wouldn't have considered becoming a chef! And as for Paris, discovering its monuments, museums and perspectives has been a source of fascination for me. Paris is a theatre, where I've been happy to perform for years; my dishes are my stage and my ingredients are my script. As of the end of 2011, I'll be acting out my role at the Hôtel de la Monnaie, a magnificent building on the Quai de Conti, which has been an integral part of the landscape of the Seine and the Louvre since 1775.'
Guy Savoy

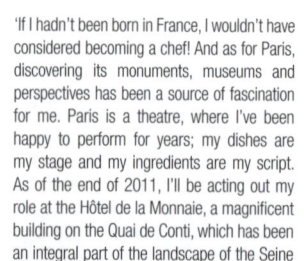

PARIS VI⁰
LE SELECT
EVERY DAY
99 boulevard du Montparnasse
01 45 48 38 24
-

Two round and proud pots, one large and one small, find their way to your table. First comes the rich, heady melted dark chocolate. Then the caress of frothing milk. This is the traditional hot chocolate served at Select, thick as a plush pile woollen carpet and as comforting as a roaring fire. A little of the Dadaist soul of Montparnasse still lingers at the bottom of the pot.

PARIS VII⁰
HÔTEL THOUMIEUX
EVERY DAY
79 rue Saint-Dominique
01 47 05 49 75
www.thoumieux.fr

PARIS XII⁰
LE TRAIN BLEU
EVERY DAY
Place Louis Armand
01 43 43 97 96
www.le-train-bleu.com

PARIS VII⁰
LE VOLTAIRE
TUESDAY – SATURDAY
27 quai Voltaire
01 42 61 1 7 49
-

Jean-François Piège has, together with Thierry Costes, taken over this hotel in the 7th arrondissement. The menu of the new Thoumieux has two parts: 'Room Service' for classic dishes such as squid carbonara and *lièvre* (hare) *à la royale*; and 'Ma Cuisine' for the chef's more audacious offerings, such as live langoustines with coconut and puffed pizza with tuna and rocket. The desserts are exquisite. Upstairs there is a small dining room for exclusive cuisine, and ten hotel rooms.

Stationary travellers set off for a realm of gilt and frescos. When studying the ceiling, their imaginations wander the Île de France, sleepily cross the Rhône and awake at the seaside. The trains are outside, and there is noise and bustle, with people arriving, departing and staying behind. On the table, in the shadow of the huge booths, a *baba chantilly* glows.

An egg is cut in half. Then things become complicated. A few slices of radish, a small bunch of green beans and sliced fresh button mushrooms. Followed by a beautiful mayonnaise made with cream and mustard, coating the eggs with a new shell. A sprig of chervil forms an exclamation mark between two tomato smiles. This is how we like our egg with mayonnaise.

PARIS XVIII⁰
WEPLER
EVERY DAY
14 place Clichy
01 45 22 53 24
www.wepler.com

PARIS IV⁰
YACHTS DE PARIS
EVERY DAY EXCEPT FOR PRIVATE BOOKINGS/EVENTS
Port Henri IV
01 44 54 14 70
www.entreprises.yachtsdeparis.fr

What is there to see here? There's the atmosphere and the setting; this is a genuine Parisian brasserie. Everyone from Bonnard to Picasso, from Henry Miller to Blier and Truffaut, who filmed a scene from *Les Quatre Cent Coups* (The 400 Blows) here, were wild about the authenticity of the place. What is there to eat? Oysters – this establishment was the first to make them its speciality over a century ago – and choucroute, or Béarnaise grilled pig's trotters. It's authentic, we say.

We embark on the privately booked *Cachemire* for an intimate gourmet cruise. Guy Krenzler, holder of the Meilleur Ouvrier de France award, is in charge of the food. Citrus-marinated scallops, avocado in suzette sauce, foie gras confit, peppered grapes and walnuts and black truffle emulsion are served. There is Baccarat crystal glassware and a marble fireplace, all of which makes this the sophisticated way to appreciate Paris and the Seine.

PARIS
HOME TO THE REGIONS

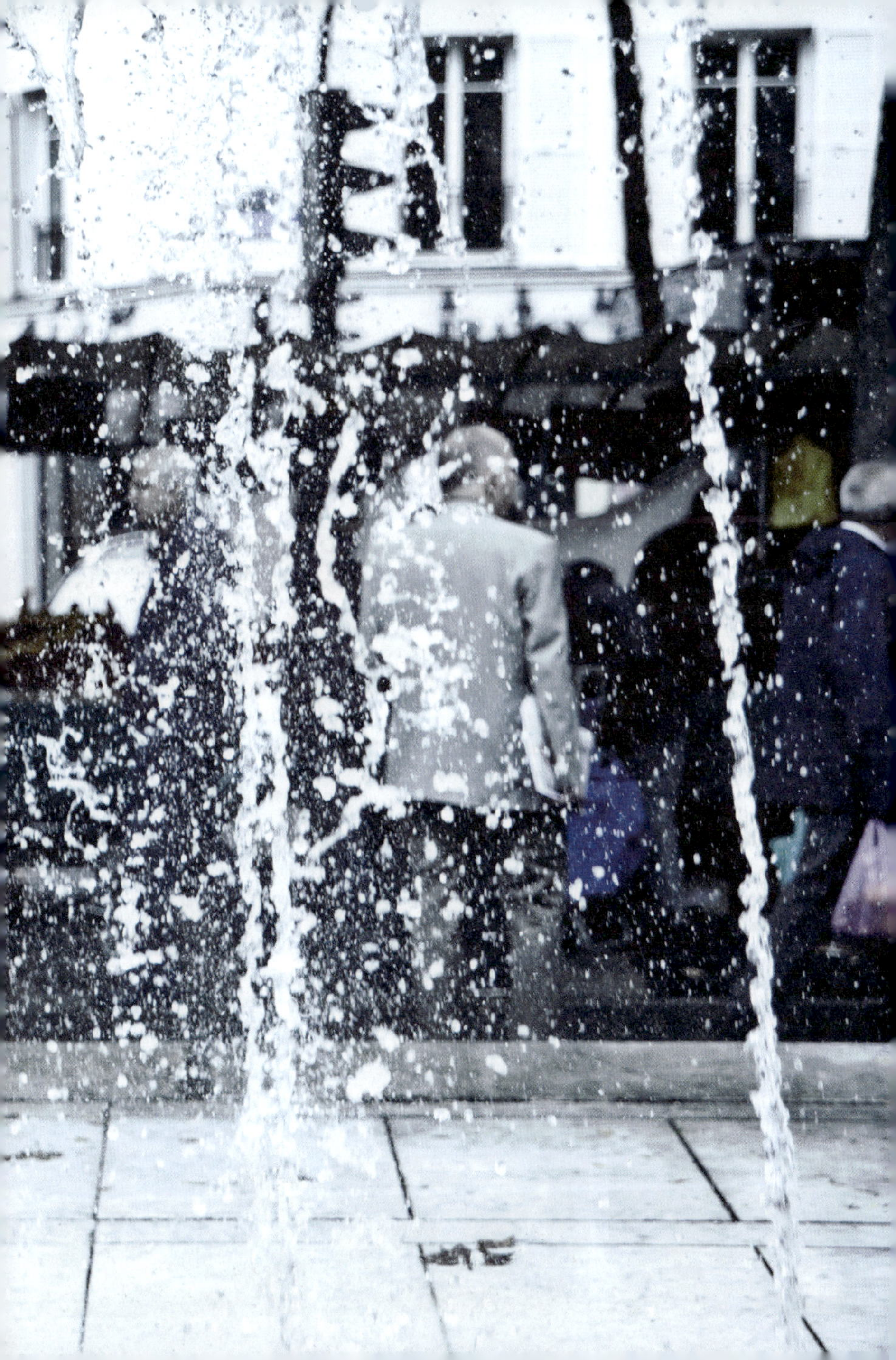

PARIS XII⁰
MARCHÉ D'ALIGRE
TUESDAY – SUNDAY
Rue d'Aligre
www.marchedaligre.free.fr

This is one of the oldest markets in Paris – the market building dates from 1779 – and also one of the most popular. Open every day except Monday, it is home to Michel Brunon, a butcher selling aged and marbled meats. Nearby is Sur les Quais, a *delicatessen* selling products from around the world and an absolute treasure trove. The other side of the square is like being on another planet. Here you will find the oldest seed shop in Paris, with its selection of pulses and herbal teas, country tableware.

PARIS XVII⁰
FROMAGERIE ALLEOSSE
TUESDAY – SUNDAY
13 rue Poncelet
01 46 22 50 45
www.fromage-alleosse.com

Under the shop there is a cellar; actually, there are four cellars, one each for storing bloomy rind cheese, washed rind cheese, goat's cheese and tomme cheeses. This establishment is unique in Paris, as is the know-how of its master cheesemaker. There is a host of specialities from everywhere, with a preference for goat's cheese, and extra-fresh *burrata* at weekends.

PARIS XI⁰
AUBERGE PYRÉNNÉES-CEVENNES
MONDAY – FRIDAY, SATURDAY EVENING
106 rue de la Folie-Méricourt
01 43 57 33 78

Gargantuan feasts take place under a ceiling hung with cold meat products. On the brown checked tablecloth, the cassoulet is XXL, the pork trotter is breaded and the veal liver is legendary. Round off your meal with a baba or profiterole, if you have room. Like being between Lyon and the south-west, here you will soon find yourself among friends. The welcome you will receive is warm and light-hearted.

PARIS VIII⁰
AUBRAC CORNER
MONDAY – FRIDAY
37 rue Marbeuf
01 45 61 45 35
www.aubrac-corner.com

'From farm to fork' is the fate of Christian Vallette's 320 cows. He makes them into hamburgers in his kitchen. Wait! Don't stop reading yet! This juicy and firm meat from Aubrac is mixed with wholegrain mustard mayonnaise. The bun, made from a combination of wheat and linseed, is as soft as white bread but with less sugar. There is just enough time for it to absorb the meat juices as you bite into the filling. You don't even need fries…

PARIS II⁰
AUX LYONNAIS
TUESDAY – SATURDAY
32 rue Saint-Marc
01 42 96 65 04
www.esprit-bistrot.com

There was once a typical Lyonnais *bouchon* (bistro) in the heart of Paris. There was no need to change anything, only to perpetuate its traditions. Each of the specialities prepared by Frédéric Thévenet, from the *pot de la cuisinière lyonnais* to the *île flottante* and pink praline tart. There is also a second, less-heralded legacy. There was once a young chef, Alain Ducasse, he grew fond of the noble region of Lyon and its iconic chefs Paul Bocuse and Michel Troigros. Aux Lyonnais is a *bouchon* deserving of praise.

PARIS XVII⁰
BALLON ET COQUILLAGES
EVERY DAY
71 boulevard Gouvion Saint-Cyr
01 45 74 17 98
www.groupe-menut.com/BallonsEtCoquillages

With its feel of a designer fishing cabin, the décor of this place takes you on holiday. The philosophy of this establishment is clear: it's a seafood bar. Over the large round wooden bar, a plate of oysters is being prepared – what a good idea it was to serve them in threes. The seafood platters, individual or for two, consist of dog cockles, Indian prawns and beautiful crab claws.

PARIS XVIᵉ
BAR À PATATES
WEDNESDAY AND SATURDAY
**Marché de l'Alma,
Avenue du Président Wilson**
-

Alain Ducasse: What is your advice for making a good Parisian frite?
Carine Bars: Actually, I recommend a Sicilian potato: the Spunta. For sautéed potatoes, the very thin and very tasty Île de Ré variety is better. Otherwise, we also have Rubis potatoes this morning. You don't normally peel them.

PARIS VIIᵉ
FROMAGERIE BARTHÉLEMY
TUESDAY – SATURDAY
**51 rue de Grenelle
01 45 48 56 75**
-

Madame Nicole is recommended for her Mont d'Or cheese, and also for her Époisse and vieux saler varieties. I fell in love immediately with her amazingly light Fontainebleau cream cheese, wrapped in gauze resembling a hat veil. It goes perfectly with the first raspberries and wild strawberries of the season. A little sugar in the whipped Fontainebleau crunches on my teeth, as it should.

PARIS XIᵉ
MARCHÉ BASTILLE
THURSDAY AND SUNDAY
Boulevard Richard Lenoir
-

This is one of the largest markets in Paris, bringing together around a hundred stallholders. You are spoilt for choice with such reasonable prices. The products sold here are often of good quality, like the fish at the stall run by Jacky Lorenzo, a popular figure at the market. Tourists come to admire the regional produce, while we appreciate the lively atmosphere in this genuine neighbourhood market.

PARIS XXᵉ
FROMAGERIE BEILLEVAIRE
TUESDAY – SUNDAY MIDDAY
**140 rue de Belleville
01 46 36 90 81**
-

Ripe cheeses, homemade unpasteurised butter and *crémet nantais* cream cheese drive your taste buds wild at the Fromagerie Beillevaire. You receive such good advice there that you'll want to buy these high-quality products, which you'll dream about having on your plate.

PARIS XIIᵉ
BOUCHERIE MICHEL BRUNON
TUESDAY – SUNDAY
**Marché couvert Beauvau, 12 place d'Aligre
01 43 40 62 58**
-

The carcass swings along a rail as if in a train crash. There is a roar of sirloins, ribs and legs. 'This is a product for the initiated,' laughs Michel Brunon with a perfectly aged rib steak in his hand. It can be cut with a fork. 'I age all my meat myself, otherwise I won't eat it. And if I don't eat it, I won't sell it to my customers. I'm a butcher, not a meat seller.'

PARIS VIIᵉ
FROMAGERIE MARIE-ANNE CANTIN
EVERY DAY
**12 rue du Champs de Mars
01 45 50 43 94
www.cantin.fr**

Daughter of Christian Cantin, founder of the Cheesemakers' Guild, Marie-Anne runs this business with her daughter and her husband Antoine. Holder of the Meilleur Ouvrier de France award, she is leading the fight against the standardisation of taste. Her cheeses are carefully chosen, having been produced in limited quantities by small-scale operations. Marie-Anne matures them in her own cellar, for several months in the case of the Beaufort and Comté cheeses. If you're passionate about cheese, you can arrange a tasting, which will be tailored to suit your palate.

Ramón Peña
SARDINAS
En Aceite de Oliva
SARDINILLAS
en aceite de oliva
DE LAS RÍAS
CALIDAD EXTRA
VENTRESCA
DE ATUN CLARO
en aceite de oliva
CHIPIRONES
en su tinta
MEJILLONES
fritos en escabeche
Kaspia
SOUPE DE HOMARD
LOBSTER SOUP

PARIS Iᵉʳ
CHEZ FLOTTES
EVERY DAY
2 rue Cambon
01 42 60 80 89
www.flottes.fr

Monsieur Gérard brandishes his big knife, the plump loaf pressed against his body. He slices the fresh Poilâne bread by hand. 'The secret is to slice it thinner than usual to enhance the flavour of the products. If you don't, you have nothing but bread in your mouth.' During his time feeding nocturnal Parisians, Gilbert Flottes, together with Lionel Poilâne, invented a simple but tasty gem: the Poilâne *croque-monsieur*. Today, his son Olivier manages the family brasserie.

PARIS IIᵉ
CHEZ GEORGES
MONDAY – FRIDAY
1 rue du Mail
01 42 60 07 11
-

This establishment has been popular since 1926. It's a real brasserie with classic brasserie fare, taken over by the owners of La Grande Cascade and L'Auberge du Bonheur. A trolley displays the daily specials, the quintessential dishes: artfully carved leg of lamb with beans and steaming *pot-au-feu* with amazing vegetables. A warm welcome and a good wine list await you. This is a place to enjoy a memorable experience. Good old Menut!

PARIS Vᵉ
CRÊPES ET GALETTES
MONDAY – FRIDAY EXCEPT JUNE – SEPTEMBER
37 rue Linné
-

There's a queue here even when it rains. In front of us, a couple of students order a caramel crêpe with salted butter and Speculoos cream. Behind, a grandfather has come to treat his grandchildren to the compote and cinnamon crêpe. An Emmenthal and hazelnut galette (buckwheat flour pancake) gets underway. The neighbourhood has a foster mother in Christiane Hérouard, who for 25 years has been spoiling the locals in Place Jussieu with fresh ingredients and gourmet recipes. She even thickened her homemade batter a little to satisfy 'her' students.

PARIS VIIᵉ
AUBERGE D'CHEZ EUX
EVERY DAY
2 avenue de Lowendal
01 47 05 52 55
www.chezeux.com

Tableside carving? That *is* rare! The duck is served this way with its fig or pear accompaniment, depending on the season. Laurent and Catherine Brenta, from L'Évasion, manage this restaurant with its feel of the France of bygone days. Under the 1950 brine tub, diners attack the sausages, the starters trolley, the legendary cassoulet and the outstanding calf's head, but they surrender to the Paris-Brest.

PARIS XIVᵉ
BOUCHERIE HUGO DESNOYER
TUESDAY – SATURDAY
45 rue Boulard
01 45 40 76 67
www.regalez-vous.com

'I left high school early and I didn't know what to do. Then my father put me in an apprenticeship with a butcher in Mayenne, my hometown. That was a revelation. It was just the thing. One thing led to another and here I am in rue Bolard, Paris. I travel 60,000 kilometres a year, crossing France from top to bottom to find lovely well-bred animals: lamb from Lozère, farmhouse pork from the Dordogne and prize-winning Corrèze calves. Today, breeders know what my customers – chefs and individuals – expect from them: the best.'

Hugo Desnoyer

PARIS XIVᵉ
LA POISSONNERIE DU DÔME
TUESDAY – SUNDAY
4 rue Delambre
01 43 35 23 05
www.poissonneriedudome.com

This is the equivalent of a five-star beauty salon for fish! Wild fish caught using artisanal techniques are pampered and delicately placed over waxed paper to prevent them from being burned by the ice. Chosen every night in small quantities from the best stalls, the fish barely have time to jump into the van before landing on your plate. This purveyor supplies the leading Parisian establishments with the finest catches: elvers, spider crabs and line-caught sea bass, among others.

PARIS Iᵉʳ
L'ÉCUME SAINT-HONORÉ
TUESDAY – SATURDAY
6 rue du Marché Saint-Honoré
01 42 61 93 87
-

You can hear the cry of seagulls in the distance. There is a notice on the blackboard: 'For dessert, raw scallops, soy sauce! Tender, tasty!' Opened and cut in front of you, the beauty reveals itself to be sweet and flowery, the ideal dessert to round off an outstanding tasting. Because here, the large selection of oysters, clams, mussels and shrimp comes with freshness and optimum flavour.

PARIS IIIᵉ
MARCHÉ DES ENFANTS ROUGES
TUESDAY – SUNDAY
39 rue de Bretagne
-

The orphanage founded here by Queen Margot and the red uniforms of its occupants have given way to a neighbourhood market. When it opened in 1777, there was even a well and a cowshed. Today, the little market is housed in a glazed hall. It is like a village square and has the same charm. It's peaceful during the week, but bustling on Sundays. You can have a light snack at one of the stallholders' tables or in the pretty square surrounding the market.

PARIS XVᵉ
ÉPICERIE DU PÈRE CLAUDE
EVERY DAY
4 rue du Général de Castelnau
01 47 34 04 04
www.lepereclaude.com

Alain Ducasse: What boneless ham is this?
Ludovic Perraudin: 'Prince de Paris' – it's a ham from Brittany made in the traditional way. It isn't treated or chopped; the brine is injected into the ham, which is then rubbed in coarse salt. Only 250 hams are made this way each week, free from colouring, preservatives or gelatine.
AD: It has a fine, silky texture. Excellent. And it also smells like real ham. It's so unusual.
LP: How about a pickle?
AD: Of course not! That would ruin it.

PARIS XIIᵉ
GRAINETERIE DU MARCHÉ
TUESDAY – SUNDAY MIDDAY
8 place d'Aligre
01 43 43 22 64
-

José watches over the seeds in his seed shop after hours... The shop's been in existence since 1895 and it's still going strong. Probably the most useful thing you can get there is advice on preparing and cooking their produce. You are overcome by the urge to buy everything. They have an amazing selection of pulses: *haricots tarbais*, tiny tender green flageolet beans, Soissons beans with taut skins and bulk pasta and rice in wooden crates – it's so hard to resist.

PARIS XVIᵉ
MARCHÉ GROS-LAFONTAINE
TUESDAY AND FRIDAY
Rue Gros, rue Jean de La Fontaine
-

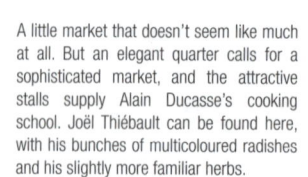

A little market that doesn't seem like much at all. But an elegant quarter calls for a sophisticated market, and the attractive stalls supply Alain Ducasse's cooking school. Joël Thiébault can be found here, with his bunches of multicoloured radishes and his slightly more familiar herbs.

PARIS Vᵉ
ITINÉRAIRES
TUESDAY – SATURDAY
5 rue de Pontoise
01 46 33 60 11
www.restaurantitineraires.com

It's a fitting name, evoking a bistro that has toured the world. In the frying pan, together with the artichokes and chanterelles, are soya bean flowers and toasted hazelnuts. You can taste chef Sylvain Sendra's marvellous creations, such as his green asparagus with foie gras and dried tuna dressing. The place is absolutely packed – we wonder why!

PARIS XVIe
MARCHÉ PASSY
TUESDAY – SUNDAY
Angle des rues Duban et Bois-le-Vent
-

Behind the white facade and glass bricks, the tall retro building houses a good neighbourhood market. Classic quality: greengrocers, butchers, fishmongers. The advantage for residents is that it's open until evening. You can pass by on your way home from work to pick out the makings of a super-fresh dinner.

PARIS XVe
LE PÈRE CLAUDE
EVERY DAY
51 avenue de la Motte Piquet
01 47 34 03 05
-

Now this is a true rotisserie. Which do you prefer: roast free-range chicken – plump with crispy skin – rotating before your very eyes, or its heavenly homemade purée? Red and white meat of noble origin, Burgundy snails, mushrooms *a la plancha* are selected and prepared for the gourmet elite with the precision of a Swiss watchmaker. Carnivore friends, don't miss the roast meat platter: lamb, beef, sausage, pork tripe sausage, black pudding. Unforgettable foie gras.

PARIS IXe
POUSSE POUSSE
MONDAY – SATURDAY
7 rue Notre-Dame de Lorette
01 53 16 10 81
www.pousse-pousse.eu

A whole-living-foods specialist, Lawrence Aboucaya owns a small deli-restaurant. Using sprouts, young shoots and wheatgrass, juice is made with a special extractor so as not to 'break up the molecules'. The same principle is applied to quiches, salads, vegetable or fresh fruit juices, all presented in an ornate, warm and cosy ambiance.

PARIS VIIe
FROMAGERIE QUATREHOMME
TUESDAY – SATURDAY
62 rue de Sèvres
01 47 34 33 45
-

In the business for 25 years, Meilleur Ouvrier de France Marie Quatrehomme family-manages three Parisian boutiques. She also supplies the hotel Le Meurice, Pierre Gagnaire and Guy Savoy. We are well aware, too, that as early as 20 years ago the team had no qualms in unveiling Roquefort Carles, less popular, less expensive and less salty than its well-known rivals. The range of refined cheeses satisfies almost every palate.

PARIS XIIe
LE QUINCY
TUESDAY – FRIDAY
28 avenue Ledru-Rollin
01 46 28 46 76
www.lequincy.fr

Come rain, hail or shine, you'll find a bow tie on the menu. Appearing just above is Bobosse, the down-to-earth owner of a mountain inn right in the middle of Paris. Enormous plates, fresh produce, French recipes. It's crayfish season, real 'red claws'. As the innkeeper would say: 'You just have to peel them apart for yourself'!

PARIS IIe
RACINES
MONDAY – FRIDAY
8 passage des Panoramas
01 40 13 06 41
-

Formerly from L'Arpège, Restaurant Laurent and Le Divellec, Nicolas Gauduin prepares his produce with talent and simplicity, under the watchful eye of owner David Lanher, a man with exacting standards. Fattened chickens and ducks, completely plucked, cooked whole in their skin, accompanied by fabulous crunchy seasonal vegetables from Alain Passard's kitchen garden. There is a good selection of 'natural' wines, now also including other varieties.

PARIS VIe
MARCHÉ RASPAIL
CURRENTLY TUESDAY, FRIDAY, SUNDAY
Boulevard Raspail
-

A market that offers three full meals: the all-day menu stretches the length of Boulevard Raspail. For breakfast: English muffins, home-baked with a smile, and poached eggs. At lunch, it's very tempting to send the entire array of organic vegetables to the roasting pan. And for dinner, roast suckling pig, very good farm cheeses, citrus salad. If we could, we'd cook this way all year round.

PARIS Ve
RIBOULDINGUE
TUESDAY – SATURDAY
10 rue Saint-Julien le Pauvre
01 46 33 98 80
www.restaurant-ribouldingue.com

The menu is all-consuming: whole kidneys with *gratin dauphinois*, sweetbreads, brains, oxtail and *sabodet* just like you'd find in Lyon. There's even snout, and cow's teats. The restaurant is welcoming, the team young and totally involved in this respectful, modern cuisine. Nadège, the owner, trained at La Régalade in the Yves Camdeborde era, and selects her bottles with precision.

PARIS IIe
SATURNE
MONDAY – FRIDAY
17 rue Notre-Dame des Victoires
01 42 60 31 90
-

It's good to go down into the cellar, where the air is quite crisp and charged with emotion. For their new chapel, Ewen trusts only artisan winemakers – men who make wine on a human scale, men who work the ground and their land in tune with the living world. And Sven Chartier cooks with extreme roughness, similar to wine production; the best produce handled only in large quantities and served with just a touch of seasoning – nothing more!

PARIS Xe
SCHMID TRAITEUR
MONDAY – SATURDAY
76 boulevard de Strasbourg
01 46 07 89 74
www.schmid-traiteur.com

When they say the whole of Alsace, they really mean the whole of Alsace. From horseradish to Black Forest cake, you pass through an ocean of cooked-meat cuts. There is turnip pickled in brine, which can be served just as you would sauerkraut, and both plain liver sausages and truffled ones that can be used as a spread. You can chew on a pretzel while awaiting your turn. It's Christmas under a cloud of icing sugar, and this has lasted for a full century.

PARIS Ier
SPRING
TUESDAY – SATURDAY
6 rue Bailleul
01 45 96 05 72
www.springparis.fr

Daniel Rose, a native of Chicago, is an atypical chef, a self-taught man dedicated to gastronomy. His open professional kitchen is located on the ground floor of the courtyard, serving approximately 20 covers. In the basement, an arched room – pure 18th century style – with a bar serving snacks. Underground, a cellar storing bottles of the day with a selection displaying more than just natural wines. An absolute must-see right next door, Spring Boutique: it offers 100 per cent organic artisan wines for sale as well as a deli.

PARIS XVIe
JOËL THIÉBAULT MARAÎCHER
CURRENTLY WEDNESDAY AND SATURDAY
Marché de l'Alma, Avenue du Président Wilson
www.joelthiebault.fr

Unbeatable for roots, the man lays out a vast vegetable rainbow. Heritage carrots, green, yellow and purple radishes, multicoloured Swiss chard exuding the celebratory spirit of a Tuscan pie. An amazing aromatic selection, including sage-tarragon which gives off a certain astringency that lasts through the cooking process. Joël Thiébault is one of the very first to have offered Vitelotte potatoes, and provides long-forgotten vegetables to starred chefs.

PARIS VI⁰
GILLES VÉROT – CHARCUTIER
TUESDAY – SATURDAY
3 rue Notre-Dame des Champs
01 45 48 83 32
www.verot-charcuterie.fr

Champion of France for his brawn; an award for best liver pâté – the list goes on: Gilles Vérot is doing justice to his pigs. We really like his ham pasties and his pistachio meat pie intended 'for the purists'. Excellent quality of parsley-garnished jellied hams and sausages. A very good pork butcher – just the way we like them – who is also winning over New Yorkers with Daniel Boulud.

PARIS X⁰
LE VERRE VOLÉ
EVERY DAY
67 rue Lancry
01 48 03 17 34
www.leverrevole.fr

Alain Ducasse: So, what are we eating today?
Cyril Bordarier: A rib steak from Desnoyer, or sea bass that comes directly from an auction in the Channel. The cauliflower is Annie Bertin's. The capers come from La Tête dans les Olives and dessert is from Desmoulins, in Boulevard Voltaire. Do you want to try it?
AD: Of course.
CB: Enjoy, it's today's menu. It'll change tomorrow.

PARIS I⁰ʳ
WINE BY ONE
TUESDAY – SATURDAY
9 rue des Capucines
01 42 60 85 76
www.winebyone.com

That's it. You're no longer lost in a sea of labels. You slot your smart card into a machine, you choose the size of your glass – 30, 60 or 120 ml – and let the computer tell you about the grape variety, pull up the tasting cards, suggest food–wine pairings. You can choose from over 100 references, to be savoured in a space-shuttle setting designed by the Nespresso space designers. The wine merchant's section sells the same bottles, which you can sample before buying.

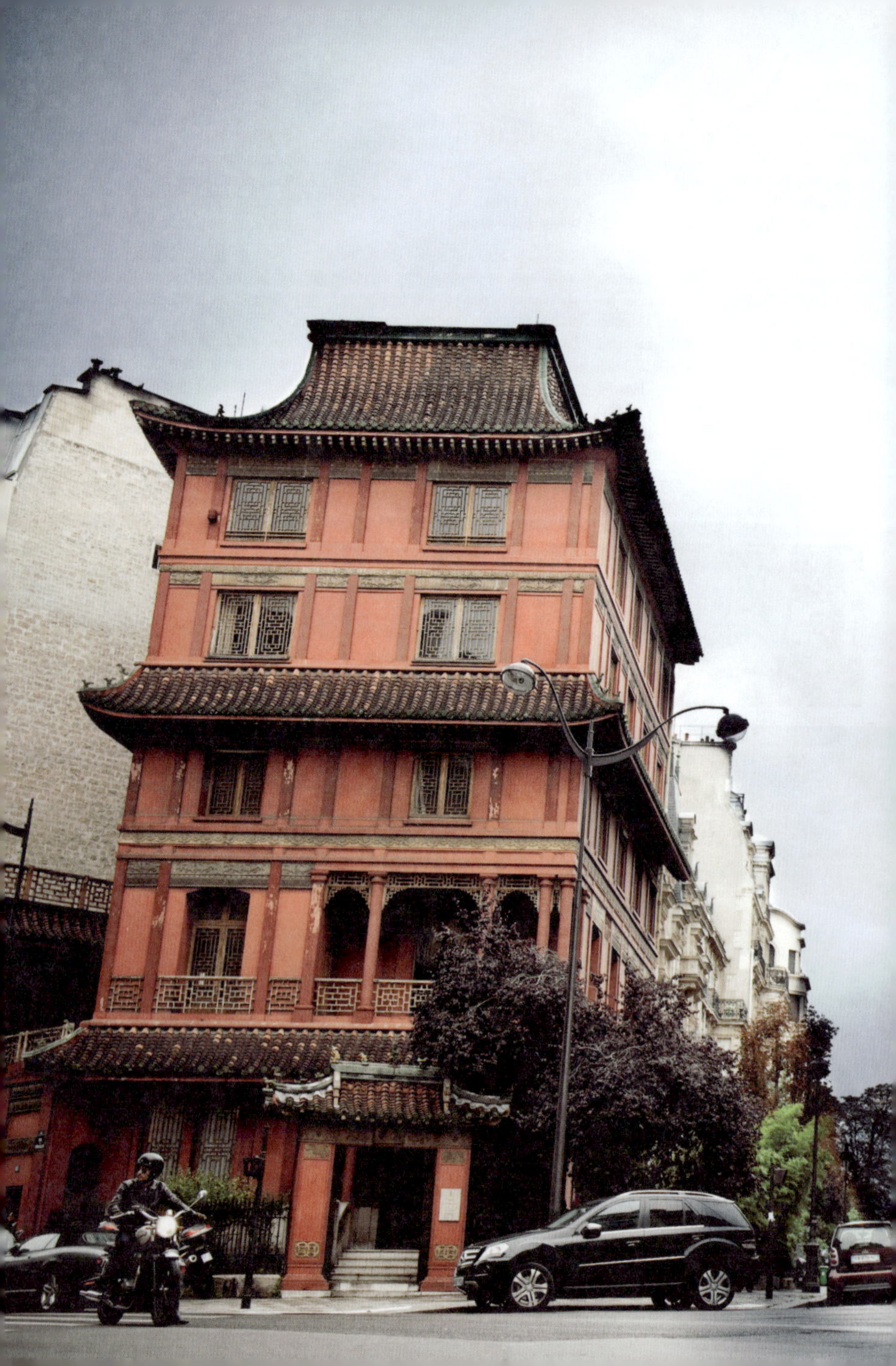

PARIS, WHERE THE WORLD MEETS

PARIS XI°
ASIE ANTILLES AFRIQUE
TUESDAY – SUNDAY
88bis–90 rue du Faubourg du Temple
01 43 57 24 63
-

The whole world contained in a hessian bag. One slaloms between the mountains of rice from all continents, legumes, yams, sweet potatoes in a variety of colours. It's packed with African mamas and Chinese papas. A West Indian man has come to choose his pork in vinegar and his 'bonda Man Jacques' or 'the behind of mother Jacques' peppers, in Creole. Fans of the exotic, and taste adventurers, leave with two different types of plantain bananas to sample.

PARIS XV°
AFARIA
MONDAY – SATURDAY
15 rue Desnouettes
01 48 56 15 36
-

The cuisine of the Pyrenees – chef Julien Duboué is of Basque origin – surfs on the fusion wave. Seasonal produce, themed menus, a sought-after offering. Rockfish roasted with chorizo, foie gras pan fried with raisins, apple black pudding in mustard pastry, or small pasta shell paella. Book the communal table with a group of friends to fully enjoy the heady atmosphere.

PARIS XI°
AMICI MIEI
TUESDAY – SATURDAY
44 rue Saint Sabin
01 42 71 82 62
-

People don't go there only for the owner, an authentic Sardinian, but rather for the pizzas. The *à la rucola* option delights the regulars, some of whom are food critics whose offices are right next door. We also love their *pizza bianca* (thin, crispy base, drizzled with spicy olive oil and *fleur de sel*), to be shared with companions while you wait, as well as the *radicchio* (Treviso) option. And if you're not in the mood for pizza, sashay over to the seaside: the small fried fish are divine and the baby squid. To die for.

PARIS IV°
L'AS DU FALAFEL
MONDAY – FRIDAY MIDDAY, SUNDAY
34 rue des Rosiers
01 48 87 63 60

Are they giving their falafels away? You'd almost think so, considering the queue that forms when it's close to eating time. Polite customers abound, even with staff seemingly detached from this world. Not a very exotic look – judging by the red canteen tray – but for nothing in this world would we go anywhere else. The crispness of their herb balls creates, for a minute, the illusion that we all have an Israeli grandmother. With a glass of lemonade – incredibly sweet, incredibly acidic – we're on holiday.

PARIS XI°
AUX COMPTOIRS DES INDES
MONDAY – SUNDAY MIDDAY
50 rue de la Fontaine au Roi
01 48 05 45 76
-

Even the little sauces – the minted green one, the strong yet delicate red one – are homemade. They showcase the care the chef takes in preparing his South Indian cuisine. The tenderness of lamb with almond and cashew nut cream steeped in its 45 different spices. The milky smoothness of a *kulfi*, a pistachio ice-cream with a hint of salt.

PARIS VII°
BETSY, BERNARDAUD
-

Betsy Bernardaud shops in the Jewish quarter. In her warm kitchen, perched on the countertop, you share a special moment among friends. A sandwich, quite simply. But not just any. It's called a 'Reuben', originating in Eastern Europe, with a detour via New York. *Yiddish broït*, a white bread with cumin, lightly browned in butter in the pan; very good, thinly sliced pastrami with a Panzer sauerkraut. Simple and delicious. Moments of friendship need nothing more.

PARIS VIIIe

BYZANCE CHAMPS-ÉLYSÉES BELLOTA / BELLOTA RIVE DROITE

MONDAY – SATURDAY
11 rue Clément Marot
09 62 00 25 02
www.bellota-bellota.com

'Alain, you were one of my very first clients to have my Ibérico Spanish ham, in May 1995. When I offered you my very best Bellota hams, I almost needed to know the pig's first name! I found that very stimulating, and so I travelled extensively around Spain, looking to understand, in a scientific way, why these hams were the best, how one chooses them, when, with whom…'

Philippe Poulachon

PARIS V^e

CAFÉ MAURE DE LA MOSQUÉE DE PARIS

EVERY DAY
9 rue Geoffroy Saint Hilaire
01 43 31 18 14
www.mosquee-de-paris.org

The sun warms the fig trees, with the sweetish aroma drifting through the courtyard. Much self-control is needed to walk past the pastries counter. Behind the door lies the Orient. You glide under the trellis archway for a mint tea, or a Turkish coffee on its hammered-copper tray. It's an oasis, a Mediterranean microcosm, an endless summer, perfumed with honey and almonds.

PARIS XIe

CAFFÈ DEI CIOPPI

MONDAY – FRIDAY
159 rue du Faubourg Saint-Antoine
01 43 46 10 14
-

Delicacy, your name is *sbrisolona*. A little dry biscuit that doesn't look like much, really, or maybe just like a biscuit! Powdered almonds, cornflour. Sink your teeth into it, though, and it's just like Verdi at La Scala, or a dive into the Trevi Fountain – in this case, into a little mascarpone cream pot. Fabrizio and Federica don't stop at the sweets, of course. They prepare pure, simple trattoria cuisine with great panache.

PARIS VIe

LE CHERCHE-MIDI

EVERY DAY
22 rue du Cherche Midi
01 45 48 27 44
www.lecherchemidi.fr

The antipasti of the house, fish of the day and carpaccios are of unquestionable freshness. They go hand in hand with remarkable olive oil and very good mozzarella. No pizzas, nor any combination of unusual products, just the produce prepared in a traditional way, with simplicity. You'll find a warm atmosphere in the small, tightly packed room, as well as a terrace, which is chock-full in good weather.

PARIS VIe

DA ROSA ÉPICERIE FINE

EVERY DAY
62 rue de Seine
01 45 21 41 30
www.restaurantdarosa.com

The roughness of natural stone walls. The rasping of a Portuguese accent burning up in the summer, icy in winter. The pungent and intoxicating aromas of Iberian hams curing along the ceiling. But, under the surface, the complex fruitiness of the *bellota*, which lasts in the mouth as long as a juicy tomato on some hot bread, the pepperiness of a cheese. In this deli-canteen that looks like none other, we settle in, as if in the Mediterranean…

PARIS IVe

BOUCHERIE DAVID

TUESDAY – FRIDAY, SUNDAY
6 rue des Ecouffes
01 42 78 15 76
-

Brooklyn delicatessens may as well go back to where they came from. In variety and quality, David's place has few rivals. He offers us tastes of his take on chicken liver with onions, as silky as a foie gras. He thinly slices his Podze calf's tongue, complex and delicate. Next to traditional fare lie the house dishes: duck pastrami, hazelnut sausages. Carried along by the enthusiasm and generosity of its owner, we'd happily taste the whole shop.

PARIS Ier
E. DEHILLERIN
MONDAY – SATURDAY
18–20 rue Coquillière
01 42 36 53 13
www.e-dehillerin.fr

The old washed parquet floor squeaks under our feet. Entering behind us, a ray of sun bounces off the copper, stainless steel and tin saucepans. Floors above, floors below; kitchen utensils everywhere, couscous sieves stacked up so high up you need a mountaineering permit. The house is almost 200 years old; you can feel it in the care that has gone into the duck press and *hâtelets*, into the schoolchildren's grey pinafores, in the traditional style of domestic staff. For a beautiful copper preserving pan, this is the place to come.

PARIS XVIII°
MARCHÉ DEJEAN
TUESDAY – SATURDAY; SUNDAY EVENING
Rue Dejean
-

Tilapia, thiof and capitaine – or even sinking your teeth into a barracuda? A live chicken or an agouti? Chewing on a golden cob – hot, corn, hot! – we let ourselves get carried away by the wafts of amazing aromas, the vibrant colours of the pepper stalls, the almost unimaginable look of a zebra-striped kettle. You bounce from one stall to the next: 'Dabou's market', 'Exotic Ivory', 'Abidjan is Great'. Under the beams of the elevated section of the underground, you feel the urge to crack open a ginger beer.

PARIS VI°
EL FOGON
TUESDAY – SUNDAY
45 quai des Grands Augustins
01 43 54 31 33
www.fogon.fr

'El Temperador' is the name of the glass-fronted counter displaying hams. It is visible from every corner of the room. Your mouth begins to water even before the arrival of the garlic-almond gazpacho. Followed by '*a banda sin banda*' rice, a gastronomic *pièce de résistance*. Alberto Herráiz has earned a star from the Red Guide. His cuisine, like his tables, holds many secrets.

PARIS IV°
FLORENCE KAHN
MONDAY, TUESDAY, THURSDAY – SATURDAY
24 rue des Ecouffes
01 48 87 92 85
www.florencekahn.fr

Creative variations on chicken liver mousse and smoked fish, fine cooked meats. Succulent cheesecake, little onion breads still warm from the oven, just waiting to be stuffed. Generous sandwiches as an alternative to falafels. Of course, this is all homemade, prepared on the day, flavoursome. On the shelves, we find a packet of *ferfels*: handcrafted pasta twice-baked in the oven, which gives it its characteristic flavour; we'll try it that very night.

PARIS V°
FOYER VIETNAM
MONDAY – SATURDAY
80 rue Monge
01 45 35 32 54
-

Fans of peace and quiet, sophistication and elegance might prefer to go somewhere else. In the Vietnamese Student Association's canteen, vegetables are eaten in deafening noise on outdated Formica tops. The cuisine is typically Vietnamese: beef *tung choy* salad or chicken salad with banana flowers, *pho* soup in stainless steel bowls, and famous *balut* (with a chick inside) – this, at least as much as the modest prices, ensures that word of the place spreads between generations of students.

PARIS XII°
LA GAZZETTA
TUESDAY – SATURDAY
29 rue de Cotte
01 43 47 47 05
www.lagazzetta.fr

This place is cosy-cosmopolitan, ideal for a lunch after returning from the market. Established and managed by the team of Le Fumoir, the restaurant has given chef Petter Nilsson, a Viking super-brilliant in heritage vegetables, carte blanche. Petter is an author, his universe unforgiving: *bonito tartare* and barbecued leeks, radishes and horseradish, celery braised with bay leaves, green tomato preserve, watercress and chanterelles…

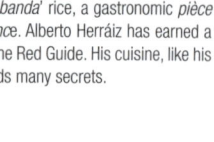

PARIS IIIe
GOUMANYAT
TUESDAY – SATURDAY
3 rue Charles François Dupuis
01 44 78 96 74
www.goumanyat.com

In 1809, the Thiercelin family established the first saffron-processing company in the world, at Pithiviers-en-Gâtinais, in an enceinte tower dating to the Middle Ages. Goumanyat is their Parisian outlet and Jean Thiercelin, master craftsman, represents the seventh generation. Ancient cabinets and jars contain a whole range of spices, among which the house blends of the Sultan and the Pharaoh. Oils and syrups are also found here, as well as Ayurvedic teas and granules for molecular gastronomy.

PARIS IXe
I GOLOSI
MONDAY – SATURDAY
6 rue de la Grange Batelière
01 48 24 18 63
www.igolosi.com

The chef is Venetian, but not sectarian. His fish from Laguna and his risottos go hand in hand with Tuscan game and oxtail *à la romaine*. Wine by the glass is selected from a very sophisticated menu which gives the house its reputation, to accompany the dishes that change each week. All of the restaurant's products can be found at the deli next door. A place one never grows tired of.

PARIS XIe
IDEA VINO
TUESDAY – SATURDAY
88 avenue Parmentier
01 43 57 10 34
www.ideavino.fr

Capers from Pantelleria in Sicily, balsamic vinegar as good as a love potion, citrus oils. 'We always aim to find entertaining recipes for our guests. In summer, I use saffron-infused tagliatelle, garnished with scampi and orange zest, with a touch of *piment d'Espelette*,' explains Rita. This dish should be accompanied by a glass of white wine from the slopes of Etna, selected in a cellar that single-handedly succeeds in embodying Italian unity.

PARIS IIe
IL CAMPIONISSIMO
MONDAY – SATURDAY
98 rue de Montmartre
01 42 36 40 28
www.ilcampionissimo.fr

'We could spend two months in search of the perfect balance of colour, crunchiness and softness for a pizza – sheer perfection! On top of that, our thing is the cooked and the raw. We often add raw ingredients to the pizza as soon as it comes out of the oven to add freshness, without spoiling the flavour. When I go into my lab to make a dough, I come out six hours later. I am constantly in search of the perfect recipe. Even my wife tells me to stop, but our guests are happy, and that's my aim…' **Gino Jaskula Toniolo**

PARIS VIIe
IL VINO
EVERY DAY
13 boulevard de la Tour Maubourg
01 44 11 72 00
www.ilvinobyenricobernardo.com

On the menu, wines, nothing but wines! Choose your bottle, and Enrico Bernardo, top sommelier in the world, will serve you the food that best accompanies it. The maestro is a purist who has designed his own line of Schott Zwiesel glasses, and his Laguiole corkscrew. You will be guided through the one and a half thousand labels from all corners of the world.

PARIS IVe
IZRAËL
TUESDAY – SATURDAY
30 rue François Miron
01 46 44 43 95
-

Alain Ducasse: What is the product that is unique to your place?
Françoise Izraël: Well, just one of them is cumin… there is cumin and then there's cumin. If you take mine… come, give me your hand, sniff and see. We have everything and nothing, whatever you want; you must come, smell, see!
AD: I see you also have fresh produce and cooked meats as well?
FI: Yes, of course. If it's good, it fits in here. That's our only condition.

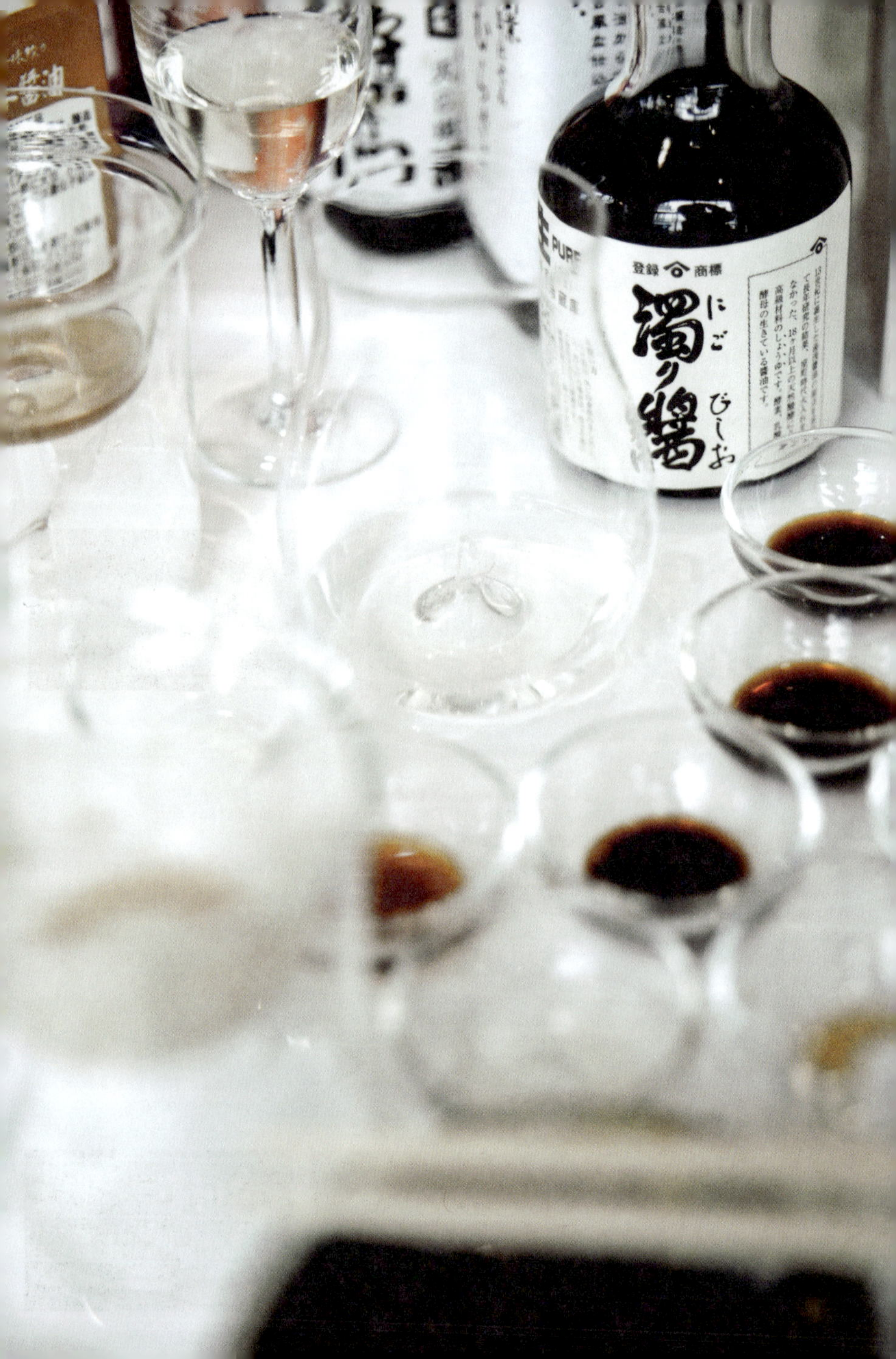
PURE
登録 商標
にご
濁り醤
びしお

PARIS XVe
KAISEKI
MONDAY – SATURDAY
7bis rue André Lefebvre
01 45 54 48 60
www.kaiseki.com

'Takeuchi sensei' holds his breath. He gathers impetus. He throws himself on the salmon. Filleted in a few precise attacks. Dye on his knife; a red, yellow and then green line appears on the mauve rice. He comes to a halt. We breathe and admire the unusual work of Hissa Takeuchi, master of 'dripping': beetroot juice coulis, the tinted lines of squid ink, trails of Matcha tea, cherry juice droplets, raw scallops in their shell, drizzled with olive oil and passion fruit pulp. This is just the beginning.

PARIS XVIIIe
MICHELANGELO
TUESDAY – SATURDAY
3 rue André Barsacq
01 42 23 10 77
–

Every morning, under the shade of the Montmartre cable car, Michelangelo Riina, a straightforward Sicilian, goes to the market and composes the menu. Every evening, he – alone – paces up and down the few centimetres that separate the open kitchen from his 15 or so guests. Between his hands, Sicilian cuisine bursts with flavours and colours, like his Gorgonzola *arancini*. Imagination, too, such as his giant prawn and pistachio tagliatelle. A well-mastered and modern Mediterranean experience.

PARIS Ier
MORA
MONDAY – SATURDAY
13 rue Montmartre
01 45 08 19 24
www.mora.fr

From Constantinople to St Petersburg, for just under two centuries Mora house has been supplying the world's top cooks and pastry chefs. It's simple: they have everything. From pink eggcups to the 'K5 Super' mixer with earth-shattering movement, valve-funnels, refractometers and the 'Sultan' decorating tube. For the impossible, they would probably only ask for a few days' grace.

PARIS XIXe
MOUSSA L'AFRICAIN
EVERY DAY
2527 avenue Corentin Cariou
01 40 36 13 00
www.moussalafricain.com

For some, Paris–Dakar means jeeps roaring through the dunes. For gourmets, it's more likely a *yassa* chicken. Or a *tiep*, a traditional Senegalese dish, or an *ndolé*, a Cameroonian bitterleaf stew – the heart wavers. Alexandre Bella Ola, Cameroonian chef-cook, invites you on a trip through darkest Africa. To start off, Malian, Ivorian, Senegalese and Cameroonian specialities, accompanied by delicious piping-hot plantain banana fritters.

PARIS IVe
BOULANGERIE MURCIANO
MONDAY – FRIDAY AND SUNDAY
14 rue des Rosiers
01 48 87 48 88
–

The Murciano bakery-patisserie lies in rue des Rosiers, in the heart of the traditional Jewish quarter of Paris. People go there to buy *challah*, the famous plaited bread, made with poppy seeds or raisins. The 'plain' one is ideal for endlessly soaking up *molokheya*, a type of ragout made from Kerria powder, an aromatic herb with a spinach-like taste. The apple strudel is delicately flavoured with cinnamon; it makes you want to sink your teeth into it. Everything here is kosher.

PARIS XVIe
NON SOLO CUCINA
TUESDAY – SATURDAY
135 rue du Ranelagh
01 45 27 99 93
–

You imagine yourself in Sicily here, with the chef as guide. Today, it's sautéed mussels and clam chowder, followed by spaghetti with sardines and wild fennel, the whole dish washed down with a full-bodied Sicilian wine. For dessert, you indulge in the amazing sweet courgette tart or the delicious cannoli with sweetened ricotta. Everything begs to be tasted and you return without any arm-twisting. It's hearty, it's cheerful, it's good.

PARIS XVIIIᵉ
NON SOLO PASTA
MONDAY EVENING – SATURDAY
50 rue du Ruisseau
01 42 55 09 33
www.nonsolopastaparis.com

You'll find a family ambiance at this quarter's canteen-dinette-caterer. Light wood tabletops, a welcoming smile, lunch during the week, dinner at the weekend. Francesco offers authentic Italian cuisine: *penne all'arrabbiata* and *fusilli alla matriciana*, tuna and tomato *galletti* that melt in the mouth, delicately flavoured with lightly spiced virgin olive oil. Try the *panna cotta* served with caramel. The Nutella mousse is just the thing to accompany a *ristretto*.

PARIS XIIIᵉ
LA NOUVELLE MER DE CHINE
MONDAY, WEDNESDAY – SUNDAY
159 rue du Château des Rentiers
01 45 84 22 49
-

Brave the less than attractive street and the wind that gusts in. As if on the shores of the China Sea, a light, subtle cuisine is being prepared. Melting prawn fritters, crunchy at first, then juicy, with a delicate lemon-garlic-salt-pepper sauce in perfect harmony; green apple salad prepared in julienne strips like a papaya; duck's tongue, salted and peppered; chicken cooked at low temperature or lemon duck. The large, calm plates are at the mercy of a gentle breeze.

PARIS XIIIᵉ
PAKKAI
TUESDAY – SUNDAY
71 avenue d'Ivry
01 45 83 47 40
-

Absolutely…frozen foods! This most demanding Asian mama is not afraid to make use of them herself, because it's not always possible to go to Singapore in search of soft-shell crab during the three weeks of its moulting. At Pakkai, you'll find a wide range of fish and shellfish, as well as steamy mouthfuls as good as any you'd get from the quarter's main rivals. A variety of Thai dishes which are a dream come true for every single time-pressed person. Free tastings on Sundays.

PARIS IVᵉ
CHARCUTERIE PANZER
MONDAY – FRIDAY, SUNDAY
26 rue des Rosiers
01 42 72 91 06
www.charcuteriepanzer.com

The shop window greets us with the sight of famous Cracow sausages. They have the same smile as Mr Panzer junior. Obviously, everything is kosher, from the Tunisian salami to the duck foie gras and cured saucisson. Self-restraint is needed not to plunge a hand into the barrel of dill gherkins. You'll find yourself inspired by the beef jerky carpaccio, calf's shoulder in herbs and spices, pickled pork tongue and paprika turkey, making up an English platter with an Ashkenazi influence.

PARIS XIIIᵉ
PARIS STORE
TUESDAY – SUNDAY
44 avenue d'Ivry
01 44 06 88 18
www.parisstore.com

One of the largest Asian supermarkets in the capital. Here you'll discover what delights the connoisseurs and takes the aspirant novice by surprise: century eggs, lemongrass sausages, banana leaves, liquorice-infused prunes…a large fresh-food department, dragon- and sugar-apple fruit, Thai basil and bitter gourds. Amusing legumes and cereals, such as brown rice that turns to a lilac colour on cooking. Modest prices, but sometimes an unnerving choice – it's wise to know what you've come to seek out.

PARIS XIᵉ
PHO DONG HUONG
MONDAY, WEDNESDAY – SUNDAY
14 rue Louis Bonnet
01 43 57 42 81
-

The ideal would be to have a huge paper serviette for a more comfortable tasting experience. As soon as you're seated, the waiter brings a mysterious-looking brown and creamy sauce to the table, with a plate of extremely fresh herbs and spices. If you're a beginner, do what the person sitting next to you does – dip the crunchy soya bean sprouts in the sauce. As simple as that! Pho Dong Huong is a legendary family-run Vietnamese temple. Special mention goes to the frittered crêpe and the *bo bun cha gio*.

PARIS XIII⁰
PHO TAI
MONDAY, TUESDAY, THURSDAY – SATURDAY
13 rue Philibert Lucot
01 45 85 97 36
-

The goddess of delicacy, who has descended to earth to seduce men, knows where to get her supply of ammunition. Divine spring rolls with slightly warmed beef, melt-in-the-mouth grilled chicken just like in Hanoi – huge portions and subtle flavourings are served with a crafty smile. In his previous establishment in rue de Longchamp, chef Te Ve Pin, the man who made the very first *pho* soup in Paris, earned himself the nickname 'the Chinese Robuchon'. Today, his menu offers the same prices as the neighbouring greasy spoons. The bargain of the century.

PARIS IX⁰
PICCOLA TOSCANA
MONDAY – SATURDAY
10 rue Rochambeau
09 51 04 46 35
www.piccolatoscana.com

You push open the deli's door and, just like in Florence, you order a *tramezzino alla porchetta* – a roast suckling pig sandwich. While it's being prepared, immerse yourself in the refined pecorinos or the Margherita *panforte*, a Siennese nougat with candied citrus fruit. Let yourself be tempted by the communal table for dining guests and the little terrace, for a plate of truffled pasta.

PARIS VIII⁰
LA RÉGINETTE
MONDAY – FRIDAY
Galerie 66, 49 rue de Ponthieu
01 83 56 65 55
-

A jam-packed canteen at Régine's – it closes when Paris starts waking up and is run by Nathalie Bénézeth and her younger brother Alexis. Inside, it's like a Streamline yacht. What light, crispy dough! The pizza man is a master craftsman, putting on a show; throwing the dough up towards the ceiling and catching it in midair, just centimetres above your head! There's even a mini Nutella pizzetta – don't even think about denying yourself dessert.

PARIS XI⁰
RINO
TUESDAY – SATURDAY
46 rue Trousseau
01 48 06 95 85
www.rino-restaurant.com

Giovanni Passerini was Petter Nilsson's sous-chef at La Gazzetta. Prior to that, he dabbled at L'Arpège and was Chateaubriand's meat slicer. He spread his wings in a micro bistro where you only see the kitchen – tomato red – and plates. Italian influences are evident in the pearl barley risotto with orange preserve or the pear *baba* with ricotta; instinct and market freshness in the yellow pollock with green cabbage and hazelnuts or hake with Swiss chard and olive oil. It's what we call an authentic kitchen.

PARIS XII⁰
SARDEGNA A TAVOLA
MONDAY EVENING – SATURDAY
1 rue de Cotte
-

We're sort of looking out for the pickpockets and the idyllic beach. That's the only thing missing, otherwise we'd be in Sardinia. Dionysian pastas, shellfish prepared with precision, a fresh take on classics such as tripe with beans, and a semi-tyrannical, semi-benevolent host. King crab claws served on a board with rocket – we'd even eat them off the bald head of a mafioso! Everything takes place in the shade of melancholic hams – we're captivated by the experience.

PARIS V⁰
SOU QUAN
MONDAY – SATURDAY
35 place Maubert
01 43 26 80 39
-

You go down the little steps at Place Maubert. Lam will take you under his wing. He knows how to choose imported mangoes, ultra-fresh vegetables, lychees that are to perfume Pierre Hermé's *Ispahan*. Amid a wide variety of produce, you can sometimes find spicy soft fish roe (*maitenko*), so take advantage.

PARIS VIIIe
LE STRESA
MONDAY – FRIDAY
7 rue Chambiges
01 47 23 51 62
www.lestresa.com

Cuisine originating from all corners of Italy: Roman artichokes, truffles from Alba, Venetian veal with onions, *parmigiana* asparagus. The mini pizzas are enjoyed by the mini mafiosi who find themselves among connoisseurs. People also come to the Stresa's pretty terrace for the three sculptures of Cesar and the hope of dining in the shadow of some celebrity, surrounded by a décor of red velour which has retained its 1950s charm.

PARIS XIIe
SUR LES QUAIS
TUESDAY – SUNDAY
7 place d'Aligre
01 43 43 21 09
www.surlesquais.com

The wooden shelves show off the little things that make us love to go 'to the quay'. A counter of sweets displayed in front of you, another a little further away also offering treasures…how can you resist? Paul Vautrain knows how to awaken your senses. Over here is an unbeatable quince paste cooked to perfection to accompany a flavoursome Manchego cheese. Over there, a pleiad of olive oils in cruets, sold by the litre, self-service-style, providing delicate seasonings.

PARIS X^e
LA TÊTE DANS LES OLIVES
TUESDAY – SATURDAY
2 rue Sainte Marthe
09 51 31 33 34
www.latetedanslesolives.com

Cédric Casanova: So, chef, what are you going to make from my olives?
Alain Ducasse: *Mamma mia*, they're very salty! I'll start by soaking them for 48 hours in fresh water. Afterwards, I'll add olive oil – but which one?
CC: Preferably the Bianca one. It's light and refined, with lemon aromas. In the large tin cruet.
AD: Good idea. Pass me the fennel seeds, in the basket over there, and the pink pepper.
CC: *Buon appetito!*

PARIS X^e
VOY ALIMENTO AU BAR DES ARTISANS
TUESDAY – SUNDAY
23 rue des Vinaigriers
01 42 01 03 44
www.voyalimento.fr

On the vegan Sunday brunch menu: blinis with almond purée and alfalfa bean sprouts, half-cooked, half-raw soup, banana-milk rice-lacuma-maca milkshake, the traditional *xocolatl* of the Aztecs, with cinnamon. Pascal, a dietician and druid from time to time, willingly introduces 'superfoods'. At the same time, Jean-François goes to meet Parisians at the organic markets. You can shop there, eat on the premises and leave armed with the day's menu.

PARIS X^e
VT CASH & CARRY
TUESDAY – SUNDAY
11–15 rue Cail
01 40 05 07 18
www.vtcashcarry.com

To get your hands on cardamom, mustard seeds or green lentil flour essential for poppadoms, this Little India address is the place to go. Connoisseurs will fill their pockets with custard powder, packets of agar-agar and textured soy protein. Also offering a variety of spices positively 'Bollyfoodian'.

PARIS IIe
WORKSHOP ISSÉ
MONDAY – SATURDAY
11 rue Saint-Augustin
01 42 96 26 74
www.workshopisse.fr

Japanese sensations. Opalescent *konnyaku* spaghetti, lifted with a touch of super-fresh *wasabi* and light soy sauce. The delicacy of soya tofu, the explosive intensity of a *mirin* that's consumed like a liqueur. Magical *miso*, yuzu juice, incomparable soya milks. Master Toshiro Kuroda instructs on the top bouillons, everything about *kombus*, the complexity of soya. Even the dog, the temple's guardian, has a place among the porcelain and Senchô pepper tree bonsais.

PARIS Ier
YAM'TCHA
WEDNESDAY – SUNDAY
4 rue Sauval
01 40 26 08 07
-

Potatoes? Just like that, in the wok, 45 seconds, almost raw? The high priestess of the flame officiates, and the spud, prepared like green mango, is ennobled. Also transformed: steamed aubergines enhanced with fermented black beans, wedge clams in the wok, duck in all its guises. Sit at the bar for a bird's-eye view over the clever and skilful work of Adeline Grattard.

PARIS VIe
ZE KITCHEN GALERIE
MONDAY – SATURDAY
4 rue des Grands Augustins
01 44 32 00 32
www.zekitchengalerie.fr

'My definition of cuisine is freedom of expression. I function between different desires, moods, passions, discoveries, travels. My inquisitiveness is the source of the cuisine I prepare today. I am also privileged to work with fabulous market gardeners – Joël Thiébault and Asafumi Yamashita – my goldsmith market gardeners, each of whom, with their own sensibility, brings me vegetables of incredible freshness and taste. I get on well with them: in fact, they're just like me, they feel and explore…'

William Ledeuil

PARIS X^e
ZERDA CAFÉ
MONDAY EVENING – SATURDAY
15 rue René Boulanger
01 42 00 25 15
-

Jaffar Achour: Here is the vegetable Berber couscous. You must oil the semolina as soon as it comes out of the steam – burning your hands in the process – otherwise it becomes oily. It's a spring couscous. On the side are finely sliced, crunchy onions.

AD: In fact, there is a whole range of different types of couscous…

JA: As far as we know, almost 450…We also prepare *berkoukes*, with larger rolled grains. It's prepared with or without meat. Here, we also serve it with shellfish.

PARIS,
SWEET
PARIS

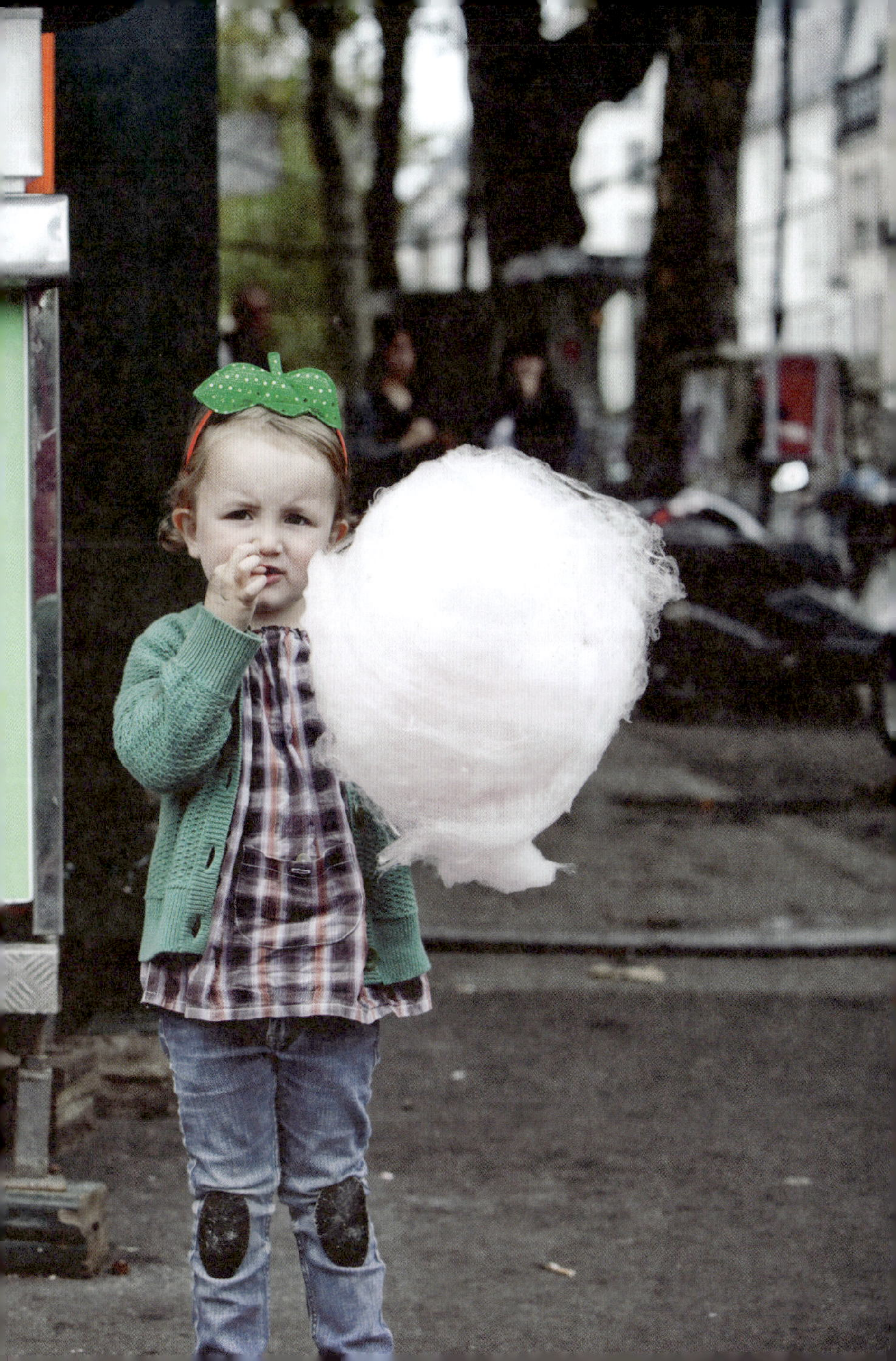

PARIS IVe
GLACIER BERTHILLON
WEDNESDAY – SUNDAY
29–31 rue Saint-Louis en l'Île
01 43 54 31 61
www.berthillon.fr

A biting-cold winter has hit Paris. In an empty tearoom, the entire Berthillon team, huddled together as if round a fireplace, is carefully crumbling a glistening mountain of candied chestnuts. Who eats ice-cream in this weather? The Parisians, it seems. They patiently await their turn, captivated by candied chestnut with a Christmas Eve scent. In summer, the chestnut gives way to wild strawberries, and the Parisians are joined by gourmets from around the world. We can understand why!

PARIS V^e
LE BONBON AU PALAIS
TUESDAY – SATURDAY
19 rue Monge
01 78 56 15 72
www.bonbonsaupalais.fr

The taste of a memory nestles in gleaming glass jars. The sweet slips from the tongue at the Palace – a 'Sucre de pomme', a multicoloured 'Froufrou', a 'Negus', a caramelised nut – and childhood sets off on its magic carpet ride. Each jeweller's marvel comes from the artisan who created it, sometimes a few centuries ago, sometimes according to a secret recipe still fiercely guarded by protective nuns.

PARIS IVe
LA CAFÉOTHÈQUE
EVERY DAY
52 rue de l'Hôtel de Ville
01 53 01 83 34
www.lacafeotheque.com

Here, we talk about Grand Crus. *Terroirs*. Fruit and floral notes, honey and spicy aromas. Soil acidity and pluviometry. Here, we turn up our noses at all types of blends, even if they're from the region. We are purists and proud of it. This is a coffee house. A house of stories. Once upon a time, there was a coffee bean that was picked up after it had been digested by the Jacu bird, somewhere in the Amazonian rainforest. Here, we begin our initiation.

PARIS XVIe
LE CHALET DES ÎLES
EVERY DAY
Lac Inférieur du Bois de Boulogne
01 42 88 04 69
www.chalet-des-iles.com

Travelling to a restaurant by boat does not happen every day in Paris. It's a short trip, but the passengers are already enjoying these moments of escape from Parisian life. At the edge of the lake, the weeping willows form a shield, impenetrable and gentle. In this soothing setting, orangeade suddenly takes on a totally different taste.

PARIS IVe
DAMMANN FRÈRES
EVERY DAY
15 place des Vosges
01 44 54 04 88
www.dammann.fr

In the shade of the archways of the elegant Place des Vosges, the Dammann Frères tea house is a haven of peace. From selecting to importing teas, as well as creating new blends, this family business has been perpetuating its know-how for the past three generations. Besides original teas sold loose, in sachets or in balls, cold-infused teas and herbal infusions make you forget the goings-on in the Marais quarter and beckon you to distant travels.

PARIS XVe
CHOCOLATERIE JACQUES GÉNIN
MONDAY – SATURDAY
18 rue Saint-Charles
01 45 77 29 01
-

Caramel. Or chocolate. A chocolate éclair with a plain caramel, or a caramel éclair with a chocolate toffee? Or maybe a hot chocolate, with some nougat…In the end, it's a tiny millefeuille. It's out of the question to even think about passing by the rainbow of fruit jellies, offering a splashing dive into the texture and scent of fruit. Come on, let's keep it simple: a toffee, made with salted butter and sprinkled with nuts.

PARIS II

HARRY'S NEW YORK BAR
EVERY DAY
5 rue Daunou
01 42 61 71 14
www.harrys-bar.fr

It's in the crowded red velour basement, on the very same piano that Gershwin composed *An American in Paris*. The partitioning was burnt during the war, to light the stove. Americans in Paris still come here to delight in the legendary Irish coffee. Vibrant evenings are held here when the American presidential elections are drawing near.

PARIS VI

PIERRE HERMÉ PARIS
EVERY DAY
72 rue Bonaparte
01 43 54 47 77
www.pierreherme.com

Pierre Hermé: So, would you like to taste a macaroon? This one is jasmine-flavoured. There's also cinnamon-cherry-pistachio, rose, chocolate, caramel, wasabi-strawberry, apricot-pistachio and milk chocolate-passion fruit, among many others...
Alain Ducasse: You know that I like them hard, without fillings!
PH: Personally, I like them soft, creamy, smooth as can be, with just a light crunchy crust. There are many different palates!

PARIS Ier

JEAN-PAUL HÉVIN CHOCOLATIER
MONDAY – SATURDAY
231 rue Saint-Honoré
01 55 35 35 96
www.jphevin.com

Jean-Paul Hévin's chocolates are unique. His extra-dark chocolate cream fillings, Grand Cru beans, and not overly sweet creations could make you fear a slightly dry approach. But this doesn't emanate from coolness. It's elegance. He plays on chocolate-cheese-herb and spice combinations, such as Époisses cheese-cumin, Pont-l'Évêque with thyme, goat's cheese-hazelnut and Roquefort-nut. Pure fine art.

PARIS VI

JUGETSUDO
TUESDAY – SATURDAY
95 rue de Seine
01 46 33 94 90
www.jugetsudo.com

The wall seats taken from a space station meld in with bamboo – the Zen shadowy-light cast by a video screen. This tearoom is a branch of the Tokyo house Maruyama Nori which has been combining *nori* seaweed with Japanese tea for the last century and a half. A *cha-zen* approach is practised here – a marriage of Zen and the tea ceremony. *Sencha* or *Genmaicha*, early crop or *Gyokuro* are consumed on the premises, or sold in exquisite packaging.

PARIS VI

LADURÉE
EVERY DAY
21 rue Bonaparte
01 44 07 64 87
www.laduree.fr

The Ladurée house remains true to its name. For almost 500 years, 16 rue Royale – one of the capital's very first tearooms – has been welcoming gourmets, regulars and tourists. In the heart of Saint-Germain-des-Prés, a special mention goes to the boutique on rue Bonaparte. Capturing the art of living the French way, Ladurée perpetuates the great patisserie tradition, while at the same time innovating through the blackcurrant-violet macaroon and the divine rose éclair.

PARIS XVIII

PÂTISSERIE ARNAUD LARHER
TUESDAY – SATURDAY
53 rue Caulaincourt
01 42 57 68 08
www.arnaud-larher.com

Trained at Fauchon and Pierre Hermé, this man did not wait for his tricolour stripe, achieved in 2007, to write his name in gold dust in the world of delicacies. His creations – such as his chocolate marshmallow or his 'Frisson', lime-pulp ganache – remain both in mouth and memory for a long time. Arnaud Larher creates a pink poppy éclair, and revisits the pistachio macaroon. Ices in summer; hot chocolate, old-style, in winter ends up drowning its taster in sinfulness. Too cute.

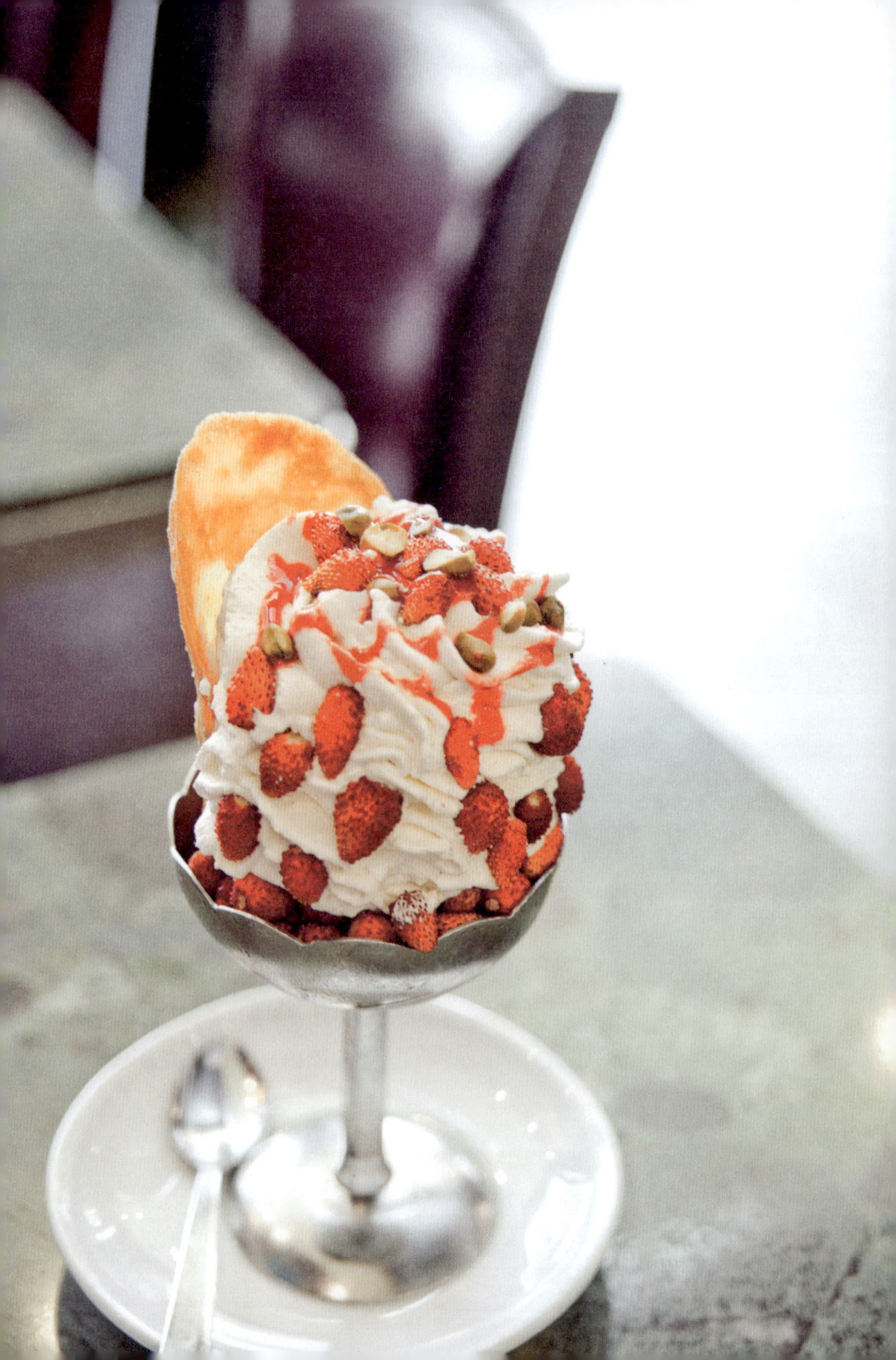

PARIS XVIᵉ
LENÔTRE
EVERY DAY
48 avenue Victor Hugo
01 45 02 21 21
www.lenotre.fr

Gaston Lenôtre, a true leading chef of his generation and creative genius, knew how to break the traditional mould of patisserie-making. Over 40 years ago, this tasteful ambassador opened the first school for gastronomic training and improvement in France. Today, his know-how is upheld by the Lenôtre house, which continues to promote the French culinary heritage.

PARIS XVIIᵉ
PÂTISSERIE RAOUL MAEDER
TUESDAY – SUNDAY
158 boulevard Berthier
01 46 22 50 73
www.raoulmaeder.fr

Apricot bread for white meats. Truffle bread to delight two scrambled eggs. Aniseed and orange-flavoured bread for teatime. Black hazelnut bread as a cake. And if you manage to escape from the fascination of breads, it's only to fall under the spell of a savoury *kugelhopf* with morsels of bacon, almonds and pistachios. Maybe even a pretzel, from pure Alsace stock. It's an absolute must to return in the really cold season for the delicious hot chocolate.

PARIS Vᵉ
MAISON DES TROIS THÉS
TUESDAY – SUNDAY
33 rue Gracieuse
01 43 36 93 84
www.troisthes.com

You ring the bell, and wait for the door to open. In the Chinese tea temple, enveloped in silence, the ritual is already underway. You discover the infinite universe of the magic leaf, the green teas of spring, just picked, Pu-Erh on tap for large pots. Shoes are removed before taking a place in the tearoom where you taste the precious water as part of the *zhong* (simple Chinese ceremony) or the *gong fu cha* (sophisticated ceremony), thanks to Master Tseng's infinite knowledge.

PARIS IVᵉ
MARIAGE FRÈRES
EVERY DAY
30 rue du Bourg-Tibourg
01 42 72 28 11
www.mariagefreres.com

It responds to the gentle name of number 419. Strange, this administrative numbering system, here, among this chocolate wood panelling, in this chocolate-box setting. But then again, 'Tamaryokucha' is rather unpronounceable. However, its pretty dark green twisted leaves, its extremely delicate keynotes, its silky texture and *umami* taste make for a brilliant tea. And as a wrapped parcel, accompanying a fillet of white fish, it's an aromatic revelation.

PARIS VIIIᵉ
MIELE
55 boulevard Malesherbes
01 42 93 72 01
www.miele.fr

Miele's greatest challenge is the sustainability of its business and the appliances it sells. 'Always better' is its currency, dedicated to innovation: materials that are constantly more eco-friendly and resistant for safe, durable and high-performance products. The key mission of this business, while protecting its reputation, is the assurance of high-quality and long-lasting household appliances with reduced environmental impact.

PARIS VIᵉ
MULOT
TUESDAY – SUNDAY
76 rue de Seine
01 43 26 85 77
www.gerard-mulot.com

Seasonal fruit tarts, clafoutis, desserts, sumptuous melting tarts – nothing has been left out. Right in front of you, a variety of generously filled sandwiches make your mouth water. On your right, amid the delicious scents, choose from among the collection of refined chocolates and heaps of macaroons. Unless you prefer to have a bite to eat on the premises. It's not by chance that Mulot patisserie has been operating in the heart of Saint-Germain-des-Prés for 25 years.

PARIS XX°
NANI
EVERY DAY
102 boulevard de Belleville
01 47 97 38 05
-

At first sight, it's a Maghreb patisserie just like the many others the area houses. In reality, Nani is Paris' first kosher patisserie. This is where it's a must to be tempted by a Tunisian millefeuille, an 'Idéal' or an almond 'Boulou'. However, the best of the best – the Holy Grail – are the opalescent glass jars lining the shop window. Since 1962, the establishment has been making its own almond-flavoured *orgeat* syrup, as creamy as the Milky Way on a starry evening.

PARIS III°
PAIN DE SUCRE
MONDAY, THURSDAY, FRIDAY, SATURDAY, SUNDAY
14 rue Rambuteau
01 45 74 68 92
www.patisseriepaindesucre.com

Didier Mathray, the master of the house – a former pastry chef for Pierre Gagnaire – greets us. He doesn't lack humour or imagination. His *'Pain de sel'* exudes pirit and his buckwheat dough with foie gras is an irresistible specimen. Don't miss the *'Pirouette Pomme'*, a caramelised apple tart with rosemary and almond, pistachio and lime cream – a dazzling combination. All the scents of the scrubland find their way into your mouth. Only one desire remains: to return.

PARIS III°
LE PALAIS DES THÉS
EVERY DAY
64 rue Vieille du Temple
01 48 87 80 60
www.palaisdesthes.com

At the centre of the light-wood boutique, a large samovar is on the boil. Help yourself: the tasting of the day encourages finding a favourite. A well-considered selection of Asian Grand Crus, discoveries from the ends of the earth, light and floral blends. Patience is advised: if it takes an hour to find the perfect tea, so much the better!

PARIS VI°
LA PÂTISSERIE DES RÊVES
TUESDAY – SUNDAY
93 rue du bac
01 42 84 00 82
www.lapatisseriedesreves.com

A millefeuille, theoretically, is crispy. On the other hand, it's not. This one melts in your mouth. It fades away like an aristocrat, in a rustle of vanilla-flavoured cream, which lasts until the last puff, thanks to the pastry chef's unrelenting technique in corsetry. Only on Sundays, otherwise people would no longer go to work. Following the rue du Bac, Philippe Conticini, one of the greatest pastry chefs of his generation, invested in rue de Longchamp. Finally!

PARIS XVI°
PERENE
16 avenue Mozart
01 46 47 47 14
www.perene.fr

The kitchen is a living space where people like to come together to share happy moments. Deeply emotional moments, in a fitting environment. At the cooking school, Perene and his talented staff have dedicated their expertise to meeting expectations, both in terms of taste and requirements. Experienced artisans, they know how to translate this excellence into kitchen-studios dedicated to sensory pleasure, and aligned as closely as possible to domestic needs, ensuring they remain true to the home environment. This is the fruit of valuable interaction.

PARIS XVI°
RÉGIS CHOCOLATIER
EVERY DAY
89 rue de Passy
01 45 27 70 00
www.chocolats.net

The fruit jellies border on the sublime. Sophisticated artisan preparation, with a recipe containing up to 80 per cent fruit pulp. The *marron glacé* is imperial, the transalpine chestnut preserved and lacquered, hiding a hint of sugar syrup at its centre, the jewel at the heart of the lotus. As for the chocolates, they are prepared each day with infinite care. A good destination for the last half a century.

PARIS VI
PATRICK ROGER
TUESDAY – SATURDAY
108 boulevard Saint-Germain
01 43 29 38 42
www.patrickroger.com

A grand master chocolate-maker, nothing scares Patrick Roger. This Meilleur Ouvrier de France is an eccentric and highly inspired artist. In his search for excellence, he makes no concessions. His 'Coloured' chocolate sweets offer delicate combinations: creamy toffee, verbena and yuzu for the 'Wild' slate colour, or caramel, vinegar and raisin for the 'Rafale' golden button. Unless you succumb instead to the chocolate morsels that answer to evocative names such as 'Jealousy', 'Insolence', 'Fantasme' or 'Marie Galante'...

PARIS V
THE TEA CADDY
EVERY DAY
14 rue Saint-Julien le Pauvre
01 43 54 15 56
www.the-tea-caddy.com

The street has an air of spring about it, the cosy tearoom having won over English gourmets. Beside a tea flower served in a 'Blue Willow' cup, Olivier Langois offers scones with whipped cream and homemade strawberry jam, or a divine apple pie. For the incurable eggs and bacon brigade, an English breakfast can also be ordered.

ALPHABETICAL INDEX

	D	B
1728	4	21
21	4	13
39V	4	17
58 Tour Eiffel	4	25

A
	D	B
A.A.A. Asie Antilles Afrique	32	401
Afaria	32	405
Alain Ducasse au Plaza Athénée	4	29
Alfred	4	37
Aligre (Marché d')	22	391
Alleosse (Fromagerie)	22	391
Amici Miei	32	501
Arôme (L')	5	281
As du Falafel (L')	32	501
Assiette (L')	5	39
Atelier de Joël Robuchon (L')	5	43
Auberge du Bonheur (L')	5	281
Auberge Pyrénnées-Cévennes	22	392
Aubrac Corner	22	299
Aux comptoirs des Indes	32	502
Aux Deux Amis	5	47
Aux Lyonnais	22	301

B
	D	B
Bain Marie (Au)	5	51
Ballon et Coquillages	22	307
Balzar	6	55
Bar à Patates	23	392
Bar aux Folies	6	59
Baratin (Le)	6	63
Barthélemy	23	311
Bastille (Marché)	23	393
Bateaux Parisiens	6	283
BE	6	67
Beillevaire (Fromagerie)	23	315
Bellechasse (Hôtel le)	6	282
Benoit	7	71
Berthillon (Glacier)	44	517
Betsy Bernardaud	32	409
Bidou bar	7	77
Bistrot Paul Bert	7	81
Bonbon au Palais (Le)	44	521
Brasserie Lipp	7	283
Brunon (Boucherie Michel)	23	319
Byzance Champs-Élysées Bellota / Bellota Rive Droite	33	413

C
	D	B
Café Constant	7	85
Café de Flore	7	89
Café de la Nouvelle Mairie	8	93
Café Maure (de la Mosquée de Paris)	33	417
Caféothèque (La)	44	525
Caffè dei Cioppi	33	421
Camondo (Musée Nissim de)	15	223
Cantin (Fromagerie Marie-Anne)	24	393
Carré des Feuillants (Le)	8	95
Cave de Joël Robuchon (La)	8	284
Cave de l'Os à Moelle (La)	8	284
Cave des Papilles (La)	8	285
Caves Augé (Les)	8	99
Chalet des Îles (Le)	44	579
Chapeau Melon	9	285
Chardenoux (Le)	9	103
Chartier (Restaurant)	9	107
Chateaubriand (Le)	9	111
Cherche Midi (Le)	33	502
Chez Flottes	25	323
Chez Georges	9	286
Chez Georges	25	394
Chez l'Ami Jean	9	115
Chez l'Ami Louis	10	119
Citrus Étoile	10	123
Closerie des Lilas (La)	10	127
Costes (Hôtel)	10	131
Cour Jardin (La)	10	135
Crémerie (La)	10	139
Crêpes et Galettes	25	394

D
	D	B
D'Chez Eux (Auberge)	25	327
Da Rosa épicerie fine	33	425
Dammann Frères	44	529
David (Boucherie)	33	429
Dehillerin	34	433
Dejean (Marché)	34	503
Desnoyer (Boucherie Hugo)	25	331
Deux Magots (Les)	11	286
Divellec (Le)	11	143
Dôme (La Poissonnerie du)	26	335
Dôme (Le)	10	287
Drouant	11	147
Du Pain et des Idées	11	151

E
	D	B
Écailler du bistrot (L')	11	155
Écume Saint-Honoré (L')	26	339
El Fogón	34	437
Enfants Rouges (Marché des)	26	395
Épicerie du Père Claude (L')	26	343

F
	D	B
Fines Gueules (Les)	12	287
Flaubert (Le)	12	288
Florence Kahn	34	441
Fontaine de Mars (La)	12	157
Forum (Le)	12	161
Fougères (Les)	12	165
Fouquet's	12	288
Foyer Vietnam	34	503
Frenchie	13	169

G
	D	B
G. Detou	13	289
Garde Manger (Le)	13	289
Gazzetta (La)	34	445
Génin (Chocolaterie Jacques)	44	533
Goumanyat	35	504
Gourmets des Ternes (Les)	13	173
Graineterie du marché (La)	26	347
Grande cascade (La)	13	177
Gros-La Fontaine (Marché)	26	351

H
	D	B
Harry's New York Bar	45	579
Hermé Paris (Pierre)	45	537
Hévin chocolatier (Jean-Paul)	45	580

I
	D	B
I Golosi	35	504
Idea Vino	35	449
Il Campionissimo	35	453
Il Vino	35	505
Itinéraires	26	395
Izraël	35	455

J
	D	B
Jadis (Restaurant)	13	290
Jeu de Quilles (Le)	14	181
Jugetsudo	45	541
Jules Verne (Le)	14	189

ALPHABETICAL INDEX

	D	B
K		
Kaiseki	37	459
Kei	14	185
L		
Ladurée	45	581
Larher (Pâtisserie Arnaud)	45	581
Lasserre	14	195
Laurent (Le)	14	199
Ledoyen	15	203
Lenôtre	47	545
M		
Maeder (Pâtisserie Raoul)	47	549
Maison des Trois Thés	47	553
Mama Shelter	15	207
Mariage Frères	47	557
Meurice (Le)	15	211
Michelangelo	37	505
Miele	47	575
Mon Vieil Ami	15	215
Mora	37	463
Moulin de la Vierge (Le)	15	219
Moussa l'Africain	37	506
Mulot	47	582
Murciano (Boulangerie)	37	506
N		
Nani	48	582
Non Solo Cucina	37	507
Non solo pasta	38	507
Nouvelle Mer de Chine (La)	38	508
P		
Pain de Sucre	48	559
Pakkai	38	508
Palais des Thés (Le)	48	583
Panzer (Charcuterie)	38	509
Papilles (Les)	16	291
Paris Store	38	509
Passy (Marché)	27	396
Pâtisserie des Rêves (La)	48	563
Pavillon de la Reine (Le)	16	291
Père Claude (Le)	27	396
Perene	48	577
Petit Moulin (Hôtel du)	16	227

	D	B
Petit Vendôme (Le)	16	292
Petrossian	16	292
Pharamond	16	231
Pho Dong Huong	38	510
Pho Tai	39	510
Piccola Toscana	39	511
Poilâne (Boulangerie)	17	235
Poule au pot (La)	17	293
Pousse Pousse	27	353
Pré Verre (Le)	14	290
Prunier (Restaurant)	17	239
Q		
Quatrehomme (Fromagerie)	27	396
Quincy (Le)	27	357
R		
Racines	27	361
Raspail (Marché)	28	365
Rech	17	243
Régalade (La)	17	293
Réginette (La)	39	511
Régis Chocolatier	48	567
Relais Louis XIII (Le)	17	294
Relais Plaza (Le)	18	249
Repaire de Cartouche (Le)	18	294
Restaurant Joséphine ('Chez Dumonet')	18	295
Ribouldingue	28	397
Rino	39	512
Roger (Patrick)	49	569
Rosa Bonheur	18	253
S		
Sardegna a Tavola	39	513
Saturne	28	369
Savoy (Restaurant Guy)	18	257
Schmid Traiteur	28	373
Select (Le)	18	261
Sou Quan	39	467
Spring	28	375
Stresa (Le)	40	513
Sur les Quais	40	471
T		
Tête dans les olives (La)	40	473

	D	B
The Tea Caddy	49	583
Thiébault maraîcher (Joël)	28	379
Thoumieux (Hôtel)	19	265
Train bleu (Le)	19	269
V		
Vérot – Charcutier (Gilles)	29	383
Verre volé (Le)	29	387
Voltaire (Le)	19	273
Voy Alimento (au Bar des Artisans)	40	477
VT Cash and Carry	40	481
W		
Wepler	19	295
Wine by One	29	397
Workshop Issé	40	485
Y		
Yachts de Paris	19	277
Yam'Tcha	41	489
Z		
Ze Kitchen galerie	41	493
Zerda Café	41	497

INDEX BY AREA

	D	B
PARIS Ier		
Alfred	4	37
Carré des Feuillants (Le)	8	95
Chez Flottes	25	323
Costes (Hôtel)	10	131
Dehillerin	34	433
Écume Saint-Honoré (L')	26	339
Fines Gueules (Les)	12	287
Hévin chocolatier (Jean-Paul)	45	580
Kei	14	185
Meurice (Le)	15	211
Mora	37	463
Pharamond	16	231
Poule au pot (La)	17	293
Spring	28	375
Wine by One	29	397
Yam'Tcha	41	489
PARIS IIE		
Aux Lyonnais	22	301
Chez Georges	9	394
Drouant	11	147
Frenchie	13	169
G. Detou	13	289
Harry's New York Bar	45	579
Il Campionissimo	35	453
Petit Vendôme (Le)	16	292
Racines	27	361
Saturne	28	369
Workshop Issé	40	485
PARIS IIIE		
Chez l'Ami Louis	10	119
Enfants Rouges (Marché des)	26	395
Goumanyat	35	504
Pain de Sucre	48	559
Palais des Thés (Le)	48	583
Pavillon de la Reine (Le)	16	291
Petit Moulin (Hôtel du)	16	227
PARIS IVE		
As du Falafel (L')	32	501
Benoit	7	71
Berthillon (Glacier)	44	517
Caféothèque (La)	44	525
Dammann Frères	44	529
David (Boucherie)	33	429
Florence Kahn	34	441
Izraël	35	455
Mariage Frères	47	557
Mon Vieil Ami	15	215
Murciano (Boulangerie)	37	506
Panzer (Charcuterie)	38	509
Yachts de Paris	19	277
PARIS V{E}		
Balzar	6	55
Bonbon au Palais (Le)	44	521
Café de la Nouvelle Mairie	8	93
Café Maure (de la Mosquée de Paris)	33	417
Crêpes et Galettes	25	394
Foyer Vietnam	34	503
Itinéraires	26	395
Maison des Trois Thés	47	553
Papilles (Les)	16	291
Pré Verre (Le)	14	290
Ribouldingue	28	397
Sou Quan	39	467
The Tea Caddy	49	583
PARIS VI{E}		
21	4	13
Brasserie Lipp	7	283
Café de Flore	7	89
Cherche Midi (Le)	33	502
Closerie des Lilas (La)	10	127
Crémerie (La)	10	139
Da Rosa épicerie fine	33	425
Deux Magots (Les)	11	286
El Fogón	34	437
Hermé Paris (Pierre)	45	537
Jugetsudo	45	541
Ladurée	45	581
Mulot	47	582
Pâtisserie des Rêves (La)	48	563
Poilâne (Boulangerie)	17	235
Raspail (Marché)	28	365
Relais Louis XIII (Le)	17	294
Restaurant Joséphine ('Chez Dumonet')	18	295
Roger (Patrick)	49	569
Select (Le)	18	261
Vérot – Charcutier (Gilles)	29	383
Ze Kitchen galerie	41	493
PARIS VIIE		
58 Tour Eiffel	4	25
Atelier de Joël Robuchon (L')	5	43
Bain Marie (Au)	5	51
Barthélemy	23	311
Bateaux Parisiens	6	283
Bellechasse (Hôtel le)	6	282
Betsy Bernardaud	32	409
Café Constant	7	85
Cantin (Fromagerie Marie-Anne)	24	393
Cave de Joël Robuchon (La)	8	284
Chez l'Ami Jean	9	115
D'Chez Eux (Auberge)	25	327
Divellec (Le)	11	143
Fontaine de Mars (La)	12	157
Il Vino	35	505
Jules Verne (Le)	14	189
Petrossian	16	292
Quatrehomme (Fromagerie)	27	396
Thoumieux (Hôtel)	19	265
Voltaire (Le)	19	273
PARIS VIIIE		
1728	4	21
39 V	4	17
Alain Ducasse au Plaza Athénée	4	29
Arôme (L')	5	281
Aubrac Corner	22	299
BE	6	67
Byzance Champs-Élysées Bellota / Bellota Rive Droite	33	413
Camondo (Musée Nissim de)	15	223
Caves Augé (Les)	8	99
Citrus Étoile	10	123
Cour Jardin (La)	10	135
Forum (Le)	12	161
Fouquet's	12	288
Gourmets des Ternes (Les)	13	173
Lasserre	14	195
Laurent (Le)	14	199
Ledoyen	15	203
Miele	47	575

	D	B
Réginette (La)	39	511
Relais Plaza (Le)	18	249
Stresa (Le)	40	513

PARIS IXE

	D	B
Chartier (Restaurant)	9	107
I Golosi	35	504
Piccola Toscana	39	511
Pousse Pousse	27	353

PARIS X[E]

	D	B
Du Pain et des Idées	11	151
Schmid Traiteur	28	373
Tête dans les olives (La)	40	473
Verre volé (Le)	29	387
Voy Alimento (au Bar des Artisans)	40	477
VT Cash and Carry	40	481
Zerda Café	41	497

PARIS XIE

	D	B
A.A.A. Asie Antilles Afrique	32	401
Amici Miei	32	501
Auberge Pyrénnées-Cévennes	22	392
Aux comptoirs des Indes	32	502
Aux Deux Amis	5	47
Bastille (Marché)	23	393
Bistrot Paul Bert	7	81
Caffè dei Cioppi	33	421
Chardenoux (Le)	9	103
Chateaubriand (Le)	9	111
Écailler du bistrot (L')	11	155
Idea Vino	35	449
Pho Dong Huong	38	510
Repaire de Cartouche (Le)	18	294
Rino	39	512

PARIS XIIE

	D	B
Aligre (Marché d')	22	391
Brunon (Boucherie Michel)	23	319
Garde Manger (Le)	13	289
Gazzetta (La)	34	445
Graineterie du marché (La)	26	347
Quincy (Le)	27	357
Sardegna a Tavola	39	513
Sur les Quais	40	471

	D	B
Train bleu (Le)	19	269

PARIS XIIIE

	D	B
Nouvelle Mer de Chine (La)	38	508
Pakkai	38	508
Paris Store	38	509
Pho Tai	39	510

PARIS XIVE

	D	B
Assiette (L')	5	39
Cave des Papilles (La)	8	285
Desnoyer (Boucherie Hugo)	25	331
Dôme (La Poissonnerie du)	25	335
Dôme (Le)	11	287
Jeu de Quilles (Le)	14	181
Moulin de la Vierge (Le)	15	219
Régalade (La)	17	293

PARIS XVE

	D	B
Afaria	32	405
Cave de l'Os à Moelle (La)	8	284
Épicerie du Père Claude (L')	26	343
Génin (Chocolaterie Jacques)	44	533
Jadis (Restaurant)	13	290
Kaiseki	37	459
Père Claude (Le)	27	396

PARIS XVIE

	D	B
Auberge du Bonheur (L')	5	281
Bar à Patates	23	392
Chalet des Îles (Le)	44	579
Grande cascade (La)	13	177
Gros-La Fontaine (Marché)	26	351
Lenôtre	47	545
Non Solo Cucina	37	507
Passy (Marché)	27	396
Perene	48	577
Prunier (Restaurant)	17	239
Régis Chocolatier	48	567
Thiébault maraîcher (Joël)	28	379

PARIS XVIIE

	D	B
Alleosse (Fromagerie)	22	391
Ballon et Coquillages	22	307
Bidou bar	7	77
Chez Georges	25	286

	D	B
Flaubert (Le)	12	288
Fougères (Les)	12	165
Maeder (Pâtisserie Raoul)	47	549
Rech	17	243
Savoy (Restaurant Guy)	18	257

PARIS XVIIIE

	D	B
Dejean (Marché)	34	503
Larher (Pâtisserie Arnaud)	45	581
Michelangelo	37	505
Non solo pasta	38	507
Wepler	19	295

PARIS XIXE

	D	B
Chapeau Melon	9	285
Moussa l'Africain	37	506
Rosa Bonheur	18	253

PARIS XXE

	D	B
Bar aux Folies	6	59
Baratin (Le)	6	63
Beillevaire (Fromagerie)	23	315
Mama Shelter	15	207
Nani	48	582

INDEX BY ESTABLISHMENT TYPE

	D	B
BAKERY		
BE	6	67
Du Pain et des Idées	11	151
Moulin de la Vierge (Le)	15	219
Murciano (Boulangerie)	37	506
Poilâne (Boulangerie)	17	235
BAR		
Bidou bar	7	77
Cave de l'Os à Moelle (La)	8	284
Forum (Le)	12	161
Harry's New York Bar	45	579
Voy Alimento (au Bar des Artisans)	40	477
BRASSERIE		
Aux Deux Amis	5	47
Balzar	6	55
BUTCHER		
Brunon (Boucherie Michel)	23	319
David (Boucherie)	33	429
Desnoyer (Boucherie Hugo)	25	331
BUTCHERY		
Panzer (Charcuterie)	38	509
Schmid Traiteur	28	373
Vérot – Charcutier (Gilles)	29	383
CAFÉ		
Bar aux Folies	6	59
Café Constant	7	85
Café de Flore	7	89
Café de la Nouvelle Mairie	8	93
Café Maure (de la Mosquée de Paris)	33	417
Deux Magots (Les)	11	286
Select (Le)	18	261
COFFEE OR TEA SHOP		
Caféothèque (La)	44	525
Dammann Frères	44	529
Jugetsudo	45	541
Maison des Trois Thés	47	553
Mariage Frères	47	557

	D	B
Palais des Thés (Le)	48	583
The Tea Caddy	49	583
CONFECTIONER		
Bonbon au Palais (Le)	44	521
Génin (Chocolaterie Jacques)	44	533
Hévin chocolatier (Jean-Paul)	45	580
Régis Chocolatier	48	567
Roger (Patrick)	49	569
DELICATESSEN		
A.A.A. Asie Antilles Afrique	32	401
As du Falafel (L')	32	501
Betsy Bernardaud	32	409
Byzance Champs-Élysées Bellota / Bellota Rive Droite	33	413
Crêpes et Galettes	25	394
Da Rosa épicerie fine	33	425
Épicerie du Père Claude (L')	26	343
Florence Kahn	34	441
G. Detou	13	289
Garde Manger (Le)	13	289
Goumanyat	35	504
Graineterie du marché (La)	26	347
Idea Vino	35	449
Izraël	35	455
Pakkai	38	508
Papilles (Les)	16	291
Paris Store	38	509
Piccola Toscana	39	511
Restaurant Joséphine ('Chez Dumonet')	18	295
Sou Quan	39	467
Sur les Quais	40	471
Tête dans les olives (La)	40	473
VT Cash and Carry	40	481
FISH MONGER		
Ballon et Coquillages	22	307
Dôme (La Poissonnerie du)	25	335
Écume Saint-Honoré (L')	26	339

	D	B
FROMAGERIE		
Alleosse (Fromagerie)	22	391
Barthélemy	23	311
Beillevaire (Fromagerie)	23	315
Cantin (Fromagerie Marie-Anne)	25	393
Quatrehomme (Fromagerie)	27	396
HOTEL		
Bellechasse (Hôtel le)	6	282
Pavillon de la Reine (Le)	16	291
Petit Moulin (Hôtel du)	16	227
ICE CREAM PARLOUR		
Berthillon (Glacier)	44	517
KITCHEN SUPPLIES		
Bain Marie (Au)	5	51
Camondo (Musée Nissim de)	15	223
Dehillerin	34	433
Miele	47	575
Mora	37	463
Perene	48	577
MARKET		
Aligre (Marché d')	22	391
Bar à Patates	23	392
Bastille (Marché)	23	393
Dejean (Marché)	34	503
Enfants Rouges (Marché des)	26	395
Gros-La Fontaine (Marché)	26	351
Passy (Marché)	27	396
Raspail (Marché)	28	365
Thiébault maraîcher (Joël)	28	379
PATISSERIE		
Hermé Paris (Pierre)	45	537
Ladurée	45	581
Larher (Pâtisserie Arnaud)	45	581
Lenôtre	47	545
Maeder (Pâtisserie Raoul)	47	549
Mulot	47	582
Nani	48	582
Pain de Sucre	48	559
Pâtisserie des Rêves (La)	48	563

INDEX BY ESTABLISHMENT TYPE

RESTAURANT

	D	B
1728	4	21
21	4	13
39 V	4	17
58 Tour Eiffel	4	25
Afaria	32	405
Alain Ducasse au Plaza Athénée	4	29
Alfred	4	37
Amici Miei	32	501
Arôme (L')	5	281
Assiette (L')	5	39
Atelier de Joël Robuchon (L')	5	43
Auberge du Bonheur (L')	5	281
Auberge Pyrénnées-Cévennes	22	392
Aubrac Corner	22	299
Aux comptoirs des Indes	32	502
Aux Lyonnais	22	301
Baratin (Le)	6	63
Bateaux Parisiens	6	283
Benoit	7	71
Bistrot Paul Bert	7	81
Brasserie Lipp	7	283
Caffè dei Cioppi	33	421
Carré des Feuillants (Le)	8	95
Cave de Joël Robuchon (La)	8	284
Chalet des Îles (Le)	44	579
Chapeau Melon	9	285
Chardenoux (Le)	9	103
Chartier (Restaurant)	9	107
Chateaubriand (Le)	9	111
Cherche Midi (Le)	33	502
Chez Flottes	25	323
Chez Georges	9	394
Chez Georges	25	286
Chez l'Ami Jean	9	115
Chez l'Ami Louis	10	119
Citrus Étoile	10	123
Closerie des Lilas (La)	10	127
Costes (Hôtel)	10	131
Cour Jardin (La)	10	135
Crèmerie (La)	10	139
D'Chez Eux (Auberge)	25	327
Divellec (Le)	11	143
Dôme (Le)	11	287
Drouant	11	147
Écailler du bistrot (L')	11	155
El Fogón	34	437
Fines Gueules (Les)	12	287
Flaubert (Le)	12	288
Fontaine de Mars (La)	12	157
Fougères (Les)	12	165
Fouquet's	12	288
Foyer Vietnam	34	503
Frenchie	13	169
Gazzetta (La)	34	445
Gourmets des Ternes (Les)	13	173
Grande cascade (La)	13	177
I Golosi	35	504
Il Campionissimo	35	453
Il Vino	35	505
Itinéraires	26	395
Jadis (Restaurant)	13	290
Jeu de Quilles (Le)	14	181
Jules Verne (Le)	14	189
Kaiseki	37	459
Kei	14	185
Lasserre	14	195
Laurent (Le)	14	199
Ledoyen	15	203
Mama Shelter	15	207
Meurice (Le)	15	211
Michelangelo	37	505
Mon Vieil Ami	15	215
Moussa l'Africain	37	506
Non Solo Cucina	37	507
Non solo pasta	38	507
Nouvelle Mer de Chine (La)	38	508
Père Claude (Le)	27	396
Petit Vendôme (Le)	16	292
Petrossian	16	292
Pharamond	16	231
Pho Dong Huong	38	510
Pho Tai	39	510
Poule au pot (La)	17	293
Pousse Pousse	27	353
Pré Verre (Le)	14	290
Prunier (Restaurant)	17	239
Quincy (Le)	27	357
Racines	27	361
Rech	17	243
Régalade (La)	17	293
Réginette (La)	39	511
Relais Louis XIII (Le)	17	294
Relais Plaza (Le)	18	249
Repaire de Cartouche (Le)	18	294
Ribouldingue	28	397
Rino	39	512
Rosa Bonheur	18	253
Sardegna a Tavola	39	513
Saturne	28	369
Savoy (Restaurant Guy)	18	257
Spring	28	375
Stresa (Le)	40	513
Thoumieux (Hôtel)	19	265
Train bleu (Le)	19	269
Voltaire (Le)	19	273
Wepler	19	295
Workshop Issé	40	485
Yachts de Paris	19	277
Yam'Tcha	41	489
Ze Kitchen galerie	41	493
Zerda Café	41	497

WINE MERCHANTS

	D	B
Cave des Papilles (La)	8	285
Caves Augé (Les)	8	99
Verre volé (Le)	29	387
Wine by One	29	397

LEGEND

café	bakery	restaurant	patisserie	bar
ice cream parlour	coffee shop	delicatessen	confectioner	butchery
butcher	hotel	wine merchants	brasserie	kitchen supplies
fromagerie	tea	market	fish monger	